MARRIAGE FOR MODERNS

MARRIAGE FOR MODERNS

Fifth edition

HENRY A. BOWMAN
Department of Sociology
The University of Texas

with a foreword by
David R. Mace
Executive Director
American Association of Marriage Counselors

McGRAW-HILL BOOK COMPANY

New York   St. Louis   San Francisco   Toronto   London   Sydney

MARRIAGE FOR MODERNS

*This book was set in Linofilm
Primer. The display type is Trade
Gothic Bold. The photographs
were taken especially for this
book by Marvin Lichtner.*

To E. K. B.

LIST OF CORRELATED FILMS

The eight motion pictures described below have been produced in collaboration with the author of this text. The films may be purchased from the Text-Film Department of the McGraw-Hill Book Company.

WHO'S BOSS? *(Chapter 2)* Portrays a young married couple, both of whom are individualists, their differences, and their decision to adjust their differences through co-operation. TIME: 16 MINUTES. FOLLOW-UP FILMSTRIP: 36 FRAMES.

MARRIAGE TODAY *(Chapter 2, 11, or as end-of-course summary)* Dramatized portrayal of two couples who made their marriages work through an understanding of their mutual aims and their need to work together to reach them. TIME: 22 MINUTES. FOLLOW-UP FILMSTRIP: 35 FRAMES.

THIS CHARMING COUPLE *(Chapter 3)* Dramatized presentation of the problems of two young people who are "in love with love" and not with each other and are unable to evaluate each other's good qualities and shortcomings. TIME: 19 MINUTES. FOLLOW-UP FILMSTRIP: 39 FRAMES.

CHOOSING FOR HAPPINESS *(Chapter 5)* Portrays through dramatized situations the reactions of a girl to various boy friends and her rejection of all of them—and they of her; and suggests that the girl should reevaluate herself and her demands on others. TIME: 14 MINUTES. FOLLOW-UP FILMSTRIP: 38 FRAMES.

IT TAKES ALL KINDS *(Chapter 5)* Portrays a series of young couples reacting to tense situations; relates their reactions to their possibilities for marriage success or failure; and emphasizes the point that marriage partners should be carefully chosen. TIME: 20 MINUTES. FOLLOW-UP FILMSTRIP: 37 FRAMES.

IN TIME OF TROUBLE *(Chapter 11)* Portrays the family minister counseling a young married couple and helping them understand the reasons for their disagreements and ways in which satisfactory adjustments can be made. TIME: 14 MINUTES. FOLLOW-UP FILMSTRIP: 36 FRAMES.

JEALOUSY *(Chapter 11)* Portrayal of a young wife, jealous of her husband, and her gradual realization that her behavior is an expression of her dissatisfaction with her role as homemaker. TIME: 16 MINUTES. FOLLOW-UP FILMSTRIP: 38 FRAMES.

WHO'S RIGHT? *(Chapter 11)* Dramatization of a quarrel between husband and wife, caused by her seeing his forcefulness as "bossism" and by his labeling her good taste as extravagance. TIME: 18 MINUTES. FOLLOW-UP FILMSTRIP: 36 FRAMES.

In addition, three other motion pictures from the McGraw-Hill Text-Film Department are especially suitable for use with this text.

HOW MUCH AFFECTION? *(Chapter 4)* Dramatized presentation of situations and questions concerning the extent of physical affection between a couple who are going steady. TIME: 20 MINUTES.

IS THIS LOVE? *(Chapter 3)* Contrasts the romances of two college girls, one impulsive and eager to get married, the other wishing to go more slowly through the stages of dating, courtship, going steady, and engagement. Concludes with open-end questions directed to the audience. TIME: 14 MINUTES.

WHEN SHOULD I MARRY? *(Chapter 8)* A minister advises a young couple, eager to marry, by describing the experiences of two other couples who married at an early age. TIME: 19 MINUTES.

FOREWORD

"No man," said Plutarch, "ever wetted clay and left it, as if there would be bricks by chance and fortune."

Yet today in these United States young men and women by the million are coming together in marriage, drawn by mutual attraction, on the assumption that satisfactory interpersonal adjustment will happen of its own accord. The available evidence suggests that not more than half of these young couples will find the kind of happiness they seek and expect.

It must be recognized, of course, that until quite recent times interpersonal adjustment was not considered necessary for a successful marriage. So long as children were born to continue the family line and the couple were forced by social pressure to stay together, the purpose of marriage was considered to have been achieved.

Indeed, elaborate devices were set up to *avoid* the development of a close interpersonal relationship between husband and wife, presumably because such involvement was known to generate explosive conflict. The two principal means employed were to condition women to a submissive role in which as wives they responded quiescently to their husbands' unfettered self-expression, and to divide the spheres of influence of husband and wife into almost completely separate compartments with the minimum of overlapping. These devices are still in widespread operation in the East.

Today in the West, however, these ancient barriers to full interpersonal involvement of husband and wife have been swept away in the campaign for individual freedom and autonomy. The result is that marriage offers, to the average couple, greatly increased possibilities of harrowing conflict.

When conflict cannot be resolved, frustrated men and women are refusing to stay together in marriage. If family life is to be a stable institution in our society in the days ahead, therefore, marriages will have to be held together by cohesion from within and not by coercion from without.

One way of achieving this is by the provision of marriage-counseling services. Good counseling can do a great deal, under reasonably favorable conditions, to steady and strengthen a marriage in trouble. The increasing provision of such services is certainly one reason why the high divorce rates in many Western countries are at last slowly going down.

However, there is something strangely irrational about a policy of waiting till people get into serious trouble and then offering to help them out. Long hours of counseling time are consumed in the attempt to correct false ideas and attitudes that should never have been allowed to develop. These ideas and attitudes were the result of miseducation for marriage.

The obvious answer is to provide all young people with education for marriage. The logic of this is so self-evident that, if human communities behaved rationally, it would have been undertaken on a vast scale many years ago. For what is at stake is nothing less than the most fundamental source of individual happiness and of social stability — good family life.

Communities do not, however, behave rationally. They follow established custom. Consequently, although interpersonal mutuality has become the central criterion for marital security, we continue to treat marriage as it was treated in an age when such mutuality was considered to be peripheral.

We do not act thus merely because we are obtuse. Our problem is a complex one. Education for marriage is not education in the traditional sense. It is certainly concerned with facts and ideas. But it is much more concerned with feelings and attitudes. Consequently, educators have found themselves hesitant about entering this new and uncharted region. Their hesitation has been increased by the fact that some highly delicate and controversial questions are involved.

The presence of difficulties is no excuse, however, for inaction. It is true that we have still a great deal to learn about the marriage relationship. But we are not as ignorant about it as some people suggest. And even if our knowledge is limited, this does not absolve us from the moral obligation to make it available, such as it is, to those who can use it to make life happier and more fruitful. It is ridiculous to say, or to imply, that those who have learned something about the art of achieving a good marital relationship will be no better off than those who know nothing about it.

Our society is greatly indebted, therefore, to those pioneering educators who have ventured into this complex field, and by dint of skill and effort, have achieved success in it. They have appeared as lamplighters passing down a dark and dangerous path, making the way safe and clearer for all who travel there.

Among this band of pioneers the author of this book holds an honored place. I have known him, and admired him, for almost twenty years. A gifted scholar and teacher, he has devoted the greater part of his life to helping college students to achieve successful marriages. His former students, whom I have encountered in many places, regard him with reverence and affection. His influence in their lives has been deep, dynamic, and enduring.

In *Marriage for Moderns* we have a distillation of the sound wisdom which Henry Bowman has accumulated in more than thirty years of teaching marriage courses. He has striven conscientiously to keep his teaching in balance between two focal points: the scientific facts as study and research brought them to light and the needs of his students as he came increasingly to understand them.

This book has been eminently successful because it has forthrightly set its goals and held to them from start to finish. The author's aim is to deal, in the framework of the marriage course, with those issues that perplex and disturb students as they move toward personal involvement in the man-woman relationship. As a wise and experienced guide of youth, he presents objectively what should be known and considered, leaving the reader to arrive at his own conclusions once he is satisfied that all the relevant facts have been presented.

In the study and in the classroom, this book has already stood the test of time. I have always considered it to be one of the very best of our marriage texts for college use. May this fifth edition make a further significant contribution to the great cause to which Henry Bowman has dedicated his life: the extension of happy and successful marriages.

David R. Mace

PREFACE

This book is addressed primarily to college and university students who are contemplating marriage in the near or distant future within the context of present-day American culture. It is addressed to them as concerned persons who are confronted with crosscurrents of attitudes, practices, and values produced by rapidly changing times but who are motivated to learn something about marriage in order to make it more meaningful. To this end they will need to acquire factual information and develop objectivity relative to empirical data. They will also, however, need to gain insight, develop attitudes, and make value judgments.

In this "age of science," with its emphasis upon research, quantification, and objectivity, the inevitability of making value judgments in day-by-day living and in interpersonal relationships often escapes our attention. Science can tell us how the gun operates, so to speak; but science can neither tell us what target to shoot at nor motivate us to pull the trigger.

Typically, teachers are older than students. And because they are older, the philosophical framework of their lives has usually progressed farther toward mature integration than that of students, whose philosophical framework is in process of formation and is probably in a state of flux due to the multiplicity of ideas and influences emerging from the campus situation. In the educational process, therefore, the objectivity of the teacher, when translated by the student, sometimes results in indifference or apathy rather than a perpetuation of objectivity. The student's erroneous conclusion may be that if all ideas and practices are to be examined only objectively, without bias, emotion, concern, or value judgment, then all are on the same level of acceptability, so it makes no difference what one does or believes. For the scientist such a point of view is appropriate. For the individual concerned about making marriage meaningful it is, by itself, insufficient.

In general, to arrive at his own point of view regarding marriage, the student utilizes two types of "data." He uses empirical data brought to light through research. Hence I have included in this edition some of the findings of research studies when these appeared to be pertinent. But the student's "data" also include the experience, observations, points of view, attitudes, and insights of persons who communicate their impressions to him in some way other than through research reports. These two types of "data" are not mutually exclusive. At the present stage of knowledge neither type is so nearly incontrovertible as might be hoped, since research in the area of marriage is young and studies are fragmentary, and since impressions and insights are necessarily incomplete. Each type of "data," however, has some validity; the difference in validity is one of kind rather than of degree. I have, therefore, included in this edition reflections of the thinking of persons, including myself, who are concerned about marriage, but reflections of such a nature that they cannot be expressed numerically. They are included not to indoctrinate the reader but to give him food for thought. He is called upon to evaluate both types of "data" equally critically. Neither is the "last word."

Some of the reflections mentioned above have been incorporated into the text. Others have been included as Correlative Readings. There are nineteen such readings, and their inclusion constitutes one of the major differences between this fifth edition and earlier ones.

There are also other differences which, because of a special timeliness or the utilization of recent research data, will, it is hoped, increase the usefulness of this edition. For example, there is an extensive discussion of premarital sexual permissiveness, which is a live issue in student thinking and discussion. A new section on contraception has been added, including discussion of oral contraceptives. The discussion of cultural factors affecting sex differences and the roles of the sexes has been expanded. The chapter on reproduction has been updated by the inclusion of recent research data and also by the inclusion of materials not readily available to either instructors or students unless they have access to specialized publications. For instance, among numerous such items included, there is a discussion of decompression as a form of pain relief in labor, the vacuum extractor as a possible substitute for the obstetrical forceps, artificial insemination with frozen sperms. All statistics have been brought up to date. The tables of marriage and divorce laws have been revised in the light of recent changes. The results of research studies of the employment of mothers, premarital sexual intercourse, time of ovulation as related to the "safe period," and other problems are presented. A new picture story depicting the role of the wife has been added. At the end of each chapter is a new annotated list of selected readings including recent publications.

I have now been teaching, counseling, and lecturing in the field of marriage and preparation for marriage for thirty-one years. During this time I have had some ten thousand students in my classes, and I have had some thirty-five hundred personal conferences with students having premarital or marital problems. In addition, I have talked with a great variety of nonclass groups. During 1963, on an assignment from the U.S. Department of State and a research grant from the University of Texas, I spent six months in Australia and New Zealand working in the programs of the Marriage Guidance Councils and studying Australian marriage and divorce law. From this total experience impressions have been gained and insights achieved that I hope will contribute at least some degree of validity to what I have written. Such impressions and insights cannot be expressed quantitatively. Indeed, they would lose something if they were. Rather they are expressed as a distillation of endeavor to understand, as one "datum" for the reader's consideration in his effort to make his marriage more meaningful.

Henry A. Bowman

CONTENTS

CORRELATIVE READINGS

Title

MARRIAGE FOR MODERNS

part 1

THE BACKGROUND
OF MARRIAGE

In all known peoples—contemporary, historical, prehis-
torical—human societies have regulated the relations
between the sexes through some type of marriage. Thus,
marriage is an ancient, venerable, and universal institu-
tion. It has survived all the ups and downs and has weath-
ered all the vicissitudes of mankind's long existence. It
is not likely soon to become obsolete, as some suggest.
Marriage changes slowly, but it does change. It changes
because the various elements of a culture are integrated,
and change in one is reflected in change in others. Mar-
riage changes in response to basic social and economic
conditions. It changes as new ideologies emerge, as new
opportunities arise, as new demands are put upon it, and
as a culture produces new kinds of people to participate
in it. As marriage changes, elements of the old are carried
along as new elements develop. On the one hand, this con-
tributes to the strength of the institutional structure. On
the other hand, it produces problems. Marriage in modern
America exhibits both old and new elements. Some of the
reasons for which present-day Americans marry—for
example, division of labor by sex—are as ancient as mar-
riage itself. Other reasons—for example, romantic love—
are relatively new arrivals on the cultural scene. As new

reasons for marriage emerge in the process of cultural change, new questions arise: What should the roles of the sexes be? What is meant by "love," and how can it be recognized? At what level of maturity are young people ready for marriage? What is involved in the choice of a marriage partner? Is it possible to prepare for marriage? If so, how? What is successful marriage, and how may it be achieved? In order to answer such questions, marriage must be analyzed in the light of certain underlying factors which may be considered the background of marriage.

chapter 1

A POINT
OF DEPARTURE

THAT THE HUMAN RACE is composed of beings of two types—male and female—is one of the fundamental facts of existence. It is a fact that at first glance may seem too obvious to mention. Yet it is often ignored or overlooked in our efforts to raise the plane of satisfaction in living. This fact of bisexuality is one of the foundation stones of life. Out of it grows much of the world's beauty in art, literature, drama, and human relations. Out of it, also, grow some of life's most trying problems, bitterest disappointments, deepest hurts, and most distasteful ugliness. It is one of the inescapables which everyone must face and to which everyone must orient himself. Members of the opposite sex, with their attributes, their roles, and their expectations, are part of the natural and cultural environment in response to which and within which personality develops. Each of these two types of being, male and female, must in some way take into account the existence of the other. This implies a continuous process of adjustment.

Adjustment is the fundamental thread running through the relations between men and women. It is the fundamental thread running through marriage; it is the very essence of marriage. It is the point of departure, the springboard, for the discussion in this book.

Throughout this discussion two words, "adjustment" and "problem," will be used frequently. It is very important that the first not be interpreted as implying something static and the latter as implying only something negative. Human life is replete with problems—situations in which individuals are confronted with possible alternatives and hence face a need for making choices, decisions, and judgments which may be made more effectively on a basis of information, understanding, and insight than on a basis of ignorance, irrationality, and obtuseness. But these choices, decisions, and judgments are also made with relation to goals, values, attitudes, and assumptions which may not be established on a factual basis. They often have a strong individual emotional coloring. They are also tinted by the cultural climate in which the individual lives. Complete objectivity, however essential to scientific understanding, is not possible in many aspects of day-by-day living. Facts alone cannot tell an individual what alternatives to choose. Facts can tell him, so to speak, how the gun operates; but they cannot tell him what target to shoot at. Hence he is called upon to consider possible flaws in his assumptions, the extent of his biases, and the possible limitations of his factual data. In the last analysis, however, he must make choices, decisions, and judgments in order to continue to live — unless, of course, someone makes them for him, as in the case of an infant, an incapacitated person, a person who is subjected to physical force. As he goes through this process of choosing alternatives, the individual seeks to move toward a type of adjustment that will, from his particular point of view, make his life more satisfactory — not necessarily more pleasant or happier, but more acceptable. Because life conditions are in a state of constant flux and the human individual is in a state of continuous development, whatever equilibrium is achieved is unstable. Adjustment is never complete, and we may think of it as dynamic rather than static.

Are men and women equal?

One often hears the questions: Are men and women equal? If not, which is inferior; which, superior? Taken as it stands, the first question is unanswerable. Equal in what respect? Two things cannot be just equal; they must be equal with respect to a given set of qualities. Even then, the answer depends in part on the connotation of "equal." Men and women are equal as to number of hands. They are unequal as to muscular strength. They are equal in intelligence, though unequal in brain size. Do they have equality of opportunity for self-expression? Some would answer in the affirmative, others in the negative. Certainly they do not have identical opportunity for self-expression. Are the roles of husband and wife equally important? They are; but this does not make them interchangeable. When either men or women talk of wanting equality with the opposite sex, for example, when women say they would like to have men's freedom or men say they envy women their preferential treatment in courts of law, what they both usually mean is equality of opportunity rather than identity of role or similarity of responsibility.

To speak of one sex as being inferior to the other is nonsensical unless some standard of superiority-inferiority is set up. If a masculine standard is used, women become inferior by definition. If a feminine standard is used, the reverse is true. We have a strong traditional tendency to set up a masculine standard; therefore, for centuries there have seemed to be more respects in which women were inferior to men than in which men were inferior to women.

Actually each sex should be judged in terms of its own functions, not in terms of the functions of the opposite sex. One sex may be considered superior to the other, not when it performs its own functions better than the other can perform them, but only when it can perform the functions of the other or common functions better than the other can perform them. If, for example, one were to compare the men and women engaged in a given occupation, one might set up a standard of proficiency in that occupation and determine whether one sex was superior or equal to the other. But to say that women are inferior to men because there have been more male than female geniuses is absurd because in fulfilling their traditional role women have had neither the need nor the opportunity to exhibit the particular type of genius that men exhibit in science, inventions, and the arts. It would be just as sensible to reverse the definition and say that men are inferior to women because throughout history men have been inferior homemakers.

The sexes are complementary

Together a lock and key that fit form a functioning unit. Together they can accomplish something that neither acting alone can accomplish. Nor can it be accomplished by two locks or two keys. Each is distinct; yet neither is complete in and of itself. Their roles are neither identical nor interchangeable. Neither is superior to the other, since both are necessary. They are equally important. Each must be judged in terms of its own function. They are complementary. A lock and a key that do not fit, or two locks, or two keys represent a simple sum—one plus one equals two. But a lock and a key that fit add up to more than two because they represent one plus one plus function.

So it is with men and women; together they form a functioning unit. Either alone is in a sense incomplete. They are complementary. Though separate with the possibility of independent existence, they are at the same time mutually dependent parts of a functioning whole. This complementariness is not 100 per cent complete and does not apply to all traits, functions, drives, or goals. When men and women engage in the same occupations or perform common functions, this complementary relationship may break down. The sexes are not complementary for such things as number of appendages, need for food, and so on, but in many important respects they are.

"Complementary" connotes more than merely quantitative difference. It is not the same as "supplementary." It connotes completion, a combination of differences that creates a new entity rather than simply an additive process. For example, a wife's earnings might be thought of as supplementing her husband's income. But if he is the breadwinner and she is the homemaker, they complement each other, since their relationship represents a combination of role differences to form a functioning unit.

One aspect of complementariness is simultaneity and reciprocity. A complementary relationship does not arise automatically, though the ingredients for it are in part natural attributes and in part characteristics produced by culture and uncritically accepted. Such a relationship is established only when individuals of opposite sex are simultaneously and reciprocally interested in accepting and utilizing their differences, this interest being conditioned by the cultural pattern within which they live. Thus complementariness is not only observed and recognized but also created.

A complementary relationship is reciprocal in another sense, also. "Supplementary" may connote interest by, or advantage to, only one person. "Complementary" connotes reciprocal interest and advantage on the part of two persons who simultaneously derive benefit from their differences.

To live together in a complementary relationship implies cooperation. In many cases, when a woman enters the business or professional world, she must learn to compete with men. If she marries and becomes a homemaker, she needs not to compete but to cooperate. She and her husband need to establish not a competitive but a complementary relationship. The woman who leaves her temporary occupational pursuit when she marries but who carries with her the competitive attitude that she has learned and that she needed in her occupation, the gainfully employed married woman who cannot successfully exhibit a cooperative spirit at home, the husband who carries competition into his relationship with his wife – these persons prevent the development of that complementary relationship in marriage which spells mutual happiness.

To speak of the sexes as complementary does not suggest that one be a satellite of the other, that they be diametrically opposite in all traits, that one merely correct the deficiencies in the other's personality, or that the wife direct all her energy toward furthering the occupational success of her husband. It implies merely a recognition of difference between men and women and a utilization of this difference for the furtherance of common ends.

Benjamin Franklin compared a single man to the odd half of a pair of scissors [Rosenbach, 1932]. In *Hiawatha* Longfellow likened a woman to the cord on a bow, bending the bow yet responding to it, "Useless each without the other." In many aspects of their association with each other, men and women are like dancing partners. In ballroom dancing involving face-to-face contact, a couple can neither make progress nor enjoy themselves unless they establish a complementary relationship.

When the man steps forward, the woman steps backward. When he moves to his right, she moves to her left. One leads, the other follows. If both try to step forward simultaneously, if each attempts to move to his right at the same time, or if they both lead, trouble ensues. Without implication of inferiority or superiority, each can, indeed must, assume a role complementary to that of the other in order that they may dance together with any degree of mutual pleasure.

Franklin's comparison is oversimplified and Longfellow's may seem at first glance to relegate women to a position of useful inferiority. Our comparison of men and women to dancing partners leaves out many important considerations. But each serves to clarify the point we have been trying to make, namely, that men and women are complementary, that together they can form a functioning unit. In the typical American marriage a more or less normal man is married to a more or less normal woman. The former has the major responsibility for breadwinning, and the latter has the major responsibility for homemaking. Both are parents of the same children. In such a marriage their biological and widely accepted roles are different, and their mutual satisfaction is increased by cooperation and decreased by competition. We live in a world of reality, a world of the present and the immediate future, on which there rests the heavy hand of the past, a world in which tradition still carries considerable weight and the mores exert a stronger influence than the theorist, a world in which boys and girls are trained for roles that are different but at the same time changing and in some respects becoming more nearly alike, a world in which new wine is being put into old bottles but in which many bottles are being left empty, a world in which most men and women do marry and in which most married women are homemakers. To disregard these facts, to talk about what might be done if tradition and the mores were radically changed or what may come about by the year 3000 may be interesting mental gymnastics, but it does not help the young people of today to adjust to the inevitabilities of life or to raise their marriages to a higher plane of mutual satisfaction.

Some differences between men and women

We shall not attempt a complete inventory of all the differences between men and women. In fact, at the present stage of knowledge such an inventory is impossible. We can, however, indicate some of the more apparent and more commonly assumed differences in order to make a point.

SIZE

One of the most obvious differences is that of size. Taken as a group, men are larger than women. This is a matter not only of common observation and statistical fact but also of traditional expectation. Men are expected to be larger than women; husbands are expected to be larger than wives. The contortions of the taller girl in accommodating herself to a shorter dancing partner, the frequent references to size in girls' discussions of boys, the efforts of the very short man to "inflate" his ego so that he seems (to himself, at least) to be as large as other men and larger than women—all these and many other common observations bear witness to the fact that men and women differ as to size and that society expects them to do so.

It is important to note, however, that though men as a group are larger than women as a group, some women are larger than some men. There is a good deal of variation within each group; individuals range from relatively tall to relatively short, with the majority clustering around the average. If the sizes of the two groups were plotted on graphs, these graphs would overlap. Size, then, though constituting a rather obvious difference between the sexes, does not make possible the drawing of a hard and fast line between them, and so it is with other traits.

BONY FRAMEWORK

Man's skeleton is not only larger than woman's but also more heavily constructed, and various parts have different relative proportions. In man the areas to which the muscles are attached are rougher and hence can accommodate larger muscles. In woman the pelvis is broader and shallower, so her legs are inclined somewhat to form a V while a man's are inclined to be more nearly parallel, a difference that is important in athletics. Furthermore, the shallower pelvis makes the woman better adapted for childbearing than she would be if her bony framework were like man's. Women are more likely than men to have a "back bend" in the elbow. When the arm is fully extended, palm up, the forearm goes beyond straight, and the arm forms an angle greater than 180 degrees, while a man's arm is more likely to be straight. Again, this is a difference that is important in athletics, especially in those sports involving throwing. Try as they will, many women cannot learn to throw a ball the way a man does. A woman's skeletal structure also tends to be more flexible than a man's. This is shown, for example, in the ease with which women can button a garment down the back, something which many men cannot do.

MUSCULAR STRENGTH

Here again the difference between men and women is obvious and traditionally expected. This difference depends on something more fundamental than training, for in almost all the major competitive sports the best men surpass the best women. There is a tendency for the women who are most successful in sports to be among those who are constitutionally least feminine [Greenhill, 1945a]. In men, muscle tissue constitutes a relatively larger proportion of the body weight than it does in women.

HAIR DISTRIBUTION

Not only do men tend to have more noticeable body hair than do women but there is a typical distribution characteristic of each sex, especially with regard to the pubic hair. Men have beards and also have a greater tendency to become bald. Here again there is an overlapping of the traits of the two groups, and there is also a certain traditional expectation. Many a man is made the butt of jest because his chest lacks hirsute adornment, and occasionally one hears of a woman who has to shave her moustache or who earns her living as the "bearded lady" in a side show.

BIRTH AND DEATH RATES

There are more male than female babies born alive. Over a long period in this country the rate averages about 105 boys to 100 girls. Fluctuations occur from year to year, but there are always more boys than girls.

There are more male babies among those born dead. More males die in infancy. In fact, the death rate for males exceeds that for females for all ages. Men are more subject to hazardous occupations and to warfare. All major causes of death strike down more males than females. There are just about three times as many male suicides as female suicides [U.S. Bureau of the Census, 1964]. The average expectation of life is about seven years greater for women than for men [*Statistical Bulletin,* July, 1963]. The result of the combination of these birth-rate—death-rate factors is that after age eighteen the sex ratio drops below 100; that is, there are fewer males than females in the population [U.S. Bureau of the Census, 1960*a*]. Adding the fact that women marry at an earlier age than do men, we find that there are four times as many widows as widowers [*Population Bulletin,* 1963].

This is a rather interesting situation in view of men's traditional claim that they are the stronger sex. When it is a question of muscular strength, men are undoubtedly the stronger. When it is a question of living long, living well, and withstanding the vicissitudes of existence, men must yield the place of honor to women. Men are stronger, but women are more durable.

DEVELOPMENT

Physically and emotionally girls develop more rapidly than do boys. Boys, however, develop over a longer period. Consequently, in their "teens" girls are likely to be further advanced than boys of their own age, but by the time they both reach their twenties, the boys have caught up and are on similar levels. Nevertheless, neither can acquire more than twenty years' *experience* in twenty years.

SEX DRIVE

Generally speaking, men's sex drive is characterized by greater urgency than women's. Men are more compulsive with regard to sex; and sexual interest is more nearly ever present. Women's interest is less compulsive and more likely to be periodic; and women are more likely to be restricted by inhibitions. As a group, women can get along more comfortably with less sexual release than can men. There are more women than men who have little or no interest in sexual intercourse. Men more readily separate sex and love, while women are more inclined to combine them.

OTHER DIFFERENCES

Men are more pugnacious than women; they are not only more prone to fight but are more inclined to enjoy fighting. They express this pugnacity in sports, in business, in warfare, and in other ways. It is said that women are more adaptable to new situations; that women are better "domesticated" in the sense that they have less tendency to form gangs and are less likely to feel the "call of the wild." Men consider women vain, and women consider men conceited. Probably they have equally sensitive egos but manifest them differently. Men have a tendency to bellow and beat upon their chests, so to speak, while women are less vociferous in exhibiting their self-esteem.

It is said that women exhibit more social intelligence than do men, that they are more sensitive to group opinion and more eager to improve their social position; but this has not been proved.

Women tend to be more subtle, more indirect in their methods and in achieving their objectives. Perhaps this technique has been forced upon them through centuries of dealing with men who throughout history have had more power. It was and is the most effective way to gain their ends for persons whose inferiority was taken for granted until only yesterday and still is taken for granted in many quarters. Women have become extremely adept at it.

In courtship men assume the role of pursuer while women assume the role of pursued. Women respond favorably to pursuit by men; men respond unfavorably to pursuit by women. This difference is the result of both biological and cultural factors. When one sex attempts a reversal of role, the other is inclined to resent it. Women almost unconsciously assume the role of the pursued, but not actually to the point of escape. They know that, with custom and men being what they are, to seem to run away invites pursuit. Men's interest in women, on the other hand, is exhibited more directly, more aggressively, and more obviously.

There are, however, indications that women are losing some of their traditional reserve and are becoming more direct and aggressive in their approach to men. Whether this is temporary or represents a permanent change in the folkways remains to be seen.

In spite of this change in female aggression in approaching the male,

American culture still sustains a male-female differential with respect to a felt need to be chosen. Actually, although they travel different routes to reach the same destination, male and female both choose and are chosen. Traditionally, however, the male's selection of a dating or marriage partner has been assumed to involve more active, more apparent choosing, while the female's has been assumed to involve more acceptance, less apparent choosing. She has not had the same freedom as he to decide whom she will attempt to choose; she has had to wait until he took the initiative, except in so far as she brought herself to his attention or made herself attractive to him. This differential is focused in the traditional assumption that it is the male who finally asks the female to marry him: the reverse has only recently become more common, but it is not yet universally approved. Because of this differential there is a difference in the reaction of the sexes to failure to date or to marry.

It is often said that women are more emotional while men are more intellectual and more logical, that men reason while women feel. When one witnesses some of the intellectual achievements of modern women, however, and observes some of the mass blunders and primitive expressions of modern men, one is prone to doubt this assumed difference in intellectual and emotional behavior. The difference between men and women is not that the former reason while the latter feel; it is one of type of emotion expressed and degree of freedom in expression.

The common and uncritical assumption is that men have greater freedom than do women. In some respects this is true. Men have greater freedom of activity and are less subject to restriction and direction. They may move about more freely, are chaperoned less carefully, and are in some ways freer to determine their own behavior. In other ways, however, men have less freedom than do women. There is some tendency for women to compare their own lot to the more superficial aspects of men's. Some women formulated their attitudes toward freedom in their adolescent years and have not since reexamined them from a more mature point of view. For example, a woman who is now middle-aged has a brother four years her senior. When she was fourteen the brother decided to hitchhike across the country. The girl expressed enthusiastic interest in going along. Her parents left no doubt as to their reaction to her plan: "You can't do that," they told her; "you're a girl." She decided then, and she still believes, that men have more freedom than do women.

There are standards of manliness to which men are in a measure forced to adhere. Women are freer to express such emotions as fear, pity, sadness, and affection for persons of the same sex. A man may feel like crying, but he may not do so for fear of being called "sissy." He may be petrified with fright, but he must put on a bold front to avoid being classified as a coward. In some respects, also, men are so overlaid with traditional restrictions and inhibitions as a result of training that they not only do not express such emotions freely but often come to experience them to a lesser degree.

Men are subject to a traditional code of chivalry which, though fading, is still extant and is directed toward standardizing men's behavior. According to this code men must show women courtesies, protect them, assist them, and accept their verbal or physical attacks without retaliation. There is no similar code for women.

Most men have no choice as to whether or not they will become breadwinners and support their families. Women may or may not have gainful employment after marriage, as they choose. In some cases, to be sure, that choice is forced upon them, but not to the same degree or in the same way as it is upon men. Men may have more freedom as to choice of gainful employment, but they have less freedom as to whether they will make that choice. When a married woman is employed, it is through voluntary choice or because of the exigencies of her individual situation. A man works partly through voluntary choice and partly because of the pressure exerted by the traditional cultural pattern.

In recent years, almost-universal required military service for men altered the freedom-restriction balance between the sexes. Women would have changed their attitudes toward their own and men's freedom if the Federal government had instituted the drafting of women.

There is a tendency for men to be more interested in facts as such or facts and their general, impersonal significance, while women are inclined to be more interested in relationships, especially in the personal aspects of those relationships. It is for this reason, among others, that communication between the sexes is sometimes difficult. If one says to a group of women, "Women are inclined to take things personally," someone in the group will probably retort, "I don't," thereby proving that she does. A young couple recently married visited one evening at the apartment of friends. During the visit the husband observed how attractively the apartment was furnished and, when they returned home, he mentioned his observations to his wife. She said little at the time but for several weeks was quiet and distant. It was apparent that she had been offended. The husband could recall nothing that he had said or done to make her react in this way. When the incident was related to a counselor, it was easily explained. The husband had made what was to him a simple statement of fact, which had no particular relation to his marriage. The wife had taken his statement personally and interpreted it as a veiled criticism of her homemaking; she had read a personal relationship into an impersonal statement. The husband's mistake lay in expecting his wife to react as a man would. If it were only a matter of home furnishings, this difference would not be worth mentioning; but it ramifies all through the behavior of the sexes.

It may be true that men are more predictable to women than women are to men. The "average" man is likely to throw up his hands and say,

"She's only a woman; you can never tell what a woman will do next."
Of course he cannot, because he has made so little effort to understand
her. By his words "she's only a woman" he implies that he believes her
somewhat inferior and probably not worth understanding. Women have
been forced through centuries of subjection to understand men, at
least in some ways. If they have not been able to control men by the
direct methods that men use on women, they have been able to exert
considerable influence, often without men's being aware of it, because
they have learned to understand men and therefore can to a certain
degree predict their behavior.

CONCLUSION

We might go on discussing numerous differences between men and
women, differences in physical traits, in interests, in attitudes both
toward things other than themselves and toward each other, in expectations which the sexes set up for each other and which are set up for
them by culture. As we intimated above, however, our purpose is not to
present a complete inventory of differences but rather to provide a
springboard for a discussion of marriage relationships. We have said
enough to show:

1. That men and women are different.

2. That, since they are different, they are called upon to adjust to
one another. The achievement of this adjustment involves not only a
general recognition of sex differences but also, in marriage, the observation of the one person with whom the adjustment is to be carried
out. Are there not traits which he exhibits just because he is masculine?
Does she not act in a particular way just because she is feminine and is
living up to the standard that society sets for women?

3. That although there are important differences, these differences
overlap, so that for almost every trait some men exhibit it more clearly
than do some women or vice versa. To avoid being tedious, we have not
mentioned this fact for every difference, but in each case we have been
able to say only "men are inclined to . . ." or "women are more. . . ."
In no case have we been able to say "only men are . . . while only
women are. . . ." In some instances there are men who for a number of
traits are more feminine than average women and some women who for
numerous traits are more masculine than average men [Terman and
Miles, 1936]. Furthermore, though there are important differences, there
are also important similarities, so that "every individual represents a
blend of male and female characteristics of varying grade" [Hoskins,
1933]. This blending extends even to the primary genital organs, men
having not only the developed organs of males but also the rudimentary
organs of females and women having not only the developed organs of
their own sex but also rudimentary male organs. The blending is apparent in the presence of rudimentary breasts in the male. In rare cases

a person is found who has the genital organs of both sexes fairly well developed or who starts life as one sex and later lives as the other—a state of affairs due largely to the fact that the unusual development made for a misinterpretation of sex at the time of birth. "Every individual is bisexual. This extends through life and is evidenced by organs which are homologous in both sexes. One sex generally dominates and the other is underdeveloped, but this preponderance can be overturned and extraordinary reversals and mix-up of sexes may occur. . . ." [Young, 1937]. However, there has never been an authenticated human case in which the same person could become both a mother and a father.

In addition to the differences between men and women taken as groups, there are individual differences regardless of sex. One might think of the sex differences as sweeping currents, while individual differences are waves rising here and falling there, superimposed but not necessarily dependent upon the currents underneath. Except for the genetic identity of one-egg twins, there are no two persons exactly alike either as to innate potentialities or as to experience. Habits, tastes, attitudes, ideas, ambitions, and a host of other things make for individual differences, which must also be taken into account in marital adjustment.

We have suggested that there are also important similarities between the sexes. There is no measurable difference in intelligence. Both men and women have sensitive egos which they seek to protect in one way or another. Both appreciate being respected as persons and resent being used as objects. Both have a desire for self-determination and have objectives for the pursuance of which they demand freedom of judgment and choice. Both are faced with the necessity of fitting their natural attributes into a cultural pattern and accepting roles which involve both opportunities and limitations. Both have a need for self-assertion and self-expression, approval, security, love, and affection. Men and women have physiological processes in some ways conspicuously different but in many ways basically similar. Their psychological processes are basically similar, and observable differences are largely a reflection of cultural expectations and restrictions rather than the product of dissimilarity of neural function. Their emotional responses exhibit many similarities in spite of the cultural framework within which emotions are expressed and in spite of presumably basic differences, as, for example, in the case of mother love. In the mutual adjustment that marriage entails it is just as essential to be aware of these similarities as it is to recognize the differences.

What causes the differences?

Several factors operate together to produce the differences between men and women taken as groups and to make individuals what they are.

DETERMINERS IN THE CELLS

Each human being begins life as a single cell. This cell is the result of the fusion of two other cells — one from the mother, one from the father — and contains within it the determiners (*genes, chromosomes*) of the individual's hereditary traits as well as the determiners of sex.

When the original cell divides into two, these two into four, and so on until in the fully grown person there are trillions of cells, the determiners of sex pass into each of the new cells in the same combination as was found in the first one. The only exception to this is the sex cells of the new individual, in which only one of the pair of determiners is found. In a sense, a person is male or female through and through. All the body cells are male or female, as the case may be.

This fact is actually not so all-important as it may seem at first glance. As Money says [Winokur, 1963], ". . . the presently observable chromosomal differences between male and female are such that by themselves and in isolation from other variables of sex they bear no relationship at all to the development of gender role and identity." Many factors operating after the new individual is formed and while he is developing may alter his development by affecting the way in which his inborn characteristics, his physiological processes, and his experience within his environment react upon one another. But the fact remains that all his cells, with that one exception, have the same genetic constitution, the same determiners; and because of this he has a tendency to fall on one side or the other of the sexual fence.

PHYSIOLOGICAL PROCESSES: GLANDS

Both sexual and individual differences are produced in part by the way one's body functions, by the physiological processes that occur, and by the way one reacts to stimuli. One of the chief factors in determining such processes is one's glandular setup. In many important respects we are what our glands make us.

One pair of glands the secretions of which play an important role in making us what we are is the *sex glands* (gonads — testicles or testes in the male, ovaries in the female). Usually only experienced horsemen ride stallions (normal males). Less expert horsemen ride mares (females) or geldings (castrated males, that is, males with testes removed). The gelding behaves more like the mare than like the stallion. Both gelding and mare are more tractable, more easily controlled, and more readily predictable. To ride in a cart hitched to a team of bulls would be almost suicidal. Not so with a team of oxen (castrated males). The difference between the behavior of the bull and that of the ox has become proverbial — "like a bull in a china shop," "mad as a bull," "dumb as an ox."

When by accident or for medical reasons the sex glands are removed from a human male, profound changes occur. Such a person is termed a *eunuch*. If the person is young at the time, he fails at the age at which puberty normally occurs to develop the typical characteristics of men.

**BIOLOGICAL AND SOCIAL
ORIGINS OF SEX DIFFERENCES**

As in the other areas of differential psychology, there has
been much discussion and controversy on the question of
the extent to which sex differences arise from basic biological factors. This problem is set apart from the rest of the
heredity-environment issue by the fact that in this case we
know that the two groups do differ through hereditary
causes in many ways—anatomical structure, hormonal
composition, and so forth. The question is, "Do these anatomical and physiological differences we know to exist
make certain kinds of psychological differences inevitable?"

It should be recognized, however, that physical masculinity or femininity is not so clearly an all-or-none quality
as many people believe it to be. Embryologically the sex
organs are practically indistinguishable for the first two
months and have corresponding structures even when
completely developed. Both main types of sex hormones,
the androgens and the estrogens, are produced in both
males and females. It is in the balance or relative proportions of these different chemicals that the sexes differ. But
this also varies considerably from individual to individual
within the same sex. Masculinity-femininity, physically
or psychologically defined, must be regarded as a continuum—or perhaps a number of continua—rather than as a
fixed entity.

The psychoanalytic writers have been the principal
defenders of the notion that differences in physiology and
reproductive functions create different emotional needs in
males and females, which are reflected in personality differences and should be taken into consideration in the
planning of a good society. Most of their writing has been
based on clinical study of patients rather than on the kind
of quantitative research with which this book is concerned.
There have, however, been a few quantitative studies supporting the psychoanalytic conclusions. Blum devised a
new sort of projective test specifically for the purpose of
measuring the kinds of psychosexual variables that the
analysts have discussed—oral and anal tendencies, castration anxiety, and the like. Having gone through standard
psychoanalytic textbooks for theoretical ideas, he made
specific predictions as to the direction of sex differences
that would appear in the various scores on the test. The

From Leona E. Tyler, *The Psychology of Human Differences*, 2d ed.,
Appleton-Century-Crofts, Inc., New York, 1956, pp. 269–275. Abridged and
reprinted with permission of the publisher.

most conclusive finding for our purposes was that for nine areas where it was possible to make such definite predictions, eight of the differences obtained from the responses of male and female college students were statistically significant in the predicted direction.

The second of Kinsey's research volumes calls into question many of the psychoanalytic generalizations but presents evidence for some kind of a basic biological difference in male and female sexuality. He stresses the fact that there is little if any difference in the anatomical or physiological bases of sex behavior in men and women. While the structures and specific sex hormones differ, the sensitive areas are the same or closely similar, and orgasm and the processes leading to it occur in the same manner. It is the *psychological* aspects of the sex response that show the clearest sex differences. Males have sex responses associated with a much wider variety of stimuli and situations than females do, so that they can be aroused in many more ways—by fantasies, by erotic pictures, by seeing male or female genitalia. Why this difference should exist is not clear to Kinsey, but it seems to arise from something deeper than differential cultural conditioning, since the same phenomenon can be observed in non-human mammals. He concludes after examining all the evidence with regard to neural and hormonal factors that there must be some sex difference in the cerebral cortex. This explanation seems hardly adequate, however, to explain the tremendous variability he reports with regard to female sexuality. A sizable proportion of women do seem to respond as strongly as men do to fantasy, sexual pictures, and so forth. It is interesting that in their range of sex behavior and attitudes, females seem to be *less* uniform than males. The theory of greater male variability does not apply here.

A somewhat different sort of biological explanation of sex differences has been proposed by Johnson and Terman. They discuss in some detail the physiological characteristics that are ordinarily included under the term *homeostasis*. They show that in the maintenance of constant body temperature, the acid-base relationship in the blood, constant blood sugar level, and gonadal activity, males are somewhat more stable than females. They propose the hypothesis that there is a difference in "mental homeostasis" that accounts for many of the psychological sex differences. Women tend to be more sensitive to external influences, more easily thrown off balance by them. It is interesting to note that this explanation, proposed so long before, fits in with some of the differences in sexuality that Kinsey outlines and with the differences in perception found by Witkin and his associates.

As evidence that sex differences are not entirely cultural, Johnson and Terman cite four facts. First, differences have been found in very young children. Second, neurotic tendencies in women have shown no relative decrease as women have been allowed more freedom. Third, institutional groups such as orphanage children whose environments have been closely similar over long periods of time show the same sort of differences as groups in the general population. Fourth, a growing body of research on animals shows plainly that sex hormones can influence behavior.

The fact that biological explanations of the origin of sex differences have become more convincing as the years have passed does not mean that cultural influences are being ignored. On the contrary, the progress of research has made it possible for us to see more clearly the ways in which the two can interact. It seems now that it is possible for any degree of "masculinity" or "femininity" to occur in an individual of either sex, but that a girl growing up does find certain attitudes, interests, and personality traits more congenial than others and tends to acquire another set. This slanting, this difference in tendency to acquire differential characteristics, is the factor that may have a biological basis.

There is little doubt that just what is acquired in the way of abilities, interests, and attitudes depends to a considerable extent on the culture in which a person grows up.

There is some evidence in a study reported by S. Smith that a general notion of male superiority develops in both boys and girls as they grow up. Girls and boys in each age group from eight to fifteen were asked to vote as to whether boys or girls possess to a greater degree each of nineteen desirable and fourteen undesirable traits. The striking fact was that the older the groups were the more favorable all the ratings made by *both* sexes were to boys. This is the more remarkable when we remember that during these school years the girls are consistently behaving better, having less trouble, and getting better marks than the boys.

Studies by Milner and by Rabban have been concerned with the interaction of sex and social status in role formation. There is evidence from both these studies that it is the personalities of the parents and the nature of the children's relationship to them that affect the learning of these sex roles. The Rabban study also shows that concepts of the sex roles develop in very young children, although there is some difference between the sexes and the social classes with regard to this. By the four- to five-year level, working-class boys show an awareness of sex roles. Middle-class boys develop it about a year later. Middle-class girls are the slowest to develop a clear-cut sex role concept.

Interest in psychological research on the topic of sex differences has grown by leaps and bounds since 1900. Tabulation of statistical information about eminent individuals has brought into sharp relief the fact that high achievement is very rare among women. In school achievement, however, girls usually excel boys. So far as tested abilities are concerned, there are some sex differences in the averages, but the distributions show a great deal of overlapping. Males tend to be higher in mathematical reasoning, spatial judgement, and science. Females average higher in verbal fluency, rote memorizing of more materials, perceptual speed, and dexterity. Careful analysis of what the distributions show has cast considerable doubt on the concept of greater male variability.

In interests, attitudes, and personality characteristics, much larger differences have been shown to exist, although even here there is considerable overlapping between distributions for the two sexes. Males show greater aggressiveness, females more symptoms of neuroticism and instability. Sex differences in likes and dislikes, in emotional and ethical attitudes, in the kind of success that is desired, in perceptual habits, and in sexual responsiveness to psychological stimulation have been shown.

There is evidence that the emotional differences are more closely tied in with fundamental biological differences than the ability differences are. In all these areas, however, concepts as to what the sex roles are seem to be of considerable importance.

Voice remains high-pitched. Beard and body hair do not appear in normal amount. Muscles have a tendency to be flabby and weight usually increases. The primary genital organs fail to develop normally, and, of course, the person is sterile. Male aggressiveness often fails to appear. If the glands are removed later in life, masculine traits change somewhat, and characteristics such as those mentioned above appear. In addition, the sexual impulse and interest in the opposite sex decrease considerably or disappear entirely [Bremer, 1959]. In short, the person becomes "feminized"; or, perhaps more accurately, he becomes something part way between masculine and feminine but not entirely either.

Equally profound changes occur when the ovaries are removed from females (termed *oöphorectomy* in humans, *spaying* in lower mammals), who then become "masculinized," or fall part way between masculine and feminine. The difference between the stallion and the gelding, the stallion and the mare; between the bull, the ox, and the cow; between the normal man and the eunuch or the normal man and the normal woman is caused in large measure by the presence or absence of the hormones secreted by the sex glands.

However, "presence or absence" does not necessarily imply "all or none." Here again, we must think in terms of blending. The hormones which play so important a part in masculinizing the male are normally found in smaller quantity in the female. On the other hand, the hormones which play so important a part in feminizing the female are normally found in smaller quantity in the male. Thus, masculinity or femininity is in large part a result of hormonal balance and may vary in degree as that balance varies. There is even some evidence to suggest that "there is no such thing as a specifically male or female hormone," that is, that these hormones are bisexual in nature, producing changes in both sexes [Robson, 1947].

But the changes they produce are relative to the character of the tissues and organs on which they act; and these, in turn, are basically masculine or feminine. There is even evidence suggesting that "part or parts of the central nervous system are masculine or feminine, depending on the sex of the individual" [Young, Goy, and Phoenix, 1964].

Maleness and femaleness, masculinity and femininity constitute a continuum. A continuum connotes differences of degree rather than simply "all or none." Maleness is not the same as masculinity, nor femaleness the same as femininity, though there is an overlap of terms as well as an overlap of anatomy and behavior. Generally speaking, "maleness" and "femaleness" refer to genetic constitution (determiners in the cells) and to primary sex organs, while "masculinity" and "femininity" refer to secondary sexual characteristics and, as discussed below, to learned behavior. "Maleness," "femaleness," "masculinity," and "femininity" all connote something positive; none represents merely a lack of its paired opposite.

An individual having ovaries, a uterus, and other typically female elements of genital anatomy is classified as female. If the individual also has a deep voice, the voice may be referred to as being masculine; but it will be *she* who has the masculine voice. An individual having testes and other typically male elements of genital anatomy is classified as male and referred to as *he*; but if *he* has scanty facial hair and small features he may be described as having a feminine appearance. If the individual exhibits a number of secondary characteristics ordinarily attributed to the opposite sex, he or she may be referred to as a feminine or masculine person, as the case may be. As a sidelight on our traditional attitude toward the two sexes in this connection, it is interesting to note that there is a special term, *effeminate*, applied to males as an expression of disapproval, with no similar special term applicable to females, for whom the term *masculine* does not connote quite the same type or degree of disapproval.

CULTURE AND EXPERIENCE

"Masculine" and "feminine" also apply to learned behavior, as suggested above. Because of genetic constitution (the determiners in the cells), anatomy, physiology, and hormones, typically each individual, as indicated earlier, begins life more or less "leaning" in the direction of masculine or feminine behavior. But with a few possible exceptions, biological differences do not by themselves determine such behavior. Biological differences do present possibilities for, and impose limitations upon, learning.

Each individual is born into a cultural framework which from birth onward determines to a considerable extent the manner of his life, the direction of his development, and the definition of what he is expected to do and become, depending upon his sexual classification. It is because of this fact of cultural framework within which the individual develops and the fact that culture varies among peoples, and even among groups within a people, that males or females do not exhibit identical behavior the world over or through time among a given people. Definitions of masculinity and femininity differ as culture varies and changes. For example, in colonial times in this country men wore clothing that would be considered highly effeminate today. In this country slenderness for women is considered to be more attractive than larger size, but in some countries a buxom woman more nearly meets the ideal. In the United States feminine modesty demands that in public a woman conceal her genital anatomy; in some countries she must cover her face. When life conditions change, alterations in behavior may ensue. For example, during the Second World War the balance between the sexes was upset because so many young men were in military service and hence unavailable to girls in their home communities. As a result, many girls became quite "unfeminine" in the degree to which they became aggressive in taking the initiative in arranging dates and lowered their standards as to acceptable appearance and manners of boys. In present-day America the population is so large and so varied, and our culture is changing so rapidly (though not at a uniform rate in all respects or in all subgroups), that there is considerable confusion and difference of opinion as to what standards of masculinity and femininity are acceptable.

But whatever the differences developed or permitted, in every known culture there are generally understood and expected means, such as clothing, hair styling, ornamentation, names, and terms of address, for readily distinguishing between the sexes. Deliberately to conceal sexual classification, intentionally to use misleading insignia, or effectively to disguise oneself as a member of the opposite sex so that others are deceived is considered a serious offense. Anything which produces only superficial camouflage rather than true disguise, as, for example, costuming in a masquerade or in a play, does not fall into the same category.

THE ROLES OF WOMEN:·QUESTION OF VALUES

Objectivity is one of the first requirements of scientific study. But who is qualified to make an objective investigation of women? Merely being a woman is not in itself a promising qualification. First, nobody seems quite sure what a woman really is. Second, any favorable statement about women by a woman is suspect as either wishful thinking or blind loyalty to her sex. But any negative statement about women by a woman is suspect as cattiness or sick self-hatred. On the other hand, merely being a man, that is, not being a woman, is hardly a more likely qualification. If a man speaks well of women, he is suspect as uxorious. But if he speaks out against them, he is neurotic or worse. Not being female, moreover, men are necessarily excluded from direct access to some of the primary data. Yet, every investigator is either a man or a woman, whatever those terms designate.

Objectivity in the study of women will then be, at best, difficult to achieve. In this, however, the study of women is not essentially different from any study of human beings by human beings. The dilemma is the same: How can we be objective about our own kind? How can we really understand those from whom we are very different? The resolution is in the selection of a suitable frame of reference and suitable objectives and methods of inquiry. The necessary degree of objectivity can be achieved by attending to the object studied. Making explicit the assumptions of inquiry is prerequisite to clarity, and cross verification by different investigators neutralizes the distorting effects of the personal equation. Sufficient progress in the study of humanity has now been made to justify optimism as to the possibility of objective studies of women. Despite the expression of misgivings and doubts by some, women are human, and the study of women is part of the study of human behavior and human nature. The same techniques can be and are being used. Qualified observers *may* be either male or female; they *must* be well trained in the methods and theory of their specialization.

Instead of attempting to relate the different ways of approaching the question of woman's nature, let us attempt to relate the investigation of woman as such to other inquiries that have started from some biological characteristic as the basis for the description and prediction of

From Ethel M. Albert, "The Roles of Women: Question of Values," in Seymour M. Farber and Roger H. L. Wilson (eds.), *The Potential of Woman*, McGraw-Hill Book Company, New York, 1963, pp. 105–115. Abridged and reprinted with permission of the publisher.

behavior. Perhaps "pseudobiological" is the better term in the present context. For, biology as science is very different from traditional notions associated with simplistic theories of biological determinism. Specifically, we are confronted by an ancient and honorable but naive and unscientific way of classifying human beings according to easily visible differences and with a causal theory that such visible differences as those of gender, or skin color, or height of forehead, or other physical traits are a reliable index to intelligence, artistic ability, mechanical aptitude, emotional stability, leadership skills, and other critical characteristics of persons.

Some categories are less useful than others for scientific purposes, when we mean by scientific purposes adequate description and prediction, and when the utility of a category is defined as follows: the characteristic chosen to define the category is a good predictive index of other shared characteristics. We can be quite sure that red hair is not a reliable index to ill temper; that fatness does not predict jollity; that skin color, while it is a useful index to probable color of eyes and hair, proportion of limbs to body, and the like, has no predictive value for intelligence, skills, or any other personal or behavioral characteristics. A study of woman, conducted on the assumption that gender predicts significantly no non-sex-linked phenomena is almost certain to be a scientific failure. What do we know about a human being, when we know the gender? We can assert with confidence that if any person is a mother, that person is surely a woman, or at least, is surely female. The same certainty attaches to statements about individuals designated as wife, sister, daughter, aunt, mother-in-law, daughter-in-law. They are bound to be female—though a few seem to have arrived at this enviable status via Copenhagen and the surgeon's knife. But we cannot judge whether any of them are intelligent or stupid, mentally well or ill, tenderhearted or tough as nails, industrious or lazy, attractive or ugly, happy or wretched. And if we do not know these things, we do not know much of value. With femaleness, as with skin color or height of forehead or other external signs, we cannot learn about persons from appearances.

Let me hasten to offer this reassurance. I am not at all asserting, as did overzealous egalitarians of a generation ago, that there is no difference between male and female. This is rather to overstate the case. I am unconditionally on the side of those who say, "Vive la différence." That males and females are different from each other at least physiologically is one of the few relatively clear and simple facts of life. But the male-female difference is a difference, not the difference. What remains problematic is this: for any physical-biological difference, what difference does the difference make? This is the crucial question for interpreting the behavioral significance of any physiological characteristic singled out for special study. And it is here that the simplistic pseudobiological categories fail.

The rejection of broad, obvious categories like race or sex or body type is perfectly compatible with the view that physiological factors are indispensable elements in the description and prediction of human nature and behavior. Long-standing arguments about biological determinism as opposed to some sort of antibiological or nonphysical determinism only get in the way of clarity. All human behavior is biological; but it is never only that. Mankind is a sociocultural being. Biological variations and sociocultural variations, not simplified stereotypes, are the object of serious, scientific inquiry. What any individual becomes depends in part on nature and in part on sociocultural values and ideal role-models, as these are worked out in the specific circumstances of each individual life history. For the study of sex differences, we may say that nature—biology, if you will—makes us male or female; the values and norms of the society in which we develop make us men or women; and the interrelations of these factors with the other biological, sociological, and situational components of experience make us the kinds of persons we become. No single factor explains the complex totality of any individual personality or of the human species.

No human society overlooks so patent a biological contrast as that between male and female. But we find cross-cultural differences of great magnitude in what various societies think is female nature, as distinct from male nature; in what different societies construct as the ideal woman and the ideal man; and, if that were not diversity enough, we find that everywhere actual behavior is permitted to diverge to a greater or lesser degree from society's ideals and role-models.

First things first. Let us start with this question: is the male or the female by nature the more sexually aggressive? As every nice girl in Western culture knows, it is the male who is the aggressor, while the passive female submits with good or bad grace. But if we ask this question of Africans or of American Indians, we do not get the same reply. Obviously, they tell us, women are more driven by sex than men. Among the Zuni Indians as among ourselves, there are stories of fearful newlyweds facing up to the terrors of the first night of marriage. But the Zuni stories feature the groom, not the bride, in a state of fear. I suspect that not a few males from other societies, possibly even our own, understand the Zuni groom's sentiments very well, but unlike the Zuni, they have been brought up to believe that the male is the fearless aggressor and that any display or feeling of fear is unmasculine. Now, I do not know which version is "biologically" true. Perhaps social expectations work on nature's endowment, which is probably variable to begin with, so that some grow up hot, some grow up cold, and those fare best whose biology is in harmony with the prevailing sociocultural notion about what is natural.

Emotional stability is another axis of variation. It is obvious, to some, that women are by nature less stable emotionally than men, that it is natural for women to cry easily and otherwise to show their feelings, whereas men are more easily able to control and conceal them. But again, the belief about what is natural and whether observed behavior corresponds to belief depend on where we happen to be. Edward T. Hall, in his book, *The Silent Language*, offers as his illustration of this point the views of male-female difference in Iran. There—in a thoroughly patriarchal society, where men are deemed the superiors of women—it is expected that women will be practical, cool, and calculating, whereas men are expected to show emotions, to be sensitive and intuitive, to prefer poetry to logic. And so it is.

To present further cases would only be to labor the point: there is universal recognition of differences between males and females—let us be thankful for small favors—but whatever the differences, they are not so strikingly uniform that human beings everywhere must come to the same conclusions about them. We have, moreover, a hint of part of the answer to the question "What differences does a difference make?" What is believed to be true of the nature of males and females influences significantly the content of ideal models constructed for the formation of character. Within a given society, there is a statistical tendency to develop according to socially defined ideals of appropriate behavior. But viewing humanity on a world-wide scale, we find no consensus. Again, nature makes us male or female, but the beliefs and values of our society make us the kinds of men or women we become. It would nonetheless be again erring in the direction of oversimplification to assert, as some social scientists have done, that observed behavior is fully explicable by social definitions of roles. Each individual perforce has a multiplicity of biological characteristics, sexual and otherwise, which may or may not be compatible with role expectations. Actual behavior is the product of complex and usually unconscious negotiations among the demands of diverse roles and diverse individual characteristics. In the dynamics of everyday life, there is much more room for individuality than is suggested by descriptions of societal norms and ideals. Permissiveness with respect to departures from established norms varies from one place to another. However, in no society is there a demand for complete conformity. Secondary norms are regularly set up to permit scope to the multiplex character of any concrete individual.

An adequate descriptive account of women would have to include the variety of beliefs about the nature of women, the variety of ideal role-models assigned to women as women but also to women as persons, and the crooked course of the flow of actual behavior relative to ideal models. Even within one society, there is so high a degree of heterogeneity in the actualities that one is led to suspect that although there are millions of females in this world, there is no such thing as "woman." To study "woman," or even "women," is to study a figment of our traditional classification of humanity. For, if anything is true of "woman," it must be true of women in all times and places. To study women as female persons is another matter. Specifically feminine roles and characteristics can then be viewed in their relationship with other types of roles and characteristics, and these all add up to meaningful totals.

Studies of women in Western culture encounter a peculiar problem. In most societies, ideals are kept within hailing distance of realities. They are understood as prescribing and proscribing behavior, thus as limiting development by channeling it. In the Western tradition, however, ideals tend to be so far above and beyond common reality that their realization is not likely, except in the rare instance.

Extravagant glorification is not the remedy for traditional degradation. Exploration of the potential of women is part of the world-wide exploration of the potential of humanity generally. Ideals too easily realized do not sufficiently spur us on to optimum growth. But we must distinguish between ideals which stimulate constructive action and the fictional products of dreams and unfulfilled needs. Impossible ideals do not bring out the best in us. They are as restrictive and deforming as the worst kind of tyranny. The construction of viable ideals for the future requires reliable factual information about humankind, male and female, not to cut down ideals to what has been achieved or can be done without much effort but rather to fit them to what can be achieved in fact, rather than in fancy, and to provide some assurance that we will be protected against the disappointments that flights from reality almost surely bring in their train. Being fully human is a high enough ideal for all; it contains the potential for woman and the potential for man, inextricably linked together. By all means, let imagination and hope soar, but untrammeled by false notions and untroubled by false problems.

In short, one of the factors making us what we are and contributing to the development of differences between the sexes is experience within a given culture. But "experience within a given culture" implies more than merely experience within a given environment which leaves the individual largely the same personality that he was before the experience, as, for example, an experience in the mountains, in another city, or in a foreign country. "Experience within a given culture" implies the molding of the individual within a framework, the formation of habits, attitudes, conditioned responses, beliefs, values, and patterns of behavior which together determine in large part the individual's way of life. The culture becomes *internalized*; it becomes part of the individual's personality, so to speak.

Some experience is sexually colored; some is not. From infancy boys and girls are subjected to different educative processes. Their games and toys are different and reflect their future adult roles. The stories they read or hear tend more and more as they get older to have a definite masculine or feminine coloring. The standards set for them by their parents and by society at large differ. There is a selection of experience so that different environmental factors act upon the two sexes. Each is encouraged to do certain things and prohibited, or at least strongly discouraged, from doing others. Each has restrictions on freedom but in different ways. Girls are given more protection, and they grow to expect it. Boys are allowed more independence, and they grow to take it for granted as a masculine prerogative.

When we think of the development of social life through a long period of time, we see that certain fundamental, unchangeable differences between the sexes could constitute forks in the road leading to the emergence of different patterns of life, different standards, different expectations, and different attitudes of each sex toward the other. Take, for example, the fact that women are physically vulnerable, not only because of their size and strength, but also because their structure permits the possibility of imposing sexual intercourse upon them against their will, something for which there is no parallel in men. On the other hand, men's vulnerability lies in the urgency of their sex drive and their susceptibility to sex appeal. Take the fact that pregnancy and childbearing encumber women but that there is no similar encumbrance among men. Or take the fact that maternity is subject to proof but paternity is not. In the light of such differences and others like them, it is not surprising that there are somewhat different patterns of life that constitute the mold into which individuals are not only squeezed but also into which they are assumed to fit "naturally."

The differences in standards of behavior set up by the group are expressed in exaggerated fashion in the old nursery rhyme: "What are little boys made of? Snips and snails and puppy-dog tails. And what are little girls made of? Sugar and spice and everything nice." "He's a real boy," says the proud father, implying that there is a standard of "boyness" and that his son is living up to that standard. The half-shocked mother who says, "Boys will be boys," implies that being a boy is different from being a girl. The words "tomboy" and "sissy" show that there are rather well-defined roles of behavior even for children and that deviation from those roles is not socially approved. In short, each sex tends to learn to act as it is expected to act. Masculinity and femininity are cores around which the structure of personality develops [Terman and Miles, 1936]. An individual is born male or female, but he or she learns to be masculine or feminine, as the case may be. Sex is genetic, but gender is acquired.

There is another aspect of the problem, however. It is true that the child is faced with two more or less distinct patterns of life—masculine and feminine—and is expected to adopt one of them. But masculinity and femininity are not entirely distinct; they overlap. Some individuals have more difficulty than others in living up to the standard set for their sex. A confusion in roles may result, and the integration of personality sometimes becomes difficult [Terman and Miles, 1936]. On the other hand, because learned differences do change, and because masculinity and femininity do overlap, in some respects our society is becoming more tolerant of the overlap. Increasingly in this country we are accepting with approval—even at times expecting—either sex exhibiting characteristics and types of behavior which have been traditionally associated with the opposite sex. Take, for example, women's increased directness in their approach to men, as already mentioned, women's engagement in competitive occupations, men's increased interest in children and increased participation in child care, and women's smoking cigarettes and wearing trousers.

Besides the sexually colored experience to which a person is subjected there are innumerable experiences that are entirely individual. They are so obvious as to need no further explanation, but they play an ample role in making us what we are.

No one of these three types of factors—inborn traits, physiological processes, or experience—is sufficient alone to determine individual or sex differences. They all react one upon the other, making the individual as well as the group the product of nature plus nurture.

Possible reactions and attitudes

There are several possible attitudes that one may assume toward the differences between men and women. It is important to note, however, that one must assume some attitude; one cannot continue to exist without taking some stand, more or less consciously, on the fact that the human race is divided into two sexes.

DENIAL

One may attempt to ignore or deny the differences. The early feminist did this. She believed that there were no really important differences between men and women and that the apparent differences were the result of training. Why not, then, let women follow in men's footsteps? Why talk about things masculine and things feminine? Why should not men and women be duplicates of one another? The feminist made a worthy contribution to the raising of woman's social position and the achievement of long-needed rights and privileges, but she did overlook some fundamentals.

Many educators have ignored the differences between the sexes. In some colleges and universities, for example, the curriculum is one traditionally designed for men. They are men's schools which women are permitted to attend. Some of these schools make little or no allowance for the fact that the roles of the sexes will be different after graduation. Whether or not they should be different is beside the point; they are different. Difference of role is in a sense a sex difference, and it makes for sexually colored experience. Such schools may have fine departments to give occupational and cultural training to both sexes; but they too often neglect the girl who is to become wife-homemaker-mother. Training for her comparable in quality and extent to that provided for an occupation is all too frequently lacking. The great majority of women become homemakers. Yet there is often an assumption that no difference exists between the needs and interests of men and the needs and interests of women; and many curricula are designed for neuter celibates.

Husbands who expect their wives to react as men and wives who are surprised when their husbands act in masculine fashion ignore sex differences. Mothers who fail to realize that when sons marry they tend more than do daughters to drift away from the parental family and consequently chafe at the bit when the mother attempts to hold them close to her as if they were still boys; men who have no understanding of a woman's desire for motherhood; men and women who do not see that there are deep-set differences in attitude toward sexual experience both marital and premarital; the father who wanted a son and had a daughter but who tried to rear her as a son only to see her fall between two chairs instead of sitting on either—these and innumerable others ignore or deny that there are differences between men and women.

"MASCULINE PROTEST"

A second possible reaction is what Adler termed the *masculine protest*. There are women who at some time in their lives have been made to feel inferior because they were female. They have, therefore, grown to resent the fact that they are women. Because they dislike being women, they wish they were men. Some of them strive in a way to be men.

On numerous occasions the writer has asked groups of girls these questions: How many of you are glad you are girls? How many of you would like to be men? In every group of any size there have been individuals who said they were sorry they were girls and wished they could be men. In one study the writer procured from college girls anonymous written replies to the question, "Have you at any time during the past year wished that you were or could be a man?" Of 393 girls, 145 (37 per cent) answered in the affirmative. No doubt such girls confuse somewhat being men and having the privileges of men, for the reason most frequently given for wishing to be a man was that men have more freedom of activity than do women. The second most frequent reason was menstruation. For many girls the wish was not very strong, and they were aware of it only occasionally. There was scarcely a full-fledged "masculine protest." Nevertheless, it is apparent that they were to some degree dissatisfied with their feminine role and status. One rarely finds a similar reaction among boys or men who are asked whether they would like to be girls or women.

The result is that women, some of whom are discontented and question the desirability of being women, and men, who rarely question the desirability of being men, are expected to work out an adjustment in marriage as if there were no difference in attitude toward role or status. There are, of course, many women who are as wholeheartedly enthusiastic about being women as any man could be about being a man. But since there are also women who do have reservations about their sexual classification, it is clear that men who lack insight or whose attitude and behavior accentuate the very differences that these women resent may contribute to the maladjustments both seek to avoid.

Women who exhibit the "masculine protest" to an extreme degree sometimes set out to surpass men in one way or another. Sometimes they try to demean men by becoming economic leeches. Sometimes they encourage affection of men, only to humiliate them, never forming enduring emotional attachments with any man.

There are instances in which men exhibit a "masculine protest." If a man is doubtful of his ability to fulfill the masculine role and to live up to the standards that the group has set for men, he may overstress the importance of being manly and may try to avoid being put to any test that might possibly bring to light his supposed inadequacy [Adler, 1937].

REFORM

Another possible attitude toward sex differences is that of reform. This one overlaps with others; in fact, all these attitudes overlap. A person may recognize that there are sex differences and set out to do something about them. This is similar to, but not identical with, the attitude of the person who refuses to admit that there are basic differences and sets out to change those superficial ones which seemingly exist.

CONFLICT

Another possible reaction is one of perpetual conflict. This is exhibited in the "masculine protest" but also in the person who recognizes the differences and takes his stand as defender of the fort in such a way that the sexes seem to be perennially at odds. They are considered lifelong antagonists, with no chance of ever successfully combining forces in a cooperative venture.

ADJUSTMENT

The most potentially fruitful attitude is one of mutual adjustment. The fact that men and women are different is recognized and accepted. Then let them adjust to each other in a way that promotes their mutual satisfaction in life and makes possible the fullest use of their resources.

Whether the differences are inborn or acquired through training and experience is beside the point. If they exist, and we have assumed that they do, they are part of the world of reality in which we live, a world in which the greatest satisfaction comes through most intelligent adjustment. We live with people as they are, not as we should like them to be or as they may be years hence when society has become different from what it is at present.

This same need for adjustment exists in marriage. Women marry men; men marry women. Whether or not they have identical possibilities is an academic question. They are different both because they were born that way and because they have been made that way. So far as the individual and his marriage are concerned, the question of nature versus nurture is unimportant. He must adjust to the other person as that person is. Individual differences as well as sex differences must be taken into account.

Adjustment does not imply that one person shall change to suit the whims of the other, that one shall do all the adjusting, or that one shall be imposed upon by the other. It implies merely that on the basis of the understanding of difference those things be done that increase the mutual satisfaction of the persons concerned.

WHAT DO YOU THINK?

1. What are some of the more important similarities and differences between the sexes, other than those listed in this chapter?

2. Which of these differences are inborn? Which acquired?

3. What part does culture play in creating sex differences?

4. Would it be possible for a given culture to be of such a nature that sex differences and roles were completely reversed? What would be the limitations on such a possibility?

5. Which of the similarities and differences between the sexes make it easier for men and women to get along together? Which make it more difficult?

6. In what fields of activity are men superior? In which are women superior?

7. If you were to set out to improve the experience and education of the two sexes, what changes would you make in American social life?

8. Nowadays, do women need more protection by law than men do?

9. Do women really want equality with men? Do men want women to have such equality? Do men want equality with women?

10. If women continue to get more rights and privileges, what is the result likely to be "in the long run"?

11. Should women strive to be as much like men as possible, as different from men as possible, or complementary to men? What would be the probable result of each of these alternatives?

12. What are some of the false assumptions that the sexes make about each other?

SELECTED READINGS

Anshen, Ruth Nanda (ed.): *The Family: Its Function and Destiny*, rev. ed., Harper & Row, Publishers, Incorporated, New York, 1959, chap. 19. This chapter by Erich Fromm supports the thesis that "the character typical of men and women in Western culture is determined by their respective social roles."

Cavan, Ruth Shonle (ed.): *Marriage and the Family in the Modern World*, Thomas Y. Crowell Company, New York, 1960, chap. 5. A discussion of the differences between the sexes and why women live longer than men.

Landis, Judson T., and Mary G. Landis: *Building a Successful Marriage*, 4th ed., Prentice-Hall, Inc., Englewood Cliffs, N.J., 1963, chap. 2. A discussion of the differences between the sexes.

Landis, Paul H.: *For Husbands and Wives*, Appleton-Century-Crofts,

Inc., New York, 1956, chap. 3. The author suggests that men and women are "equal but different."

—— : *Making the Most of Marriage*, 2d ed., Appleton-Century-Crofts, Inc., New York, 1960, chap. 3. The native endowment, drives and appetites, and emotional and psychological differences between the sexes.

Mead, Margaret: *Sex and Temperament in Three Primitive Societies*, New American Library of World Literature, Inc., New York, 1950. An anthropologist's study of the role of culture in the development of masculinity and femininity.

Scheinfeld, Amram: *Women and Men*, Harcourt, Brace & World, Inc., New York, 1944. An analysis of a great variety of sex differences: physical, psychological, achievement, etc.

Seward, Georgene H.: *Sex and the Social Order*, McGraw-Hill Book Company, New York, 1946, chap. 9. The role of culture in determining masculinity and femininity.

Terman, Lewis M., and Catherine Cox Miles: *Sex and Personality*, McGraw-Hill Book Company, New York, 1936. A study of masculinity and femininity based upon a masculinity-femininity test administered to various kinds of persons of both sexes.

Tyler, Leona E.: *The Psychology of Human Differences*, 2d ed., Appleton-Century-Crofts, Inc., New York, 1956. A discussion of the origins of sex differences and of differences in tested achievements, in personality, in motivation, etc.

chapter 2

MARRIAGE IN MODERN AMERICA

IN THE PREVIOUS CHAPTER the point was made that men and women are complementary but that this complementariness is not manifested uniformly throughout their numerous and varied characteristics and relationships. The complementary nature of the sexes is most clearly apparent in connection with affectional, sexual, and reproductive behavior. Except in the case of deviants with regard to the first two and except in the case of hypothetically possible experimental parthenogenesis with regard to the third, this aspect of complementariness may be considered universal and permanent.

In other respects, however, the complementary nature of the sexes is more flexible and more sensitive to cultural influence. It is, therefore, subject to change. Nowhere is this more apparent than in the roles of the sexes in present-day American social and occupational life and in marriage and family living. The roles of the sexes, both as expected and as played, exhibit variations relative to socioeconomic class and educational level. However, since this book is addressed primarily to college and university students, most of whom are either middle-class members or middle-class aspirants, a discussion of roles — and perhaps later of other topics — with, at times, some degree of middle-class orientation is not entirely inappropriate.

American marriage in earlier times

In earlier times in this country, for example, in colonial days, the family exhibited more prominently than it does today what are termed its *institutional aspects*. Such elements as the support of the family by the husband-father, the maintenance of the home and the bearing and care of children by the wife-mother, mutual protection, and the production of goods were considered criteria for evaluating the success or failure of marriage and family life. The man was accepted as the head of the family. He had considerable authority over both his wife and their children. This authority was supported by the mores and to some extent by the law. There was a clear-cut division of labor by sex both in the home and in the occupational world outside the home. One could accurately speak of "men's work" and "women's work."

There were couples who developed deep conjugal love and devotion. But love, especially love with a romantic coloring, was not considered the *sine qua non* which it has approached today. The sexual aspect of marriage was tolerated by women as essential to childbearing and as unavoidable in fulfilling the function of wife. We may safely assume that fewer women than at present either achieved or were aware of the possibility of achieving satisfaction in their sexual relations. We may be sure that fewer women expressed such interest and awareness and that still fewer demanded such satisfaction as an essential criterion for the evaluation of marriage.

In their activities leading up to the wedding, young people had, of course, to get acquainted. But their contacts were restricted both by the mores and by the common practice and probably universal acceptance of chaperonage. There were at least some rules governing propriety relative to discussion, so there were restrictions not only on the topics a young couple might discuss but also upon the content and extent of their discussion. Undoubtedly young people made some appraisals of each other in terms of personal attractiveness and had romantic inclinations toward each other. There was a place for romantic love, but it was not allowed to overshadow other considerations.

Under such circumstances the answer to the question, "What are the qualities of a good husband or a good wife?" would reflect the emphasis upon the institutional aspects of family life. One might well imagine that many an American woman in the early days set up criteria not dissimilar to those expressed by a Boer woman who lived on the African frontier. Said she, "I am sick of all this talk of choosing and choosing. . . . If a man is healthy and does not drink, and has a good little handful of stock, and a good temper, and is a good Christian, what great difference can it make to a woman which man she takes? There is not so much difference between one man and another" [Leyburn, 1935, p. 129]. Such an attitude makes choice of marriage partner relatively easy because the criteria of choice are readily observable and do not depend largely on personal taste. It therefore permits both more help in making the choice and more control of the choice on the part of the young couple's families.

In those early days many a couple considered their marriage to be successful in the absence of love. Because of this and also because of the widespread opposition to divorce and the division of labor which made husband and wife economically necessary to each other, the divorce rate was low. In a sense, in earlier times the marriage was considered more important than the persons in it. The couple were expected by society to perform duties, make sacrifices, and accept circumstances, unless extreme, for the good of the marriage. Now the marriage is considered less important than the persons in it, dissolvable when it ceases to meet their personal expectations. When the marriage is considered less important than the persons in it, this appraisal is the outgrowth of individual judgment and voluntary perspective rather than the result of law and custom.

To a considerable extent, education, religious worship, recreation, and manufacturing were carried on in or through the family. Because communities were small and travel to and communication with the outside were both slow and difficult, the pressure of primary group control was considerable. That is, the same group lived together, worked together, traded with one another, worshiped together, played together, and banded together for mutual aid in time of crisis. Hence each family was an integral unit in a face-to-face society. Therefore, whatever the conditions and relationships within a marriage, the marriage was held together in part by forces exerted from the outside.

Changes in American marriage

Present-day American marriage still entails an ample economic element, and the institutional factors in family living are far from absent. Division of labor by sex, support, protection, mutual aid, and child-bearing and rearing still exist. There are still manufacturing activities, education of children, recreational pursuits, and religious worship carried on in the home or through the family. But the picture is changing. Many of these activities, at least to a considerable degree, increasingly center in nonfamily agencies, as shown diagrammatically in Figure 1. The increase in urban and suburban living has broken down the primary face-to-face groups, thus removing some of the societal support from marriage, not in the sense of reducing societal approval of marriage but rather in the sense of there being fewer external, societal, and institutional forces acting to hold marriages structurally intact. There is increased emphasis upon how persons of opposite sex feel about one another and what kind of interrelationships they establish. In short, in present-day America, there is much less emphasis upon the institutional aspects and much more upon the personality aspects of marriage and family life. This change is manifested in numerous ways. It is important to note, however, that at no known period in history, among no known people, has marriage succeeded on the basis of emotion alone. There is always found some degree of cooperation, through division of labor by

(a)

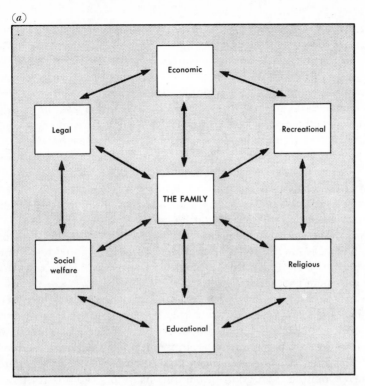

(b)

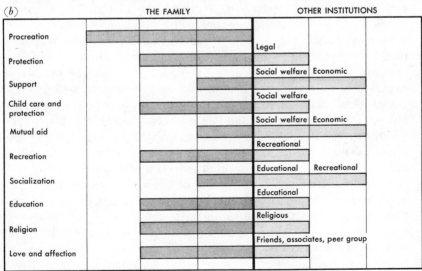

Figure 1. (a) Diagrammatic representation of the interrelatedness of social institutions, showing the family as an integral part of the social structure. (b) The way in which nonfamily agencies have taken over traditional family functions. (The proportions indicated are not intended to be exact.) One problem of the present-day American family is to develop personality functions to replace those lost to institutions.

sex, in the maintenance of a way of life. American marriage is no exception.

In the activities and events preceding the wedding, young persons have a degree of freedom not so great as that found in some cultures but conspicuously greater than that which existed in this country in earlier days. Chaperonage is not yet entirely passé, but it is much less commonly expected or accepted and is often somewhat perfunctory. Some degree of physical contact between individuals of opposite sex is widely and casually accepted, although there is far from universal agreement on the matter of premarital sexual intercourse. Discussion is almost, but not quite, unrestrained. There are young persons of college and even high school age who discuss topics such as sex and reproduction more freely and with less embarrassment with dating partners than married couples of yesteryear discussed such topics with each other after the birth of their first baby. It is to be expected that such freedom would have some bearing upon the criteria set up and the judgments made relative to the choice of marriage partner.

In marriage and in choosing for marriage, that element given greatest prominence is love. Today in this country most people "marry for love," although physical appeal is an often undetected counterfeit. "Marrying for love" implies a primary emphasis upon emotion, upon how two individuals feel about one another, and upon personal satisfaction, and a corresponding reduction in emphasis upon the institutional aspects of marriage. Hence, new criteria of success in marriage are established. New qualities desirable in a husband or wife are highlighted. New opportunities are presented for richness of living and completeness of sharing in marriage. But along with those opportunities go new problems, for when people do not find in marriage the personal satisfaction that they anticipated, they feel justified in seeking escape. Other social changes which we shall discuss in a later chapter have made such escape easier than it used to be. One of the side effects of "marrying for love" is an increase in marital instability and hence of divorce. This is not meant to imply that more marriages are unhappy today than in earlier times, for there is no known way of making such a comparison. "Unhappy" and "unstable" are not synonymous.

When marriage is based upon love and when personal satisfaction is given more weight than institutional factors, the responsibility for wise choice of marriage partner rests upon the shoulders of the individuals making the choice. Today they can and do get little help from their families. Often the help that is volunteered is rejected. In a way this makes choice of marriage partner more difficult than it used to be because the elements upon which it is based are less readily observable, depend upon personal taste rather than a cultural standard, rest upon an appraisal of another personality largely extracted from that individual's background, and are so variable that each individual who makes such a choice assumes it to be unique. One can hardly imagine a young American college student of today saying anything even remotely approximating the statement of the Boer woman quoted earlier.

As contrasted with marriage of the past, present-day American marriage presents both sexes with a changed and expanded concept of the roles expected of husband and wife. Put another way, each sex is expected to play a greater multiplicity of roles, to do a wider variety of things. In a sense, each individual is expected to be a larger number of different persons.

THE ROLE OF THE HUSBAND

American society gives evidence of moving toward an equalitarian type of family life. But not all groups and subgroups are moving toward this end at the same rate. There are differences among the various segments of society; and within groups families are not necessarily uniform. The result is that, while many men are assuming the new husband-father role as described below, there are other men whose roles are more nearly traditional and whose wives, with themselves, accept and are happy in a patriarchal or semipatriarchal type of family life. Hence, the generalizations below are not universally applicable. They do, however, represent a trend.

The male is still expected to be the primary provider for the family. In some states his wife may sue for divorce on the ground of nonsupport should he fail to do so. However, he is not necessarily the only provider. There is a rapidly increasing number of families in which that role is shared by both spouses.

According to census definition the husband-father is head of the family. But functionally he is not head of the family in the traditional, authoritarian, patriarchal sense. His expressed judgments relative to family behavior and welfare may be given considerable weight, but they are not necessarily considered the last word. He has the legal right to determine domicile for his family, and in some states he may sue his wife for divorce on the ground of desertion if she refuses to join him in the residence he has established. To a considerable extent the demands of his occupation take precedence over those of the wife's occupation or desires in determining where the couple will live and to what socioeconomic level their common life will be geared. There is an increasing inclination for family decisions to be made by husband and wife, or even by all family members, jointly rather than by strictly masculine decree. Yet there are many males who still assume that the husband has some natural or inborn right to a majority of the family votes. They sometimes express this as "If a husband and wife cannot agree on a particular issue, shouldn't the husband, because he is the male, have the last word, the right to make the final decision?" Such a statement reflects a traditional assumption taken for granted rather than insight into the new

SOME CONFLICTS IN ROLE CONCEPTS

Social changes in American society have brought with them changes in roles. These changes are particularly apparent in the sexual roles expected of young men and women, for the new expectations find themselves side by side with the old. Modern concepts of masculine and feminine roles have not yet replaced but coexist with the traditional ones. Moreover, they are often mutually exclusive, so that the young person trying to fulfill his role finds himself in conflict. Although somewhat exaggerated, the following examples suggest some of the opposing attitudes toward dual sexual roles that young people face today. Each individual must find his own solution.

The young husband recalls that in the home of his parents his mother happily waited on his father, who enjoyed the service, and he believes that theirs was a successful marriage relationship . . .

sort of interrelationship toward which American marriage is moving. It also suggests entering marriage with the objective of getting one's own way, assuming that one is naturally better qualified than someone else to make decisions, imposing one's will upon another person rather than making a mutual contribution through acceptance, giving, and the recognition of variation in competence depending upon the issue under consideration. Masculine dominance is a point of view to which many modern wives do not subscribe.

In his role as father, the present-day male is more than a biological parent, a provider, and a disciplinarian. Many a man shares the lives of his children, understands them and openly shows affection for them, plays a part in their rearing, and participates in infant care. He may attend classes for prospective fathers, read books on child psychology, participate in the PTA, and force his growing bulk, softening muscles, and queasy stomach through the "survival test" of a boy scout hike and cook-out in order to prove that he is a pal to his son. He not only does not expect his children to be "seen but not heard" but is more likely to resign himself to being neither seen nor heard when his children reach adolescence and begin to date. He is often unashamed to be seen pushing a baby carriage or hanging out a baby's laundry which he himself has done. If his children attend college, he may willingly continue their financial support beyond the point at which they have become emotionally and socially independent of him and resistant to whatever remnant

yet in the new concept of "togetherness" he is expected to participate in household activities traditionally assigned to the wife.

of paternal authority he has sought to retain. In some cases such financial support continues after the wedding. In earlier times financial independence and personal independence were more likely to occur simultaneously, thus drawing a sharper line of demarcation representing the termination of parental control. Nowadays that line of demarcation is often ragged, and the parent-child relationship is equivocal, making for problems with which neither side is well prepared to cope.

There is a growing feeling that the home is no longer only a place of comfort and refuge for the male; it is becoming an area of participation. This means that there is not only sharing of family life on the part of the husband-father but also more participation in the tasks of housekeeping. Clear-cut division of labor by sex within the home is breaking down. We can no longer speak of "men's work" and "women's work" with the simple accuracy of earlier days. The shift is far from complete. There are still many males who resist housekeeping and participate reluctantly, if at all, or participate only in emergencies. Their resistance is often most apparent when the task in question is symbolic and doing it regularly might seem to indicate acquiescence in a change in masculine status or authority. For example, preparing his own breakfast is for many a man such a symbolic task. In earlier times when a man did pre-dawn chores on the farm, he could well expect his wife to have a substantial breakfast ready for him when he returned to the house. Nowadays breakfast tends to precede work rather than follow a part of it, and is often light, requiring little or no preparation. Yet, not because of inability to do it or because of time or energy limitations but rather because a carryover of attitude has made breakfast symbolic, many a man insists that it be prepared by his wife. In his estimation, "getting up to get my breakfast" is an indication of wifely commitment and effectiveness. There are some women who do not want their husbands to take any part in housekeeping. On the other hand, however, there is an increasing number of husbands who willingly do household tasks.

Exactly how much housekeeping a particular man will do must be determined by a number of factors: the time available to each spouse; how much of the total housekeeping job must be done after the husband's regular work hours; how the job may best be done, given the skills and interests of the husband and wife; the attitude of each person toward his own role and toward the other person and that person's role; what kind of marriage the couple expect to achieve; and how much they appreciate leisure time together. Too broad generalizations as to what responsibility a modern husband should assume are likely to be less than helpful. What is needed is not generalization but rather particularization. The question is, "What is the best arrangement for this couple with their personalities and abilities and their specific situation?" A problem often arises when an attempt is made to impose in advance a traditional pattern of family living without taking into account emerging and shifting variables.

Textbooks and contemporary
magazine articles instruct him to
be warm, loving, and gentle with
his wife, remaining always
sensitive to her needs . . .

yet his male friends reflect
and support a traditional concept
of masculinity in which the
husband directs the marriage
relationship with a strong hand
and largely controls the social
pattern of the family.

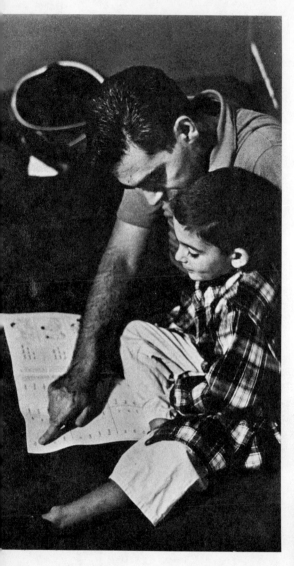

He should be a pal, or a buddy, to the children, meeting them at their own level and offering wise, gentle guidance in the development of their interests . . .

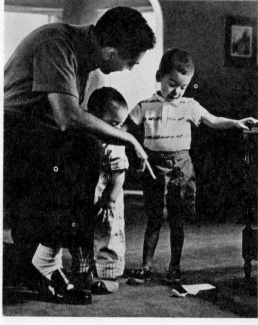

yet he is expected to be the authority figure in matters of discipline, to clamp down on the child from his superior position as an adult male.

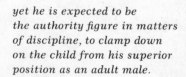

The husband of today is expected to be a companion to his wife, to share leisure time with her and to engage with her in social activities and recreational pursuits. This creates a problem for both marriage partners, since it implies not only sex-limited interests on the part of each but also common interests. With the present-day awareness of women's affectional and sexual nature, the male is expected to be both a lover and a sexual partner in a sense somewhat different from that of earlier times. The difference emerges from a new insight into female sexual respon-

A modern father is expected to be active in community activities which make heavy demands on his time . . .

yet tradition, based on male strength and economics, expects him to devote full time to providing his family with ample physical comforts and financial security. Time and energy place limits on his activity, so that he must be selective.

He is expected to encourage his wife in her own self-fulfillment, which may mean simply admiring her ceramic work. However it may also mean his wife's involvement in a career . . .

yet he has been brought up to value financial independence and regards being the family's sole provider of goods as essential to his feeling of manliness.

siveness and the possible means through which it may be evoked. This recognition that women may achieve, and in increasing numbers seek, sexual satisfaction presents the male with a new problem of understanding and a new orientation for his sexual drive, for it is no longer a simple matter of directing his efforts to his finding sexual release himself through the use of a female partner who derives no comparable release herself, but rather one of his finding his greatest satisfaction both through and simultaneously with the sexual satisfaction of his wife. This means that his sexual drive must be oriented toward giving pleasure as well as toward getting pleasure. Hence a new demand for understanding, insight, self-discipline, and the combining of sex and love is placed upon the husband.

In the last analysis, the final appraisal of a man's success or failure as a husband is made by only one person, his wife. This appraisal rests primarily, but not entirely, on what kind of person he is and what her feelings about him are. It is at its core a personal appraisal and to a considerable degree strips the husband of cultural props and the protective coloration of overt conformity to cultural norms and relative success in meeting the criteria which reflect the institutional aspects of marriage. A man may be admirable in the eyes of his friends or even of his wife, have prestige in his occupation, supply his family with all that is necessary to maintain a more than adequate standard of living, be moral, law-abiding, and active in the church; yet if his wife no longer loves him and they do not get along happily together, the assumption is made that he has failed as a husband. The converse may also be true.

This suggests that the expected role of husband or wife is defined only in part by society at large. It is also defined in part by the tastes, attitudes, hopes, expectations, assumptions, and biases of one other person, the marriage partner.

THE ROLE OF THE WIFE

The expectation that a wife will be a homemaker and, if biologically possible, a mother is probably as ancient as marriage itself. In spite of the present-day increase in the number of gainfully employed married women, it is still commonly taken for granted in this country. Even when a wife has full-time gainful employment and has hired housekeeping help, she is expected to take major responsibility for household planning and for the supervision of such help. Whereas typically the family's socioeconomic level is determined largely by the husband's occupation, the tone of family living is determined to a considerable extent by the wife's contribution to homemaking, using the word "homemaking" as involving many intangibles not included in the concept of "housekeeping." Homemaking is an economic as well as a cultural and emotional contribution to family living. What a wife does as a homemaker may not involve a salary, but it has money value.

A woman's choice of role is complicated today by the fact that she is caught between the pressures of three forces. On the one hand, there are the weights of tradition and her biological nature pushing her in the direction of homemaking and motherhood. On the other hand is the open door of new-found opportunity in the world of gainful employment. Her choice is complicated by the fact that the four elements—marriage, homemaking, childbearing and childrearing, and employment—may be considered separable, so with one exception a woman may have any element or combination of elements with social approval. She may marry without becoming a homemaker. Control of conception makes it possible for her to marry but have no children, whether or not she becomes a homemaker. She may have a home of her own without marrying. Employment may be combined with the other three elements in a variety of ways. The only element she cannot have with social approval is motherhood without marriage, although a few unmarried women adopt children. As a result of this separability of the four elements mentioned, women face a greater number of alternatives than formerly, and their choice is therefore more complex. In one respect, however, it is easier because the choice is made among more alternatives, with the result that there is less compulsion exerted by any one of them, whereas in earlier times there was more inclination to squeeze all women into the same mold. In those earlier days, though there were the same four elements involved, three of them—marriage, homemaking, and childbearing—were combined and accepted as a constellation, much as a man accepts the combination of marriage and breadwinning today, so actually a woman's choice was limited to two alternatives. Most women chose to marry, and social expectations supported their singlemindedness. Relatively few married women were gainfully employed.

A wife has not only an economic function of her own, so to speak; she also has a socioeconomic role as the marital partner of a man with a particular occupation. For example, the differences in roles of the wife of a farmer as compared with the wife of a traveling salesman, the wife of a clergyman as compared with the wife of a businessman, the wife of a writer as compared with the wife of a physician, and the wife of a politician as compared with the wife of a banker are readily apparent. This matter of occupationally determined role requirement is coming more into prominence. Large corporations are giving it attention. The unusual demands which the young husband's military service has made on thousands of wives ill-prepared to meet them highlight this problem. Books written to meet the needs of wives attest to the slowly growing attention being given to it.

The wife has a role as "social director" in the family for which there is no parallel for the husband. Although he may participate in this function, the burden of the responsibility falls upon her shoulders.

Whereas in earlier times the wife was expected to be able to produce many of the goods used by the family, her role has now shifted from that of producer to that of consumer. She is expected nowadays to be skilled in the art of purchasing. By economical and careful expenditure she "stretches" the purchasing power of her husband's income. The shift in role is not complete, however. Many wives make clothing or raise and preserve food products, and the traditional attitude toward "good home cooking" is still in our cultural climate.

In other ways, too, the wife's role is somewhat mixed. She has more independence, is given less direction and supervision, and has more freedom of choice than formerly. At the same time, through both law and public opinion, she is accorded more protection and in some circumstances may make demands upon her husband which a man very seldom makes upon a wife, such as suing him for divorce on the ground of non-support, making him responsible for her debts, or having the right to be awarded alimony.

While the wife is expected to fulfill a socioeconomic role equivalent in contribution if not in content to that of the wife of yesterday, she is also expected to be something not expected of the wife of the past, namely, an enthusiastic, responsive sexual companion who accepts her own femininity, her husband's masculinity, and the sexual aspect of their relationship with uninhibited pleasure rather than reluctant tolerance. The modern wife is expected not only to love her husband but also to like to love him. It is assumed that she will be a companion whether they are alone in the privacy of their home or at a social affair where the impression each makes is reflected upon the other. There are, of course, individual and class differences as to how fully such expectations are taken for granted. In the last analysis, the wife's role, too, as we said was true of the husband's, is in part, at least, a matter of his definition of her role and his appraisal of the degree of success or failure she exhibits in fulfilling it. She, too, may seem to meet all the cultural criteria and norms of a "good wife." But if her husband is disappointed in her and does not love her and they do not get along happily together, she is assumed to have failed as a wife.

Gainfully employed married women

A phenomenon which simultaneously reflects the wife's changing role and contributes to it, and which is also affecting the role of the husband, is the rapid increase in married women's gainful employment in recent years.

The actual number of married women who are gainfully employed is increasing. Also the proportion of married women among the employed is increasing. In 1890 about 1 in 22 married women was gainfully employed [U.S. Bureau of the Census, 1960b]. By 1900 it was 1 in 18. By 1930 the proportion had become 1 in 9 [Breckinridge, 1933]. By 1940 it was 1

THE MANY "LIVES" OF THE MODERN WIFE

Millions of words have been written about the problems of modern women. The new freedoms that women have gained through cultural change have opened to them a wider range of roles than that of the traditional wife-homemaker-mother. In the wake of their new freedoms, however, have come increased and varied responsibilities, plus complex, and sometimes perplexing, problems of setting appropriate goals and of fulfilling their personalities as women. Perhaps no one feels the combined pressures of tradition, biological nature, new marital and social expectation, and occupational opportunity more acutely than the young wife-homemaker-mother with a career of her own. Scholars, as well as columnists, are continually describing—or decrying—the multiple roles that she is expected to play, many of them within the span of one day. In a sense, she is expected to be a variety of persons and to live many "lives."

Culture and her biological nature predispose her to motherhood and concern for family living. Her morning typically begins with responsibility for starting family members off in various directions according to schedule. Only after playing the role of family organizer can she concentrate on other roles.

in 7 wives eighteen years old or older living with their husbands [U.S. Bureau of the Census, 1940a]. By 1963 about 1 married woman in 3 was gainfully employed [U.S. Bureau of the Census, 1964]. This ratio varies with number of years married, however. About 1 wife in 2 is employed during the first year of marriage, as compared to 1 in 5 after five years [Statistical Bulletin, 1951]. This indicates that women tend to give up employment while their children are very young, resuming it after the children enter school or become independent. It also suggests that many girls who plan to continue working after the wedding have their plans interrupted. In 1900, 15 per cent of all employed women were married; in 1930, 29 per cent [Breckinridge, 1933]; in 1940, 35 per cent [U.S. Bureau of the Census, 1940b]; by 1963, about 57 per cent [U.S. Bureau of the Census, 1964].

REASONS WHY MARRIED WOMEN ARE GAINFULLY EMPLOYED

Opportunity. Married women are gainfully employed for a variety of reasons, some of which are highly individual. All reasons must necessarily represent two sides, so to speak. One side is the personal desire or situational imperative that motivates the woman to work. The other side is the opportunities open to her. Opening a door does not necessarily motivate people to walk through it. But it does give new opportunity to some who have previously hoped for it, and it suggests walking through to some who had not previously thought of it. In recent years, and especially since the Second World War, many new opportunities have opened to women. It is not surprising that so many have availed themselves of these opportunities. Now that they have learned what this means to them personally and economically, there is no turning back the tide no matter how much some persons may wish to do so.

Money economy. Our money economy plays a part in women's desire for gainful employment. In this country money is set up as a standard of judgment applying to things as diverse as human life and works of art. If a person is killed in an accident, his relatives may sue the guilty party and the court may award a sum of money, as if that could fully compensate for loss of life. If an employee loses a finger in a factory machine, he collects money for it. If a person commits a minor criminal offense, he may satisfy the state by paying a fine. Money is one of the bases on which the population is divided into classes. It can gain prestige for dullards while geniuses starve and go unrecognized. One of the questions most commonly applied in America to the things that we do or make or acquire is "How much did it cost?"

In a culture in which money has so prominent a place it is not surprising that those pursuits involving wages or profits should by some persons be considered more desirable and more respectable than others. Occupations for men and employment for women outside the home in-

A complete change in attitude and appearance is required if she is to be a successful entrepreneur in the world of business and industry, furthering her own occupational interests.

At midmorning she is a competitor in the full swing of intersexual business activity. To promote effectively her custom-crafted products, she depends upon talent, education, and specialized training, not the exercise of charm and feminine guile.

In early afternoon when she interrupts her business schedule to attend a PTA meeting, she assumes still another role as participator in community service. Activity of this type, involving her children and their welfare, is expected to take precedence over her career.

volve wages and profits; homemaking does not. One would expect some women to be so influenced by our attitude toward money that homemaking would seem to them something inferior and undesirable.

Masculine ideology. Another reason—one that overlaps that just considered—is our masculine ideology. Traditionally, things masculine are considered superior to things feminine. The idea is so ingrained in our thinking and attitudes that it is only now beginning to change. It is still effective enough to make some women want to follow in men's footsteps because that course seems preferable to fulfilling the traditional feminine role.

Success in competition. The competitive spirit so common in this country plays a part in women's seeking remunerative employment. From infancy, children are trained in competition. Competition permeates schools, sports, the building of homes, the ownership of automobiles, church congregations and their activities, business, and the professions. In discussing our persons, our activities, our possessions, our natural resources, and our achievements, we have an unabashed affinity for superlatives—best, largest, richest, longest, costliest, prettiest, oldest, newest, strongest, and so on ad infinitum. We like to "get into the game," and usually we play to win. Many remunerative occupations offer the zest of competition and are therefore more attractive to some women than is homemaking.

A birthday party is an event of special social importance when one is five or six years old. And who but a mother can make sure that party clothes and gift packages are as they should be? In "shifting gears" from her role as a competent professional in the business world to that of an understanding mother in the home, she tries to make the transition with grace and apparent lack of strain.

The highly competitive occupational area that she has selected to work in requires her to be both an efficient manager *and a careful* supervisor. *These same roles are necessary in her family life if she is to be a resourceful homemaker.*

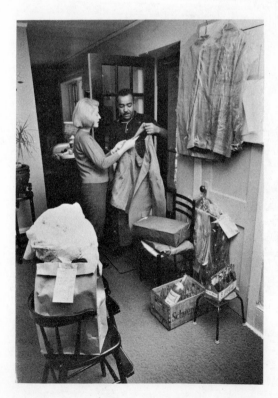

In regular performance of the ordinary tasks of housekeeping she must be a knowledgeable consumer *of goods and services in order for the household to function smoothly. Her family naturally assumes that her role in providing for their comfort and wellbeing will be given priority.*

As is the case in many homes, she must carry out the preparations for the entertainment of guests with simultaneous responsibility for routine family schedule. She is always expected to be a skilled behind-the-scenes coordinator.

Her image and effectiveness as a charming hostess are important to a successful relationship with her husband. Her social abilities may have a direct bearing on her husband's advancement and may affect materially the family's ultimate socioeconomic status.

*Although she is called upon to compete with men in her oc-
cupation, she is still expected to be an understanding and
cooperative* companion *in her personal relationship with her
husband. The aggressiveness that helps her in one situation
may hinder her in another. Despite some feelings of ambivalence and doubt regarding the multiple roles she has fulfilled
during the day, she recognizes that the final appraisal of her
success or failure as a* wife *rests with her husband.*

Necessity.   In many cases the married woman is gainfully employed
because the husband's income is insufficient to maintain subsistence.
This may be due to illness, incapacity of some other form, unemploy-
ment, low wages, or unusually heavy expenses. These are the women
who work because they are face to face with the basic elements in the
struggle for existence.

"Necessity."   Some women are gainfully employed because their husbands' incomes, while sufficient to maintain subsistence and even sub-

sistence plus, are not sufficient to maintain a desired standard of living. They work to provide luxuries, surplus, travel, automobiles, education for the children, or something else over and above maintenance. These are the women engaged in a struggle for a standard of living rather than a struggle for existence. Of course, all organisms engage in a struggle for existence; but these women do not feel the immediacy of that struggle as do those mentioned above. Nevertheless, some of these women may feel the pinch of their "necessity" almost as keenly as their less fortunate sisters feel the pinch of actual necessity.

In recent years there has arisen a new "species" of gainfully employed wife, who may, in a sense, be classified in both of the above groups. She is the woman who works to "put her husband through school." So common has she become that at commencement time some colleges and universities, half-facetiously but half-admiringly, award such wives the degree of PHT (Putting Husband Through).

Personal desire. Some married women are employed for one or more of the following reasons:

1. To escape homemaking duties.

2. Because of interest in the activities, subject matter, or contacts connected with an occupation. The woman may feel that she can carry on such activities more effectively than she can make a home, and she wants to do what she can do best.

3. To seek "self-expression." In many cases it would be more nearly accurate to speak of "self-determination" rather than "self-expression" because many women, like many men, have nothing to "express." They merely want the freedom to make their own choices and decisions. A wife's employment may cause marital problems, but so may straining at the tether if she longs for "self-expression," believes that employment is the outlet she needs, and yet feels tied to her home.

4. To escape boredom. If a woman has a small apartment or if she does only the barest minimum with her homemaking, and if she is not skillful in the use of her own resources, she may become bored and decide that the only solution for her is to seek work outside the home.

5. To escape the care of children. A woman who has employment outside the home has what seems to her in many instances an acceptable excuse for having no children.

6. To work with the husband in his business or profession.

7. To prevent stagnation. Some women feel that homemaking eventually makes for the stagnation of personal development. Consequently they seek to avoid it.

8. Because of dissatisfaction with their marriage relationships. In some cases working outside the home is a symptom of dissatisfaction with the marriage. Work is an escape from an unpleasant situation.

9. To be independent, especially financially.

10. To render service to mankind.

In some cases the woman's personal desire represents what might be termed a "true" reason for her seeking employment. That is, she actually does have skill which she wants to put to use or interest which she wants to satisfy or a desire to build an enterprise with her husband. In other cases, however, the woman's apparent desire is a surface manifestation of some underlying cause of which the woman herself may not be aware and having its roots in early experience, such as parents' ambition for their daughter, the fact that the parents wanted a son and the daughter was reared with this knowledge and consequently developed an urge to prove herself, a subtle rejection of her role as a woman, or something similar.

PROBLEMS AND DEVELOPMENTS GROWING OUT OF MARRIED WOMEN'S GAINFUL EMPLOYMENT

When two related parts of culture change at different rates and the independent element changes so much more rapidly than the dependent element that the latter lags considerably behind, social problems are likely to arise during the period of lag. This situation is referred to as *cultural lag.* For example, in Figure 2, let A represent the development of the automobile as a machine. Today in this country we have the most

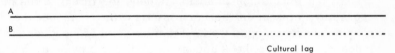

Figure 2. Diagrammatic representation of cultural lag.

cars and the largest, fastest, most powerful cars in the world and in history. But control of the automobile, as represented by B, though improving through the construction of superhighways, the testing and licensing of drivers, the move toward uniformity of traffic signals, required liability insurance, and so on, lags behind. The result is a series of problems, such as a high accident rate, difficulties in parking, and often no protection for the innocent victim of an accident. Both the automobile as a machine and control of the automobile are subject to relatively ready objective evaluation. When A or B in the diagram above is not subject to objective evaluation, for example, when A represents something not readily measureable—such as an activity—and B involves attitudes toward, and reactions to, that activity, cultural lag is likely to be less apparent but more persistent.

Let the rapid increase in the number of gainfully employed married women be A in the diagram above. Let B represent our attitudes toward, and adjustment to, this new phenomenon. There is evidence of cultural lag, with its resultant problems. Some of these problems and developments are as follows:

Double income. At first glance one would assume that a couple could live on two incomes twice as readily as they could live on one. In some cases, however, even when the couple need the additional money, the wife's income presents a problem. Our traditional cultural pattern, with its attendant attitudes, is adapted to a one-income family arrangement with the husband as the breadwinner. When the wife also has an income, new questions may arise. Is her income joint property or her own private property? Should her income be pooled with the husband's to purchase necessities for the family, or should it be used for luxuries or for meeting the wife's personal needs, or should it be saved as a "nest egg" for the proverbial "rainy day"? Who should determine how the wife's income will be used?

Wife's income too large. There is still extant a sufficiently persistent remnant of a traditional assumption of women's inferiority to create a problem in some cases in which the wife earns more than the husband. If her larger income is interpreted by the husband as a threat to his ego, the couple may not get along so well with more money as they would with less.

Husband's attitude. The point mentioned immediately above suggests a not uncommon problem, namely, the threat to the husband's ego. Many a present-day husband asserts with vehemence that "no wife of mine is ever going to work." From his point of view her earning is a reflection on his manhood and on his ability to provide for her. Her employment may also be a subtle source of fear that she will not be able to make the sort of home he envisages. He may resent her being away from home or what he considers neglect of her duties. The actual or imagined attitude of friends may concern him. He may protect himself by developing a patronizing attitude toward her work. He may consider her work less important than his, thus setting the stage for a clash of egos.

New type of husband. We referred earlier to the wife who works to put her husband through school as a new "species." Similarly there is a new "species" of husband developing. The type of husband who objects to his wife's employment is not uncommon. The type who willingly accepts or reluctantly tolerates it is becoming more common. A third type has arisen, namely, the husband who insists that his wife work. He may do this in advance for some reason, such as completing his education. Or she may have been working but now wants to stop in order to become a full-time homemaker and begin to have her children, only to find that her husband is adamant and insists that she continue.

Wife's attitude. The wife may use her employment as a rationalization for the rejection of homemaking or for remaining childless. On the other hand, she may vigorously resist employment even in the face of economic necessity and blame her husband for failing to take care of her.

Care of children.   Although many wives cease gainful employment, at least temporarily, when their children are young, many do not. In 1960 almost one-fifth of employed mothers had children five years of age or younger. In 1948 the proportion of such women was only slightly over one-tenth [Nye and Hoffman, 1963]. Often the wife who is working to put her husband through school cannot afford to stop except, perhaps, for a very brief time after the birth of each child. The result is an unprecedented problem of providing daytime care for small children outside the home by persons other than parents. Opinions differ as to whether such care is beneficial or harmful.

Breakdown of division of labor outside the home.   This has not been the result exclusively of married women's employment but rather of the great influx of women in general into remunerative occupations, many of which had previously been monopolized by men. But married women have contributed abundantly to this influx. There has been infiltration from both sides; in recent years men have entered occupations previously assumed to be restricted to women, and women have entered occupations previously assumed to be restricted to men. Today one is hard put to find an occupation exclusively reserved for one sex or the other. One may find segments of occupational areas, but to find an entire occupational area reserved for one sex is another matter.

In 1836 Harriet Martineau, a visitor to this country, wrote that earlier than that year there were only three remunerative occupations open to women, namely, teaching, needlework, and keeping boarding-houses or hotels but that by that year (1836) women were also employed in mills and factories, in printing offices and domestic service, and in a few other occupations. The list was not long. By 1940, of the 451 types of jobs listed by the Bureau of the Census, women could choose any except that of railroad conductor, engineer, baggageman, switchman, fireman, brakeman, or mechanic; automobile mechanic; fireman in a fire department; soldier; sailor; Marine; or Coast Guardsman. By 1951 women had entered all but two of these occupations, namely, those of locomotive engineer and locomotive fireman [Ogburn and Nimkoff, 1955].

As the division of labor has broken down, the old concept of "men's work" and "women's work" as distinct entities has begun to disappear. As men and women have found themselves in the same occupations, intersexual competition has increased. In earlier times when their occupational lines were clearly drawn, the sexes did not compete. Nowadays they seek the same jobs and at times accept different rates of pay for those jobs, thus sharpening the edge of competition.

Comparative prestige. In earlier days a woman's prestige depended upon her doing "woman's work." There was no problem for her in choosing that channel of activity which in her judgment would lead to greatest prestige. Today she may choose, and there has arisen the problem of the prestige accorded homemaking as compared to the prestige accorded gainful employment. Many women choose the latter. Many other women accept the former reluctantly. Women often complain that men do not give enough prestige to woman's role as homemaker. That may be true. But many women make the same mistake they attribute to men in that they underrate their own importance as homemakers and accord homemaking too little prestige. Some women have no problem in this connection. They appreciate the importance of their homemaking role, and for prestige which comes from the "outside" they substitute conviction which comes from the "inside."

Status of women. As women prove themselves in new areas of endeavor and increase their financial independence, it is inevitable that their status will change. Many concepts of woman's nature, ability, role, and relationship to men and to the family are either reexamined and modified or slowly changed without deliberate intent on anyone's part by a subtle, evolutionlike process. But, though progress is being made, American women are still subject to occupational discrimination. Differentials in pay between men and women for the same kind of work are common. Women do not have such ready access as men to more highly paid jobs. Advancement rates differ. In white-collar occupations about three-fourths of the men are in grades reached by only one-fourth of the women. Women applicants for employment are often not considered on their merits; the fact that they are women is often given more weight than their competence [President's Commission on the Status of Women, 1963].

Divorce rate. Whether or not the increase in women's gainful employment actually contributes to the divorce rate in the sense of contributing to failure in marriage is still an open question. There are both protagonists and presumably objective evidence on either side. In interpreting statistics on the relationship between wives' employment and the failure of marriage, caution must be exercised in diagnosing cause and effect. Undoubtedly there are some cases in which a marriage is damaged by the wife's outside employment. On the other hand, there are also cases in which a wife's dissatisfaction with her failing marriage motivates her to seek outside employment. In the over-all picture it is difficult to be sure which is the cart and which is the horse.

The financial independence that women may find through earning may be a factor contributing to the divorce rate in the sense that a woman need no longer be tied to an unhappy marriage in order to gain support. If she has had employment during her marriage and thus tasted financial independence and in a sense made a break from the home, making the break complete through divorce becomes less radical than such a step used to be. The popularity of alimony as money paid to an ex-wife for her own support, as distinct from money paid to her by her ex-husband for child support, is decreasing. This, too, may reflect women's new-found independence.

Breakdown of division of labor within the home. The traditional clear-cut line of demarcation between "women's work" and "men's work" within the home has not disappeared, but it is gradually growing less clear. This has come about through myriad factors, one of which is married women's employment. The question, "How much should a husband be expected to participate in housework?" does not arise only because of wives' employment. But such employment sharpens the issue. It constitutes an additional push in overcoming the inertia of tradition and in increasing the momentum of social change.

In the present-day family, especially that in which the wife is employed, there is no accurate way of determining in advance and on the basis of tried and known traditional practice what portion of the total homemaking responsibility each spouse will accept. A problem arises when one spouse assumes that this can be done while the other spouse expects to have the housekeeping tasks apportioned on a functional or opportunistic basis rather than a traditional one.

The problem is not only one of the amount of work a given spouse does in the home. The problem is also one of attitude. For example, some wives complain that their husbands do not help enough with housekeeping and child care. Other wives, however, are not so much concerned with how much the husband does as they are with the reasons he gives for not doing more. An employed wife, for instance, can accomplish a great deal, even handling the two jobs of earning and housekeeping, if her husband is doing his best, granting time and skill limitations. On the other hand, if her husband does little because he rests his case on tradition and therefore resists doing "woman's work," the total task may prove too much for her. Conversely, the husband may face a similar problem of attitude in his wife's success or failure in her role as homemaker as he defines it. From his point of view it may be one thing for her to "let the house go" because of time and energy limitations involved in the twofold task of homemaking and employment. It may be quite another thing for her to neglect housework because of lack of interest or slovenly habits.

New expectations for marriage partner. It goes almost without saying that the rapid increase in married women's gainful employment with its resultant effects on family living has helped to highlight, even though it has not by itself initiated, a new and more flexible set of criteria for evaluating marriage partners either in actuality or in prospect. What is a "good wife" or a "good husband," in terms of present-day conditions and expectations, becomes a live question neither readily nor uniformly answered.

Pattern of family life.   There is no longer a standard pattern or class-determined standard pattern of family life in this country as there used to be. Many factors have contributed to this change. One of them has been the increase in married women's employment outside the home. With variations in patterns of family living, any one of which may be "best" for a given couple, each couple must answer the question, "What pattern is best for us?" When people are given new alternatives from which to choose, some will find in their new freedom of choice new opportunities for enrichment of living that contributes to marital success. Others will find new opportunities for making errors in judgment which contribute to marital failure.

When the pattern of family life was imposed largely by society, there was little room for conflict. But nowadays, when it is determined to a greater extent by each couple, there is the possibility of one spouse's imposing a pattern on the other, with conflict frequently the result.

One of the prominent characteristics of American society has been and still is a striving in the direction of upward mobility, that is, a striving to better one's socioeconomic status, to move from one class level to that above it, to acquire at least the observable "outward" appurtenances, if not the unobservable "inner" philosophy, of the "next floor up." American society, unlike certain older societies, has been sufficiently fluid and uncongealed to permit such upward mobility to become one of our most commonly noted traits. At its best such striving may result in general cultural improvement. At its worst it may mean superficial "keeping up with the Joneses." One new tool that may be used to advance the process of upward mobility is the increased income derived from the wife's employment.

Consistency.   If, as mentioned above, married women's employment is one important factor in both the reflection and the causation of social and family change, there arises the problem of achieving a reasonable degree of consistency in expectations and demands which marital partners set up for one another. For example, can a young husband expect his wife to finance his education, bear babies, keep house, be an enthusiastic sexual partner, and be an interested and stimulating companion at the same time? Can the wife expect the husband simultaneously to provide for her, agree to her freedom to have employment outside the home, participate in housekeeping, be a sexual partner, be a companion, be a father to her children, and accept traditional legal protection for her while she demands new rights? Perhaps so. We are only raising the question.

COMMON ARGUMENTS FOR AND AGAINST MARRIED WOMEN'S GAINFUL EMPLOYMENT

The following is intended to present various sides of the issue as expressed in commonly heard arguments pro and con. It is intended as food for thought, not as a defense of a position. In considering these arguments, it is well to keep in mind that many of them should be weighted, depending upon whether a woman is employed full time or part time and when her work hours come with relation to her husband's time schedule and her children's school schedule.

The wife's employment may permit a young couple to marry earlier than they could otherwise. If the man is preparing for a profession, his income may be small and his expenses great for a considerable period.

The wife may derive great satisfaction from her occupation. Why should not a woman do what she is most interested in and can do best, just as a man does, whether this be homemaking or work outside the home? The traditional assumption is that most women are interested in the same occupation, homemaking. We do not make a similar assumption for men.

It is said that employment keeps the woman mentally alert, so her husband, therefore, does not "leave her behind." If she is sincerely interested in keeping mentally alert, there are plenty of opportunities to be found in homemaking. Many women feel that employment out of the home will be a ready-made solution of their problem because the demands of the job are an impetus to effort and define the area into which their activities are to fall. On the surface this seems easier than does drawing on their own resources and making the most of their marital and domestic opportunities. Although there are many women who have marked time while their husbands have marched ahead, there are others who only think that they have, because they have confused development and promotion. Their own development is not easy to measure and is less obvious, while the husband's promotion in his occupation is readily apparent.

Employment, it is claimed, makes a woman keep up her appearance. This may be a good argument if one is thinking of women in general, for there are many wives who neglect their appearance. As far as the individual wife who is weighing the pros and cons of her own employment is concerned, this is shifting responsibility. It puts the responsibility for keeping up her appearance on something outside herself instead of on her own pride and self-respect and her attitude toward husband and marriage.

Some argue that there is not enough in homemaking to keep a woman occupied and interested. The young woman looking forward to marriage tends to think of her homemaking as occurring on a relatively small scale because her dwelling will not be large and there will be no children at first. She also anticipates having much timesaving equipment. So she is inclined to insist that in the early years of marriage, at least until the arrival of a baby, homemaking cannot be a full-time occupation. There is truth in her argument. Yet there is another side to the problem. In the early part of marriage, many young women have only small skills with which to make their small homes, if we may put it thus. It may seem easy to a more experienced homemaker but does not necessarily seem equally easy to a bride. Most brides need to learn much, but not all see this need equally clearly. Besides further learning in the domestic skills, there are many other areas of a young woman's life in which learning can and should continue after the wedding. If a woman thinks of her life in terms of continued growth and learning, she will always find interests to occupy her. She will not be bored whether she is single or married, has a small home or a large one, is employed or a full-time homemaker.

If a woman devotes her time to homemaking and child rearing, to the exclusion of other interests, she too often finds herself stranded when her children leave home. There is no more pathetic person than the middle-aged woman who is lost and floundering because that to which she has devoted her life has been taken away. A woman's outside interests do not of necessity have to involve earning. It would seem absurd for a man to pursue two occupations so that when he retired from one he could follow the other. Some men devote so much time and thought to their occupations, to the exclusion of all other interests, that when they retire they are discontented and restless and gradually drift back to "the office." They are in much the same position as the woman whose family has grown up and left home. Other men keep up extraoccupational interests, and to them retirement means not boredom and pointlessness but opportunity to do more fully and more leisurely some of the things that they have always wanted to do.

Remaining employed after marriage permits a woman more readily to readjust herself if her husband dies or is incapacitated. If she does not remain employed and is thrown again on her own resources, she finds herself out of touch with her occupation and often has to take an inferior job. Fundamentally, the situation is not dissimilar to that of a man. If a man prepares for an occupation and devotes part of his life to it and then through technological change, illness, accident, business depression, or age he finds that he can no longer pursue his chosen occupation, he must make a readjustment. For many men this means accepting inferior jobs. There are no statistics available, but one would guess that there are as many men who have to readjust occupationally at some time in life as there are women who give up their occupations to devote themselves to homemaking and later have to reenter gainful employment with the "cards stacked against them." Most men do not try to follow two occupations at once in order to ensure themselves against such emergency.

On the other hand, a responsible man uses a portion of his income, which ultimately means a portion of his life, to protect his family through the purchase of life insurance. If a woman uses a portion of her time to keep abreast of her occupation so that in an emergency she may protect her children, there is a fundamental similarity.

The woman may neglect her home. The employed wife is subject to both the demands of the home and the demands of the job. Since the latter is likely to be more uncompromisingly urgent and less flexible, she must neglect the former if time limitations and fatigue make it necessary to neglect one.

The employed wife may neglect her husband. We do not mean to suggest that the wife is guardian, caretaker, or nurse for her husband. Since, however, the sexes are complementary in some important respects and to some extent are trained for complementary roles in life, there is a possibility that there is greater opportunity for happiness if the husband and wife complement each other than there is when there is duplication of function or of contribution. Would society not consider it neglect of the wife if a husband were gainfully employed only part of the time and spent the rest of his time doing something he wanted to do because for some reason he did not derive sufficient satisfaction from his occupation? There is no more logical reason for a man's being subject to traditional pressure toward full-time breadwinning than there is for a woman's being subject to traditional pressure toward full-time homemaking. If a man does engage in a full-time occupation in order to support his wife and home, may he not expect that his wife give whatever time is needed to making that home?

Women can have freedom to choose or not to choose gainful employment only so long as men do not have similar freedom. So long as men are subject to social pressure to be breadwinners, women may or may not be employed, as they choose. If men were given freedom of choice as to whether they would be breadwinners, women's freedom would be both modified and threatened. Would women be willing to give men the freedom of choice which they demand for themselves?

The gainfully employed woman may neglect her children. The adequate rearing of children requires a great deal of time, effort, interest, and information. A mother is in a position similar to that of a student who spends fifteen hours per week in classes but must spend at least twice that much in preparation in order to maintain a high level of academic work.

Children obviously do not ask to be born, so whoever bears them has a responsibility for them regardless of other interests. None of us approves of anything that is damaging to children. Not all the facts are known, but research indicates that it is not the mother's employment per se that is detrimental to children. The critical considerations are the quality of person that she is, the quality of the relationship that she establishes with her children, the quality of care which the children receive, and whether or not the woman enjoys her work [Nye and Hoffman, 1963]. In a study of some 13,000 high school students, Moore and Holtzman found that students whose mothers were better educated and employed were aware of no more problems of adjustment than children of similarly educated, nonemployed mothers [Ramsey, Smith, and Moore, 1963]. Another consideration is whether the mother's employment affords her children an opportunity for cooperation and learning in the home or prematurely imposes upon them too heavy adult responsibilities. If we condemn wholesale the gainful employment of mothers, as some persons do, we indict unjustly those women whose circumstances give them no alternative to employment. Many widowed or divorced women, and women whose husbands do not earn enough to meet family needs, must be gainfully employed. Yet they do an excellent job of child rearing. On the other hand, there are many nonemployed mothers who do a poor job of child rearing. The presence of the mother in the home does not guarantee the quality of her relationship with her family. As Iscoe says [Ramsey, Smith, and Moore, 1963], "the mere passage of time with a child does not constitute 'good motherhood.'" If the woman has a strong desire to be employed and feels that her children keep her from it, her relationship with her children may be adversely affected.

It is often maintained that gainfully employed married women take jobs from married men and single women who must work to support themselves or their families. The argument is often especially barbed when directed against wives whose husbands earn enough to maintain the family but who seek to raise the family's standard of living. It is obvious that if a job is held by one person, it cannot be held simultaneously by another. But it is illogical to criticize women for attempting to do the very thing men are encouraged to do, namely, to work to raise the family's standard of living. In a country where one of the basic tenets of democracy is the right to equal opportunity in the utilization of personal resources for the improvement of life, such discrimination has no place.

CONCLUSION

We have discussed the reasons that married women are gainfully employed, arguments for such employment and those against it, and problems arising from it. The only reasonable conclusion is this: we cannot generalize except to say that the employment of married women is here to stay; there are indications that it will continue to increase. Hence it behooves both sexes to learn to live with it. In so far as a given family is concerned, however, it is not a question of whether married women should be employed. It is a question of whether a particular married woman, with her particular skills, personality, opportunities, interests, and tastes, with her particular husband and home situation, should be employed in a particular occupation. The effects of her employment on herself, her husband, her children, and her home will depend upon many factors, such as time, fatigue, type of work, and income, which no one but she and her husband can fully evaluate.

Granting that whether or not a given married woman will be employed is an individual matter, we may still raise questions about her (1) if she rejects the fact that she is a woman and is overwhelmed by the traditional masculine ideology, (2) if her home and children are neglected, (3) if she is too much influenced by material values, (4) if she depends upon factors outside herself to prevent boredom and neglect of appearance when such prevention should arise from her own personal resources, and (5) if she does not know what she wants. There is a vast difference among the married woman who must work because of economic necessity, the woman who chooses to work and has an intelligent, integrated plan for combining marriage and employment, and the woman who has not sorted out her values and therefore cannot make a choice. This last woman does not really have a plan to combine marriage and employment. What appears to be a plan is actually a lack of plan. She attempts the combination because, unable to make a choice, she wants everything in sight. Such a woman is likely to be restless, dissatisfied, and ineffective because she is an immature and poorly integrated personality.

May homemaking be considered a career?

Housekeeping is only part of homemaking. A house is a dwelling place, usually containing furniture and equipment. A home is a state of mind, a cluster of attitudes and relationships, which center in a dwelling and the persons living in it. In the following discussion we shall think of *homemaking* in the broad sense, as involving marriage, homemaking, housekeeping, and parenthood.

A career involves knowledge and skills. Consider what is involved in homemaking. A woman who is an effective homemaker must know something about teaching, interior decoration, cooking, dietetics, entertaining, consumption, psychology, physiology, social relations, community resources, clothing, housing, household equipment and maintenance, hygiene, first aid, and a host of other things. They make an impressive list. She is a "general practitioner" rather than a specialist.

The common attitude toward the knowledge and skills involved in homemaking as compared with those in work outside the home is somewhat incongruous and paradoxical. If a woman teaches someone else's children, she is accorded professional status; if she teaches her own children, she is "just a mother." If she follows interior decoration as an occupation, she has a career; but if she applies the principles of interior decoration to her own home, she is "just a housekeeper." If she studies dietetics and has charge of a large kitchen in a restaurant or institution, she has a profession; but if she applies dietetic facts and principles to the feeding of her husband and children, she is "just cooking."

There is some drudgery, some routine, some uninteresting detail in every occupation. Many of the patients who visit a physician have something less than interest-stimulating ailments. A lawyer has to prepare numerous dull papers. A musician has more drudgery and sometimes less genius than his audience, as a rule, can realize. In comparing homemaking with a career outside the home, the better aspects of the one should be measured against the better aspects of the other; worse against worse. Too frequently the routine element in homemaking is compared with the glamor and stimulation of a career, and naturally homemaking is thus shown in an unfavorable light.

Young women contemplating marriage often fail to see the possibilities in homemaking because their understanding goes only as far as some of the routine tasks of housekeeping. They talk about dishwashing and dusting as if these were synonymous with homemaking. It is conceivable that such activities may never be stimulating and interesting to a given girl. On the other hand, what seems drudgery under one set of circumstances may appear in a different light when conditions change. Washing and polishing a car are one thing to a garage assistant, quite another to a boy who has received a new convertible as a graduation gift. Taking care of one's own baby is not the same as just taking care of babies. A girl who has done housework in her parents' home during their absence and found it uninteresting may develop another attitude toward it when she does it in her own home and in part to please her husband. An activity is or is not considered drudgery, depending upon the reasons for which one engages in it, the attitude he has toward it, the ends which he expects to be achieved through it, and the conditions under which he carries it out.

In a career there is opportunity for long-time growth and development. So is there in homemaking. Compare the young woman with her incomplete knowledge, small apartment, and first baby to the middle-aged woman whose home has atmosphere, who is recognized in the community, whose children are well-reared and form a successful family group. Growth and development are not lacking; but of course there is no promotion in the business or professional sense.

In homemaking there is a degree of independence and freedom from supervision found in relatively few occupations. The homemaker is her "own boss," does her own planning, and budgets her time largely as she sees fit. There is opportunity for social contacts. The homemaker performs a most important service to her family and to society; but since this service is usually not accompanied by publicity, it is often taken for granted. She has opportunity for long-time, deep satisfaction in doing well what she undertakes. She can see results. Her work is constructive and creative. She has ample opportunity for exercising organizing ability. She has considerable responsibility for planning family recreations, the life within the home, and the family's relations with other families and community groups.

There are standards of quality and achievement in homemaking, but they are not so definite as those in other careers. Mediocrity is more readily tolerated. There is not the competitive element found in business and the professions, though there is a comparative element. Some persons hold this to be one of the major obstacles to considering homemaking a career. Yet the fact that there are standards, however ill-defined, cannot be dismissed. We do have at least a vague idea of what we mean by the American home; and women are subject to recognition or criticism on the basis of their success in creating it.

Homemaking may be considered a career. The unmarried young woman's problem is not that of homemaking versus career but that of choosing among a number of careers, one of which is homemaking. Drawing such a conclusion may seem like fencing with a windmill; its purpose is to balance emphases more equitably and to get away from the not uncommon notion that to choose homemaking rather than another career is to relegate oneself to the class of the might-have-beens. The young woman who decides upon homemaking as her career need have no feeling of inferiority. In spite of loud and vociferous protests from various quarters, she need not feel that she is making no contribution or that her contribution is less than her husband's. Wife and husband together make a contribution to family and society that neither can make alone.

This husband-wife relationship may be looked at in several ways. One may say, as some do, "Men can have careers because women make homes." One may say that women are released from the necessity for earning and are free to devote their time to the extremely important matter of homemaking because men specialize in breadwinning. Or one may say that together the breadwinner and the homemaker form a complementary combination second to none.

The position of women in modern America

Much water has passed under the bridge since 1863, when a man wrote the following in a memory book presented to a young woman: "The mission of woman—to light her home with smiles and to strew flowers along her husband's path," and since 1870, when Queen Victoria wrote to a Mr. Martin [Markun, 1930, p. 281]:

The Queen is most anxious to enlist everyone who can speak or write to join in checking this mad, wicked folly of "Woman's Rights," with all its attendant horrors, on which her poor feeble sex is bent, forgetting every sense of womanly feeling and propriety. Lady . . . ought to get a *good whipping*. It is a subject which makes the Queen so furious that she cannot contain herself. God created men and women different—then let them remain each in their own position.

That the good queen was herself maintaining a status involving rights and privileges which her more humble sisters were in their lesser ways striving to attain and that she assumed that differences between men and women were all God-made and necessarily implied inferiority of status for the women does not alter the fact that she reflected the common attitude of the times and the fact that that attitude is now becoming passe.

It is not difficult to say that woman's social position has changed and still is changing. More and more women are gainfully employed both before and during marriage. As we have seen, this affects their relative position by giving them a type of independence that they did not have formerly. Technically, at least, a large proportion of the nation's wealth is "in the wife's name." Men are still expected to contribute to the support of their wives after the marriage tie is broken by divorce, but not to the same extent as formerly, for in many quarters there is a growing opposition to alimony.

Women have achieved suffrage. They have educational opportunities almost equal to those of men. As a group they have made intelligent use of those opportunities. Mothers have been somewhat emancipated from their children and are gradually being freed from bearing a greater number than they desire or can care for adequately. In earlier times when less was known about, and there was not such widespread use of, contraceptives, to an appreciable degree the number of pregnancies a woman had depended upon her husband's interest in sexual intercourse and the exercise of his legal right to such intercourse, regardless of her interest. More recently contraceptives have permitted control of conception regardless of frequency of intercourse but with the husband's cooperation or at least with his knowledge, due to the difficulty of a wife's concealing from her husband the fact of her using a contraceptive even when his cooperation is not required. Now for the first time in history, with the development of oral contraceptives a wife can prevent conception without her husband's knowledge.

With the development of modern warfare women have lost some of the inviolability in war which they formerly had. Men are still the chief participators in warfare, both as fighters and as victims, but women are playing a more extensive role, especially as victims.

Woman's social influence is increasing. Women are making progress in the professions but have not yet achieved professional status equal to men's. They are also making progress in other occupations, but there is still a tendency for them to be given subsidiary jobs with lower salaries. Women still receive more social and legal protection than do men.

Both employed women and housewives are gaining an increased amount of leisure time, but one wonders whether they have as yet learned to use it to best advantage, though progress is being made.

For centuries, regardless of the proportion between the sexes, there has been an inclination for men to treat women as if they were a minority group. Women have been the victims of groundless generalizations; uncritical stereotypes; implications of inferiority; personal, social, political, and economic discrimination; legal and social restrictions; superstitious fear; occupational stratification; moral inconsistency; exploitation; lack of understanding and appreciation in much the same manner as Negroes, Jews, immigrants, and other minority peoples. So long as women "kept their place," men, in their more idealistic moments, were willing to "put them on a pedestal" and gloss over their inferior status with a code of chivalry. The present trend is toward thinking of men and women as integral parts of the same group on a more nearly equal footing. Men's attitude toward women and treatment of them are changing. Today women are thought of as individuals more than they ever were formerly. There are still married men who treat their wives as if those wives were minors under the guardianship of the husband, but the trend is toward equalitarian marriage.

Perhaps the most important change that has occurred—the one that in a way epitomizes the others—is increased freedom of choice. Women have more freedom of choice—in educational, social, and occupational matters; in choosing a husband; in getting married; in escaping an unhappy marriage; in bearing children—than they have ever had before. They are coming to play a larger part in determining their own destinies.

THE RELATION OF THE INDIVIDUAL WOMAN TO STATUS, MEN, AND MARRIAGE

There are a number of things that the individual modern woman must do if she is to adjust to this new and evolving set of life circumstances. She must in most instances prepare for gainful employment. In earlier days she passed directly from her parental home to that of her husband. What she learned about homemaking she learned chiefly from her mother. Now she usually prepares for at least temporary employment, a stopgap to bridge the transition from school and parental home to marriage. In rapidly increasing numbers she is continuing to work after the wedding. If she does not marry, she has greater occupational freedom of choice than women have ever before had. If her husband dies, she usually must earn her own living.

She must have a knowledge of life and social affairs, for she has increased independence and freedom of choice and decreased protection and direction. She takes a more extensive part in community life.

She must know something about science and other fields of knowledge. Whether married or single, she must be more or less familiar with calories, vitamins, hormones, nuclear weapons, fall-out, what it means to put a satellite into orbit, and a host of other things. She cannot read or converse intelligently without knowing the identity of Einstein, Freud, Madame Curie, and similar persons.

She must learn new techniques, for example, the technique of driving a car, the technique of consumption, the technique of applying modern psychology to child rearing.

She must understand herself, her resources, her goals, for she no longer has someone else to guide her or to dictate her mode of living; and traditional patterns are in a state of flux. The modern woman needs to learn how to avail herself of the new opportunities that have opened to her without at the same time overlooking the opportunities for, and losing the qualities prerequisite to, making a contribution in the noncompetitive areas, such as marriage and homemaking.

She must decide what she wants, what her objectives are to be. She cannot afford merely to drift. Nor can she expect to have everything in sight. Failure to decide leaves her confused, frustrated, restless, and discontented.

She must carefully study modern morals so that she does not confuse freedom with license.

She must understand men in a way different from formerly, for she is now on a different level with respect to them. She has more varied contacts with men and more freedom of choice in her associations. Men expect more from her. She is no longer an inferior, studying men in order to wheedle out of them the means to her own ends. She is a teammate in a new sense.

She must develop a more enlightened attitude toward sex in marriage, realizing that inhibitions that were considered appropriate in times past are all too frequently a barrier to successful marital adjustment now. She must substitute intelligently balanced attitudes for blind resistance, enthusiastic participation for disinterested tolerance in the sexual aspects of marriage. She must learn to accept wholeheartedly her own sexual classification and capacity and the masculinity and sexual interest of her husband.

She must prepare for a new type of marriage relationship involving new attitudes of husband and wife toward each other, new expectations, new demands, but a relationship in which roles are no longer so clearly defined as formerly. Lack of clear-cut cultural definitions makes necessary greater insight, a higher degree of adaptability, and more carefully focused motivation if she is to contribute to the success of her marriage.

The position of men in modern America

In recent decades so much attention has been given to the question of the status of women that almost none has been given to that of the status of men. There are even some persons who assume that there can be no problem of men's position. Actually men, like women, can have a problem of definition of status, of determination of position, when and as social changes occur that upset traditional roles and expectations and make new definitions necessary. Helen Mayer Hacker [1957] writes of the "new burdens of masculinity." Furthermore, members of a dominant group may have as great a problem in maintaining a given status as members of a dominated group have in improving theirs.

READING 3 **THE NEW BURDENS OF MASCULINITY**

In the field of intergroup relations it has often been ruefully remarked that there is no Negro problem, but only a white problem, no Jewish problem, but a Gentile problem; in short, no minority group problem, but a dominant group problem. And the problem of the dominant group was not only that its attitudes perpetuated the minority group, but also placed limitations on its own development. Amusingly enough, when men are the dominant group, they are quick to admit that their chief problem is women. This answer may be in part defensive, in part facetious, but it is true that inadequate attention has been paid to the sociology of dominant groups, and the strains imposed by the burdens of their status.

Indeed interest and research in changes in men's social roles have been eclipsed by the voluminous concentration on the more spectacular developments and contradictions in feminine roles, and changes in masculine roles have been treated largely as a reaction and adjustment to the new status of women. Possibly one reason why masculine social roles have not been subjected to scrutiny is that such a concept has not clearly emerged. Men have stood for mankind, and their problems have been identified with the general human condition. It is a plausible hypothesis, however, that men, as well as women, suffer from the lack of a generally accepted, clearly defined pattern of behavior expected of them, and that their interpretation

From Helen Mayer Hacker, "The New Burdens of Masculinity," *Marriage and Family Living*, vol. 19, no. 3, August, 1957, pp. 227–233. Abridged and reprinted with permission of the editor and the author.

of the masculine role varies according to individual personality needs and social situations. The massive social changes initiated by the Industrial Revolution have not only affected the complementarity of the sexes, but posed new problems of personality fulfillment for both men and women.

Analytically, contemporary masculine problems may be viewed as arising from three sources, which may prove difficult to disentangle. First, we may consider those burdens of masculinity which have survived from earlier periods, but which modern conditions may have aggravated. Men in their traditional role of breadwinners have always encountered difficulties, but it may be that recent developments in our occupational structure have added new tensions. Pertinent to this problem would be studies of occupational mobility and the increasing importance of education as both barrier and base to economic success, of vocational adjustment and the new personality traits, such as skill in politicking, needed for high level positions. Then, too, from Adam on, men have had their troubles with women, but can we distinguish the enduring from the variable in their complaints?

Secondly, it may be useful to distinguish conflicts engendered by feelings of inadequacy in fulfilling role expectations from those stemming from feelings of uncertainty, ambiguity, or confusion regarding role expectations. A man may have no doubts concerning the criteria of masculinity, but feel that he does not live up to them, or he may be unsure concerning the requirements for validating manhood. Preliminary interview materials reveal that the ideal man is considered by men as being, among other things, a good provider, the ultimate source of knowledge and authority, and strong in character so that he may give a feeling of security, not only financially but emotionally, to his wife and children, and it was evident from their further responses that the respondents found themselves deficient in meeting these demands.

The norms of masculinity, however (and, conversely, those of effeminacy), may vary among social groups, and multiple group participations may set up contradictions and inconsistencies in outlook. For example, it was only after several months of counseling that a skilled mechanic developed the courage to dust off some old Caruso records he had stored in the attic, and find that listening to them was no threat to his manhood. The group memberships of a professional man, however, would hardly produce this particular conflict.

The third source or way of examining the problematic aspects of masculine social roles is interpreting them in terms of accommodation to the new freedoms and responsibilities of women.

The chief obstacle so far experienced in efforts to collect data as a basis for the formulation of precise hypotheses has been men's reticence, which may be attributed in part, as mentioned previously, to the lack of cultural focus of attention on men's problems, as revealed in the defensive answer, "women." More important, though, is an element of the traditional masculine role which proscribes admission and expression of psychological problems, feelings, and general overt introspection, as summed up in the stereotype of the strong, silent man. True he may be permitted moments of weakness, some faltering in his self-appointed task, when he falls back on a woman for emotional support, but such support is in the nature of ego-building rather than direct participation and counsel. The ideal American male personality has been described by John Gillin as a "red-blooded, gentlemanly, go-getter" and any confessions of doubts, uncertainties, or insecurities would tarnish this image, any sign of weakness might be taken for effeminacy. Perhaps this is the greatest burden of masculinity our culture imposes.

Nevertheless, there are objective indices that all is not well with men. Most obvious is the widespread expression of resentment toward women in conversation, plays, novels, and films.

Let us try to apply the notion of ethical consistency to some of the main statuses which men occupy in our society.

As a man, men are now expected to demonstrate the manipulative skill in interpersonal relations formerly reserved for women under the headings of intuition, charm, tact, coquetry, womanly wiles, et cetera. They are asked to bring patience, understanding, gentleness to their human dealings. Yet with regard to women they must still be sturdy oaks. As I heard on the radio recently, a woman wants a man to be "big and strong, sensitive and tender, the sort of person on whom you can rely, and who leaves you free to manage things the way you want." This contradiction is also present in men's relationships with men. As Riesman points out in *The Lonely Crowd*, now that the "softness of the personnel" has been substituted for the "hardness of the material" men must be free with the glad hand, they must impress others with their warmth and sincerity (rather than as formerly with their courage and honesty and industry), they must be trouble shooters on all fronts. Yet they are not thereby relieved of the necessity of achieving economic success or other signal accomplishment, nor are they permitted such catharses as weeping, fits of hysterics, and obvious displays of emotionalism. Of course, it may be objected that as women are increasingly allowed male privileges, they, too, are restricted in their emotional expression. Yet in the present era of transition women may still on the basis of the unpredictability of their sex, which is vaguely linked to biological functioning, have greater recourse to moodiness and irrationality.

In the status of husband, a man must assume the primary responsibility for the support of the home. A man who marries for money is exposed to more social opprobrium than a woman, and there is scanty social support for the expectation that the wife should shoulder half the financial burden. The self-respecting male has no choice but to work. Rarely do marriage and homemaking offer an alternative! Yet his responsibility does not end there. Although he should excel his wife in "external creativity" he is also called upon to show some competence in "internal creativity" in developing the potentialities of the husband-wife relationship, and sharing the physical and policy-making burdens of maintaining the home.

As a father, he bears the chief responsibility in law for the guardianship of the children, but often in practice plays a subordinate role. He may wistfully long for or stormily demand the respect of his children, but his protracted absence from the home makes it easy for them to evade his authority and guidance. Moreover, he is increasingly reproached for his delinquencies as a father. He is urged to strengthen his friendly, democratic relationship to his family without in any way lessening the primacy of his occupational role, though he is made to feel guilty for his efforts to support the home to the extent that they remove him from it. Indeed, the conflict between home and job is more salient and universal for men than for women. He has lost the security of the old *paterfamilias*, who was the autocrat of the breakfast table, and experiences difficulties in establishing a satisfying new role.

Father is no longer the chief mediator between the outside world and his family.

Dr. Leo Bartemeier has pointed to a further conflict in the father role. In accordance with the cultural ideal of the he-man, fathers may feel that to be loving and gentle is consciously or unconsciously regarded as psychological failure, and indeed it may be difficult to make the transition from the attitude of ruggedness and toughness developed in schools, businesses, colleges, teams, and clubs to "the guiding light of paternal solicitude, love, and affection."

The requirements of the father role are further obscured by recent over-emphasis on the mother-child relationship, especially in infancy. Father is relegated to the role of mother-substitute or nursery assistant, and receives little help in becoming an effective member of the parent team.

We turn now to a consideration of men in the status of lover. In one sense this role strikes at the heart of the problem of masculinity. The ability to perform the sexual act has been a criterion for man's evaluation of himself from time immemorial. Virility used to be conceived as a unilateral expression of male sexuality, but is regarded today in terms of the ability to evoke a full sexual response on the part of the female. Men as the dominant group feel the strains of accommodating to the changing status of the minority group, and meeting the challenge presented by the sexual emancipation of women.

In general, it can be said that masculinity is more important to men than femininity is to women, and that sexual performance is more inextricably linked to feelings of masculine selfworth than even motherhood is to women. As stated previously, our cultural heritage has identified masculine with human, and both men and women aspire to masculine values. If a man is not masculine, not a "real man," he is nothing. But a woman can be unfeminine, and still be a person. There is a neuter category for women, but not for men.

By implication, if not directly, in the foregoing we have referred to men's occupational role, and we may now turn explicitly to this area. The problems which men, more than women, experience on the job have already been mentioned: (1) the greater compulsion to success, if not from themselves, then from their wives; (2) the lack of an alternative to gainful employment; (3) the identification of economic success with masculinity (one woman of my acquaintance has told me that a man's success is an important component of his sex appeal, both directly and indirectly; that men who feel themselves failures lack confidence in their dealings with women); (4) the new need for politicking or using traditionally feminine forms of behavior for ingratiating superiors, customers, et cetera; and (5) the feeling of being threatened by women in industry, who are seen as limiting opportunities for men, diminishing the prestige of jobs formerly held only by men, and casting a cold eye on masculine pretensions to vocational superiority. Also to be mentioned, although not new and not confined to men, are the problems of obtaining recognition, usually phrased in terms of earning more money, and job satisfaction in the sense of feeling that one is making a vital contribution to society.

The presence of women in industry is a disturbing fact on several grounds. First, it is frequently felt that women are not gentlemen, that is, they compete unfairly by using sexual attractiveness and other tactics closed to or beneath men. If the distribution of the sexes in positions of power were more equitable, this objection would lose its basis. Secondly, women who have ample opportunities of observing men on the job are not so likely, in the words of Virginia Woolf, to reflect their image double lifesize. The man's occupational role loses its mystery, and women need no longer depend on men as a link to the world outside the home. This problem, too, is one of transition, and should disappear when through habituation to working women both men and women no longer expect masculine superiority and establish casual, workaday relationships on the job. And if through propaganda and education the presence of women in the occupational world, like other minority groups, can be shown to raise levels of productivity and shorten working hours for men, then their competition will not be regarded differently from that presented by other men.

If we can return to our dominant group, minority group analogy, we can say that men are paying a price for the past lack of reciprocity between the sexes, and the future solution need not be the reversal of the caste line in a matriarchal society as some men fear, but rather the collaborative effort of men and women in evolving new masculine and feminine identities which will integrate the sexes in the emotional division of labor so that the roles which men and women play will not be rationalized or seen as external constraint but eagerly embraced as their own.

One of the problems men face today is that there seems to be a widely accepted, clear-cut conception of what it means to be a "real he-man" in terms of the highly individualistic, frontier, sexually bisected society of the past, but there has not as yet been formulated a universally accepted concept of what it means to be a "real he-man" in the competitive, industrialized, urbanized, sexually blended society of the present. The individual man is expected to meet simultaneously both the traditional and the contemporary criteria of masculinity. How can a man satisfy his ego needs in this country today if there is lack of agreement on what a man is supposed to be and if he is expected to be at the same time more than one kind of person? For example, a man is expected to be simultaneously "red-blooded and two-fisted" on the one hand, gentlemanly and peace-seeking on the other. He is under one type of pressure to "get ahead," under another type of pressure to avoid giving too much weight to material success. He is supposed to feel sorrow and sympathy but not give way to crying. He is expected to cooperate with women as equals at the same time that tradition tells him that at times, especially in times of crisis, he must "take charge" and under no circumstances ever let a woman dominate him or "get the best" of him. And so it goes.

There cannot be such penetrating changes as those which have swept over the feminine world without correlative changes in the masculine world. The point is that the worlds of both sexes are in transition. There is no immediate prospect of a crystallization of these worlds into a static *status quo*. There is no way of knowing what the ultimate outcome will be. In the meantime there will remain an active issue concerning the position of men.

THE RELATION OF THE INDIVIDUAL MAN TO STATUS, WOMEN, AND MARRIAGE

Factors irresistible as glaciers are at work to make a new woman out of the partially developed material passed on by tradition to the modern age. She is making increasingly better use of her resources. Her training is improving continually. Her social status is more nearly on a level with that of man. An assumption of woman's inferiority is as outmoded as a belief in evil spirits. Men's attitude toward women, though changing, tends to lag somewhat behind the modern scene; it is highly colored by tradition. If some men were to dress in a manner appropriate to their attitudes toward women, they would have to wear suits of armor.

A man needs to face the facts and exhibit some of the objectivity and logical thinking for which men have a reputation. Men need to sweep their minds of cobwebs and look at women as they are, not as the voices of those long since dead have claimed that they are.

Men need to adjust to the unalterable fact that a new type of intersexual competition has arisen in a way previously unknown. They cannot afford to let the attitudes of their early male ancestors so color their thinking and so determine their course of action that they find themselves either in the position of a man standing on the shore trying to stop the tide by shouting at it or in the position of a player who seeks to win a game by haranguing his opponent or refusing to let him play.

Men need to introduce consistency into their treatment of women. A man who strikes a woman violates a code of chivalry and is branded a coward and a cad. But a man who uses a woman for selfish purposes, who exploits her sexually, is assumed to be merely "sowing his wild oats." Men need to realize that they cannot "have their cake and eat it too." They cannot expect to prepare themselves for marriage while they think of women as fair prey for sexual exploitation. They cannot justify their criticism of women's sexual fears and inhibitions when men's sexual irresponsibility contributes to the establishment of those fears and inhibitions as a means of women's self-protection.

Men need also to change their attitude toward homemaking and to improve their preparation for participation in it. The day is past in which homemaking was solely a wife's responsibility, with the husband in the role of permanent guest who assumed he was head of the family because he supported it financially. As we have seen, the trend today is for the family to have no head or two heads, and homemaking is becoming a joint responsibility of husband and wife. This does not mean necessarily that they divide equally between them all aspects of housekeeping, family feeding, purchasing, and child rearing. It does mean that a man has a new role to play in the home and that he can no longer assume that domestic illiteracy is the only preparation he needs for it. It means also that a man recognize that homemaking represents a total job to be done. How the various aspects of it are apportioned between husband and wife may change as time goes on or even from day to day. But a problem arises when a man assumes that this apportionment can be arbitrarily determined in advance and permanently fixed solely on the basis of tradition.

A concluding observation

There is confusion on the part of men and women both as to their own role and as to the role of the opposite sex. There is confusion as to definitions of masculinity and femininity. Generalizing broadly without research data to substantiate the generalization, we may speculate that to some degree this confusion leads men and women to arrive at the same point through diametrically opposite means.

With new opportunities for employment open to them and with attendant increased financial independence, occupational prestige, higher standard of living, and personal satisfaction, to some degree at least many married women reject women's traditional role as full-time homemaker-mother and engage in out-of-home pursuits. On the other hand, in the absence of a clear-cut, universally accepted definition of masculinity consistent with present-day urban, industrial society, but still wanting to prove themselves "real he-men," contemporary males often shy away from new opportunities, such as participation in homemaking and child care, and fall back upon criteria of the past. They become overly absorbed in work, in itself an unquestioned criterion of manliness throughout history. Some spend much time in the development of physical strength even when such strength has no direct functional value in their particular type of life. Some take pride in sexual exploits. In either case, male or female, the result is often a reduction in the individual's personal involvement in family living—in the case of the male through overemphasis of the old, in the case of the female through overemphasis of the new. Working out a better balance in this connection is one of the unsolved problems of modern family life.

WHAT DO YOU THINK?

1. Is women's status going up or down? What is likely to happen in the future? Could women's status become too high? Could men's status become too low?

2. What suggestions do you have for the solution of the problem of "the new burdens of masculinity"?

3. If husbands continue to participate in homemaking, will men eventually become feminized?

4. At what points does the difference between the traditional pattern of family life and the modern pattern of family life create conflict?

5. By what criteria should an individual be judged a "real man" or a "real woman" in America today?

6. Is there any evidence to prove what some persons suggest, namely, that America is becoming a matriarchy?

7. What is involved in being a "good wife" or "good husband" in this country today as compared to the past? As compared to other countries?

8. How much participation in housekeeping should be expected of a husband?

9. What is the full significance of the fact that there is no longer a standard pattern of family life in this country?

10. In present-day America, can homemaking be considered a career for a woman?

11. What must a couple do in order that the wife may successfully combine marriage, employment, homemaking, and motherhood?

12. A woman wants to devote full time to her husband, home, and children without having gainful employment. Yet she does not want to find herself "high and dry" when the children have grown and left home. What suggestions would you give her?

13. Is there any sound reason for men having more authority in marriage than women have? If a couple cannot agree on something, who should have the "last word," the deciding vote? Why?

14. Some people speak of the man as a "leader" in family living. Is this valid?

SELECTED READINGS

Bassett, Marion: *A New Sex Ethics and Marriage Structure*, Philosophical Library, Inc., New York, 1961. A woman's analysis of the sexual nature of women, the differences between the sexes, and the assumption of male superiority.

Bell, Norman W., and Ezra F. Vogel (eds.): *A Modern Introduction to the Family*, The Free Press of Glencoe, New York, 1960, chaps. 11, 13, 29, 41. Changes in family structure in the nineteenth century, the effects of married women's employment on the family power structure, the effects of mothers' employment on children, and how various types of role conflict may be resolved.

Bernard, Jessie, Helen E. Buchanan, and William M. Smith, Jr.: *Dating, Mating and Marriage*, Howard Allen, Inc., Cleveland, 1958, chaps. 1, 9, 10. The changing family; changing roles of men and women. Includes many case-documentary materials.

Burgess, Ernest W., Harvey J. Locke, and Mary Margaret Thomes: *The Family*, 3d ed., American Book Company, New York, 1963, chaps. 3–5, 16, 17. The family in transition; family life of yesterday on the farm and in early America; family mobility; the Negro family; the urban family.

Calhoun, Arthur W.: *A Social History of the American Family* (3 vols.), Barnes & Noble, Inc., New York, 1917, 1918, 1919, reprinted 1960. A study of sex codes, role and status, and family change from the colonial period to 1919. Contains many interesting quotations from writings of this period.

Farber, Seymour M., and Roger H. L. Wilson (eds.): *The Potential of Woman*, McGraw-Hill Book Company, New York, 1963. A symposium. The objective "was to gather together a group of people, from as many professions as possible, to talk about the potentialities of women and the hazards they confront in their search for the most meaningful of freedoms, the freedom to be oneself."

Foote, Nelson N.: "New Roles for Men and Women," *Marriage and Family Living*, vol. 23, no. 4, pp. 325–329, November, 1961. A discussion of what is occurring relative to sex roles in the United States.

Francis, Philip: *The Legal Status of Women*, Oceana Publications, Inc., Dobbs Ferry, N.Y., 1963. A summary and analysis of the laws affecting the status of women, their rights and property, problems they may have relative to marriage, divorce, maintenance, etc.

Friedan, Betty: *The Feminine Mystique*, W. W. Norton & Company, Inc., New York, 1963. A journalist discusses the modern woman's confusion and conflict of roles. She says, ". . . something is very wrong with the way American women are trying to live their lives today."

Glick, Paul C.: *American Families*, John Wiley & Sons, Inc., New York, 1957. A statistical analysis of the changing family in the United States.

Goode, William J.: *World Revolution and Family Patterns*, The Free Press of Glencoe, New York, 1963, chaps. 1, 2. The effects of industrialization on the family; the trend toward equalitarianism; the meaning of changing family patterns; dating; premarital sexual intercourse; divorce; the rights of women; other related topics.

Gruenberg, Sidonie M., and Hilda Sidney Krech: *The Many Lives of Modern Woman*, Doubleday & Company, Inc., Garden City, N.Y., 1952. The authors are "especially concerned with the women who have some choice about the way they spend their lives and some scope in which to create new designs for living." Women's problems and dilemma.

Kephart, William M.: *The Family, Society, and the Individual*, Houghton Mifflin Company, Boston, 1961, chaps. 5, 8. The American family heritage; emergent marriage and family values; changes in courtship, marriage, etc.

Knopf, Olga: *The Art of Being a Woman*, Blue Ribbon Books, New York, 1932. The author is a woman physician. The book is "an attempt at a natural history of women in present-day society." The author holds that "women can reach the highest development of all their possibilities by refusing to fight against their sexual role." She feels that "the psychological differences between the sexes are entirely artificial."

Komarovsky, Mirra: *Women in the Modern World*, Little, Brown and Company, Boston, 1953. A discussion of women's roles.

Landis, Paul H.: *For Husbands and Wives*, Appleton-Century-Crofts, Inc., New York, 1956, chaps. 1, 4, 5. What it means to be a husband or wife today.

Lindbergh, Anne Morrow: *Gift from the Sea*, Pantheon Books, a Division of Random House, Inc., New York, 1955. An expression of a sensitive, insightful writer of a search for new meaning in the life of woman and an answer to the problem of how to remain whole in the midst of the distractions of life.

Lundberg, Ferdinand, and Marynia F. Farnham: *Modern Woman: The Lost Sex*, Harper & Row, Publishers, Incorporated, New York, 1947. A psychiatrist and a social scientist examine the role and problems of modern women whom they consider to be "one of modern civilization's major unsolved problems."

MacKenzie, Norman: *Women in Australia*, F. W. Cheshire, Pty. Ltd., Melbourne, Australia, 1962. The changing role and status of women in a country in some ways different from the United States but in other ways going through changes similar to those this country has experienced in the recent past and is experiencing today.

McCall, Milton L., and Robert J. Trace: "Effects of Pregnancy on Women in Industry," *Pennsylvania Medical Journal*, ser. 63, pp. 1773–1778, December, 1960, abstracted in J. P. Greenhill (ed.), *The Year Book of Obstetrics and Gynecology, 1961–1962*, pp. 29–31, The Year Book Medical Publishers, Inc., Chicago, 1961.

Mead, Margaret: *Male and Female*, William Morrow and Company, Inc., New York, 1949. A noted anthropologist analyzes the roles of the sexes. "How are men and women to think of their maleness and femaleness in this twentieth century, in which so many of our old ideas must be made new?" Have men been overdomesticated? Has education done something disastrous to women?

Menninger, Karl: *Love against Hate*, Harcourt, Brace & World, Inc., New York, 1942, chaps. 3, 4. A psychiatrist discusses the frustrations of women; husband-wife relations; the depreciation and repudiation of femininity.

National Manpower Council: *Work in the Lives of Married Women*, Columbia University Press, New York, 1958. The proceedings of a conference on womanpower; the employment of married women; the effects of mothers' employment on children.

Nye, F. Ivan, and Lois W. Hoffman (eds.): *The Employed Mother in America*, Rand McNally & Company, Chicago, 1963. The chapters were written by various investigators of many aspects of mothers' employment, effects on children and husband, etc.

Ogburn, W. F., and M. F. Nimkoff: *Technology and the Changing Family*, Houghton Mifflin Company, Boston, 1955. "Our objective is to learn why the family in the United States has been changing."

Oliver, Bernard J., Jr.: *Marriage and You*, College and University Press, New Haven, Conn., 1964, chap. 1. The changing definition of marriage and family life; a summary of the differences between American marriage in colonial times and today.

Queen, Stuart A., Robert W. Habenstein, and John B. Adams: *The Family in Various Cultures*, 2d ed., J. B. Lippincott Company, Philadelphia, 1961, chaps. 13, 14. The colonial family in North America: family structure, status of the sexes, choice of marriage partner, family controls, sex mores, divorce; the transition to the present.

Riesman, David: "Permissiveness and Sex Roles," *Marriage and Family Living*, vol. 21, no. 3, pp. 211–217, August, 1959. Some consequences of the spread of permissiveness in creating educational, sexual, and other problems.

Scott-Maxwell, Florida: *Women and Sometimes Men*, Alfred A. Knopf, Inc., New York, 1957. A woman psychologist discusses what women are becoming "now that they have a new ability to change." The author believes that every woman has both masculine and feminine feelings and that the pressures of modern life cause many women to be dominated by their masculinity. Penetrating and illuminating.

Seward, Georgene H.: *Sex and the Social Order*, McGraw-Hill Book Company, New York, 1946, chap. 10. Changing sex roles in Western culture.

chapter 3

TO MARRY OR
NOT TO MARRY

MARRIAGE IS NOT something that "comes naturally." It is not the product of inborn behavior patterns sometimes called "instincts." It is an institution. It is a cluster of mores and folkways, of attitudes, ideas, and ideals, of social definitions and legal restrictions. One of its focal points is the "sex instinct"; but marriage is much more than that. It is much more than mating. If marriage and mating were the same, there could be no illegitimate children. Human beings mate, but they *also* marry. In their marrying, "instinct" plays a relatively minor role. If, then, they do not marry "instinctively," why do they marry?

Why people marry

People marry for a combination of reasons. Such reasons as love, economic security, the desire for a home and children, emotional security, parents' wishes, escape from loneliness or from a parental home situation, money, companionship, sexual attraction, protection, notoriety, social position and prestige, gratitude, pity, spite, adventure, and common interests are obvious.

In some cases in which a person has been disappointed in love, had an engagement broken, or suffered some similar painful experience, he transfers his affection from the first love object to a second, feeling toward the second as he felt toward the first even though the second may be a quite different sort of person and even though he has not known the second long enough to be really in love with that person. He makes a choice before he has sufficiently regained his emotional balance to make a wise one. This is marriage on the rebound.

There are still weddings resulting from pressure—"shotgun weddings"—but there is less pressure than formerly. There is a growing feeling against forcing a couple to marry, even if there is a premarital pregnancy. A forced marriage gives a child a legal father but cannot give him a loving father or the advantages of having happily married parents. Sometimes when there is neither love nor social pressure a man feels honor bound to marry the mother of his child. But such a feeling is hardly a substitute for love and is difficult to sustain throughout marriage.

In some cases the more parents object to a marriage, the more determined the young couple become and the more attractive they seem to each other. They marry not so much because they want to marry as to assert themselves.

Law and custom play a part. Our social life is such that people are expected to marry. If they do not, society is inclined to wonder why, and they themselves may feel "different." Many a person marries because others in his circle of friends are marrying and he does not want to be the last one to do so. In recent years this reason for marriage has become frequently apparent as the age at marriage has declined and an increasing number of adolescents of high school age, sensitive to the pressure of the peer group, have become involved.

The law prescribes certain types of behavior for men and women and places restrictions upon them. The law does not force people to marry; but it does force them to marry if they want certain rights and privileges.

In the last analysis, people marry because marriage is the socially accepted pattern through which they can most satisfactorily achieve certain desired ends and satisfy certain innate or acquired urges, some of which may be achieved or satisfied to a degree without marriage. It is these desires and goals that may be thought of as the reasons for marriage. Whatever the individual elements involved, they must be fitted into the cultural pattern. Marriage is a societal as well as an individual matter. Hence no two people marry for one reason alone.

Love

If you were to ask a group of married people why they married, probably the majority of them would say, "Because we were in love." They "married for love." No doubt they would be at least partly correct. They did marry because they experienced a feeling that they interpreted as love. It is difficult, however, to state with any great degree of precision just what the feeling is. We use the term *love* in a great many different senses. You say, for example, "I love my parents," "I love my fiancé," "I love God," "I love my country," "I love animals," "I love nice clothes," "I love to hunt." It is obvious that you cannot love your mother in the same way that you "love" hunting. You do not have the same emotional experience with your country that you have with a fiancé.

We might qualify the term *love* by such adjectives as "filial," "parental," "conjugal," "romantic"; but that would still not explain precisely what we mean when we say we "marry for love," or we "fall in love." Furthermore, love means different things to different people, depending upon their background and experience, and it has various meanings at different periods of life.

What distinguishes the love into which we "fall" from the other types of love is the obvious sexual element, the fact that it grows out of a recognition of sex differences. This is not the same as saying that love is entirely on a physical basis, for it is not. Sex is more than physical; it ramifies all through an individual's life. But in romantic love, the love into which we "fall," the love that leads up to and over into marriage, there is a centering of attention on the other person as a focus of biological urges and a means of relief from biological tension. Such love, however, involves not only the desire for relief from tension but also the desire to increase it, so that unmarried lovers may exhibit the strange paradox of enjoying nearness to each other, fondling each other, and dreaming of each other, when these activities are both bitter and sweet at the same time.

MISCONCEPTIONS CONCERNING LOVE

There are a number of common misconceptions concerning love that play a part in our thinking about it and add to the confusion of the individual who is attempting to determine whether what he is experiencing is genuine love or one of the counterfeits that often pass for it. Some of these misconceptions are as follows.

The expression "fall in love" gives the impression that love is a pit covered with branches to camouflage a trap set to catch the unwary. Of course, if a person "*falls* in love," he may easily convince himself that he is the victim of a fate over which he has no control and for the results of which he therefore has no responsibility.

We assume that we "fall in love" only with our "hearts," but that is not true. We do "fall in love" with our "hearts" but also, it is hoped, with our "heads." In addition, the process is colored by the traditions, customs, standards, ideas, and ideals of the group in which we live and out of which our attitudes spring.

It would be much better to say that we grow into love. That would be nearer the truth, but it sounds unromantic. Although one may fall precipitously into a condition of violent infatuation, it takes time for love to develop. Love is a complex sentiment. It does not strike suddenly or fall unexpectedly like manna from heaven. It comes only when two individuals have reoriented their lives, each with the other as a new focal point.

Some persons believe that when an individual is experiencing what he interprets to be love his immediate experience outweighs all other considerations. He is sometimes almost expected to lose his perspective. There is also an assumption that what an individual feels at a given moment cannot and will not change and that therefore it must be love. These misconceptions go hand in hand with the uncritical assumption that love is largely a physical experience.

Some persons attribute to love an almost unlimited power of off-setting or eradicating individual shortcomings. The assumption seems to be that, if feelings are sufficiently intense, personality traits will affect neither the couple's relationship nor their marriage, or else that undesirable traits will be molded to fit the ideal merely through the healing balm of love.

There exists a similar misconception relative to love's ability to solve problems. Individuals supposedly in love often blithely disregard problems connected with parents, income, possible babies, employment, the completion of their education, and so on.

Some individuals believe that somewhere in the world is *the* one, the only person with whom they could fall in love and with whom they could find happiness. They are depending upon a kind fate, plus a certain amount of seeking on their own part, to bring the two predestined lovers together. This is a very romantic conception, but it cannot be squared with the facts. The assumption that only people suited to each other will fall in love is false. Since Americans are born at the rate of one about every seven to eight seconds, it would be somewhat difficult to keep one's seeking abreast of the population.

What happens to make it seem as if the above theory were true is probably this: Two persons have certain ideas concerning an ideal marriage partner. They meet and fall in love. During this process each revamps his ideal to fit the other person, and consequently each has fallen in love with the ideal partner. But before that happened, they might as readily have fallen in love with any one of a number of persons. After the ideals have been revamped and centered around given individuals, however, this fact colors their attitude toward other persons and might make it impossible to fall in love with anyone else.

There is a misconception that when love does come it can be instantly recognized. In one case that illustrates this point clearly because it is extreme, a serviceman wrote to a college girl whose picture he had seen in a newspaper. She responded. Through correspondence they presumably became acquainted, fell in love, and became engaged. On his first leave, the boy came to meet his fiancée for the first time. He was scheduled to arrive on Thursday. The wedding was to take place on Friday. On Wednesday the girl was asked how she could be sure that she was in love with a boy whom she had never seen. She answered, "As soon as he steps off the train, I'll know."

There is a common assumption that a person marries only another individual and that therefore only his feelings toward this individual are important; other considerations may safely be disregarded. In one sense, of course, a person does marry only an individual. In another sense he "marries" that individual plus that individual's family, background, social status, occupation, financial condition, moral standards, friends, past, and everything connected with him.

The above misconception leads to another with which it overlaps, namely, that love is the only and entire basis for marriage. Yet associated with this misconception is another partially contradictory one. There are persons who believe that falling in love is the only prerequisite for getting married, but at the same time they believe that most couples fall out of love sooner or later after the wedding and settle down to a more or less humdrum marital existence in which each takes the other for granted.

HOW CAN ONE TELL WHETHER ONE IS REALLY IN LOVE?

There is no simple formula for determining the presence of love. One cannot say, "$a + b = c$; therefore, I am in love." Hence, with the possibility of their overlapping, we have chosen to do two things: first, to present a brief series of contrasting attributes of love and infatuation; second, to present a series of questions to aid in self-analysis. The items mentioned below represent tendencies. One cannot say consistently, "Love is always like this, while infatuation is always like that." These items are intended only to help the individual reach a conclusion regarding his own experience.

Love and infatuation. Love grows, and all growth requires time. Infatuation may come suddenly. The question of whether or not there can be love at first sight is often raised. What usually happens in "love at first sight" is that the couple are strongly attracted to each other, perhaps infatuated, from the very beginning. Then this strong attraction develops into love without any break in the process. It seems as if it were love at first sight; but that does not prove that it was.

"Love at first sight" may also be compulsive in nature. The individual has a strong urge to love someone, and this urge becomes focused on a particular person. What should be expressed as "This is the individual I must love" is expressed by the person concerned as "This is the individual I do love" [Waller, 1951]. Such an urge to love is not uncommon in adolescence, when new emotions, with which the young person has not yet learned to live and which are largely the result of his own physiological development rather than of his experience, begin to well up within him.

Such "love" may also be an outgrowth of an individual's feeling of inferiority or his fear that because of personal unattractiveness or inability to meet members of the opposite sex he may never marry. Seizing upon the first opportunity to be attractive when someone exhibits interest in him, he convinces himself that it must be love at first sight.

Usually an individual reaches a sound conclusion that he is in love after seeing the other person under a variety of circumstances. An individual may become infatuated after seeing the other person in relatively few situations or even in only one and reach a premature decision about love.

Love grows out of an appraisal of all the known characteristics of the other person. Infatuation may arise from an acquaintance with only a few or only one of these characteristics.

When an individual is genuinely in love, he is in love with the other person as a total personality; his feelings grow primarily out of his relationship with that other person and his total estimate of him. An infatuated individual may be "in love with love." His feelings are primarily self-generated and grow only in part out of his relationship with the other person. The other person is a hook on which these self-generated emotions are hung.

Love is other-person-centered. It is outgoing. It results in sharing. Infatuation is self-centered. The other person is a means of self-gratification. An individual in love feels identified with the other person; they seem to be a team or pair. An infatuated individual is inclined to think of the other person as separate from himself but to be used for his own satisfaction.

Genuine love is centered on one person only. An infatuated individual may be "in love" with two or more persons simultaneously. These persons may be quite different as to personal qualities. The following is a not unusual situation. A girl is "in love" with two boys and cannot choose between them. One is relatively mature, stable, ambitious, thrifty, responsible, and reserved. The other is relatively immature, unstable, uninhibited, irresponsible, fun-loving, and a free spender. At times she likes to be with one, at other times with the other. When she thinks of marriage, neither boy seems to have all the qualities that she would want in her husband. What is the explanation of this seemingly incongruous situation? It is unlikely that a girl could be genuinely in love with two boys who are so different. One possible explanation is that the girl is relatively immature and is in the midst of emotional transition between late adolescence and early womanhood. In so far as she is a woman, she seeks the qualities represented by the first boy. In so far as she is still adolescent, the qualities of the second boy appeal to her. She is "on the fence" emotionally, and her experience has not yet permitted her to find one man who exhibits all the qualities she seeks. To get what she wants she must combine the qualities of two quite different boys. Hence she is "in love" with both. Many such individuals eventually marry persons whom they had not yet met at the time the above problem arose.

An individual in love tends to have a sense of security and a feeling of trust after considering everything involved in his relationship with the other person. An infatuated individual tends to have a blind sense of security based upon wishful thinking rather than upon careful consideration, or he may have a sense of insecurity that is expressed as jealousy.

An individual in love works for the other person or for their mutual benefit. He may study to make the other person proud of him. His ambition is spurred, and he plans and saves for the future. He may daydream, but his dreams are reasonably attainable. An infatuated person may lose his ambition, his appetite, and his interest in everyday affairs. He thinks of his own misery. He often daydreams, but his dreams are not limited to the attainable. At times the dreams become substitutes for reality, and the individual lives in his world of dreams.

Love leads to idealization, but because the ideal is partly an outgrowth of understanding of and appreciation for the other person, it may be checked against reality without loss. In infatuation there tends to be idealization accompanied by a disregard of reality. A certain amount of idealization may be desirable, for none of us can look at a love object with complete impersonality; but the idealization should be continually checked with reality and not depart so far from it that sight of the real person is lost and a true appraisal is impossible.

A couple in love face problems frankly and attempt to solve them. If there are barriers to their getting married, these barriers are approached intelligently and removed. Those that cannot be removed may be circumvented, but with the knowledge that what is done is deliberate circumvention. In infatuation, problems tend to be disregarded or glossed over. Barriers to the couple's getting married may be lightly set aside, and circumvention may be confused with solution. If, after the wedding, these same problems again arise to harass the marriage, the couple may not have foreseen that this would occur. A couple in love intelligently anticipate such problems.

Love tends to be constant. Infatuation often varies with the "distance" between the couple. There may be greater attraction when they are separated because they idealize each other but less when they are together because they see each other as they are and are more critical. Or there may be greater attraction when they are together because of overwhelming physical appeal that beclouds judgment and less attraction when they are separated because physical responses are less intense and they see each other from a different point of view. There may be less attraction when the couple are apart because each sees the other in total perspective and the situation becomes more complex, but when they are together physical presence seems all that is necessary and the situation appears simpler.

Physical attraction is a relatively smaller part of their total relationship when a couple are in love, a relatively greater part when they are infatuated. Let us imagine, for illustration, that physical attraction is represented by a 3-inch square. In infatuation this square is, say, part of a 4-inch square; in love it is part of a 12-inch square because there are other considerations.

When a couple are in love, any physical contact that they have is likely to have meaning as well as to be a pleasurable experience in and of itself. It expresses what they feel toward each other. In infatuation, physical contact is typically an end in itself. It represents only pleasurable experience, devoid of meaning.

In love an expression of affection may come relatively late in the couple's relationship. In infatuation it may come earlier, sometimes from the very beginning.

Love tends to endure. Infatuation may change suddenly, unexpectedly, unpredictably. When love changes, the reasons are usually more or less apparent. Infatuation may change for no apparent reason, and the cause of the change is to be found in the physiological and psychological processes of the individual in whom the change first appears rather than in what the other person has done or become.

Love is "tough"; it is resilient. It can absorb personality conflicts and adverse circumstances without being unduly threatened. Even when there is conflict, the individual in love accepts the other person and is concerned about that person as well as about himself. Hence a person who is in love is not readily provoked to impulsive rejection or to impatient lashing out with criticism designed to demean the other person in order to protect self. Infatuation is more brittle. An interpersonal relationship based upon it, though intense, hangs by a slender thread. It is easily threatened. Relatively minor events or bits of personal behavior can upset it. Since infatuation is so largely a type of self-gratification, the infatuated individual is inclined either to gloss over or to be blind to the other person's faults or to attempt to change for his own increased comfort even relatively insignificant traits of the other person. Love is not blind, contrary to the old adage. It is infatuation that is blind. Love sees but accepts. "A friend," someone has said, "is one who knows all about you and loves you." If this be true of friends, how much more true it is of persons in love!

A person who is genuinely in love is concerned about his relationship with the other person. His concern is about the relationship, not just about the contribution of the relationship to his own pleasure. He does not deliberately do anything that might damage that relationship. He is alert to possible means of strengthening it, preserving it, and furthering its development. An infatuated individual is more likely to lack awareness of the role he can play in furthering the relationship. He may do things to please the other person, but these things are designed to increase the other person's acceptance of him and therefore to increase his own self-gratification rather than to strengthen the interpersonal relationship.

A person who is in love seeks to please the other person but also has the concern, insight, and courage to do what is best for that person even when that person himself does not understand what is best for him and demands only what is pleasant to him. This is not intended to imply making another person's decisions for him but making one's own decisions on the basis of love-induced concern. For example, take the case of a girl who, in spite of a boy's impatience and in spite of her desire to be married, refuses to agree to an early wedding date in the face of a boy's need to prove himself occupationally before assuming the responsibilities of a family.

A couple in love are not indifferent to the effects of postponing their wedding and do not prolong the period of postponement unduly, but they can wait a reasonable time; they do not feel an almost irresistible urge toward haste. They may think of the period of postponement as one of further preparation so that when it does occur their marriage will be on a sounder basis than if they married immediately. An infatuated couple often feel an urge toward immediate marriage. Postponement is intolerable to them, and they interpret it as deprivation rather than as preparation.

Questions for self-analysis. The questions listed below are intended as an aid in self-analysis. They are for the person who has doubts; they are not meant to undermine the confidence of anyone who feels sure. The reader may answer each question for himself. In many instances no one can tell him what the answer should be. He must determine the significance of an affirmative or a negative answer in his own case and weight each answer in the light of his own personality, the other person's personality, and the whole situation. Not all the questions necessarily apply to every person, and there is no single criterion by which he can solve his problem. One might answer all of them and still be in doubt if in his case there were special considerations that are not included.

Above all, these questions are not to be scored as a test, as in the case of a list of similar queries that appeared in a popular magazine. The questions were useful, but the author of the article suggested that each "yes" answer count 5½ and that the total score would indicate the degree of infatuation or love. Such a suggestion is absurd. Who can say that a "yes" answer means the same for everyone? Moreover, not all "yes" answers would necessarily be of equal value; and the configuration of answers, that is, which ones were answered "yes" and how they were related, as well as the number of them, would be significant.

"No" answers are not necessarily undesirable in the light of a total situation. Being in love cannot be expressed by a mathematical average.

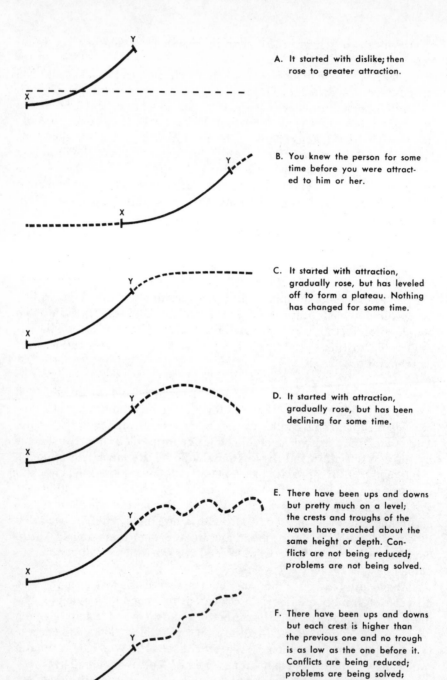

A. It started with dislike; then rose to greater attraction.

B. You knew the person for some time before you were attracted to him or her.

C. It started with attraction, gradually rose, but has leveled off to form a plateau. Nothing has changed for some time.

D. It started with attraction, gradually rose, but has been declining for some time.

E. There have been ups and downs but pretty much on a level; the crests and troughs of the waves have reached about the same height or depth. Conflicts are not being reduced; problems are not being solved.

F. There have been ups and downs but each crest is higher than the previous one and no trough is as low as the one before it. Conflicts are being reduced; problems are being solved; progress is being made.

Figure 3. Possible changes in a couple's relationship to be considered in diagnosing love. The X-Y portion of each line may look the same as that portion of the others, disregarding the oversimplification. The direction the line will take after point Y can be determined only through time.

Furthermore, a person cannot make himself be in love by "going through the motions" of the things suggested in the questions. Following, then, is the list of suggestions to aid the individual in analyzing himself to determine whether or not he is in love.

1. Do you like to be in the company of the other person? Do you prefer that person's company to anyone else's?

2. Is the individual personally attractive to you? Do you feel inclined to apologize for his or her appearance, manners, ideas, conversation, or language? Are you confusing admiration with love and assuming that your relationship is the platonic variety, involving no physical elements? It is as unwise to attempt to rule out physical attraction as it is to permit such attraction to be the entire basis of your relationship.

3. How do you make up after a quarrel or difference? How do you go about reestablishing your relationship?

4. As you look back over your relationship from the first meeting, how has it changed? Which of the diagrams in Figure 3 most nearly describes it, and what does this mean in your case? Notice that all the possibilities may show considerable resemblance to one another in the earlier stages. Only increasing acquaintance over a period of time makes it possible to distinguish among them.

5. Do you have common interests? Did you have these interests before you met? Or did you develop them together? Or did you become interested in the other person's interests? If the last is the case, are your interests sincere, or are they a means of being attractive to the other person?

6. Has enough time elapsed to tell? The sooner after meeting the couple consider themselves in love, the greater the probability of infatuation.

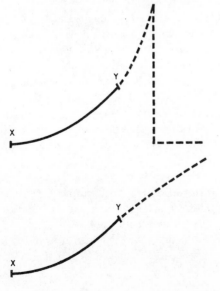

G. It started with a great swish of enthusiasm, exploded in mid-air with spectacular effects, then skyrocketlike, it began to fall rapidly toward the earth, a mass of cooling ashes. Many "war marriages" were based on this sort of relationship and unfortunately, in many cases, the wedding occurred just before the rocket reached its highest point and started to descend.

H. It started with attraction and has become steadily richer and deeper. You can conceive of its continuing to do so indefinitely.

7. Is there anything more than physical attraction in your relationship? How soon after your acquaintance began did you begin to be affectionate? If you feel strong attraction toward the other person, become stirred up when you are together, dream about him or her constantly when you are separated, even though you have known the individual only a very short time, there is a possibility that the attraction is largely physical. At least the possibility is great enough to make postponement of marriage desirable until you can be more sure. What proportion of your time is taken up with close physical contact? How intense is such contact? Does it dominate your relationship? Is it characterized by such urgency that it leads you to disregard time, place, circumstances, other people, or appropriateness? Is it preventing the two of you from getting to know each other in a way conducive to the development of love? Is it furthering your total relationship, or are you letting one aspect of your relationship get out of perspective?

8. Do you love the individual as a person, or do you like merely your feeling about him or her? Are you in love with a personality or "in love with love"? The boy or girl in early adolescence is inclined to be attracted to persons of the opposite sex in general. Almost anyone passably acceptable will serve as the focal point for the new emotions that have sprung up within the child. At that stage the child is "in love with love." Some persons develop beyond this stage sooner than others. Where do you stand? Are you still in the stage of being "in love with love"?

9. Are you attracted to the individual for what he or she is or for what you read into him or her? Have you overidealized the person to the point of blindness so that you pick out those traits that seem to fit your picture of an ideal spouse and close your eyes to others? Is the individual like an oil painting, attractive because of what is on the canvas, or like a motion-picture screen, reflecting only what is projected onto it?

10. Does the person "wear well" with your friends and family? You may see qualities that your friends do not appreciate or have not had opportunity to observe. On the other hand, your friends may be more objective and unbiased; they are not likely to be blind to shortcomings. Your parents may not know the person as well as you do, they may be biased in their appraisal, and they cannot weigh all the subjective elements involved in your choice. On the other hand, however, it is highly likely that your parents know more about marriage than you do.

11. Are you attracted to the person for what he or she is or for what he or she can give you or do for you?

12. Over what matters and how frequently do you have conflict? Is the conflict open or suppressed? Is it superficial or fundamental?

13. Are you willing to make concessions, or do you always expect the other person to do the pleasing, agreeing, and adjusting?

14. Do you have any doubts about your love? A certain amount of doubt while love is developing is not at all unusual. When, however,

the question is whether or not to marry, the old adage, "When in doubt, don't," is apropos. Marrying to escape a doubt-ridden situation does not resolve doubts; it merely puts them out of mind temporarily.

15. How do you weather a crisis together?

16. Do you feel that you want to love the other person or that you have to fight against it? Is yours a case in which strong physical attraction tends to draw you toward the other person at the same time that careful appraisal of personality makes you resist the physical appeal?

17. Do you feel that, if you "let yourself go" and loved the other person as much as you might, you would become submerged in his or her personality and lose your individuality?

18. Are you sufficient stimulus for each other when you are together, or do you require external stimuli, such as movies, dancing, or a group of people, to prevent boredom? To what degree is your stimulus for each other limited to physical appeal?

19. Do you love the person in your calmer moments, or do you seem to be in love only when your temperature and blood pressure are high and your heart is palpitating?

20. In your mind, how does the individual fare in competition with others? As comparisons are made with others, is he or she always at the top of the list? Or are you constantly looking for "greener pastures"?

21. How readily and how frequently do you publicize what ought to be private? Calling attention to the other person's weaknesses, recounting embarrassing experiences, or disclosing confidential information may indicate a disregard of the feelings of the other party.

22. What is the relationship between your enthusiasm and the presence or absence of the other person?

23. Do you feel that your relationship hangs on a very slender thread and could be easily broken?

24. Do you willingly permit the person to date when you are separated for an extended period? What is the reason for your answer and what does it mean with regard to your relationship with the other person?

25. Do you forgive, tolerate, accept, overlook, or resent faults and shortcomings? Do you love the individual "faults and all," or are you holding yourself in check pending reform?

26. What is the effect of separation after it is over?

27. Have you seen the individual in enough different types of situations and observed enough different facets of personality to know that you are in love? In some ways students in a college are like animals in a zoo. If you wanted to study lions, you might learn a good deal about them by observing them in a zoo. You could, for example, see their size, shape, and color. You might watch them eat the food that the keepers provided or do the tricks that the keepers taught them to do. But after you had observed the lions as carefully as you could in the zoo, your knowledge of

them would still be limited. If you wanted seriously to study lions, you would have to observe them in their natural habitat. There you would see them procure their own food in competition with their kind. There you would see how protective coloration can make even a large animal inconspicuous. There you would see animals survive or die in a struggle for existence that is reduced in captivity. In many respects, a campus represents an artificial environment. In such an environment certain aspects of an individual's personality and life pattern may escape notice and others may be magnified. Or the other individual may base his judgments of another person upon words rather than upon direct observation of behavior. Take, for example, the matter of an individual's family and his relationship to it — so important because in a real sense, as suggested earlier, when a person marries he marries a family as well as a spouse. If an individual has not been observed in his family, is it safe to base one's judgments upon what he says about family when what he says must of necessity be biased and incomplete?

28. Do you see the person's faults *and* their significance? Or do you merely see faults in a distant, detached way, without realizing what those faults would mean in marriage?

29. When you are with other men or women without this person present, do you think more or less of him or her, as to both frequency and intensity?

30. If he has told you in no uncertain terms that he is sure he loves you and will love you forever, what part does this certainty play in making you feel that you love him? If she seems indifferent, has it caused you to confuse love with the "spirit of the chase"? Are you under the pressure of some "test" of love, such as "If you love me, you will do thus and so"?

31. To what extent do you feel identified with this person? Do you think of yourselves as a pair or as isolated individuals?

32. How much are you concerned about the individual's welfare and happiness?

33. Is there anything or anybody in life that you consider more valuable to you than this other person or that you love more than you love him or her? If so, what or who is it, and what does that fact mean?.

34. Do you have a desire to escape an unhappy home, school, or work situation? Such a desire to escape often "makes the grass on the other side of the fence look greener." Marriage looks like the way out. Under such circumstances, it is easy to confuse infatuation and love.

35. What has been your reaction to these questions? Have you found it difficult to be honest with yourself? Have you rationalized any of your answers? Have you dismissed the use of such analysis on the assumption that questions cannot help you anyway? Have the questions put you on the defensive, as if you were afraid they would undermine something not fully secure?

The reader may wonder whether there can be any genuine love. Doubts about his own feeling may have increased. This may be temporarily confusing, but it is not dangerous. Let him remember that a love that cannot stand the test of thirty-five questions could never stand the test of thirty-five years of marriage or, for that matter, even thirty-five months of marriage.

In many cases, try as he will, an individual cannot reach a conclusion as to whether or not he is in love. Sometimes the more he tries the more confused he becomes, and the more confused he becomes, the more he feels impelled to reach a conclusion, until the vicious circle into which he has been precipitated absorbs a large portion of his time, energy, and attention. There is no simple prescription that may be administered to such a person to rid him of the problem that plagues him. Probably the answer is time and the explanation of his plight is this: He is trying to reach a conclusion by intellectual processes alone, when that conclusion must be based at least in part on a growth process, and growth requires time. His experience up to date in his relationship with the other person has contributed certain "data" that form part of the basis upon which a conclusion will eventually be reached. But the "data" are incomplete and, although the individual goes over them, examines them, "digests" them again and again, he arrives nowhere. What he needs is more experience, more contact with and observation of the other person, more "data." This will require time. Since it is indecision that is plaguing him, and since any decision will aid him in breaking the vicious circle, the individual may "make a decision to make no decision"; that is, he may definitely make up his mind to suspend judgment until he has more "data" and for the time being stop trying to reach a conclusion.

Putting all that we have discussed up to this point into a nutshell, we may say that two individuals are in love not only when they have certain strong emotional responses to one another and have for each other a particular type of regard. They are in love when their mutual relationship fosters the growth of each individual and is itself likely to increase in depth and satisfaction. They are in love when they begin to merge their patterns of life into one common pattern that will eventually represent a new entity of which each individual is a complementary part.

In discussing love, we may well raise one further question. On what basis does any individual have the right to assume that he will be loved by someone else? To be loved is a great privilege. To be loved is also a great responsibility. When an individual allows himself to be loved, he holds in his hand the happiness, perhaps even the destiny, of another person. Shall he expect to be loved because he is so lovable? Or shall he expect to be loved because the other person is so loving? As we shall see in a later chapter, upon his answers to these questions may rest his approach to one of the basic aspects of marital adjustment.

The marriage rate

HOW MANY MARRY?

The marriage rate (the number per 1,000 population who marry in a given year) fluctuates from year to year. It decreases during a depression, for instance, and tends to increase at the beginning and at the end of a war. More than a year before the United States entered the Second World War, when Selective Service was under consideration, the marriage rate rose. After Pearl Harbor the rate reached another peak. Then, while millions of men of marriageable age were in the service, many of them abroad, the rate decreased. It rose again after the surrender of Germany and Japan, reaching an all-time high in 1946. By 1955 it had settled down to approximately what it was in 1930 [U.S. Public Health Service, 1957]. A marked upswing of the rate is expected between 1965 and 1970, when large numbers of young people from the "baby boom" of the middle 1940s reach marriageable age [Lunde, 1963].

There has been an upward trend in the amount of remarriage. About two-thirds of the women and about three-fourths of the men who obtain divorces eventually remarry [Glick, 1957]. Of the persons who married in 1961 about one-fifth had been married before [U.S. Bureau of the Census, 1964].

THE NORMALITY OF MARRIAGE

Statistically marriage is normal; more than nine out of ten of the persons who live to be fifty or older eventually marry [Glick, 1957]. In a sense, therefore, marriage is normal and the minority who never marry are abnormal. On the other hand, if at a given time everyone of marriageable age in this country were married, that would be an abnormal situation. So we may think of a certain amount of singleness as normal, also. Thinking in terms of the whole group, the normal is variation. Therefore, we are not justified in thinking of every individual who does not marry as being abnormal in the sense of necessarily "having something wrong with him." Yet often in everyday life that person must justify his choice, and sometimes he himself comes to think of his own state as one which brands him as "different" or "peculiar."

Since 7 to 8 per cent of the population never marries and this amount of nonmarriage is a normal expectation in the group, and since the individual considers the two alternatives of marriage and nonmarriage before choosing either, the unmarried, their reasons for remaining single, and the problems they face are integral parts of the composite whole.

Reasons for not marrying

LACK OF OPPORTUNITY

Disproportion of the sexes. As we have seen, both the birthrate and the death rate are higher for males than for females. There has been relatively little change in the proportion of the sexes at birth in recent years. Death rates for both sexes have decreased, but the rate for females has decreased more than that for males.

In recent years immigration has decreased in quantity and has changed in type. Before 1930 it was predominantly male. Since that time it has become predominantly female. Life expectancy has increased, and there is an increasing proportion of older persons in the population. The result of these changes has been a gradual decline in the sex ratio, that is, a gradual decrease in the number of males per 100 females in the population. As we have seen, at present the ratio falls below 100; that is, there are fewer males than females in all age groups above the eighteen-year level [U.S. Bureau of the Census, 1960a].

In the last analysis some persons must remain single because there is no one for them to marry. However the disproportion of the sexes does not operate alone to prevent marriage. Probably other factors, such as lack of interest in marriage and unattractiveness, play a part in sifting the population, so the statistical excess includes many persons who are even otherwise unlikely to marry.

The type of community in which one lives. The disproportion of the sexes is not evenly distributed through the country. There are community and sectional variations. There are also community factors unrelated to statistics, since the mere presence of members of the opposite sex is no guarantee that they will be considered attractive.

Responsibilities which prevent the meeting of eligible marriage partners. For example, the care of invalid parents.

Occupation. The missionary, the explorer, the herder, a person whose occupation requires nightwork, and many others may find that their occupations prevent their meeting eligible marriage partners.

Unattractiveness.

Ignorance of means of approaching the opposite sex and getting acquainted.

Open aggression on the part of women. There are some women who do not marry because they are too anxious. They pursue men so obviously that men avoid them.

Too long delay in earlier years.

Career interest. If an individual has a greater interest in a career than in marriage, or if he feels that career and marriage cannot be successfully combined, he may remain single. The priesthood is a case in point.

LACK OF INTEREST IN MARRIAGE, HOME LIFE, AND THE OPPOSITE SEX

There may be persons who lack interest in marriage, though it need not be assumed that there is anything "peculiar" about them. There are also other persons, and *the two types should never be confused*, who lack interest in marriage because they have stronger leanings toward members of their own sex than toward persons of the opposite sex.

Hereditary defects. Persons who are aware that they may be carrying inheritable defects which, though they are not observable in themselves, could be transmitted to their children sometimes hesitate to marry. Or one person may hesitate to marry another who is the carrier of the defect.

Distorted ideas. If a person has ideals so unattainable that he seeks a perfect marriage partner and refuses to marry until he finds one, the result is apparent, for there is no such thing as a perfect husband or wife.

If a girl feels that by marrying she will submerge her personality in that of her husband or that she will become a satellite revolving around her brilliant mate and shining only by reflected light, she may shun such an existence.

"Single blessedness" is a commonly used phrase reflecting an attitude that leads some people to avoid marriage. Many unhappily married persons are the victims of what Frederick Knight has termed the "old oaken bucket delusion." Discontented, disappointed, unsuccessful people, persons subject to this delusion, are inclined to glorify the past. They think of it as the golden age to which they would gladly return. They remember only those parts of the past that are pleasant to remember; they forget the unpleasant ones. This attitude leads some persons to assume that singleness is preferable to marriage.

Disinclination to assume the responsibilities of marriage.

THE "PHANTOM LOVER"

In some cases when a sweetheart or a fiancé dies, the other person remains "true to the memory" of the deceased, idealizes him or her to such an extent that no living person could possibly reach the ideal and compete with the deceased one, and remains in love with an individual who is to a considerable extent the product of the living lover's imagination. Such an idealized individual is termed a "phantom lover." The loved one need not have died, however, to become idealized to the point of becoming a "phantom lover." There are persons who commit themselves only once and remain true to a first love for life even though the other individual marries someone else.

Disappointment in love. This may result in the "phantom lover," but it may also result in a bitterness or discouragement that militates against marriage.

PARENTS

Some persons remain single because parents prohibit marriage at any time or because they prohibit marriage to a particular individual and the son or daughter never desires marriage with anyone else.

Care or support of parents sometimes prevents marriage. The individual feels that, since his parents have done so much for him, he cannot desert them in their time of need. Occasionally one finds a parent who feigns illness or is subject to psychosomatic illness (illness that has physical symptoms but an emotional basis) in order to dominate the child and prevent his marriage.

Parent fixation is another factor preventing marriage in some instances. It often plays a part in the filial "devotion" explained above. We shall return to this matter of fixation when we discuss emotional maturity. At this point a brief explanation will suffice. Every child goes through a stage in his development when his first love is his mother or father. If he fails to develop beyond this stage, if his emotional growth becomes fixated at an immature level, he becomes the victim of parent fixation and he cannot experience normal love for a person of his own age.

A man with a mother fixation may not marry because he cannot bear to have another woman take first place in his life, that is, take the place of his mother. He may marry a very young woman who will seem like a child in his family and will not disturb his attachment to his mother. Or he may marry a woman who will be more like a mother than like a wife to him. If he does marry and his mother fixation remains intact and his wife cannot accept the role that she must play, his marriage is put on a precarious footing and may fail. No one is ready for marriage who cannot put his spouse before his parents, no matter how much he may love the latter.

FEAR

Fear of sex is not uncommon, especially but not exclusively among women. Fear of sex may be due to early conditioning, that is, early experience or teaching that makes sex seem unclean, repulsive, or sinful. If a child has had a traumatic experience, if his parents made much ado over his naïve and sincere questions about childbirth, if a girl was not prepared for her first menstruation, if a boy is told that masturbation will be followed by horrible consequences, or if a parent has had an unhappy marriage and continually tells a child to remain single, such a child may grow to fear sex. Fear of sex may also be due to misinformation or lack of information. Frequently Christian teachings are distorted so that sex is made to seem sinful and unclean.

Fear of uncertainty is not unusual. Marriage does involve a chance element, an element of uncertainty. It is not possible to predict in advance exactly how a marriage will work out. If an individual has evolved a fairly satisfactory adjustment to the *status quo*, he may hesitate to leave it to plunge into something untried and, to a degree, uncertain.

Fear of the opposite sex may be due to ignorance, distorted information, or unfortunate experience early in life. For similar reasons a person may develop a *fear of marriage*, the unfortunate experience in some cases being the parents' marriage.

There is also *fear that the other person may not be adequate* or may not "measure up." He may have a physical defect or a personality quirk that would seem to put marriage to him on a precarious basis.

Finally, there is *fear of one's own abilities and capacities.* If an individual feels inferior, if he feels that he may not be able to reach the standard set for a marriage partner, he may hesitate to marry. Such an individual sometimes becomes a "Don Juan." To the poet, Don Juan was the great lover who captivated feminine hearts wherever he went. To the psychologist, Don Juan is often the fearful lover, the lover who is insecure and lacks confidence in his own abilities. Therefore, in order to prove his adequacy to himself and to others he must make repeated conquests but no permanent attachments.

GUILT

An individual who feels guilty because of some sexual or other indiscretion may hesitate to marry, either because he feels unworthy of marrying a person whose record is presumably clear or because he fears that his past may come to light and shatter the love and confidence of the other person and thus destroy the marriage.

FALLING IN LOVE WITH A MARRIED PERSON

This experience prevents marriage in many cases. In some instances such a love is bona fide; in others an individual falls in love with a married person because he is "safer." If an individual is afraid of marriage, falling in love with a single person may result in a chain of developments leading to the very thing he wants to avoid. By falling in love with a married person he may have the love experience without the same danger of its leading to the altar.

Compensations for not marrying

There are both compensations and problems involved in remaining single, just as there are advantages and disadvantages in marrying. In one sense the single person does not "put all his eggs into one basket"; in another sense he does. He does not build his life around another person, running the risk of having the bottom drop out of his world if that other person dies or disappoints him. On the other hand, in depending for his happiness upon himself rather than on himself plus another person, he misses the contribution that the other person may make.

We cannot say that married or single persons have more freedom. One neither gains nor loses freedom in marrying; he merely changes its form.

A single person usually has no children to care for, worry about, or contend with, as the case may be. The single person who fears sex, childbirth, or something else connected with marriage does not have the fear stimulus constantly plaguing him. His income is less committed, so he may use it as he sees fit. His success or failure depends more largely on himself than does the married person's. The single person feels he has more control over his own life.

Problems to be faced

There is a problem of companionship. As the single person's friends marry, he has to make readjustments. There is often the matter of being the odd person at social gatherings. The question of satisfactory companionship with members of the opposite sex is at times difficult to work out.

There is the problem of preventing inflexibility. The single person who lives alone has his own way most of the time. He is not so often called upon to make concessions to others. Sometimes an individual's life pattern becomes so inflexible that he expects to have his own way at all times. He may cease to be aware of the importance of considering others. When this unawareness spills over into his social and occupational relationships, he becomes difficult to get along with. In order to prevent such crystallization, some single persons avoid living alone.

There is the problem of understanding marriage. The single person often has little understanding of marriage and little appreciation of the husband-wife relationship. He may not see that married persons are not entirely independent like himself and do not want to be treated as if they were. Lacking insight into a couple's desire for privacy, he may become intrusive. If he is a member of one spouse's family, he may not understand how the bond between husband and wife can be different in both degree and kind from the bond between siblings. He may therefore set up expectations which the married person cannot readily meet.

There is the problem of avoiding interference in other people's affairs. This problem is, of course, not limited to single persons. But the single person is often a ready victim of it for a particular reason. Most people are interested in the affairs of others. The married person fits into a pattern in which such interest is expected. The unmarried person does not have this approved outlet for his interest in others. If he becomes as interested in the affairs of others as if they were his spouse or his children, his interest is likely to be resented.

An unmarried woman sometimes has a problem of preventing masculinization. If her occupation necessitates competition with men, she may develop masculine characteristics in order to succeed. Some such women have relatively little social contact with men in a way that motivates them to be feminine. We must be careful, however, not to leap to conclusions and put the cart before the horse when a single woman exhibits masculine characteristics. Some women who exhibit such characteristics enter occupations where there is competition with men. The masculine characteristics contribute to, rather than result from, both the competition and singleness.

The single person must adjust himself to the attitude of society toward celibacy. It is commonly assumed that when a man remains single it is through his own choice but that when a woman remains single it is through someone else's choice — the result of necessity, lack of opportunity, unattractiveness, or some similar factor. This, of course, is only a common assumption; it is not necessarily true. Yet it is enough to produce a feeling of inferiority in some persons who do not marry.

The single person usually has a problem with regard to the giving and receiving of love and affection. Almost everyone wants to love and be loved. The most efficacious scheme thus far discovered for the fullest development of love is marriage. The single person who has the desire for love and its expression must find a substitute method or have his life somewhat cramped.

A problem related to the one mentioned immediately above is that of sexual satisfaction in the more specific sense. There are both men and women, especially the latter, who feel no very strong sexual drive. At least, they have no experience that they definitely distinguish as a specific interest in sexual satisfaction. Such persons may have no apparent sex problem. Others have a sexual urge of which they are not clearly aware because it has been repressed; but it affects their behavior, nevertheless. Still others are aware of sexual desire but know of no adequate means of satisfying it and hence must hold it in check or resort to incomplete substitutes.

The unmarried person has a problem of maintaining a balanced personality in a world organized for the controlled expression of natural desires and in a culture built in large measure around marriage and the family. To maintain his emotional balance, the unmarried person, like everyone else, must face reality. But in facing reality he faces a world in which life is organized largely for persons unlike himself. How can he adjust himself to the world instead of continually trying, as some do, to adjust the world to himself?

Singleness as adjustment

One does not avoid problems by remaining single; one only changes their form. Neither does one solve problems by refusing to face them. Life is full of situations involving adjustment, whether the individual is married or single. Furthermore, one cannot gain the satisfactions of marriage by avoiding the problems of marriage. Singleness admittedly has certain compensations; but it cannot and does not produce the impossible situation of having the joys of marriage without its perplexities.

If a person remains single, he should face the facts, maintain his friendships and interests but not force them to the saturation point, avoid self-pity, make use of his opportunities, and never think of himself as inferior or peculiar. If he is unhappy, anxious, or depressed, he should look for and seek to remove the cause in his situation or within himself rather than fruitlessly project the blame onto singleness as such. Being an "old maid" or an "old bachelor" is a state of mind rather than a legal status. There are well-adjusted single persons; there are married "old maids" and "old bachelors."

Marriage is no cure-all. It is not a panacea for human ills. It is not a creator of a utopia. Marriage is only as good as the persons in it.

WHAT DO YOU THINK?

1. How did marriage originate?
2. Which of the similarities and differences between the sexes might have contributed to the origin of marriage?
3. Do human beings have any instincts that could have contributed to the origin of marriage?
4. What are the basic functions of marriage? Of the family?
5. What does marriage contribute to the individuals in it and to society which nothing else contributes?
6. Is love a sufficient basis for successful marriage? What else is needed?
7. What factors in present-day American life sometimes make it difficult to distinguish between love and infatuation?
8. What is common-law marriage? Should it be continued as legal marriage in this country?
9. What is the difference between singleness and celibacy?

10. Are there any factors, other than those mentioned in this chapter, which operate to keep people from marrying today?

11. A friend tells you that he or she plans to remain permanently unmarried and asks for suggestions as to how to make his life useful and happy. What would you suggest? Would the same suggestions apply to both sexes?

12. Are there any considerations besides those mentioned in this chapter that might be of help in distinguishing between love and infatuation?

SELECTED READINGS

Bee, Lawrence S.: *Marriage and Family Relations*, Harper & Row, Publishers, Incorporated, New York, 1959, chap. 6. The meaning and varieties of love.

Bell, Robert R.: *Marriage and Family Interaction*, The Dorsey Press, Inc., Homewood, Ill., 1963, chap. 5. Love and the courtship process.

Blood, Robert O., Jr: *Marriage*, The Free Press of Glencoe, New York, 1962, chap. 4. The nature of love; conditions for, varieties of, and elements of love; pseudo-loves.

Burgess, Ernest W., Harvey J. Locke, and Mary Margaret Thomes: *The Family*, 3d ed., American Book Company, New York, 1963, chap. 11. Changes in courtship and romantic love in the United States.

Cavan, Ruth Shonle: *American Marriage*, Thomas Y. Crowell Company, New York, 1959, chap. 6. The nature of love; love as a basis for marriage.

_____(ed.): *Marriage and the Family in the Modern World*, Thomas Y. Crowell Company, New York, 1960, chap. 8. The role of love in human development; the nature and expressions of love; the dialogue of courtship in popular songs.

Duvall, Evelyn Millis, and Reuben Hill: *When You Marry*, rev. ed., D. C. Heath and Company, Boston, 1962, chap. 2. The difference between love and infatuation; learning to love.

Goode, William J.: "The Theoretical Importance of Love," *American Sociological Review*, vol. 24, no. 1, pp. 38–47, February, 1959. "I suggest that love is a universal psychological potential, which is controlled by a range of five structural patterns, all of which are attempts to see to it that youngsters do not make entirely free choices of their future spouses," says the author.

Kephart, William M.: *The Family, Society, and the Individual*, Houghton Mifflin Company, Boston, 1961, chap. 11. The definition of love; sex differences in love; love and sex.

Landis, Judson T., and Mary G. Landis: *Building a Successful Marriage*, 4th ed., Prentice-Hall, Inc., Englewood Cliffs, N.J., 1963, chap. 10. What is love? Mistaken conceptions of love; love at first sight.

Landis, Paul H.: *Making the Most of Marriage*, 2d ed., Appleton-Century-Crofts, Inc., New York, 1960, chaps. 6, 7. The genesis of love; elements of love; "Romantic Love: Can One Count on It?"

Lantz, Herman R., and Eloise C. Snyder: *Marriage*, John Wiley & Sons, Inc., New York, 1962, chaps. 5, 6. The nature and significance of love; the development of the capacity for mature love.

Magoun, F. Alexander: *Love and Marriage*, rev. ed., Harper & Row, Publishers, Incorporated, New York, 1956, chaps. 1, 2. An extended analysis of the definitions, nature, and expression of love.

Martinson, Floyd M.: *Marriage and the American Ideal*, Dodd, Mead & Company, Inc., New York, 1960, chaps. 7–10. The meaning of love; criteria for distinguishing love.

Oliver, Bernard J., Jr.: *Marriage and You*, College and University Press, New Haven, Conn., 1964, chap. 5. The meaning and nature of love; the definition of love in marriage.

Peterson, James A.: *Education for Marriage*, 2d ed., Charles Scribner's Sons, New York, 1964, chap. 3. The meaning of love; studies in romantic idealization; what mature love is.

Waller, Willard: *The Family: A Dynamic Interpretation*, rev. by Reuben Hill, Holt, Rinehart and Winston, Inc., New York, 1951, chap. 7. The various conceptions of love; the experience of falling in love.

part 2

MARRIAGE PREPARATION AND PARTNER SELECTION

In some cultures in which young persons have little to say about the choice of their marriage partner, the prerequisites for marriage may, in a sense, be relatively simple and consist chiefly of arrangements made by parents after the young persons have reached marriageable age. In this country today, on the other hand, young persons have great freedom of choice in selecting a marriage partner, and their choice is prefaced by unprecedented freedom of contact and communication in premarital activities. Hence, such activities need to be described and analyzed, both in terms of their nature and in terms of change; but they also need to be evaluated in terms of their possible contribution to, or detraction from, the objective of successful marriage which young people set up and which society encourages. Questions such as the following arise: What constitutes effective dating? What are the pros and cons of premarital physical contact, affectionally and/or sexually? How long and how well should a couple know each other before they choose each other as marriage partners? What is involved in such choice? What may be said about choices involving special problems, for example, when the couple represent different religious faiths? What is meant by "maturity"? When are young people ready for marriage? What is the best age for marriage? The answers to these and similar questions constitute part of the foundation upon which a couple's marriage is built.

chapter 4

DATING PRACTICES AND STANDARDS

Dating

THE IMPORTANCE OF DATING

When one realizes that normally dating is eventually brought to a focus on one of the most significant decisions of life, the decision to marry a given individual, one sees how important dating activities are. Yet there is a common tendency to divorce these activities from preparation for marriage and to think of them as incidental and to some extent as ends in themselves. We are prone to see the close connection between dating and marriage only when a couple are beginning to think of each other more specifically in terms of possible husband and wife. For this reason some persons draw a distinction between dating and courtship. But since the line between these is so indistinct, one shading imperceptibly into the other, and since it is so difficult to determine where dating ends and courtship begins, we have chosen to use the term *dating* to include both.

No matter who the date or what the activity, dating is an integral part of life experience leading to marriage. The importance of dating becomes apparent when its several aspects are considered. Dating is fun. It affords special association with a person of the opposite sex which provides elements of interest not to be found in association with one's own sex. Dating is a universal expectation; young people are expected to date when they have reached a given age. Questioning, wondering, and worry result when they do not. Dating may be a source of prestige, either because of the frequency with which it occurs or because of the persons dated. On the other hand, it may be a source of dissatisfaction or give rise to feelings of inferiority when an individual has difficulty in dating sufficiently often or in attracting acceptable dates. Dating is an educational process, since it affords opportunity to become better acquainted with persons of the opposite sex and with the social opportunities, demands, and restrictions surrounding the activities of couples. Dating is in part a trial-and-error process. It usually involves numerous false starts in the process of choice that will eventually result in the selection of a marriage partner. Frequent dating or avoidance and disparaging of dating are sometimes used as camouflage for a feeling of insecurity. Dating is a proving ground for maturity.

Dating should involve getting acquainted not only with one person of the opposite sex but with many. The object of dating may ultimately be to prepare for marriage but not necessarily marriage to a particular individual, at least not at first. A woman cannot know her husband, or a man his wife, well without also knowing a number of other persons for comparison and contrast. To focus love and affection upon a single individual may be an indication of maturity. The process of maturing, however, must follow its natural course; it cannot be reversed. One does not make himself mature by prematurely centering his love on a particular individual and going with that person exclusively before he has had sufficient acquaintance with others to determine that it is this individual upon whom he desires permanently to center his attention.

In dating not only does each "put his best foot forward" but often each sees everything, including the other person, through rose-tinted spectacles. There is much idealizing and wishful thinking. Sometimes, because of this, promises are made that cannot be kept, and expectations are built up that cannot be fulfilled. Marriage then seems like a "letdown." The reason is not that marriage is less interesting or exciting than dating but that in marriage there is inevitable impact with reality; and in dating reality may be temporarily obscured by imagination. Much is said about how people change, often for the worse, after they marry. The greater change is in dating. Before marriage the persons put on a false front, and each sees the other from a favorably biased point of view. Then, after the wedding, each returns to the real self and the spouse sees that self as it is, not as it was thought to be.

Much is written and said about failure in marriage. Relatively little is mentioned concerning dating failures except in connection with failure to date or to have a good time. Yet, in a significant sense, many "marriage failures" are in reality dating failures. These failures include the failure to allow sufficient time to become acquainted, failure to make intelligent decisions, failure to correlate values with behavior, failure to make wise choices—they occur before the wedding but become apparent only afterward. Lack of recognition of this fact makes for a disregard of the problems and processes of dating and a somewhat uncritical attitude toward the activities involved. This tendency is accentuated by the fact that never before in history have so many persons dated so much through such a long period in their lives with so few recognizable guideposts, such ill-defined social patterns, such a wide variety of standards, and so few socially imposed controls.

DATING AND SOCIAL CHANGE

A complete analysis of the effects of social change upon dating will not be attempted here. A few generalizations may serve to point out that dating does occur in a cultural milieu and does have social forces brought to bear upon it.

The automobile, commercialized amusements, the growth of cities, the shrinkage of dwelling size, the increased use of apartments, the changed status of women, new expectations with regard to marriage, and myriad other factors are making of dating something that it used not to be. As noted already, today there is less social and parental control; this fact puts a new responsibility upon the shoulders of the young persons making their own plans and choices.

We have reached a period of national development when the old is no longer adequate and the new is in the process of being established. There are confusion, transition, and lack of clear-cut definition. Standards are ill-defined. Young people must rely upon their own judgments, their own conclusions, their own definitions of objectives, and their own self-discipline more than before. Many of the admonitions of their parents are of the "don't" variety and have their roots in a cultural period somewhat different from the present. Survivors of a previous era cannot be expected to set the standards for this one. If modern young people want happy and successful marriage, they will have to work for it and through intelligence adapt their dating to the exigencies of the day. Abandoning the old without substituting an improved new, rushing blindly through an open gate just because it is open and without ascertaining where it leads, cannot help playing a part in making the marriages of the future no better than those of the past.

CONCLUSION

In seeking to make dating activities contribute to his preparation for marriage, there are several things that the individual may do.

He may carefully define his goals. After defining them, after setting his objectives in life, he may work toward them, doing those things that contribute to reaching them and avoiding those that impede his progress or sidetrack his efforts. If one of his major objectives is successful marriage, this may be kept in mind as he makes choices among various possible dating activities. It is important to avoid losing perspective.

EVALUATING THE DATING RELATIONSHIP

Following are five controversial statements, each of which requires some degree of qualification. To what extent do you agree or disagree with each? If you feel there is some truth in a statement, support your opinion with examples from your own experience or from the text. How would you qualify each to bring it nearer the truth? After you have modified the statements, reexamine them and compare with the opinions of other students. Can you, from this process, arrive at a personally satisfying answer to what dating can and should be for you?

"Dating is an artificial relationship in which each participant tries to show only the best side of his personality."

"Dating is the most romantic period in one's life because
one can have many of the pleasures of marriage
without any of the tedious responsibilities."

He may plan and prepare, not drift. This implies not only what was
suggested in the point above but also the integration of dating activities with other aspects of life and the improvement of his understanding
of the requirements for marriage.

He may develop a positive attitude toward sex. This suggests an understanding of sex as one of the basic elements in life and the means

"It is impossible for two young persons of opposite sex to have a close friendship without physical attraction's playing a prominent part in their relationship."

"In the dating period one concentrates on himself, building his experience in interpersonal relations; during engagement he centers all his interests on the other partner."

"Radical changes in dating patterns have occurred over the last few years, for example, opportunities for unchaperoned socializing. Any person who is really concerned can find, through study and by examining his conscience, clearly defined social standards for dating."

by which it may be utilized in making life adjustment in general and marriage adjustment in particular more satisfying and successful, rather than mere awareness of sexual impulses without seeing how they fit into the scheme of life.

He may put into effect in the dating period the standards and ideals that he wants to be permanent. He cannot expect to be two individuals, one with a set of questionable, poorly adapted, incompletely thought-out standards before marriage, the other with a set of intelligently derived, highly acceptable standards that suddenly develop after the wedding, entirely without premarital exercise and growth. But putting into effect standards and ideals that he wants to be permanent does not necessarily imply engaging in types of behavior that he expects later to become part of his permanent pattern of life.

He may establish a reasonable correlation between his attitudes and behavior and his age. What might be excusable in a very young adolescent who is just beginning to date may not be excusable in an individual who is almost ready for marriage.

He need not act as if he were unattractive. This does not preclude his making a fair, accurate, and objective appraisal of himself or continued effort toward self-improvement. He need not, however, confuse his own feeling of insecurity with personal unattractiveness, reading his inaccurate appraisal of himself into the judgments of other persons. He need not leap to the conclusion that he must compensate for his supposed lack of appeal by lowering his standards of behavior, fearing that unless he did so he would be unattractive to others.

Petting

There is more freedom of contact between the sexes today than there was a generation or so ago. There are, however, no conclusive data available to indicate how that freedom is being used. No one knows fully what the present situation is. There are many guesses, many questionable deductions, many broad generalizations based upon incomplete evidence, and some useful studies. There are persons who generalize upon their own limited experience or their own restricted observations. There is moralizing. But there is no proof of what actually exists. Youth likes to exaggerate and to impress. Given half a chance, he will tell a good story even though he has to embellish the facts in order to do so. On the other hand, many persons are hesitant to let their behavior become known to others.

This new freedom of physical contact between the sexes creates a problem of discriminating between the degree of contact that is wise, beneficial, and emotionally healthful and that which is unwise, risky, and emotionally unhygienic. Young people living in the twentieth century cannot be expected to behave as if they were Puritans living in the seventeenth century. But it is not too much to expect that they will apply intelligent, critical judgment to their premarital activities and evaluate such activities in terms of the goal of successful marriage which young people set up for themselves. This process is similar to, and as sensible as, the process by which a student evaluates his academic and extracurricular activities in terms of such goals as grades, degree, and occupational training.

There are many terms that apply to physical contact that stops short of sexual intercourse. Without difficulty and without attempting to make a formal study, the author has collected more than four hundred such terms from his own students. None of them is specific. Some are picturesque. Some are geographically so highly localized that they are meaningless to persons from other parts of the country. The great variety of such terms is one side light on the widespread distribution and frequency of the activity they are designed to describe and indicates, too, the casualness with which this activity is currently accepted. We shall use the term *petting* because it is probably the most widely understood.

Physical contact between the sexes may extend from holding hands to sexual intercourse. It is difficult to draw an arbitrary line on one side of which will fall contact that one would not define as petting and on the other side of which is petting as we shall discuss it. Surely hand holding or a single good-night kiss would not be considered petting. Some persons distinguish between necking and petting on the basis of intensity, areas of anatomy involved, and extent of fondling or bodily exploration in addition to kissing. Such distinctions have value, but there is another side to the problem. Different criteria may be used in differentiating among terms for the purpose of discussion on the one hand and for the purpose of evaluating the activities to which the terms apply on the other. An individual reacts as a whole, not as an agglomeration of disconnected parts. His behavior must be evaluated in terms of what happens to him as a person, not merely in terms of the parts of his anatomy involved. This suggests that necking and petting are phases of the same process, that they are variations of degree rather than of kind. We shall define "petting" as physical contact for pleasure as an end in itself, usually involving some degree of bodily exploration, arising from sexual desire in one or both parties but stopping short of intercourse, and of such nature that in one or both there is produced an increased sexual sensitivity and response, a stirring up of sexually colored emotions, and an increased tension that can be relieved immediately only by intercourse or some substitute therefor. In the absence of relief, the tension has a tendency to persist for a time.

To fall within the bounds of our definition, petting need not be promiscuous; it may be limited to one person. We shall not, however, include the physical contact of couples who have bona fide engagements, because in their case caressing is presumably not only a pleasurable end in itself but is also an expression of affection and part of a growing meaningful relationship. If, however, the engagement is not bona fide and was entered only as a means of rationalizing petting, the activities of such a couple may be included in our definition.

It is impossible to generalize on the consequences of petting, since so much depends upon the attitudes of the two persons, their backgrounds, the degree of promiscuity, the intensity, the extent and frequency, the specific individual reactions and responses elicited, the meaning that the couple read into their experience, and what they do about the tension generated. It may serve in part as an outlet for sexual desire as well as a stimulator of such desire. When petting is continued to the point of orgasm, there is sexual pleasure and release. On the other hand, there are possible arguments against it.

The reader is cautioned to remember, when reading the following items, that they apply to petting as we defined the term, that they apply to premarital relationships and not to physical contact between husband and wife, and that we are speaking in terms of possibilities, not statistical probabilities.

Most dates are brief, and time limitations necessitate centering attention upon relatively few activities. If attention is centered on petting, a false focus is created. Other activities that would help the couple to become better acquainted are neglected. Their problem of distinguishing between love and infatuation is made more complicated. They may commit themselves to marriage prematurely.

Some girls pet as a price for popularity. They often forget that such popularity is insubstantial. In boomerang fashion it may strike back at a girl. If she pets to be popular, she may be popular because she pets. She deceives herself into thinking that she is liked for herself and her personal qualities, whereas she is only an attractive and convenient means to an end. In such cases the petting is exploitive. Some girls assume that all boys expect all girls to pet. But studies of the dating behavior and attitudes of students do not substantiate such assumptions. If petting is considered a price for an evening's entertainment, it becomes a commercialized relationship similar to that which exists when a youthful secretary dates her middle-aged employer because he presents her with expensive gifts.

A girl may acquire a reputation for petting. Then she is likely to attract boys who expect to pet rather than those who prefer to be interested in a girl for more substantial reasons.

For some persons petting is an outgrowth of insecurity, loneliness, or hunger for affection. Individuals who feel themselves to be unattractive, whose shyness makes it difficult for them to extend friendships, whose early life was characterized by lack of affection and love in the home may seek an answer to their need in petting. For such persons petting may provide a temporary relief, a sedative that seems to remove their distress; but actually it cannot serve as a solution to their underlying problem.

Petting tends to become cumulative. It tends to be one-directional. It gathers momentum, and the couple's emotions become more and more intense. It is a principle of biology and psychology that with repetition the effect of a stimulus tends, under certain circumstances, to decrease. In order, then, to produce the same effect as at first, the stimulus must be increased. This principle operates in petting. In order that the individual may continue to derive a given degree of satisfaction, the amount and intensity of the petting must be increased. There are, however, limitations upon this process. Petting cannot be increased indefinitely; it cannot even be increased considerably without risk of its getting out of bounds. The alternative is to broaden the base and improve the quality of the interests, activities, and contacts upon which the couple's relationship rests.

Petting may cheapen affection in the minds of the couple. It may deprive of its meaning an expression of real affection.

A boy interested in a girl because she pets may stop dating her without warning if a more attractive girl appears on the horizon. The boy turns to "greener pastures."

A girl may confuse her physical responses with love. In some cases the girl alone seems to fall in love. Some girls do not experience any arousal of responses that they identify as sexual until their late teens or thereabouts. The first time that she becomes conscious of such responses a girl may be almost overwhelmed. The boy, on the other hand, has typically had identifiable sexual reactions for some time before his relationship with this particular girl began. He may not be deceived into thinking he is in love, though some boys are misled.

A girl who has frequently petted without any desire on her part because boys wanted her to do so may generalize on her own limited experience and conclude that all boys are interested in girls for physical satisfaction alone. She may awake to the fact that she has been only a means to an end and may resent that. At any rate, the attitude that grows from such a conclusion is not likely to be favorable for marriage.

The couple may become sexually aroused with no prospect of adequate release, as if they were "all dressed up with no place to go." This may make for nervous tension that may extend past a particular date. Sometimes this tension produces hypersensitivity and increased irritability which strain the relationship of the couple or prevent the development of a relationship that might have eventuated in marriage.

There is the possibility of an emotional stoppage at an immature level instead of the development of more mature response. Petting may become a permanent substitute for fuller sexual experience in marriage later. Constant exercise of control under stress in order to prevent going beyond petting may create lasting inhibitions.

Petting may be either a cause of or a result of an inclination to appraise members of the opposite sex primarily in terms of their physical attributes. Such an attitude is conducive to neither effective preparation for marriage nor successful marital adjustment.

In the white heat of sexual excitement, perspective may be lost. When emotion goes up, reason and self-discipline go down. Many couples start with petting and end with sexual intercourse when the latter was not intended. They reach a "point of no return." They are like a man whose rowboat is caught in the irresistible current at the brink of the falls. If such a man would row to shore, he must start to do so upstream while he can still pull against the current.

For a couple to pet when either is under the influence of alcohol is like driving a car without brakes. Alcohol is a depressant and reduces control. Standards and consequences are often forgotten. A man's muscular strength may be temporarily increased because of the removal of restraint. Many a girl has found herself in an embarrassing or even dangerous predicament because she dated a boy who drank too much, permitted him to take her away from the company of other people to a place where her control of the situation was reduced, allowed him to take the first steps toward petting, and found that once he was aroused there was no way of dissuading him. Cases in which girls have been seriously upset emotionally by such an experience are not uncommon. In one case a girl who attended a party at which everyone drank more or less intemperately and where everyone petted indiscriminately found herself later with only a vague memory of what had happened for part of the evening. There was evidence that she had had intercourse with several boys, but which ones she was not sure. She spent some frightful weeks worrying about pregnancy, which fortunately did not occur.

The couple may rationalize sexual intercourse. Protracted, intense sexual stimulation without release may produce pain in the region of the testes in the boy. Such pain may be uncomfortable, but it is not dangerous and disappears in a short time after the stimulation ceases, even in the absence of release. Knowledge of the possibility of such pain on the part of the boy who has the prospect of it and on the part of the girl who does not understand its nature and is afraid that it may be harmful to the boy sometimes makes for rationalization of intercourse.

CONCLUSION

There is no evidence to prove that petting is invariably either beneficial or detrimental. People who have petted promiscuously and excessively have later married successfully. On the other hand, some persons have been harmed by petting. In considering the question of whether or not to pet, each person should carefully weigh the disadvantages against the advantages. He should also consider the possible as well as the probable results. Since his ultimate objective is happy marriage, he should ask himself whether petting contributes to his preparation for such marriage or is an impediment to his achieving the sort of marriage he wants. Since petting often involves a limitation on activities that would help a couple to become better acquainted, a misplaced emphasis on physical appeal and a false assumption that intense physical response is equivalent to love, it leads some couples to premature, ill-founded marriages. A couple should therefore make every effort to retain their perspective, appraise their situation realistically, and avoid rationalizing an assumption that their relationship is not subject to any of the traps that plague some other couples.

Prevention of petting. Students, especially girls, often ask how they may prevent petting. The following are suggestions; they cannot automatically solve every problem. Some of them have been deduced from the writer's observations and discussions with students; others have been suggested to him by persons who found them useful under given circumstances.

Avoid situations in which occasion for petting may arise and those where time hangs heavy and there seems nothing else to do. Some petting arises from boredom.

Stating one's attitude frankly but without ill feeling and then firmly adhering to the position one has taken may be a satisfactory solution. This need not be done at the very beginning of the first date without any provocation on either person's part; but some persons appreciate knowing where the other person stands. In refusing to pet, it is not so much the fact of refusal as the method of refusal that is likely to irritate the other person.

Directing conversation away from topics associated with sex and petting, engaging in interesting activities together, and other devices which will suggest themselves to couples with ingenuity may be helpful.

Kissing seems to be acquiring new meaning. In an earlier period in history, kissing tended to occur relatively late in a couple's association, to express affection or to signify that their relationship was becoming or had already become one based upon love. Today there is a tendency for kissing to occur earlier in the couple's association and to imply mutual pleasure in each other's company, a girl's obligation, a boy's prerogative, conquest, or the opening of a door to further development of the couple's relationship either in the direction of petting or in the direction of love. In either period, kissing represents a line crossed; but it is not the same line today as formerly. Since interpretations of the meaning of kissing vary in different periods of time, in different localities in a given period, and among different individuals, a couple should know what this symbol means to each other when they employ it. Otherwise, each may misunderstand the other's motives.

Avoiding symbols and experiences that suggest sexual experience and arouse sexual interest may help. The individual knows what these are for him and may plan accordingly. He may control his behavior by controlling stimuli as well as by controlling responses.

Finally, but by no means least important, he may carefully think through his code of values and, by means of self-discipline and perseverance, adhere to those standards that he believes to be of greatest worth in a long-range perspective.

Premarital sexual intercourse

IS THE PROBLEM NEW?

The problem of premarital sexual intercourse is not new. It has existed since time immemorial. Premarital intercourse is a problem in all cultures except those in which such intercourse is expected or accepted within the mores. Today in this country, however, there is more open discussion of premarital intercourse than there used to be. There is more expressed concern. There is more known about it. All this undoubtedly contributes to an impression of newness.

THE EXTENT OF THE PROBLEM

Various studies arrive at different conclusions as to the frequency of premarital intercourse. Kinsey and his associates report that, among the 5,300 males in their sample, 92 per cent of the total group and 67 per cent of those who ever went to college, had premarital intercourse at some time. By age 20, 83 per cent of those who never went beyond grade school, 75 per cent of those who went to but not beyond high school, and 44 per cent of those who ever went to college had such intercourse [Kinsey, Pomeroy, and Martin, 1948]. Among the 5,940 females in their sample, almost 50 per cent of the total group and 60 per cent of those who ever went to college had premarital intercourse at some time. The seeming discrepancy in these figures is due to the fact that girls who do not go to college tend to marry earlier than girls who do, and thus there is less time for premarital intercourse to occur. By age 20, 25 per cent of those girls who never went beyond grade school, 26 per cent of those who ever went to but not beyond high school, and 20 per cent of those who ever went to college had such intercourse [Kinsey, Pomeroy, Martin, and Gebhard, 1953]. In Terman's [1938] study of 792 couples, just over 60 per cent of the men and 37 per cent of the women admitted premarital intercourse. Burgess and Wallin [1953] found that almost 68 per cent of 580 men and 47 per cent of 604 women reported such intercourse. In a sample of 841 university students Ehrmann [1959] found that 65 per cent of the males and 13 per cent of the females reported premarital intercourse. In a study of 177 wives of university students, Kanin [1960] found that about 44 per cent indicated having had premarital intercourse with the men they later married, but with variation as to social class as follows: upper middle class, 31 per cent; middle class, 42 per cent; lower class, 83 per cent. Clark [Pillay and Ellis, 1953] found about 60 per cent of 113 never-married women who were given pelvic examinations to be nonvirgin. Landis and Landis [1963] found that, among 3,000 students from 11 colleges and universities, 9 to 12 per cent of the girls reported such intercourse. Hamilton [1929] found that among 100 men and 100 women 54 per cent of the former and 35 per cent of the latter admitted premarital intercourse. Dickinson and Beam [1934] report 12 per cent of 350 single women. Bromley and Britten [1938] report 52 per cent of 470 college males and 25 per cent of 618 college females. Davis [1929] reports 9 per cent of 2,200 women.

In interpreting percentages such as those mentioned above, it is very important to note the wide variation and to keep in mind that they represent "cumulative incidence," that is, lifetime figures, the percentage of a given sample that *ever* had premarital intercourse. Compared to this there is "active incidence," the percentage of a given sample *currently* having premarital intercourse. Cumulative incidence includes more and is therefore higher than active incidence. For example, as indicated above, Ehrmann [1959] found that 65 per cent of the male students and 13 per cent of the female students reported that at some time in their lives they had had premarital intercourse, but only 38 per cent of the males and 9 per cent of the females reported that they were currently having it. Furthermore, cumulative-incidence percentages as given do not make allowance for frequency of intercourse. An individual who, let us say, had intercourse once at age 16 would be included in the cumulative incidence even though he has not repeated the experience during his four years in college. Similarly a girl who during her high school and first two college years had had intercourse numerous times with fifteen boys and had had two pregnancies terminated by criminal abortion, but who resolved to stop having intercourse and has not had it for about a year, would be included in cumulative incidence but not in active incidence.

All studies of premarital intercourse up to date involve shortcomings of one sort or another, such as inadequate sampling, methodological errors, debatable interpretations, or time-relative validity (data gathered years ago). They provide useful insights. They present a more helpful picture of cumulative incidence than of active incidence, with the result that though the picture of cumulative incidence is incomplete, the picture of active incidence is sketchy indeed. Some of them corroborate and document what experienced counselors have long suspected. They do not, however, constitute the last word on the extent of premarital sexual intercourse. But they do suggest at least three generalizations:

1. Premarital sexual intercourse is more frequent than some persons have insisted or feared and not as infrequent as others have demanded or hoped.

2. There is some difference in both frequency and acceptance of premarital intercourse relative to social class and educational level. In the less well-educated groups there is greater acceptance of premarital intercourse and less of petting, while in the better-educated groups the reverse is true; in the latter groups there is a greater acceptance of petting and less of premarital intercourse.

3. There is some evidence of a shift in the type of female involved. The data suggest that males in this country have about as much premar-

ital sexual freedom now as formerly. In earlier times, however, the females with whom the males had their premarital experience more often belonged to a group from which the males did not choose their wives. Nowadays there is an increasing tendency for the females to belong to the group from which the males do choose their wives. Many present-day females have premarital intercourse only with their fiancés. This point will be discussed more fully later.

THE NATURE OF THE PROBLEM

Sexual intercourse is not merely a quantitative extension of petting, different from it only in degree. It is true that when an attempt is made to distinguish between "heavy petting" and intercourse, they are found to be separated not by a sharp, clear-cut boundary line but rather by a boundary zone, since the distinction may depend upon details of anatomy or fine-spun definition. Yet, when an act such as intercourse is directly related to the possibility of conception and hence to a third person as well as to the couple, a qualitative as well as quantitative difference is introduced. Sexual behavior is an integral part of life activity. Hence, premarital sexual intercourse is not an isolated phenomenon, unrelated to the rest of life. Whatever an individual's premarital sexual behavior may be, it is part and parcel of the fabric of his life, not a patch upon that fabric which he may apply or remove as whim suggests or circumstances permit. If one thinks at all about premarital intercourse, one cannot avoid relating it to other areas of interest and concern.

There are several such broad areas: the nature of human life, the culture in which we live, and the objectives which the individual establishes for himself. In other words, if his attitude is to be critical and considered rather than uncritical and naïve, whatever conclusions an individual reaches regarding premarital intercourse should be human-nature derived, culturally relative, and goal-oriented. To some degree these overlap.

THE NATURE OF HUMAN NATURE

Because all human beings have lived as members of society and thus from birth onward have been subject to cultural influences, there is much about human nature per se that is still unknown. Man is a mammal. As a mammal he has biological drives, including a sex drive. But man is not merely a mammal; he is a mammal plus. It is this "plus" element which distinguishes him from all other known organisms.

Other mammals function largely on a basis of instinct, with intelligence playing a minor role. Man functions to a much greater extent by intelligence, exhibiting few, if any, instincts. This means that other mammals "take life as it comes" except in so far as they exhibit automatic, instinctive patterns of behavior which enable them to alter it to some extent, these patterns passing from generation to generation through heredity. Man is not content with the world as he finds it. He embellishes his existence with culture which is passed from generation to generation through learning. Other mammals have hunger. They eat whatever food nature provides. Man has hunger, but he also plays a part in increasing his food supply through science and agriculture. Only he makes an art of cookery and food service. Some other mammals have prehensile paws. Only man uses his hands to make and employ complicated tools and to create works of art. Other mammals employ sounds for instinctive cries or for simple means of communication. Only man has conceptual language. Some mammals have group living. Only man lives in groups upon which there is imposed a moral structure. Other mammals make simple choices. Only man can make value-oriented judgments.

Other mammals exhibit responses that are sometimes complex. But such mammals only "do." Man "does," but he also knows what he "does." He has self-awareness. More than this, he relates what he does to a concept of what he feels he ought to do. He is the only organism that consciously reaches out beyond his immediate experience, that seeks to discover and explain reality, that conceives and attempts to predict the future, that sets up values which he considers worth striving for, and that establishes hypotheses based upon incomplete observation. It is part of man's nature to believe in something. In reaching out beyond his experience, he sets up ideals which he knows he can never reach. Among mammals, he is the only one that interprets life in terms of values and meaning. Hence, man, though he has a sex drive that is in some respects similar to that of other mammals, has the unique capacity to interpret this drive in terms of such values and meaning.

None of this is meant to imply that ideals must be uniform for all human beings regardless of time, place, culture, or circumstance. There is, however, a universal human process of idealizing which underlies the specific and varying ideals which it produces. The thinking individual can no more readily escape the human tendency to relate practice to ideal, to interpret life in terms of values and meaning, than he can escape the influence of the culture in which he has lived or the hunger which all mammals feel. But he must also examine the place and validity of idealism in an age of science in which so much emphasis is placed upon testing, experimentation, measurement, and objectivity.

When the individual does relate practice to the ideal, he finds that there is no necessary relationship between *what is* and *what ought to be*, however the latter may be defined. *What is* is a matter of observation. *What ought to be* is a matter of value-oriented judgment. Culturally *what is* and *what ought to be* may be the same; philosophically they may be quite different. For example, there is a reasonably high degree of correlation in this country between observed fact and the approved standard relative to monogamy and freedom of worship. On the other hand, there is a considerable discrepancy between observed fact and the approved standard relative to honesty or traffic safety. Kinsey and his associates [1948, 1953] found that about one-half of the males and about one-fourth of the females in their samples admitted extramarital intercourse, that is, marital infidelity, or adultery. What is the relationship of such substantial percentages to the problem of *what is* versus *what ought to be*? To what degree should frequency of practice be allowed to color concepts of what is considered ideal?

The problem the thoughtful, critical individual faces with regard to premarital sexual intercourse is one of imputing to it some kind of meaning, of correlating practice with some sort of ideal, and of deciding whether *what is* and *what ought to be*, as he understands them in his own behavior and in that of his group, are consistent or inconsistent. Because of all this, there emerges one of the basic problems of being human, namely, the problem of being continually confronted with an unresolved and unresolvable dilemma growing out of the perennial conflict between what man knows that he does and what he is convinced he ought to do, between ideals and practice.

Sex, per se, is neither good nor bad, beautiful nor ugly, moral nor immoral. Man imputes to it one or the other of each of these pairs of attributes through the application of value judgments. In like manner he makes decisions regarding chastity, promiscuity, monogamy, and polygamy. Allowing for the pressure of the cultural pattern and the impact of environment upon the development of such a pattern, man has some degree of freedom in choosing the type of sexual behavior which he deems most desirable. Hence, he can commit himself to a given pattern of sexual activity both premaritally and maritally. In fact, he must commit himself to some pattern because there is no society known in which sex is entirely free from personal and cultural regulation.

RELATION TO CULTURE

We said above that whatever conclusions an individual reaches regarding premarital intercourse should be culturally relative. If the individual is a member of a simple, uncomplicated society that has been isolated for a long period and which, therefore, represents a homogeneous population with uniform folkways and mores universally accepted within the group and exhibiting little or no change from generation to generation, his problem is easy. In fact, he may have none, since he takes for granted the culture in which he has been reared. But if the individual is a college student living in the highly complex, urbanized culture of the present-day United States, his problem is at the opposite extreme. Standards of approval vary according to class, region, generation, and the myriad subgroups and cross-classifications that constitute modern America. The population is mobile and heterogeneous. There are no unquestioned universally accepted norms for many things, including sexual behavior.

A large university exhibits many of the characteristics of an urban community. Whatever its location, it represents, in a sense, an urbanized population. The student body is heterogeneous and is composed of secondary rather than primary groups. The phenomena of large numbers are observable. As the size of a population increases, the individual's concern and felt responsibility for the total group decreases. It is difficult for the individual to form a strong loyalty to the total group. Impersonality and anonymity increase. Standards of the various secondary groups within the total population often conflict. Hence there is less pressure to conform because there are no universal norms to which to conform. There is a degree of individual freedom of action and belief not found in smaller groups. Outside control of the individual tends to come not from the entire group but from specialized sources. Hence the need for control from within the individual is increased. Family pressure tends to be replaced by pressure from nonfamily organizations. The university population, like an urban population, is mobile. It is even more temporary. The individual is often judged on the basis of impressions and externals rather than on the basis of thorough and intimate acquaintance. He is appraised less as a total personality and more as a specialized performer in a particular, temporary group.

In such a situation how does the individual decide which standards and practices to accept and which to reject? For example, how does he decide to accept or to reject women smoking cigars, "dutch dating," married women's employment, campus marriage, and premarital sexual intercourse? He may decide on the basis of one or a combination of the following:

1. By assuming that the new is better than the old
2. By assuming that the old is better than the new
3. By choosing what is thought to be best for self
4. By choosing what is thought to be best for others
5. By choosing what is thought to be best for all "in the long run"
6. By doing uncritically "what everybody's doing"
7. By weighing values
8. By relating behavior to principles and ideals
9. By relating behavior to moral and religious precepts

But his decision is not entirely free, since his thinking is colored by cultural influence. The practices he chooses must be fitted into some sort of cultural milieu.

As mentioned above, there are class differences with regard to premarital sexual intercourse so far as both attitudes and practices are concerned. In discussion of this problem, objections are sometimes raised to a standard of premarital chastity as being "middle class." It may be true that such a standard is more nearly middle class than any other. This is no argument either for or against it. The sociologist looks objectively at the entire scope of class structure. But the individual in his living must arrive at some sort of self-classification. He cannot belong simultaneously to all social classes and live simultaneously by all varieties of class standards. As we said earlier, it would be a fair guess to say that most college students are either middle-class members or middle-class aspirants. It is on this level that they expect permanently to live. This, then, might be taken into account in a student's decision regarding premarital intercourse.

No matter what the conclusion at which the student arrives, in reaching that conclusion he might keep several other considerations in mind. One of them is that sex is an integral part of life, so sexual behavior is subject to the same kind of logic as other human behavior. Sex is not an isolated, unrelated part of life that is subject to some special logic of its own.

FOLKWAYS AND MORES OCCUR IN CONFIGURATIONS

Folkways and mores, though they may seem to be isolated from other aspects of culture, are not so isolated. Typically each one is part of a configuration of related customs. When a new element of culture is introduced into one segment of the configuration, related changes occur in other segments. The process might be compared to a chain reaction or to the concentric circles of ripples that move out from the point of contact when a pebble is dropped into a pool of water. For example, the introduction of the automobile provided more than a piece of mechanical equipment to be used for transportation. As the concentric circles of change occurred, dating practices, family recreation and problems of use, vacation travel, suburban living, industrial concentrations and developments, the death rate, law, standards of conspicuous expenditure, and numerous other aspects of culture were affected.

It is for reasons such as this that sometimes one element of a culture cannot be isolated from other elements and transferred to another culture, or that new elements cannot be introduced into a culture as readily as some persons assume. Individuals who learn about other cultures often wonder why we cannot extract certain of their apparently desirable elements and introduce them into our own culture. We can do so if we are willing to accept the related changes that may accompany such introduction, if we are ready to go along with the concentric circles no matter how far they may extend. For example, the cultivation and use of both corn (maize) and tobacco were borrowed from the American Indians. Except in so far as the production of intoxicating liquor from corn is disapproved in some quarters, it would be difficult to find a "concentric circle" emerging from the introduction of corn that is not widely, if not indeed universally, accepted. With tobacco, on the other hand, although millions of persons use it, in some quarters there is still resistance to its use on grounds other than those of hygiene, some persons consider its use immoral, some church groups condemn it, smoking it is prohibited in some public places, physicians advise against it, and in the light of recent research governmental restrictions have been placed upon it, there is a double standard relative to its use by men and women.

If premarital sexual freedom were made a universal norm in this country, would we be willing to accept the related changes that would come about? For example, would all men be willing to marry nonvirgins? There are seldom circumstances such that a man has proof that his wife's child is also his biologically. He accepts it as his own because of his confidence in his wife and a degree of assurance produced by the partial safeguards of chastity and legitimacy that our culture sustains. If premarital intercourse were a universal practice, would newly wed American husbands be willing to accept the first child with even less certainty of paternity than they now have? What would eventually happen to American family life under such circumstances?

INDIVIDUAL FREEDOM AND SOCIETAL GOOD

How and where is the line to be drawn between individual freedom and societal good? To illustrate, a man with his wife and baby in his car is driving at night on the open highway at 100 miles per hour. Is such a man committing a dangerous, unwise, unlawful, antisocial, or immoral act? A man draws a gun and shoots toward a crowd of people "just for fun." Must we wait to judge his act until he shoots someone? Or may we judge his act by its potentialities as well as by its consequences? An individual is arrested while selling narcotics to high school students. He argues that the students purchase voluntarily, that this is a free country, that we protect freedom of enterprise, and that, therefore, society is unjust in depriving him of his chosen means of livelihood. How much weight should his argument be given? On the one hand, we protect the sanctity of the home. On the other hand, we permit the state, by its right of eminent domain, to force a family to sell its home so that the state may use the land in connection with a public works project. Is this consistent? An individual has no living relatives. He is dying of an incurable disease. The pain is excruciating. There is no known means of helping him. He asks his physician to administer a drug that will quickly and painlessly end his life. Should the physician be permitted to accede to his patient's request? An individual sees a person about to commit suicide. Should he let the person go ahead on the assumption that the person has a right to do as he wishes with his own life? Or should he try to stop the person on the assumption that there is a societal element involved? A hopelessly deformed baby is born but does not breathe spontaneously. Should the obstetrician let it die or try to get it to breathe?

Hypothetical cases such as those mentioned above point up the pertinence of the issue: How and where is a line to be drawn between individual freedom and societal good? Could something be good for the individual and not good for society, or good for society and not good for the individual? Is premarital sexual intercourse entirely a matter of individual freedom and choice, or is there involved in it in some way a question of societal good? If the latter, where should a line be drawn between individual freedom and societal good? Since, with a few exceptions in cases of sterility, every act of sexual intercourse may be considered as potentially procreative, this fact, as mentioned earlier, makes sexual intercourse different from petting in kind as well as in degree, qualitatively as well as quantitatively. Pregnancy is not merely a condition in a woman's body, to be treated only according to medical need or personal desire. It is a social situation involving three persons, all of whom are considered members of society. Since sexual intercourse involves a third person, a child, as well as the couple, it has societal as well as personal implications.

NEED AND RIGHT

A problem related to the one of individual freedom versus societal good is this: To what degree does an individual's felt need to do something establish his right to do it? For example, there is widespread agreement that an individual has a right to kill in self-defense. In an emergency, say, to get a bleeding accident victim to a hospital, does a person have the right to violate traffic laws? For their own convenience many people assume the right to tell "white lies" with no feeling of having actually lied. In order to get to work on time an individual insists that he has to exceed the speed limit. Does a student's need to pass a course give him the right to copy during an examination? Or a student says to an instructor, "I need a B in this course to get the necessary grade points to graduate." Should the instructor modify the grading plan so that, instead of recording a grade that represents the student's achievement, he records a grade that meets the student's need? Does the answer to this question depend upon how close to a B the student's actual grade is? For example, suppose a numerical average of 80 per cent is represented by a B. The instructor rounds off fractions of one-half point or higher to the next digit, so 79.5 per cent would also be a B. Suppose the student's average is 78.0 per cent; should he be given a B? 79.0 per cent? 79.4 per cent? Is there a principle involved? Or is the entire matter one of convenience, opportunism, need? Where does premarital intercourse fit into this picture? To what degree does an individual's felt need or want establish a right to assume that he should have such intercourse?

To what degree does an individual have a right to do something which affects another person just because that other person requests it? For example, a news item tells of a driver pinned under an overturned, burning gasoline truck and begging onlookers to shoot him. Does this give one of the onlookers a right to do so? Does an individual have a right to provide transportation to a minor running away from home, to furnish information during an examination, to locate an abortionist for a pregnant, unmarried girl, to repeat a known untruth, or to procure prohibited foods for someone on a strict diet or cigarettes for someone trying to stop smoking, merely because he is requested to do so? What is the responsibility in such cases, and with whom does it rest? Are these questions pertinent to the matter of premarital intercourse?

DOUBLE STANDARD

In many aspects of life in this country we are moving toward equality of the sexes. In the specifically sexual sphere, however, there are remnants of a double standard. Infidelity is considered to be more serious for a wife than for a husband. In cases of premarital pregnancy there is more severe criticism of the woman than of the man. The assumption that males should have more premarital sexual freedom than females should have is made by numerous members of both sexes. Some males set up a "double double standard" – a standard of premarital sexual freedom for themselves, a similar standard for females with whom they will have their premarital intercourse, and a standard of premarital chastity for the group of females from which they will choose their wives. Such a position is logically untenable because, if it were universalized, it would result in all females being virgin, in which case no males could have premarital intercourse, or else in all females having premarital intercourse, in which case there would be no virgins to marry. The double standard is so deeply ingrained traditionally in this country that our language contains no word for the equivalent of virginity in the male. This lack implies cultural acceptance of premarital sexual freedom for males in much the same way as the lack of a word applicable to wives that would be equivalent to "henpecked" implies an acceptance of the husband's domination of the wife and a resistance to the wife's domination of the husband.

Some individuals interpret present-day practices as movement in the direction of a single standard of premarital sexual freedom for both sexes. Some persons advocate such a standard. Others insist that there should be a single standard of premarital chastity. There is much confused thinking and still more confused assertion on this issue. At some place in the formulation of his own point of view, each individual must come to some conclusion on this issue if his philosophy is to be integrated and consistent.

GOAL ORIENTATION

Most college students either expect someday to marry or are already married. We may assume that they want marriage to be happy and successful. What constitutes marital happiness and success is determined in part by cultural standards, in part by the attitudes of the persons involved. At any rate, it is reasonable to suggest that premarital sexual intercourse be evaluated in the light of the almost-universal goal of happy marriage which students set for themselves. When this is done, such questions as the following arise: Is premarital intercourse a contribution to the achievement of this goal? Or is it neutral? Or is it an impediment? As preparation for marriage, is it necessary or unnecessary?

Statistical studies of premarital intercourse sometimes fall into the trap of merely recording frequency without qualifying the results in any way. A correct and complete appraisal of such intercourse includes the answers to such questions as: When did it occur? How often? With whom? At what age? Under what circumstances? Is it entirely past? Is it current? Is it likely to be repeated? Will it prevent or create problems in marriage? What were the attitudes of the couple? What was their relationship other than sexual? What did their sexual intercourse do to the quality of their total relationship? Did it make that relationship more or less satisfactory? What meaning was imputed to the experience? Did they learn anything? If so, what? What is their present attitude toward premarital sexual intercourse? Such a qualified appraisal is especially important when one person is seeking to interpret the significance of the premarital sexual experience of the other, a fiancé or a spouse.

We are inclined to make a similarly qualified appraisal of, say, honesty. We do not classify as a liar or a thief everyone who has at some time uttered an untruth or taken something that did not belong to him. We ask: Did he do this when he was a child or recently as an adult? Does he currently and habitually lie or steal? As a boy did he jump a fence and steal an apple or did he as a college student enter someone's room and steal money? With some exceptions, the important consideration in such cases is less what an individual has done and more what he now is. Similar qualification is called for in appraising premarital intercourse.

MARRIAGE REPRESENTS A VALUE SYSTEM

Providing that he does not victimize another person in the process and providing that he does not violate the law and the mores, each individual is free to decide what kind of marriage he wants. If he can find a marriage partner with a point of view similar to his own, they may work out what they consider to be a happy and successful marriage even though it may be of a type that would be intolerable to the great majority of people.

Many present-day Americans, however, are working out a type of marriage somewhat new in history. It is new in its emphasis on interpersonal relationships and personal satisfaction, in the feelings and attitudes involved in assuming that love is its cornerstone, in its mutuality, in the degree of sharing anticipated, and in its expectation of sexual exclusiveness. Marriage is inextricably bound up as an integral part of the idealism of thoughtful people who want life to be meaningful. Such idealism is true realism because it rests upon a continual reaching out for the values that endure rather than for transient satisfaction. Hence, thoughtful persons of both sexes may make successful marriage one of their major goals in life. When they fail to achieve it, the whole structure of their lives may be profoundly shaken.

In order to achieve the sort of marriage we are discussing, an individual must first decide that he wants it and then determine, with perseverance and courage, to get it. If the times are contributing factors that are inimical to such marriage, he must rise above the times. He cannot afford merely to stumble blindly along without ever raising questions about premarital behavior, without ever reexamining it to see whether it is contributing to the establishment of the kind of marriage he wants. He cannot afford to assume, as some do, that what is, is good, that all one needs to do is to conform to the pattern of the group or "get by" with the minimum required or the most tolerated, as the case may be.

This new type of marriage rests upon a system of values involving love, trust, monogamy, family unity, the oneness of which husband and wife are parts, respect for human personality, the sharing, mutuality, and sexual exclusiveness mentioned above. Such a value system tends to be integrated. When one element is disturbed, the whole system is affected, like earthquake shock waves that radiate from a center of shift and may destroy buildings miles away from the place at which the quake originated, or like removing a stone from an arch. Therefore, disturbing one of the elements becomes of major importance—not only in and of itself but as part of the value system.

If sexual exclusiveness is one of the expectations in this value system, it is clear that the kind of marriage we are discussing cannot be achieved if sexual intercourse is considered a casual experience of the moment, if it is disconnected from long-time goals and perspective. Sexual exclusiveness is not something that begins after the wedding. It is something that reflects an individual's point of view regarding the value system of marriage and the meaning of life. If marriage as we are discussing it involves the most profound sharing of which human beings are capable, that sharing is rendered incomplete to the degree that an individual has "shared" himself with another before the wedding.

Married couples, neither of whom had premarital intercourse, sometimes report a subtle satisfaction in having reserved "something" for each other. Neither is plagued by the question as to what the person with whom the spouse had premarital intercourse was like or what the spouse's reaction to and attitude toward that person were. Both have, rather, a sense of unique exclusiveness.

This concept of exclusiveness is deeply ingrained in our thinking. It is not merely an outgrowth of fear of pregnancy or, as some imply, of property rights in females. Both sexes are aware of it, though not always to the same degree. Most Americans look upon marital infidelity with disfavor. Typically, engaged couples who are temporarily separated do not approve of each other's having sexual intercourse or even petting with someone else. Many nonengaged couples think in similar terms.

Some couples even object to each other's dating during separation when there is no suspicion of petting or sexual intercourse. Most students will express strong disapproval of affectional and sexual freedom among a hypothetical group of parents all the women of which are by definition past the menopause and therefore sterile. Undoubtedly there is some possessiveness, perhaps some insecurity, at the root of such attitudes. But there is also a concept of exclusiveness that is one of the ramifications of the standard of ideal monogamous marriage as established in our culture, fuzzy and beclouded as that standard may be at times.

Exclusiveness is one of the cluster of values upon which many present-day marriages rest. Since this exclusiveness is not merely an outgrowth of fear of pregnancy, the introduction of 100 per cent perfect, guaranteed, "foolproof" contraception would undoubtedly have some effect upon the frequency of premarital pregnancy, but it is questionable whether it would result in complete sexual freedom, as some persons assume, so that eventually sexual intercourse would be considered no more serious than kissing. The frequency of premarital pregnancy suggests that in spite of the ready availability of contraceptives there is much intercourse without adequate contraceptive precaution. Today more is known about contraception than ever before, and contraceptives are more readily available than ever before, yet the illegitimacy rate continues to rise. On the other hand, there are many persons who assume that modern methods of contraception are 100 per cent effective and yet refrain from premarital intercourse.

Sharing loses its mutuality to the degree that one individual has an attitude of exploitation and uses another person for his own satisfaction alone. Such sharing must rest upon a wholehearted desire to share. If the premarital attitudes and behavior of men contribute to women's resisting the idea of sexual sharing in marriage and to their developing fears and inhibitions relative to it, then men defeat themselves in achieving the sort of sexual relationship in marriage and the degree of enthusiasm and responsiveness on the part of their wives that they so much desire.

Marriage, as many are trying to work it out, rests in part upon mutual respect—not a simple verbal statement of "respect," but a manner of treatment of another person. One individual cannot respect another if he subjects that person to risk with no assurance of security except a verbal one or a vague assumption, as in premarital intercourse, instead of protecting that person from risk and guaranteeing security through a public acceptance of responsibility.

Because so much is involved in marriage, marriage does not eliminate the need for maintaining balance and perspective regarding sex. The attitudes upon which balance and perspective depend do not arise spontaneously at the time of the wedding. They must be developed and toughened through exercise before the wedding.

If a man insists, as some do, that the male *must* have sexual intercourse and that sexual restraint is dangerous, and on this basis he rationalizes premarital intercourse, what will he do when he is married? If his wife becomes ill, if she is away for an extended visit, if he is in military service, or if for some other reason there is an unusually long period during which he cannot have normal marital intercourse, what will he do about the urgency of his sexual needs? Will he assume that the sexual needs of a married man are less demanding than those of the unmarried? Or will he be consistent and rationalize infidelity? Or will he accept the need for restraint? Studies suggest that this insistence that the unmarried male *must* have sexual intercourse is a rationalization. If such intercourse is an essential answer to a need, rather than a means of satisfying a want, it would seem that it would occur relatively more frequently. Yet Kinsey and his associates [1948] found that, in their sample, premarital intercourse was included in the histories of 42 per cent of the males 16 to 20 years old who go to college, and for college males age 20 to 30 such intercourse accounted for only about one-fifth of the total "outlet"; that is, these males had four times as frequent sexual release of some other sort, such as masturbation and/or nocturnal emissions.

In innumerable aspects of life some restraint is necessary. One cannot live happily in society if he goes about expressing all his natural impulses at any time, in any place, with anyone. Control of many impulses is essential to civilized living. This applies to the sexual impulse as it does to numerous others. The individual must learn to fit his impulses into the pattern of social life. Often this necessitates learning to live with frustration. Most people eat regularly; they do not graze like cattle. They control the concomitants of digestion. They refrain from satisfying the impulse to take another's property when it appeals to them. They do not give free vent to their pugnacious propensities. They obey the rules of etiquette, even when obedience produces discomfort. They submit to the laws of the state, even when submission is unpleasant. In countless ways they suppress natural impulses.

One of the factors accentuating the "sex problem" today is the fact that several generations of persons have developed the notion that they must satisfy their desires and natural urges the moment they become conscious of them. We sometimes lose sight of the whole of life because we think of its parts singly or one after another, instead of together. We overeat and overdrink. We advocate sexual freedom. We rear children without discipline because we are afraid they will become repressed, with the result that they have adult privileges but are not subject to adult restrictions. We plunge into installment buying with little thought beyond the immediate satisfactions arising from our purchase. We drive too fast and, forgetting all rules of courtesy, curse other drivers for their misdemeanors. Without seeming to advocate puritanism, a broader philosophy of living than that based upon impulse may be suggested.

In the last analysis, the problem of sexual restraint for the ordinary young person sums up to a problem of control, guidance, management, and direction. We have for too long thought of chastity in terms of either absence of desire or suppression of desire. We may better think of it in terms of present control in order to contribute to future achievement. This is a positive rather than a negative approach to the problem.

When an individual thinks of what he wants life to mean in the "long pull," he finds, as suggested earlier, that he cannot separate premarital sexual intercourse from the rest of life as if it were an entirely distinct, isolated phenomenon. Whether or not he has such intercourse is due in part to the pattern of values that characterizes him and upon which his life is being built. If this is to make possible the establishment of sound marriage, the pattern of values itself must be sound and consistent. Sex can most readily be built into a permanent plan of life when it is integrated into the value system upon which marriage rests, whatever that value system may be as determined by the persons whose marriage is under consideration.

In addition to the above there are other practical considerations for the individual who is seeking to make his premarital sexual behavior goal-oriented. It is difficult, if not impossible, to obtain accurate statistics on items such as the following. But each item has come to light in one way or another in counseling. The individual who seeks to make his premarital sexual behavior goal-oriented must consider possibilities as well as probabilities.

The future husband or wife may be unwilling to accept the fact of premarital sexual intercourse with someone else. There are many people who overlook previous intercourse. A large proportion of men, however, still insist upon virginity in their fiancées. There are innumerable women who expect the masculine counterpart of virginity in their fiancés or accept the lack of it only with reluctance. The question of whether or not it is justifiable for people to maintain such an attitude is academic. The real question is, "Can one be happy in marriage with an individual who does maintain that attitude?"

Withholding knowledge of premarital intercourse from the other person entails a type of misrepresentation the moral implications of which some persons consider serious. There is also the possibility that the knowledge may reach the husband or wife by indirect channels. If this happens, trust may be destroyed. Sometimes failure to tell about premarital intercourse is considered more serious than the intercourse itself.

Let us suppose that an individual who insists upon premarital chastity marries one who has had sexual intercourse but does not tell about it. Some time after the wedding the fact is discovered. The first impulse may be to take some imprudent step, since in disillusionment marriage and love are thought to be permanently and irremediably destroyed. Nothing would be gained by such a course of action, except the salving of pride. The two married because they were in love. Sexual intercourse had already occurred, but the individual was chosen for other qualities. He is still that same person. He has had no more premarital experience now than when they fell in love. He should be judged for what he is, not for what he was. The thing that should be saved is not pride, but the marriage.

This suggestion applies only to cases in which the spouse's experience occurred before the couple became engaged—not to those in which it occurred with someone other than the fiancé during engagement. It is not to be interpreted as condoning premarital intercourse. It is meant as a practical suggestion to face the facts, weigh values, and put marriage and the happiness of two persons above one person's pride or hurt.

If before marriage the other person is made aware of the premarital intercourse, he may then make his own choice. If he chooses to marry and accept it, he should do so without reproach and make an unbreakable rule never to flaunt the fact before his spouse by recalling the premarital experience in a critical or vengeful way.

During sexual excitement moral and religious considerations may be temporarily suspended, only to reappear to haunt one after his return to the somewhat cooler state of normalcy. One cannot remove his biography as he takes off his coat. Early training makes a lasting imprint upon personality. As a result, premarital sexual intercourse is sometimes followed by a sense of guilt. This sense of guilt may produce conflict, worry, and strain, which in some cases are inordinately damaging to personality and emotional health. The individual may hesitate to marry because he feels unworthy. He may have an acute sense of sin. He may be afraid to meet people, lest by some subtle means they suspect his offense. He may withdraw into a semi-imaginary world, in which he feels more secure. He may develop a feeling of inferiority for which he compensates in some less acceptable way. The distastefulness and risk of either confession or deceit may annoy him.

In a specific case, a girl had had intercourse when she was in her early teens. It had occurred only once, but the feeling of guilt that was engendered persisted into her college years. She thought other girls disliked her; yet there was no ground for that belief. As her closest friends she chose less attractive girls. She was shy and reticent. In discussing her problem with a counselor she became very much wrought up, betraying the conflict and emotion ordinarily hidden by her reserve. Her thoughts constantly turned to her guilt, and she felt that she was unworthy of marriage. The prospect of marrying without confessing to her husband made her worry lest he make the discovery for himself. On the other hand, the prospect of telling a fiancé before marriage caused her to shudder. The boy in the case lived in her home town, and every time she went home from college she was terror stricken lest, when she refused to date him, he might become angry and divulge the secret. She finally grew so sensitive that she believed that a person might detect her guilt by merely conversing with her. Such a strong sense of guilt may warp a personality, and there was evidence that hers had not escaped entirely unscathed.

It is impossible for an individual to predict in advance of premarital sexual intercourse what his attitudes will be afterward. He is not the same person afterward. Something has occurred that involves innumerable ramifications. He will look at it through different eyes.

It must not be assumed that only girls are subject to the upsetting of one's sense of self-worth. A boy may feel that he has taken advantage of a girl, had a regrettable experience, or put a relationship on an undesirable level. Girls as well as boys take the initiative in instigating intercourse, although not so frequently [Ehrmann, 1959; Kirkendall, 1961]. Many times a girl encourages a boy, communicates her desire verbally or otherwise, or stimulates him through close contact, fondling, or exposure of her body. Intercourse occurs, and it is then the boy who regrets it. Such regret is sometimes very poignant if the boy feels he has "let down" another girl whom he loves and plans to marry [Kirkendall, 1961].

An individual may have no sense of guilt immediately after premarital intercourse, but later on, when he has fallen in love and contemplates marriage, he may begin to fear exposure, regret may begin to gnaw at his conscience, and the bravado he exhibited in his earlier years may be lost.

A couple who start with the idea that their sexual intercourse will bind them closer to each other may find that their experience serves as a means of separating them. If one or both regret the episode, they may lose respect for each other and build up a barrier between themselves, even though they are engaged. Communication, instead of becoming freer, becomes more restrained. The interpersonal relationship they expected to be strengthened is weakened. Sometimes it is damaged beyond repair. At other times the relationship seems to be strengthened by intercourse; but there is reason to suspect that in such cases what actually happens is that the intercourse does not damage a relationship that is already strong [Kirkendall, 1961].

The relationship is often one-sided because the boy seeks only his own satisfaction, with no thought for the girl or her feelings. She may be left emotionally stirred up but frustrated, or she may be left with the attitude that sex is masculine only. For her it is all give and for him all take. This depersonalizes a relationship that should be highly personal. The girl, instead of being wanted for all her personal qualities, is wanted only because she is female. Some girls contribute to this situation by making femaleness so conspicuous that they obscure femininity.

There is often little or no preparation of the girl for intercourse. This may be due to the boy's thoughtlessness, as indicated above, to his ignorance of what such preparation involves, to haste, or to the difficulty of preparing her if she is having intercourse reluctantly. Girls much more frequently than boys engage in sexual intercourse unwillingly [Ehrmann, 1959]. Therefore, the girl's experience is more likely to be incomplete and unsatisfactory. Many girls "get nothing out of" premarital intercourse. Some have discomfort due to resistant tissues or reluctant participation. It is not difficult to understand why some such girls conclude that men are interested primarily in their own sexual satisfaction and that sex in marriage holds little promise of mutuality.

The relationship may mean more to the girl than it does to the boy. She may yield to him because she loves him, whereas he is interested only in physical satisfaction and has no wish to fall in love or to marry her. If this is the case, he may drop her when his appetite has become satiated or when he discovers that she is in love with him. If the relationship does mean more to the girl than to the boy, even though the experience does not cause the boy to lose interest in her she may be deeply disappointed because it does not increase his interest. She assumes that it will make him care for her more, and he does not change. She makes the mistake of assuming that there is no difference between the sexes. She has intercourse with him because she feels she loves him. Therefore, *ipso facto*, since he suggested intercourse, it must indicate that he loves her. She is caught in her own trap.

This trap becomes even more serious when the boy deliberately misleads the girl into believing that he loves her, knowing that she feels she loves him, and in this way persuades her to have intercourse. This is illustrated in the following case, in which the girl thought she was in love, though the time element involved would make this unlikely. The girl was virgin. The boy had had frequent intercourse with numerous girls. The couple met on the fourth of the month. On the sixth the boy told the girl that he loved her. She felt that she was falling in love with him and agreed to intercourse. No contraception was used. On the ninth he asked her to marry him a month later. She agreed. Intercourse without contraception occurred again. That was the last time she ever saw the boy. Fortunately she had not become pregnant.

The relationship may mean more to the girl than to the boy in another way. For some girls premarital intercourse is a means to an end: marriage. They agree to intercourse, or even initiate it, with the hope of leading the boy toward marriage either through his interest or his sense of obligation.

In the first chapter we indicated that the male more readily separates sex and love than the female, who more readily combines them. Ehrmann [1959] states that probably the single most important empirical finding in his study of 841 university students is the difference between the sexes in this regard, female sexuality being directly related to love and romance and male sexuality being more indirectly and less exclusively associated with love and romance. Females are more concerned with romanticism, while males are more concerned with eroticism. He states that the difference is ". . . so marked that there are distinct male and female subcultures" [p. 270]. Of course, eroticism is important to females, just as love and romance are important to males. But love comes to the male within a strong erotic orientation, while erotic interest in the female is likely to be aroused within a romantic complex [Ehrmann, 1959].

There is still another way in which the relationship may be one-sided. The argument is often advanced that if a girl does not want to have sexual intercourse, a boy who respects and loves her will not expect her to do so. To this a counterargument is sometimes expressed to the effect that if a boy wants sexual intercourse, a girl who loves and respects him and is aware of the male's sexual drive will have intercourse with him for his sake rather than her own. What is overlooked in the counterargument is the fact that the boy's restraint and the girl's yielding may involve different "costs" which cannot be equated. The situation is similar to that in which a boy asks a girl to drop out of school in order to marry him immediately but she insists upon postponing their marriage in order to complete her education. His "cost" in waiting and her "cost" in giving up her degree cannot be equated.

Sometimes a woman focuses her life on the man with whom she first has intercourse. The fact that with him she passes a milestone in her life causes her to develop a strong attachment to him. This attachment may be accentuated if she feels that, being no longer virgin, she would not be worthy of another man. If the man to whom she develops the attachment happens to be a loving husband, this attachment contributes to a happy marriage. If, however, he is a man she would not want or cannot get as her husband or a man with whom she could not be happy in marriage, her attachment may distort her whole future.

A girl who has intercourse to gain popularity or to do a man a favor destroys the mutuality of the relationship and may reemphasize in her own thinking the traditionally accepted but spurious belief that sexual desire is a masculine prerogative only. Eventually, if we are to found our attitude toward sex on facts instead of fables, we must get over the notion that women are neuter, that intercourse is something that men demand and to which women reluctantly submit. The girl who submits voluntarily but reluctantly, in order to become popular or to get dates, commercializes the relationship and is in a class with any woman who yields to masculine impulses for economic return.

If a girl fears that she will lose the man unless she agrees to premarital intercourse, she might ask herself whether that would really be as bad as it seems at first thought. If he would give her up as a person because he cannot have her as a sexual partner, how highly does he regard her as a person? How much respect does he have for her feelings? Does he have a sort of attitude toward her that she would want in a husband? After the wedding would he have more concern for himself than for her? To establish a sound marriage she must have a husband she does not fear losing every time he and she disagree on something. So if the girl can lose the boy over the matter of premarital intercourse, she may well be glad to lose him, having discovered in time the kind of person he is. It might be said, on the other hand, that through her refusal he discovers what kind of person she is and might be glad to lose her. Perhaps. But as indicated above, there are two quite different sets of considerations underlying his demand and her refusal.

There is overemphasis upon physical satisfaction. The couple may believe at first that there will be more than this in their relationship; but circumstances often make the development of the other aspects difficult. In premarital intercourse the physical is so obtrusive that the couple may be blinded to other important considerations and to the whole personality of the other person.

Sexual experience may be compared with eating. The glutton eats for taste alone. The person who eats only to fill his stomach or to get calories can do so with poorly prepared food. For that sort of eating, place and associates are inconsequential. A curbstone is as effective as a dining room, and solitude is no worse than company. Imagine a dinner table beautifully appointed, the food delectable, the guests congenial. Appetites are satisfied. Caloric content is provided. But the meal is not an end in itself. It is something that draws friends closer, warms conversation, prefaces an evening of good fellowship in which lasting, growing values are subtly reiterated and more firmly established. In this sort of eating the physical is only part of the larger picture and is combined with the social and the emotional. Sexual experience in marriage has greater possibilities for being like this type of eating. Intercourse before marriage is often more like the curbstone variety.

Overemphasis on the physical may also lead to premature commitment. The couple confuse their physical experience with love and marry before they are ready to do so, before they are well acquainted with each other's total personality.

Sex may be cheapened in the eyes of the two persons.   Instead of its being something through which love is expressed, something that is an essential part of a deep and growing oneness in marriage, it may become only a means to satisfy an appetite.

Fear of discovery often leads the couple to seek out-of-the-way rendezvous, which are not conducive to the better type of romance.   This fear also makes for haste, uneasiness, apprehension, and emotional strain. At the particular time of their rendezvous the couple may have complete privacy in the temporary, geographical sense of being safe from immediate detection. They do not have what might be termed psychological or social privacy. Society considers the sexual affairs of the unmarried a topic for public discussion more so than it does the affairs of married persons. Since there are two persons involved, there is the possibility of the secret's being divulged. Hence there cannot be complete privacy, with its attendant feeling of security. Fearing that what one has done will be discovered, being unable to talk about it, lying about it upon occasion, side-stepping the topic in discussion for fear a slip may be made, or marrying another person whose impression is that one has been chaste when one knows that this is not true may produce conflict and tension.

An individual may acquire a reputation for promiscuity.   If the individual is a girl, boys may come to think of her in one way only, instead of considering her as a possible wife. If a boy gets a reputation for sexual promiscuity, it may be difficult for a girl to trust his expression of love before marriage or to be convinced that he will maintain strict fidelity afterward. His sexual demands may put a girl so on guard that a barrier is put in the way of what otherwise might develop into a sound relationship.

There is the possibility of contracting venereal disease.   Figures are not available, but probably the incidence of venereal disease is not so high among college students as in the general population. Nevertheless, there is usually no simple way of telling which ones are infected. Certainly, even with the incidence low among students, one has a somewhat greater chance of contagion with an individual to whom one is not married than with a husband or wife about whose background and condition of health more is known. There are college men who cohabit with prostitutes, and many prostitutes are diseased. Is there any way of being certain that a man who suggests intercourse is not also one whose impulses lead him to other women?

Premarital testing of sexual responsiveness.   Persons of student age, battered as they are by the present-day affinity for sex discussion, bombarded continually with what often amounts to exaggerated emphasis upon both its normal and its perverted expression, are aware that sex is an important aspect of human life and is one of the basic essentials in marital adjustment. Many of them leap to the conclusion that, with sex so important in marriage, one should not enter wedded life blindly and the best test of fitness and preparation for marriage is premarital intercourse.

Sexual responsiveness is not something to be tested. It is something to be developed, through time and experience. This can be done most readily in a setting of love and security. Sexual adjustment is something to be "built."

The idea of testing disregards the sexual nature of women, that is, as women are to be found in our culture regardless of whether this "nature" is inborn or acquired. Many women are not spontaneously responsive. They must learn to be responsive. Therefore, sexual responsiveness is not something which a woman either does or does not have, as she has or has not blue eyes or a certain blood type, which may be ascertained by means of a simple test or by direct observation. If a couple have premarital intercourse with the idea of testing and the girl proves to be responsive, admittedly they have learned something. But if, for any one of a number of reasons, personal or circumstantial, the girl proves to be unresponsive, what will they conclude about her probable responsiveness in marriage? In such a case, the couple have learned nothing. They may even be worse off than they were before the test if they leap to conclusions on the basis of it or if some unexpected consequence emerges, as in the following case.

A young woman said she was interested in the physical aspects of sex, seemed to have normal sexual desire, and often became stirred up when her fiancé caressed her. The couple decided not to wait until after the wedding to have intercourse. An attempt was made. In spite of her other feelings favorable to sexual adjustment, the girl subconsciously feared the consequences. The result was that intercourse was impossible because of involuntary contraction of some of the muscles associated with her genital organs, a reaction termed *vaginismus*. Further attempts were followed by like results. The girl at length became much concerned over her continual failure, worried about it, and became upset emotionally. She feared that she was unfit for marriage and that she could never be a wife to the man she loved. This worry cast her into a vicious circle: the more she worried, the more she failed; and the more she failed, the more she worried. She felt that it would be unfair to marry unless she proved her adequacy, and this could not be proved without marriage. She finally learned from a counselor that her solution was to marry. The probability was that, as soon as the risks entailed in premarital intercourse were removed, her adjustment would make rapid progress. If, however, she had not sought counsel and had broken her engagement, she would have brought great unhappiness to herself and her fiancé. If, on the other hand, her premaritally generated fears had become so firmly established that they carried over into marriage, adjustment might have become difficult, if not impossible.

Even though no reaction so extreme as that described above occurs as a result of a couple's premarital intercourse, they may find that their experience is not all that they anticipated. The girl especially may be disappointed, as we have already indicated, and she may conclude that she is unfit for marriage or that, if marriage entails this sort of disappointing experience, she wants none of it. It takes time to develop a full sexual adjustment in marriage. For many couples the gates of heaven do not swing wide at the first experience. If this first experience is based too largely on physical appeal, the gates may remain closed and locked. One cannot learn all there is to know about sex in a fleeting, abbreviated episode. Since there is so often no time in premarital sexual experience to develop adequate adjustment, premarital intercourse is not a test of sexual responsiveness or of fitness for marriage.

If through the test the couple find that the girl is sexually responsive, they have not proved that they could live together happily in marriage because in marital adjustment more is involved than physical responsiveness. Such a couple may develop a false sense of security because they base their prediction of marital success on only one factor in the total situation.

A well-known physician writing under the pseudonym of Hotep [1938, p. 83] says:

. . . there is no question but that even one night together before marriage would save many a couple from years of suffering, with eventual divorce, and there are some countries in which such short periods of trial marriage are approved by custom if not by law. There is much to be said in favour of such a custom in this country for persons who feel the need of it.

In making this statement he shows that in his own thinking he has oversimplified the matter of marital adjustment and has fallen prey to the common fallacy, mentioned above, of thinking of sex as something to be tested rather than as something which the couple work out and build together.

In some cultures fertility is tested before the wedding. Proved ability to become pregnant contributes to a girl's marriageability. In our culture the suggestion of such a test of marriageability would seem worse than ridiculous and would be greeted in most quarters with uncompromising opposition. Although we put great emphasis upon family life, the sexes take each other on faith, assuming that they will be able to have children and that, if they cannot, they will adopt some or learn to live without them. Taking each other on faith sexually, assuming that they can work out a satisfactory sexual adjustment based upon affection, love, understanding, and a will to succeed, many couples feel is a sounder approach to sex than is inadequate testing.

PREMARITAL INTERCOURSE AS PREPARATION FOR MARRIAGE
In an attempt to determine whether an individual's premarital sexual experience prepares him for marriage, there must first be established the reasons for that experience. It is not only an act that counts but also the motives and conditioning factors back of it. A voluntary act cannot be separated from the attitudes that lie behind it. If premarital intercourse is due to immaturity, lack of standards, an exploitive attitude, insufficient self-discipline, an effort to prove manliness, rebellion, pressure by the peer group, meager understanding of sex and its role in marriage or of marriage itself, an inclination to satisfy appetite without thought of consequences, a selfish lack of appreciation of the feelings of the other party, an attempt to provide a solution to a problem of insecurity, loneliness, or hunger for affection as mentioned earlier in connection with petting, then it is apparent that it will not be preparation for marriage.

Research findings are far from conclusive with regard to the effect of premarital intercourse on marital adjustment [Burgess and Wallin, 1953; Davis, 1929; Hamblin and Blood, 1956; Hamilton, 1929; Kanin and Howard, 1958; Kinsey, Pomeroy, and Martin, 1948; Kinsey, Pomeroy, Martin, and Gebhard, 1953; Kirkendall, 1961; Locke, 1951; Terman, 1938]. The reasons for this inconclusiveness are the difficulty of getting the data and of separating the variables involved. Premarital intercourse can affect a marriage only in so far as the two persons with their particular attitudes react to it. It is also difficult to determine cause and effect. For example, if more women who have had premarital intercourse than women who have not had such intercourse are sexually responsive in marriage, does this indicate that premarital intercourse increases responsiveness or that responsive women are more likely to have premarital intercourse [Kinsey, Pomeroy, Martin, and Gebhard, 1953]?

We must beware of taking uncritically at face value the statements of persons who claim to have no regrets regarding their premarital intercourse. Some do have no regrets. Others merely say they have none. Some rationalize. Some are the kind of persons who think only of their own pleasure and have no concern for others. "No regrets," as Kirkendall [1961] suggests, is more a measure of individual satisfaction than an appraisal of a total relationship. There may be more validity in "no regrets" when expressed by two spouses who had premarital intercourse only with each other. Some women claim to have no regrets for having had an illegitimate child or a criminal abortion. Kinsey and his associates [1953] found that 83 per cent of the women who had premarital pregnancies and 84 per cent of those who contracted venereal disease expressed little or no regret regarding these two exigencies (see also Vincent, 1961). Such an attitude indicates much about the women, but it proves nothing about the phenomena toward which it is directed.

Some persons maintain that a girl may find advantage in being initiated into sexual experience with a man who is not her husband so that the first steps are associated with someone else and dissociated from her marriage. This can occur only if her experience does not cause her to react unfavorably and does not condition her against sexual relations with her spouse. Furthermore, such a suggestion disregards women's inclination to combine sex and love, as discussed earlier.

Through premarital intercourse some persons may learn the art of love, but these persons could learn the same art equally well or better in marriage with the right spouse. With the wrong spouse they would be no worse off in marriage than with the wrong partner before marriage, as far as their attitudes toward future sexual experience would be concerned. To argue that intercourse before marriage enables a girl to avoid the risk of psychological shock during the honeymoon is fallacious, since she must have her first experience with some man and shock is not dependent upon the performance of a wedding ceremony.

The argument that continence before marriage makes for a poor choice of mate because, in that choice, physical appeal plays too large a role, the couple being anxious to marry so that they may satisfy their sexual cravings, may be countered by the argument that intercourse before marriage would make an individual minimize the role of physical appeal in choosing a mate or give rise to an appetite for variety, either of which would contribute toward a desire for extramarital liaisons. Neither argument can be proved; one is as good as the other.

If an individual is promiscuous before marriage and has intercourse with many persons in turn throughout a considerable period, there may be either established or exhibited a behavior pattern that would carry over into marriage and prevent completely "monogamous" adjustment. For example, Kinsey and his associates [1953] found that women who had had premarital intercourse were about twice as likely to have extramarital intercourse as were women who had not had premarital intercourse. In these promiscuous relationships each partner in turn is chosen for qualities that, at best, are only partial contributors to successful marriage. How can a promiscuous individual be sure that his spouse will always satisfy him any more than any of the other persons with whom he had sexual relations and soon found unenticing? How can he be sure that marriage will not prove to be just a more prolonged episode in a series of temporary unions? He is in no better position with respect to making his marriage successful than is the person who has had no premarital experience. No matter how much experience an individual has had before marriage, to make his marriage succeed he must work out an adequate adjustment with a particular person.

Some women express the desire that the men they marry will have had premarital intercourse on the theory that through the experience the men will have learned something that can be applied to the wife's initiation into the sexual aspects of marriage. But premarital intercourse per se teaches a man little, if anything. He can learn from sexual experience only as he understands and applies himself to the development of the relationship, an important element of which is the woman's responsiveness. Since in premarital intercourse, as mentioned earlier, there is often neither time nor inclination on the part of the man to prepare the women to respond (and for the man the experience so often involves sex separated from love), he does not necessarily learn what he needs to know to initiate and promote his wife's responsiveness. In fact, in some cases, where a man approaches his wife as he approached the woman or women with whom he had premarital experience he defeats the very thing they both hoped would develop.

PERMISSIVENESS

In an earlier connection it was pointed out that there is an increasing tendency for males' premarital sexual partners to be females who belong to the group from which the males choose their wives, and that many present-day girls have premarital intercourse only with their fiancés. A shift is occurring in premarital sexual behavior and attitudes toward it. Promiscuity, exploitation, mere voluntary consent, irresponsible "hit-and-run" sexual episodes, and intercourse in the absence of love are one thing. This problem is still to be found. But in addition something else is emerging—intercourse by mutual consent among young people who accept responsibility for their behavior, are in love, and plan to marry. This is not promiscuity. It is not exploitation. It is not "hit-and-run." It represents true mutuality, not merely voluntary consent. It is coming to be thought of as a special kind of permissiveness. What are the pros and cons? Students often ask something to this effect: "Imagine two university students. They are mature. They are genuinely in love. They are engaged, and the engagement is accepted by their families. They plan to marry in the near future. They are informed with regard to contraception; but if the girl did become pregnant, they would simply move their wedding date forward. They respect and have concern for each other. They have a sense of responsibility for each other and for their relationship. Marriage will be very meaningful to them. They want to express their love completely and in every way. They would both like to have sexual intercourse. Why shouldn't they?" This question is not answered either positively or negatively so easily as supporters of either side of the issue often assume. Man's life would be simpler if his choices were always between clear-cut good and clear-cut bad. But his life is complicated by his having to make choices between degrees of good on the one hand and degrees of bad on the other.

Arguments in favor of permissiveness run as follows: Times are changing. American people and their culture are changing. Attitudes and practices relative to sex are changing. Inhibition and fear, moralizing and condemnation of sex carried over from the past are no longer appropriate and contribute to personal maladjustment and marital failure. We should get away from these and accept sex as natural, desirable, and healthful. We are accepting with approval greater freedom in many aspects of human relationships. Why should the sexual relationship be a conspicuous exception? If a couple are old enough to marry, they are old enough to take responsibility for their sexual activities. If they are informed about contraception and are the kind of people who would take responsibility for a pregnancy, then the threat of the possibility of pregnancy, one of the most frequently used arguments against premarital intercourse, may be dismissed as no longer applicable. The possibility of pregnancy becomes a calculated risk, much like the risk of driving or flying, and intercourse becomes largely a personal rather than a societal issue. There is no conclusive evidence to prove that premarital intercourse jeopardizes marital success. Many couples who have had such intercourse are happily married. Many who have not had such intercourse are unhappily married.

Arguments against permissiveness are: Love and the meaning of sex are best expressed not merely by a personal, private act of sexual intercourse but within a societal context as well as through an interpersonal relation. An expression within a societal context involves the couple's doing at least the minimum that society expects them to do to express such meaning, namely, to have a wedding. A couple who want to express their love "in every way" cannot do so short of this. To a private expression of love and responsibility, a wedding adds a public expression of meaning and responsibility recognized and supported by others as well as the couple. Premarital intercourse does not express the meaning of the couple's love and relationship; it shortcuts that meaning. Through marriage within a cultural framework the couple feel assured that they can realize a cluster of values which they seek, and which they cannot achieve without marriage. With regard to the man's supporting the woman and possibly the woman's contributing to the man's support while he is a student, and in living together, making a home, and having children, a couple subscribe without question to the common assumption that there is a difference between engagement and marriage. Is it sound to assume that sexual intercourse is in a different category? If a couple have a wedding not only because the law requires it, in which case a minimum ceremony would suffice, but also because they want to, as indicated by the preparation, pageantry, guest list, publicity, cost, sentiment, and religious context, they indicate that they believe a wedding will add meaning to their relationship. Conversely, they must believe that shortcutting the wedding will detract from the meaning of their relationship. Furthermore, not all engaged couples marry. There are many broken engagements. Occasionally unforeseen circumstances make necessary the postponement of the wedding, or one of the engaged pair dies. There is always the possibility of pregnancy except in cases of complete sterility. Even responsible couples sometimes take a "long chance," especially if intercourse becomes frequent. If the couple do not marry, the complications of a premarital pregnancy are obvious. If they do marry, the fact that the pregnancy necessitated a change in plans may give their marriage a poorer start than they had anticipated. Premarital pregnancy will be discussed further in the next section.

An engagement is only as substantial as the two people in it. It may have the approval of families and friends. Society at large approves the fact of engagement as a social process. But society does not give an individual engagement the degree of support and protection that it gives an individual marriage. Engagement involves folkways, but marriage involves mores. This is shown by the fact that a couple may enter an engagement through no more than mutual agreement; it may be broken either by mutual agreement or by the decision of one person. There are no legal or societal demands in connection with either process, except in so far as there may be almost obsolete legal remnants of bygone days, such as seldom-used provisions for breach of promise. Hence engagement does not provide a couple with the complete framework within which to engage in an activity which may eventuate in a condition, namely, pregnancy, which needs fullest societal support. Consequently cases like the following, though not common, are possible.

The couple were engaged. The man had given the girl a ring. Parents and friends were informed of the wedding date. The couple attended universities some distance apart. During vacations they returned to the same home town. On one of these vacation visits the girl became pregnant, but the pregnancy was not diagnosed until after she and her fiancé had returned to their respective campuses. When she became aware of the pregnancy, the girl notified the man. A few days later she received the following note:

Dear Jane:
    I am terribly sorry to hear the news that you are pregnant. My advice to you is to see a doctor and get some pills to get rid of it. Don't try to force me to marry you because I am already married. How far along is it? If you can't get the pills, get the boy who is responsible for it there to get them. Sorry. A blood test won't prove anything.
                                        Yours respectfully,
                                        Bill

Investigation showed that the boy had written the truth. After receiving word of the pregnancy, he hastily married a girl he had dated a few times at his university. They were both of legal age for marriage. Nothing could be done about it. The pregnant girl had her baby at term and placed it for adoption.

It is true, of course, that had this couple been married before the girl became pregnant her husband might not have taken responsibility for her and the baby and might even have divorced or deserted her. Yet the difference in her status and that of the child, the degree of societal support accorded her, and the alternatives available to her in the two situations are obvious.

With the development, publicizing, and dissemination of oral contraceptives, some students have leaped to the conclusion that herein is to be found a simple, universal, and almost automatic solution to the problem of premarital intercourse in general and the special permissiveness we have been discussing in particular. Such is not the case. Knowledge of effective methods of contraception has been available in this country for some time. Yet Americans continue to have hundreds of thousands of premarital pregnancies each year. Why? Because not all the means of contraception known can prevent even one pregnancy unless they are applied with knowledge, intelligence, foresight, and self-discipline. Oral contraceptives are no exception. In the last analysis, the only effective means of contraception known is a sense of responsibility. There is no more guarantee that oral contraceptives will be used responsibly in the future than there has been evidence of responsible use of other means up to date. Granting the desirability of preventing premarital pregnancy, to assume that the use of contraception is the entire solution to the problem misses the central issue and creates a false focus. It is like assuming that the solution to the problem of safe driving is to carry a first-aid kit in one's car.

In a word, all this suggests that the issue facing young people today is not only one of freedom versus restriction or of preventing pregnancy but also one of deciding upon what meaning they want to express through sex and how this may best be accomplished. Without meaning, present-day freedom is no better than traditional restriction and makes no greater contribution to human personality or happiness. Nowadays whatever meaning is imputed to sexual intercourse comes from the persons involved, with, of course, cultural coloration; it is not imposed by the cultural pattern. Freedom undirected toward carefully thought-out goals and devoid of meaning can in the "long run" be disappointing. The consequences of freedom unseeingly used can be as binding as the results of restriction blindly applied.

THE PROBLEM OF RISK

All of life entails risk. Some risk is unavoidable, for example, the risk of inhaling harmful bacteria while breathing. Some risk is practically unavoidable in our type of living, for example, that involved in riding in an automobile. Some risk is avoidable, for example, that involved in speeding. Each individual has, on the one hand, the problem of reducing necessary risk and, on the other hand, that of deciding how much unnecessary risk he is willing to undergo. In doing this he must reach some conclusion as to what possible price he is willing to pay for what possible gain. He does not solve the problem by assuming that risk is something to which only others, not himself, are subject.

In this connection, perspective and the "long view" are basic. How much would be gained at what cost? Since neither can be predicted in advance, could the greatest possible gain and the greatest possible cost be out of proportion? Could it be like burning a cathedral to fry an egg in order to satisfy a ravenous appetite? Would the future be mortgaged for the present? Would the end result be the purchase of complex problems with the currency of simple pleasure? Or would it be the purchase of an enriched relationship with the coin of risk? Or would the risk element not be great enough to be given serious attention?

Risk may be considered in two ways: (1) What is the statistical risk; that is, how frequently is it incurred relative to the frequency of premarital intercourse? (2) What is jeopardized if the consequence does occur, and what can be done about it? The individual's problem is not merely the achievement of the scientist's objective understanding of a statistical analysis of a situation. His problem is also the subjective one of evaluating and assimilating what may be for him a world-shaking, life-encompassing experience, even though he may be only one inconspicuous statistic in the over-all picture.

Each individual also has the problem of deciding how much avoidable risk he is willing to impose upon another person and for what reasons. If a person wants to play "Russian roulette" with the gun pointed at his own head, that is one thing. If, however, he wants to play "Russian roulette" with the gun pointed at someone else's head, it becomes an entirely different issue. In premarital intercourse the woman does not assume the entire risk; but she does assume the greater risk, because in a case of premarital pregnancy the woman more often shoulders the burden. We may safely assume that more often than not premarital intercourse occurs primarily on male initiative. In such premarital intercourse, who plays "Russian roulette" with the gun pointed at whose head? Let us imagine that a study is made of the restaurants most frequented by students at a given university. The study reveals that the most popular restaurant serves 10,000 meals per month. It also reveals that on the average 2 persons per month who eat at that restaurant contract ptomaine poisoning and die. That is 1 death per 5,000 meals. Would you eat there? Would you take your fiancé, husband, wife, or parents there? What about premarital intercourse, which involves a risk greater than 1 in 5,000?

In premarital intercourse, then, both parties assume risk. For the man the risks are as follows:

Accusation of rape by force.   Cases are not at all unknown in which a woman voluntarily has premarital intercourse, and afterward, because she feels guilty, or to get attention, or because the fact is discovered, or for some similar reason, she claims rape. Usually there are no witnesses to premarital intercourse. Hence it is the man's word against the woman's. She may not succeed in making her accusation hold up in court. But even after the fire is put out, so to speak, the odor of smoke remains in the air, and there may be people who still wonder whether the man was guilty and justice miscarried.

Accusation of statutory rape.   Typically, state law specifies an "age of consent." This is the minimum age which an unmarried girl must have reached in order legally to give consent to sexual intercourse. If she is below the age of consent, she cannot legally consent to having intercourse even though she voluntarily says the words agreeing to it. A comparable situation is found in an individual's inability to sign a valid legal contract before age twenty-one even though he writes his name on the contract form.

Let us assume that in a given state the age of consent is sixteen. A physically well-developed fifteen-year-old girl claims to be seventeen. A twenty-one-year-old man takes her at her word. She voluntarily has sexual intercourse. Her parents discover this fact and make known her correct age. The man with whom the girl had intercourse is liable to prosecution for statutory rape, which is not considered to be quite so serious a crime as rape by violence but which nevertheless constitutes a felony.

Accusation of paternity.   If a girl becomes pregnant, any man who has had intercourse with her within a given time span is a possible candidate for an accusation of paternity. Cases such as the following have come to this writer's attention:

1. The man admitted intercourse but disclaimed paternity, asserting that the girl had confessed to intercourse with other boys. His family paid a considerable sum of money to the girl's parents on their promise not to institute a paternity suit and not to put pressure on the boy to marry the girl.

2. A pregnant girl tried to force a man to marry her after they had had intercourse. The man resisted. The girl finally admitted that she knew that this man could not be the father of her child because she was already pregnant when the intercourse occurred; but he was a more desirable candidate for marriage than any of the other men with whom she had had intercourse.

3. A girl claimed pregnancy and almost succeeded in forcing a

man to marry her. Before the wedding she admitted that she was not pregnant. They had had intercourse and she was using the "pregnancy" as a means of exerting pressure because she wanted to marry this particular man.

Contrary to common assumption, paternity cannot be unequivocably ascertained by means of blood tests. It is true that blood types are hereditary. Blood tests made upon man or men, mother, and child can ascertain whether a given man could or could not be the father. That is not equivalent, however, to determining that a given man is the father. For example, suppose Miss X has a child. She admits having had intercourse with three men, namely, A, B, and C. Blood tests are made on all five persons. The tests indicate that Miss X could not have had that child, with its particular blood type, with A or B. She could have had that child with C. That still does not prove beyond all doubt that C is the father. Miss X may not have mentioned D, with whom she also had intercourse and whose blood type is the same as C's.

Pressure to marry in case of acknowledged paternity. Pressure to marry in such cases may be "external" or "internal." It may come from parents, fear of gossip, or concern for reputation. Or it may come from a sense of honor and responsibility.

If the couple are engaged, there may be no pressure in the usual sense of the term because they are in love and, therefore, plan to marry anyway. Their problem is relatively simpler, involving only actual or asserted change of wedding date. In some cases, however, marrying earlier than they had expected is a serious upset to a couple's families and to their educational and occupational plans.

If, on the other hand, the couple had not planned to marry or would not be good choices as marriage partners for one another or do not know each other well enough or are not in love, marriage to camouflage a pregnancy or to give a child a legal father and a name may be damaging to all three persons. We shall discuss this problem further in the paragraphs below.

For the woman the risk of pregnancy is serious and ever present. What happens to the woman's reputation, to her sense of self-worth, to her attitudes, to her relationship with her family and with the man involved all constitute elements of risk for her. These are compounded by the serious and ever-present risk that she may become pregnant. At the present stage of knowledge there is no 100 per cent perfect contraceptive. Employed with care and intelligence in marriage where circumstances are conducive to their most efficacious use and based upon the advice of a physician, contraceptives assure a degree of security that enables the couple to control conception and have no worry about unwanted pregnancy. The circumstances under which premarital intercourse occurs are often not conducive to careful, cautious, intelligent use of contraceptives, even when the devices themselves are of the better types. Hurry, apprehension, inadequate preparation, and especially lack of cooperation and responsibility on the part of the man make the risk of pregnancy always imminent. When this is coupled with the fact that in many cases the contraceptive devices used are not those recommended by a physician, but are rather those purchased on the recommendation of drugstore clerks, filling-station attendants, or magazine advertisements, the risk may clearly be seen. As suggested earlier, neither contraceptive information nor contraceptive devices alone can prevent conception. Information must be applied. Devices must be put to use. In premarital, as in marital, intercourse, many couples take a chance because emotion befogs caution or contraception seems too troublesome.

Frequency of premarital pregnancy. There is no way at present to get a complete and accurate picture of premarital pregnancy. But there are useful studies giving some indication of frequency. These studies include such items as the number of babies born alive to unmarried mothers, the number of unmarried women who have criminal abortions, the number of babies conceived before the wedding but born in marriage, the number of women who report premarital pregnancy regardless of the termination of such pregnancy.

In studies made by Gebhard and his associates [1958] in a sample of 5,940 women, it was found that among girls who had reached age 15, *including all girls who had reached this age disregarding whether or not they reported that they had had premarital intercourse,* 1 in a thousand had already become pregnant; among those who had reached age 20, 33 in a thousand; among those who had reached age 25, 75 in a thousand; and among those women who had reached the thirties and forties and were still unmarried, 100 in a thousand, or 10 per cent, had become pregnant. The above figures are for all the women and make no allowance for differences relative to educational level. By age 25, 8 per cent of those who had attended college and 11 per cent of those who had attended high school had become pregnant. By age 30, 10 per cent of the college group and 13 per cent of the high school group had done so. Among the women *who had had premarital intercourse,* 25 per cent of the high school group and 17 per cent of the college group had become pregnant by age 25, almost 29 per cent of the former and more than 20 per cent of the latter by age 30. Generalizing, these investigators assert that among women who have premarital intercourse, 1 in 5 becomes pregnant at some time before marriage. Of the women in the sample who had become pregnant before the wedding, 13 per cent had done so twice, 5 per cent three times, 2 per cent four or more times.

It is estimated that in this country in 1962 there were 245,100 children (about 1 child in 17) recorded as having been born out of wedlock; 176,800 (72.1 per cent) of these were born to women under 25 years of age. The total number was almost three times as large as in 1940. Part of the reason for this increase is that in cases of premarital pregnancy there is less pressure put upon couples to marry than there used to be. The number of children born out of wedlock per 1,000 unmarried women aged 15 to 44 years (the illegitimacy rate) was 21.5, more than three times as high in 1962 as in 1940. In 1962 there were 58.8 illegitimate births per 1,000 live births—the highest ratio on record in this country [U.S. Bureau of the Census, 1964]. Gebhard and his associates [1958] found that 3 per cent of the ever-married women in their sample were pregnant at the time of the wedding. In a study of 1,531 marriages in a county in Indiana, Christensen [1953] used the method of "record linkage"; that is, he compared dates for first births with wedding dates, making an allowance for premature deliveries. In this study he found that one-fifth of all first births within these marriages were the outcome of conceptions that must have occurred before the wedding. It would not be safe to generalize too far on Christensen's findings and assume that they were applicable to the country as a whole, and Christensen never implied that they were. Approximately one-fourth of all live births, or currently about 1 million annually, are first births. Hence, if Christensen's findings are at all representative, they would suggest that each year some 200,000 babies are born within marriage after having been conceived before the wedding.

Figures such as those above are subject to question because there is no way of being certain that findings emerging from a study of a sample of the population are descriptive of the entire population. But if we assume a reasonable degree of validity in the studies mentioned and others like them, some of which bear out these findings, and we combine and generalize upon the figures for births recorded as illegitimate and children born within marriage but conceived before the wedding, assuming the addition of an unknown number of premarital pregnancies terminated by criminal abortion before or after the wedding (Kinsey reported that among the women in his sample from 88 to 95 per cent of the premarital pregnancies were terminated by induced abortion before marriage) [Calderone, 1958], an unknown number of such pregnancies ending with a stillborn child, and an unknown number of illegitimate infants killed immediately after birth (some of which are discovered, and in some cases the mothers are apprehended), we arrive at approximately a half million. If there are anywhere near a half million, or even several hundred thousand, premarital pregnancies in this country each year, this constitutes a problem of major proportions and suggests a risk in premarital intercourse that is not to be ignored.

On the basis of their studies, Kinsey and his associates [1953] estimated that there was 1 premarital pregnancy for each 1,000 acts of premarital intercourse among the women in their sample. Even if we accept such an estimate as approaching accuracy, and there is ample reason for questioning it, we must be cautious in interpreting it. It certainly does not suggest that a girl may have premarital intercourse 999 times without risk of conception. There is undoubtedly some ratio of premarital pregnancies to instances of premarital intercourse, but this ratio cannot be ascertained with accuracy. In one sense this ratio means that a girl has one chance in a given number of becoming pregnant. In another sense, however, such an interpretation is misleading. The figure above makes no allowance for use or nonuse of contraceptives, for relative fertility or infertility, for the time during the menstrual month that intercourse occurred. Each time a girl has such intercourse, in a sense she assumes not a portion of the risk but the entire risk. But the probability of pregnancy increases with repeated exposure to the risk.

Suppose you flip a penny nine times and each time it turns up heads. What is the probability that it will turn up tails on the tenth throw? We know that if you flip the coin often enough, you will get an approximately equal number of heads and tails. Eventually, then, if you continue to flip the coin it will turn up tails. But the fact that it turned up heads nine times in succession has no effect on the tenth throw. Because the coin has two sides, on the tenth throw as on every other throw there is a 50–50 chance of its turning up tails, just as if it were flipped only once. In other words, each throw is independent of all the rest. Each time intercourse occurs the entire risk of pregnancy is assumed. Some girls become pregnant the first time they have intercourse. Other girls have frequent intercourse through months or years without contraception and without becoming pregnant. But the more often a girl has intercourse, the more likely she is to conceive. Averages here mean little or nothing. One is reminded of the man who carefully calculated the average depth of the river and found it to be 4 feet. Being 6 feet tall, he started to wade across but drowned in the process because the depth ranged from a few inches at the shore line to many feet over his head in midstream.

The number of children born out of wedlock does not by itself present the entire picture of illegitimacy. In one study made in New York City it was found that more than 20 per cent of the mothers had no prenatal care until the seventh or eighth month, and 17 per cent (as compared with 3 per cent of married mothers) had no prenatal care at all. In another study, also made in New York City, it was found that the maternal death rate among the unmarried was almost twice as high as among the married. The infant death rate was more than twice as high for children born out of wedlock as for those born in wedlock. Among children born out of wedlock the death rate for those born to mothers who had no prenatal care was 3½ times as high as for those born to mothers who had such care. Almost twice as many children born to unmarried mothers as compared to those born to married mothers were premature [Oettinger, 1962].

When a girl has a premarital pregnancy, there are relatively few alternatives open to her.

1. She may marry. If she was engaged when the pregnancy started and her fiancé is the father of the child, the situation is as favorable as it could be under the circumstances. If she marries a man whom otherwise she would not marry, the marriage gets an inauspicious start. If she marries a man she knows is not the father of the child and does not apprise him of the fact of pregnancy, in some states the man has ground for annulment or divorce should that fact become known after the wedding. At best such a procedure is a serious form of misrepresentation. The girl may, and in some cases does, marry a man who accepts the child even knowing that he is not the father. In one case the girl had already become pregnant before she met a particular boy. On their first date she told him about the pregnancy. He became so enamored of her and had such a compulsive desire to protect her that he married her within a month after their meeting in order to legitimate the child.

If a couple have premarital intercourse because they are not ready to marry, will they be more ready to marry if a pregnancy leads them to marry earlier? There is evidence to suggest that marriages entered into in order to camouflage a premarital pregnancy are more than ordinarily unstable. In one study it was found that the divorce rate was more than twice as high for those marriages in which conception occurred before the wedding (with the child born after the wedding) as it was for those marriages in which conception occurred after the wedding. Of the latter 8.95 per cent ended in divorce; of the former 18.54 per cent ended in divorce [Christensen and Meissner, 1953; see also Christensen, 1963].

2. The girl may remain unmarried and have the baby at full term. Some girls keep their babies. Others place them for adoption. One estimate places the number of such cases at 50,000 per year [Oettinger, 1962]. Some girls sell their babies illegally on "black market." Because of antagonistic public opinion some girls who keep their babies disguise their situations. A few girls—as we suggested above there is no way of ascertaining how many—destroy their babies after birth. Such destruction is, of course, a felony.

3. The girl may have a criminal abortion, performed either by herself upon herself or by an abortionist. In either case there are ethical, legal, religious, and psychological considerations, as well as physiological risk. This matter of abortion will be discussed more fully in connection with the topic of reproduction.

THE INDIVIDUAL WHO HAS HAD PREMARITAL INTERCOURSE

Whatever may be the exact percentage of students who have had premarital intercourse, we may assume that in every college or university population there are likely to be some. Each of these students, though he may be interested in the over-all issue and its pros and cons, is almost sure also to approach the issue personally and subjectively. As such a student reviews and scrutinizes his sexual experience, he must of necessity fall into one of two categories. Either he accepts his experience or dismisses it from his thinking and thus has no problem, or he is torn by some degree of conflict and thus does have a problem. This conflict may arise from a sense of regret or guilt, fear that his experience will not be accepted by a fiancé or spouse, a feeling that he has "let someone down," fear of discovery, confusion due to the crosscurrents produced by a variety of points of view to which he has been exposed and which he has not as yet been able to think through sufficiently to "be at peace with himself," embarrassment at recognizing that he was once what he now considers so immature and shortsighted, a self-imposed judgment of immorality or sinfulness, apprehension lest he be unable to have a successful marriage, or any of a number of similar factors, some of them highly individualized products of human ingenuity in achieving self-condemnation. What may such an individual do? The following are some points to be considered. These items are not to be construed as either condemning or condoning premarital intercourse but only as facing the reality of the situation.

His marriage is not necessarily doomed. What he takes to his marriage is both his past experience and his present attitude. Of the two, the latter is the more influential so far as contributing to marital success or failure is concerned, unless in failing to recognize this fact one spouse gives past experience too much weight or unless the past events have an unusual bearing on the present marriage.

What is done is done. This does not necessarily excuse the past. On the other hand, there is no way of changing it. In the discussion of maturity in a later chapter, it will be pointed out that a mature person faces the unchangeables in life with poise and a minimum of defeat.

Regret and guilt are not identical. Either implies that the individual is sorry for what he has done. But regret is directed primarily toward the act — "I am sorry that I did thus and so." Guilt is directed primarily toward oneself, the person who committed the act — "I did thus and so for which I am sorry, and the fact that I did it indicates that I am weak (or immoral or sinful or whatever it may be)." An individual who regrets his act but still has confidence in his own integrity and ability to redirect his future behavior can rise above his past. On the other hand, the individual who brands himself through guilt may so lose his self-confidence that he remains permanently chained to his mistakes.

Self-appraisal must be particularized. As suggested earlier in this chapter, a given overt act does not always have the same significance so far as the evaluation of an individual is concerned. Questions such as when, why, how often, and so on, need to be answered before an accurate appraisal can be made. If, in his earlier days, an individual did something which more mature judgment now suggests was unwise and he would not therefore repeat it, what he did should be recorded against immaturity rather than permanently against the person who has now grown beyond that immaturity. Without implying that "anything goes," there are cases in which a similar thing may be said of circumstances. One may think of exceptional circumstances under which an individual might exhibit behavior which he would not exhibit if the circumstances were different. This does not necessarily suggest lack of moral fiber, and it does not necessarily constitute an excuse. The fact remains, however, that under exceptional circumstances an individual may exhibit what for him is exceptional behavior that he does not repeat when circumstances are more commonplace. If under such exceptional circumstances an individual had premarital intercourse but has not continued to have it under more nearly "normal" conditions, he may not thereby excuse his earlier behavior or automatically remove all regret, but the exceptional circumstances may certainly be taken into account in evaluating both his behavior and his personality.

Almost everyone has regret about something. There may be individuals whose self-righteousness leads them to assume that they are perfect and that, therefore, they have never done anything for which regret would be appropriate. Most people, however, have at some time done something in their lives for which they feel regret. The "something" does not have to be sexual. Most of these persons somehow find a way to live with that regret. A problem arises when the assumption is made that an individual can commit no offense worse than a sexual offense; anything else may eventually be forgiven and assimilated, but not that. In other words, in evaluating sexual behavior perspective is often lost.

Values are not easily achieved. The individual who is concerned about his past sexual behavior is a thinking person, else he would not be concerned. Therefore, his concern is part of a process of working out a set of values that will fit his needs. For the thinking person such a set of values is the outgrowth of one of the most difficult of all human activities — careful, analytical, critical thought. Hence the individual who is concerned about his premarital sexual behavior may utilize that concern as a step in the process of working out a set of life values, a life philosophy. He and his marriage may be the better for that process.

No one is bound to his past. In one sense what is past cannot be changed; it becomes a permanent part of the individual's personality and biography. In another sense, however, no one is inextricably bound to his past. At any point in his life he may change; he has the inalienable human right to turn a corner if he desires to do so.

Counseling may help. If the individual will talk over his problem with a counselor in whom he has confidence, he may often obtain help. This help may come from the counselor's understanding and suggestions in assisting the person to attain self-understanding. The individual may also be helped by the process of discussing his problem, "getting it off his chest." "Bottling up" regret, guilt, conflict, or confusion plays a part in increasing it. "Getting it out into the open" often has the opposite effect.

Religion may help. If the individual is religiously inclined, he may find a source of help in his faith. The predominant religious point of view in this country, the Judeo-Christian, makes ample provision for help for the person who finds the weight of his own shortcomings so great that he cannot lift himself by his own bootstraps.

WHAT DO YOU THINK?

1. What is the difference, if any, between dating and courtship?
2. To what extent should girls take the initiative in dating?
3. What are the pros and cons of "dutch dating"?
4. What do you consider acceptable standards of behavior in dating? Appraise present-day practices in the light of such standards.
5. What suggestions would you give to a couple who are in love and are affectionate but do not want their expression of affection to get out of control?
6. In your judgment what should the standard be with regard to premarital sexual intercourse? Give the reasons for your answer.
7. What is meant by the term *value*?
8. How are a given individual's values determined?
9. How does an individual or a group determine *what ought to be* as compared to *what is*? How do you?
10. To what degree should common practice determine norms or standards of behavior?

11. How and where should the line be drawn between individual freedom and societal good?

12. What are the arguments for and against a single standard of premarital sexual freedom, as opposed to the present double standard? Is America moving toward a single standard whether it is approved or disapproved?

13. What are the arguments for and against forcing marriage in a case of premarital pregnancy?

14. An individual had premarital sexual relations with someone other than his (or her) present fiancée. This fact is unknown to the fiancée. What are the arguments for and against the individual's making the fact known to the fiancée?

15. In your judgment, what are acceptable standards with regard to petting?

16. What are the similarities and differences between controlling one's sexual drive and the following: dieting, stopping smoking, saving money, studying to learn as compared to studying to get a degree, refusing to "use" one's friends, refraining from shoplifting when walking through a store, controlling speed when in a hurry, failing an examination instead of cheating, telling the truth even when it hurts, controlling drinking, disregarding safety signals when driving, engaging in "shady" practices to make money?

17. There are some situations in social life in which people cannot function satisfactorily, freely, and effectively without some sort of legal protection in addition to personal agreement. For example, a man takes a job in a business organization. After he has worked for a while, the employer decides to back out of the agreement and not pay him. Or a student takes a course on the assumption that he will receive credit if he makes passing grades. What if the university refused to give him such credit? Or two friends start on an automobile trip and agree to share expenses. They have an accident, and one friend does not follow through in assuming his share of the cost. What are the similarities and differences between such situations and the premarital sexual situation in so far as the matter of legal protection via a wedding and personal agreement to have intercourse are concerned?

SELECTED READINGS

Allen, Frederick Lewis: *Only Yesterday,* Harper & Row, Publishers, Incorporated, New York, 1931, chap. 5. "The revolution in manners and morals" in America during the 1920s, including the rapid change in premarital sexual frankness and freedom.

Bassett, Marion: *A New Sex Ethics and Marriage Structure,* Philosophical Library, Inc., New York, 1961. A discussion of the sexual nature of women; sex practices before and in marriage; laws relating to abortion and illegitimacy.

Beach, Waldo: *Conscience on Campus*, Association Press, New York, 1958, chap. 9, "The Morality of Romance." A discussion of premarital sexual relations from a Christian point of view.

Bell, Robert R.: *Marriage and Family Interaction*, The Dorsey Press, Inc., Homewood, Ill., 1963, chaps. 4, 7, 8. Dating and the courtship process; premarital sexual behavior and attitudes.

Bernard, Jessie, Helen Buchanan, and William M. Smith, Jr.: *Dating, Mating and Marriage*, Howard Allen, Inc., Cleveland, 1958, chaps. 2–4. Dating; the effects of military service on dating. Includes many case-documentary materials.

Bertocci, Peter A.: *The Human Venture in Sex, Love, and Marriage*, Association Press, New York, 1949. "These chapters are addressed to young people who want to work out . . . a reasoned answer to their questions and doubts, who want to satisfy the rational urge to understand and not merely rationalize their strongest desires."

Blood, Robert O., Jr.: *Marriage*, The Free Press of Glencoe, New York, 1962, chaps. 1, 5. Dating as preparation for marriage; premarital sexual relations, consequences and control; the course of sexual involvement.

Bowman, Henry A.: *A Christian Interpretation of Marriage*, The Westminster Press, Philadelphia, 1959, chaps. 1, 3. A discussion of the nature of sex and premarital sexual relations from a Christian point of view.

Cavan, Ruth Shonle: *American Marriage*, Thomas Y. Crowell Company, New York, 1959, chaps. 5, 10. College dating: characteristics and codes; the nondater; evaluating premarital sexual relations—why students approve or disapprove; premarital pregnancy.

——— (ed.): *Marriage and the Family in the Modern World*, Thomas Y. Crowell Company, New York, 1960, chap. 9. Attitudes of students toward premarital intercourse; the problem of premarital intercourse and its implications.

Cole, William Graham: *Sex and Love in the Bible*, Association Press, New York, 1959. A discussion of sex before and in marriage; biblical teachings; sexual deviations.

Duvall, Evelyn Millis, and Sylvanus M. Duvall: *Sex Ways in Fact and Faith: Bases for Christian Family Policy*, Association Press, New York, 1961, chaps. 7–9. Teen-agers' sex attitudes and behavior; premarital pregnancy—record linkage studies; illegitimacy.

Ehrmann, Winston: *Premarital Dating Behavior*, Holt, Rinehart and Winston, Inc., New York, 1959. A study of the sexual attitudes and practices of university students.

Hiltner, Seward: *Sex Ethics and the Kinsey Report*, Association Press,

New York, 1953. An appraisal of the Kinsey report on the male from a Christian point of view.

Himelhoch, Jerome, and Sylvia Fleis Fava (eds.): *Sexual Behavior in American Society*, W. W. Norton & Company, Inc., New York, 1955. A critical appraisal of the Kinsey reports. Chapters written by persons in the fields of sociology, psychiatry, law, medicine, and theology.

Kephart, William M.: *The Family, Society, and the Individual*, Houghton Mifflin Company, Boston, 1961, chaps. 10, 12, 13. Dating behavior and problems, including lack of attractiveness; parental influence; premarital sex codes and activity; the attitudes of the churches toward premarital sex; legal complications; the relation between premarital sexual intercourse and marital adjustment.

Kirkendall, Lester A.: *Premarital Intercourse and Interpersonal Relationships*, The Julian Press, Inc., New York, 1961. A study of premarital sexual behavior and attitudes based on interviews with hundreds of university students; includes many quotations from these interviews.

———: *Sex Adjustments of Young Men*, Harper & Row, Publishers, Incorporated, New York, 1940. This book grew out of the author's experience in teaching and counseling male university students; a discussion of their problems and attitudes.

Martinson, Floyd M.: *Marriage and the American Ideal*, Dodd, Mead & Company, Inc., New York, 1960, chaps. 5, 6, 14, 15. "The primary purpose of this book is to show how the major value themes in American culture and the findings of social science relate to problems and decisions of marriage and family living." A discussion of dating and premarital sex.

McPartland, John: *Sex in Our Changing World*, Holt, Rinehart and Winston, Inc., New York, 1947. A history of changing sex practices and attitudes in America in the twentieth century.

Merrill, Francis E.: *Courtship and Marriage*, rev. ed., Holt, Rinehart and Winston, Inc., New York, 1959, chaps. 6–8. Dating in America: theory, patterns, complications, norms, and functions; "rating and dating."

Mueller, Gerhard: *Legal Regulation of Sexual Conduct*, Oceana Publications, Inc., New York, 1961. A digest and analysis of state laws regulating various types of sexual conduct and offenses.

Neville-Rolfe, Sybil: *Sex in Social Life*, George Allen & Unwin, Ltd., London, 1959. A compilation of articles giving views of a number of British writers on various aspects of sex before and in marriage.

Pilpel, Harriet F., and Theodore Zavin: *Your Marriage and the Law*, Holt, Rinehart and Winston, Inc., New York, 1952, chap. 7. Laws relating to paternity tests and illegitimacy in the U.S. Includes case materials.

Reiss, Ira L.: *Premarital Sexual Standards in America,* The Free Press of Glencoe, New York, 1960. An analysis of sexual standards rather than a statistical analysis of sexual practices; a discussion of the emergence of "permissiveness with affection" – what will the future trend be?

Simpson, George: *People in Families,* Thomas Y. Crowell Company, New York, 1960, chaps. 4, 6, 24. The unmarried mother and father; why premarital pregnancies occur; dating, petting, and premarital intercourse. Psychoanalytic emphasis.

Turner, E. S.: *A History of Courting,* E. P. Dutton & Co., Inc., New York, 1955. A history of courtship practices in Europe and America, including petting, premarital sex, and the decline of chaperonage. Contains many excerpts from literature and personal letters.

Vincent, Clark E.: *Unmarried Mothers,* The Free Press of Glencoe, New York, 1961. A study of unmarried mothers: their personal characteristics, family backgrounds, attitudes toward their pregnancies, and what they did with their babies.

Waller, Willard: *The Family: A Dynamic Interpretation,* rev. by Reuben Hill, Holt, Rinehart and Winston, Inc., New York, 1951, chaps. 8–10. The impact of middle-class mores on dating; rating and dating; courtship as trial and error; exploitation; courtship as an interactive process.

Young, Leontine R.: *Out of Wedlock,* rev. ed., McGraw-Hill Book Company, New York, 1963. A study of the problem of premarital pregnancy based on the author's experience in working as a social worker with 350 unmarried mothers.

chapter 5

CHOOSING A MARRIAGE PARTNER

A WISE CHOICE is "half the battle." One person cannot tell another whom to choose or even how to choose. But the importance of choice can hardly be overemphasized. Of all the choices an individual is called upon to make in his entire life, the choice of marriage partner can go as far as any, and farther than most, toward determining his happiness. It is safer and easier to choose well than to attempt to alter personalities after the wedding. It is better to match than to patch. Change may occur through experience, self-effort, or the influence of one's spouse; but it can take place only on the foundation of personality traits present before it began.

Personality traits are types or aspects of behavior. They are abstractions deduced from observation of concrete, overt acts. Traits themselves have no actual existence within an individual. His behavior does not express his traits; his behavior *is* his traits. Changing those traits is not a process like that of changing one's clothes, taking off one garment and putting on another. It is, rather, a process of change in behavior, which entails the development of new habit patterns. As a rule people do not like to be changed, especially when the suggested alteration implies inferiority and they are made the subject of a reform program concocted by someone else.

Each of a person's traits is relative to all others and is manifested against the background of his total personality. None ever stands alone, isolated from the rest of the individual. Each is also relative to the attitude of every individual who makes a judgment of it. Besides, traits are not always constant. A person may exhibit a given trait under one set of circumstances but not under another. He may, for example, be honest when he is trusted but dishonest when subjected to suspicion. He may control his temper at home but lose it on the golf course.

The same trait may appear in different light as circumstances vary. If a man has fought his way to the top in business, we must expect him to be aggressive. Aggression, however, is more acceptable at a meeting of the board of directors than at the family dinner table. Absorption in his work may be commendable in a man; but if he cannot escape it long enough to spend some time with his wife or friends, it becomes an annoyance rather than a virtue. An individual cannot be two personalities simultaneously — one with his family, another with other persons. If he seems to be so dually constituted, it is because the basic traits in his personality appear differently under different circumstances.

Qualities of marriage partner

It would be an interesting and perhaps provocative exercise to attempt to list all the qualities desirable in a marriage partner. The end result would probably be an inventory of all the virtues and some of the vices, depending upon one's point of view, of which the human race is capable. Our difficulty in presenting such a list would be that we should be attempting to catalogue the desirable traits to be found in marriage partners in general. Actually, there is no such thing as a generalized husband or wife; there is only some particular woman's husband, some particular man's wife. It is useless to talk about the qualities of a spouse until we answer the question, "Whose spouse?" The qualities held to be desirable are variable and depend upon the personality and expectations of the individual making the choice. Qualities are not absolutely desirable or undesirable. They are relatively so and are weighted according to the attitudes of the maker of the list.

One author asked a thousand couples to state types of behavior that they felt contributed to the success or failure of their marriages. In the published list of those items most frequently mentioned are to be found such things as "She always has meals on time. She sews very well. She always has clean clothes for me to wear. She washes my back. He helps me with the dishes. He loves nature. He does not overtell old jokes. He gladly rubs my back" [Burkhart, 1937]. The list contains many items more commonly desirable than the ones quoted here. These are cited to show how weighted by individual points of view the qualities considered desirable in a husband or wife may become. It is apparent at a glance that for one man whose marital happiness rests to an appreciable degree on the washing of his back there must be thousands who are quite content to make their toilet single-handed.

We suggest, therefore, that the reader carefully and thoughtfully make the following study. (1) List in writing all the qualities desired in a husband or a wife, as the case may be—all that come to mind or that may be suggested through discussion or reading. (2) Select the ten most essential qualities from the list. Be sure that in your judgment these are actually the ten most essential and not merely ten most clearly exhibited by a person in whom you are interested. (3) Rank these ten qualities from most important to least important. (4) Go through the list again and mark with a plus sign those qualities which he himself has, with a minus sign those which he does not have or which he needs to develop further, with a zero those that a spouse of his sex cannot be expected to have, but for which he may substitute the correlative quality pertaining to his sex. (For example, a man is not expected to be a good homemaker; he is expected to be a good provider.) This will call to his attention what he has to give in marriage as well as what he hopes to get. Choice is two-sided, and an individual should not expect his choice of partner so to counterbalance his own shortcomings that he interprets preparation for marriage only in terms of search, to the exclusion of self-improvement. The better choice one is, the better choice he can make. The use of personality rating scales may be helpful if administered and interpreted by an expert, but they are not to be used indiscriminately by amateurs.

No matter to what extent romance may seem to have created the illusion, no one has ever yet found a perfect spouse. No man or woman will have all the good qualities included in the reader's list. This is fortunate, because anyone who is aware of his own limitations must realize that to have a perfect spouse would give rise to an inferiority feeling, which would make wedded life unbearable. No one need be pessimistic because he cannot find a perfect spouse. Rather should he be optimistic, because happy marriages can be made by persons like himself who fall somewhat short of the ideal. Successful marriage is not a matter of two faultless human beings finding each other. It is a matter of the mutual adjustment of two persons possessing good qualities, but considerably less than perfect, who are willing to work for success.

Some other objectives in making the list of qualities suggested are:

1. It may serve as a frame of reference in the light of which possible marriage partners may be judged. This is, to be sure, a rough standard and the technique of analysis is not scientifically refined. But we do "size up" people, and it is well to have some sort of matrix within which to form a judgment. If the reader thinks through his list carefully, his future judgments may be affected, even though he does not consciously recall the list while associating with other people. It is not necessary to carry a notebook and pencil—if we may exaggerate to make the point clear—and to check off qualities as they are observed, in order to improve one's choice. Neither does one need to assume the proverbial attitude of the Canadian Mounties, who always succeed when they set out to "get their man."

2. The list should make the reader realize that individuals of the opposite sex have many personal qualities in addition to the few that first attracted attention. Judgment should be based upon all those qualities, not upon a limited number only. Those that are fundamental, as well as those that are superficially apparent, should be taken into consideration so that the individual may be judged as a whole personality.

3. Listing the qualities desirable in a husband or a wife may play some part in assisting the reader to marry with his "head" as well as with his "heart," if we may so express it. To marry with "heart" only is to be swept away by romance. To marry with "head" only is to be cold and calculating. In making marital choices, as in adjusting to life in general, a combination is needed.

In choosing a marriage partner further considerations are also important, such as the following: (1) The type of person one wants. This person may be either a reflection of an ideal or the individual to whom one has already developed an emotional attachment. (2) The type of person one needs, that is, the person one can best get along with, who will complement one's own personality and round out one's life, who will prove stimulating, who will afford emotional and economic security, to whose life one can make a contribution, and with whom one can maintain a desirable standard of living. (3) The type of person one is likely to be able to get. In this connection we are making no necessary implication of superiority or inferiority but only of difference, and we do not mean that one's standards should be low. Individuals who fall in love with married or engaged persons, who in hero-worshipping fashion fill their daydreams with visions of movie stars or other celebrities to the exclusion of more mundane contacts, who seek to attract persons who are obviously not interested in them, who refuse to consider any but a very wealthy person—these and numerous others are thinking only in terms of what they want and overlooking the important question of what they are probably able to get. One person cannot choose another unless that other person is available. Availability is determined not only by existence, proximity, and acquaintance but also by interest in and inclination toward the individual hoping to make the choice. There must be reciprocal attraction, which in its turn increases attractiveness. One cannot make a choice without simultaneously being a choice.

In some cases, however, individuals do have higher aspirations than their personal assets seem to warrant. Less attractive persons have the same sorts of impulses, hopes, and ambitions as more attractive ones, but they seldom have an objective point of view with regard to their own traits. They do not see themselves as others see them. In some cases awareness of their unattractiveness makes them more than ordinarily eager to win an attractive partner in order to compensate for their own feeling of inferiority. But being eager to win such a partner is not the same as winning him. Not infrequently the unattractive person makes himself unhappy and discontented because he persists in shooting at a target that is out of range. A more serious type of case in which the individual wants someone that he cannot get is the one in which an individual takes a "her or nobody" attitude and goes through life disappointed, despondent, and disillusioned because the person of his choice refused to marry him.

A good choice may be "half the battle," but it is only half; it is the beginning, not the end, of marital adjustment. The situation is not dissimilar to that found in choosing an occupation. No matter how wise one may be in making an occupational choice, no matter how well he is adapted or prepared, there still remain many adjustments to be made and much work to be done before success in that occupation is achieved.

One chooses a marriage partner not only for the immediate future but, in most cases, for life. Therefore, the qualities to be sought should be those that will stand the test of time and contribute to the couple's happiness in years to come as well as during the honeymoon and the exciting freshness and adventure of the first few months after the wedding.

Choice involves not only the personality of the other person but also things associated with him, the circumstances under which the couple will live, the demands of the husband's occupation, the place of residence, and the type of in-laws. This is in some ways more true of a woman's choice of husband than of a man's choice of wife, because, as suggested in an earlier connection, the nature of the husband's occupation, the "long arm of the job," reaches so far into their family life and plays such a large part in determining the wife's role and the kind of personal qualities she needs to fulfill that role successfully. The husband's occupation also plays a large part in determining the couple's place of residence and status in the community. There is a tendency for the wife to assume the social position of the husband rather than vice versa. The divorce rate varies according to occupations, tending to be higher for men who are away from home a good part of the time and lower for men whose occupations permit them to spend more time with their wives. In thinking of marriage to a particular man, any woman would find it well worth while to make a careful analysis of the circumstances under which she would live and the demands that would be made upon her and then frankly to ask and sincerely answer the questions, "Can I adapt myself? Have I the personal equipment to succeed under these circumstances? Will I be happy in this type of life twenty years after my wedding?" A man, thinking of the demands that his occupation would put upon a wife, would do well to ask himself whether a particular woman was prepared to meet those demands successfully.

When a person chooses a marriage partner, he chooses "an area of operation." This "area of operation" defines, at least in part, the opportunities that will be presented by and the limitations that will be imposed upon his marriage. In a sense, he puts himself in the position of an artist who, in choosing the material with which he will work, is henceforth limited by the limitations of that material. No matter how great the artist's skill, no matter how far-reaching his vision, no matter how penetrating his insight, no matter how high his hopes, he still cannot make wood do the work of stone nor make paint behave like clay. When, for example, there is a discrepancy between actual role and expected role, this point becomes clear. If a man wants his wife to be very domestic but marries a woman who neglects homemaking because of her career interests, if a woman wants a husband interested in participating in shared family recreation but marries a man who prefers strictly masculine pastimes "with the boys," if a woman expects a husband to participate in housekeeping and marries a man who shuns "woman's work," there is almost sure to be antagonism. Conflict in marriage is normal. In some marriages, of course, there is more than in others. Some conflicts are at least hypothetically resolvable. For example, a couple might resolve conflict over money by earning more, spending less, or making alterations in the handling of funds. On the other hand, conflict growing out of a difference in religious faith, moral standard, age, or cultural background may prove to be unyielding. When an individual chooses a marriage partner, to a considerable degree he chooses the conflicts that his marriage will entail.

OTHER QUALITIES

In two rather extended studies of marital adjustment certain significant factors have come to the fore. Space and the nature of this book prohibit mention of more than a few of the generalizations at which the investigators arrived. Readers who are interested in examining the statistical data on which the conclusions were based are referred to the original publications.

On the basis of his study of 792 couples Terman [1938] concludes:

Happily married women, as a group, are characterized by kindly attitudes toward others and by the expectation of kindly attitudes in return. They do not easily take offense and are not unduly concerned about the impressions they make upon others. They do not look upon social relationships as rivalry situations. They are cooperative, do not object to subordinate roles, and are not annoyed by advice from others. Missionary and ministering attitudes are frequently evidenced in their responses. They enjoy activities that bring educational or pleasurable opportunities to others and like to do things for the dependent or underprivileged. They are methodical and painstaking in their work, attentive to detail, and careful in regard to money. In religion, morals, and politics they tend to be conservative and conventional. Their expressed attitudes imply a quiet self-assurance and a decidedly optimistic outlook upon life.

Unhappily married women, on the other hand, are characterized by emotional tenseness and by ups and downs of moods. They give evidence of deep-seated inferiority feelings to which they react by aggressive attitudes rather than by timidity. They are inclined to be irritable and dictatorial. Compensatory mechanisms resulting in restive striving are common. These are seen in the tendency of the unhappy wives to be active "joiners," aggressive in business, and overanxious in social life. They strive for wide circles of acquaintances but are more concerned with being important than with being liked. They are egocentric and little interested in benevolent or welfare activities, except in so far as these offer opportunities for personal recognition. They also like activities which are fraught with opportunities for romance. They are more inclined to be conciliatory in their attitudes toward men than toward women and show little of the sex antagonism that unhappily married men exhibit. They are impatient and fitful workers, dislike cautious or methodical people, and dislike types of work that require methodical and painstaking effort. In politics, religion, and social ethics they are more often radical than happily married women.

Happily married men show evidence of an even and stable emotional tone. Their most characteristic reaction to others is that of cooperation. This is reflected in their attitudes toward business superiors, with whom they work well; in their attitude toward women, which reflects equalitarian ideals; and in their benevolent attitudes toward inferiors and underprivileged. In a gathering of people they tend to be unself-conscious and somewhat extroverted. As compared with U [unhappy] husbands, they show superior initiative, a greater tendency to take responsibility, and greater willingness to give close attention to detail in their daily work. They like methodical procedures and methodical people. In money matters they are saving and cautious. Conservative attitudes are strongly characteristic of them. They usually have a favorable attitude toward religion and strongly uphold the sex mores and other social conventions.

Unhappy husbands, on the other hand, are inclined to be moody and somewhat neurotic. They are prone to feelings of social inferiority, dislike being conspicuous in public, and are highly reactive to social opinion. This sense of social insecurity is often compensated by domineering attitudes in relationships where they feel superior. They take pleasure in the commanding roles over business dependents and women, but they withdraw from a situation which would require them to play an inferior role or to compete with superiors. They often compensate this withdrawal by daydreams and power fantasies. More often than H [happy] husbands, they are sporadic and irregular in their habits of work, dislike detail and the methodical attitude, dislike saving money, and like to wager. They more often express irreligious attitudes and are more inclined to radicalism in sex morals and politics.

The above descriptions apply to husbands and wives as they were found to be and are based partly on the subjects' self-analysis. The traits mentioned may be the result of marital adjustment or they may be factors contributing to it. It is difficult to be sure that the cart and the horse are in their proper positions. The descriptions apply also to persons who were happy or unhappy in their marriage, rather than to the persons who made someone else happy or unhappy. The study is based on a large group; there is no allowance for individual difference in the summary way in which we lifted the above excerpts from their contexts. Nevertheless, one may safely assume that in many instances the traits mentioned contributed to marital happiness or unhappiness for both parties and that, therefore, these traits are worth considering, at least, in making marital choices, provided that adequate allowance be made for individual situations and desires and the adjustment of two persons, rather than the description of two groups.

Terman [1938] also concludes that background circumstances are frequently the bases upon which marital success may be predicted. Among these background factors those that he considers most important are: (1) The happiness of parents. There seems to be a direct correlation between parents' marital happiness (as estimated by children) and the happiness of the children's own marriages. Individuals whose parents were or are happy in marriage are more likely to have happy marriages. (2) Childhood happiness. Persons who had a happy childhood are more likely to be happy in marriage than persons whose early years were unhappy. (3) Lack of conflict with mother or father. (4) Home discipline in earlier years. The most favorable type was firm but not harsh or too frequent. (5) Amount of attachment to mother or father. (6) Parental frankness about matters concerning sex. (7) Premarital attitude toward sex that is free from disgust or aversion. He concludes that the "subject who 'passes' on all . . . of these items is a distinctly better-than-average marital risk."

In their study of 526 couples, Burgess and Cottrell [1939] stress the importance, among other things, of (1) background factors, such as a child's relation to his parents, the happiness or unhappiness of the parents' marriage, and the relation of the child to his brothers and sisters, and (2) the degree of socialization of the individual, that is, his education, his religious activities, the number and sex of his friends, his participation in social organizations, his conformity to social rules, his respect for convention, and his stability of character.

The reader is cautioned against leaping to unwarranted conclusions on the basis of this brief summary, especially if the above conclusions seem to "prove" what he had previously hoped. Our purpose in mentioning these studies is not to give the reader an infallible method of predicting success in marriage or a ready-made means of making a wise choice, for at the present stage of knowledge that is impossible. Our purpose is to call to his attention items that are worth considering in making a choice; but that choice must ultimately be based not upon a printed scale but upon an intelligent understanding of the total individual situation.

It is risky to assume that broad generalizations based on large numbers of people apply with equal vigor to each individual. If, for example, we studied a thousand persons who came from very happy home backgrounds, and another thousand who came from very unhappy home backgrounds, we should find more unsuccessful marriages among the second group than among the first group. But we should also find some unsuccessful marriages among persons coming from happy backgrounds and some successful ones among persons coming from very unhappy backgrounds. Family background is not the only factor which determines an individual's adjustment to life. Many an individual learns from his parents' experience, and observation of their unhappiness increases his determination to succeed. A similar thing may be true of any of the other factors mentioned above.

PHYSICAL ATTRACTION

Physical attraction is important in choosing a marriage partner. We do not wish to give the impression that it may safely be disregarded. Nevertheless, it is very obtrusive, overshadowing other considerations more often than being overshadowed by them. In choosing a marriage partner, one cannot depend upon sex appeal alone, or too much, or too long. Most men and women are married to beings whose exterior falls somewhat short of the classic beauty of Venus or Apollo, yet they may be happy in their relationships. Increasing age is bound to have some effect upon youthful appearance. There are so many aspects of marriage besides the physical that it is essential to keep the latter in its proper perspective.

In spite of our emphasis upon the fact that the qualities deemed desirable in husband or wife are heavily weighted by individual hope and expectation, there are traits and circumstances so commonly influential upon marital success and failure that we may discuss them and call attention to the importance of taking them into consideration.

Health and choice of marriage partner. Health is an important consideration. Although one may not choose another *because* of a healthy body, he may refrain from choosing someone because of lack of health. At any rate it is important for both persons to know what they will have to face in marriage so far as health is concerned. For this reason each one should have a premarital medical examination more extensive than that required by state law. The function of such an examination is six-fold: (1) to ascertain the state of general health and to point out, if necessary, any symptoms that might affect the couple's choice or their future conjugal relationship; (2) to discover details of anatomy that might affect the couple's sexual adjustment; (3) to discover, if possible, any anatomical characteristics that would make it inadvisable for the woman to become pregnant; (4) to test for the presence or absence of the Rh factor in the couple's blood; (5) to give the couple an opportunity to talk over their marriage and their initiation into it with the physician and to have questions answered; (6) to permit the couple to get advice, if they so desire, on some method of controlling conception that would be acceptable to them.

The purpose of the premarital medical examination is not to ascertain whether the couple can have children. The physician may make observations that suggest possible relative infertility, but many of the conditions contributing to infertility are not taken into account in the premarital medical examination at all. At the present stage of knowledge there is no way that a physician can tell that a given couple can have a child, unless, of course, they have already had one. Nor is the purpose of the medical examination – as is often supposed – entirely negative, that is, to prevent the marriage of the unfit and perhaps to make it advisable for two persons who are in love to relinquish the idea of marrying. Its chief purpose is to assist marriage in getting a better start and to enable couples to make the best possible adjustment.

HEREDITARY TRAITS AND MARRIAGE

In choosing a marriage partner, one chooses not only an individual and his relatives but also, in a sense, his more distant ancestors in so far as he exhibits hereditary traits or carries the determiners of them in his germ plasm with the possibility of passing them on to his children. Consequently, the question of heredity is important. This matter not infrequently comes to the attention of the counselor via the worries of some person in love who is concerned about the advisability of marriage or parenthood, because of either his own hereditary constitution or that of the other person.

Reliable data on human heredity are not so plentiful as one might wish. Those that are most uncontestable apply to such traits as eye color, skin color, supernumerary fingers or toes. The average young person, however, wants to know about the inheritance of such things as insanity, feeble-mindedness, cancer, tuberculosis, syphilis, and criminality. Sometimes the data are conclusive, sometimes inconclusive. There are frequent apparent exceptions. The whole matter of human heredity is more complex and less well understood than the arithmetic ratios of coat type in guinea pigs or color in peas, often employed to illustrate Mendelian laws to the beginning student, might lead one to suppose. So many human "traits" are not simple. They are complex combinations of traits that result from multiple hereditary determiners acting together, and they are eventually manifested in a social environment. The problem is so complicated and ramifies in so many directions that in this book we can do no more than touch upon a few broad generalizations and then make a suggestion.

Although some investigators are reopening the question of the inheritance of acquired traits, for our purpose we may assume that such traits are not inherited. In order to be inheritable a trait must be carried in the genes, that is, in the germ plasm. If an external influence, such as X ray, affects the genes of a given individual, mutations may be produced and the traits of his offspring affected. External influences that affect only the body tissues of an individual do not affect inheritable traits. Yet reports of the inheritance of acquired traits are common. Everyday experience ought to show, however, that such reports are unfounded. Women who have had permanent waves for years have children with straight hair. Men who have all their lives had their hair cut have sons who in their turn must visit the barber. People who have lost parts of their bodies in accidents, through disease, or by means of surgery have offspring with normal anatomy.

Hereditary traits are passed down to us not only from our immediate ancestors but from all our ancestors. Many of us would probably find wormy fruit on our family trees if we examined them carefully and traced back far enough. The purpose in saying this is not to minimize the importance of heredity or to pass lightly over those cases in which it is a serious consideration with regard to a given marriage. Our purpose is rather to remove some of the unnecessary fears with which persons looking forward to marriage are sometimes plagued.

In deciding whether or not to marry an individual in whose family line there are known to be defects which may possibly be inheritable, or in case there are such defects in one's own line, a distinction must be drawn between the advisability of marrying and the advisability of having children. If the individual with whom marriage is contemplated is himself free of the defect, then marriage may be safely planned. If the defect is of such nature that it may be manifested later in life, this possibility may be taken into consideration. If the individual manifests the defect, then the decision must be made with this knowledge in mind. If he does not manifest it but there is reason to believe that he carries it in his germ plasm and may pass it on to his children, then marriage may safely occur, with the possibility of taking adequate steps to prevent conception. These steps should be taken upon the advice of a physician. There are also cases in which inheritable defects may be corrected.

In any case, the solution to the problem lies in knowledge and intelligent planning, not in worry. Worry over the inheritance of defects sometimes causes more damage than the defects themselves. It is conceivable that worry might precipitate mental illness which is not inherited and which the individual would not have acquired if he had not worried lest he had inherited it. Worry that a defect will be exhibited by one's children often leads to expecting that it will be manifested and to such continual "reading into" the child's behavior that the environmental stage is set for his developing the trait one hopes he will avoid.

If there is reason to believe that one party has in his family line a questionable hereditary trait that might make marriage or parenthood inadvisable, there are four things to be done before a final decision is made. (1) Gather all available information about the individual's background. (2) Submit the data to the best authority available, telling the whole truth in so far as this is possible. Students are especially fortunate in this connection because they may submit the data to an instructor in a marriage course, in biology, in genetics, in psychology, or to a college physician who is likely either to know the answer himself or to know where it can be found if it is known at all. In some cases, such as with certain types of mental deficiency, our knowledge is such that the couple may be assured that the likelihood of their children's inheriting the trait is no greater than that of children in general. In other cases a less favorable answer would have to be given, but it could be given with reassurance. In still other cases, the possibilities are not so clear-cut, so it would be advisable to get the judgment of more than one expert. (3) Draw a careful distinction between traits that would make marriage inadvisable and those that would make parenthood inadvisable. (4) When the judgment of the experts has been communicated to the couple and accepted by them, the latter should consider it carefully, to be sure that they understand it and all its possible implications and ramifications, then draw their own conclusion, make a plan for the future, adhere to it, and stop worrying.

COMMON INTERESTS

In one sense the term *common interests* connotes such things as hobbies; interest in sports; and taste in music, art, and drama. It is important that the couple have some such interests in common. It is also important that they have individual interests. In addition, each person needs to have understanding of, tolerance of, and appreciation for, the other person's interests, that is, "an interest in the other's interests." Each one's interests must be compatible with and acceptable to the other. When such interests are not mutually acceptable, they may wedge a couple apart instead of drawing them together. A hobby may be an intruder instead of a binder.

The term *common interests* also connotes common purposes and sense of purpose, common goals, similar ideas concerning the couple's activities, similar expectations concerning the role of each, similar interpretations of life in general and of their life together, similar attitudes toward such things as children, home, religion, values, sex, people, money, and property. It is apparent without explanation how profoundly significant such common interests are in marriage. Yet many young people assume that recreational interests are the only common interests they need.

The more enduring common interests are, the more important they are likely to be in marriage. Pursuit of them must also be sincere and well founded. Sometimes, as has been suggested, in order to advance the courtship process, one individual will superficially take up the interests of the other, only to drop them again after the wedding and thereby dissolve what the other person had assumed would be a bond between them. This temporary pursuit of an interest is not always insincere, as the individual may confuse interest in the other person with interest in what that person does. One of the best tests of supposedly common interests is to compare them in retrospect, that is, before the two individuals met, as well as after.

Common dislikes as well as common likes may draw a couple together at first, but dislikes are too negative and too much something to avoid rather than to pursue to take the place of common interests in marriage.

STANDARDS OF BEHAVIOR

It is important to consider a disparity in standards of behavior because it indicates a difference in attitude toward something that at least one of the couple considers a value. Difference in attitude is often accompanied by difference in behavior, and this may be fertile soil in which to grow the seeds of friction. There are things of such nature that difference in attitude and behavior with regard to them may cause serious and even irremediable conflict. These should be carefully considered in making marital choices. One of these is extramarital sexual freedom. Another is honesty, interpreted broadly. A third is the use of alcoholic beverages. The reader may add others.

In spite of the fact that at some time many Americans have extramarital sexual intercourse, such intercourse is generally disapproved. Not even all the persons who have such intercourse approve it. In many cases there is only a single experience or a brief episode, and often special circumstances are involved. Guilt frequently follows past experiences or accompanies current ones, even if they continue in spite of it. Hence having extramarital intercourse and believing that one should have the freedom to have such intercourse, though they overlap, are not identical.

Most people enter marriage with the expectation of sexual exclusiveness, as discussed earlier; extramarital intercourse is a direct antithesis. Such exclusiveness bolsters the confidence, trust, and security on the basis of which they can make their fullest contribution to family living. When children are born, fundamental values are reiterated and the couple assume not only responsibilities for the children but also new responsibilities for each other. In our culture there is no place in this constellation of values for extramarital intercourse.

So we may wonder whether an individual who believes in extramarital sexual freedom is ready for marriage. His attitude indicates that he thinks in terms of partial rather than complete commitment and that he expects to be partly single and partly married simultaneously. There are, of course, many cases in which one of the spouses overlooks and forgives the other's infidelity. There are cases in which a wife, for example, because of her incapacity or lack of interest, urges her husband to have extramarital sexual intercourse. But such cases are beside the point. We are considering the expectation of extramarital sexual freedom as an attitude to be taken into account in choosing a marriage partner.

Honesty, broadly interpreted, connotes not only truth telling and refraining from stealing and cheating but also integrity, the degree to which an individual "holds together." In turn this connotes a predictability that is important in the establishment of enduring interpersonal relationships. Given a set of circumstances, one can be confident of what an honest person will do. On the other hand, the behavior of a dishonest person is shifty because it rests not on oneness of personality but on multiplicity, depending upon whim, selfish interest, the misleading of others, shady deals, partial truths, broken promises, and lack of correlation between what is affirmed and what is done. If there is any relationship the success of which requires that it be built upon a rock rather than upon sand, it is marriage.

No matter what one's personal views upon the use of alcohol may be, and no matter what the degree of his indulgence, from total abstinence to dipsomania, the fact remains that there is the assumption of possible risk in marrying an individual who is addicted to the habitual and excessive use of intoxicating liquor because so frequently such addiction is a symptom of poor personality adjustment. The behavior of such a person is not readily predictable. His assumption of responsibility may be perfunctory or intermittent. His behavior may upon occasion prove embarrassing or humiliating. Friendships may be limited. Social activities may be restricted because such an individual often leans toward those that have an alcoholic accompaniment or injects a sometimes unacceptable alcoholic element into the activities of more temperate groups. If the person uses alcohol in order to escape problems, to bolster his courage, or to remove inhibitions and make himself more sociable, then in many cases the risk is increased because the indulgence is a symptom of immaturity, fear, feeling of insecurity, or some equally significant underlying difficulty, which may militate against the success of the marriage both directly as an undesirable personality trait and indirectly through its alcoholic disguise.

In contemplating a marriage in which there is a difference in standards of conduct, an individual should answer one important question to his own satisfaction: What does this difference mean to me? If he lets judgment become clouded by romance, he may make an unwise choice that will not stand the test of time. If he rests his decision on a verbal promise to reform made in response to a request to change or an expression of disapproval, when the other person's intent is merely to remove a barrier to getting married, his decision may be precarious indeed. If he depends upon reforming the other person after marriage, he is falling into the trap of wishful thinking. It often happens that the person with the lower standard drags the other down rather than that the person with the higher standard raises the other.

ECONOMIC ELEMENTS IN PARTNER SELECTION

In an earlier connection we pointed out that at no known period in history, among no known people, has marriage succeeded without some degree of cooperation, through division of labor by sex, in the maintenance of a way of life. In the present-day United States this involves the husband's occupation and earning, the wife's homemaking, and sometimes her earning as well. But between earning and the maintenance of a way of life there is the intermediate step of spending. This involves a complex of attitudes, objectives, knowledge, choices, and activities that do not come naturally to a young couple when they fall in love and contemplate marriage. The effective handling of this intermediate step requires the development and focusing of skills and processes on objectives that have been mutually agreed upon. Hence it would seem appropriate for two individuals considering each other as possible marriage partners to begin to explore this intermediate zone together.

Such exploration might include a consideration of such questions as the following: At the time of marriage will the man's income be sufficient to maintain a home and provide for the arrival of a possible child? If not, how will his income be supplemented? Will the girl continue employment? Would she be able to do so if she became pregnant? Will they receive a subsidy from their parents? Is the man really interested in, and does he have aptitude for, the occupation which he has chosen? Is he industrious and ambitious? Does the girl have the interest and skills necessary for effective homemaking? Has she taken advantage of opportunities available in her school to increase her homemaking skills? How do the two persons use their present incomes? For what does each spend beyond necessities? Do they manage to save anything? Is either wasteful? Do they budget their money and stay within the budget? Do they spend without plan until their money is exhausted and then borrow or appeal to their parents? Do they exhibit similar degrees of generosity? What is their attitude toward home ownership? Toward cars? Toward insurance? Toward going into debt? Toward installment buying? Do they agree on how and by whom the family income will be handled? Do they know how to shop wisely? If they have had ample allowance from parents, would they be prepared to take a possible step down in their standard of living when they marry? Have they worked out trial budgets based on realistically projected family income and a realistic understanding of the cost of living? If in attempting to do so they ran into snags, did this motivate them to get further information or to sidestep the problem and say, "We'll find a way. We'll cross that bridge when we come to it"?

"LIKES" AND "OPPOSITES"

Proverbially, "Likes repel, opposites attract," as if human beings were the poles of a magnet and their behavior were governed by relatively simple forces. Such a broad generalization might easily be carried to ridiculous extremes. If opposites attract, then the intelligent should marry morons, large persons should marry small ones, and college students should marry illiterates. If likes repel, similar interests, values, temperaments, or backgrounds would produce discord rather than harmony. Husband and wife should have complementary rather than clashing characteristics, enough similarity to be mutually agreeable and enough dissimilarity to be mutually stimulating. Even this is a broad generalization. In the last analysis all depends upon the two personalities involved and their mutual adjustment. In some cases likes, in others unlikes, have very happy marriages.

There are combinations of traits, however, that merit caution. We may mention a few by way of illustration. A meticulously neat individual and one who carelessly leaves his clothes and other things lying about, a person who is punctual and one who disregards time, two individuals whose tempo of life is different, a person who pays particular attention to manners and one whose manners are crude, a person who is affectionate and one who does not like to touch or be touched, a person who is interested in acquiring things and one who would like to sacrifice things to travel and states of mind, an individual whose rhythm of life makes him nocturnal and one whose rhythm makes him diurnal, one who is gregarious and one who does not like to be with groups of people, a very modest individual and one who is uninhibited, a person with a sense of humor and one lacking it, a conventional individual and one inclined to be conspicuously unconventional—such combinations can, of course, be successful when the differences are accepted or are offset by other traits and circumstances; but such combinations can also contribute to perennial conflict, especially when the differences crystallize as focal points of irritation.

With human nature so variable and so complex and with the final judgment to be made by the reader anyway, we might never strike exactly the combination of traits that is in his mind as he thinks of his possible union with some particular person. We cannot even go so far as to say that it is always essential that the husband be masculine and the wife feminine, although this is the most commonly accepted and expected type of "opposites" that attract. It is better to suggest to the reader that he make his own careful analysis than to give him the impression that a short list of generalizations will pigeonhole his particular problem and yield a ready-made judgment. Furthermore, it is not only the difference or similarity in one or a few particular traits that counts but all the traits of each person. A sense of humor may offset a quick temper, a lovable disposition may counteract the impracticality of the dreamer.

CHOOSING A PARTNER LIKE ONE'S PARENT

Not uncommon is a tendency to seek a marriage partner like one's father or mother, as the case may be, the parent of opposite sex having been an adolescent ideal. It may be well to desire that a husband or a wife possess some of the admirable qualities of one's parent, and the latter's qualities may form a good basis upon which to found an ideal that will grow as time goes on. But to set up one's parent as an ideal and to insist that one's spouse conform is to establish an impossible standard and to set an unattainable goal, for several reasons. There are no two persons exactly alike. Parents and future spouse were born in different cultural eras. Typically, the former are also some twenty to thirty years ahead in their development. Twenty-five years from now one's husband or wife may be more like one's father or mother, but at the moment it is impossible to eradicate the age difference. Furthermore, an individual does not know firsthand what his parent was like when the parent was the age of the future spouse. Because parents love one another and have a happy marriage does not prove that the child could duplicate their experience with one of them. In order to live with one of the parents as the other has, the child would have to be that parent rather than himself. In many cases, it is not the actual qualities of the real person that are set up as the standard but rather the idealized image of the parent. Actually, not even the individual himself completely attains this unreal standard. Naturally, then, no other person could be expected to attain it.

If a child's relationship with the parent of opposite sex has been unpleasant, he may seek a marriage partner having quite different qualities. This is understandable and not unreasonable, as long as he allows for difference of degree in various personality traits and realizes that traits may be exhibited differently under varying circumstances, judges by the whole individual, and knows at least in part which of his parent's traits were present at the time of marriage and which developed because of the marital situation.

QUALITIES OF A DATE

The qualities desirable in husband or wife and those desirable in a date are not necessarily identical. In dating, some of the more superficial and inconsequential qualities play a prominent role. For example, the ability to dance is put more into the foreground in judging a date than in judging a husband. A date is expected to be a free spender, but he need not be occupationally ambitious. In dating it is more important for a girl to be attractive in appearance than to know how to keep house. When students are asked to list the qualities that they like in a date, and those that they desire in a husband or a wife, heading the first list are likely to be such things as ability to dance, ability to carry on a conversation, good manners, consideration, pleasing personality. In the other list the qualities most frequently mentioned are likely to be such things as companionship, ability to provide, understanding, love, ambition, intelligence.

Somewhere in the welter of each individual's personal attributes are those traits that will contribute most abundantly to his success or failure in marriage. They may not be fully developed in the earlier part of the dating period. A youthful individual must be judged by his possibilities as well as by his achievements, provided that one does not confuse observation of possibilities with wishful thinking and the other person does not expect possibilities permanently to substitute for actualities. Like saplings, these traits and potentialities of husband or wife may be partially shaded and hidden by the already grown trees and underbrush of more readily apparent traits of dates. To seek them out and clear the land around them so that one may see the nature of the growth that will form the new forest, as well as the components of the present one, is the process of intelligent choice of a marriage partner.

Typically, people do not marry until they have dated each other for a more or less extended period. This would suggest that, as dating progresses and it becomes increasingly marriage-oriented, the standard of what constitutes desirable traits in a date may well be reappraised. An individual may consciously begin to ignore those aspects of our dating system that are temporary and unrelated to successful marriage and begin to give more attention to those qualities of a date and those aspects of our dating system that are related to successful marriage. In this way a person may have a more functional dating experience. When the need for such a transition is not recognized, an individual may base his choice of marriage partner on an inappropriate set of qualities.

Reasons for poor choice of marriage partner

Many of the factors making for poor choice of marriage partner have already been implied. Confusing infatuation with love; hoping to reform the other party; judging by too few qualities; marrying before tastes and attitudes are well developed; overemphasizing money; acting under the stimulus of rebound, spite, habit, pity, and similar attitudes are obviously contributory to errors in judgment. Among other factors are those that follow.

Some persons make a poor choice of partner because they marry in haste — to repent at leisure and perhaps in misery. Less care and intelligence may be exhibited in choosing a husband or a wife than in choosing an occupation, registering for courses, or even selecting new garments. Marrying the first person who is willing, without waiting for experience broad enough to give ground for comparison and contrast, sometimes makes for poor choice. This does not mean that the first person is invariably a poor choice. It suggests only the exercise of caution and judgment and a clear understanding of the fact that it is false to assume that, if the first person is not accepted, there will be no other.

There are individuals who are not sufficiently conversant with the requirements of marriage. They do not understand what marriage involves, not realizing that it is a most intimate relationship and that there are responsibilities as well as pleasures. Some go so far as to think only up to, rather than beyond, the wedding or even to think of marriage as if it were a lifelong date. Some persons gloss over problems or irritating personality traits because they do not recognize the difference in the time element in dating as compared to marriage. Suppose, for example, a couple have personality traits that cause them to annoy one another. In dating, they are aware of this annoyance; but dates are limited in time, and after each date there comes a time of temporary separation, after which another date is voluntary. In marriage there is no similar separation with similarly voluntary reunion; therefore there is no respite from the annoyance. Also, because of the nature of marriage and attitudes toward it as compared to dating, there is a greater feeling of "ought" read into the behavior of the marriage partner — "She ought not do this to me, because I'm her husband" — and this makes the annoyance two-pronged: there is the annoyance produced by the trait itself plus the annoyance produced by her continuing to do it when she "ought" not do so. The result is that the annoyance tends to be cumulative unless, in time, the couple immunize themselves against it. A personality trait that is annoying may be like a pebble in one's shoe. If you walk across the room with a pebble in your shoe, you will notice it, but it will not be either excessively painful or injurious. If, however, you walk 20 miles with the same pebble in the same shoe, at the end of your trip you will have either an open wound or a callus. Dating is like walking across the room. Marriage is like taking a 20-mile hike.

Marrying to please one's family rather than oneself is risky, since the individual rather than the family has to live with the person chosen. In some cultures where more emphasis is put upon institutional factors in marriage, such as support, protection, and reproduction, and less upon personal factors, such as companionship and love, families may make better choices than individuals, since what is sought is stability rather than personal satisfaction. In our culture, where the personal factors are held in such incomparable esteem, only the individual himself can make the final choice, although he may, of course, give weight to his family's opinions.

The marriage of childhood sweethearts does not always turn out so satisfactorily as storybooks lead one to suppose. The common assumption is that, if persons have liked each other since childhood, they must know each other well enough to marry successfully. In some cases this is true. The couple have developed along parallel paths and, in spite of contacts with other persons, they find each other most attractive.

In other cases, however, childhood sweethearts marry because they have been afraid of people and have lacked social experience. They cling to their earlier choice because their fear or lack of contacts prevents their making another. Such persons are emotionally immature and, in a sense, theirs is a child marriage. Since marriage is for adults rather than children and should be the outgrowth of adult experience, and since it succeeds or fails to the degree to which it can survive in an adult world, the marriage of such childhood sweethearts is sometimes a precarious one. It may not fail in the sense of ending in divorce; but it may fail in the sense of falling far short of the possibilities of which marriage is capable. For a similar reason, cousin marriage is sometimes ill-advised. Disregarding for the moment the biological considerations in connection with consanguineous marriage, if relatives are attracted to each other because they have been thrown together, have known each other from childhood, and are too shy or too fearful to make wider social contacts, their marriage falls into a class similar to that discussed above.

In one sense, everyone who marries does so to escape something as well as to achieve something. He wants to escape the various unpalatable elements in his unmarried state. But to marry to escape circumstances that are unusually unpleasant, such as an unhappy home situation, the irksomeness of earning one's own living, or the demands of a school program that is not to one's liking, when the factor of escape carries more weight than the relationship with the other person, is a precarious basis upon which to make a choice of marriage partner. One case will serve to clarify the point. The parents of the girl in this case were divorced when she was an infant. When she was ten years old, her mother married an alcoholic. The daughter never got along with him. There were frequent quarrels, especially when he had been drinking, and there was perpetual ill feeling. The girl had for some time felt a desire to leave home. At the age of seventeen she became engaged to two boys and accepted a ring from each. Because she could not make up her mind as to which she loved more, she wavered between them. Usually she was partial to the one who was present. Her decision was made for her when one of the boys left town. Soon afterward, she married the other. An impersonal observer could recognize almost immediately that the girl was deeply infatuated with both boys and not ready to marry either. Her desire to escape from home was so great that she could not resist and blindly made her choice. Two years later she obtained a divorce.

Marrying merely to satisfy an urge to marry rather than a desire to marry a particular individual may lead to poor choice because requirements are relaxed.

PARENTAL OBJECTIONS

Burgess and Cottrell [1939] and Locke [1951] found that parents' approval and successful marriage adjustment tended to go hand in hand, while in cases in which there was parental disapproval there was a higher percentage of poor adjustment. When there is parental disapproval, it is essential to ascertain first the nature of the objection. Do the parents insist upon lifelong celibacy, or do they object to the child's marrying immediately or in the near future? They may later approve of a marriage to which they now object because of the age element involved. Or is opposition due to the fact that they do not approve of the individual chosen? They do not like him or they feel that he will not be the sort of spouse that they wish their child to have.

When parents object to a child's ever marrying, there are only two alternatives. One is for the child to acquiesce in his parents' wishes and remain celibate for life. This is too much for parents to expect. Sometimes they sincerely believe that the child will avoid unhappiness by remaining single. They assume that the child will have the same marital disappointments that they had. At other times their wish to have the child remain celibate is entirely selfish, although they may not be aware of that fact. They want the child to remain with them, to keep the family intact, or to take care of them in their old age or infirmity. The other alternative is for the child to marry against his parents' wishes. Before he does so, however, he should be sure of his decision and know that he is mature enough to take a step so drastically affecting his relationship with his family.

If the parents object to their child's marrying immediately or soon, it may be worth while to wait a bit longer, especially if the child is of about student age. It means so much to a young couple to have their parents on their side that a brief wait may prove a good investment in future happiness. At times a student's parents object so strongly to his marrying immediately that their objection overflows and spreads to his dating, especially if he wants to go steady or become engaged. Such a student often fails to understand his parents' attitude. The parents, on the other hand, fail to understand that the student's talk about marriage does not make the wedding so imminent as it appears, and the probability is that their fear that he will elope or do something equally rash is not well founded. The parents' motives are good. Because of their own experience, cases that they have observed, or their distrust of the judgment of youth, they fear that their child will do something to jeopardize his happiness.

In such cases the student could make his relationship with his parents smoother and prevent argument if he would reassure them that he is not going to marry too soon, sincerely mean it, and by his behavior prove to them that he means it. The more he argues about the theory of the thing, the more he tries to convince them that it would be all right for him to marry now if he wanted to, even though he has no intention of doing so, the more he attempts to show them that "things are different from what they were when you were young," the more fearful and suspicious they will become. They will wonder whether he is hiding his true feelings and intentions in order to trap them into agreement.

If the objections are not directed against marriage as such or the time of marriage but apply only to a particular individual chosen, they should not be disregarded until one is certain that he understands the reasons behind them. If the objections are the outgrowth of prejudice or incomplete knowledge, they may be given little weight if the parents remain immovable, or they may be altered by arranging contacts between the parents and the individual in question so that the former will see the latter in a different light. Sometimes parents see things that their children, in the throes of romance, overlook. Older persons are often better able to judge those qualities that will further and those that will impede marital adjustment than is the younger person, who has no firsthand experience of marriage. In such cases objections should be given weight and the opposition should not be lightly dismissed on the basis of wishful thinking or attributed to prejudice when the disapproval is actually the outgrowth of careful, balanced observation. It is easy to describe a person as biased when his only fault is disagreement with us. Children who term their parents prejudiced often do so because they themselves are strongly prejudiced in the opposite direction. Two persons in love are never completely unbiased.

When parental disapprobation is directed toward a specific individual, the child in love sometimes exhibits negativistic behavior. The objections have an effect opposite to that intended; instead of making the love object seem less attractive, they make him seem more so. The young person may confuse his attitude toward the other individual with his reaction against his parents. Since many an ill-advised choice is made for this reason, it might have been included among the reasons for poor choice listed above. Let us examine a specific case.

The girl was a college student with a pleasant personality who did superior academic work. At a high school party she had met a boy who was a star athlete and, therefore, very popular; but he was a poor student and unrefined. The girl decided then, at that high school party, that he was the boy she was eventually going to marry. After graduation from high school he got a job and she went off to college. They corresponded and saw each other occasionally.

As soon as the girl's parents realized that this affair was not going to burn itself out as others had done, they raised objections. Through a period of two or three years their objections grew into arguments and their arguments generated quarrels, until the family could scarcely be together without suffering violent emotional upsets and venomous recriminations. All three protagonists were obstinate, and their conflicts, instead of making one side yield, served only to entrench them more deeply in their antagonistic points of view. The daughter was forbidden ever to see the boy. This led to clandestine meetings.

As the girl's college experience progressed, while the boy marked time, it became readily apparent to an impersonal observer that the two young people were growing farther and farther apart. Intellectually the girl could see that. She could see that their interests were different. She was aware of the unrefined elements in his personality. She knew that he would never go very far occupationally and that his income would always be too small to maintain the standard of living she wanted for herself and her children. He was a Catholic, and her parents were much opposed to his religion, but the girl talked glibly of joining his church. The parents threatened to disown her if she married the boy, and she knew they would not attend her wedding. Yet in spite of all this, she felt that she loved him and was determined to marry him in the not-too-distant future. The parents by their very opposition were forcing her into a marriage about which even she herself was doubtful in her more lucid moments. In her revolt against her parents she had to have some focal point for her reaction; one cannot revolt in a vacuum. Since marriage to this boy had become the focus for her revolt, she could not retreat.

If the parents had ceased their opposition and let the daughter see the boy as frequently as she wished and let her talk about marriage if she cared to, she would have lost her reason for revolt and would probably soon have seen the boy in his true light and changed her mind. As matters stood, however, it appeared that she would marry him in spite of all the unfavorable factors. If, as the old adage says, "Forbidden fruit is sweeter," it is not because the fact of its being forbidden raises its sugar content but rather because the person who eats it allows his perception of taste to become affected by his wishful thinking and enjoys the satisfaction of having trespassed without being detected and thus having proved himself superior to the individual who bade him let the fruit alone.

Although there are exceptions, by and large parents do have some understanding of a child and some appreciation of the sort of person who would make a satisfactory marriage partner for that child. Also, some children are more like their parents in their attitudes toward basic values and acceptable ways of life than they consciously realize. Although again there are exceptions, typically parents are less likely to idealize a child's prospective spouse than the child himself is because the parents are not subject to the loss of perspective due to romance. Parents are often also more attentive to considerations other than the personality of the prospective spouse, whereas the child in love may depend largely upon subjective judgment of personality separated from the things connected with it. Parents, too, though they may be biased by their own marital experience, have at least had marital experience, while for the child such experience is ordinarily only a matter of observation and imagination rather than participation. For reasons such as these it is worth while to seek parents' judgments. The child is not bound to abide by these judgments. But at least he should not hesitate to subject his choice to such a test.

WHAT DO YOU THINK?

1. Should everyone be permitted to marry? If not, on whom should restrictions be placed, and by what means?

2. What are your observations as to why some people make a poor choice of marriage partner?

3. To what degree should heredity be considered in choosing a marriage partner?

4. A couple marry after knowing each other for only a brief time. Soon after the wedding they discover that they have made what appears to be a poor choice. What suggestions would you give them?

5. Studies show that, as a group, the children of happily married parents are more likely to have happy marriages than are the children of unhappily married parents. Does this mean that, if an individual's parents are unhappily married, his own marriage is necessarily doomed? If not, what can he do to prevent his falling into the pattern set by his parents?

6. Compare the qualities considered desirable and undesirable in a husband or wife with those desirable and undesirable in a date.

7. To what degree can written tests, personality rating scales, elec-

tronic devices, and similar means assist an individual in making a wise choice of marriage partner?

8. An individual's parents object to his choice of marriage partner. What suggestions would you give him?

9. What are the advantages and disadvantages of making a choice of marriage partner only on the basis of campus contacts?

SELECTED READINGS

Adams, Clifford R., and Vance O. Packard: *How to Pick a Mate*, E. P. Dutton & Co., Inc., New York, 1946. "In this book we have tried to include those findings which should be helpful and interesting to all people involved in love and marriage. . . . It is not our intention to lay down a set of rules. . . . We hope that . . . you will be more enlightened in your hunches. . . ."

Blood, Robert O., Jr.: *Marriage*, The Free Press of Glencoe, New York, 1962, chap. 2. Standards of compatibility; testing for compatibility.

Bowerman, Charles E., and Barbara R. Day: "A Test of the Theory of Complementary Needs as Applied to Couples during Courtship," *American Sociological Review*, vol. 21, no. 5, pp. 602–605, October, 1956. The report of a study that does not support the theory of complementary needs.

Burgess, Ernest W., Harvey J. Locke, and Mary Margaret Thomes: *The Family*, 3d ed., American Book Company, New York, 1963, chap. 12. Choosing a marriage partner.

Cavan, Ruth Shonle (ed.): *Marriage and the Family in the Modern World*, Thomas Y. Crowell Company, New York, 1960, chap. 6. Do "opposites" or "likes" attract? Should men marry older women?

Farber, Bernard: *Family: Organization and Interaction*, Chandler Publishing Company, San Francisco, 1964, chap. 5. Courtship and the selection of a marriage partner in present-day society; mixed marriages; early and late marriage.

Fishbein, Morris, and Ruby Jo Reeves Kennedy (eds.): *Modern Marriage and Family Living*, Oxford University Press, Fair Lawn, N.J., 1957, chap. 8. Factors affecting the choice of marriage partner and factors affecting success in marriage.

Kephart, William M.: *The Family, Society, and the Individual*, Houghton Mifflin Company, Boston, 1961, chap. 9. Choosing a marriage partner; the college situation; the theory of complementary needs.

Landis, Paul H.: *Making the Most of Marriage*, 2d ed., Appleton-Century-Crofts, Inc., New York, 1960, chap. 11. Selection of a marriage partner by impulse or insight? Personality types that have difficulty in marriage.

Magoun, F. Alexander: *Love and Marriage*, rev. ed., Harper & Row, Publishers, Incorporated, New York, 1956, chap. 6. Considerations in choosing a marriage partner; the "need for more analysis and less romance."

Merrill, Francis E.: *Courtship and Marriage*, rev. ed., Holt, Rinehart and Winston, Inc., New York, 1959, chaps. 9, 10. Complementary needs; personality needs; the "ideal mate."

Peterson, James A.: *Education for Marriage*, 2d ed., Charles Scribner's Sons, New York, 1964, chaps. 8–10. The social process of selection of a marriage partner: psychological, social, and economic factors involved.

Waller, Willard: *The Family: A Dynamic Interpretation*, rev. by Reuben Hill, Holt, Rinehart and Winston, Inc., New York, 1951, chap. 11. Subconscious and rational elements in choosing a marriage partner; marriages of the maladjusted.

Winch, Robert F.: *Mate Selection*, Harper & Row, Publishers, Incorporated, New York, 1958. Analysis and exposition of the "theory of complementary needs in mate-selection."

chapter 6

ELEMENTS OF DIFFERENCE IN CHOOSING A MARRIAGE PARTNER

Mixed marriage

Let us define as mixed a marriage in which there is a considerable, obvious, significant, and unusual difference between the spouses. This excludes sex difference because it is universal in marriage. In all marriages there are some differences. Many of these if accentuated would be sufficient to classify the marriage as mixed. Sometimes in a mixed marriage there is more than one element of mixture. Take, for example, a case such as the following. At the time of the wedding the man was twenty-five years old, the woman was thirty-two. He had never been married before. She had been married twice before, the first time at age fourteen, and had a son aged seventeen. The man was Protestant, the woman Catholic. He had had two years of college. His father had a college degree; his mother had attended high school. The woman had completed only elementary school, and her parents were uneducated. The couple dated for three weeks before they married. Within two weeks after the wedding the wife started dating other men. Before the two weeks had elapsed the couple began to talk of divorce; but somehow the marriage lasted for two years before the husband finally obtained a decree.

Usually there is little hope of changing the elements of difference in a mixed marriage. The couple, to make their marriage successful, must adjust to them. Too often the young person swept away by romance forgets the first point and assumes that the second is easier than is actually the case.

Theoretically there is no *type* of marriage that contains within itself the germs of its own inevitable failure. Any *type* can be made successful if the couple face and solve the special problems involved. This is not the same as saying that any marriage can be made successful. At times the *if* is practically insurmountable. There are individual marriages that seem hopelessly doomed from the beginning.

In a sense, what was just said about mixed marriage is true of marriage in general. There is no single element that is always present in successful relationships and always absent in unsuccessful ones, or vice versa. Success or failure depends upon one whole personality reacting with another whole personality and both reacting to the whole marital situation.

In mixed marriage, too, success or failure depends upon total adjustment rather than upon merely the elements of difference. For example, in a Catholic-Protestant marriage, success or failure depends not only upon the religious difference as such but also upon the husband's attitude toward the wife's religion and her attitude toward his; upon their personal qualities; and upon numerous other elements, such as sex, money, in-laws, children, recreation, which compose the total situation. A mixed marriage presents the problems of regular marriage plus those due to the fact of mixture. In a mixed marriage, as in any other, differences and similarities must be weighed one against the other. In every marriage there are both; success depends upon the relative proportion between them, the weighting given to them, and the degree of sharing that they permit.

Mixed marriage presents a problem to both spouses. If a Protestant is contemplating marriage to a Catholic, the former tends to think of Catholic-Protestant marriage as only a Protestant problem. It is just as much a Catholic problem.

Although the success of mixed marriage depends upon the total situation and the two personalities involved, rather than upon only the elements of mixture, those elements sometimes become the focal point for conflict or are blamed for conflict which is due to other causes. Suppose, for instance, that there is conflict between a husband and wife because their personalities are incompatible. Their ideas, tastes, and habits are at variance. Suppose that to this situation there is added a disparity in religion—one is Catholic, the other Protestant. Unconsciously the couple seek an explanation of their poor adjustment. From their point of view the simplest, most obvious explanation is the religious difference. Consequently, they fasten upon that. They feel that if they could resolve the conflict over religion their problems would be solved. As a matter of fact, the religious difference is only one among many contributing factors playing a part in their marital disharmony. In almost every case, disharmony, discord, and failure in marriage are the result of multiple causation. There is almost never only one single, simple cause. We must beware of oversimplified explanation.

Let us examine several types of mixed marriage and attempt to ascertain the special problems that each type may add to marital adjustment.

Age difference

We shall consider as mixed a marriage in which there is a considerable and unusual age difference between the persons but where both parties are old enough to be ready for marriage. This will serve to differentiate marriage mixed as to age, from child marriage. In the latter there may be great discrepancy in the ages of the two individuals, but at least one of the persons is too young to be ready to marry at all.

Recent news articles mention a bridegroom of 78 and a bride of 26, a man of 82 with a 21-year-old wife, a woman of 62 who seeks a divorce from her 30-year-old husband, and a man of 24 who married a woman of 75. In this country in 1959, in 29 reporting states, there occurred 15 marriages in which the groom was 70 or over and the bride was 20 or under, 6 in which the groom was 15 or under and the bride was 20 to 30, 139 in which the groom was 20 or under and the bride was 30 to 39, 16 in which the groom was 20 or under and the bride was 40 or over, and 1 in which the groom was 19 and the bride over 65 [U.S. Department of Health, Education, and Welfare, 1959]. There are many other instances in which the age difference is not so great but in which the motives and problems are similar. It is difficult to draw an arbitrary line separating marriage with normal age difference from that classifiable as mixed. Some difference, especially toward the seniority of the husband, is not only accepted but usually expected. Let us say only that (1) the greater the difference, the more likely it is that there will be problems; and (2) the greater the difference is in proportion to the ages of the two persons, the more likely it is that these problems will be accentuated. A wife of 20 and a husband of 35 would probably find adjustment more trying than a wife of 40 and a husband of 55. In either case, the absolute difference is 15 years; but fifteen is larger in proportion to 20 and 35 than it is in proportion to 40 and 55. In some instances in which there is considerable, or even extreme age difference, the marriage appears to be very happy. This is because the couple have particular needs which such a marriage can meet. Their experience and judgment cannot be taken as a basis for generalization.

In connection with marriage mixed as to age, there are four questions to be answered: (1) Why does the younger person want to marry the older one? (2) Why does the older one want to marry the younger one?

(3) What special problems are they likely to face? (4) Will this kind of marriage meet their individual needs better than one with less age difference?

Many of the reasons for which people in general marry will, when given special emphasis, serve as answers to the first two questions. The desire for emotional or economic security, money, inheritance, social position and prestige, the satisfaction of making a conquest, pity, grati-tude—these may motivate the younger individual. Parent attachment and emotional immaturity of such nature that a parent substitute, rather than a husband or a wife, is sought may play a part. If a girl fears sex or childbirth, she may feel that there is less chance of having her fear realized if she marries an older man. Hero worship may be confused with love. A girl may rationalize infatuation by stating reasons why she believes a husband should be a good deal older than the wife.

Either person may have failed to meet an eligible mate of an age more nearly comparable with his own. Either may be subject to flattery. A young woman may be flattered by the attentions of an older man be-cause she assumes that he has chosen her from among many alluring women whose hearts he might easily have captured. Either may be moti-vated by a desire to dominate. The younger may accomplish this because of the elder spouse's gratitude for having a young person marry him. The older individual may accomplish it because of his age and experience. Such a person may have a parental attitude toward the youthful spouse.

There is sometimes a desire to regain lost youth. This desire may be the rationalization of emotional regression. There may also be fixation. The older person may have stopped his emotional development at the stage at which he was interested in very young persons of the opposite sex. In extreme form, this type of fixation is classified as perversion and is subject to legal penalty. It is legalized to the degree to which we per-mit child marriage. In its milder forms it may appear as the basic reason for some cases of mixed marriage.

In the case of an older man and a younger woman, there may be a special sexual element. Some older men find younger women physically more attractive than they do women of their own age. Men do not ex-perience a menopause; only a person who has *men*struated can have a *men*opause. Among investigators, there is no unanimous opinion re-garding a male climacteric, or change of life [Oliven, 1955; Walker and Strauss, 1941]. Men do, of course, pass through a process of aging. But if there is a male climacteric, the symptoms are not so clear-cut as those in women and are far from universal. Nevertheless, in later life some men do exhibit a flare-up of interest in sex, as if they were making one last grasp at youth before settling down to older age.

If a man happens to be unmarried, widowed, divorced, or willing to destroy his existing marriage, he may marry a woman much younger than himself. A man may apparently be happily married and yet for a year or two show a silly and incongruous interest in young women. In such cases, however, there is reason to suspect that his marriage is not so satisfactory to him as it appears on the surface and that the presence of deep-set problems, especially sexual ones, is highly probable. This does not excuse his action; it does help to explain it. Usually his interest fades shortly, and many a wife realizes that it is too evanescent a matter to serve as a reason for divorce. Her attitude may be such that she can never again feel toward him or their marriage as she had previously; nevertheless, there is a possibility of their working out a good marriage even though it may not be the best or one that can fulfill all her expectations.

The wife should also examine herself to see to what degree she has contributed to the man's loss of interest in her and the shifting of his interest to some younger person. In many instances a share of the fault rests with her. He is as much a victim of neglect of appearance, absorption in housework and child rearing, stoppage of personal growth, loss of enthusiasm and spontaneity, sexual indifference or rejection, or lack of affection on her part as she is a victim of his indiscretion. Again, this does not excuse his action; it merely helps to explain it. In fact, the failures and shortcomings of the wife may be partly due to earlier failures on the part of the husband. The situation is two-sided and complicated. Causation is complex. It is not a simple matter of either-or. In looking forward to marriage, the individual should not let himself become prey to broad assumptions that husband or wife will inevitably be or do thus and so twenty years after the wedding. Each individual should consider his own responsibility and role in prevention. He should not enter marriage fearfully, certain that something will go seriously wrong, and hence concentrate on the negative aspects of the relationship. But he should enter marriage with the realization that, if something does go seriously wrong, the probability is that he himself shares the blame.

WHAT SPECIAL PROBLEMS MAY THE COUPLE FACE?
The greater the age difference, the greater is likely to be the disparity in the couple's patterns of behavior. There may be variation in tastes, in interests, in recreational pursuits, and in attitude toward life.

There is likely to be a difference in degree of "habit set." The younger person will probably be more flexible and adaptable than the older. As a result, they will not change together or at the same rate. This may necessitate more adjustment on the part of the younger person, because the older one persists in his habitual ways. In the day-by-day contact of husband and wife this may become extremely irksome.

Older persons, especially those who have had no children in a previous marriage, are often inclined to indulge a young child in a grandparental way or to be very strict in their discipline because their habit patterns are too inflexible to be adapted to the demands a young child puts upon parents.

An older husband may assume a paternal attitude toward his wife. If there are plans or decisions to be made, he makes them because she is too inexperienced and he feels that he knows what is good for her. He may be impatient with her because of her inexperience. He is not seeking a wife who will be a copartner in all respects. He expects her to fulfill only part of the wifely role. Sharing is incomplete. Consequently, he does not anticipate her taking responsibility for things financial. In some cases she is in a measure an outsider who steps into an already functioning establishment and is accepted partly as wife and partly as permanent guest. Some women find this situation difficult to adjust to; they do not want to be patronized. They are likely, too, to feel the sting of public opinion because they realize that friends are aware of their equivocal position.

An older person may have reduced physical capacity. An older husband may be unable to meet the sexual expectations of a young wife; but there is no such reduction in sexual capacity in women with increasing age as there frequently is in men. Fertility may be so low in either case that the couple cannot have children; and, of course, a woman becomes completely infertile after completion of the menopause. If the younger person is interested in active sports, the older one may not be able to keep up. An older man may not be able to get enough life insurance to protect his family.

While still in the prime of life the younger person may have to care for a senile spouse. Cases are not unknown in which the younger person has an extramarital affair in such an eventuality and rationalizes it on the basis of the one-sidedness of the marriage. As stated in an earlier chapter, on the average women live longer than men; wives tend to outlive their husbands. In a marriage in which the wife is considerably younger than the husband, she is almost sure to face years of widowhood. If the couple have children, they may be left fatherless at a critical stage in their development.

If the husband is considerably younger than the wife, their problem of adjustment during the wife's menopause may be accentuated. At that period some women become nervous, change in appearance, and put on weight. With the traditional masculine affinity for feminine youthfulness, it is not difficult to see how adjustment in such cases might become complicated.

There is often a problem with regard to common friends. The very young wife trying to assume a matronly role in order to fit into a group of women of her husband's age has difficulty because the older women do not readily accept her as one of their company. She may appear younger and more inexperienced than is actually the case. The older husband trying to keep pace with the friends of a very young wife has an equally difficult problem. They can scarcely accept him as one of their own companions, and he must often force upon himself interest in their recreations. Instead of his appearing more youthful, his age is accentuated. In many cases there is no group into which both husband and wife readily fit as a couple.

Since tradition is more favorable to the marriage of an older man and a younger woman than to one in which the age difference is reversed, an older wife and a younger husband have the problem of adjusting to an attitude that places their marriage in the category of the unusual. People look askance at them, wonder why they did it, and become over-curious.

There is the necessity of the couple's assuming an intelligent and well-balanced attitude toward their own marriage. They should, of course, face and solve as objectively and as rationally as possible the special problems involved. But there is danger of putting too much emphasis on the problems and of exaggerating them beyond the limits indicated by the facts.

A seniority of six years on the part of the wife is worth considering; but it is not serious enough to damage a marriage if considered intelligently and without exaggeration. One couple exhibiting such an age difference had known each other for some time, were in love, were both well-educated and apparently well-adjusted persons, and had similar interests and backgrounds. The husband, however, started on the wrong tack. Immediately after the wedding he began seeking information as to how to surmount the obstacle in the path of their happiness. He searched through books for suggestions. He asked physicians what to do when his wife reached the menopause. Before two months of marriage had passed, he visited a counseling agency to ask for advice. Fundamentally his attitude was sound. He wanted to attack the problem with as much knowledge as he could accumulate. But he was exaggerating the problem and worrying about it out of proportion to its importance, until his attitude, rather than the age difference, was rapidly becoming the obstacle to happiness.

In contemplating marriage to an older person who has never married before, a younger individual should be certain that some important questions are satisfactorily answered before the final decision is made. Is there something about him that makes him an undesirable choice?

Has he lacked interest in marriage? Is he well adjusted? Has singleness been due to economic, educational, or military factors or to factors involving his personality and emotional maturity? How and why did he get so far along in life without marrying? If these questions cannot be adequately answered, then marriage may be a risk.

Difference in size

Tradition decrees and society expects that a man shall be at least as tall as his wife, preferably taller than she is. Ordinarily girls dislike dating boys smaller than themselves and vice versa. As was seen in Chapter 1, men are on the average taller than women. If, then, a husband is taller than his wife, even though he may be much taller, we shall not consider it a mixed marriage. On the other hand, if the wife is conspicuously taller than the husband, it may constitute a mixed marriage because the difference between them is significant and unusual. This sort of difference is not infrequently depicted in cartoons and newspaper comics; and people readily carry over their attitude from the comic strip to an actual couple.

A more serious problem, however, is that of the man's own reaction to his size. Small men sometimes become domineering, bossy, and egotistical in order to compensate for their size. This inclination on the part of the small man is likely to be accentuated if he marries a woman taller than himself because, with tradition decreeing that he should be the taller of the two, his size stands out in clear relief. Hence, such a husband may become domineering and overbearing toward his wife. He orders her about, reprimands her in public, belittles her, and may take the credit for her achievements.

In other cases, however, a small man may become excessively meek, spiritless, and submissive. Such a man is easily dominated by a larger wife, and this sometimes occurs, making the marriage more or less one-sided.

Many women prefer a man to be somewhat masterful. In discussing this point with numerous groups of women students it was found that in every instance the girls who said they wanted a man to be masterful said also that this would be acceptable only if he were taller than they, or at least as tall. They could not accept it in a much shorter man.

Difference in nationality

Nationality difference implies variation in customs, standards, and points of view. The greater the contrast in the backgrounds of the two spouses, the greater is the possibility of there being special problems of adjustment. If there is also a language difference, the situation is rendered even more complicated.

In some ways difference as to nationality and difference as to family background are similar; but the latter is a difference that occurs in a single matrix of custom, while the former involves the more basic ways of life. Every people believes its accepted way of life to be superior and right. It is more or less intolerant of other peoples' ways. In their dealings with each other, peoples set out with preconceived ideas and prejudices. Inevitably individuals reflect the attitudes of the group, and many of these have a direct bearing upon the marital relationship.

One of the most pertinent differences between this country and some other nations, as far as marriage is concerned, is the dissimilarity in attitude toward women, in their status, in their role, in the degree of restriction placed by custom upon their behavior, in women's attitude toward their own position and toward men. Attitudes toward authority in the home, toward the organization of the family with respect to relatives and in-laws, toward morality and aesthetics, and toward myriad other things may vary. Such differences may make a contribution to marriage. On the other hand they may make adjustment difficult, depending upon which spouse is American and where the couple live.

The problem of deciding whether or not to marry a person of another nationality is not uncommon among students who are in a position to meet young men and women from other countries. If an American meets a foreign student who is taking college work in this country, knows the language, is partly assimilated through his school experience, and plans to live here permanently, the problem of adjustment in marriage is one thing. But for the American who plans to marry a foreign student and reside permanently in the latter's homeland without first having experience in that country it may be quite another. Let us remember, however, that the potential problem is relative to the degree of difference between the two nationalities. One would scarcely consider mixed the marriage of a citizen of this country and an English-speaking Canadian.

It is exciting and romantic to fall in love with someone whose foreign extraction casts a halo and stimulates the imagination. If residence abroad is contemplated, the thrill of travel is added. In cases that have come to light in conferences with college students, the thrill, excitement, and glamor have often tended to becloud sober judgment and to make the wedding the limit of foresight. Furthermore, there is usually no way of checking on the credentials of one whose roots and attachments are abroad. Like everyone else, he is biased. He may make exaggerated claims about himself or his family; the American must judge only by his word and his own attitude toward his own importance. In rare cases there is deliberate falsification. For illustration let us consider a specific case.

The girl was an American college student who "fell in love" with an Iranian. They planned to marry when he graduated and to return to Iran to live. The thought of travel and residence in a foreign land seemed like a thrilling adventure to the girl and, as subsequent events proved, the glamor camouflaged her infatuation and made it seem like love. About Iran, about the man's family, and about his way of life she knew nothing except what he had told her. There was no reason to doubt his sincerity, but even sincere persons can look at life only through their own eyes. He saw Iran and his people through the eyes of an Iranian, not through the eyes of a young American girl thousands of miles away from relatives, friends, familiar scenes, and customary ways of life.

In the discussion of her contemplated marriage, it soon became apparent that there were several questions that she had never sought to answer. Would the day-by-day existence of an Iranian wife be agreeable to her? What is the position of women in that country? Would her relatives-in-law accept her? Would she like them? Could she learn the language quickly enough to prevent the beginning of an unbridgeable gap between herself and her husband's people? Would she become homesick? Would she be satisfied to see her children reared as Iranians? Would the economic structure and her husband's place in it exactly be as he had described them? Would the Iranian standard of living be acceptable? Is there any prejudice in Iran toward Americans?

The answers to these and similar questions she did not know. To marry without knowing them would be to take a plunge in the dark. The more she thought about it, the more she realized that there was little in favor of her plan and much against it. At length she decided to break her engagement, and she has not regretted doing so.

We do not mean to imply that a marriage such as this can never succeed. However, the problems are complex. Not everyone is equipped to make a satisfactory adjustment.

Difference in race

Up to the present in this country there has been more racial intermixture (miscegenation) than racial intermarriage. This has been due in part to the intermixture which occurred between white males and Negro females before the abolition of slavery. It is thought that, because of that intermixture, a large proportion of American Negroes have some white ancestry. As mulatto-white and mulatto-mulatto intermixture continued, many instances of gradual lightening of skin coloration from generation to generation have occurred, until some mulattoes, though they carry Negro genes, have become as light as whites. Because mulattoes are accorded Negro status, many of these very light mulattoes have "passed"; that is, they have crossed the color line and passed as white. Their children may not be aware of this passing. No one knows exactly how many such persons there are in the general population. Estimates of the number of persons who change their racial classification in this way each year range from a few thousands to tens, even hundreds, of thousands [Drake and Cayton, 1945; Davie, 1949; Simpson and Yinger, 1958]. Through the years the cumulative effect would be appreciable. Hence the very problem which prejudice, discrimination, and legal restriction have been intended to prevent, namely, racial intermarriage, has become complicated by the fact that a special group is involved in it without this fact being known by one person, both, their children, or society at large.

There has also been more racial intermixture than racial intermarriage because in some states marriage between a white person and a member of another race is unlawful. Not only is the marriage void in such states but in some there are legal penalties imposed besides.

The greatest barrier to racial intermarriage lies in the mores, the established customs of the group that are deemed to be essential for societal welfare, together with the attitudes and prejudices to which such mores give rise. But mores and attitudes are subject to change. There is no natural, inborn, instinctive, biological aversion to racial intermarriage, as some persons assume. This is shown, for example, by the acceptance of racial intermarriage in some countries. Fundamentally, a considerable portion of the "racial problem," rather than being one of difference in physical characteristics, is one of social status of which physical characteristics are erroneously assumed to be natural, universal indications. This is shown, for example, by the difference in acceptance of the marriage of a white person and a light mulatto as compared to that of a white person and a very dark native of India.

In recent years in this country there has been an increase in racial intermarriage due to such factors as the Second World War, during which many American servicemen married Oriental girls; urbanization, with its attendant indifference and impersonality relative to individual behavior so long as such behavior does not encroach directly upon the freedom and welfare of others; the influx of foreign students and other visitors; the extension of American business and political interests throughout the world; and the increased intermingling of peoples. To these factors may be added two others. One is the Negro "revolution," which has been proceeding apace in this country and elsewhere and changing both Negro-white relations and, as its reverberations have spread to other groups, the relations between whites and all colored peoples. The other factor is the cause-and-effect relationship between social change and acceptance of it. Repeated exposure to a phenomenon and increased familiarity with it tend to further acceptance of it. In turn, growing acceptance of it facilitates increased frequency. To some degree a social phenomenon is the cause of its own proliferation. The more racial intermarriage occurs, the more it is likely to occur.

There is still another factor that has entered the picture of Negro-white intermarriage, not in a great many cases as yet, but nonetheless found. There have long been whites who have made Negro-white inter- marriage the ultimate reason for continuing insistence upon racial discrimination—"Would you want your daughter to marry a Negro?" There is now beginning to emerge a small number of whites who are going to the opposite extreme and making such a marriage the ultimate test of their own racial acceptance—"My greatest contribution to racial equality is to marry a Negro." In either case perspective is lost. Mar- riage to a particular individual is confused with dedication to a "cause" involving a group. Entering any type of marriage to "prove" something is not likely to prove anything except that the individuals involved mar- ried for a reason that is difficult to sustain and that is unrelated to the factors which contribute to marital success.

In the light of all this, a gradual increase in racial intermarriage of various types may be anticipated. This increase, however, is not likely to occur suddenly. Most thoughtful persons, regardless of racial classifica- tion, are not pressing for it. Furthermore, numerical increase will not automatically remove problems and make success easier to achieve. During the period in which the reader of this book will make his choice of a marriage partner and for some time thereafter, racial intermarriage will entail special, complicated problems with which many mixed cou- ples will be ill prepared to cope and which only some will be able suc- cessfully to solve. A sociologist examines social change objectively and impersonally describes his observations. But a young couple contemplat- ing marriage must work out a highly personalized relationship within the undercurrents and crosscurrents of a social milieu. They are not called upon to use their marriage as a contribution to the solution of a complex social problem.

Racial intermarriage, like all types of marriage, does not occur in a vacuum. It occurs within a societal matrix. Many persons other than the couple are involved. No matter what the couple's attitude toward each other may be, the attitudes of family, friends, and members of society at large seep into their marriage; they cannot be completely walled out and disregarded. One of the criteria of success or failure in marriage is the degree to which a given marriage facilitates or erects barriers to the as- sociation of people. In present-day America, even in the light of recog- nized social change, racial intermarriage perhaps more than any other type contains stone and mortar for the building of walls between people. In many communities a racially mixed couple have difficulty in finding friends who are sufficiently unprejudiced to accept both spouses without hesitation or discrimination. Many families are not prepared to accept a child-in-law of another race. The spouse belonging to the majority race may find himself the target of prejudice and discrimination directed by segments of society toward the minority race, in much the same way as individuals are made to suffer through guilt by association. Also, to fall into the trap of attributing to racial difference the marital problems that are the result of nonracial factors is easy, especially during emotional upset, as in a quarrel. The thoughtless use of vernacular expressions and reference to popular misconceptions can produce lasting hurt, and perhaps even lifelong scars.

There is also the problem of offspring. Life is seldom smooth for the hybrid child. His associates are inclined to relegate him to the status of whichever one of the two racial groups he represents that is held in lower esteem. Often he is not fully accepted in either group, becoming a quasi-outcast, torn by conflicting loyalties. A very small admixture of yellow, brown, red, or black "blood" can throw the balance to the side of the colored race; usually no amount of white ancestry seems to counter-act this imbalance. Hence we may find a hybrid child with white aspira-tions, not understanding why he is shackled by public opinion and social pressure to colored status. His *salient identity*, the particular kind of person he conceives himself to be, becomes confused. He is ambivalent about his identity. His ambivalence creates an inner dilemma, for he does not know who or what he really is [Broom and Selznick, 1963]. Even when the child is accepted by friends, there may be a tendency for them to consider him "different." As he has associated with whites, his amorous proclivities are directed toward whites. But there he may strike an obstacle, for whites may hesitate to date him and refuse to marry him.

Racial difference per se is not the basic problem in racial intermar-riage. The basic problem is one of degree of acceptance or rejection of each other on the part of the two races involved and hence the degree of acceptance or rejection of the racial intermarriage in a given commun-ity. For example, in one part of this country a marriage between a white and an American Indian may be fully accepted, even glamorized. In another part of the country such a marriage may be considered anath-ema or "lower class," and the couple may be ostracized.

There are instances of intermarriage which, strictly speaking, are not racial. Yet, by the general public in some communities, they are treated to some degree as if they were, and in a given social setting they may present the problems of racial intermarriage. In some parts of the country where there is a large Latin-American population, a marriage of a Latin-American and an Anglo-American may be put into such a quasi-racial category. The false assumption underlying such classification is that all persons of darker skin belong to non-Caucasian races. Actually skin color is only one criterion of racial classification, and a not-too-accurate one at that. There are darker-skinned peoples, such as Latin-Americans or the peoples of India, who are "white," and lighter-skinned people, such as light mulattoes, who are classified as "colored."

Difference in economic status

In storybooks the princess marries the page, the heiress marries the chauffeur, the millionaire marries the chorus girl, and they "live happily ever after." In real life, too, there are occasional similar cases. But to marry a person of radically different economic status and make that marriage succeed is not so simple as it seems to the young person in love or to the individual whose materialistic approach to romance leads him to seek a wealthy spouse. Wealth involves responsibility as well as pleasure, restriction as well as privilege. Economic status, cultural background, tastes, and habits of life are so interrelated that there is more involved than merely the use of money. Let us discuss briefly some of the possible problems that may be faced by spouses of different economic status.

Some sensible, practical financial arrangement must be worked out if the marriage is to be successful. It is probably somewhat easier if the man is the wealthier, because then the marital situation more nearly approximates the traditional one, where the husband is the provider. If the wife is wealthier, various possible plans for the use of her money are not of equal merit, and their acceptability and practicality vary according to the two personalities involved. The couple might create a common fund, or the wife might let the husband control her money. She might buy luxuries, while he provided support. She might retain control of her money, using it only occasionally or saving it for the future. The couple might live on the husband's income only or on the wife's money.

If the husband is the poorer and accepts part of the wife's money or the benefits therefrom, there arises the problem of the effect of such a procedure upon his personality and upon the wife's attitude toward the husband and the marriage. Some men are so deeply influenced by tradition that a plan of this kind would prove humiliating. Some would be hypersensitive to the actual or imagined opinions of friends. Others have personality quirks which through such a plan might produce the equivalent of pauperization. Still others have the personality by means of which such a plan could be made a success. If the wife became domineering or demanded gratitude from the husband, conflict might easily result.

If the husband is the poorer and refuses to accept any part of the wife's money, even though she is willing to have him do so, a barrier may be erected between them. Furthermore, living on the husband's income may prove trying to the wife, who has been accustomed to a high standard, and may give rise to feelings of guilt, regret, or inferiority on the part of the husband who forces her to do so.

If the wife is the poorer, she may have some difficulty in adjusting to the husband's way of life. Most girls from families of moderate income are not prepared to direct a household of servants or to manage a large household budget. There is also the temptation to spend too freely because of the sudden rise in standard of living – an indulgence that may not be accepted by a husband who is thrifty though wealthy.

In one case an intelligent girl of the middle economic class married a wealthy man. The husband allowed the wife $30,000 a year for household expenses alone. The girl was not equipped to operate a household on that sort of budget, and at the end of the first year she found herself in debt. Only expert budget assistance finally helped her to solve her problem.

A special problem is found in some cases in which the two persons have a similar financial status at the time of marriage and immediately after marriage live on the husband's income or their combined earnings, but one of the spouses anticipates a large inheritance at the time of parents' death. This anticipation leads the couple to be careless about their expenditures, to go into debt, or even to lose occupational ambition. They may fail to develop the very qualities they will still need when they receive the inheritance.

Another problem sometimes encountered is that of the congeniality of the spouses' families and the degree to which each family accepts the child-in-law or makes demands beyond the ability of the child.

Some persons, given without effort on their part what less favored individuals have had to work for, fail to develop such traits as ambition, industriousness, and concern for others which characterize the mature, well-balanced personality. Knowing of this possibility and knowing that the success of her marriage would depend upon an interpersonal relationship, not upon money alone, one girl, for example, refused to marry a wealthy boy whom she loved until he had proved himself occupationally.

Whatever the case may be, success in this sort of mixed marriage is not so easily achieved as might at first glance be supposed. As indicated above, some sensible, practical scheme for the use of money must be worked out, and this should be done before the wedding. Just because one of the parties is wealthy, the future cannot be left to chance or hope.

Difference in family background

As everyone knows, there are superior individuals who have sprung from seemingly poor family backgrounds and inferior persons who have derived from apparently very good ones. The basic question in this connection is not only the nature of the family background of the person with whom marriage is contemplated but also how much it has affected him. Not all persons are affected to the same degree by similar circumstances; but in many cases environment leaves its mark, and an individual's family experience is carried into his marriage.

Difference in family background may seem relatively innocuous to

DIFFERENCES IN BACKGROUND

As higher education becomes increasingly accessible to greater numbers of young adults, more students of different backgrounds come into contact with one another. Though only one of many factors in the selection of a marriage partner, difference in background must be neither exaggerated nor ignored. The reader who is concerned about either his own background or the background of another person who is a possible choice as a marriage partner may find help in the following suggestions.

The quality of a personality is more important than the background from which that personality comes. There is no regular and direct correlation between personality and background; well-adjusted individuals can come from apparently poor backgrounds and poorly adjusted persons can come from apparently good backgrounds.

college students who are temporarily isolated from such background and are in circumstances conducive to making judgments of other people somewhat unrelated to family circumstances and extraction. But difference in family background may imply dissimilarity in any number of things taken for granted as part of an acceptable and appropriate way of life by one or the other spouse, for example, food tastes and levels of quality in cookery; degrees of neatness and cleanliness; table manners, polished or unpolished; English usage, correct or careless; types of recreation; definitions of husband and wife roles; attitudes toward arguing, quarreling, or a husband's striking a wife; standards relative to the use of alcohol, tobacco, or even coffee; scales of values; the celebration of holidays; definitions of authority within the family; and prejudices and biases of one sort or another.

Differences in background do not doom marriage to failure nor does similar background guarantee success. The individual's motivation, his degree of determination to work for the success of his marriage, and his level of commitment to marriage as a major life goal may counterbalance the effects of differences in background.

Consider two examples. In the first, the wife was an only child in whose parental family birthdays and holidays had always been days of special celebration and gifts. The husband was one of eight children in a family that was too poor to give special attention to any holiday except Christmas. On the couple's first wedding anniversary, the wife surprised the husband with an attractive, expensive gift. The husband gave the day no thought and bought nothing for the wife. His reaction to her disappointment was, "I felt so small that I could have left the room through the keyhole."

In another case the husband came for counseling with a written list of thirty-eight complaints against his wife. One of the major complaints was that their sexual adjustment was unsatisfactory. Another was that when they married she had agreed to continue working until he received his degree. These two problems proved to be related, in that continual bickering over the wife's employment, housekeeping, and money had seriously cooled the wife's interest in sexual intercourse

Much may be gained by realistic self-appraisal and similar appraisal of the other party in shared activities. Has his background permanently anchored him to a fixed set of values, attitudes, and habits that he accepts uncritically? Or has he the necessary objectivity to accept new learnings and values not rooted in his own background?

with her husband. The husband assumed that the wife was breaking a bargain in wanting to give up her job. In a sense she was. But the basic cause of her attitude was not personal; it was cultural. It was a reflection of a family background deeply ingrained in her personality. Her parents were native-born but of European stock. The family lived in a small community of families of similar extraction, so that attitudes were subject to relatively little change. In the wife's family it was taken completely for granted that women did not have gainful employment after they married. It was "simply not done." By a devious route, then, the family background of this wife had crept into the couple's sexual adjustment.

In some cases a problem arises because one of the couple "bends over backward" in an effort to get as far as possible from his family background. For example, a husband whose mother was a careless house-

If there are unanswered questions regarding background, this fact might indicate the need for taking more time to make the final choice of marriage partner.

keeper demands that his wife be overly meticulous, or a wife whose parents used poor English continually badgers her husband because of his careless speech.

Another pertinent reason for taking background into consideration is that, whether we wish it or not, the wedding delivers to each spouse free of charge a complete set of in-laws. These in-laws will visit and be visited, will make demands of one sort or another, and in many cases will try to hold the child to their own pattern of life, even though he has departed from it. Much depends upon proximity of residence; but geography does not always eradicate family bonds or extricate a child from the cultural pattern that has been woven around him.

Difference in education

The question of whether to marry anyone of considerably different educational experience is not uncommon, in the public at large or among college students who are away from the home town, where the fiancé, who is not planning to attend college, has remained after graduation from high school. The answer is not simple, because there is a distinction to be made between real and formal education. Usually these two types overlap; but they are not necessarily identical. There are many self-educated persons who have never attended college; and there are many poorly educated men and women who have been awarded degrees.

Where the need is recognized, an individual may further his preparation for marriage by utilizing counseling resources available to him, some of which may be found in most colleges and universities. The counselor may be able to help the individual's appraisal of self or of the other person and help formulate a plan for solving the problem.

A distinction must also be made between technical, specialized, occupational, or professional training and education for living. A girl with a bachelor of arts degree has three or four years less formal schooling than a man with a medical, engineering, or law degree; but so far as education for living is concerned, they have approximately equal amounts. Two high school graduates may have about the same amount of education for living, even though one of them goes on after graduation and takes several years of specialized business training.

When there is considerable disparity of education between husband and wife, there are in general four possible courses that their marital life may take. (1) They may make a satisfactory adjustment, with little actual change on either side. (2) There may be formed between them an unbridgeable chasm. (3) The one with the better education may assist the other to raise himself to the higher level. (4) The one with the lesser education may drag the other down to the lower level. The last is the path of least resistance and is not infrequent in actual experience.

In his intensive study of 200 married persons, Hamilton [1929] found that for persons in whose marriages both spouses had an equal amount of formal education there were more cases of high happiness score than of low happiness score, but for persons in whose marriages one spouse had more formal education than the other the opposite was true. When the husband had more education than the wife, there were more men and more women with low scores than with high ones. When the wife had more education than the husband, there were more men with high scores than with low ones, but more women with low ones than with high ones.

Difference in intelligence

Difference in intelligence and difference in education are not necessarily concomitant. Some individuals, by good fortune, devious means, or misplaced charity, zigzag through the maze of hurdles that better students jump, escaping academic elimination and receiving degrees that are insignia of neither ability nor achievement.

In uncommon cases couples of noticeably different intelligence get along well in marriage because, as we have said, success is in part relative to expectations. A genius and a dullard may make a mutually satisfactory adjustment if the former is not unhappy in intellectual isolation, enjoys a pleasant home, and has his emotional needs satisfied, and if the latter finds it agreeable to serve the superior spouse and bask in reflected brilliance with hero-worshiping admiration. Still, such marriages of genius and dullard are not common enough to furnish the basis for generalization.

In more ordinary unions in which there exists a difference in intelligence between the spouses, there is danger that the two may grow apart. Intellectual isolation may prove irksome and unsatisfying to the superior individual. They may both discover that in marriage mental stimulation is as important as emotional satisfaction, that exchange of ideas and contact of minds are as essential as exchange of caresses and contact of bodies. Intellectual isolation may result on the one hand in withdrawal, so that the superior spouse becomes less and less a part of the total marital situation, or on the other hand in his seeking elsewhere for the stimulation and intellectual contacts that the other spouse cannot supply. Either condition may produce a loneliness that makes marriage disappointing.

The less intelligent spouse, if he is keen enough to sense the real situation, may develop a feeling of inferiority. If he is not so keen, he may aggravate the difficulty by his very apathy and blindness. If the former occurs and he does grow to feel inferior, that too may produce loneliness that will eventuate in withdrawal or the seeking of companionship upon a more acceptable level. A feeling of inferiority may produce unhappiness, insecurity, and frustration. The inferior spouse aspires to keep pace with his superior partner but comes to realize that his mental legs are not long enough to maintain the stride.

Adjustment is not impossible, however. Hart and Hart [1935] suggest that it can be done (1) if the couple both recognize and face the facts, (2) if they find common ground in certain areas of their lives where they are on a more nearly equal footing, (3) if one partner is allowed to excel in some respects and the other partner in other respects, (4) if they adopt a definite leader-follower relationship, or (5) if the less intelligent spouse accepts a role of subordination.

Difference in previous marital status

Although the divorce rate is higher in marriages in which one spouse has been married before than it is in those which represent first marriage for both persons, among the remarriages that do endure the level of success is about the same as in first marriages that endure. Yet marrying a widowed or a divorced person is not the same as marrying one who has always been single, no matter how similar the external conditions may seem to be. When such a union is contemplated, answers to a number of important questions might well be ascertained to the satisfaction of the person to whom marriage will be a new experience. If the other individual's previous marriage was happy, that fact is likely to affect his attitude toward his new relationship. If it was unhappy, that experience will have left a mark. There is also the fact that marriage gave him a social status that cannot readily be eradicated from the memories of those who know him, especially if they also know or knew his spouse. It is inconceivable that anyone with normal human sensitivities could be completely indifferent to a marital experience.

Whether the previously married person was widowed or divorced, there is the question of rebound. Is he marrying in an attempt to fill an unfillable void in his emotional life and doing so before he has become sufficiently readjusted to make a wise choice based upon sound judgment? Is he marrying in desperation? How much time has elapsed since his divorce or bereavement?

What is his attitude toward his first spouse? Is there any possibility of that person's coming between you, either actually or in the imagination of one or both of you? In particular, why is he contemplating marriage with you? Is it because you are you and he loves you for yourself, or because you are so much like the previous spouse with whom he was happy, or because you are opposite in type and personal qualities from the person with whom he was unhappy? Does he love you or his first spouse in you? Does he continually compare you with the other person? How do you react to this comparison? Could you tolerate it over a long period in the close contacts of wedded life? Does he continue to display reminders of his past experience; if so, might they become barriers between you or make you self-conscious in your new relationship?

Will you, when you marry this person, step into a home already furnished and established by the previous spouse? Or will the two of you begin an entirely new home together? Could you make an adjustment if the former were the case?

After the wedding, where will you stand in the estimation of his friends and relatives, especially those of the former who were friends of both husband and wife? This problem becomes more than usually complicated if the friends and relatives feel that he remarried too soon.

What are his knowledge of and attitude toward sex as compared with yours? Some individuals are so abysmally ignorant of sex, even after marriage, that their marital experience makes no appreciable difference in their attitudes. In other cases marital experience, especially when coupled with some ignorance and lack of consideration, leads a person to make demands that the uninitiated, inexperienced spouse cannot meet. In still others, it produces deeper understanding, fuller appreciation, and greater consideration. At best there cannot be the same element of new adventure together when to one spouse sexual experience in marriage is a repetition of something familiar.

There are further special questions applying to marriage with a divorced person. One of the most important considerations is the real cause of the divorce. Almost all cases of divorce are two-sided; neither partner is solely to blame. Nevertheless, sometimes one, sometimes the other is more at fault. In any case, the real situation out of which the divorce grew is important. Unless he understood that situation, one could scarcely marry a divorced person without risk. Yet such marriage in darkness is sometimes contemplated.

Knowledge of the grounds for divorce alleged in court is, as we shall see in a later chapter, not sufficient, because causes and grounds are seldom identical. The grounds are worked out to satisfy the requirements of the law and may have little relation to the couple's actual relationship. Furthermore, there is a tendency for more divorces to be sought by and granted to wives. To ascertain who sued for divorce would not render the information desirable in contemplating marriage to one of the divorced partners.

Whether or not the other person was more at fault than his first spouse, there is the possibility of a problem's developing. If he was more at fault, he may repeat his mistakes. He may also still be in love with the former spouse. There is reason to believe that some divorced persons fail in completely overcoming their "fixation upon the former mate" [Waller, 1951]. If he was less at fault, he may be bitter and disillusioned. He may even marry for revenge. In either case, he may regret the divorce. It is important to know whether he has become soured and pessimistic about marriage or is still optimistic and looking for the best that marriage has to offer.

It is essential to know, too, whether he has readjusted himself after the divorce crisis. The concept of successful divorce is provocative in this connection. Was he at odds with his former spouse, with marriage, or with life in general? If the first is true, then marriage to another person may prove successful. If the second is the case, previous maladjustments may again develop, or a new start may make for better adjustment because the first marriage and its termination, though painful, were instructive. If the individual was and is at odds with life, of which marriage is only one maladjusted part, a second marriage will in all probability eventuate in some such way as the first unless those personality traits or circumstances that set him at odds with life are readjusted. This is not a simple, quick process. A divorced person may also develop an attitude of self-protection inconsistent with freely outgoing love for a second spouse so that his capacity to love another person wholeheartedly is permanently impaired.

Another pertinent question is the number of former marriages and divorces. One may be more hopeful of a person who has been divorced but once. When the process is repeated over and over again, that is fair evidence that the individual is seeking something that quirks in his personality or the nature of married life will not permit him to attain. Jessie Bernard [1956] speaks of the "divorce prone." Marriage to such a person would probably be a temporary affair.

For obvious reasons, in marriage to a divorced person the possibility of the former spouse's becoming a disrupting factor is greater than in widowhood. There is not only a possible emotional bond but the very real possibility of appearance or communication. The former spouse may be met at social gatherings. News is spread through common friends. The person may have trouble and ask for assistance, as in one case in which the husband did not hear from his former wife until several years after his second marriage, when she had some difficulty and wrote for money. There may even be an attempt to rewin the divorced spouse who has remarried. Whether or not a marriage can withstand the pressure of such circumstances depends upon the personalities of the two spouses. Some persons maintain their balance; others cannot do so.

If a divorced man pays alimony to his former wife, this fact may serve either to maintain the tie with the earlier marriage or to keep alive the old bitterness and disappointment. In either case, the economic problem of living on a reduced income may be irksome, especially since it is easy to project the blame for it onto the recipient of the alimony.

If the divorced individual had children by the first spouse, they may serve as a tie to the past, even though they live with the other person. A marriage may be so unhappy that divorce is a release and the two persons are gladly rid of each other. But one can scarcely be divorced from his children. Seldom do they contribute to the cause of marital failure. Parental attachment is usually too strong to be severed by court decree. If there are children through the new marriage too, the whole situation becomes complicated, as the relationships between the two sets of offspring become tangled, equivocal, and sometimes hypersensitive.

In cases of marriage to a widowed or a divorced person whose children live with him there is the problem of determining whether one has been chosen chiefly to become a husband or a wife or mainly to become a stepparent. In either case, there is stepparenthood with its ensuing adjustments. Under the best circumstances this in not easy. In general, the younger the children are, the less difficult the adjustment becomes. If they are very young, little difficulty is encountered unless the stepparent resents them. If they are old enough to have known both their natural parents, there is not only the problem of the mutual adjustment of new parent and children and the latter's acceptance of the former but also the problem of the children's adjustment to the new relationship between their natural parent and the stepparent. In many cases, the children are on the defensive. The new parent is an outsider intruding into a hitherto closed family group, and acceptance is difficult. In other cases the children are eager for the parent to remarry. If there are children by the second marriage also, there is the problem of maneuvering the adjustment of the two sets of offspring and at the same time preventing favoritism and discrimination.

The stepmother, like the mother-in-law, has been subjected to a great deal of suspicion and caricaturing. Some of it has been deserved. Much of it has not. There are stepmothers who show favoritism, who resent the children of some other woman, and who use them as focal points for all the pettiness and cruelty of which their personalities are capable. But there are also others who courageously and with self-abnegation assume the arduous task of rearing the children of the men they love and do as well by them as their personal resources would permit their doing by their own offspring. Some women eagerly desire stepchildren. In one case a plan was evolved by which a prospective stepmother made frequent visits to the home of the child's grandparents for the express purpose of winning the child's confidence and affection and of gradually weaning it away from the unofficial guardians who had kept it for so long that they were reluctant to give it up.

In attempting to overcome the one-sided stepmother tradition and also the possible prejudice of the children toward her, the woman may overstress her care and attention. If she disciplines the children, she may feel that she will be blamed for doing it because they are not her own. This may make her feel awkward and self-conscious toward them, even jealous of them. The woman may feel that she gives the impression of loving the children too little, and this may lead her to indulge them too much.

Difference in religion

Religion is more important in marriage than many young persons in love are inclined to think. It may be a uniting force or a disrupting influence. It may be the prop that supports a couple during a crisis, or it may precipitate a crisis. It may make for peace and happiness or for dissension and ill will. It may serve as a means of dissipating potential conflict or as a focal point upon which incipient conflict may crystallize. It may be a common interest orienting husband and wife in the same direction, or it may produce a divergence of interests, drawing husband and wife toward opposite poles. It may make possible a profound sharing in one of the most important areas of life, or it may militate against sharing.

An interesting side light on the possible role of religion is provided in a study of 13,528 young people in Maryland between the ages of 16 and 24. About 1 in 22 (4.6 per cent) of the Jews came from homes broken by divorce, separation, or desertion. There was little difference between Catholics and Protestants; approximately 1 in 16 (6.4 per cent) of the former and 1 in 15 (6.8 per cent) of the latter came from such homes. Of the individuals whose parents' marriage was mixed as to religion, 1 in between 6 and 7 (15.2 per cent) came from broken homes. When the parents had no religious affiliation at all, the ratio became 1 in 6 (16.7 per cent) [Bell, 1938]. No doubt there were factors other than religious affiliation that played a part in the breakdown of these families, but the figures are provocative, nonetheless.

The young sometimes fail to realize the importance of religion in marriage because their relatively short-time perspective does not permit a final judgment. As Howson [Folsom, 1938] points out, college students often abandon religion and the church temporarily, only to return to them later in life, when the sober responsibilities of marriage and parenthood awaken them to a new sense of religious values. When this occurs, early training often reasserts itself. The apple seldom falls far from the tree. If the religious backgrounds of husband and wife are basically different, that difference may again come to the fore, especially in time of crisis, even though in earlier years it was somewhat over-shadowed by youthful romance. Religion often plays relatively little part in dating. The result is that young people may become emotionally involved with each other before questions of religious difference arise, since such questions assume importance in their thinking only when marriage is contemplated. Young people in love often fail to realize, too, that it is not only religion as such that is important but also what people do in connection with it. If religion involved only faith, entirely separate from life activities, religiously mixed marriage would present few problems. But differences in faith entail differences in practice, in verbal expression, and in attitudes toward children, foods, holidays, and numerous similar things. They also involve families and other people with divergent attitudes and patterns of behavior. These can result in tugs, pressures, and conflicts as each family attempts to hold one member of a couple to the pattern which the family has set.

When there is a difference in faith and church affiliation, there may be not only a negative effect on the marriage but a lack of positive effect. If religion means something to a couple, then their having common experiences through participation in the activities of the same church will mean something. If their religious difference deprives them of these common experiences, a bond which strengthens many marriages is lacking.

When marriage to anyone of different religious background and affiliation is being contemplated, there are several questions that ought first to be answered satisfactorily.

How much does religion mean to you? Is it something of little importance, in which your interest is superficial, or is it something so vitally important that you could not conceive of living without it? Do you believe that your particular faith is the only right one, or are you tolerant and broad-minded? Do you have a driving zeal to convert others to your belief, or are you willing to let each adhere to the belief of his choice?

How great is the religious difference between you and the other person? Is it a Catholic-Protestant difference, Jewish—non-Jewish, Christian—non-Christian (such as Buddhist or Mohammedan), fundamentalist-liberal, religious-nonreligious, denominational (such as Baptist-Methodist), or a matter of degree, one of you being more religious than the other but both adhering in general to the same faith? How tolerant and broad-minded is the other person? There are Protestants and Protestants and Catholics and Catholics, just as there are individuals of various degree and type in every religious group. Furthermore, in each group there are good ones and bad ones, intelligent ones and stupid ones, well-informed ones and ignorant ones, tolerant ones and intolerant ones, well-adjusted ones and maladjusted ones. The common tendency is to lump together persons of a given religious affiliation and assume that they are all alike. Protestants often discuss Catholics as if the latter were all fashioned from the same pattern and were as identical as the proverbial peas in a pod. The same is done with other groups. There is great variation within groups, as well as among them. A very liberal Christian, for example, may be more similar to a very liberal Jew than he is to an ultraconservative member of his own group. In the contemplation of marriage, individual differences as well as group differences must be taken into account.

Would either or both of you make religion a bone of contention? How did you deduce your answer to this question? Have you ever discussed religion together? Do you argue about it and find yourselves emotionally wrought up and unable to find any common basis for agreement? Do you contemplate avoiding an interfaith marriage by having one person accept the faith and join the church of the other? Would she expect you to change your religion, or did you offer to do so? Would you expect him to change his, or did he suggest it? Has either of these alternatives been discussed? If so, when you discussed them, did you mean change in religion or change in church affiliation? It is easy to talk glibly about the latter when romance casts a rosy hue upon problems. But is the former really, at least readily, possible? If one changed, would it be because of conviction or to remove a barrier to marriage? Is your plan for the eradication of the religious difference the choice of a compromise church which both persons will join? For two persons who are affiliated with somewhat similar Christian denominations this may not be too difficult. But for the Catholic-Protestant, Jewish–non-Jewish, or Christian–non-Christian couple a truly mutual compromise is quite another matter. There is no church "between" Catholic and Protestant, for example. Each church is either one or the other, or it is neither. The other types mentioned are similar. Hence in some cases what is suggested as a compromise is actually a somewhat one-sided concession. Have you planned that each will retain his own faith and affiliation? If so, have you carefully thought through the problems that this might involve in later life, when there are children to be reared?

Children can scarcely adhere to two divergent faiths; some choice must be made. To plan to let the child make his own choice when he reaches the age of discretion is more easily said than done. Either he must be subjected to some religious influence in early life and thus have his choice colored or he must be allowed to grow to the age of discretion without having any religious influence exerted upon him, and thus be expected to make a choice with no foundation upon which to make it. Frequently the husband and wife who are intelligently tolerant of each other's religion find themselves unable to agree upon the training of offspring. The child may be pulled simultaneously in two directions; if, then, he goes the way of one parent, the other may feel resentful. The problem can be worked out, but a satisfactory solution requires all the personal resources that the two parents possess.

This is a discussion of marriage, not of theology. We are interested in the role of religion in marital adjustment, especially in the part that religious difference may play and in the problems that such difference may create or accentuate. Our discussion is not to be interpreted as a criticism of any religious group. In this discussion all faiths are considered of equal merit and are on an equal footing. "Many are the paths which lead in shadow up the side of the mountain; but from the cloudless summit all who climb behold the selfsame moon." So says an old proverb, and such will be our attitude toward religions in the discussion that follows.

CATHOLIC – PROTESTANT MARRIAGE

Protestant and Roman Catholic church organizations have evolved such dissimilar tenets and countenance such different modes of behavior that marriage adjustment between their adherents involves special problems. Neither the Catholic Church nor Protestant churches encourage interfaith marriage. The latter are more tolerant of it than the former, which definitely discourages it and permits it only after certain conditions have been fulfilled. These conditions are itemized in the "Ante-nuptial Contract and Promises," a sample of which is reproduced on p. 226. The existence of such an agreement suggests that the Catholic Church is able to bring pressure to bear upon the young couple in a way neither possible for, nor desired by, Protestant churches and that, therefore, the Catholic individual is likely to be more unyielding, while the Protestant spouse is expected to make concessions. It is the latter's freedom that is the more restricted. When the various promises are examined objectively, it becomes apparent that the agreement is onesided. By and large the Catholic agrees to do what he would do anyway. Most of the items to which the Protestant agrees he would not do were he not marrying a Catholic. It is not surprising, then, that the Protestant is often the breakdown point of the agreement. In some instances, however, the Catholic party makes gestures of broad-mindedness or agrees to generous compromises. In any case, there is a tendency for the couple to be unrealistic. They make promises under a set of circumstances

ANTE-NUPTIAL CONTRACT AND PROMISES

To be signed in duplicate in the presence of the priest by the parties entering a mixed marriage, and by two witnesses.

To Be Signed by the Non-Catholic Party

I, the undersigned, not a member of the Catholic Church, wishing to contract marriage with the Catholic party whose signature is also hereinafter affixed to this mutual agreement, being of sound mind and perfectly free, and only after understanding fully the import of my action, do hereby enter into this mutual agreement, understanding that the execution of this agreement and the promises therein contained are made in contemplation of and in consideration for the consent, marriage and consequent change of status of the hereinafter mentioned Catholic party, and I, therefore, hereby agree:

1. That I will not interfere in the least with the free exercise of the Catholic party's religion;

2. That I will adhere to the doctrine of the sacred indissolubility of the marriage bond, so that I cannot contract a second marriage while my consort is still alive, even though a civil divorce may have been obtained;

3. That all the children, both boys and girls, that may be born of this union shall be baptized and educated solely in the faith of the Roman Catholic Church, even in the event of the death of my Catholic consort. In case of dispute, I furthermore, hereby fully agree that the custody of all the children shall be given to such guardians as to assure the faithful execution of this covenant and promise;

4. That I will lead a married life in conformity with the Law of God and the teaching of the Catholic Church regarding birth control, realizing fully the attitude of the Catholic Church in this regard;

5. That no other marriage ceremony shall take place before or after this ceremony by the Catholic priest.

In testimony of which agreement, I do hereby solemnly swear that I will observe the above agreement and faithfully execute the promises therein contained, and do now affix my signature in approval thereof.

_____
Signature of the non-Catholic party

_____
Address

_____
City or Town

To Be Signed by the Catholic Party

I, the undersigned, a member of the Catholic Church, wishing to contract marriage with the non-Catholic party whose signature is affixed above to this mutual agreement, being of sound mind and perfectly free, and only after understanding fully the import of my action, do hereby enter into this mutual agreement, understanding that the execution of this agreement and the promises therein contained are made in contemplation of and in consideration for the consent, marriage and consequent change of my status, and I, therefore, hereby agree:

1. That I shall have all my children, both boys and girls, that may be born of this union, baptized and educated solely in the faith of the Roman Catholic Church. I understand that in case of my death, or in the event of a dispute, the custody of all the children shall be given to such guardians as to assure the faithful execution of this covenant and promise;

2. That I will practice my Catholic religion faithfully and will strive, especially by example, prayer and the frequentation of the Sacraments, to bring about the conversion of my consort;

3. That I will lead a married life in conformity with the Law of God and the teaching of the Catholic Church regarding birth control, realizing fully the attitude of the Catholic Church in this regard;

4. That no other marriage ceremony shall take place before or after this ceremony by the Catholic priest.

_____
Signature of the Catholic party

_____
Address

_____
City or Town

Signed in the presence of:

_____   _____
Witness   Witness

I, the undersigned, do hereby attest that the parties whose signatures are affixed to the above agreement and promises appeared before me personally on the given date, and fully understanding the import and meaning of the aforementioned agreement and promises, freely entered into this agreement and signed the above in my presence.

_____
(Pastor-Assistant)

Date:_____

TWO COPIES of this form should be filled in and sent to the Chancery. One copy, when duly signed, dated and sealed by the Chancellor, will be returned to the priest to be kept in the parish archives; the other copy will be retained in the Chancery. See "Synodus Dioecesana Sancti Ludovici Septima – 1929" (Page 54 No. 95 under 2).

highly colored by romance and the desire to marry. They are expected to carry out those promises under other circumstances, face to face with reality and beyond their present experience and therefore beyond their ability to foresee reactions.

The obligation to fulfill the terms of the ante-nuptial agreement is a moral rather than a legal one. If it were violated, there would be no suit for breach of contract. Nevertheless, for a non-Catholic to accede to such an agreement insincerely would not only involve a serious violation of his personal integrity but would put his relationship to his spouse upon an equivocal and insincere footing. The marriage would begin with dishonesty, and there would almost certainly be conflict as the Catholic spouse attempted to carry out his own agreement. Furthermore, the Catholic Church holds that, if a Protestant signs the ante-nuptial agreement and it is later proved that he had no intention of keeping it, the marriage, so far as the Church is concerned, is null and void. This does not annul it legally, however.

READING 4 # CATHOLIC—PROTESTANT MARRIAGE AND THE ECUMENICAL COUNCIL

Canon 1102, 2, forbids any sacred rites to be performed at mixed marriages. This legislation appears severe to Protestants. If the Church does permit a mixed marriage and the non-Catholic partner is a believing Christian, then it would seem that the Church would want to call the divine blessing on the couple, and stimulate in them the common faith in Christ and the desire for a holy union.

How could this be done? Many Catholic pastors believe that some ceremonies should be permitted at mixed marriages. While solemn nuptial Mass and blessing are proper to the wedding of two members of the Church, simpler blessings and the Mass of the day could be granted for mixed marriages. Many Catholics feel that once the Church has given the dispensation for a particular mixed marriage, the pastoral and liturgical action should be such as to induce a deep Christian commitment.

Canon 1062 tells the Catholic partner in a mixed marriage that he is obliged to work for the conversion of his spouse. While a believing Protestant agrees that a Catholic will want to witness to his faith and, by word and example, make his Church understood to his family, the formula-

From "Mixed Marriages and the Council," *The Ecumenist*, Gregory Baum (ed.), vol. 1, no. 2, December, 1962, pp. 23–25. Reprinted with permission of the Paulist Press, New York.

tion of the canon does not exclude methods of persuasion which invade the freedom of the individual conscience and employ questionable means such as threats, complaints, constant lamentations, etc. Here again a new formulation might be found. It could indicate that the Catholic partner must not only give witness to the faith and desire to share it with the non-Catholic partner, but he must also manifest a real respect for the Christian conviction of his partner and not despise his faith which he regards as his most precious link to Jesus Christ.

At present, the promises which the Church demands of the non-Catholic party must be put down in writing and signed. To many Protestants this is objectionable. If they make a promise, they intend to keep it. In some countries inner integrity of conscience is the heart of Protestant holiness. It is desired, therefore, that Church legislation give the priest permission not to insist on the signing of the promises, if he feels that the Protestant partner has made a sincere promise from his heart.

The points mentioned so far have been of secondary importance. They deal mainly with terminology and the range of application of the present legislation. There is one law of the Codex, however, which is most offensive to Protestant Christians. Its change would affect the lives of many people and alter the ways of pastoral care.

Since the Council of Trent, the Church has demanded that all Catholics must observe the form of marriage laid down in canon law. Any Catholic who attempts marriage neglecting this form is not validly married. This legislation invalidates secret marriages among Catholics. But it also implies that a Catholic marrying a Protestant "outside the Church" does not enter into a valid marriage. His marriage is not only illegitimate; it is null and void in the eyes of the Church.

VALID MARRIAGES

To Protestants this legislation appears very severe and almost arbitrary. The Catholic Church regards the marriage of two pagans or two Protestants as valid and permanent. Why then does she consider invalid a marriage of a Catholic and a Protestant performed "outside the Church"? A Protestant's confusion increases when he learns that the Church teaches the essence of the marriage union to be the mutual consent between two parties. He does not easily see how an act of law could intrude into such a consent, rendering it incomplete.

Prior to the new C.I.C. of 1918 the Church, in certain parts of the German Empire, regarded as valid, though illegitimate, mixed marriages performed "outside the

Church." Protestants desire that in countries where Catholics and Protestants live together and mingle freely, this decree would again come into force.

What is the Catholic attitude to this proposal? It is far from uniform. Many pastors are in favor of the strict legislation, believing that this is the strongest method of deterring Catholics from entering a marriage outside the Church. Other pastors believe that the more lenient legislation would, in the long run, be more beneficial to souls. They think that stigmatizing a mixed marriage performed "outside the Church" as illegitimate and imposing a censure on those who attempt it, should be sufficient penalty to deter Catholics from such unions.

Many Protestants are inclined to be offended by the "Ante-nuptial Contract and Promises." They argue that the Catholic Church has no right to impose such an agreement on Protestants. That is one side of the coin. The other side is the fact that the Catholic Church is by definition and history an authoritarian church whose right to regulate the lives of its members is taken for granted by Catholics but not understood by Protestants, whose frame of reference is quite different. In one sense the Catholic Church imposes the agreement on Protestants. In another sense it decrees how Catholics must be married if they marry Protestants.

Protestants are also offended by the fact that the agreement has to be signed and by the fact that it precludes a Protestant's having a wedding in his own church, which implies a disregard for both his convictions and his church. In recent years the Catholic Church has become increasingly aware of these two points of grievance. Reflecting the attitudes of two liberal popes and a growing number of clergy, there are "straws in the wind" which suggest that, in the not too distant future, these strictures may be mitigated to make the agreement oral and to permit the couple to have a second wedding ceremony in a Protestant church.

Protestants also resent being asked to promise to refrain from remarriage during the lifetime of the Catholic in case there has been a civil divorce. They feel that once the marriage has been legally terminated, they are no longer under obligation to the Catholic Church.

According to one Catholic writer, who presumably reflects official opinion, the Catholic Church opposes interfaith marriage not because it holds non-Catholics in low esteem but because it is solicitous of their welfare as well as that of its own adherents. The Church has found through centuries of experience that interfaith marriage contains elements that are threatening to the happiness of both parties [O'Brien, 1937].

Catholic-Protestant dating. Another Catholic writer goes so far as to say that in some cases even keeping company with a non-Catholic is a sin. It is not always sinful, because under some circumstances the Church does permit interfaith marriage. If, however, the Catholic is already rather "weak in the Faith" and keeps company with a non-Catholic who "makes no secret of harboring gross prejudices and hostile sentiments against our Faith, and expresses them openly and sneeringly" and they plan marriage, the Catholic party commits a grievous sin. In any case, this same writer asserts that when a Catholic keeps company with a non-Catholic, there is always the possibility of its eventuating in marriage, and this is dangerous to the faith and to the happiness of the Catholic party. Hence, the latter should be very careful to tell the confessor of the "hazardous courtship" in order to obtain advice and perhaps to avert disaster [Meyer, 1934].

Howson [Folsom, 1938, p. 223, reprinted by permission] feels that "under the circumstances, a union between a devout and faithful Roman Catholic and a convinced member of any other religious group lacks that equality of spiritual status that is essential to the highest reaches of marital adjustment." Catholic writers share this point of view. For example, Miller [1960] says that "there is something radically wrong with any Catholic who sees no obstacle to happiness in a mixed marriage" and [1961] that mixed marriages "lack the unity of belief and outlook necessary for happiness in marriage." Lord [1952], another Catholic writer, says that mixed marriage is not fair to the Protestant and that "I advise my Protestant friends . . . never, if they can avoid it, to fall in love with Catholics."

Validity of marriage. Protestant churches accept as valid a wedding performed by a Catholic clergyman; but the Catholic Church recognizes as valid only a ceremony performed by a priest. Marriage by a Protestant clergyman is not recognized by the Catholic Church. Of course, the ruling of the Catholic Church is not imposed upon Protestants unless they want to marry Catholics, and the Pope does not presume to legislate concerning the validity of Protestant weddings performed by Protestant clergymen [Conway, 1929b]. If the couple are allowed to have a Protestant ceremony, as mentioned above, this would follow the Catholic ceremony; it would not replace that ceremony, which is the only one considered valid for the Catholic.

The Catholic Church takes this stand with regard to the validity of marriages of its adherents because it considers itself the only true church. To recognize as valid a ceremony performed by a Protestant clergyman would be putting churches founded by mere men — Luther, Calvin, Wesley, and others — on the same level as the church founded by Jesus Christ, namely, the Catholic Church. Such an act would be a commission of the sin of apostasy. Catholics who deliberately violate this ruling are subject to excommunication because they are guilty not published as they are when both parties are Catholics. The blessing of the ring is omitted. There is no nuptial Mass [Conway, 1929b].

In order to show disapproval of interfaith marriage, the banns are not published as they are when both parties are Catholics. The blessing of the ring is omitted. There is no nuptial Mass [Conway, 1929b].

In some cases, because of these details as to ceremony, Protestant parents refuse to attend, and there is family friction even before the wedding. Parents who are ardent opponents of Catholicism may not yield even for so important an occasion as a child's wedding. It is unlikely that the Catholic would break faith and be married in a Protestant church. A Catholic who has a wedding ceremony performed by a civil officiant, such as a justice of the peace, commits a sin. He does not contract a valid religious marriage but is not subject to excommunication, since he has not committed the sin of apostasy, or breaking away from the faith [O'Brien, 1937].

Conception control. One weighty problem in Catholic-Protestant marriage is that of conception control. Officially, the Catholic Church is in unalterable and irrevocable opposition to what it terms "unnatural" methods of family limitation, that is, mechanical or chemical contraceptives. The opposition to contraception is not due to the fact per se that it may prevent conception but rather the fact that it is a perversion of a natural process, a violation of natural law, and a deviation from right order. The intensity of this opposition is reflected in the vehement denunciatory statements made by Catholic writers. Pope Pius XI [*Encyclical Letter*, 1930] referred to contraception as "intrinsically against nature," a practice that is "shameful and intrinsically vicious," a "foul stain," and a "grave sin." Edgar Schmiedeler [1946], former Director of the Family Life Bureau of the National Catholic Welfare Conference, terms it an "immoral practice" and a "most powerfully disintegrating and destructive force" in family life today. Another writer says that "God condemns it"; he describes it as a "deadly sin," an "unnatural vice," and a "crime against nature." He says further that it "degrades those who practice it," that such persons "in their sane moments despise themselves," and that they are "not good sportsmen" but rather "shirkers" who want the "favors of nature without its burdens." He goes on to assert that contraception is one of the causes of an increase in women's diseases and that the wife is reduced to the "status of a kept woman" [Scott, 1930]. Still another writer asserts that contraception is "desexing" and "approximates homo-sexuality," that as a method of family limitation it is "riotous, morally anarchic, and perverted" and is "utterly detestable" [Cox, 1936]. Another writer claims that contraception leads to the degradation of women, that it is injurious to women's health, "lowers their dignity and self-respect," and often causes broken homes [Conway, 1929a]. Another blames contraception for economic decay and says that the increase in its practice and the rise in the divorce rate stem from the same cause, namely, the number of married couples who are sensual and averse to sacrifice [Pruemmer, 1934]. Still another [Quay, 1961] says, "Contraception is wrong because it is a fictitious symbol of love, a substitution of what, in truth, symbolizes shared selfishness for what symbolizes utter self-giving."

The Catholic Church does not insist that a woman bear all the children that unlimited sexual intercourse might provide or bear them at grave risk to her life or health. But in one utterance Pope Pius XII threw new light on the common assumption that the Church fully condones the "safe period" or "rhythm." He made it clear that there is no objection to a married couple's having intercourse at a time when conception could not occur but that if they deliberately restrict intercourse to that period exclusively, "then the conduct of the married couple must be examined more closely" [1951]. Such restriction of intercourse is acceptable only when there are serious reasons for desiring to prevent conception. These reasons are termed *indications* and fall into several categories [Clemens, 1957; Thomas, 1957; Tobin, 1962]:

Medical, for example, the process of childbearing involves unusual difficulties for the wife; the wife is unable to carry pregnancies to term; the mother suffers unusual strain in rearing her children; prolonged illness among the children or the presence of a defective child requiring special care.

Eugenic, for example, a child is likely to exhibit inherited defects; in a case of demonstrated Rh incompatibility a physician advises that subsequent children may be seriously affected.

Economic, for example, the father is unemployed; the father is incapacitated and unable to fulfill his role as breadwinner; the couple desire to avoid indebtedness by spacing pregnancies.

Social, for example, the couple are faced with a long separation due to the husband's military service; the husband and wife are students; the couple cannot find adequate housing.

In the absence of such serious reasons "the determination to avoid habitually the fecundity of the union while at the same time to continue fully satisfying their sensuality, can be derived only from a false appreciation of life and from reasons having nothing to do with proper ethical laws." Pius XII went on to say that, in cases where conditions are such that pregnancy absolutely must be avoided because of the risk to the woman, and dependence upon the "safe period" would not give her "sufficient security," "there is but one way open, that of complete abstinence" from sexual intercourse [1951].

If a couple are contemplating use of the "safe period," or "rhythm," it is recommended that they do not themselves alone make the final judgment but rather that they consult a spiritual adviser, who would typically be a priest. The adviser's function is not to give them information concerning methods and techniques of practicing this method of family limitation. His function is to help them understand and appreciate "the vocation of marriage" and to assist them in interpreting and applying moral principles [Good and Kelly, 1951; Kane, 1952; Thomas, 1957].

It is clear that the Catholic Church's approval of the "safe period," or "rhythm," is not so unqualified and the decision to use it is not dependent upon the couple's own judgment as is true in most Protestant churches. So far as official Church expectation is concerned, it is not so fully a matter to be decided by the couple's choice as is commonly assumed.

As we said in an earlier connection, however, there is variation among Catholics just as there is among Protestants. Not all Catholics are equally devout. Not all adhere to the precepts of the Church with monolithic steadfastness and unswerving consistency. Catholics, like Protestants, often exhibit a discrepancy between expectation and practice. Such discrepancy is a matter of concern to the Catholic Church, a concern which is an indication that the discrepancy exists.

In spite of official statements of the Catholic Church, in the last analysis, a couple's decision to use the "safe period," or "rhythm," rests upon their own judgment and is a matter of their own conscience. It has only been recommended that they consult a spiritual adviser, never required that they seek permission. Many Catholics use contraceptives and visit birth control clinics or raise no objections when a Protestant spouse does either of these. In one study of 2,713 white married women it was found that Catholics did not use contraceptives so freely as non-Catholics. Catholics, as compared to others, more frequently relied on the "safe period" only and tended to begin to use contraception later in married life. It was found that in mixed marriages the religion of the wife tended more often than that of the husband to determine whether any method was used and, if so, which. Altogether, however, 30 per cent of all the Catholics, and 50 per cent of those Catholics who used any type of contraception, had adopted methods considered unacceptable by the Church. In some cases of mixed marriage the issue of contraception was found to be a source of serious marital conflict [Freedman, 1959].

Sterilization. The Catholic Church is opposed to direct, intentional sterilization under any circumstances [Bonnar, 1937; Fremantle, 1956; Pope Pius XII, 1951; Thomas, 1957]. Protestants are inclined to accept sterilization in cases such as that in which a woman has had several Caesarean operations and her obstetrician advises her to have no more pregnancies or that in which there are known hereditary defects that may be passed on to the children. Many Protestants hold that sterilization is entirely a matter of an individual's or a couple's judgment for whatever reason they may desire it, even in the absence of such considerations. But the Catholic Church in no uncertain terms condemns direct, intentional sterilization as sinful and immoral. It does not, however, condemn indirect, unintentional sterilization, as in a case in which a woman has a tumor which can be removed only by having the entire uterus removed.

Artificial insemination. In spite of its emphasis upon the importance of reproduction, the Catholic Church condemns artificial insemination, whether the donor of the seminal fluid be the woman's husband or an anonymous male chosen by a physician or both. The reasons given for such disapproval are that artificial insemination involves the perversion of a natural faculty, since sexual intercourse is naturally a cooperative act, and that such insemination typically involves the collection of the seminal fluid either through the use of a contraceptive device or through masturbation, which is considered to be grievously sinful [Bonnar, 1937; Good and Kelly, 1951; Pope Pius XII, 1951]. The Catholic Church is not alone in disapproving artificial insemination. Many Protestants assume it to be a matter of personal decision. But some Protestant clergymen have vigorously expressed objections to such insemination involving a nonhusband donor on the ground that such a procedure savors of adultery. Some courts have raised questions regarding the legitimacy of a child when the father is a nonhusband donor. The question of whether the woman's husband should be required to adopt the child in order to make it his legal heir has still not been answered to everyone's satisfaction.

Therapeutic abortion. Once a woman becomes pregnant, there are considered to be no circumstances whatever that justify the deliberate, direct destruction of the fetus even to save the life of the mother [Pope Pius XII, 1951]. Thus, Pius XII expressed unalterable opposition to therapeutic abortion, which is commonly accepted by Protestants as an unfortunate necessity in extreme cases. Exceptions are sometimes made, however, when the destruction of the fetus can be rationalized as being indirect. For example, in the case of a tubal pregnancy, when in all probability the tube would eventually burst and the fetus would die anyway, the surgical removal of the tube may be considered a direct solution of a medical problem, the objective being to save the mother from the serious consequences of the burst tube. In such a case, the destruction of the fetus may be considered indirect and unintentional rather than direct and deliberate. But Protestant physicians are inclined to label this as hairsplitting and evasion of the issue. In other cases, for example, those in which a pregnant woman has acute heart or kidney disease, such rationalization of the indirect destruction of the fetus would not be possible.

This position of the Catholic Church on therapeutic abortion is extremely difficult, if not impossible, for the typical Protestant young woman to accept. Protestant thinking and Catholic thinking rest upon different premises. The girl knows that she is unlikely to develop any condition in which therapeutic abortion would be called for. Yet she wants to feel secure in knowing that if such a condition did arise, the various persons concerned — her husband, her obstetrician, her clergyman, her parents, her parents-in-law — would all, unhesitatingly, decide to try to save her life even at the sacrifice of the baby, tragic as this may be. Actually, medically speaking, therapeutic abortion is rarely necessary literally to save the life of the mother. Yet the Catholic Church's position on what she interprets as a definition of the importance of her as a person is what the young woman resists.

The couple's problem. In a marriage in which both partners are Protestant they are free to do as they see fit with regard to spacing children or limiting their number. In a marriage in which both spouses are Catholic they have a similar point of view and are subject to the same restrictions and twinges of conscience. But when one is Protestant and the other Catholic, there is ample ground for conflict over this vital question of procreation. Often the problem does not arise until the couple have had several children, and this fact makes it difficult for the unmarried to predict accurately what their attitudes will be later.

The solution of the problem is sometimes simpler if it is the wife who is Catholic. She then is the one who opposes conception control and she is also the one who must bear the babies. There are husbands as well as wives who wish to limit the size of their families, so even in such cases there may be cause for conflict. If, however, the husband is a Catholic and the wife is a Protestant, if she wants no more children but his religious scruples will not permit the practice of conception control and his natural impulses make it difficult for him to refrain from intercourse, there may be a crisis. In the study of 2,713 white married women mentioned earlier, it was found that in mixed marriages the religion of the wife only tended more often than that of the husband to determine what the couple did about contraception; her religion was not always the determining factor. In this study it was also found that in some mixed marriages there was serious conflict over contraception [Freedman, 1959]. Take a case such as the following. The couple have had four children. Since the birth of the last child the wife has been in poor health. She cannot safely bear another child, she does not want another, and they cannot well afford to have one. She is Protestant and would use some sort of control of conception if her husband would permit it. He is Catholic, is virile, and is somewhat inconsiderate. He opposes conception control and insists upon intercourse. The result is that the couple are growing apart. Estrangement from her husband is the only form of self-defense the wife has thus far been able to devise.

If the couple are willing to accept all the children that the nonuse of control of conception might provide, or if they can work out some satisfactory solution not inconsistent with Catholic ideals or not painful to their own consciences, the matter of conception control may not be an obstacle to successful marital adjustment.

The rearing of children. Both parties are expected to agree that any children of their particular union will be reared as Catholics. Protestant students sometimes express the erroneous belief that the Catholic Church approves of the couple's rearing boys in the faith of the father and girls in that of the mother. One of the chief reasons for which the Catholic Church disapproves interfaith marriage is the danger that the children will be lost to the faith and to the Church. The influence of the non-Catholic parent may prove a hindrance to the child's acceptance of Catholic doctrine and his devotion to Catholic ideals unless this influence is counteracted by the Catholic parent, the Church, and the parochial school. The Catholic parent may die, leaving the other to rear the children as non-Catholics [Conway, 1929b].

Even though the agreement be kept and the children be reared as Catholics, the problem is not automatically solved. It is one thing to agree to a plan for the training of one's future children, which are not yet born; it is another thing to carry out such a plan without reluctance or regret. Protestants usually do not want their children to be Catholics any more than Catholics want theirs to be Protestants. Suppose, however, that the children are reared as Catholics without either reluctance or regret on the part of the Protestant parent. There still remains the problem of the children's reconciling themselves to having a non-Catholic parent, who cannot participate in their church activities — at least, not on an equal footing with themselves — and who by the very faith they profess is a foreigner to the spiritual fold.

Divorce. The Catholic Church does not recognize divorce for any cause. If a Protestant spouse secures a divorce from a Catholic, that divorce is legal and the two persons are legally free to remarry; but the Church will not permit the Catholic to remarry unless the Protestant has died. Nor will the Church permit a Catholic to marry a divorced person unless the person's ex-spouse has died or unless the Church considers the first marriage of the divorced person invalid.

Although the Catholic Church holds that husband and wife should live together, under unusual circumstances it may allow them to separate, even permanently. Such separation, however, does not dissolve the marriage bond; neither party may remarry because they are still married to each other.

Under certain circumstances a Catholic couple or a Catholic-Protestant couple may find that their marriage is not valid according to the rules of the Catholic Church; there were certain impediments that prevented their establishing a valid marriage. In such cases the couple may secure a religious annulment. They would also have to secure a civil annulment or divorce because the Church cannot administer state law. But if they secure a civil divorce under such circumstances, it would not be considered a divorce so far as the Church is concerned because the couple had never had a valid religious marriage. After a religious annulment a Catholic is free to marry, since, by definition, he has not been married. This would be true even if he had had to secure a civil divorce as mentioned above.

Most people enter marriage with the idea of permanence. Relatively few think of possible divorce, and still fewer marry feeling that the bond will probably be temporary. In a survey of the opinions of 1,151 college students, approximately 91 per cent said that when they married they would consider it to be for life. Only 7 per cent said that they would feel free, if the marriage did not succeed, to get a divorce. These opinions do not show what the students would actually do if their marriages failed; they show only the present attitude of those who made the statements. Why is the Catholic attitude toward divorce something to be taken into consideration in contemplating an interfaith marriage when persons about to be married do not think of divorce anyway? It is important because it is a reflection of the whole Catholic point of view concerning the nature of marriage and its relationship to the spiritual existence of the couple.

Prevention of Catholic-Protestant marriage. The problem of Catholic-Protestant marriage is one thing if a couple are already married and adjustment is the only alternative, and quite another thing if they are in love but as yet unmarried and must either agree upon their plans for the future or discontinue their relationship. The latter may mean permanent regret. For those persons who are neither married to, nor in love with, nor even going with individuals of the other faith the question has still another aspect. If one is not in love with a Catholic, or with a Protestant, as the case may be, he may avoid complications by allowing an acquaintanceship to go no further as soon as he discovers the other person's religious affiliation. He may nip the relationship in the bud before he falls in love.

Preparing for Catholic-Protestant marriage. If Catholic-Protestant marriage is seriously contemplated, there are two things to be done, preferably before a definite engagement is agreed upon. These are the *sine qua non* of common sense and successful adjustment. (1) As much as possible should be learned about the other person's religion. This may be done through reading, church attendance, and conference with both the minister and the priest. It must be admitted that such a process is easier for the Protestant than it is for the Catholic, since the latter's church disapproves of his conferring with a Protestant clergyman or attending a Protestant church. (2) The couple should agree upon a practical, workable plan, which should be much more than an easily entered and equally easily broken compromise. This plan should be discussed with both clergymen and, if possible, with both sets of parents. We are assuming, of course, that both parties are the type who will adhere to agreements once made.

In cases in which students have fallen in love, or what they momentarily diagnose as love, and are more or less definitely thinking in terms of Catholic-Protestant marriage, there is often a tendency to talk glibly but understand slightly, to make broad statements of intention or ability that pass beyond the limits of practicality and probability. Such students agree so readily to become Catholic or to believe that the other person can do so that it is obvious that the difficulty, if not the impossibility, of this process has entirely escaped them. They are inclined to discount or overlook the influence of bias, to forget parents and their role after the wedding, to minimize the problem of child rearing or even to have a sort of temporary amnesia with regard to the fact that reproduction is still a part of human life. In examining briefly a few specific cases, we shall see why the prognosis was pessimistic.

READING 5   **SIMILARITIES AND DIFFERENCES BETWEEN CATHOLICS AND PROTESTANTS**

Since Roman Catholicism and Protestantism are in the same course of Christian history up until the Reformation, there are many points at which they come together in agreement. Without taking account of the special refinements developed by the theologians on both sides, it can be said in general that there are points of agreement relating to: The Apostles' Creed; the Nicene Creed; redemption as indicated in the incarnation and Cross of Christ;

From Stanley I. Stuber, *A Primer on Roman Catholicism for Protestants*, Association Press, New York, 1953, pp. 261–268. Abridged and reprinted with permission of the publisher.

the doctrine of the Trinity; the events in the earthly ministry of Christ; the manifestation of the Holy Spirit; the existence of sin; atonement through Christ's death upon the Cross; the reality of God; the forgiveness of God; the justice of God; the presence of grace; the need of salvation; the assurance of eternal life; the Bible as the Word of God; the frequent use of the Lord's Prayer; the existence of the Christian Church; the basic requirements of worship; the nature of prayer; the scriptural authorization of at least two sacraments; a Christian way of life; a missionary motivation and program.

While Protestantism has kept, as its very own, much of the Christian belief and practice which is the common inheritance of all Christendom, there are certain pronounced disagreements. While attempting to be as factual as possible, we will list some of the chief differences which exist between Roman Catholicism and Protestantism. (Although an attempt has been made in the following listing to be as specific as possible, the reader may want to place "some" before Protestants.)

1. Protestants believe that the Church belongs to all true Christians and is "a community of forgiven sinners"; Roman Catholics believe that the Church belongs only to those who are members of the Roman Catholic Church, either knowingly or unknowingly.

2. Protestants believe that only "Christ is head of the Church which is His Body"; Roman Catholics believe that the pope is head of the visible Church on the earth as the Vicar of Christ.

3. Protestants believe in justification by faith—that salvation comes only by the grace of God; Roman Catholics believe that salvation is secured by faith plus good works—only as channeled through the Roman Catholic Church.

4. Protestants believe that the Protestant Reformation was a return to the creative principles of the New Testament; Roman Catholics think of the Reformation as something forced upon a self-reforming Church and as alien to the true Christian faith.

5. Protestants believe that the democratic inheritance of America was created and nurtured almost exclusively by Protestantism; Roman Catholics claim a large share in the democratic nature of America.

6. Protestants believe that no human being is, or can be, infallible; the Roman Catholic Church teaches that when the pope speaks ex cathedra he is infallible.

7. Protestants believe that Peter was one of Christ's chief apostles; Roman Catholics believe that he is "the Rock" upon which the Church is founded.

8. Protestants believe that the Ten Commandments are the basis for individual and social morality; Roman Catholics add to the Ten Commandments the six Precepts of the Church.

9. Protestants believe in voluntary church attendance; Roman Catholics demand Church attendance.

10. Protestants believe that the financial support of the church and the clergy should be on a purely voluntary basis; Roman Catholics stress the obligation of making financial contributions.

11. Protestants believe that "while there are indications of diversity in worship in the New Testament, nevertheless the preaching of the Word and the administration of Baptism and the Lord's Supper were everywhere marks of the Church's unity," and therefore Protestants have only two sacraments or ordinances, namely, Baptism and the Lord's Supper; Roman Catholics have seven sacraments: Baptism, Confirmation, Holy Eucharist, Penance, Extreme Unction, Holy Orders, and Matrimony.

12. Protestants believe that Baptism is not absolutely essential to salvation; Roman Catholics hold that all who are not baptized will go to hell.

13. Protestants believe that both elements of the Lord's Supper, that is, bread and wine, should be received by the communicant; the Roman Catholic Church reserves the wine exclusively to the clergy.

14. Protestants of various denominations believe that Christ is present at the Lord's Table in spirit, along with the elements; Roman Catholics believe that the bread and wine are actually changed by the miracle of transubstantiation into the *real* flesh and blood of Christ.

15. Protestants believe in the priesthood of all believers and that the clergy, although specifically called and commissioned to special Christian service, is not of different nature than the Christian laity; Roman Catholics make a sharp distinction between clergy and laity.

16. Protestants believe that no one has the right or power to forgive sins save God alone; the Roman Catholic Church teaches that the priest can and does forgive sins.

17. Protestants believe that clergymen have the right to marry; the Roman Catholic Church enforces clerical celibacy.

18. Protestants believe that the Christian life is a "vocation" in the highest sense of that term and that the laity should have a prominent and official part in the life of the Church; Roman Catholics stress the sanctity of the priesthood and place the entire management and control of the Church in the hands of the hierarchy.

19. Protestants believe, for the most part, that all people after death enter either the state of heaven or hell; Roman Catholics also believe in heaven and hell, but add an intermediary stage to heaven known as purgatory.

20. Protestants claim the right to discipline both clergy and laity for infractions of doctrine and practice; the Roman Catholic Church exercises the power of anathema and excommunication.

21. Protestants have no single ecclesiastical body which can adopt doctrines or church practices that are binding on all Protestant churches throughout the world; the Roman Catholic Church either through the pope, or councils called by him, can define dogmas which are absolutely binding upon every Roman Catholic throughout the world.

22. Protestants believe that most of the Bible existed before the organized Church; Roman Catholics believe that the Church is the mother of the Bible.

23. Protestants believe that the Scriptures are all-sufficient for Christian life and practice; the Roman Catholic Church teaches that tradition must be accepted along with the Scriptures as interpreted by the Church.

24. Protestants have a Bible of 66 books; Roman Catholics have a Bible of 72 books.

25. Protestants believe that they have a right to read any version or translation of the Bible; the Roman Catholic Church forbids its members to read any version or translation not specifically authorized by itself.

26. Protestants give the individual the right to interpret the Scripture; the Roman Catholic Church insists upon being the interpreter for the individual.

27. Protestants believe that Mary was the mother of Jesus; Roman Catholics believe that Mary is the "Mother of God."

28. Protestants believe that Jesus had brothers and sisters; the Roman Catholic Church teaches that Mary had no other children save Jesus.

29. Protestants teach in their creeds that Christ was born of the Virgin Mary; Roman Catholics believe not only in the Virgin Birth of Christ, but also in the immaculate conception of Mary.

30. Protestants believe that Mary's body was natural and must wait for the general resurrection of the dead in Christ; the Roman Catholic Church teaches that Mary's physical body has already ascended into heaven.

31. Protestants honor Mary as the mother of Jesus; Roman Catholics venerate Mary and direct their prayers to her.

32. Protestants credit Mary with no miracles; Roman Catholics believe that Mary has performed and does perform miracles.

33. Protestants believe that marriage is a holy institution and a sacred bond; Roman Catholics believe that the marriage of baptized persons constitutes a sacrament of the Church.

34. Protestants warn against the dangers of mixed marriages, but have no specific church laws forbidding the marriage of Protestants to Roman Catholics; the Roman Catholic Church forbids mixed marriages and they are allowed only by special dispensation.

35. Protestants, under certain circumstances, permit divorces; the Roman Catholic Church teaches that a couple united in the sacrament of Matrimony can never, by any human power, be divorced.

36. Protestants have no moral or spiritual laws forbidding the practice of birth control; the Roman Catholic Church forbids the use of any method of artificial birth control.

37. Protestants believe that Christ suffered "uniquely in His once-and-for-all death"; Roman Catholics believe that in the sacrifice of the Mass "Christ through the ministry of the priest, offers Himself to God in an unbloody manner under the appearance of bread and wine."

38. Protestants practice a form of worship which is largely fluid and individual . . . ; in the Roman Catholic Church worship is largely fixed and objective. . . .

39. Protestants are free to worship where they please; Roman Catholics are forbidden to worship in Protestant churches.

40. Protestants, in the main, believe that God will receive to Himself unbaptized babies who die in infancy; the Roman Catholic Church teaches that an infant, dying unbaptized, will never be able to enter heaven.

41. Protestants believe that full forgiveness of sins may be received from God and that it is not necessary for those who are forgiven to pay for sins after death; Roman Catholics believe that some sins cannot be entirely atoned for upon earth and that the granting of indulgences helps to alleviate the unpaid debts of temporal punishment in purgatory.

42. Protestants believe that the Communion of Saints consists of "the fellowship of the whole company of believers on earth and in heaven"; Roman Catholics believe that it is "the union of the faithful on earth, the blessed in heaven, and the souls in purgatory."

43. Protestants believe that good works should result

from the faith of the Christian, but that they are not an essential part of the process of salvation; the Roman Catholic Church teaches that "one can earn the eternal reward of heaven by performing the corporal works of mercy."

44. Protestants believe that it is proper to confess sins to God and to each other, but that only God through Christ has the power to forgive sins; the Roman Catholic Church believes that in the Confessional the priest himself can absolve those who confess their sins.

45. Protestants believe that prayer should be from the heart, directed to God Himself, and thus encourage personal, impromptu prayers; the Roman Catholic Church believes that prayer can be directed through saints and has an elaborate system of formal prayers to be recited.

46. Protestants believe that true worship is of spirit and truth, and is devoid of physical objects having spiritual benefits; Roman Catholics have "sacramentals" such as blessed beads, crucifixes, images, candles, holy water, medals, and scapulars.

47. Protestants, because they believe that "the Church by its very nature is an evangelizing fellowship," have a missionary program which is directed to all those outside the Christian churches, but Roman Catholics are not specifically included; the Roman Catholic Church definitely includes Protestants in its missionary enterprise.

48. Protestants freely permit their children to attend secular public schools; the Roman Catholic Church forbids the attendance of Roman Catholic children at "non-Catholic, neutral or mixed schools," and they can do so only by special ecclesiastical permission.

49. Protestants take the stand, on the basis of the separation of Church and State, that public tax money should not be used to support religious or parochial schools; Roman Catholics encourage the use of public funds for parochial schools on the principle that it is the duty of the State to help support the cause of true religion.

50. Protestants have no legal and binding arrangements with governments; the Roman Catholic Church has an arrangement of treaties or "concordats" with specific governments.

51. Protestants have no independent and sovereign government of their own; Roman Catholics have the Vatican City State of which the pope is the absolute ruler and to which representatives of other governments are accredited.

52. Protestants believe in, and practice, religious freedom for all faiths and for those of no particular faith; the

Roman Catholic Church allows "equality of *civil* rights for all denominations," but it only "tolerates" what it considers to be false religions.

53. Protestants believe the conscience of the individual Christian should be the guide in the reading of books and the viewing of plays, movies, and television; the Roman Catholic Church has a formal system of censorship for all its members.

54. Protestants have a world fellowship through various world alliances and through the World Council of Churches, but they have no central system of government or control; the Roman Catholic Church is organized as a hierarchy, with the pope as its supreme authority.

55. Protestants believe in Christian co-operation and are making progress toward various forms of church unity, although denominational bodies retain autonomy; the Roman Catholic Church believes itself to be "the one true Church," and will consider union only on the basis of a return to its own fold.

In one case the girl was Protestant, and her "boy friend" had intimated that he would expect her to become a Catholic if they married. She could not conceive of doing this, and it was apparent that she knew very little about the Catholic religion. The man was trying to hurry her decision. Her parents were prejudiced against Catholics, although they liked the man personally. Her father had threatened to disown her if she married a Catholic and had refused to attend the wedding.

In the second case a sensible, intelligent girl was trying to think through marriage to a Catholic man with whom she was much in love and whom she held in high esteem, as he seemed to her to be the personification of her ideal. They had frequently discussed religion but always unsatisfactorily. He insisted that she become a Catholic if they married and that all their children be reared in that faith. She had done some reading and considerable thinking about the Catholic point of view, and there were many things that she felt she could not accept. Her personal integrity was too great to permit her to change only her church affiliation and to turn Catholic only externally. She was afraid that if they married and she retained her own faith (provided that she could persuade the man to allow her to do so), her children, being reared as Catholics, might not respect her. She had asked the boy about birth control, but he refused to discuss it and said she would have to trust him. He had also taken a now-or-never attitude with regard to her deciding to marry him and had given her a month in which to make up her mind.

In the third case the girl was a Catholic. In her opinion the man had no idea as to what Catholicism means or involves. He had attended church with her upon occasion and had told her that he would become a Catholic. She was intelligent enough to realize that this was just empty talk on his part, for he continually scorned and disparaged her religion.

In each of these instances the girl was sure of her love for the man and was confident that their marriage would be successful. These are only three cases among many, but they represent a common situation in so far as this writer's observation permits a conclusion. In his experience in student counseling and in dealing with hundreds of students yearly in group discussions of this topic, there have been very few student cases about which he could sincerely feel optimistic as far as the religious mixture was concerned.

In one instance, to illustrate this type of case, the Protestant girl was an unusually intelligent, well-balanced honor student. She was a leader in campus nondenominational religious activities, was very broad-minded, and had a type of religious experience and attitude that transcended outward form. She understood the attitude of the Catholic Church toward interfaith marriage, so she agreed to make the adjustment required of a Protestant. She read about Catholicism, attended the Catholic Church occasionally, and had a number of conferences with the local priest, with whom a sincere friendship developed. In the Catholic religion she found many things that appealed to her, although she was not yet ready to accept it entirely and become a Catholic. She would not object to having her children reared in their father's faith. The man was intelligent about the whole matter and made no arbitrary demands. Instead of hurrying her, he urged her to take her time in reaching a decision and did all that he could to help her to understand his church. He was willing to marry her whether she remained a Protestant or became a Catholic. Both sets of parents were agreeable to the marriage. Her parents liked the man and had no prejudice against his religion. In a case such as this there is still a problem, but it appears that a workable solution is imminent. The couple were making progress in working out their differences before marriage; they were not postponing solutions until after the wedding and substituting wishful thinking for actual agreement.

JEWISH – NON-JEWISH MARRIAGE

Among the problems to be confronted in Jewish – non-Jewish marriage are many of those already met in the Catholic-Protestant type, and we shall not elaborate upon these again. The reader may readily make his own inferences. There is, however, no well-organized, centrally controlled, world-wide church hierarchy to bring pressure to bear upon the individual Jew and to mold his thinking, as there is in the case of a Catholic. This leaves the Jew freer and also permits a wider range of variation among Jews than among Catholics. Officially, the latter tend to be more nearly uniform, and those who do deviate from the commonly accepted tenets of the Church do so without the Church's sanction. With Jews there is a great variety of points of view, each represented in one or more organizations, ranging from the strictly orthodox group, who adhere closely to ancient Hebrew belief and custom, through the conservative, to the most liberal or "reformed" Jews, who dispense with ancient ritual and freely reinterpret the Scriptures. As a group, Jews hold marriage and family life in very high esteem. Their attitude toward contraception is similar to that found among Protestants. Among Jews there is no celibate priest class as there is among Roman Catholics. Rabbis may marry as Protestant clergymen do. Among some Jews, Jewish – non-Jewish marriage is prohibited. Some rabbis will not officiate at a Jewish – non-Jewish wedding but, nevertheless, do recognize the marriage as valid.

Perhaps no group of people is more carelessly lumped together than are Jews in the thinking of the average white, non-Jewish American, unless it be Negroes. To him a Jew is a Jew, and he makes little or no allowance for individual differences. In this attitude of careless indiscrimination our average American is all too prone to let prejudice color his feeling toward the whole people, whereas he does not fall into the same trap and as thoughtlessly generalize where non-Jews are concerned. Furthermore, he is not aware of the social stratification that Jews recognize among themselves, just as all groups do.

Prejudice does form one of the important elements in the background against which Jewish–non-Jewish marriage takes place. This problem is not one-sided, however. Jews are often prejudiced against non-Jews, just as the latter are often prejudiced against the former. Prejudice, no matter who exhibits it, is unfortunate enough. But prejudice on the part of members of the majority group against members of the minority group contains the seeds of greater hurt. Try as he may to prevent it, and sincere as he may be, the non-Jew in a mixed marriage does in some cases find himself subjected to anti-Semitic prejudice because of his Jewish spouse and in other cases is put on the defensive, developing a type of inferiority feeling. It is easy, too, for the non-Jew to attribute to the other's Jewish extraction sources of marital conflict resulting from quite un-Jewish causes. If, in a moment of emotional uncontrol, as in a quarrel, the non-Jew, reflecting the worst sort of public opinion, uses the term *Jew* as if it were an epithet, there may be inflicted a wound hard to heal or there may be created a breach difficult to close.

In Jewish–non-Jewish marriage there is sometimes difficulty in making common friends. In some of the more orthodox Jewish families a non-Jewish child-in-law is not readily accepted. There is, also, the often disheartening problem of rearing children who, because of their mixed ancestry, are subjected to the same prejudice as Jews.

Prejudice and discrimination are painful to Jews. But somehow through the centuries they have learned to live with them and at times even to survive persecution. Hence, when the mixed child of a Jewish–non-Jewish marriage is the victim of prejudice and discrimination, the Jewish parent is not surprised. The non-Jewish parent, on the other hand, never having had to learn to live with this sort of social pressure, is ill-prepared to meet the situation when his child is the target of such hurt. This parent, being a member of the majority group, takes his rights and privileges for granted. Often he assumes that his child will have the same rights and privileges. When the child is classified as a member of a minority group and is treated accordingly, the non-Jewish parent may be at least nonplused and at most may be deeply and perhaps permanently hurt.

OTHER TYPES

A couple need not represent such radically divergent points of view as those discussed above in order to have marital conflict over religion. People seldom have friction over true religion, but they are continually at odds over all sorts of dogmas and practices. Suppose, for example, one spouse believed that Jesus was the product of natural reproductive processes and had a natural biological father, while the other spouse believed that His birth was unique in that He was the child of a virgin. To many persons this is a fundamental theological contention, and it could be the source of endless argument and perennial friction. The theory of evolution has proved its power to generate dissension and ill will. Women's smoking may by devious route be brought under the religio-moral banner and become a thorn in doctrinal flesh. Even the quantity of water necessary to initiate a convert into the company of the elect may be permitted to separate believers who ought to be united in common purpose. Some churches frown on such commonly accepted things as movies, instrumental music, and drinking coffee. In one case, one of the focal points of conflict in the marriage was the wife's interest in roller skating, which the husband's church disapproved. A couple may easily ground their marriage in the shallows of denominational difference.

Persons of different faith have at least a minimum common orientation in that they are both religious and are likely to have some appreciation of the importance of religious values even though they disagree on particular items of belief and practice. But a religious and a nonreligious person do not have even this minimum common orientation. A nonreligious individual, by definition, could hardly be expected to appreciate religious values. Therefore, the marriage of a religious and a nonreligious person may provide fertile soil for conflict. On the other hand, two tolerant individuals who are willing and able to give each other freedom of both thought and action may well work out a faith–no-faith marriage.

Conclusion

As was said at the beginning of this chapter, theoretically any *type* of marriage can be made to succeed if the special problems involved are faced and solved. We have attained some slight insight into the possible magnitude of this *if* and should have reached the conclusion that in real life the problems are more obtrusive than a brief written exposition might seem to indicate. It would be trite to say that the problems of mixed marriage are most readily avoided by avoiding mixed marriage. Yet this is true; and it may be well to impinge this platitude upon the thinking, unmarried, unengaged reader who is still free to make his choices without hurting anyone else or causing himself damage or pangs of conscience. In many cases mixed marriages turn out to be happy and successful. But the reader should be sure that he has taken a careful personal inventory of himself and the other person before he blithely assumes that they will fall into the category of the favored.

Mixed marriage may be approached in one of two ways. Looking at it from the point of view of the sociologist, it is apparent that whenever groups of people are brought into contact over a long period of time there will be intermixture and in many instances intermarriage among them. If they are groups within a highly mobile population, such as that in the United States, this process will be accelerated. But the process itself appears to be inevitable.

On the other hand, mixed marriage may be approached from the point of view of the couple contemplating such marriage within a given social milieu, with its attendant pressures, expectations, customs, attitudes, and prejudices. The couple are concerned about the success or failure of one marriage, not about a sociological process. They feel no obligation to contribute to social change. Therefore, what, on the one hand, the sociologist assumes is inevitable, on the other hand, a given couple may decide is for them unwise.

WHAT DO YOU THINK?

1. Think of an instance of mixed marriage with which you are familiar. What factors, attitudes, behavior, points of view, practices, and persons other than the spouses have contributed to its success or failure, as the case may be?

2. How much difference in values, standards, codes of behavior, and so on, could a couple exhibit and yet work out a successful marriage?

3. In a proposed marriage of two persons of different religious faiths, would you suggest that they give up church entirely, both join a compromise church, one join the church of the other, or each continue to attend his own church? Give reasons for your answer.

4. What part does or can religion play in the success or failure of marriage?

5. With traditional roles of breadwinning for the husband and homemaking for the wife, is the employment of married women creating a new type of mixed marriage?

6. With increasing urbanization in this country, are mixed marriages likely to become more numerous? More widely accepted? Easier to work out?

7. Is television having the effect of making the traditional stereotype of marriage more deeply ingrained in our thinking? Or is it opening a door to the wider acceptance of new types of marriage? The acceptance of mixed marriage? Or does it have no effect on our thinking about marriage?

8. Should all laws prohibiting racial intermarriage be rescinded? If you answer in the affirmative, why? If you answer in the negative, which ones should be retained and why? (See Appendix.)

9. Just as there are laws setting a minimum age at which persons may marry, should there be laws setting the maximum permissible difference in the ages of two persons who want to marry?

10. Since clergymen act as agents of the state in officiating at weddings and are licensed to do so, should they be required to "marry" any couple who request them to do so? If not, how much discretion should they have in refusing to do so, and in what kinds of situations?

SELECTED READINGS

Banahan, John S.: *Instructions for Mixed Marriages*, The Bruce Publishing Company, Milwaukee, 1957. Suggestions by a Catholic priest on how to reduce the chance of failure in Catholic-Protestant marriage. To this end the author's objective is to help Protestants understand the Catholic point of view.

Bernard, Jessie: *Remarriage*, Holt, Rinehart and Winston, Inc., New York, 1956. Motivation for and success in remarriage; courtship in remarriage; remarriages with and without children; families and remarriage.

Blanshard, Paul: *American Freedom and Catholic Power*, Beacon Press, Boston, 1950, chaps. 6–8. Written by a non-Catholic. A critical appraisal of the Catholic position on marriage, divorce, contraception, and related topics.

Bonnar, A.: *The Catholic Doctor*, P. J. Kenedy & Sons, New York, 1952. A discussion of the position of the Catholic Church on sex, birth control, artificial insemination, sterilization, ectopic pregnancy, mercy killing, and similar topics.

Bossard, James H. S., and Eleanor Stoker Boll: *One Marriage, Two*

Faiths, The Ronald Press Company, New York, 1957. A discussion of interfaith marriage.

Bowman, Henry A.: *A Christian Interpretation of Marriage*, The Westminster Press, Philadelphia, 1959, chap. 9. A discussion of interfaith marriage.

Brav, Stanley R. (ed.): *Marriage and the Jewish Tradition*, Philosophical Library, Inc., New York, 1951. A discussion of Jewish values and the meaning of marriage.

Burma, John H.: "Interethnic Marriage in Los Angeles, 1948–1959," *Social Forces*, vol. 42, no. 2, pp. 156–165, December, 1963. A study of 3,200 interethnic marriages. The author found an increase in such marriages during the period mentioned. He also found that the largest number of interethnic marriages were Negro-white.

——: "Research Note on Measurement of Interracial Marriage," *American Journal of Sociology*, vol. 57, no. 6, pp. 587–589, May, 1952. The report of a study of racial intermarriage in Los Angeles after the nullification of its antimiscegenation law.

Cahnman, Werner J. (ed.): *Intermarriage and Jewish Life*, Taplinger Publishing Co., Inc., New York, 1963. A symposium discussing various effects of intermarriage. Most of the contributors are Jewish.

Cavan, Ruth Shonle (ed.): *Marriage and the Family in the Modern World*, Thomas Y. Crowell Company, New York, 1960, chaps. 16, 23. Problems of the children of divorced parents and of stepchildren; attitudes of college students toward interfaith marriage; a suggested solution to the problem of interfaith marriage.

Chancellor, Loren E., and Thomas P. Monahan: "Religious Preference and Interreligious Mixture in Marriages and Divorces in Iowa," *American Journal of Sociology*, vol. 61, no. 3, pp. 233–239, November, 1955. The report of a study of interfaith marriages in Iowa. One of the findings was a higher divorce rate for mixed than for non-mixed marriages.

Cheng, C. K., and Douglas S. Yamomura: "Interracial Marriage and Divorce in Hawaii," *Social Forces*, vol. 36, no. 1, pp. 77–84, October, 1957. Changing patterns and history of racial intermarriage in Hawaii.

Clemens, Alphonse H.: *Design for Successful Marriage*, 2d ed., Prentice-Hall, Inc., Englewood Cliffs, N.J., 1964. Discusses various aspects of dating, sex, marriage, and parenthood. The author is a sociologist and is director of the marriage counseling center at the Catholic University of America.

——: *Marriage and the Family: An Integrated Approach for Catholics*, Prentice-Hall, Inc., Englewood Cliffs, N.J., 1957. The nature and purpose of marriage; marital roles and adjustment; sex before and in marriage; parenthood.

Colacci, Mario: *Christian Marriage Today*, rev. ed., Augsburg Publishing House, Minneapolis, 1959. A comparison of Catholic and Protestant points of view; the nature of marriage; mixed marriage.

Davie, Maurice R.: *Negroes in American Society*, McGraw-Hill Book Company, New York, 1949, chap. 18. Racial intermixture and intermarriage.

Drake, St. Clair, and Horace R. Cayton: *Black Metropolis*, rev. ed., Harper & Row, Publishers, Incorporated, New York, 1945, chap. 7. Racial intermarriage and "passing."

Duvall, Evelyn Millis, and Sylvanus M. Duvall: *Sex Ways in Fact and Faith: Bases for Christian Family Policy*, Association Press, New York, 1961, chaps. 3, 5. What Protestant churches say about family life, contraception, artificial insemination, divorce, remarriage, and related topics. Research findings on mixed marriages.

Emerson, James G., Jr.: *Divorce, the Church and Remarriage*, The Westminster Press, Philadelphia, 1961, chap. 6. The position of various Christian churches on the issue of remarriage after divorce.

Fishbein, Morris, and Ruby Jo Reeves Kennedy (eds.): *Modern Marriage and Family Living*, Oxford University Press, Fair Lawn, N.J., 1957, chaps. 4, 33. Marriages mixed as to religion, race, nationality; remarriage and the problem of stepchild-stepparent.

Ford, John C., and Gerald Kelly: *Contemporary Moral Theology*, vol. 2, The Newman Press, Westminster, Md., 1963. An analysis of Catholic doctrine on a variety of topics relative to sex and marriage, including oral contraceptives.

Genné, Elizabeth, and William Genné: *Christians and the Crisis in Sex Morality*, Association Press, New York, 1962. The views and proceedings of a Protestant church conference on sex, marriage, interfaith marriage, contraception, abortion, sterilization, etc.

Good, Frederick L., and Otis F. Kelly: *Marriage, Morals and Medical Ethics*, P. J. Kenedy & Sons, New York, 1951. The Catholic position on the nature of marriage, sex, control of conception, ectopic pregnancy, etc.

Hallett, Paul H.: *What Is Catholicity?* The World Publishing Company, Cleveland, 1955. An explanation of Catholic faith and doctrine by a convert to Catholicism.

Kane, John J.: *Catholic-Protestant Conflicts in America*, Henry Regnery Company, Chicago, 1955. Written by a Catholic. "Much of this book is an attempt to explore the inside of Catholicism in America, clerical-lay relations, the social structure of American Catholics and such."

——: *Marriage and the Family (A Catholic Approach)*, Holt, Rinehart and Winston, Inc., New York, 1952. Discusses a great variety of topics related to marriage and family living.

Kelly, George A.: *Birth Control and Catholics*, Doubleday & Company,

Inc., Garden City, N.Y., 1963. A discussion of birth control from the Catholic point of view.

Mayer, John E.: *Jewish-Gentile Courtships*, The Free Press of Glencoe, New York, 1961. "Identification of the factors which lead an individual to marry someone he formerly considered ineligible constituted the focus of our study." Each person in this study had met parental opposition before marriage but married the other person anyway. Also the persons themselves had been negatively predisposed to Jewish-Gentile marriage.

Pike, James A.: *If You Marry outside Your Faith*, Harper & Row, Publishers, Incorporated, New York, 1954. The author is an Episcopal bishop. He discusses Catholic-Protestant marriage and also Protestant-Protestant marriage.

Quay, Paul M.: *Contraception and Marital Love* (pamphlet), The Family Life Bureau, National Catholic Welfare Conference, Washington, D.C., 1961. The Catholic point of view on contraception.

Rehwinkel, Alfred Martin: *Planned Parenthood and Birth Control in the Light of Christian Ethics*, Concordia Publishing House, St. Louis, 1959. Written by a professor of church history at a Lutheran theological seminary, "the emphasis in this book is the ethical aspect of Planned Parenthood and Birth Control."

Rock, John: *The Time Has Come*, Alfred A. Knopf, Inc., New York, 1963. The author is a Catholic gynecologist who, through his research on infertility, contributed to the development of oral contraceptives. He makes proposals for ending the Catholic-Protestant controversy over birth control and sees the possibility of reconciling oral contraception with the Catholic point of view.

Rosten, Leo (ed.): *A Guide to the Religions of America*, Simon and Schuster, Inc., New York, 1955. Chapters by different persons on "Why I Am a Baptist," "Why I Am a Catholic" (Christian Scientist, Jew, Presbyterian, etc.). Includes data on church memberships, doctrines, etc.

Sattler, Henry V.: *Two to Get Ready*, The Family Life Bureau, National Catholic Welfare Conference, Washington, D.C., 1963. A series of essays by a Catholic priest on courtship, love, engagement, and adjustment in marriage.

Simpson, George: *People in Families*, Thomas Y. Crowell Company, New York, 1960, chaps. 7, 8. Choosing a marriage partner of different religion or race — some psychological elements involved. Psychoanalytic emphasis.

Simpson, George Eaton, and J. Milton Yinger: *Racial and Cultural Minorities*, rev. ed., Harper & Row, Publishers, Incorporated, New York, 1958, chap. 17. The problems of interracial couples and their children.

Slotkin, J. S.: "Adjustment in Jewish-Gentile Intermarriages," *Social Forces*, vol. 21, no. 2, pp. 226–230, December, 1942. A study of 183 Jewish-Gentile marriages.

Stuber, Stanley I.: *A Primer on Roman Catholicism for Protestants*, Association Press, New York, 1953. An objective, nontechnical explanation of Roman Catholicism to aid Protestants in understanding. Compares the Protestant and Catholic points of view on many topics. Useful for anyone contemplating Catholic-Protestant marriage.

Thomas, John L.: *The American Catholic Family*, Prentice-Hall, Inc., Englewood Cliffs, N.J., 1956. The Catholic family today; the Church and marriage; families in trouble; interfaith marriage; Church doctrine, early and current.

———: *The Catholic Viewpoint on Marriage and the Family*, Hanover House, Doubleday & Company, Inc., Garden City, N.Y., 1958. An explanation of the Catholic position on birth control, interfaith marriage, divorce, and other similar topics.

———: *Marriage and Rhythm*, The Newman Press, Westminster, Md., 1957. A discussion of the Catholic point of view relative to "rhythm," or "safe period." The author is Catholic.

Williams, J. Paul: *What Americans Believe and How They Worship*, Harper & Row, Publishers, Incorporated, New York, 1952. An explanation of the history, doctrines, and organization of major American churches.

chapter 7

MATURITY AND READINESS FOR MARRIAGE

WHAT IS THE BEST AGE for marriage? This question is commonly asked. It is not so simple as it seems, nor is it easily answered. Before attempting any answer at all let us divide *age* into five components or types — chronological, physical, mental, social, and emotional. These are five aspects of maturity.

Common sayings show that in popular thought there are varying concepts of age. They show that chronological age is not always to be taken at its face value. "A man is as old as he feels; a woman is as old as she looks," we say. "A man is as old as his arteries." According to some women, "Men are just grown-up boys." "Act your age," says one student to another whose behavior does not seem coincident with his years. An individual may not be of the same age in all respects.

Physical age

In most persons there is a fairly close correlation between chronological age and physical age. There have been instances in which registering officials or relatives have made errors and the bones have proved more reliable indicators of age than the birth certificate or the record in the family Bible.

An individual develops according to a growth pattern, the regulators of which are, in a sense, present at birth, though the regulators at each stage affect those of the next stage in a sort of chain reaction. In some respects, growth patterns for all individuals, except extreme variants, are similar, so that an approximation of a person's relative maturity may be made by comparing him with others. In other respects, each individual's growth pattern is unique. It unfolds, so to speak, at its own rate [Aldrich and Aldrich, 1954; Stone and Church, 1957]. Parents not aware of this often make hairsplitting comparisons between their own and other people's children, growing anxious because their child does not walk at, say, fifteen months, when the child of friends walked at one year; showing unfounded pride when their child uttered his first word a few weeks earlier than a relative; or worrying because their child does not do all the things that some book mentions as typical of the average child of his age. Comparing an individual to an average is meaningless unless the fact is taken into account that an average, by definition, represents a range of variation.

PUBERTY

At puberty a child's sex organs, which have remained more or less dormant, begin to develop and to function in more nearly adult fashion. Simultaneously, secondary changes take place.

A boy's voice changes. His muscles increase in size. His shoulders broaden. Pubic hair appears. What was previously only an unimpressive fuzz becomes a shaveable beard.

In a girl, the breasts develop. Owing to fat deposits, what were angularities become more aesthetic lines. Pubic hair appears. The pelvis broadens, and the girl is prepared for childbearing. But, although there are instances of extremely early motherhood, there is evidence to suggest that in most cases a girl does not immediately become fertile when she reaches the *menarche*, that is, when she begins to menstruate [Montagu, 1946]. Some investigators, however, question this and believe that in many girls fertility is established just prior to the first menstrual period [Greenhill, 1960].

In addition to adjusting to the physical changes that occur at puberty, the child must adjust to emotional changes and learn to live with the new attitudes and new subjective experiences that spring up within him. Also, since girls reach puberty earlier than boys, there is a period in which many girls are both more mature and taller than boys of the same chronological age. The situation creates problems for both sexes. It is at this period that some girls begin to lean in the direction of older boys.

In both sexes the production of germ cells begins (sperm in the male, ova in the female). In the boy there is the secretion of seminal fluid which is stored in the seminal vesicles (see Chapter 15) and constitutes an internal stimulus or readiness to respond to sexual stimulation. Puberty is announced in part by the discharge of this fluid during sleep. These nocturnal emissions, or "wet dreams," are a normal occurrence in the male. Typically they are marked by pleasurable sensations and are accompanied by sexually colored dreams. In the girl puberty is marked in part by the first menstruation.

In the matter of puberty, too, there may be a disparity between chronological and physical age. Most children reach puberty at about the twelfth to fourteenth year, but in exceptional instances girls have menstruated much earlier. Some girls do not begin to menstruate until their late teens or early twenties. A few never do, and their condition is termed *amenorrhea*.

A person's sexual development may stop at an early level, so that he goes on getting older but some of his physical traits remain those of a younger person. The primary sex organs may remain in an immature state, producing a condition termed *infantilism*; the person may be an adult by the calendar, by his appearance, stature, and musculature, but a child by his sexual anatomy and function.

At puberty the sexes meet a fork in the road of development that is the point of departure for some of the later differences in attitude toward, and behavior regarding, sex. The changes which occur at this time further sharpen the differentiation between the sexes, lead to increased intersexual attraction, and establish more firmly the individual's identification with his own sex. To some degree these processes are already under way before puberty is reached, not only through anatomy but also through names, clothes, social groups, and differential treatment and expectations. Generalizing and recognizing the fact of variation in both groups, the sexes may be described as follows. Whether these differences are culturally or biologically determined is not our immediate problem.

MALE	FEMALE
1. Considerable interest in sex.	1. Less interest in sex.
2. Much discussion of sexual activities.	2. Less discussion of sexual activities.
3. Sexual sensitivity and response spontaneous.	3. Sexual sensitivity and response less spontaneous.
a. Little or no learning needed for response.	*a*. More learning needed for response.
b. Accumulation of seminal fluid constitutes internal stimulus.	*b*. Nothing equivalent to accumulation of seminal fluid.
c. Tend to cluster around mean; less variation; relatively few unawakened or unresponsive.	*c*. Wider range of variation; many unawakened or unresponsive; some more responsive than males.
4. Pleasurable sexual experience.	4. Pleasurable sexual experience.
a. Frequent.	*a*. Less frequent.

MALE	FEMALE
b. Tends to be "continuous"; regularly repeated.	b. Tends to be "discontinuous"; often long periods between instances of sexual activity.
c. Typically starts early in life.	c. In some cases, starts late in life.
d. Extends through greater part of life.	d. Often experienced during brief part of life; sometimes only once.
e. Practically all have some such experience at some time.	e. Some never have such experience during entire life.
f. Reaches peak of frequency and physical responsiveness in teens.	f. May not reach peak comparable to male until several years after wedding.
g. Experiences orgasm plus ejaculation.	g. Experiences orgasm; nothing equivalent to ejaculation.
h. Lesser orgasm capacity; can achieve orgasm and ejaculation less frequently in limited time span.	h. Greater orgasm capacity if responsive; can reach orgasm more frequently in limited time span.
5. Nocturnal emissions practically universal; pleasurable, frequent.	5. Nothing equivalent to nocturnal emissions.
6. Masturbation practically universal, especially among younger males.	6. Masturbation at some time by perhaps two-thirds, often extending through brief part of life.
7. Premarital sexual intercourse.	7. Premarital sexual intercourse.
a. More males engage in.	a. Fewer females engage in.
b. More frequent by those who engage in.	b. Less frequent by those who engage in.
c. Usually pleasurable.	c. Often not pleasurable, disappointing, painful.
d. More males initiate.	d. Fewer females initiate.
8. Active imagination relative to sex.	8. Less active imagination.
a. Nocturnal sexually colored dreams common; often accompanied by orgasm and ejaculation.	a. Nocturnal sexually colored dreams uncommon; sometimes accompanied by orgasm.
b. Sexually colored daytime fantasies more common.	b. Sexually colored daytime fantasies less common.

MALE	FEMALE

c. Romantically colored daytime fantasies common.

9. Much interest in tactile sensations.

   a. Readily responds to being touched by opposite sex.

   b. Seeks to touch opposite sex; interested in "exploring" female body.

   c. Because of interest and experience, more inclined to think of reproductive organs as "sexual" organs.

10. Much interest in visual experience.

    a. Interested in seeing female body.

    b. Interested in seeing pictures of female body; may have pictures of identified, conventionally clothed females, but also interested in pictures of unidentifiable, nonconventionally clothed or unclothed females.

11. Is reared with less emphasis upon modesty.

12. Nothing equivalent to menstruation.

13. More readily separates sex and romantic love.

---

c. Romantically colored daytime fantasies common.

9. Less interest in tactile sensations.

   a. Some response to being touched by opposite sex.

   b. Sometimes seeks to touch opposite sex, but ordinarily not interested in "exploring" male body.

   c. Because of less interest and experience, more inclined to think of reproductive organs as merely genital organs.

10. Little interest in visual experience; usually no interest.

    a. Little or no interest in seeing male body.

    b. Little or no interest in seeing pictures of male body; may have pictures of identified, conventionally clothed males, but usually sees no point in having pictures of unidentifiable, nonconventionally clothed or unclothed males. Likely to be aware of male's interest but not likely to understand why he has this interest.

11. Is reared with considerably more emphasis upon modesty. Modesty is a matter of convention, not a simple matter of yardage.

12. Menstruation: never pleasurable, always inconvenient, sometimes painful.

13. More inclined to combine sex and romantic love.

As a result of these differences between the sexes, which are in part an outgrowth of changes that begin or are accentuated during puberty, at the time of the wedding a couple may represent significant contrasts in their experiences up to date and their approaches to the sexual aspect of marriage. Their problem is not one of determining the statistical probability of the other person's exhibiting certain traits or reflecting certain experiences. Their problem is recognizing the possibility of such, thus opening the way to greater understanding. For example, assuming that the wedding occurs some years after puberty, the bridegroom, through one or more forms of sexual release (nocturnal emissions, masturbation, and in some cases premarital sexual intercourse), may have had hundreds of separate instances of pleasurable sexual experience, and perhaps more than a thousand. The bride, on the other hand, may approach her wedding without ever having had even one such instance. The question is not, "How many brides and bridegrooms are like this?" The question is, "What is the condition of this particular couple?" If neither individual is aware of the typical difference between the sexes relative to interest in visual experience, tactile sensations, or modesty, unintentional offense may be committed. [See Kinsey and Associates, 1948, 1953.]

MENTAL AGE

An individual's mental age depends on both his equipment and his achievement. By studying the behavior of large groups it is possible to establish norms for various age levels. Then an individual may be compared to the norm and his relative advancement or retardation determined. The extreme of retardation is found in a person who, although of adult years chronologically, has the mental equipment and achievement of a young child. From idiocy up to and beyond normal development an individual's mental age may not coincide with his chronological or physical age.

Mature behavior

An individual reacts as a whole rather than as an agglomeration of disconnected parts. It is difficult, therefore, to draw fine lines of distinction between mental, social, and emotional age when they are considered in their broader aspects. Criteria for determining these types of age overlap. Hence, we shall discuss them under the general heading of mature behavior.

There are patterns of behavior that may be thought of as mature and others that may be thought of as immature. In characterizing a given individual no single criterion is sufficient. His relative maturity depends upon a number of factors. An individual may exhibit both mature and immature behavior.

DEVELOPMENT OF THE INDIVIDUAL

In his development an individual does not pass from one stage to another, as if the stages were a flight of stairs, each previous one being left entirely behind as each new one is mounted. His development is more nearly like a series of concentric circles. As he passes from each smaller circle to the larger one that encompasses it, some of the elements represented by the smaller one remain to compose part of the larger area.

This process is clearly shown in the development of an individual's love interest. A newborn infant is a completely selfish, self-centered, unsocialized organism. His only "love" is for himself. There are no restrictions on his behavior except those imposed by biological inadequacy. The first person other than himself who enters his world is his mother. She becomes his second love. Next he discovers his father, then other relatives and friends. As he grows older he takes an increasing interest in his contemporaries, at first with no discrimination as to sex, though he may be vaguely aware that boys and girls are not the same. As his awareness of sex differences grows he leans more strongly toward segregated groups. Gradually an interest in the opposite sex takes precedence over that in the child's own sex, and, instead of shunning members of the opposite sex, the child begins to approach them. At first almost any passably attractive individual who represents the opposite sex will do; it is "boyness-girlness" which interests him. He falls in and out of "love" with amazing rapidity. Little by little his interest narrows to a smaller and smaller number of persons. He becomes increasingly selective in his dating—that is quite different from going steady prematurely, for the individual who goes steady prematurely is unselective. His dating activities more and more reflect his ultimate goal, marriage, less and less a desire for immediate pleasure as an end in itself. Finally he falls in love with one person whom he marries. When his children come, his love extends to them too.

We may readily see how each of these stages in the development of love interest includes some of the elements of previous stages. The boy who is loyal to members of his peer group still loves his mother; so does the student who has fallen in love with a girl he may marry. The woman who loves her husband may still have deep affection for her women friends. A man loves his children at the same time that he loves his wife and parents.

Comparing development to a series of concentric circles makes it appear simpler than it actually is, for not only do some traits remain in the course of normal development but others are outgrown, and the growth of some takes place unevenly. It may cease for a given trait while it continues for another. Some traits may persist in immature form into adult life. Under such circumstances there is said to be a *fixation;* that is, the person's growth with regard to a particular trait has become fixated, or stopped, at an immature level. For example, an individual may have a mother fixation because his love for his mother, instead of being of a mature type, has failed to develop beyond the infantile stage, and the person has never gone on to fall in love with another individual of his own age but of opposite sex.

An individual may also be immature because of *retardation*. Some aspect of his development, though not fixated, may be slower than other aspects and therefore may lag behind. For example, he may not be the victim of a parent fixation, but because of his family situation he may be slow in becoming independent, and this aspect of his development does not catch up with other aspects and with his calendar age until he leaves home and goes to college.

Personality is composed of numerous traits. The integration among them, as well as the degree of development exhibited by particular traits, forms a measure of maturity. Most persons are more mature in some respects, less mature in others. A personality in which a particular trait has remained at the infantile level as others have become mature is almost certain to be poorly integrated; one cannot be an adult and a child at the same time.

Adulthood is a social status; maturity is a level of development. Society is organized for both adults and children. It sets up a standard of behavior for those who have adult status and assumes that there will be a correlation between adulthood and maturity. A person who meets adult situations with attitudes and habits that were formed in childhood and failed to mature as the years passed is a child in adult guise. There is certain to be a conflict between what society expects of him and what he is able to achieve. An individual cannot become mature merely by engaging in the activities of older, more nearly adult persons. For example, the fact that getting married, going steady, beginning to date, and similar activities are moving downward in the age scale does not necessarily mean that young people are thereby becoming more mature; they may only handle these activities immaturely.

An individual may also be immature because of *regression*; that is, he may go on to a more mature level; then, finding adjustment difficult, unpleasant, or impossible, he may return to a more immature level. He becomes a backslider.

Perhaps the best-known case of regression — a case more serious than the numerous jokes about it might lead one to suppose — is that of the bride who "goes home to mother." The young woman marries with great expectations. She finds that adjustment in marriage is more difficult than she had anticipated, and she cannot carry it through. So she leaves her husband and returns to her mother. She has tried adjustment on a more mature level and failed. Instead of working it out on that level, she takes a step backward emotionally and returns to her mother, because with the latter she finds security, affection, and the solution of problems.

Another common case of regression is that of the homesick student who leaves school. He tries adjustment on a more mature level but cannot succeed. So he goes back home, where familiar circumstances, proximity to parents and friends, and a situation that his habit patterns fit make adjustment easier.

One may observe numerous instances of temporary regression that are quite harmless; in fact, they are sometimes beneficial. Consider the middle-aged alumnus who returns to his alma mater for the twenty-fifth reunion of his class. It happens to be the week end of the homecoming football game. As soon as he reaches the campus he sheds the cloak of reserve and poise that characterizes him as the stern business executive or the dignified professional man and becomes collegiate with a vengeance. He feels an obligation to cheer most loudly at the game. He may saturate himself with alcohol. He stays up all night "with the boys." On Monday he returns to his office, his temporary regression over, tired perhaps but none the worse for wear and possibly even benefited by his emotional release.

Criteria of mature and symptoms of immature behavior

Maturity is relative, and there is no quick and easy way of determining whether an individual is mature or immature. However, certain traits or the lack of them may be used as criteria. It is important to understand that many of these traits may be indications of immaturity in one individual, but in another they may be the result of some other cause. They are symptoms. One might compare them to fever. Fever also is a symptom; it may be caused by measles, diphtheria, influenza, the common cold, or any of a number of diseases. When a physician is diagnosing a patient's ills, he takes into account all symptoms. He does not base his judgment on one alone; and in so far as possible, he studies the patient's history.

In making marriage successful there is probably no single factor more important than maturity. There are thousands of child brides in this country, that is, brides who are chronologically children. There are many more thousands of child brides and child bridegrooms, if they are judged by their behavior. They do not make sensational newspaper copy, but their marriages are almost sure to suffer because of their immaturity.

If an individual is immature in one or several respects, he might be expected to react in immature fashion to some of the situations in marriage. Since marriage is for adults rather than children, such a person makes difficult the realization of the full possibilities of marriage or makes necessary an undue amount of adjustment on the part of his spouse. If the adjustment cannot be made and if the other person persists in his immaturity, the marriage may fail.

SOME CRITERIA OF MATURE BEHAVIOR

The question, "When should one marry?" cannot be answered only in terms of chronological age; emotional age is an equally important factor. The emotional maturity of the person will largely determine the wisdom with which he selects a marriage partner and the success of his subsequent marriage relationship. The mature person:

does not blame his failures on others, but takes full responsibility for his own mistakes and profits from them . . .

can look at himself with honesty and some objectivity . . .

is interested in other people and gets along well with them . . .

neither overemphasizes nor negates sex, but regards it as a natural, satisfying aspect of life . . .

accepts his chronological age and the responsibilities it entails . . .

is at ease with members of both sexes . . .

Let us list and discuss, then, some of the criteria of maturity and some of the symptoms of immaturity. We shall permit some overlapping in order to make various emphases. In judging maturity and immaturity we must base our conclusion on the traits that typify an individual's personality and beware of being misled by behavior exhibited very rarely or only once.

A MATURE PERSON HAS INTELLIGENCE COMPARABLE TO HIS CALENDAR AGE AND USES THIS INTELLIGENCE ON A MATURE LEVEL IN DAILY LIFE

He develops a reasonably objective point of view toward both himself and things and persons other than himself, determining a considerable part of his behavior on this objective basis. The person who goes through life with blinders on, who cannot see himself even in part as others see him, who is not aware of his own limitations, whose behavior

functions effectively within the framework of society's codes . . .

is founded too largely on emotions, prejudices, and his own imagination, is immature. The mature person has perspective. The immature person is inclined to assume that his own experience and observation encompass the world and therefore form an adequate basis for broad generalizations.

He profits by his own experience and the experience of others. So does a child. But if a person reaches a plateau in his mental development so that he fails to go on to further utilization of his possibilities, he may be considered immature.

He integrates what he knows and lives by that integrated knowledge. An individual whose "mind" contains "watertight compartments" holding inconsistent contents, with no seepage from one compartment to another, is living among the paradoxes of a child's world, in which im-

*accepts the present as given
and works from the motivation
of his own convictions
toward the future.*

possible incongruities continually occur but are accepted without question. The man who does not see, for example, that democracy and class discrimination are incompatible is little different from the child who believes that Santa Claus with his abdominal rotundity comes down the chimney.

He sees various sides of a problem, studies it carefully, seeks a thorough solution. The immature person resorts to ready-made cliché solutions. These are applied with confidence because they rest on the assumption that all problems are soluble and fall into simple categories and that a simple and ready-made solution may be drawn from the correct pigeonhole. The mature person learns to live with problems that he recognizes as insoluble.

    This same evidence of immaturity is found in persons who accept a life philosophy ready-made from other persons without thinking through to one of their own. Those who do this have no true philosophy at all because they merely repeat words without assimilating ideas. This is often the case of a student who labels himself something extreme, mouthing the utterances of others but failing fully to understand their points of view.

The immature person is highly suggestible and easily influenced by others. He is especially liable to the influence of one around whom there is cast an aura of hero worship and is inclined to be uncritical as to the effect of such influence upon him. The mature person is open to suggestion, but he accepts it critically and does not put it into effect without examination. The influence of others bears upon him, but he does not become an always-empty vessel ready to have suggestion poured into him. His behavior is an outgrowth of his own personality rather than the reflection of some other.

A MATURE PERSON SEES HIMSELF AS PART OF A LARGER WHOLE

He has an appreciation of man's relation to the universe and has worked out a philosophy of life which includes things cosmic and eternal as well as things earthly, temporary, and immediate. In working out such a philosophy he relinquishes childish concepts and infantile symbols and in place of them substitutes others, arising from his expanding knowledge of the world and his deepening insight into life. He has no fear that science will destroy his philosophy or undermine his faith, for he realizes that the more man knows, the broader his horizon becomes.

He has some knowledge of social life, how it is organized, and what the requirements are for living in a society. He seeks his own advancement through cooperation with and service to other members of the group, but the group is not a gang. The immature person does not know what is expected of him socially. He seeks his own ends through the self-centered insistence of the infant, who expects others to contribute toward his satisfactions but does not consciously give anything in return. The mature person takes social responsibility. The immature person tends to let others worry about the community and, even when there is opportunity for assuming responsibility, he, childlike, lets others do it. He expects to receive the benefits of group living without making a contribution to group living.

A student group entails some aspects of social living, and students show their relative maturity by the degree to which they voluntarily assume responsibility for the welfare of the group and the maintenance of its buildings and grounds. The student who litters the campus with wastepaper, who throws cigarette butts on the floor, or who writes on walls or carelessly damages furniture exhibits immature behavior. He is like the infant, who depends upon someone else to change his clothing and pick up his toys and whose interest span is limited to the satisfaction of his own wants.

A mature person also takes responsibility for his own welfare. He does not expect others to make decisions for him. He is willing to work for what he wants. He takes care of his own possessions. He exercises whatever caution is necessary for personal safety. The immature person frequently says, "Tell me what to do." He lets others do his work for him; for example, he plays while others study and, at the last minute before an examination, hastily crams from borrowed notes. He drives without regard for others or for ordinary rules of safety, assuming that others will protect him. The immature person's approach to life is "You take care of me."

He understands the finesse of social relations. He knows the details of etiquette which make social life more agreeable to the greater number. The person who is constantly offending others by his lack of tact, his poor manners, or his uncouth behavior is like a child who thinks only of his own satisfaction without regard to other persons and who is too young to have had his natural responses polished into social niceties.

He makes concessions to others, but he does not become too dependent upon them. A mature person lives partly by intelligent compromise but maintains his own individuality and integrity. There are, of course, some things on which an individual cannot compromise without sacrificing integrity, ideals, values, or principles. Refusal to make such a sacrifice is not an indication of immaturity. When, however, the refusal to compromise takes the form of obstinate failure ever to meet other persons halfway, it indicates immaturity.

He has a reasonable respect for authority and tradition. In his development, an individual passes through a stage in which he is inclined to revolt against authority and tradition. It should be a temporary, transitional stage. Eventually, if he is to become mature, the individual must learn to compromise between obedience and independence, between conformity and progress.

In order to make it as agreeable and as smooth as possible for the great majority, life in a group must be defined and to some extent limited by standards of behavior. Society at large has laws. Student groups have rules. The mature individual finds true freedom through obedience and self-discipline. By conforming in certain required matters he is free to do as he wishes in others not limited by regulation. The immature person seeks freedom through disobedience, only to find that eventually his disobedience brings upon him the pressure of the group and limits his freedom more than it would have been limited by the original regulations.

A MATURE PERSON LIVES IN A WORLD OF REALITY

In so far as he is able to discover reality he faces it. He distinguishes between the real and the unreal; and, though he is interested in the products of creative imagination, he does not confuse them with actuality. The mature person faces reality when he is confronted with a problem. He accepts it without unreal components, and the solution constitutes a direct attack. The immature person is inclined to embellish his problems with imaginary elements and to seem to solve them by retreating from the world of reality to a world of his own making. The former adjusts himself to the world; the latter adjusts the "world" to himself.

A common example of this tendency to escape reality is one type of daydream. There are two types of daydream: (1) the type in which the individual sets goals for himself, but the goals are possible of achievement, and in his dreams he makes plans and orients himself toward those goals — for example, plans for occupational achievement or the building of a home; (2) the type in which the individual sets goals impossible or at least improbable of achievement, or in which the individual confuses the contents of his daydream with reality and acts as if the wish had already become fact. The second type is escape from reality.

Another retreat from reality is found in the exaggeration of symptoms of illness or in the creation of them. An athlete who limps off the field after making a poor play, pretending that an injury impaired the exercise of his skill, evades reality. The following is a more serious case. A boy in high school found himself ready to go to class without having prepared an important assignment. As he was hanging up his wraps in his home room, he inadvertently bumped his head slightly on one of the clothes hooks. That gave him an idea. He hurried to his seat and smeared ink on the "wound." Then he reported to the school nurse and said that the injury had left him with a headache. She gave him a class excuse and he went home. He knew that his mother would detect his trick, so he sneaked into the house and actually bumped his head against the wall until it was black and blue and there was a noticeable swelling. He stayed home from school for the remainder of the day and had time to complete his assignment.

In college he was confused and discouraged by a love affair that was not progressing as he hoped it would. He could see no ready solution for his problem, so he shot himself. Fortunately his life was saved. Again he had tried to solve his problem by escaping from reality. He was no more mature when he pulled the trigger than when he found a loophole of escape in the bump on his head.

There are innumerable others who, like this boy, exaggerate actual physical symptoms or exhibit physical symptoms that have an emotional cause, that is, psychosomatic symptoms. Some of these are classed as "neurotic"; all are in a sense immature.

Another type of escape from reality is intoxication. Some persons drink because alcohol makes them less inhibited and more sociable. They are dissatisfied with reality, dissatisfied with their own personalities. Instead of developing new and more desirable traits, they resort to alcoholic escape and to the creation of an unreal "world," in which they seem different from what they really are.

The mature person realizes that change is part of the world of reality. He adapts himself to change and expects it. The person who will not accept the fact of change is one who would, if he could, hold the world back so that it might remain permanently on the level at which he feels most comfortable. This means that he refuses to go beyond a level that represents something short of his possibilities.

He lives in a world in which past, present, and future are balanced and integrated. The infant lives in the present. Although past experiences influence him, he is not aware of the past and certainly is not aware of the fact that the experience of the human race extends back further than his birthday. He cannot know that there is a future because the concept of a future and to a considerable extent the concept of the past depend upon language. The person who attempts to escape reality tends to live in the past or the future instead of the present. The mature person lives in the present as well as the past and the future.

He faces an unalterable situation in which he has a deep interest with poise and a minimum of conflict. He accepts the inevitables in life without a feeling of defeat. There are, of course, many unalterables and inevitables to which he is indifferent because they do not affect him. An individual who struggles against a fate over which he has no control is like a child whose kicks and screams do not prevent his mother from dragging him across the room.

Everyone must face the prospect of his own death. He need not assume, as the fatalist does, that the date and manner are prearranged and that nothing can alter them. But he must face the fact that man is mortal and that life at best is short. He may enjoy life to the full and wish it could be interminable. Nevertheless, when death comes, he is ready because he has developed a philosophy of life that includes his own decease and that of his loved ones. He has accepted an unalterable fact, an inevitable situation, with a minimum of conflict and defeat.

A failure or a disappointment once passed becomes an unalterable situation. One cannot go back and relive what has become part of history, though it may be possible approximately to duplicate a previous situation and direct it toward a new outcome. The immature person often stops with his failure. He goes through life explaining and excusing himself. He is knocked down and lies there. The mature person is knocked down and bounces as high as he fell. He rises above failure. He builds on the shoulders of failure.

He depends upon adult accomplishments for prestige.   The businessman who can neither forget nor let others forget that he was a star fullback in college, the professional man who too conspicuously displays the emblem of a college honorary fraternity, the college student who continually reminds friends that he was elected to the honor society in high school, these and others like them graduated academically but never graduated emotionally. Excellence in any field of endeavor is not to be depreciated, and recognition for such excellence and insignia to symbolize it are not without their place; but as one grows older, he has to prove himself over and again. To rest on his oars is an indication that development has been blocked. It is not the recalling of early achievements but rather the depending upon them for prestige in adult life that indicates immaturity.

He uses the present rather than the past as a point of departure.   An inclination similar to the one mentioned immediately above, but not identical with it, is noticeable in a person who uses some earlier period of life as the point of departure for all comparisons and all judgments of things present. The past becomes a point of reference that does not change as time goes on. People are friendly or unfriendly, morals are loose or strict, homes are beautiful or ugly, it is good to do this or not good to do that, all as compared to the life and affairs of the earlier period. In his way, anyone who takes this point of view is a sort of missionary, dwelling in a strange land, resisting the cultural influence of the group in which he resides, willing to change them to his way of life if possible, harking back to his native land for his standards, leaving his loyalties and fidelities at home while he goes forth among the heathen, whose customs because they are different he considers inferior.

He accepts his chronological age for what it is.   He may not wish to grow old, and his behavior and attitudes may be more youthful than his years. However, that person is immature who will not admit his chronological age even to himself, who without acceptable reason tries to deceive others because he strives to hold onto his youth.

THE MATURE PERSON IS INDEPENDENT
He can fulfill his economic role in life.   If the individual is a man, he can support himself, his wife, and his family. If the individual is a sin-

gle woman, she can support herself. If she is a married woman, she can adequately fulfill her economic responsibility as homemaker. The person who cannot or will not carry his share of the economic load is immature. This does not include those who through illness, accident, or other factors beyond their control are prevented from assuming the role they are willing to assume.

The person who expects something for nothing, who depends upon luck rather than effort, or who thinks that the world owes him a living is immature. He is like the child who takes for granted his parents' care and believes that in some way, without effort or explanation, the things he wants will be given to him.

He is relatively independent of his parents. With the great increase in college enrollments in recent years, the tendency to extend formal education through a longer period, and the fact that as enrollments have increased, student populations have become cross-section groups rather than highly selected groups of the elite, a new situation has been created. For some of the problems arising out of this new situation neither students nor their parents are very well prepared. One of these problems arises from the fact that many students are at least partially dependent upon their parents financially at a period in their development when they have a strong desire to be independent socially and emotionally and when they would probably be "on their own" were they not in school. Because of the child's financial dependence, parents often feel that they have a right to continue to control the child's behavior. Because of the child's growing emotional independence, he tends to resist such control. Both young person and parents are caught in a sort of "lame-duck session" of parent-child relationships. The conflicts arising from the "lame-duck session" are often difficult to handle. The student caught in the crosscurrents of such conflict might well give the following serious consideration:

1. Will you ever again live at home with your parents permanently? Or will you live at home only on a temporary basis, for example, during vacations? If the latter is true, it would seem unwise to approach every problem as if you were going to live at home for the rest of your life. You can afford to make concessions in the interest of family harmony. Although your situation is not exactly like that of a week-end guest in someone's home, there are similarities. If you went home with a friend for a week end and when you arrived you found that there were differences of opinion between you and your friend's parents, you would not spoil the week end by argument and conflict. You would make concessions in the interest of harmony.

2. As an individual grows more mature, his relationship to his parents becomes more nearly like that of friend to friend and less like that

of child to adult. Most persons realize that they do not always have to agree with their friends in order to get along with them. They work out ways of enjoying friendships in spite of differences of opinion or of behavior.

3. Parents are sometimes right in their judgments and children wrong. No matter how poor their judgment, no matter how great their mistakes, almost all parents have good motives when their children are involved. What parents do, whether it be wise or unwise, they do for the sake of the child's welfare as they see it. It is a rare parent, indeed, who deliberately plans to hurt his child. When we judge people by their motives, as well as by their action, we often find it easier to accept their action.

4. Whatever can be done within reasonable limits to preserve parents' good will is a worth-while investment. Such good will is a fine asset in establishing a new marriage.

5. Conflict is more readily handled when there is a distinction made between more important issues and less important issues. For example, many a family has conflict over an engagement ring or a wedding date, though these are relatively unimportant issues as compared to parental approval of choice of marriage partner or parental acceptance of intent to marry.

6. Some families establish an over-all pattern of perpetual conflict. Then everything that happens is out of perspective, and every difference, no matter how great or how small, is equally effective in setting the whole pattern in motion. The continuance of such an over-all pattern of conflict is often an indication that both parents and child have failed to mature.

7. If there is change called for in order to resolve a conflict between parents and child, it is more likely that the child will have to change than that the parents will change. This may seem to the reader like an unfair statement because he so strongly desires his parents to agree with him. It is not meant to be unfair. It is merely realistic. By change, however, we do not necessarily imply that the student will agree with his parents. We imply only that in some way he must either rise above, or immunize himself against, the conflict. The reader may not be able to change his judgments, behavior, or plans. But perhaps he can change his attitudes toward his parents.

8. If the conflict has taken the form of open rebellion of student against parents, the student should try to understand something which at first may seem incongruous to him. His tendency is to resist his parents, to fight against them, to try to win out over them and try to prevent them from winning out over him. He must see that the only way he can win is to stop fighting. So long as he continues to fight, his parents are keeping him in an immature pattern of rebellion. No matter what else the student may think he is gaining, so long as they keep him in that pat-

tern of rebellion, the parents are winning out. In a very important way they control the situation. They control the student's behavior. As soon as he rises above immature rebellion and stops fighting his parents, the student begins to control his own behavior and, therefore, is moving in the direction of a true solution to the problem. Furthermore, the more the student rebels, the more he proves to his parents that his judgments are too immature to be given serious consideration – an assumption that they had made in the first place and that was one of the sources of the conflict.

Overattachment to or overdependence upon one's parents is an indication of immaturity, especially when it extends beyond the age at which an individual might normally be expected to be relatively independent emotionally. Eventually, every person should be able to "sail under his own steam"; he should be relatively independent of his family. Each individual, if he is to become mature, must be emotionally as well as dietetically weaned. Either type of weaning makes mother and child less important one to the other. Many students are content to snuggle in their parents' emotional arms, so to speak, being "mother's little girl" or "mother's little boy," as the case may be. The remedy, however, is not a sudden, cruel, superficial assertion of independence but rather a gradual, step-by-step, well-founded development.

It requires nine months of continuous development and some maternal inconvenience to produce a new individual, and his birth is a painful process for the mother. It is also a trying experience for the baby. Although he apparently feels no pain, his life hangs in the balance until he is safely launched on his semi-independent existence. Once the process has started, there is no safe retreat for either mother or child.

In a sense, each individual is born not once but twice. The first time, he is born an infant. His physical attachment to his mother is severed, and he leaves the protection of her body to struggle for existence in the outside world. The second time, he is born an adult, a mature person who has broken from his infantile emotional attachment to his mother and launched into the independent existence of adulthood. This process too involves a long period of development, and the new birth is not without pain, trial, and sacrifice for mother as well as child. But if the mother has a mature attitude, this second birth will be a source of satisfaction rather than of pain. Here again there is no safe retreat for either without endangering the emotional life of one or both.

Parent fixation may be manifested in numerous ways. Sometimes it takes the form of an unusual feeling of responsibility for the parents' welfare. At other times it is manifested in a child's tendency to blame himself for his parents' failures. Overattachment to parents may be a cause for homesickness not only among college students but also among brides and bridegrooms. Parent attachment also plays a part in marriage adjustment in the matter of the wife's or husband's assigning relative values to parents, children, and spouse. A person with a parent fixation will be in perpetual conflict, torn between loyalties. The child in him and the adult in him will be perennially at odds.

Students often ask what an individual may do if he is in love with a person who is overattached to parents or vice versa. Such a student must realize first of all that there is no simple thing to be done to remedy the situation and that he himself is probably in the least advantageous position to do anything. He may, however, understand the other person, and that is part of the solution. There are several considerations to which he may give serious attention in deciding whether or not marriage would be advisable.

How old is the parent who is overattached to the child?

Where will the young couple live with relation to the parents of the spouse with the fixation?

Does the parent use subtle means to hold the child?

Is it a case of parent being overattached to child, child being overattached to parent, or of mutual overattachment? With regard to the reader's marrying the person in question, the three situations are mentioned in order of increasing seriousness.

Will the individual have to contribute to the support of the parent after marriage?

Has there been any appreciable change in the parent-child relationship? Is the child making progress toward independence, or has his development apparently ceased on a definitely immature level? Has his falling in love had any effect on his relation to his parents?

How old is the child in question? What appears to be overattachment at eighteen may be delayed maturity rather than fixation. On the other hand, there may be fixation at this age.

Is either child or parent aware of this situation? Is either attempting to do something about it?

Are there other children to whom the parent may turn if the particular child in question marries and leaves home?

Is the parent a widow, or is the other parent living?

Who makes the child's decisions for him?

Is the person dominated by the parent, or is he squirming under the parental thumb?

Is the child afraid of the parent? Is he afraid to hurt the parent's feelings by getting married?

Is the child able to adjust himself to life away from the parent?

Persons contemplating marriage with individuals who are the victims of parent fixation naturally wish that something could be done about this condition. Sometimes something can be done. But there are limitations as follows:

A parent fixation is a pattern of behavior that crystallized in childhood and is used inappropriately to meet adult situations.

Because the pattern is one of habitual responses in the child, not in the parent, time, distance, or even the death of the parent will not necessarily remove the fixation.

An intellectual understanding of fixation will not necessarily change the individual's emotional reactions, though the former may be a step toward the latter. Because intellectual understanding and emotional reactions may be in "watertight compartments," so to speak, verbal discussion of the problem may not solve it.

An act of will alone is not the solution to the problem. The individual cannot say, "I will no longer have a parent fixation," and thereby remove it, though here again such determination may be a step toward solution.

Threat, force, shame, shock, and similar factors will not remove the fixation.

A wedding is not an automatic solution. It does not suddenly change the participants' emotional reactions to parents.

The solution to the parent-fixation problem requires time, further maturation, reeducation, insight, a desire to remove the fixation, and the provision of life circumstances that encourage or call for the formation of new and more mature habit patterns. But in many cases no solution is possible because the fixation is of too long standing, is too "deep-set," and involves too large a proportion of the individual's personality and behavior.

A MATURE PERSON DOES NOT DEPEND TOO MUCH UPON FLATTERY, PRAISE, AND COMPLIMENTS

Everyone finds pleasure in knowing that his position is secure and that his behavior is approved by members of his group. The person who needs too frequent bolstering up by his associates and leans too heavily upon them for a definition of his status is immature. An immature person is inclined to judge himself in comparison with others. A mature individual is inclined to judge himself in the light of his own greatest possibilities.

He does not easily take offense at what he interprets as slights. The immature person often feels that the world is against him, that nobody understands him, and that his parents are especially lacking in this highly desirable virtue. If the adolescent is walking along the street and someone looks at him in passing, he wonders why. He may say to a person who in all innocence looks at him during a conversation, "What are you looking at me that way for?" If anyone laughs in his presence or even within earshot, he thinks it is he who is being laughed at. If this attitude of defense and this easy offense at assumed slights persist into adulthood, the individual may be considered immature.

He accepts the responsibility for his own acts. Each person is the product of his biography. His experience up to date explains his behavior. If he is to become mature, he must say, "I am what I am because of my past; but explanation no longer constitutes excuse. From now on I take the responsibility for my own acts. I will no longer shift it to biography." Past experience is an excuse for present behavior only so long as an individual remains unaware of this fact. Once he has had it called to his attention, his awareness becomes part of his biography and should be taken into consideration in his subsequent behavior. This implies that, instead of putting the blame for his behavior on his past experience, he can, if he will, do something about his own habits and attitudes. This will require time. Eventually he may retrain himself, develop new habits, and even exercise willpower and self-discipline. A human being is not an automaton, the unchangeable product of his past.

An illustration will clarify this point. Much is written about the effects upon children of family breakdown and divorce. There is no doubt about the seriousness of these effects. Children's personalities may be warped and distorted. Their ideals and loyalties may be rendered askew. Their behavior may be colored by the conflicts, disillusionments, insecurity, and tensions of the broken or breaking home. Broken homes contribute more than their proportionate share of juvenile delinquents. All this is explanation.

Suppose that the reader is the child of divorced parents. His early home life was unpleasant. He is full of conflicting ideas and ideals. His attitude toward his own future marriage has been colored by the failure of his parents. He feels insecure when he contemplates his own assumed inadequacy, and he wonders whether he could make his marriage successful. If such a reader is to become mature, he must realize that this explanation of his attitudes, though adequate as an explanation, is no longer an excuse. There are two alternatives open to him. He may continue as he is at present, the product of his biography, blaming the past and his parents' failure for his own behavior. If he does this he remains immature. Or he may begin a new chapter in his biography. He may determine to profit by his parents' mistakes rather than to be limited by them. He may, through careful analysis of the explanation, obviate the need for excuse.

A mature person also accepts the responsibility for his own acts instead of shifting it to other persons or to current circumstances. It is the immature person who uses "He did it first" as an excuse; who follows the crowd even against his own better judgment and then says, "I couldn't get out of it"; who uses another's insistence as an alibi for his own lack of self-discipline; who seeks to explain his own thoughtlessness by asserting, "Something made me do it"; who says, "You didn't tell me," when he should have depended upon his own observation. A mature person follows through on an assignment, but he sees the difference between taking responsibility for the assignment once given and taking responsibility in the sense of making an assignment unnecessary. The immature person often confuses the two.

He applies adult criteria to his personal traits.   An individual may be considered immature if his reaction to an adult situation is represented by a habit pattern that grew out of an earlier experience and is carried into later life unchanged, so that he reacts to the present situation as if it were the earlier one. Citing common instances of this will make the point clear.

A boy is laughed at by his playmates because of his small stature. They exclude him from their games and taunt him with opprobrious nicknames, such as "shorty," "runt," "half pint." As a result he feels inferior to other boys. In an attempt to prove that he is equal to them, he becomes a bully. When he reaches manhood, he continues to be a bully. He orders his wife about in military manner. He bears an almost visible chip on his shoulder. He has carried into adult life an attitude formed in a childhood setting and has not realized that adults do not usually judge a man by his size. Yet this man behaves toward adults as if they were calling him "shorty."

A girl has been overweight all her life. She is intelligent but has never been pretty. In college she makes high grades but has difficulty participating in extracurricular activities because of her extreme shyness. She is afraid to meet people, has difficulty in carrying on a conversation, cannot speak in a group. She continually belittles herself and disparages her own achievements.

When she was six years old her parents had their second child, another girl. This second child was unusually beautiful and was accorded the devoted attention of relatives. As time went on, the younger child took her place in the limelight, and the older one was left out. It seemed that nothing she could do compared favorably with what her sister did and that it was impossible successfully to compete with the younger child. So, without reasoning it out, she gave up trying to compete, assumed that she was inferior, and withdrew from any situation that would make her inferiority apparent to others. Now she is reacting to an adult situation as if it were the one of childhood. She cannot participate in extracurricular activities because she fears that what she does will compare unfavorably with what others do, as if those others were her sister and observers were her relatives.

A MATURE PERSON CONTROLS HIS BEHAVIOR

He acknowledges possible undesirable urges and appetites in himself but tries to rise above them and to exert conscious and intelligent control. The immature person may indulge appetites that he considers undesirable and unworthy of him, doing it secretly or making excuses to himself for his indulgence. The man who opposes vice to the point of fanaticism may be hiding behind a blind of reform and deriving a vicarious pleasure from condemning in others what he himself would like to do. The man who drinks because the "boys" insist and because such "good fellowship" is supposed to make for more profitable business contacts may be giving an excuse for an appetite that he desires to satisfy, while refusing to admit the truth.

He will endure present discomfort and sacrifice for future gain. He recognizes the relation of personal effort to personal gain. The immature person expects immediate satisfaction of his desires and needs. Let us suppose that two boys are classmates in high school. Both are interested in girls. Both find study trying. One boy is so anxious to have a good time that he leaves school, gets a job with a small salary that furnishes him with spending money, buys a secondhand car, and has a good time with his girl friends. The other boy graduates from high school and goes to college and professional school. The probability is that after twenty years there will be a noticeable contrast in their economic and cultural status. One boy mortgaged the future for the present. The other was mature enough to sacrifice for future gain.

READING 6 THE SELF-ACCEPTING PERSON

The fully accepting person . . . is one who can become acquainted with the positive and negative ways he views life in order to be able to make a reasonably accurate evaluation of realities in everyday living.

The self-accepting person is a participant in life rather than a spectator.

He is inclined to be objective, spontaneous, and emotionally and intellectually honest.

He tries to understand the interpersonal and environmental problems he faces, but he also accepts his limitations in gaining true insight concerning them.

He works out the best adjustment to life of which he is capable, often without fully understanding all that is involved.

However, he is willing to experience the pleasures and discomforts of self-revelation: i.e., he accepts the mixed pain and joy that accompany each change in his attitude and feeling toward himself and others.

His claims on life are, for the most part, reasonable. If he wants to be a member of the Country Club and yet cannot afford it, he finds other social and recreational outlets in keeping with his budget.

The self-accepting person without special talent or

From Eugene C. McDanald, Bert Kruger Smith, and Robert L. Sutherland, *Self-acceptance*, 1962. Reprinted with permission of The Hogg Foundation for Mental Health, Austin, Texas, and the authors.

ability is able to share emotionally in the gifts of others without undue regret about his inborn deficiencies.

He does not brood about missed opportunities, lost causes, errors, and failures. Rather, he looks on them for what they can contribute to his doing things differently or better in the future.

He does not get stuck in the rut of irrational feelings of love, hate, envy, jealousy, suspicion, lust and greed, because he lets each feeling spell out its special message for him.

Although the self-accepting person may prefer not to be alone or isolated from family or friends, yet, in special times when aloneness or isolation is a necessity, he can endure lack of contact with his fellows.

The self-accepting person may or may not be conventional in his thinking, feeling, or behavior. But when he is unconventional, it is not for the purpose of flaunting convention but rather for the sake of expressing or fulfilling a valid personal or public need.

He is not rigidly guided by rules and moralisms; hence he is willing to alter values in keeping with new insights.

He grants to others their right to values not identical with his own.

The self-accepting person puts himself into life in terms of his highest insights. Yet he accepts the fact that, in its essence, it remains the mystery of mysteries.

Self-acceptance, then, in the ongoing sense of the term is a task demanding maturity. The rewards of this process are manifold—the adjustment to or reduction of personal difficulties in living and a greater realization of one's potential as a person. With this realization, one can reach out to become a reasonably productive member of the larger world of which he is a part.

His behavior is determined in part on the basis of principles rather than pleasure or pain. He does certain things because he considers them values. The immature person does the same things because someone forces him to do them. Take, for example, the matter of honor system versus faculty suspicion and supervision. A student who refrains from cheating on an examination only when the instructor is present to detect violations is immature. He is honest only when he is forced to be so by fear of penalty. The mature student is honest whether the instructor is present or absent. He does not cheat on examinations because he considers honesty a value worth preserving and would rather fail the course than violate his personal integrity.

He exhibits adult restrictions upon his behavior. Often younger persons feel that to become adult is to do away with all restrictions on behavior. The mature adult does not live without restrictions; he substitutes adult restrictions for those of childhood. The type rather than the quantity is changed.

Behavior typified by showing off is like that of a child who disrupts his mother's tea party by turning somersaults on the living-room floor. Excessive use of cosmetics, gaudy clothes, noise for noise's sake, sometimes hysterics are means of bidding for attention in rather juvenile fashion. The immature person demands attention to please himself rather than to gratify those who give the attention.

The person who habitually exaggerates the expression of emotions, who pretends to collapse when he is told something that could by no stretch of imagination be sufficient cause for collapse, who punctuates his conversation with open-mouthed, starry-eyed grimaces, whose vociferous expression of surprise is out of proportion to the stimulus is play-acting, like the child whose meager world, in order to seem satisfying, requires the embellishments of a free imagination.

The child does not mind his own business. He asks questions about matters that do not directly concern him, except in so far as he is curious about them. He draws no distinction between "no trespassing" areas and public property. He respects no privacy of thought, word, or deed. The adult who continually intrudes into other people's affairs and infringes on other persons' privacy is immature.

The man or the woman with an uncontrolled temper is like an undisciplined child. He expresses his emotions explosively or by sulking, without regard to the feelings of those about him. He may also threaten another with his displeasure. The mature person studies other people to determine what reactions on his part will best influence them. He also exhibits what may be termed "selective anger." He directs his anger only toward the particular person who precipitated it, instead of making the innocent suffer with the guilty.

Cruelty may be the result of various types of conditioning factors, but it may also be a symptom of immaturity. Children often tease and torture animals, deriving pleasure from observation of the creatures' reactions. They do not mean to be cruel; they do not fully understand that the animals feel pain. The cruelty is a result rather than a motive. When a grown person derives pleasure from the discomfiture of others, he may be considered immature, especially when he causes the discomfiture. The practical joker is such a person. He produces discomfort, pain, embarrassment, or fear in his victim and finds his childish, act amusing.

Not all practical jokes are indications of immaturity, however. Much depends upon appropriateness of circumstance. Practical jokes are out of place at a wedding. At a Halloween party they are not. Persons attending such a party expect them. Much, too, depends upon whether the victim as well as the perpetrator enjoys the prank. At the party both enjoy it, but there is no pleasure for the dinner guest whose chair is pulled from under him, for the freshman who is hazed by upperclassmen, for the "pledge" who is made ill by the corporal application of fraternal love, or for the bride who starts her honeymoon with worry, disappointment, and nervous exhaustion.

There must be a trace of this type of cruelty in most of us, however, for we often find enjoyment in the harmless discomfiture of others, an enjoyment that quickly changes to sympathy if the discomfiture becomes pain. Suppose a very fat and very pompous gentleman strutting along the street suddenly slips and falls. Unless he is injured, observers will probably laugh. Perhaps it is the incongruity of the situation rather than the fat man's predicament that makes us laugh at his plight. We laugh at the antics of motion-picture comedians, when in real life their experiences would be most unpleasant. In animated cartoons cruelty may be carried to extreme, yet the audience's reaction is one of laughter.

"Sadism" is a word often used carelessly to designate any sort of cruelty. Strictly speaking, however, it refers only to cruelty from which the perpetrator derives sexual pleasure. Since it is probably due to a fixation of response plus an exaggeration of certain aspects of sexual behavior, it is considered perversion and is not to be confused with immaturity.

A mature person is not preoccupied with his own biology. Early in life, a child exhibits an extraordinary interest in his bodily processes and the various parts of his anatomy. His world is small, and each new discovery is of prime importance. He plays with his toes and may even put them into his mouth. He is fascinated by his own movements. He touches his genital organs. Excretion becomes a process in which he finds not only pleasure but also, on occasion, a source of pride. This stage is usually transitional. As the individual grows older, other interests should supersede his interest in his own anatomy and physiological functions. His interest should take a mature form and his bodily parts should appear to him in adult perspective.

He has an integrated personality. His life is focused. There may be several focuses, but they are more or less constant. If they change, they do so gradually and in orderly fashion. They do not continually shift. Within the mature personality there is a minimum of friction but not to the point of stagnation. In choosing a career, in going to college rather than to work, in making a choice of husband or wife, in spending money, normal people experience conflicting motives. In the mature person, most of these conflicts are eventually resolved. The person typified by permanently conflicting motives and perennially clashing drives is like the proverbial man who leaped upon his horse and rode off in all directions. Such a case follows.

A woman now thirty-five was outstandingly successful in her college days and had high academic ambitions. She loves her husband and children and wants her marriage to be successful and her home attractive. But she has never been able either to choose between the academic and the domestic roles or to work out a compromise between them. Her life is a series of partially blind dashes. For a while she takes work at the university and neglects her home. Then there is a period during which she neglects her academic work and becomes ultradomestic. There is continual trial with seemingly continual error. The same conflict of drives is noticeable in her pursuit of other interests, such as music, sports, hobbies. She never carries anything to completion. Her life is typified by indecision, with slight, short-lived thrusts first in one direction then in another, like the flare-ups of interests found in a young adolescent.

A MATURE PERSON HAS AN ATTITUDE TOWARD SEX, LOVE, AND MARRIAGE COMPATIBLE WITH ADULTHOOD

He is heterosexual. He is interested in and associates with individuals of the opposite sex as well as his own. He is at ease in a segregated group, a mixed group, or one in which he is the only representative of his sex. He finds satisfaction in normal adult sexual life.

Nature provides each individual with hunger but does not determine in advance what menu he will eat to satisfy it. As a result, individuals and groups learn to eat a great variety of foods to meet the same basic needs. In a similar way, Nature provides each individual with a sex drive and a desire for love and affection. Again, however, Nature does not determine in advance the means of satisfaction upon which the individual learns to depend. As a result, individuals arrive at different means to achieve the same end. Most, but by no means all, individuals eventually settle upon the opposite sex as the means of satisfying their basic needs.

In his early life a boy may be so identified with his mother that his emotional life becomes feminized. He may be so attached to his father that the father becomes the pattern for his future love objects. Parents who wanted a boy and had a girl may attempt to make her seem like a boy and so distort her development that she focuses her love interests on other girls instead of on boys. In some cases such individuals may be classified as homosexual. In many student cases it is not only safer and more hopeful but also more nearly accurate to classify the individual as preheterosexual or immature. The term *homosexual* implies fixation; *preheterosexual* implies a stage of development, perhaps retarded, which will eventually be superseded by more mature heterosexuality.

There are cases in which two persons of the same sex are unusually closely associated because they feel insecure, shy, or lonely, or are starved for affection. They readily turn to anyone who will give them affection, companionship, and security. In such instances there may be no homosexual elements, and serious harm may be done such individuals if their behavior is misinterpreted. If associates immediately leap to the erroneous conclusion that they are homosexual and begin to shun them and gossip about them, if school authorities take disciplinary action as if homosexuality were involved, the individuals may be drawn still more closely together in self-defense and may be forced more deeply than ever into the very type of relationship that they need to outgrow.

He has a healthy, well-balanced, informed attitude toward sex and marriage. He is reasonably well informed regarding sexual anatomy and physiology. He has some understanding of reproduction. He is free from fear, inhibition, repression, and aversion; in place of these he is characterized by intelligent self-control, an optimistic, constructive attitude, and natural responsiveness. He is interested in expanding his knowledge of sex but is not overly curious. He puts sex appeal into its proper perspective; he is not overwhelmed by it. Successful marriage is one of his major objectives and he anticipates marital sexual experience.

He carries into marriage the desirable elements of courtship but not the elements of uncertainty. For either spouse to "keep the other guessing" is to undermine the other's security, for there is an assumption that the wedding ceremony involves a permanent decision. Such a person is likely to rationalize his conduct by saying that this is the only way to keep the other interested; but there are more mature ways of doing it.

He is adequately prepared for marriage. There are regional and class differences as to what constitutes adequate preparation. That needed by a college graduate who will live a complex life in a progressive urban center is not the same as that of the unschooled, naïve person who dwells in a backward community. Since success in the former's marriage depends upon the utilization of well-developed personal resources, he is not ready to assume what is obviously an adult role if his social and emotional growth has been stunted.

Sometimes *sexual maturity* is assumed to be synonymous with *puberty* and to imply only a level of physical development. But, as we shall use it, *sexual maturity* is a more inclusive term, implying more than physical maturation alone. An individual may reach puberty yet not go on to become sexually mature. On the other hand, puberty is a prerequisite for sexual maturity. Assuming, then, that normal puberty has occurred, the sexually mature individual may be described as follows.

He is nonpredatory, nonexploitive. Instead of considering members of the opposite sex as things to be used, he considers them as persons with whom meaningful relationships may be established.

He is able to combine sex and love. He no longer requires a variety of love affairs or of individuals of the opposite sex to satisfy his needs. He finds the answer to his needs in one person, such as his spouse.

He accepts responsibility for his sexual behavior. He does not expect privilege without responsibility. He has developed a moral code which he follows without supervision by others, a set of values through which his behavior is self-governed.

He has a reasonable degree of understanding of the psychology, responsiveness, needs, and problems of members of the opposite sex. He is aware of both the similarities and the differences between the sexes.

He has a reasonable degree of sexual responsiveness and gets past early inhibitions and fears relative to sex. This point is especially, but not exclusively, applicable to females, since many of them do not develop until after the wedding a degree of responsiveness comparable to that which typifies the male in his middle teens.

He understands, accepts, and incorporates into his life the changes that occurred at puberty. He accepts with enthusiasm his own sexual classification. In order to do this he must also accept the sexual classification of members of the opposite sex. This point, too, is especially, but not exclusively, applicable to females, many of whom regret the fact that they are women.

Readiness for marriage

This chapter was begun with the question, "What is the best age for marriage?" in order to focus attention upon the question itself but also to suggest that there are different types of "age" which may be thought of as aspects of maturity. These aspects of maturity have been discussed with the implication that relative maturity and readiness for marriage are closely correlated. But the question regarding age has not yet been answered. In the next chapter that question will be considered.

WHAT DO YOU THINK?

1. List instances in which you have observed immature behavior on the part of students. What can or should be done about such behavior?

2. Can there be different types of criteria for judging maturity; that is, can definitions of maturity differ? Or is maturity something like time, which is not defined differently by different people but only ascertained correctly or incorrectly?

3. In your judgment, what are the most important aspects of maturity?

4. What types of immature behavior are most likely to be detrimental to marriage?

5. What are some of the problems which college students and their parents have in getting along with each other? What suggestions can you make for solving such problems?

6. An individual complains of immature behavior on the part of the marriage partner. What suggestions would you give such an individual?

SELECTED READINGS

Bee, Lawrence S.: *Marriage and Family Relations,* Harper & Row, Publishers, Incorporated, New York, 1959, chap. 5. The nature of emotional maturity.

Blood, Robert O., Jr.: *Marriage,* The Free Press of Glencoe, New York, 1962, chap. 6. Readiness for marriage; deciding when to marry.

Landis, Judson T., and Mary G. Landis: *Building a Successful Marriage,* 4th ed., Prentice-Hall, Inc., Englewood Cliffs, N.J., 1963, chap. 9. Maturity: what it is and its relationship to marriage.

Magoun, F. Alexander: *Love and Marriage,* rev. ed., Harper & Row, Publishers, Incorporated, New York, 1956, chap. 4. What emotional maturity is and its relation to courtship and marriage.

Oliven, John F.: *Sexual Hygiene and Pathology,* J. B. Lippincott Company, Philadelphia, 1955, chap. 6. The development of the sexes at puberty.

Saul, Leon J.: *Emotional Maturity,* 2d ed., J. B. Lippincott Company, Philadelphia, 1960. Emotional maturity; persistence of childhood patterns; the nature of neurosis; dependence versus independence, etc.

Strecker, Edward A.: *Their Mothers' Sons,* rev. ed., J. B. Lippincott Company, Philadelphia, 1951. The author, a psychiatrist, had wide experience with the problem of parental domination and fixation when many men were screened out of military service for psychiatric disorders during the Second World War. This book is about "moms."

——— and Vincent T. Lathbury: *Their Mothers' Daughters*, J. B. Lippincott Company, Philadelphia, 1956. Two psychiatrists discuss the parent-daughter relationship and its role in contributing to immaturity.

chapter **8**

ENGAGEMENT
AND AGE
FOR MARRIAGE

Length of acquaintance

How long should two people know each other before they marry? Studies have shown a direct relationship between length of acquaintance and happiness in marriage, longer periods of association being related to more successful marital adjustment [Burgess and Cottrell, 1939; Locke, 1951; Terman, 1938]. There is a qualitative as well as a quantitative aspect to this problem, however. It is not only a matter of how long but also of how well a couple have known each other.

When two individuals marry after a relatively brief acquaintance, they learn things about each other after the wedding that they might better have learned before. They learn them in a new atmosphere with a different "freedom" of choice. There is greater pressure toward either acceptance or conflict. They may be called upon to revise their expectations regarding one another, especially with respect to each person's role in marriage. Inability to revise such expectations and to accept the other person as he is rather than as he was thought to be is one of the factors commonly contributing to marital failure. Putting it another way, they marry before they know each other well enough to reject each other as marriage partners.

Although no one can say with any reasonable degree of definiteness precisely how long acquaintance should be, of some cases it may be said with certainty that the period is too brief. In student groups, instances of whirlwind acquaintances continually come to light. The following

289

cases illustrate this point. A couple had a "blind date" on June 9. On June 16 the boy proposed marriage, and on June 22 the girl talked with a counselor wondering whether she should marry immediately and go with the boy to another city. In another case a couple met on shipboard. The young man worked on a large plantation in China. The plantation was 60 miles from town. On it there were twelve white men and three white wives; they got into town about once a month. After three weeks with this man, ten days of this period on shipboard, the girl decided to marry him and go to China, and she would soon have done so if her parents had not intervened. In still another instance the girl's parents arranged to have her meet a boy of whom they strongly approved. With some reluctance she had a date with him. She found that she liked him better than she had anticipated. On their fourth date he gave her a ring. The wedding followed shortly thereafter.

At a campus dance two students met for the first time. The boy had had a quarrel with his girl friend on the evening of the dance. A few days before, the girl had had a serious quarrel with her fiancé. After the dance some of the students decided to go to a nearby restaurant for refreshments. By the time this couple arrived at the restaurant they were married. They had gotten the license clerk out of bed to get a license and a jeweler out of bed to purchase a ring. Another girl whom they had taken along as a witness remonstrated with them, and the jeweler tried to dissuade them. But the bridegroom was insistent, and they married after only about three hours' acquaintance. They lived together several years, had two children, and were then divorced. In such cases it is obvious that the period of acquaintance was too brief before commitments were made. One would have to possess the insight of a god to know another individual well in so short a time.

Occasionally, one of these abbreviated acquaintances prefaces successful marriage because the two persons are highly compatible and their relationship expands and deepens after the wedding. But the chance element is greatly increased, and they are successful in spite of, not because of, the brief acquaintance. Their rare experience is a very precarious basis upon which to rationalize one's own desire for haste.

Let us perform an imaginary experiment. We shall choose at random 1,000 college men and a similar number of college women, all of whom are of the same race and none of whom is married. We shall blindfold these 2,000 individuals and let them mill about in a large enclosure. At a given signal they will stand and take off their blindfolds. Then each man will marry the girl standing nearest his right hand. It is highly probable that in this group of a thousand marriages there would be some successful, just by chance. There would be persons who married without ever having seen each other before but who, nevertheless, would have fallen in love and married if they had met. By chance some individuals would make a good "choice" of marriage partner. How many people, however, would want to acquire a spouse by such a process? They would argue that the chances were against a good choice and that it was a mistake to give too much weight to the exceptions. Yet when similar exceptions occur in day-to-day life, some persons use them as a basis for broad generalizations, unfounded assumptions, and wishful thinking.

A type of acquaintance that is frequently deceiving because it gives a superficial appearance of sufficient length is that which depends largely upon correspondence. The following is a typical example. (Similar cases may readily be discovered in any school in which a large proportion of students are living away from home.) On a trip in April the girl in this case met a boy with whom she spent about two days. After separating, they corresponded for some fifteen months. During that period their letters became more personal and amorous until the couple thought they had fallen in love. By correspondence, too, they became engaged. In one way they had known each other for more than a year. In another way their acquaintance was of only two days' duration. When the boy spent two weeks at the girl's home the following summer, they found that they scarcely knew each other. Their letters had completely misled them. Before the boy departed, they had broken their engagement.

Another type, deceiving because it gives a superficial appearance of sufficient length, is that which begins relatively early in life. For example, a student says, "I have known her for five years and gone with her for three. That ought to be long enough." But they are both eighteen years old. Thus, they became acquainted when they were thirteen and started dating each other when they were fifteen. Certainly this five-year period should not be given the same weight as the period, say, from eighteen to twenty-three.

Engagement

Engagement affords added security of choice during the period prior to the wedding and provides the couple with opportunity to make final plans and to announce their intention to marry. Although it should not be a period of getting acquainted, for the couple should know each other well before the engagement, it is a period in which they grow to know each other better than was possible before and test out their reactions to a relationship more intense, more intimate, more exclusive than that which previously existed.

This engagement period gives an opportunity for the couple to experiment with the experience of being devoted to each other, or belonging to each other exclusively in certain respects. They have an opportunity to find out whether this intensified relationship will prove intellectually and emo-

tionally satisfying or irritating. They have an opportunity
of trying out the social adjustments involved—introducing
each other as their future husband or wife, seeing how
their tentative partners get on with each other's friends,
discovering whether the adjustments of emotional and social partnership really work out well or begin to chafe.
Often the period of betrothal is also a time when the couple
are building up the economic resources and status necessary to start the kind of home toward which they aspire.
The engagement might well be characterized, then, as the
period during which the idea of marriage with this particular mate is being explored as a working hypothesis [Hart
and Hart, 1935].

HOW LONG SHOULD THE ENGAGEMENT BE?

Engagement should be relatively brief. But it should come after an adequately long and effective period of acquaintance. In the studies made by
Terman [1938], Burgess and Cottrell [1939], and Locke [1951], there appears to be a positive relationship between length of engagement and
happiness in marriage; that is, the longer the couples were engaged, the
more successful their marital adjustments tended to be. These studies are, however, not such clear-cut arguments for long engagements
as they appear to be on the surface. The statistics do not allow for the
overlap between length of engagement and length of acquaintance, and
hence do not show the effect of engagement as such. Furthermore, the
studies start with married couples instead of couples contemplating
marriage. Because the more successful couples tend to be the ones who
were engaged longer does not mean that the longer an engagement, the
greater the probability of success when the problem is approached from
the point of view of the reader who is single. By the very nature of such
studies, no account can be taken of those cases in which long engagements proved so trying that they were broken.

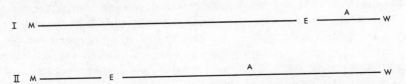

Figure 4. The relationship of length of acquaintance to engagement and
wedding.

The engagement should not in itself constitute the greater portion
of the total period from first meeting to wedding. In Figure 4, M is the
time of meeting, E is the time engagement begins, and W is the wedding.
It is better to have the engagement relatively brief, as in I, rather than
to have the period of acquaintance brief and the engagement very long,

as in II. The problem cannot be solved, however, simply by abbreviating $E-W$ and thus abbreviating $A-W$. A long engagement is preferable to a premature marriage. There is no inflexible rule with regard to the public announcement of the engagement, but usually having it near the wedding (A in I) is preferable to announcing it too early (A in II).

The question, "How long is too long for an engagement?" is a reasonable one but difficult to answer. Much depends upon personalities, propinquity, the reason for the delay in wedding plans, how often the couple see each other, whether they date other people while engaged, and other similar factors that vary in individual cases. We may, however, set up some very rough criteria and say that an engagement is too long if there is an excessive amount of nervous tension generated; if the couple experience excessive frustration; if they grow irritable; if they are getting to the point where they cannot keep petting and sex within the bounds that they originally set; if they become more than usually tired of waiting; if they grow discouraged; if they become indifferent to each other; if they begin to accept the *status quo* as a substitute for marriage and lose interest in the latter; if the engagement constitutes more than a relatively small fraction of the total period from meeting to wedding; or if they become tempted to plunge into marriage precipitously, impulsively disregarding the serious considerations that originally led them to decide to postpone their wedding. The opinion commonly expressed among students to the effect that on the basis of a few months' acquaintance a couple may safely enter upon an engagement of several years' duration is open to serious question indeed.

HOW INTIMATE SHOULD ENGAGEMENT BE?

Greater intimacy of contact is expected in engaged couples. Freer expression of affection on their part is normal. Provided that the engagement is not too long, this intimacy is acceptable because it leads toward unrestricted expression in marriage. Furthermore, some tension is expected in the engaged; otherwise, they would not desire marriage. If, however, their intimacies go so far that tension is increased to the point where it affects their emotional equilibrium, their academic or other work, and causes them to permit physical appeal to play an excessive role in their thinking and behavior, they increase the problem of delayed marriage instead of mitigating it.

Many of the queries concerning petting come from persons who are sincerely in love, have bona fide engagements, and wonder how far they should go and what to do about their intense desire for physical contact.

The following is a letter written by a college girl.

Do you give professional advice to disturbed young lovers outside the classroom? Bill and I are up against a brick wall of discussion and our answer isn't in the books.

As you know we are facing a long engagement, and, since we are well aware of the dangers involved and want to handle it intelligently, we have done a lot of thinking and talking about our particular problem, which is petting. But the books are vague. They consider either the moral issue, which has no part in our present discussion, having been worked out before, or the problem of "going all the way," which, I am sure, is not our danger. That leaves a wide realm of pleasure and fear which apparently has an answer somewhere. But where can we find it?

Of course, we pet. That, I think, is inevitable when two who are in love are thinking of and planning for approaching marriage. Our emotions become very much aroused — to the point in fact of complete satisfaction for Bill but not for me. And that is what worries Bill. He feels that stimulation without satisfaction will be too much for me. Probably he is right there. But how can we go back? Won't the nervous tension be just as bad if we stop completely?

This is Bill's theory, derived from association with a teacher at school who tried to help him work this out: if an engaged couple can stimulate their emotions to the extent that each can achieve sexual satisfaction without actual union, they will be safe from physical and mental dangers for as long as they need. Is it sound and can it be accomplished? Or are we treading on dangerous ground to attempt it?

Sublimation is not the answer either. It doesn't work when we are together and we don't need it when we are apart. You see, while school is in session, we are together only during week ends. The weekdays are easy. But, during that time, we unconsciously build up our emotions so that by Saturday night we have a head start on ourselves.

So what is the answer? We have really tried to figure this out wisely; but our judgment is biased and our knowledge limited. Our particular angle of this subject can't be unique and yet it is our angle that the books seem to avoid.

We are both inclined to do a lot of thinking in such situations, so perhaps we take this too seriously. But our marriage is going to be a tremendous thing for both of us and we do want to be wise about it.

Here are an intelligent couple looking at their problem as sensibly as they can, aware of what is involved, eager to do whatever will contribute most to their success in marriage, but withal very affectionate, sincerely in love, and unable to find a social pattern to guide them satisfactorily in their dilemma. They typify the modern, educated young pair whose marriage is unavoidably delayed because of educational preparation, military service, or economic insufficiency.

Of necessity, the solution to such a problem is highly individualized and is at best only partial, since their problem cannot be fully solved until their wedding. The problem of petting for an engaged couple is not all-or-none. It is a problem of drawing a line between that which enables them to express their affection, to know each other better, and to further the final stages of their preparation for marriage, on the one hand, and that which confuses them, disturbs them, and sidetracks or disorganizes the final stages of their preparation, on the other. The attack on the problem should be made on the basis of control rather than of complete cessation of the conditions to which they have already become accustomed. The criterion for discrimination between what is and what is not to be done should be the consequences of any particular type of behavior. Whatever makes for a happier, less strained, and less fearful relationship is to be continued. Whatever increases tension, worry, or guilt is to be discontinued. Having a degree of physical release during their engagement does not really solve the problem, but rather accentuates it, because in whirlpool fashion each instance of satisfaction only leads with greater inevitability to the next and invites a greater degree of intensity in the next. Some sublimation is possible. Absorbing interests and fascinating activities in which they engage together may aid in dissipating accumulated nervous energy. Analyzing and controlling the initial steps leading toward too much intimacy may help. There is some danger that physical appeal and contact may become almost an obsession with the couple. They think of it too much, anticipate it, plan on it, daydream about it. No matter how intimate their contact may be, short of sexual intercourse, and no matter how much of a degree of satisfaction they seem to achieve, there still may be a residue of frustration, which may as readily make for irritability as does the tension that they seek to relieve. The problem is certainly one well worth a couple's serious consideration, but thinking about it too much may defeat their purpose. They drift into an endless spiral and, instead of improving, become more confused. If either alone or with a counselor they could reach some reasonable plan and tenaciously adhere to their decision without continually reviewing the pros and cons, they might find a solution.

When an engaged couple pet excessively, there is always the possible inclination to say, "Why not go the limit, since we are going to marry anyway?" This problem of premarital sexual permissiveness has already been discussed.

SHOULD ENGAGEMENT MEAN MONOPOLY?

An engagement may be broken, but while it lasts it should signify what might be called emotional monopoly; otherwise it becomes meaningless. There should be no doubt in the mind of either party that the other is his final choice of marriage partner. If there is doubt, there should be no engagement. Engagement is not the same as an option on a piece of property, a small fee that gives a person first choice if at any time one decides to sell or the other decides to make the purchase. An engagement is more like a down payment with the signing of a sales agreement by two persons whose decision is made but whose final contract of purchase has not yet been validated.

There is a practical problem met by engaged persons, particularly when they are students attending colleges in widely separated towns or the man is in military service. Should they or should they not date other persons? Much depends upon how far separated they are, how often they see each other, how remote marriage is, what their individual attitudes are, what frequency of dating is anticipated, and what sorts of dating activities would be involved.

Many campus activities are organized around couples. One must have a partner to participate in these activities. Omission of them means relinquishing enjoyable recreation and forfeiting valuable social experience. It is important that the young person become acquainted with many individuals of the opposite sex. He will not enter a cloister when he marries. He will associate with both sexes at parties, at dances, in business and the professions, in groups of his spouse's friends. Sooner or later he must learn to accept persons of the opposite sex merely as people who are not possible husbands or wives, not competitors with his spouse. He may like them without having amorous inclinations toward them. So an engaged student may date just because he likes to be with people and to attend college functions. His engagement still means emotional monopoly, since none of his dates is considered a competitor with his fiancée. Such dating may help to relieve the strain of separation. It is also a good test of the couple's devotion, for if their love and trust cannot withstand a simple test like this, they are not ready to marry and their engagement is insubstantial. Said one girl in explaining why she did not mind her fiancé's dating when they were separated, "If I could be replaced that easily, it wouldn't be worth trying to make it work."

Engaged students frequently complain that they do not enjoy dating. The probable reason for their dissatisfaction is that, instead of accepting other individuals as people, they continually compare them with the fiancé. Naturally, in most cases the others then do not make a brilliant showing. Such students could have an enjoyable time if they ceased making comparisons.

Other engaged students express apprehension because they do enjoy dating. They conclude that if they can find pleasure in the company of a person of opposite sex other than the fiancé or if they can be interested in the activities of mixed groups without the fiancé's being present, their enjoyment is an indication that they are not in love. Again, they have failed to realize that it is possible to like other people without thinking of them as competitors with one's chosen partner.

In the last analysis, the question is not whether engaged persons date. The question is whether they are free to date if they want to do so. Who tells whom what he or she may or may not do? Do the couple have confidence in each other's judgment and trust each other? Or does one seek to control the other's behavior by imposing his own will upon that person? "I love you so much I can't stand the thought of your dating while I'm away. If you date, I'll be very uncomfortable and unhappy." In other words, "I don't want *you* to date, because if *you* date, *I'll* be unhappy." Apparently whether *you* are unhappy is not a consideration. Is such a demand an expression of love and trust upon which marriage can be built or an indication of immaturity, insecurity, and self-centeredness that suggests that the individual is not ready for marriage?

Our references above have all been to dating for pleasure and convenience, without serious interest in the other person and without petting or sexual intercourse, and to dating no one person exclusively. "Going steady" with one individual would give a fiancé justifiable reason for distrust and for assuming that the engagement no longer had meaning. Dating without the fiancé's knowledge and consent involves certain risks. Under most circumstances, that is scarcely fair play.

RINGS, PINS, AND "DROPS"

An engagement ring is a symbol of love and an insignia of intention to marry. It has a standardized meaning which is generally agreed upon. The meaning of a pin or "drop" (something a girl wears on a chain around her neck), however, is not so clearly defined. (In some schools being "dropped" is referred to as being "lavaliered.") Because of this lack of clear, commonly accepted and understood definition, a pin or "drop" may vary in significance from group to group and even from individual to individual. The boy who gives it may imbue it with a meaning different from that given to it by the girl who accepts it. There may be agreement upon meaning when the pin or "drop" changes hands; but as time goes on the meaning may become altered for one person while it remains constant for the other. The symbol remains the same, but the significance has shifted. It is for this reason, among others, that a reasonable degree of caution in giving and accepting pins and "drops" is important. It is easier to give or accept such a symbol than it is to return it or have it returned, as the case may be. Shifting meaning of which the individual himself is unaware but which is increasingly clear to the other party is the cause of many a hurt.

Another possible problem in connection with the lack of standardized meaning of a pin or "drop" grows out of the fact that the couple live in society. Their friends and families may give the symbol a meaning different from that which they themselves give it, with the result that the couple's relationship is misinterpreted.

When 178 university upperclassmen (69 male, 109 female) were asked to state in their own words what a ring, a pin, and a "drop" meant,

TABLE 1

ring	male	female	total
Official engagement	44	89	133
Intent to marry	12	8	20
"Hands off" sign	4	15	19
Going steady (class ring)	3	7	10
Enlightening period before marriage	4	3	7
Sure of feelings	2	4	6
Deep friendship	1	4	5
"Promised"	2	2	4
Agreement to marry	0	2	2
Next step to marriage	2	0	2

pin	male	female	total
"Engaged to be engaged"	35	62	97
Going steady	17	36	53
Contemplating engagement	0	14	14
Serious relationship	8	6	14
Engagement—same as ring	3	5	8
Between "dropped" and engaged	0	6	6
Informally engaged	4	1	5
Engaged—marriage in distant future	0	3	3
"Pre" or trial engagement	0	3	3
Trial period	0	1	1
Friends	1	0	1
"Socially engaged"—not necessarily leading to marriage	1	0	1

"drop"	male	female	total
Going steady	25	77	102
Do not know what it means	13	5	18
Not dating others	0	17	17
Breaking up	11	6	17
Same as pinned	3	5	8
Getting acquainted	4	4	8
Slightly more serious than going steady	3	4	7
Serious interest in each other	0	5	5
"Engaged to be engaged"	1	1	2
Nothing	2	0	2
Plan to become engaged	0	1	1
Secretly engaged	0	1	1
Good friends	0	1	1
Know each other	1	0	1
"Just a gift of jewelry"	0	1	1
Very little	1	0	1

they replied as shown in Table 1. Lack of standardized meaning is apparent. Clearly the meaning of a ring is more widely agreed upon than that of either of the other two. Note that about a third of these students did not know what "drop" meant, thought it meant little or nothing, or confused it with the ordinary meaning of *drop*, namely, to discontinue a relationship, to "break up," although this one-third were on the same campus as the other two-thirds.

When more than 1,100 college sophomore girls reported the number of fraternity pins they had accepted, the results were as follows: 328 girls had accepted one pin, 99 two pins, 32 three, 15 four, 11 five, 1 six, 2 seven, 1 eight, 2 ten, 1 eleven, and 1 fifteen pins.

PROBLEMS TO BE FACED DURING ENGAGEMENT

When a couple are contemplating marriage, there are several problems which they might well consider during the engagement at the very latest, preferably before. The answers to certain questions need to be ascertained to the satisfaction of both parties. They may be obtained through an extended period and through close observation. There need be no inquisition just prior to the wedding, no suspicious third-degree inquiry. (1) Are they going to plan to have children? If so, when and about how many? What is each person's attitude toward control of conception? (2) What is the source of the man's income? How much does he earn? What plan for the use of money will best fit their temperaments and circumstances? (3) Where will they live after the wedding? (4) Will the wife be gainfully employed? (5) What type of wedding will they have? When will it take place? Whom will they invite? (6) Will they have a honeymoon? If so, where will they go? How long will it be, and how much will they let it cost? (7) What are their attitudes toward the sexual side of marriage? Are there any facts that they should obtain from reading or a counselor? Will they have a premarital medical examination?

REVEALING ONE'S PAST

How much of one's past should be revealed to one's fiancé? No universally applicable answer to this question is possible. It depends upon a number of factors which vary in individual cases: the other person and his attitude toward oneself and one's behavior; what he volunteers about himself; what the incidents are that cause the question to be raised; how long ago they occurred; how much possibility of continuation or repetition there is; one's own present attitude toward the past; what has happened between the incidents and the engagement; how much danger of discovery there is or how much risk of information reaching the fiancé through indirect channels; how much each wishes to know about the other; the reason for which the individual feels he should tell.

One generalization is apropos: by and large it is better to let the other person volunteer information, and to accept what he volunteers as the whole truth, than it is to pry through curiosity into experiences which the other person long ago buried and does not want to disinter.

No one is under obligation to bring all the skeletons out of the closet just because he has become engaged. It is only fair play, however, to reveal anything that has bearing on the couple's future relationship. The presence of disease, previous marriage, hereditary or other defects, debts, imprisonment, and similar items should be told. Anything that may readily be learned through a third party is better told in advance.

Whatever is revealed should be told before the wedding. If it is told after the wedding, the other person may feel trapped. Great care should be exercised to avoid overstressing the facts for the sake of feeling that one has made a confession. Because of the hypersensitivity of both persons during engagement, it is easy to exaggerate either the revelation or its interpretation. What is told should be told as information that will further the marital adjustment and happiness of the couple. It should not be told only to obtain emotional release, important as this release may be. The effects on the other party, as well as the effects on oneself, should be taken into consideration.

Discussion of anything that is troubling either one may be an advantage, but not if it is going to hit off complexes in the other that will create more difficulty than the original worry. Confession for its own sake is worse than useless, since it relieves the confessor of anxiety at the expense of the confidante, who may exaggerate the offense because of the very seriousness of the remorse of its narrator, and go on to expect more terrible misdemeanors in the future. Actually not what has happened, but why and with what result, is the important question as a key to what is going to be true, and only the wisest, scientifically trained, and disinterested observer can get much of an inkling as to the real state of affairs when they are told by the person most concerned [Groves and Ross, 1936, p. 29].

Many young people struggle painfully with this question of revealing the past. They feel guilty when they think of keeping some fact secret. They feel fearful when they think of making it known. They are torn by conflict and indecision. Such persons may find help in discussing the problem in confidence with a counselor, either to bring a plan to a focus or to confirm a plan already determined upon.

BROKEN ENGAGEMENTS

Engagements entered with best intentions and sincerest motives are sometimes broken. Those entered without careful thought and after very brief acquaintance are especially ephemeral. The younger the couple are at the time of engagement, the more likely they are to change their attitudes toward one another or to be swept away by infatuation and, consequently, the greater the probability that the engagement will not endure.

Many an engagement is broken because a couple "put the cart before the horse" and expect the engagement to do something it cannot accomplish. They are insecure in their relationship and fear they will lose each other. They become engaged in order to create the security they desire. But an engagement cannot produce security. It can only express security that already exists.

Of 1,151 college sophomore girls, 287 said that they had been engaged once; 66, more than once. Since most of the girls were still in their teens, the probability is that many of these engagements have since been broken. In a study of 1,000 engaged couples, at least a third of the men and about half the women had had one or more broken engagements [Burgess and Wallin, 1953].

In a study of just over 8,000 women who had been married, more than one-fourth (26.8 per cent) had been engaged at least once before becoming engaged to the men they married; about 10 per cent (included in the 26.8 per cent) had been engaged twice before.*

A broken engagement is distressing, to say the least, but it is not so painful as a broken marriage. It is better for the couple to learn before their wedding that they are incompatible than to marry blindly and discover this later. The purpose of the engagement is to enable them to make the final adjustments before the wedding. It is inevitable that some of these attempts at adjustment will fail.

As a rule, an engagement should be broken as soon as either party wishes to break it. This does not mean that it should be broken and remade each time they have a quarrel and then patch up their differences. When either one after careful thought decides that he cannot go on with the wedding plans, the other person should be notified. This notification will be unpleasant for both parties and may be extremely galling to the one notified. Once a couple have become enmeshed in a relationship as permeating as an engagement, it is usually impossible for one to get out without hurting the other unless by uncommon coincidence both desire release. The longer the break is postponed, the greater the hurt is likely to be, and during the delay the one who is going to make the break must "put up a false front" and misrepresent himself to the other party. To marry a person against one's better judgment is only to increase the injury. It is neither a favor nor a charity to marry a person

*In this study, 20,000 questionnaires were sent to former students of Stephens College; 9,526 questionnaires were returned. Of these 9,526 women, 8,001 reported themselves as having married. Since some of the women were recent graduates and may have married later, these figures do not suggest a marriage rate.

against one's will. Neither pride, the opinions of family or friends, the fact that wedding plans are under way, nor the embarrassment of facing the other person should be permitted to act as a deterrent to the effecting of one's decision.

Another not infrequent deterrent is the fear that the disappointed individual will commit some rash act as a result of the break. Consider such cases as the following.

After a brief acquaintance and on the basis of what later proved to be infatuation, a college girl became engaged to a boy who soon afterward joined the Army. When the girl discovered that she was not in love and did not want to marry him, the boy threatened to desert the Army and do something desperate. His mother tried to prevail upon the girl to marry her son, insisting that a broken engagement would result in the ruination of his future. The girl was confused and did not know what to do.

A couple had been going together for several years. The boy was sure he loved the girl and was very persistent about their marrying. For some time she had felt that she was no longer in love with him and was convinced that she would never marry him. She had repeatedly tried to explain her attitude, but he refused to listen. The boy had periods of depression and moodiness. Once after she had told him she could not marry him he became very depressed. He went for a walk, met a friend, and the two boys decided to go hunting. When the boy in question took his gun from its rack, it went off and the bullet penetrated his chest just over his heart. At the time, it was reported as an accident and the girl accepted that explanation. Later, however, when they had talked of marriage again and once more she had told him she could not marry him, he then told her that what had passed as an accident had been an attempt at suicide. After that she was afraid that if she persisted in her refusal he would make another attempt to take his own life.

What should an individual do under circumstances such as these? There is only one feasible plan of action: break the engagement as painlessly as possible, take a firm stand, and tenaciously adhere to the decision. If the engagement was seriously entered and the break is founded upon a sincere change of heart, what the other person does, even if it be self-destruction, is not the fault of the one making the break. This may seem like a heartless statement; but it is not so heartless as it would be to suggest that the future happiness of two persons be jeopardized by plunging them into a loveless, incompatible union. Again, a counselor may be able to help the student work out a plan.

In the great majority of instances, suicide threats in this sort of circumstance never get any further than the self-pity stage, and relatively few are ever carried out. If an individual seeks alcoholic escape from problems or threatens suicide, he exhibits an instability of personality which in itself might be ample reason for breaking the engagement, even if love had not died or reason had not intervened. If he threatens vengeance, he demonstrates a type of immaturity that would be highly undesirable in a marriage partner. Most people recover from the shock of a broken engagement more readily than either of the two fiancés imagines possible at the time of the break. In a state of emotional upset it is easy to exaggerate possible consequences, most of which never occur.

Some individuals recover slowly. Some never recover. But such cases do not constitute sufficient reason for entering an undesired marriage, though they do constitute weighty argument for avoiding insincerity, short-sightedness, and premature commitment in becoming engaged.

It is to be expected that both parties, and especially the unwilling participant, in a broken engagement will be temporarily upset and disillusioned. For the latter to do something to prevent permanent bitterness and frustration is not always easy. In so far as possible he should face the facts, and, after allowing for a period of adjustment, start over. To assume a "her-or-nobody" attitude spells defeat. As soon as feasible he should begin to date and should from the beginning associate with persons of both sexes in mixed groups. In addition to permanent disillusionment, perhaps his most imminent danger and the trap into which he is mostly likely to fall is "rebound."

Early marriage

Let us define as early marriage that in which the couple are about twenty, or younger. It is not synonymous with hasty marriage. Early marriage entails a number of considerations.

There is the problem of maturity. Are the couple mature enough to marry at this early age?

The earlier the marriage occurs, the more likely it is that there will be overemphasis on sex and physical attraction. The younger the persons are, the more they are inclined to be swept away by infatuation.

Are the couple ready to have children? Among modern, educated young people there is more to having a family than merely the biological process. Babies cost money, and to rear them as the couple will want to rear them requires maturity and preparation, security of both present and future, and a readiness to devote oneself to them.

Are the couple prepared to maintain an acceptable standard of living? Is the man ready to make sufficient income to support a wife and a home? If the wife plans to have gainful employment, is she trained for anything but a routine job? What would happen to their plans if she had a baby?

Have persons so young had adequate time to make a wise choice of marriage partner? During the late teens, and sometimes during the early twenties, many individuals are still in the process of rather rapid change in attitudes, tastes, and choices. In many instances, what seems at the time like a permanent choice proves later to have been a tentative one. As we have seen, broken engagements are common. Many of them occur without warning and with no observable reason in the sense of one party's committing an offense against the other. The reason for such broken engagements is that the persons have not allowed enough time to become thoroughly acquainted or that they reappraise each other as they move from dating closer to marriage or that one individual's growth process has led him to alter his judgment of the other person, who now appears to him in a new light. Broken engagements are painful enough. When a similar change occurs after the wedding, the result is more serious. In many instances, the same immaturity that prevents an individual from making a permanent choice contributes to his unquestioned confidence that his tentative choice will be the final one.

Has one person put the other under pressure to marry? If one person does not feel ready to marry but the other feels an urgency, as the result of which pressure is exerted on the first party, the one who exerts the pressure proves thereby that he or she is not ready for marriage. This person considers marriage to be something which eventuates from persuasion and the imposition of one person's will upon the other rather than something chosen freely and entered by mutual desire and decision.

The earlier the marriage occurs, the less likely the couple are to have reached a "monogamous" attitude. As we saw when we examined emotional development, an individual is first interested in the opposite sex in general and gradually narrows down that interest to one person. If a couple have reached this "monogamous" stage, it is one thing. If they marry when they merely like each other a bit better than they like several other persons, it is quite another.

Will the couple have had ample opportunity for social development before accepting the responsibilities of a home and a possible family? We have suggested that there are class and regional differences as to what constitutes adequate preparation of marriage. Advocates of early marriage sometimes assume that all married couples will live the same type of life in the same social environment and that therefore all young people are ready for marriage when they have reached a given stage in their physical growth. Just as a person must pay a price in time, effort, and the postponement of returns in preparing for a profession rather than a job, so people are called upon to meet a certain cost in preparing for marriage if they want successfully to avail themselves of the opportunities that marriage presents and to meet the demands put upon it in modern, complex, highly urbanized society.

READING 7 THE PROBLEM OF EARLY MARRIAGE

That the timing of marriage constitutes a major concern of American society at present may be gathered from the scholarly and popular literature as well as from the concerns of PTA's, school boards and the public at large. We observe, in many instances a combination of panic and punitive reaction on the part of the responsible citizenery: panic, presumably because they sense a knotty problem which they do not know how to deal with, and a punitive response growing out of a desperate desire to reverse the trend. It is becoming increasingly clear, however, that neither panic nor punishment will solve the problem. What we need is a broad-gauged view of the problem.

What is early marriage? We can define it statistically or legally. The latter would be more simple, since the legal age for marriage without consent of the parents is, in most states, 18 for women and 21 for men. Early marriage may be viewed as those marriages in which either the male is under 21, or the female under 18, or both.

The first thing that comes to mind in connection with the alleged existence of a problem of early marriage is a very simple-minded one. It is appalling, though not surprising, that the American public and, indeed, many of the more intelligent sections thereof, have developed such concerns about early marriage, especially as a supposed causative factor in divorce. The social system in which the early marriage takes place is ignored.

The sub-culture is ignored. The family dynamics of the parties to the marriage are ignored. The individual personalities of the subscribers to the contract are ignored. And yet we blithely move along, pointing our fingers, shaking our heads and clucking that early marriage hurts the individuals and hurts society. In essence I am saying that it is patent nonsense to assess behavior or an institution on the basis of chronology alone.

Admittedly, chronology has some importance. We

From Irving Doress, "The Problem of Early Marriage," *The Bulletin on Family Development*, vol. 2, no. 1, Spring, 1961, pp. 20–23. Reprinted with permission of the editor.

would not expect a six year old to be ready for marriage. But this is an extreme case. We are not dealing with six year olds. We are dealing with individuals who are presumably biologically mature, who are capable of copulation and procreation. The question is should John and Mary go ahead and marry given this physical maturity or should they delay in order to make themselves more ready on social, psychological and economic levels. If they elect to delay marriage, how do they go about preparing for the big day? What constitutes readiness? Does conditioning oneself to a single life prepare one for marriage? Of course, the answers to these questions are not easy. One key lies in the meaning of marriage. That is, do we see marriage as primarily a legal bond or a social-psychological bond? If we choose the latter, then we have to face the possibility that no adequate preparation for marriage in this sense exists in our society at this time. The protagonist at this point might well cite the greater stability of marriages contracted in the late twenties and early thirties as evidence of the notion that marriage-preparedness does exist. Yet, this can be questioned. It may well be that couples marrying in their late 20's and early 30's (for the first time) have developed individual patterns of living their lives which are scarcely modified by marriage. In fact, the "stability" of those later marriages may be due largely to the fact that they do not involve the depth commitment of earlier marriages. There is *probably* less welding, less joining-together, less *egoisme a deux*. It follows then, that where there is less involvement, there is less vulnerability, less brittleness. In short, marriage between those approaching middle-age may have a very different meaning for the participants than early marriage does for its participants. It may be a moderate rather than a major emotional investment.

Researchers who have studied this problem agree that while a great many early marriages suffer from a variety of difficulties, there are, nevertheless, a goodly number which succeed. What is needed now is careful investigation of those marriages contracted in the teen years which manage to survive and, indeed, which manage to survive with flying colors. An intensive case-study of, say, 30 such marriages might get us off to a good start. Later, we might look for points of difference between matched samples of successful and unsuccessful early marriages. We might ask ourselves such questions as the following:

1. Is emotional and economic support from parents a factor in marital success?

2. Is the closeness of the male to his vocational ob-

jective a factor? It would appear likely that fewer problems would develop in a marriage, if the male either were supporting his family or fairly close to the capability of such.

3. Is the length of acquaintanceship a factor? The nature of the courtship process? The opportunity to come to know each other in a comprehensive way?

4. Are the couples who delay parenting better parents than those who plunge right into parental roles? It seems reasonable to suppose that those who delay their parenthood are in a lot better position. In fact, my impression is that it is *parenting* which interferes with school work and with jobs much more than marriage as such.

One could go on and on with research possibilities, but, at this point, let us examine some of the brickbats that have been flying around, pro and con, in connection with early marriage. The brickbats have been mostly con.

Anti-early-marriage experts maintain, correctly, that the divorce rate for teen-agers is much higher than for older individuals. However, we might ask: is the high divorce rate for early marriages due to factors inherent in early marriage itself or due to the fact that society, having decided early marriage is bad, proceeds to destroy it. Is it not probable that young marrieds, saturated with foreboding, start to see problems around every corner where none exist? In fact, some young couples who are reasonably well-adjusted might begin to think that there is indeed something unnatural about their relationship inasmuch as they do not live up to the model expectation of being beset with problems!

A second argument against early involvement is that tastes change, personality changes. Young people are told they will come to regret their choice. This contention is based on the assumption that changes in personality take place up to a certain age and then personality freezes. However, this assumption does not stand up in the face of new findings and modern adult personality theory. The stream of empirical research and emerging theory is leading us inescapably to the conclusion that personality growth and change is a constant throughout life. The major deterrent to change seems to be the conviction that it will not occur. Therefore, the argument that one should delay marriage until the personality settles down could require a permanent cessation of marriage plans.

The argument that marriage interferes with studies, particularly in a two-student family is plausible. It seems more plausible where there is parenthood. Yet, research to date reveals that the grades of married students run higher than their unmarried colleagues. It may well be that there is more interference with studies caused by the incessant, obsessive seeking of sexual-amative experiences by unmarried college students. The married students by virtue of being married have, in a sense, energy and time released into scholarship. Or, at least, energy and time is not consumed in the dating-courtship ratrace.

Let us consider the relationship between the timing of marriage and the existence of premarital sexual intercourse. Nominally, our society insists on chastity at the time of marriage, at least for the female. Given the earlier heterosexual socialization process in operation at present (dances in the 5th grade, going steady in the 7th, etc.), the additional demand that marriage be delayed, say, to the middle twenties, puts an unbearable burden on the backs of young people. On the one hand, we rush them into growing up. Then, we tell them to slow down. Heterosexual relationships in depth begin frequently by the sophomore or junior year in high school. Now we have to do one of two things. Either we say, all right—people—you've gone through the stages of the courtship process, you want each other, you need each other—get married and we'll help you. Or, as a society, we are going to have to come to accept full sexual relationships before marriage. The age-old conflict of biological and social man is with us yet. We are not going to solve this conflict by wagging our fingers. Of the two choices indicated above, I would prefer the former. I would encourage early marriage, since in a marital situation, there are built in responsibilities, which normally do not function in nonmarital sexual liaisons.

This paper has attempted to contribute by way of seeing early marriage on a wide screen. Since most of the written material in this area has varied from mild to violent opposition to early marriage, I have attempted to fill in the lacunae by questioning the assumptions of the "antis." At any rate, barring any massive changes in our social structure, we can expect the trend toward early marriage to continue. Why not attempt, in our research, in our teaching, in our writing, in our counseling—to make the best of it? Why not accept early marriage as a *fait accompli* and make every effort to help young marrieds?

THE FAILURE RATE

We cannot state categorically that early marriages will fail. Some persons are more ready to marry in their late teens than others are regardless of their chronological age. Such relatively mature young people may work out successful marriages and in so doing relieve the stress and strain of dating and waiting. However, there is evidence to suggest that early marriages contribute more than their proportionate share to the marital failure rate. Glick [1957, p. 110] states that there is a "very distinct negative correlation" between age at first marriage and proportion of marriages broken. In the divorces occurring in 1960, 16 per cent of the males and 45 per cent of the females had married before reaching age twenty, while in the marriages contracted in that year only 13 per cent of the males and 37 per cent of the females were under twenty [Carter and Plateris, 1963]. These investigators conclude that age at marriage "appears to have an important effect on the likelihood of divorce." In this country in 1954, women who were still in their first marriage had been, on the average, about two years older at the time of the wedding than women who had terminated their first marriage and contracted a second [Glick, 1957]. In one study of 425 women who had been divorced, it was found that the average age at the time of the wedding was "substantially younger" than that of women in the general population who were still in their first marriage [Goode, 1956]. In the Family Court Center in Toledo, Ohio, it was found that, through a five-year period, in just over two-thirds of the divorce cases heard the couple had married when the bride was "under 21" [1953]. In interpreting studies such as these, however, we must be careful to distinguish between age per se as the cause of failure and the personality and situational factors that lead to early marriage as a cause of failure. In other words, do people who marry early have a high failure rate merely because they marry early? Or do they have a high failure rate because they are the kind of people who are inclined to marry early? We have no way of knowing whether they would be more successful if they waited a year or two longer. Perhaps both types of factors are operative.

Postponing marriage

In a culture such as ours, and especially in better-educated groups, relationships are complex, and marriage makes rather heavy demands upon its participants. Periods of cultural and occupational training are being lengthened. Economic self-sufficiency is not simple of achievement. Personality is coming to play an ever-larger role in the lives of husbands and wives. As a result, marriage is usually postponed for some time beyond the achievement of physical maturity. This period of postponement is one of stress and strain, emotional incompleteness, frustration, physical restraint, and intellectual confusion for myriad young people, among whom the college student is one of the most common and most poignant sufferers. There is doubtless no single problem which causes the student more worry, which gives rise to more inquiries, which more frequently tempts to experimentation or trial-and-error methods than this. It affects his relationships with persons of the opposite sex and his social relationships in general. It may affect his grades and his occupational choice. It creates an unprecedented parent-child problem for which the solution up to date has been little more than conjecture.

It is easy to say that society should do something to solve this problem. Butterfield [1939, p. 125, reprinted with permission] voices the opinion of many writers in saying:

> When neither youth nor parents are able to exert any helpful influence on the situation, a radical change in economic or moral structure seems inevitable. Either society will have to remodel its economic structure to make conventional marriage possible to young couples, or there will certainly come a change in the marriage mores. Either of these changes involves so many radical aspects as to earn the term "revolutionary," yet anything less than that is not likely to give help. It would seem that only some form of "new deal" which will make marriage economically possible for the majority of young people in the early twenties will avert a continued increase in adolescent tension with respect to marriage and premarital sex behavior.

It may be true that society should do something about this problem. But society has not done anything. The economic structure and the institution of marriage change slowly and are more sensitive to basic evolutionary forces than to theory and injunction. If we learn anything from history, we must see that for years to come the reader of this book and thousands like him will face this problem of the postponement of marriage before society does anything about it. This does not mean that we should cease trying to improve the social situation. It means only that in our zeal for reform we should not lose sight of present reality. Is there anything that the individual may do to contribute to the solution of this problem in his own particular case? We have no easy, ready-made solution, but we can offer a few possibly useful suggestions.

The person who must postpone marriage should face reality. His problem is to make the best adjustment he can to the situation as it exists rather than to make a poor adjustment because he feels the need for change. His adjustment to the marital situation is in many ways similar to his adjustment to life in general. The economic system is not all that it should be; there are inequality of opportunity, inequitable distribution of wealth, and all too frequently insecurity of savings and investments. Yet we work and save and invest to the best of our ability. Medical science is not perfect, but we live as healthfully as possible in the light of incomplete knowledge. The individual's problem is to find the greatest happiness over a long period. The fact that society makes serious errors does not foredoom the individual to equally serious errors if he intelligently faces his handicaps.

The individual should realize that the age for mating is not necessarily the age for marriage. He may be physically and sexually mature. But is he ready to marry and assume the inevitable responsibilities and fulfill his marital role? Sometimes the desire for sexual experience is confused with the wish to marry. If a young couple plan permanently to "live on love," they need consider nothing but the factor of sex and its attendant emotions. If they are to have a home, rear offspring, maintain a standard of living, and take their place in the community, they must consider something more than the physical.

Sexual freedom is no real solution. Too often sexual freedom begun as a stopgap to carry over until hopes may be realized and plans fulfilled becomes a permanent obstacle to the achievement of those very hopes and plans. Such freedom is not an adequate substitute for marriage, even when on a temporary basis.

It is difficult for normal, healthy, vigorous young people to be sexually continent for a long period after physical maturity is reached. That some of the best things in life are difficult is a truism. Some of the things most worth-while are things for which one must struggle, strive, prepare, sacrifice, and on occasion fight. Education, occupational success, principles, and many other things fall into this category; and among these things, in the attainment of which are involved effort, foresight, and preparation, is successful marriage. Successful marriage must be won. It must be built. It is not a gift of Nature and is never reached by the path of least resistance.

Every individual is subject to the necessity for making choices. If he attends one college, he cannot at the same time attend another. If he chooses one career, he automatically eliminates others. If he spends money for one thing, he cannot spend it for something else. If he chooses to get a college education, he has made a choice that involves certain benefits but also certain costs. He cannot have his education with its future returns and at the same time have the immediate returns that would be derived from choosing to go to work rather than to school. If he intends to have a college education, he may have to forego some things until his education is completed. Marriage may be one of these.

The individual may think of the present as part of a larger picture. From the perspective of years of marriage, the present postponement will not seem so long, even though at the moment it may seem interminable. The present may be looked upon as preparation for the future rather than as an infringement upon it.

He may think forward to near events. By shorter steps he may bridge the period of waiting rather than let his interest in near events become beclouded by a fog of immediate hopeless anticipation through which he can see only the remote star of his very distant marriage.

He may do things for his marriage. By discussing and planning practical matters pertaining to their life after the wedding, a couple may bring a little of the future into the present. Many of these things done by them separately or together act as tension relievers.

He should be certain that he does not compare the best parts of marriage with the worst aspects of his present situation, forgetting that there are probably bright spots around him if he only opens his eyes to them.

What is the best age for marriage?

The previous chapter was started with the above question. We shall close this one with an attempted answer. So far as success in marriage is concerned, the question of the best age for marriage is one of how far the individual has progressed in his development, what his level of readiness is, rather than the number of leaves he has torn from the calendar. The situation is not dissimilar to that of a student entering college when he is prepared, rather than when he reaches a given age. The above concept has limitations because people tend to think in terms of chronological age, and that age is most easily measured; and the concept applies only to marriages in which both persons are of similar chronological age. One would hesitate to recommend the marriage of a person of twenty to another of sixty, no matter how relatively mature the former or how immature the latter.

If an individual's development were plotted on a graph, the graph would appear roughly like that in Figure 5. This figure is oversimplified and makes no allowance for the fact that one aspect of development

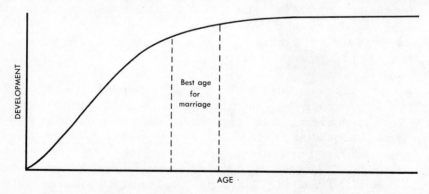

Figure 5. The best age for marriage.

may lag behind others or may be precocious. Relative change is rapid at first. As the person grows older, each year finds him changing less as compared with the previous year, so the graph tends to level off. Between the first and the second year, for example, the change is tremendous. Between the fiftieth and the fifty-first, the relative change is slight, though the time period is identical. The best time to marry is represented by that segment of the graph where the curve begins to level off but has not yet reached the level stage. It is the age at which the individual has become relatively mature, the period of most rapid change is passed, and the habit patterns that will characterize him for life have begun to form, but the process is not complete, habits are not entirely set, and the individual is still adaptable enough to adjust to a new situation. For most persons whose development has been more or less normal and in whom there is to be found a fairly close correlation between chronological age and other types of age, this period is the twenties. That is to say, for normal people some time in the twenties is the best age for marriage. If there are unusual circumstances affecting the individual's development, the best age for his marriage may be different from that for persons in general. Here again the demands of the group in which one lives must be taken into consideration.

When the ages at first marriage for all persons in this country are arranged in order from lowest to highest, the middle age is almost 23 for males and 20 plus for females. In other words, half the males who marry do so at almost 23 years of age or younger, and half the females who marry do so at about age 20 or younger. The median age at first marriage, contrary to common belief, has been declining, as shown in Table 2.

TABLE 2 MEDIAN AGE AT FIRST MARRIAGE

year	male	female
1890	26.1	22.0
1900	25.9	21.9
1910	25.1	21.6
1920	24.6	21.2
1930	24.3	21.3
1940	24.3	21.6
1950	22.8	20.3*
1960	22.8	20.3
1963	22.8	20.4†

*U.S. Bureau of the Census, 1960.
†U.S. Bureau of the Census, 1964.

Among men 20 to 24 years of age, the proportion married almost doubled (from 27 to 51 per cent) between 1940 and 1955. Among women in the same age group and during the same period, the proportion married increased from about half to more than two-thirds (from 51 to 69 per cent) [*Statistical Bulletin*, May, 1956]. Among both men and women who had had from one to four years of college experience, the proportion married in the 20-to-24-year-old age group approximately doubled between 1940 and 1950 [Glick, 1957]. Today more than three-fifths of the married men under 25 years of age have children, as compared to fewer than one-half in 1940 [*Statistical Bulletin*, March, 1957]. Almost two-fifths of present-day brides are in their teens, and more than half of these become mothers before they are 20 [Population Reference Bureau, 1962]. In 1959, 14 per cent of the babies born had teen-age mothers, and 3 per cent had teen-age fathers ["The Teen-age Mother," 1962]. It is clear from figures such as these that the number of both young marriages and young families is increasing.

Do the median age at first marriage and the best age for marriage coincide? If we take the median age just as it stands, we see a broad similarity between it and the best age for marriage. If, however, we take into account that a median by definition represents a distribution, then we may raise questions. The lower the median age for marriage, the more very young persons considerably below this median must be included in it. Many will be below the best age for marriage, as discussed above.

As the median age at first marriage declined, it was inevitable that the lower half of the distribution would increasingly overlap with the ages of high school and younger college students. In 1962 there were 79,000 high school students and 30,000 college students who were nineteen years of age or younger and married, with the spouse present [U.S. Bureau of the Census, 1964]. These represent minimum numbers, since in many cases the spouse would be absent, as, for example, in military service. In the present-day concern about high school and younger college marriages, especially the former, with the efforts of some school administrations to discourage marriage by placing restrictions on students who marry (for example, the requirement in some instances that students who marry leave school), we are hearing the supersonic boom, so to speak, of a breakthrough which is the current phase of a trend that began decades ago. The first such boom was heard when college marriages increased after the Second World War. The increase in very early marriage is not the result only of young people's immaturity, impetuousness, and caprice but also a reflection of tidelike social changes that are sweeping over Western culture. This fact does not relieve young people of responsibility for wise choice and intelligent planning. It should, rather, motivate them to seek understanding of this social trend and the reasons underlying it so that they are not caught up in a process in which they are ill prepared to participate.

There must of necessity be some stopping place for this downward trend in median age at first marriage. Where that will be no one knows.

The decline in age at first marriage not only creates problems of marital adjustment often eventuating in failure, as mentioned earlier, but it also creates unprecedented pressure toward early marriage. Early marriage produces early marriage. As more young people marry very early, more feel an urgency to marry early lest they get out of step with the peer group or fail to find a marriage partner. This in turn has reverberations in the acceptance of petting and premarital sexual intercourse, especially on the part of girls.

WHAT DO YOU THINK?

1. When should a couple start going steady?
2. How long should a couple know each other before becoming engaged? Before getting married?
3. What are possible explanations of a person's becoming engaged to more than one individual at a time?
4. When separated for an extended period, should engaged persons date others?
5. Could a couple decide to marry and yet not consider themselves engaged? What is an engagement?
6. How soon after a couple decide to marry should they tell their parents?
7. Recently there has been an increase in the number of marriages involving high school students. What criteria of judgment would you apply to such marriages? Can any generalization be made as to whether or not high school students are ready for marriage?
8. In your judgment, what is the best age for marriage? What are the reasons for your answer?
9. If you insist, as many do, that no generalization as to the best age for marriage is possible, that "it depends on the individuals," and if many of the persons who are marrying are relatively young and may be assumed to be immature and therefore make immature judgments about themselves, how can any answer to the question of the best age for marriage be reached?

SELECTED READINGS

Blood, Robert O., Jr.: *Marriage*, The Free Press of Glencoe, New York, 1962, chap. 7. The engagement: ring, showers, timing, function; interaction during engagement.

Burgess, Ernest W., and Paul Wallin: *Engagement and Marriage*, J. B. Lippincott Company, Philadelphia, 1953. A study of 1,000 engaged and 666 married couples; measuring success in engagement activities; relation of engagement to marriage.

Cavan, Ruth Shonle (ed.): *Marriage and the Family in the Modern World*, Thomas Y. Crowell Company, New York, 1960, chaps. 7, 11. Why engagements break; why there are early marriages; age for marriage.

Duvall, Evelyn Millis, and Sylvanus M. Duvall: *Sex Ways in Fact and Faith: Bases for Christian Family Policy*, Association Press, New York, 1961, chap. 4. What we know about young marriages.

Landis, Judson T., and Mary G. Landis: *Building a Successful Marriage*, 4th ed., Prentice-Hall, Inc., Englewood Cliffs, N.J., 1963, chap. 14. Engagement: why engagements are broken; danger signals in engagement; sexual intercourse during engagement.

Martinson, Floyd M.: *Marriage and the American Ideal*, Dodd, Mead & Company, Inc., New York, 1960, chap. 12. The meaning and function of the engagement.

Merrill, Francis E.: *Courtship and Marriage*, rev. ed., Holt, Rinehart and Winston, Inc., New York, 1959, chap. 11. Nature and functions of the engagement; conflict during engagement; sexual intercourse during engagement.

Peterson, James A.: *Education for Marriage*, 2d ed., Charles Scribner's Sons, New York, 1964, chap. 11. The engagement as a testing period for choice of marriage partner and as a planning period.

Waller, Willard: *The Family: A Dynamic Interpretation*, rev. by Reuben Hill, Holt, Rinehart and Winston, Inc., New York, 1951, chap. 12. The engagement: a bridge to marriage; types and functions of engagements; the engagement as a preventive of divorce.

chapter 9

BEGINNING
MARRIAGE

The wedding

Why are weddings necessary? Why is it that two persons who are in love do not start living together without the intermediate legal and religious steps? The purpose of the wedding is publicity in the better sense of the term. It is not notoriety, as some couples seem to assume when they have the ceremony performed in theaters, on horseback, at the bottom of the sea, on roller skates, or in blocks of ice. Notoriety puts the emphasis on the *how*; publicity puts the emphasis on the *fact that*. The wedding is a doorway to new status. It is the announcement of a new relationship between two persons, a relationship in which society, as well as the two individuals themselves, is interested. For this reason there are a ceremony, records, a public expression of willingness on the part of the couple, witnesses, sanction of the state and frequently of the church, and an official, impartial, disinterested representative of the state or of both church and state. There are exceptions made for some religious sects, for example, the Quakers.

The wedding does not have as its purpose the creation of personality traits that are not found in the two persons before the ceremony. It contains no magic. There is no administering of a love potion, no laying on of hands to remove evil spirits. No oracle speaks on the wedding day to communicate to the bride and groom the divine will or to teach them how to "live happily ever after." Whatever happiness they achieve is the result of intelligence, knowledge, love, and effort.

What the wedding does create is chiefly external rather than internal. It creates status, rights, and opportunity. It gives the couple the right and the opportunity to achieve a new degree of mutuality and satisfaction. It does not provide the wherewithal to make that achievement. It does play a part in crystallizing and focusing the meaning of the couple's relationship; and, therefore, it has a personal as well as a social function.

INTEREST OF STATE AND CHURCH

Society, the state, is interested in weddings for several reasons: (1) To safeguard moral standards. Society is anxious that no one shall depart from the mores, the accepted norms. (2) To protect property rights. The state is interested in knowing what belongs to whom. Whether or not the ceremony contains the phrase *with all my worldly goods I thee endow*, property rights are redefined at a wedding. According to the law of the state, husband and wife have various rights to each other's property and to property acquired jointly during the marriage while they both live, when one spouse dies and there are no children, when one dies and there are children. The wedding is a means of showing that the couple acquiesce in the laws of property. (3) To determine the legitimacy of children. Society is interested not only in biological parenthood but in what might be termed "social parenthood," that is, the assumption of social responsibility for children, their support, name, and inheritance of property. Although there is no way of guaranteeing legitimacy or proving paternity—as we pointed out in an earlier connection, fatherhood is based largely on faith—society operates on the assumption that, unless there is evidence to the contrary, the children of a given wife belong also to her husband, especially when he accepts them as such. (4) To protect persons, especially women, from abuse and exploitation. The state is anxious to guarantee status to those who marry. Hence measures are taken to prevent bigamy, fraud, the use of force, and the marriage of children and of persons seriously incompetent. When prevention fails, the state may punish the person whose infraction makes it impossible to guarantee status to the other party. (5) To guarantee the legality of contracts. The wedding ceremony is not a contract in the strict business sense; but there are similarities, and in some cases wedding agreements do involve contracts. (6) To guard against marriages within prohibited degrees of relationship. All states, for example, prohibit marriage between close "blood relatives." Some extend the prohibition to include close relatives-in-law.

The church is interested in weddings for some of the above reasons and also because in some faiths marriage is considered a sacrament. Even when marriage is not counted strictly a sacrament, it is often considered to be ordained by God, and the ceremony contains an important religious element. For this reason a representative of the church is often the officiant. This representative has another function, too, however. The state must, of necessity, depend upon people for the insurance of its requirements. A clergyman is a reliable person, one to whom this responsibility may be entrusted.

SIZE OF THE WEDDING

It is impossible to generalize or to state specifically just how large a wedding should be. A wedding, like a garment, should fit. It should be appropriate to the standard of living and social position of the couple. As is true of a garment, there is no point in having the largest one possible.

The wedding day tends to be more the bride's day than the groom's. The bride is the center of most attention. The change in her life and status brought about by the wedding is greater than that to which the groom is subjected. In most cases she changes her name, follows the groom as to place of residence because his occupation is considered more important than hers, becomes economically dependent upon the husband, assumes the responsibility for homemaking, and prepares — socially, at least — to have children. Furthermore, she is more likely than the groom to be sentimental about the wedding. She wants something to remember and wants a ceremony that will be remembered by her friends. Since this is true, the bride's wishes should within reason take precedence over those of the groom, who may want a simple ceremony, quickly performed. To have friction over wedding plans because the groom seeks to impose his ideas upon the bride is a poor way to start a marriage. On the other hand, however, the bride should be sensitive to the feelings and wishes of the groom.

COST

Size and cost are usually closely correlated, but this is not necessarily the case. Cost, too, should be appropriate to the couple's standard of living. An expensive wedding that is out of proportion to income seems top-heavy and may mean the spending of money that the couple could better use for some other purpose, such as house furnishings. There is no value in a "big splash," as such. A too expensive, too spectacular wedding tends to put the emphasis in the wrong place, namely, on the wedding instead of on the marriage. The former becomes an end in itself.

Most of the wedding expenses are borne by the bride and her family. Nevertheless, as the cost increases, the groom's expenses increase also. It is true of many college students that the bride's family is well established and can afford a relatively expensive wedding, but the groom is still in school or just recently out of school, has a small income, and in many cases has debts. A large wedding would be a burden that he could not readily bear. This situation may well be taken into consideration when plans are being made for a wedding.

PREPARATION

Preparation for a wedding involves innumerable details and activities, from the addressing of envelops to attendance at parties. The more orderly this preparation is, the more foresight and intelligent planning are applied, the less will be the fatigue and tension. Under the best circumstances there may be some fatigue, and every reasonable effort should be made to minimize it. To put off wedding preparations until the last minute, as some students do their schoolwork, is to invite the same sort of flustered haste in the former as is found in the latter, with an additional nervous element in the case of the wedding, which leads to increased irritability.

If we accept the assumption that the marriage is more important than the wedding, then we may seriously question the wisdom of the social schedule which precedes and accompanies the wedding in the case of many couples. The success of marriage does not depend solely on honeymoon attitudes and experiences. Yet, at best, the couple's first days together after the wedding, and especially their first night together, are often supercharged with emotion, sentiment, romantic expectation, and sometimes apprehension. This last is more often experienced by the bride as she contemplates her new sexual role, but is not limited to brides.

If the couple do not plan carefully and instead approach their first days of marriage "worn out" from numerous parties, receptions, receiving lines, and so on, it is not unknown for them to "get off on the wrong foot" on their honeymoon. They are victimized by well-meaning parents and friends who sometimes use the bride and groom to further their own social ambitions. Of course, they themselves may encourage this social orgy. This is not meant to imply that there should be no pre-wedding social events involving the prospective bride and groom. It is meant to suggest only that perspective be not lost.

DATE

The wedding date should be set by the prospective bride, taking into consideration, of course, the wishes of the fiancé and his occupational, military, or other responsibilities. She has to make more preparation than he and can more accurately determine how much time she will need and when her family will be able to carry out their responsibilities. If possible, also, the wedding date should not fall during her menstrual period, not only because of sexual relations but also because during that period many girls tend to be depressed, tired, or irritable. If, however, the groom is understanding and well informed, if he gives the bride's happiness and the success of the marriage precedence over the immediate satisfaction of his sexual impulses, if he is not dominated by an outworn tradition that dictates inevitable consummation of the marriage on the wedding night, the problems attendant upon menstruation are not insurmountable.

The wedding ceremony

The wedding may vary from the barest minimum with a brief statement before a civil official, on the one hand, to an elaborate church affair, on the other. It varies from church to church. It may vary within a given church. It would be impossible to reproduce here all the forms of the service in which readers may participate. Since, however, so many readers will have a religious ceremony, we have chosen to present certain statements or concepts connected with a typical Protestant, Roman Catholic, and Jewish wedding.* We cannot, of course, expect universal agreement on meaning, and the following is intended to be suggestive rather than definitive. During a religious wedding ceremony a couple utter some of the most profound intentions and acknowledge

*Statements from the several ceremonies are taken from the following publications: Protestant: William H. Leach, *The Cokesbury Marriage Manual*, 2d ed., Abingdon Press, Nashville, Tenn., 1945. Roman Catholic: Third Plenary Council of Baltimore, *A Manual of Prayers for the Use of the Catholic Laity*, P. J. Kenedy & Sons, New York, 1930. Jewish: Hyman E. Goldin, *Hamadrikh: The Rabbi's Guide*, Hebrew Publishing Company, New York, 1939. For further discussion of the Protestant ceremony, see Henry A. Bowman, *A Christian Interpretation of Marriage*, The Westminster Press, Philadelphia, 1959.

PREPARATION FOR THE WEDDING

So often the wedding preparation is a one-sided affair managed by the bride-to-be who has usually been involved in the wedding preparations of sisters or friends. The man's involvement, on the other hand, may have been minimal and he may need help in accepting forms, especially if the wedding is to be a large social occasion. The prelude to marriage and the preparation for it can be mutually rewarding and exciting for both partners participating in the things that will play a part in their life together after the wedding.

The apartment and its furnishings are about to become the possessions of both.

some of the most far-reaching responsibilities of which human life is capable. Yet circumstances are often such that their attention is directed toward what is happening rather than toward the meaning of what is said.

"Dearly beloved, we are gathered together here in the sight of God" is a commonly used opening statement in the Protestant ceremony. "The holy state of Matrimony was instituted by Almighty God in the beginning of the world" opens the instructions preceding the ritual proper in the Catholic *Manual of Prayers*. Very early in the Jewish ceremony the rabbi utters this prayer: "He who is supremely mighty; He who is supremely praised; He who is supremely great; May He bless this bridegroom and bride." Such statements affirm the religious nature of marriage, and serve to remind the couple that what they are about to do is God-related. Before they make any commitment concerning one another, they have their attention called to the fundamental orientation of their new life together.

owned in common and used in common. They will be an expression of the interests and tastes of both individuals as a couple.

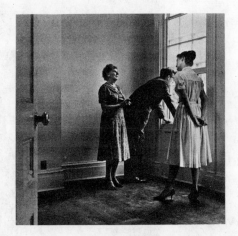

Selecting the home and furniture will be a creative experience in which differences of opinion appear, thoughtful compromises are made, and financial realities are faced.

The phrase "and in the face of this company" usually follows the statement mentioned above in the Protestant ceremony. This is more than a courteous nod in the direction of the assembled guests. It is more than a speaker's beginning with "Mr. Chairman, friends." It is a reference to the importance of marriage as a basic social institution. Because society has always been deeply interested in and concerned with marriage, it is taken for granted that representatives of society should witness a wedding. All three ceremonies include such witnesses, and the *Rabbi's Guide* specifies that they should be unrelated to the bride and groom. This same societal interest in marriage is also implied in a later statement in many Protestant ceremonies, "If any man can show just cause why they may not lawfully be joined together, let him now speak, or else hereafter forever hold his peace." Such interest is indicated, too, in the publication of the banns before a Catholic wedding, for which one of the reasons given is to "afford parents and others interested an opportunity to interpose, if needful."

Especially for the parents of the bride-to-be, the period before the wedding is often one of open rejoicing and some private sadness that a daughter is soon to leave home. During this time a little extra thoughtfulness of the bride-to-be to spend some leisurely moments with her parents can contribute greatly to their happiness. Such appreciation and consideration of others is a quality that will contribute later to the success of her own marriage.

IS THE WEDDING OR MARRIAGE A SACRAMENT?

A sacrament is defined as "an external, visible sign of internal, invisible (or spiritual) grace." Most of the major Christian churches define at least baptism and communion (the Lord's Supper) as sacraments. Two exceptions are the Baptist church (or churches) and the Disciples of Christ, in which such rituals are referred to as ordinances rather than as sacraments [Williams, 1952]. The Catholic *Manual of Prayers* frankly uses the phrase. "The Sacrament of Matrimony," and the Catholic Church combines the wedding with the nuptial Mass. This practice is held to be not merely advisable but necessary today "when the foes of religion are leaving nothing untried in their efforts to deprive . . . Holy Matrimony of all sanctity, and all likeness to a Sacrament."

Phrases such as "holy matrimony," "instituted of God signifying unto us the mystical union that is betwixt Christ and His Church," "holy estate," "God's holy ordinance" which are found in many Protestant ceremonies raise the question of whether the wedding or marriage is a sacrament in Protestant churches, too. Answers to this question among Protestants reflect considerable divergence of opinion. Some hold that marriage is a sacrament. Others hold that marriage is not a true sacrament but is sacramental; that is, it is the symbol of and means for the spiritual union of two persons. Such a view suggests that marriage may become a means by which God's love is made manifest in human life but that this does not of necessity occur at the time of the wedding. The wedding offers the couple an opportunity to participate in the sacramental possibilities of marriage. Through the wedding they indicate their readiness to do so. The wedding does not, however, force these possibilities upon them or make their participation automatic.

The idyllic existence to which the couple look forward in thinking about their days together after the wedding requires thought and planning. For each the focal point of the honeymoon will be their relationship, and together they can decide on the setting in which they will be most relaxed. By giving themselves comfortable surroundings and comparative privacy, they give the honeymoon a good chance of succeeding as a joyful transitional experience.

WHO OR WHAT MARRIES A COUPLE?

A couple may marry without a license if they can find an officiant willing to perform the ceremony. In such a case the penalty, if any, falls upon the officiant; but the marriage is usually valid. A valid marriage may occur without a ring. Except in cases of common-law marriage and in those involving the adherents of certain religious sects, there is an officiant. If the couple believe that their wedding was bona fide, only to learn that the supposed officiant was an imposter, their marriage is usually still valid. It is not necessary to include any religious element in the ceremony in order to fulfill the requirements of the law. It is impossible to escape the influence of the state. But the state merely sanctions; it does not marry people. The state, for instance, could not marry two persons against their will. Witnesses, by definition, merely observe. It is not

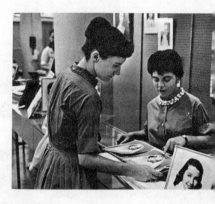

Some aspects of the preparation remain the responsibility of the bride-to-be, and often the man has little or no interest in them. Her family and female friends, though, are usually willing. . .

*and often delighted to help
her with such details.*

required that the bride be "given away." In the last analysis, then, the element without which there can be no valid wedding is found in the couple's mutual agreement, their "I do's" or "I will's." This mutual agreement is termed *consensus*. This it is that marries them, with the sanction of church and/or state. This statement cannot be taken too literally, however. A couple could not marry themselves simply by saying that they had agreed to be husband and wife, though in some states such an agreement is a legal consideration in determining their status at common law.

It is important to note that when "I will," "Wilt thou have this Woman to be thy wedded wife," "Wilt thou love her, comfort her, honour, and keep her," or "Wilt thou take N. here present" is used, as it is in the Protestant and Catholic ceremonies, it implies an act of will, not the future tense of the verb. This is expressed in the Jewish ceremony as "Do you of your own free will and consent." All of this is indication that at the core of marriage there is a deliberate, voluntary commitment to a new relationship.

A NEW STATE OF BEING

Toward the end of the Protestant ceremony the clergyman says, "I pronounce that they are man and wife." In making this statement he is not marrying the couple. He is announcing the fact that they are married and that their marriage falls within the framework defined and approved by church and state. In some Protestant ceremonies "declare" is used in place of "pronounce." Before the clergyman makes the above pro-

The content of the marriage ceremony itself can easily get lost in the shuffle of the many details of preparation. If the couple allow this to happen, they deprive themselves of one of the most meaningful aspects of the wedding. The clergyman considers his responsibility not only the performance of the ceremony but the interpretation of its significance to the participants. Many couples today, under the clergyman's guidance, make additions to or alterations in the traditional ceremony based on their own personal philosophy. Rich in symbolism, the ceremony with its meanings remains important to the couple throughout their married life.

nouncement or declaration, he summarizes what has happened with such phrases as "having consented together in holy wedlock," "have witnessed the same before God and this company," "have given and pledged their troth," "have declared the same by giving and receiving a ring and by joining hands." The use of the word *pronounce* in this connection is similar to the use of the same word by a physician when he says, "I pronounce the patient well" or "I pronounce the patient dead." This does not imply that the physician has healed or killed the patient. It is an announcement of a recognized state of being.

In the Catholic ceremony, after the bride and groom have expressed their commitment, the priest says, "I join you together in marriage, in the name of the Father, and of the Son, and of the Holy Ghost." Actually, the priest does not marry the couple at this point any more than a Protestant clergyman does, as mentioned above. But the priest, as the representative of God, performs a priestly function in connection with a sacrament.

What is this state of being that the clergyman recognizes? Is it merely a new social relationship? A partnership? A cooperative pair? A new opportunity for two people to share a common life and to have children? A common responsibility? A union of two persons in love — within the law and approved by the church? It is all of these — but also more. It is a relationship in which two individuals may find possibilities for sharing in a spiritual and, some would hold, a sacramental union. They become "one flesh."

On a certain occasion in answer to a question, Jesus quoted a statement from the book of Genesis (Gen. 2:24) as follows: "For this cause shall a man leave his father and his mother and cleave to his wife; and they two shall be one flesh" (Mark 10:7–8). The term *one flesh* implies more than sexual union. It implies that a new "body," a new oneness, has been created — an entity that is more than the mere sum of two separate and distinct units. Even the law in its most critical application recognizes that there is something unique in the husband-wife relationship and that they are not two entirely distinct persons when it provides that in court a wife cannot be forced to testify against her husband or a husband against his wife when one is accused of a felony. It would be too much like a person's testifying against himself. As suggested earlier, some churches go farther and recognize this uniqueness as the establishment of both a sacramental union and a new spiritual entity described by comparing it to the "mystical union that is betwixt Christ and His Church."

A SINGLE STANDARD

The statement to which each person says "I do" or "I will" typically is the same for both. There is no double standard of intent or responsibility. In the light of the equality implied in this statement, it is interesting to note that many ceremonies make allowance for the woman to be given in marriage, usually by her father or some relative or close friend. There is no corresponding procedure by which the man is given in marriage. Does this suggest inequality? This practice may be a carry-over from very early times when a woman passed directly from the control of her father to the control of her husband with no intermediate state of relative independence. Or it may be an indication that women are accorded more protection than men. Assuming greater vulnerability and therefore a greater need for protection of women, it is considered important for somebody besides the woman herself to approve of her marriage. If this approval can be expressed through a public act, the marriage may be given some added element of security by being tied in with the woman's parental family.

TAKING OF HANDS

At some point in the ceremony it is common for each to take hold of the other's right hand. This adds a new element, namely, personal contact. Whenever two persons bring parts of their bodies into contact in an acceptable, favorable way, they tend to break down some of the barriers that ordinarily exist between them and to begin to share one another. To some degree, however slight, a community, a union is set up between them. For example, a kiss is an expression of affection. Shaking hands is an expression of friendship. In the wedding ceremony we find community and union implied through a symbolic form of physical contact.

MARITAL ADJUSTMENT IMPLIED

In the commitments which a couple declare, there are statements that both implicitly and explicitly suggest the nature of marriage adjustment. For example, Protestant: "Wilt thou love her (or him), comfort her (or him), honour, and keep her (or him), in sickness and in health; and, forsaking all others, keep thee only unto her (or him), so long as ye both shall live?" and "To have and to hold from this day forward, for better for worse, for richer for poorer, in sickness and in health, to love and to cherish, till death do us part." Catholic: "I, (Name), take thee, (Name), for my lawful wife (or husband), to have and to hold, from this day forward, for better, for worse, for richer, for poorer, in sickness and in health, until death do us part." Jewish: The rabbi says, naming the bride or groom, "Do you of your own free will and consent, take . . . (naming the other person) to be your wife (or husband); and do you promise to love, honor, and cherish her (or him) throughout life? If so, answer Yes."

These statements suggest (1) that the couple will accept one another as they are; (2) that they will both love and respect each other in spite of possible shortcomings; (3) that they will exert continued effort to make the marriage succeed; (4) that they may well anticipate problems; (5) that marriage is an exclusive relationship; (6) that they permanently commit themselves to it.

Following the statement of commitment, there is an exchange of a ring or rings. We shall discuss rings and their meaning later in this chapter. Suffice it to say here that in the modern wedding ceremony the ring is a token, a symbol of the pledge made and of the hope that the marriage will be permanent.

IS MARRIAGE DISSOLUBLE?

In the Protestant ceremony and as part of the nuptial Mass in the Catholic Church, the clergyman reads the following statement made by Jesus: "Those whom God hath joined together let not man put asunder." This statement plus the phrases "so long as ye both shall live," "till death do us part," and "throughout life," found in one form or another in all three ceremonies, raise a basic issue. Is marriage dissoluble? Is divorce ever justified? We know, of course, that divorce is possible within the law. We know, too, that the great majority of Americans regret the occurrence of divorce but, nevertheless, accept it. But how does divorce harmonize with religious teachings? Here, again, we find far from universal agreement. Divorce is possible within the Jewish faith. The Roman Catholic Church holds that marriage once established is indissoluble because it is under the jurisdiction of God and not within the jurisdiction of any human agency. By and large, Protestant churches permit divorce, and the following is broadly representative of a Protestant point of view.

It is true that in a typical ceremony the couple say "I will" to a question that ends with the expression "so long as ye both shall live." This may be interpreted as expressing their solemn intent to the best of their ability at the time of making the commitment. It need not be interpreted as the irrevocable welding of eternal bonds merely through the saying of words. "So long as ye both shall live" does not follow a promise merely to stay married. Ordinarily it follows a commitment to "live together after God's ordinance in the holy estate of matrimony," a commitment to love, comfort, honor, protect, and be faithful to the other party. If a couple find that their marriage has ceased to be what the first part of this statement suggests, and if we recognize that no amount of insistence or force can re-create and reestablish such a marriage in the spiritual sense of the term, then it would seem that rigid adherence to "so long as ye both shall live" is a preservation of the body after life has been destroyed. In the expectation of society and in the thinking of the couple entering it, marriage is taken to be a permanent relationship. The great majority of marriages are such permanent relationships, at least until the death of one of the parties. Some persons would hold, therefore, that marriage in intent and in essence is indissoluble, and that dissolubility suggests a passive process. On the other hand, marriage is destructible, destructibility suggesting a sundering of a relationship that, by its very nature, should not have failed but somehow did.

Since the Roman Catholic Church does not recognize divorce, it cannot approve of remarriage after divorce. Such remarriage is accepted within the Jewish faith. Protestant churches vary in the degree of their acceptance of remarriage. Some raise no issue. Some accept the remarriage as valid but do not permit the wedding ceremony to be performed in the church. Some oppose remarriage. Among the last there is often an inconsistency. They deplore divorce, even though they may accept it, on the basis of children's need for two parents and whole family life. But in opposing remarriage they deprive children of the possibility of having such whole family life. Thus the children are penalized for the mistakes of the parents and become unwitting victims of doctrine.

Wedding customs

Many contemporary wedding customs are so old that their origins are lost in antiquity. In numerous cases we can only speculate as to how they started. Such customs are *survivals*; that is, they have maintained their form but have lost their original meaning and endured beyond the time when they had a function in connection with the ceremony. They might be called social fossils or be compared to vestiges, such as the appendix.

When we know nothing of the origin of one of these survivals, or when the original function, though known, is no longer acceptable, we rationalize the custom and convince ourselves that we carry it out for good luck. When doing something for luck savors too much of the superstitious, we are inclined to continue to do it "for fun." In most cases we carry it out because it is traditional and we accept tradition uncritically.

Marriage is a very ancient institution. There are no peoples known today, no matter how primitive, and no peoples known in history or pre-history without some form of marriage. We can assume that marriage is almost as old as the human race. When a twentieth-century couple marry they step into the stream of cultural history and link themselves with one of the oldest, most venerable, most tenacious, and most durable institutions known—an institution that has persisted in one form or another through all the vicissitudes of mankind's varied experience and in the face of innumerable theorists and reformers because it is the most effective means thus far discovered or evolved for ensuring the values maintained by marriage. Marriage is not the outgrowth of modern state legislation and romantic love alone. It is the product of the ages. One simple, concrete way of showing this is through a brief discussion of wedding customs.

The term *wedding* itself is a carry-over from ancient times. Originally the *wed* was the money or goods that the prospective groom gave to the father of the girl to secure or pledge the purchase of the bride.

The throwing of rice is so common as to be almost universal in this country. According to one theory, the rice constitutes a symbol of fertility. Throwing the rice is an expression of a wish that the new couple will have many children or is an offering to the spirits with this end in view. According to another theory, the rice was originally an offering to appease evil spirits bent on doing harm to the bride and groom. Or the throwing of the rice may be an outgrowth of the ceremonial eating of it [Eichler, 1925].

To show how saturated with tradition we are, how we accept tradition uncritically, and how anything different from the customary is likely to seem ridiculous, let us suggest for illustration that navy beans be substituted for rice at weddings. They are small and inexpensive. They make as much or as little impression when they strike. They have the advantage of being more readily discovered and located in one's clothing. Yet such a substitution seems preposterous. The reader's reaction to it shows how he looks at life through the colored glasses of the mores and folkways and how the use of rice has become conventionalized.

Old shoes are sometimes thrown after the couple or tied to their vehicle as they leave the scene of the ceremony. Why old shoes? In many parts of the world the throwing of shoes has been considered a means of bringing good luck. In Scotland and Ireland shoes were thrown after anyone starting a new enterprise. When Queen Victoria first went to Balmoral Castle, shoes were thrown after her for good luck. In ancient Germany, after the ceremony the bride threw one of her shoes. The person who caught it would not only be the next to marry but would have lifelong good fortune.

The most commonly accepted theory is that the shoe signifies the sealing of a bargain or the transference of authority or property ownership. This was true among the ancient Egyptians, Assyrians, and Israelites [Eichler, 1925]. In the Old Testament story, when Ruth and her mother-in-law, Naomi, returned to Bethlehem after the death of their husbands, Naomi set about planning the remarriage of the younger woman. According to the law of the levirate, it was the duty of the man nearest of kin to the deceased husband to marry the widow, the children of the union becoming the heirs of the dead man. Boaz was related to Ruth's former husband, but there was one man whose kinship was nearer. Boaz wanted to marry Ruth. So he went to the city gate and waited for the other man to appear. Then he called together ten of the town's elders and in the presence of these witnesses stated that Naomi wanted to sell some land and whoever bought the land would have Ruth as his wife.

And the kinsman said, I cannot redeem it for myself, lest I mar mine own inheritance: redeem thou my right to thyself; for I cannot redeem it. Now this was the manner in former time in Israel concerning redeeming and concerning changing, for to confirm all things; a man plucked off his shoe and gave it to his neighbor: and this was the testimony in Israel. Therefore the kinsman said unto Boaz, Buy it for thee. So he drew off his shoe. And Boaz said unto the elders and unto all the people, Ye are witnesses this

day, that I have bought all that was Elimelech's. . . .
Moreover Ruth . . . have I purchased to be my wife, to
raise up the name of the dead upon his inheritance . . .
[Ruth 4:6–10].

If the throwing of old shoes after a bridal couple is, as it seems, a carry-over of a means of sealing a bargain, one may readily see how a wedding links the couple to the past, for the story of Ruth is supposed to have occurred more than three thousand years ago, and the custom was already established at that early date.

The bride often wears "something old, something new, something borrowed, and something blue." The origin of this custom is not known. Part of it may again be attributed to the ancient Israelites, who were bidden to wear blue upon the borders of their garments, blue signifying purity, love, and fidelity.

The bride may wear a veil, or part of her costume may be what might be considered a remnant of a veil. It seems strange that on her wedding day, when she should be proud of her appearance, the bride should wear what is ordinarily a face covering. The veil may originally have been a means of indicating difference in status between an unmarried and a married woman. Typically peoples in some way indicate this difference. It may be a carry-over of the canopy held over the bridal couple during the ceremony among the ancient Hebrews and still used in the Jewish wedding [Eichler, 1925]. Or it may have originated as a means of disguise from evil spirits. All our remote ancestors were primitive and believed in such spirits. On her wedding day a girl was considered especially vulnerable to their influence, and in many parts of the world today a bride is disguised as a means of protection.

The use of a ring as a token or pledge is ancient. After Joseph had interpreted Pharaoh's dreams to the latter's satisfaction, the ruler said to Joseph, "See, I have set thee over all the land of Egypt. And Pharaoh took off his ring from his hand, and put it upon Joseph's hand . . . " [Gen. 41:41–42]. Other early peoples used rings in a similar manner. Eichler [1925] says that the ancient Egyptians were the first to use the ring in connection with marriage vows. In hieroglyphics a circle represents eternity, and the ring probably symbolized the eternal nature of marriage ties. Among the early Anglo-Saxons a ring was included in the *wed* mentioned above. This ring was worn on the bride's right hand until the time of the wedding ceremony, when it was transferred to her left hand. Wedding rings were employed by the Christians as early as A.D. 860.

There are several theories as to why the ring is worn on the fourth finger of the left hand. It is said that in early times the right hand signified power and authority, while the left signified subjection and submission. The ancient Greeks believed that there was a vein extending directly from the ring finger to the heart, the seat of love. It may be that the ring is worn on this particular finger merely because it is the least used of all fingers and ornaments worn upon it cause no inconvenience.

In many wedding ceremonies, both bride and groom have attendants. With the possible exception of the best man, these attendants no longer have any save a decorative function. This custom may have its origin in the ten witnesses required in ancient Rome, the witnesses usually being friends of the bride's family. Or the custom may be a carry-over of marriage by capture. It is thought that in very early days wives were stolen or captured and that parties of friends and relatives to protect the girl or assist the prospective husband gave rise to the custom of having attendants. Among some peoples today there is still mock capture at the wedding ceremony [Sumner and Keller, 1927, III].

Until recently the bride promised to "love, honor, and *obey*." Nowadays *obey* is commonly omitted. The status of women has changed, and the relationship of husband and wife has been considerably altered. Hence, there is no use in including superfluous words in the ceremony. It is significant, however, that the word "obey" was until recently commonly employed and is still sometimes used and also that at no time did the groom promise to obey; he promised to "love, honor, and *cherish*," or something similar.

The custom of the bride's throwing her bouquet to the young unmarried women after the ceremony is still not uncommon, although bouquets are now sometimes composed of numerous sections wired together and ready for convenient distribution. When the bride does throw her bouquet, the belief is that the girl who catches it will be the next to marry. It is said that in the early fourteenth century in France it was considered good luck to procure one of the bride's garters after the ceremony—a custom rather inconvenient for the bride. From this grew the custom of throwing a stocking, a practice that was common during the fifteenth century. This, too, was inconvenient and gave way to throwing the bouquet [Eichler, 1925].

It is believed to bring ill luck if the groom sees the bride in her wedding dress or sees her at all before the ceremony on the wedding day. The origin of this custom is uncertain. It may be that it began when parents feared elopement and consequently being cheated out of the bride price [Eichler, 1925]. It may have originated in the belief that the groom could direct evil spirits or the evil eye to the ever-vulnerable bride.

In many cases noisemakers are used before or after a wedding. A bell is rung, tin cans are tied to the couple's vehicle, or other cars follow the bridal car with horns sounding. We accept the wedding bell without question, and the other two types of noisemaking are rationalized as "fun." But one wonders what the origin of this custom was. It may have begun with the belief that noise frightens evil spirits, as many peoples still hold. It may be only a means of publicity, as we shall see later.

Often there is an element of slight promiscuity introduced into a wedding. After the ceremony proper the men are free to kiss the bride and the women to kiss the groom. The commonly accepted line drawn between those who have such freedom and those supposed to exercise restraint and to lack interest in such osculatory indulgence breaks down. There is reason to wonder whether this slight promiscuity is reminiscent of the complete license found at weddings among some of the peoples of the world whose beliefs and customs have remained unaltered for centuries.

It is not unusual for the groom to carry the bride over the threshold of their new home. In ancient Rome the threshold was considered sacred to Vesta, the goddess of virgins, and it was thought to be an ill omen if the bride stumbled over it. To prevent her stumbling, the young husband carried her into the house. What happens if he stumbles with her is not clear.

The custom of "belling" or charivari (often pronounced colloquially as if it were "shiveree," with the accent on the last syllable) is current in some communities. The practice has many local variations. In each case the twofold function seems to be the same, namely, publicity plus community acceptance of the marital status of the newly-wed pair. Newspapers and other modern means of publicity and communication make a demonstration superfluous in most communities, but the custom persists in part as a survival.

The following is a description of a small-town "belling." Upon returning from their honeymoon, the couple were met at the train by a group of friends. Almost before they knew what was happening, the bride and groom had been whisked into a truck, which had recently been used for hauling cattle to market and had reminiscences of its past strewn on the floor. Since there were no seats, the couple had to stand, balancing themselves as best they could, while the truck moved over the rough pavement, and looking in their solemn-faced embarrassment like a motion-picture version of Marie Antoinette on her way to the guillotine. At the rear of the truck was tied a large empty oil drum, which boomed in thunderous fashion as it bounced along the street. Following the nuptial vehicle was a long line of cars, each crowded with friends and each with its horn sounding continuously. Up and down the streets went the noisy procession until everyone in town had heard and had seen. After that there was no doubt as to who had been married or as to whether or not the community accepted the new status of the bride and groom. The combined function of publicity and acceptance had been fulfilled.

In one form of the charivari, friends bring noisemakers of all sorts — dishpans, shotguns, drums, horns, their own husky voices — and surround the house to which the bride and groom have retired. They set up a terrific din, which they do not permit to abate until they have been fed either on the spot or at a local restaurant. In some cases they bring their own food as well as the noisemakers. The function again is the same as with the "belling" described above. Of this function the participants may be naïvely unaware, engaging in the ceremony because it is fun and is traditional. This is an indication of the custom's being an old one and again demonstrates our tendency uncritically and unanalytically to accept tradition and to keep the ball rolling, so to speak, even after social change has removed part of the original function and meaning.

Secret marriage

There is a difference between a secret wedding and a secret marriage. The former is an elopement and the fact of marriage is made known after the ceremony. In the case of the latter, the secret is kept for an extended period and neither the ceremony nor the new relationship is made known. An elopement may also be a "runaway" wedding which is not necessarily performed secretly but is performed in a manner and in a place that carry it beyond the influence and observation of relatives and friends.

In the case of either wedding or marriage, there are various degrees of secrecy possible. The secret may be kept from everyone except the license issuer, the officiant, and the legally required witnesses. It may be kept from parents, from friends, from an employer, or from the public at large. The degree of secrecy and the persons from whom the secret is kept constitute variables that affect the arguments pro and con listed below.

There are few valid arguments in favor of either secret wedding or secret marriage, and those few apply to relatively rare circumstances. In cases where there is *unreasonable* and *unfounded* opposition, where parents insist upon lifelong celibacy, where there has been a recent death in the family that upsets wedding plans and preparation, or where similar unusual conditions obtain, secrecy may be justifiable. But such cases are relatively uncommon. A young couple should be careful not to read into their situation elements that are not there in order to rationalize their secrecy.

There are secret weddings and secret marriages that work out well, but in general the arguments against them are weightier than those in their favor. There is no opportunity for the couple's enthusiasm to be either counterbalanced or reinforced by the judgment of relatives and friends. Secrecy is all too often the outgrowth of haste; and hasty marriage frequently ends in failure. Married life is started with deception and concealment. It is not only a matter of deceiving those who might object to the marriage but also a matter of keeping secret something that one wants very much to make known. One young woman who had married secretly and kept the secret for some time explained that after the ceremony she was very happy. She loved her husband and they planned eventually to marry anyway, but they married secretly in order to do so earlier. She wanted very much to tell her family and friends how happy she was, and her emotions seemed to accumulate as time went on. But because of the administrative situation in the school that she was attending, she could not mention it. When the time came that she could tell her secret, her original burst of enthusiasm had waned somewhat, for she had then been married for several months and, much to her regret, she had missed one of the great experiences of a girl's life.

Secrecy involves the omission of many of the preparations for a wedding which when kept in balance are a source of satisfaction and an experience to look back on. Omission of these preparations naturally includes the omission of shower and wedding gifts to some extent at least and in many cases such gifts have an important place in the economy of the new household.

Secrecy is likely to offend parents and friends and often makes for enmity with in-laws. Parents are usually hurt, not only because their child has married but because their pride has been injured by their being kept ignorant of plans and events. Often, too, the girl's parents have for years dreamed of wedding plans for her. Her secrecy seems like an affront, since it has the appearance of a refusal to accept what they are eager to give or a lack of gratitude for what they would willingly have done. It may also seem to them an indication of lack of trust, in that it appears as if the son or daughter did not feel free to confide in them.

Then, too, suddenly to find that they have a new son-in-law or daughter-in-law without having gradually come to an acceptance of this state of affairs through wedding preparations is frequently something of a shock to parents and necessitates readjustment more rapid than they had anticipated. In order to gain some idea of how parents might feel under such circumstances, let the reader imagine that he is a college student who has been away at school since autumn and has not seen his parents since he left home. Letters have given no clue to any change within the family and he assumes that everything is still as it was when he last saw them. At commencement time he looks forward with eager anticipation to his parents' attending the graduation exercises. Only his mother comes, however. When she arrives, he learns for the first time that his parents have been divorced and that his mother has remarried, the new husband accompanying her to the commencement. What a shock he would experience! What rapid new adjustment would become imminent! How difficult he would find it to accept a fact so remote from his previous expectation! How his pride would be hurt because he had not been informed of the impending change!

Marriage is important enough to make it worth while to start out under the best possible auspices. Parents and parents-in-law may do much to make marital adjustment easier or more difficult. Unless it means the sacrificing of one's happiness, the cultivation of their favor is an investment that pays ample dividends.

There is sometimes a cloud of suspicion cast over a secret wedding or secret marriage. When at last the facts are made known, people naturally wonder about the reason for the secrecy. Was she afraid she would lose him? Did she not get along well with her family? Was it a forced marriage? Did they really marry when they say they did, or did they marry later and then say that they had been secretly married earlier in order to camouflage a premarital pregnancy?

The best secrets sometimes leak out, and then seemingly well-laid plans are disrupted. If the marriage as well as the wedding is kept secret, the couple find difficulty in living either as single or as married persons. If they try to live in the latter way, their behavior will be subject to question by their families and friends. If they attempt to seem unmarried, there frequently ensues a problem of dating, especially if the couple attend different colleges. It is all very well to make ambitious statements about letting each other date, but because of our expectation of exclusiveness it is difficult to work out smoothly. Husband or wife may not be able to accept in practice what seems acceptable in theory when marriage is being contemplated, and it appears that whether or not they will marry soon and secretly depends upon their willingness to be liberal and broad-minded. There is also likely to be criticism when the dates discover that the person they thought single is married and that they have in a way been duped. Public opinion is unfavorable to such dating. In one case a girl secretly married went steady with a boy for several months. She was a frequent visitor in his home and accepted by his family as a "girl friend." The boy spent many hours coaching her in academic subjects in which she had difficulties. At the end of the college semester, when his help was no longer needed, she told him that she had been married some time before. His disillusionment and his family's resentment may be imagined.

If the marriage is secret and the wife becomes pregnant, explanation is made most difficult. Friends and relatives may or may not believe that she was married at the time of conception. A person does not usually carry a certificate stating the date of the wedding so that he may show it to friends the moment their doubt and suspicion become manifest. Such a certificate, even if one did carry it, could not be made available to everyone who might have an inclination to pick up and pass on a tempting bit of gossip.

This section on secret marriage is intended for the single, not the married. We should be the last to implant doubt, apprehension, or regret in the mind of a reader already secretly married. What is done is done. Such a one needs a practical plan for the future, not criticism of the past.

Our purpose has been to provide food for thought. No one needs to marry secretly unless he chooses to do so; he is never forced to do it. Our only hope is that those contemplating secret marriage will weigh the pros and cons before making a decision.

The honeymoon

Sometimes the honeymoon as a period of adjustment immediately following the wedding is distinguished from the wedding trip as such. Since, however, the honeymoon and the trip coincide to some extent and in many cases, we shall use the terms interchangeably, recognizing that there is a period of adjustment of longer duration than the journey. In common parlance the terms are used synonymously.

Not every couple has a wedding trip, and there is no reason to assume that married life cannot have an auspicious beginning without one. More depends upon the couple than upon the fact of travel. Some couples choose to rest for a brief period before a trip is begun; and this plan has arguments in its favor. Some choose only to stay at a hotel in town for a while. Others leave for the trip immediately after the wedding. Still others go directly to their new home. Some do not miss even one day of work or classes.

FUNCTION

The function of the honeymoon is to enable the newly wedded couple to make the transition from single to married life with the greatest facility and the fewest handicaps. Hence, in so far as possible, they should promote whatever furthers this transition and avoid whatever impedes it. It is important to realize that the honeymoon is a transition period. Marriage is not just a long honeymoon. Consequently, in some respects the honeymoon is an artificial situation and must be considered as such. Regarded in this way, it is able to provide unusual opportunities as well as to exhibit certain limitations.

Although the honeymoon does present an artificial situation and is a transition period, it need not be thought of as a brief, bright interlude between the stress-imbued, painful bliss of courtship and the supposedly unromantic monotony of settled wedded existence. To marry and go on a honeymoon is not like ascending a high peak after a laborious climb in order to get a glorious view of a grand panorama, from which, after a brief stay at the summit, one returns to the commonplace, everyday, restricted views at the foot of the mountain. To marry is, rather, like climbing a gradual slope to a higher level, from which one gets a broader view but also from which one sees still higher levels to be reached in time and with patience. In well-founded marriages the couple do not return to a lesser experience after the honeymoon; the latter is the door through which they pass to greater experiences. Unfortunately not all marriages work out so satisfactorily; but marriage must be judged by its potentialities as well as by its failures. Knowing what marriage can be is the first step toward its fullest attainment.

LENGTH

In connection with the honeymoon that involves a trip there are several considerations to be kept in mind. It should not be too long. This is most indefinite; but no one can say exactly what its length should be because that depends upon a number of factors, among which are the two personalities of man and wife and their finances. It should, however, be long enough to fulfill its function and at the same time short enough so that it is terminated before enthusiasm wanes and boredom sets in, before the novelty wears off and it begins to drag. This is not the same as saying that marriage is boring and monotonous; as we have already stated, the honeymoon is an artificial situation and is subject to the limitations of any extended vacation.

Traveling has a recognized tendency to begin with enthusiasm and end with fatigue. The ordinary person is not prepared to travel indefinitely, even if he can afford it. There is, too, the probability that the bride will be eager to get back to her new home. Unless he is a student with an ample allowance from his parents or he has an independent income, the groom cannot help thinking of his work and the family income.

There is reason to believe that it is better for the couple to set an approximate rather than an exact date for their return. In this way they may avoid unnecessary explanation if they decide to return early for financial or other reasons. In this way they may also avoid too great pressure of social obligations immediately upon their return, if they care to do so.

COST

The honeymoon, like the wedding, should be of a cost commensurate with the couple's standard of living. Since it is customary for the groom to meet the honeymoon expenses, his financial condition rather than that of the bride's family should be taken as the standard. If the honeymoon becomes too expensive and too elaborate in comparison with the life that the pair will lead upon their return, it may fail to fulfill its function of enabling them to make the transition to married life and may result in what seems like a "letdown." Romantic though it may be to have an unusual honeymoon to look back upon, it is not conducive to marital happiness to have one's present and permanent situation compare too unfavorably with the first few days of marriage. To be happy, one must find pleasure and contentment in his day-by-day existence as well as in his memories.

Perhaps the best plan is to budget the honeymoon, prepare carefully so that expenses remain within the budget, and thus have a honeymoon free of financial worry. In such planning, however, some allowance must be made for unexpected circumstances so that there need be no embarrassment and no penny pinching. By careful planning the couple may avoid spending money needed for their new home. It would obviously be a mistake to spend all that they had on a trip and to return without funds, furniture, or household equipment.

PLACE

It is probably advisable for the couple to go where they are not too well known. At best, newlyweds have a way of betraying their consciousness of their recently acquired status. If they go where they are not well known, they will be better able to escape questions, knowing looks, telling smiles, and jokes at their expense. Embarrassment and self-consciousness will be decreased. They will avoid being repeatedly introduced as bride and groom. There will be no social obligations or schedules not of their own making. They can have privacy when they want it.

The honeymoon need not be a busman's holiday, but the couple should avoid going to places where life and experiences are so radically different from what they are accustomed to or prepared for that adjustment becomes difficult. This does not imply that they should have stereotyped plans or do nothing unusual and different. It implies only doing nothing which will defeat the purpose of the honeymoon. If, for example, the bride has never traveled by water, it might be unwise to plan an extended voyage. What could be more disconcerting and less conducive to a favorable introduction to married life than a seasick bride on a honeymoon? If the couple have dwelt in the city all their lives and have had no experience in roughing it, there might be risk in planning to camp in the north woods, away from town, telephone, and people. For those accustomed to crowds and noise, the quiet solitude of the forest might soon change romance into boredom. Indigestion might follow upon attempts at cooking over an open fire. Upon the heels of indigestion might come irritation. Unless the couple are unusually sure of themselves, there is some risk in depending only upon each other's company.

PLANS

The honeymoon should be leisurely; it should not have a crowded program. The purpose is to make the transition to married life, not to get to places. The honeymoon should not be a travel-bureau, prearranged, all-expense tour on which the traveler feels that unless he sees every monument and witnesses every spectacle he is not getting his money's worth. A simple plan is better. Dashing here and rushing there are almost sure to lead to excessive fatigue; and fatigue often leads to unpredictable behavior, which may leave scars on a marriage, especially when it occurs during the sensitive, idealized, self-conscious days of the honeymoon. A period so suffused with romantic expectation produces an increased vulnerability of feeling; and fatigue-induced irritability may give rise to unnecessary disillusionment during this period of transition.

ADDRESSES

The bride and groom may have to slip away after the wedding because of the childish propensities of some of their emotionally immature, practical-joker guests; but they should not leave without arranging with some reliable person for means of communicating with them should an emergency arise. To make this point clear let us take an imaginary example. A bride wants to leave a mailing address with her mother, but the groom's wish is to be completely free and arrange for no means of communication. The bride yields to the groom's wishes. They are away for ten days. When they return, they find that the bride's father has been killed in a motor accident and that the funeral is over. Her probable reaction would be to say to her husband, "If it had not been for you, it would not have happened this way." She might erect a barrier that would affect their entire future relationship. This is an extreme example, and nothing like it is likely to happen to the typical couple. Since presumably they have only one marriage at stake, however, and there is always the possibility of an emergency's arising, and since arranging for a means of communication is really a trifle, it seems short-sighted to assume the risk.

The transition from singleness to marriage

We have referred to the honeymoon as a period of transition. Actually, of course, it represents only part of such a period. The transition from singleness to marriage begins at least with the engagement and extends through the wedding and honeymoon and into marriage itself. The point is that to make their marriage succeed a couple must pass through a number of transitions. To the degree to which they fail to do so, the marriage is likely to suffer. During the honeymoon and for a while thereafter the need for such transitions is brought to a new focus. Some of these transitions are as follows.

From independence to a "team" relationship. This "team" relationship is, in a sense, unique because it involves two persons of opposite sex. When two complementary equals are united in common purpose, a new oneness, a new entity, is created. Their relationship extends not to a part of life but to a fundamental way of life. Such a transition entails concessions on either side. It requires a new perspective in that the relationship is in some ways considered more important than the individuals in it. Obviously, a person who cannot make this transition and who consequently continues to think, act, make demands, and set expectations as if he were still single is an impediment to the success of the "team."

From a premarital sexual pattern to a marital sexual pattern. For many persons, especially but not exclusively women, this involves a transition from premarital chastity or infrequent, often incomplete, sexual relations to normal, unrestrained marital sexual experience. For some women this expected rightabout-face is not easy, and the full transition takes time. But certainly it is appropriate to expect a woman who marries to redefine her sexual objective and shift it from premarital self-protection and reluctance to marital acceptance and enthusiastic sharing. A woman can hardly be married and single simultaneously. If she insists upon protecting herself from her husband, what did she mean in the wedding ceremony when she said, "I take this man"?

Depending upon his premarital experience or lack of it, the man may be called upon to make a transition from giving first consideration to his own sexual satisfaction to giving first consideration to the satisfaction of his wife through which his own satisfaction is increased. He is called upon to think of sex as a mutual rather than only as a self-oriented experience.

The couple are called upon to make a transition from thinking of sexual intercourse as having no place in their premarital behavior pattern, from treating it casually, from being subject to premarital limitations, or from the woman's reluctant acceptance for the sake of the man's pleasure, to integrating it into the totality of their common life.

From the relative irresponsibility of romance to the responsibilities associated with establishing and maintaining a home and family. For this transition many young people are not well prepared. The man may fail to understand that homemaking and family living today put demands upon him other than in his role as breadwinner. He may expect his wife to continue to wait upon him as his mother did or to perform without reciprocation on his part the personal services for which in his premarital days he was accustomed to pay and for which, therefore, he felt no call to express appreciation. The woman may be unprepared to carry out housekeeping duties with efficiency and dispatch. Her attitude toward gainful employment may lead her to resist or even to reject the role of homemaker to which, she feels, there is attributed too little prestige.

From the responsibility of carrying out assignments to the type of responsibility that makes assignments unnecessary. College students who may be considered "good students" in the sense of carrying out assignments and conforming to faculty expectation are in some cases ill-prepared to make and carry out plans without outside pressure. They fritter away time and energy and sometimes do only the minimum necessary to "get by" – or less – because in marriage they have no one to tell them what to do.

From premarital food preparation to family feeding. This applies particularly, but not exclusively, to women. Many a girl who is skilled at preparing party foods finds herself confronted with quite a different problem in preparing a balanced diet for a husband who eats 1,095 meals per year or in feeding two persons on a meager income.

From student purchasing to family purchasing. With some exceptions, college students may usually do the bulk of their purchasing in a small number of stores of relatively limited type adjacent to the campus. Family purchasing presents a somewhat different problem because of the greater variety of items to be purchased and because of the resulting greater complexity of the budget. With the exception of gifts, student purchasing involves largely items for oneself. Family purchasing requires knowledge of buying items for a home, for a member of the opposite sex, and for children.

From a single person spending pattern to a "double person" spending pattern. In some cases the man continues to think in terms of "my money," a portion of which he reluctantly doles out to his wife when her need is clearly apparent or her pleas are sufficiently convincing. The woman, in some cases, continues to spend family income as if she were still single and receiving an allowance from her parents and her own desires were the only ones to be considered.

From being a child of one's parents to being husband or wife. This raises the question, "Who will be put first in one's scale of values, spouse or parents?" The individual who cannot put spouse first is not ready to be married.

From being a child of one's parents to being a child-in-law of the other person's parents. This transition takes time and calls for understanding and effort on the part of all concerned, as we shall see in a later chapter.

From marriage to the family, that is, from having no child to having a child. For obvious reasons the arrival of the first child is most critical so far as this transition is concerned. A question arises as to the spouse's and the child's relative position in one's scale of values. In a successful family there is an integration of such nature that spouse and child are not thrown into competition for the attention of the other parent. In some families, however, the arrival of the first child means that husband or wife, more frequently the latter, allows attention to the child, in a sense, to squeeze the other party out of the marriage relationship. In other words, the woman becomes so much a mother that she is correspondingly less a wife. In occasional cases the situation is vice versa. For example, in one case the couple got along apparently happily until the birth of the first baby. Then the husband refused to go out with his wife in the evening because he would not leave the child with a baby-sitter. He objected to his wife's shopping, visiting friends, or attending church for the same reason. He would not go out or let her go out and take the child along because he feared it would contract some contagious disease. The wife felt that she was virtually a prisoner in her own home because of her baby.

From personal appearance to attract to personal appearance to please. Actually the above distinction is not complete; the two processes overlap. But there are many young people who give much time and attention to making themselves attractive during their dating days only to let their appearance rapidly deteriorate after the wedding. Not everyone can be beautiful or handsome; but everyone can, if he will, make the most of his possibilities. Neglect of appearance is sometimes a reflection of disappointment with marriage.

Even persons most attentive to personal appearance cannot be equally attractive at all times. No one is so attractive upon getting up in the morning or while doing certain types of work as he may be at other times. Marriage involves understanding and accepting this fact — which in itself is a transition for many persons with limited premarital contacts. The critical point here is the individual's attitude toward personal appearance after the uncertainty of the premarital search for a spouse is ended and the security of marriage makes no longer necessary attracting another person. The transition involved is that between attraction, on the one hand, and attractiveness, on the other.

WHAT DO YOU THINK?

1. What is the relation of a wedding to a marriage?

2. A couple attend the same university. In September they marry secretly. In December the girl finds herself pregnant. What suggestions would you give them?

3. Discuss the pros and cons of having a honeymoon.

4. If it is not possible to have a honeymoon immediately following the wedding, can a couple have a honeymoon a few weeks or months later?

5. When they marry, are there transitions, in addition to the ones mentioned in this chapter, through which a couple must pass to make their marriage succeed?

6. Analyze the wedding ceremony of a given church. Point out the elements in it which pertain to the success or failure of marriage.

7. Analyze the wedding ceremony in a given church. What elements in it suggest that marriage is a religious, moral, legal, social, traditional, and interpersonal relationship?

8. Under what circumstances is secret marriage justified?

9. Is elopement ever justified? If so, under what circumstances?

SELECTED READINGS

Blood, Robert O., Jr.: *Marriage*, The Free Press of Glencoe, New York, 1962, chap. 8. The wedding and honeymoon; the wedding ceremony and finances.

Bowman, Henry A.: *A Christian Interpretation of Marriage*, The Westminster Press, Philadelphia, 1959, chap. 4. An analysis of the Protestant wedding.

Fishbein, Morris, and Ruby Jo Reeves Kennedy (eds.): *Modern Marriage and Family Living*, Oxford University Press, Fair Lawn, N.J., 1957, chap. 13. The wedding and honeymoon, including a consideration of costs.

Richards, Sherman L., Jr.: "The Secret Marriage," *Marriage and Family Living*, vol. 22, no. 3, pp. 243–247, August, 1960. A study of secret marriages in Michigan.

part 3

BASIC COMPONENTS
OF MARITAL ADJUSTMENT

Marriage is not merely a part of life; it is a way of life. As such, for its success, it requires a continuous process of adjustment on the part of the persons in it. Such adjustment is not static. It does not imply the couple's reaching a "dead level" of equilibrium. Rather, it implies dynamic change, continuing "growth" on the part of both the couple and their relationship. In order for such "growth" to be achieved, the couple need to have an understanding of various aspects of marriage—psychological, interpersonal, social, sexual, reproductive, and financial—as well as an understanding and acceptance of each other as persons. They need to make certain transitions from singleness to marriage. They need to have an awareness of possible problems plus a commitment to the solution of the soluble ones and the acceptance of the insoluble ones. In short, they need a will to succeed. As a marriage becomes a family, with the arrival of a child, both new problems and new opportunities arise.

chapter 10

SOCIAL FACTORS AFFECTING MARRIAGE

Attitude of adjustment

Marriage is not a Procrustean bed. Procrustes was a character in ancient mythology whose favorite pastime was to capture unwary travelers and put them to bed. When the traveler was too short, he was stretched to fit. When the guest was too long, the obliging host cut off part of his legs. Procrustes made the serious mistake of thinking that there was only one variable in the situation, the traveler. Actually, there were three possible variables: the traveler, the bed, and Procrustes' own attitude. He would have proved a more congenial host if he had adjusted the bed to the size of the occupant or if he had had an attitude flexible enough to permit some slight lack of fit between bed and guest. Instead, he set out with a rigid ideal and insisted that everyone be forced to accommodate himself to it.

In marriage the concept of adjustment is fundamental. But adjustment to what? Two personalities must adjust to each other, to the marital situation in both the narrow and the broad sense, and to social conditions in general. All these elements are continually in a state of flux. Marriage is a process, not a constant. Marital adjustment is, therefore, dynamic rather than static. It does not imply one person's adjusting to another as if the other person were a fixed point and both were seeking to reach a dead level of changeless equilibrium. Being dynamic, it implies a developing mutual relationship in which resources for satisfaction are more and more fully drawn upon. Preparation for marriage is of necessity generalized. In marriage, adjustment becomes particularized through knowledge, love, discovery, effort, and ingenuity.

Adjustment does not imply that one person must do all the adjusting or that there shall always be compromise. There may be situations in which no compromise is acceptable, as, for instance, in cases of excessive alcoholism or infidelity. Even in such cases, however, a study of causes is important and readjustment may be possible.

Every problem of marriage adjustment or human relationships, with a few possible theoretical exceptions, is two-sided and occurs in a milieu, against a background of the marital and social situation. Adjustment may be achieved by one person's changing his behavior, by the other's changing his attitude, or by a change in the elements that compose the situation — such as income, housing, or proximity to relatives.

Adjustment implies relief from tension. The only complete relief is death. All life involves tension, some of which is never completely relieved, while some may be temporarily relieved. In marriage there is always some tension because marriage involves the relationship of two persons of opposite sex. A perfect adjustment, with complete relief from tension, could be achieved only by sexless automata. Continual adjustment to tension infuses zest into marriage. When adjustment does not eventuate, that same tension may produce dissatisfaction or failure.

That so much is said about marital adjustment does not mean that a couple are unpleasantly aware of it twenty-four hours in the day or that it comes automatically to those who have read and assimilated a few chapters in a book. When one considers that it takes about twenty years to become partially adjusted to life in general before marriage, the suggestion that a couple allow a few years to adjust to each other in a new relationship does not seem excessive. Marriage is not a part of life; it is a way of life. Hence, marital adjustment is a widely permeating and basically essential process.

Persons of student age discussing or reading about adjustment in marriage sometimes acquire the notion that adjustment is something that obtrudes itself into a couple's consciousness. Adjustment in marriage is similar to that in life in general. It is a continuous, never-ending process, but we are conscious of it only at intervals when changes are made, judgments are drawn, or problems are faced.

Students sometimes become apprehensive when discussing marital failure. They should keep several points in mind. (1) It is easier to talk about failure than about success. (2) We know more about failure because it is more obvious, more readily defined, and makes news. (3) Achievement in marriage varies from worst to best in the same way as achievement in any other human venture. There are many instances of success, perhaps more of success than of failure. (4) Problems are met one at a time, not all at once as one sees them in printed case studies. (5) Whatever fear one may have is lost after starting, just as stage fright is lost after a speech is begun, because then one thing at a time is concentrated upon and the individual does not look forward in more or less confused anticipation to the whole situation at once, as the unmarried young person looks forward to marriage. (6) When reading about or discussing problems of adjustment, one must realize that those are the things that happen to all couples considered as a group, not to one couple alone. No one couple faces all the problems heard or read about. It is like reading a book on medicine; no one has all the illnesses described. (7) Normal, intelligent persons who make a wise choice of marriage partners have everything in their favor. (8) There are pitfalls and mistakes that may be avoided if recognized in advance. (9) Marriage involves problems, but it is not all problems and nothing else, any more than is life in general. Their presence in marriage is hopeful because it shows that there are opportunities and possibilities, even though they are missed by some couples.

In spite of the amount of marital failure in this country and the publicity given to such failure, the fact remains that a large proportion of American marriages are at least acceptably satisfactory to the couples concerned. Much is said about the high divorce rate. Relatively little mention is made of the fact that each year in this country about 150,000 couples celebrate their golden wedding anniversaries, "and that there are nearly 750,000 surviving couples who have been married fifty or more years" [Glick, 1957]. American marriage is still a "going concern." On the whole, it may not be so good as its most optimistic participants and most hopeful observers believe. Neither is it so bad as its most pessimistic participants and severest critics insist. It is tougher and more durable than many people realize. No substitute has yet been found for the contribution that marriage makes to human life. These millions of reasonably happy marriages have not been established by perfect individuals drawn together by a kind fate and living in perpetual bliss with no cloud of problems ever to shadow their happiness. These marriages have been established by imperfect individuals like ourselves who have somehow found it possible to accept one another, who have faced and met problems squarely, solving some and tolerating others, and who have been willing to devote time and effort to building something which they consider profoundly important.

What is successful marriage?

Successful marriage is a dynamic, growing relationship in which the personalities of both partners continue to develop. It reaches a relatively high level of personal satisfaction. Both parties get at least what they expected from marriage. The more they get, the greater is the relative success. The couple achieve relatively full use of their personal resources and draw freely upon environmental resources to further their adjustment and increase their mutual happiness. There is no unusual amount of conflict, overt or covert, and the marriage endures so long as both parties live. Joint enterprise and intimate relationships are not only acceptable but attractive and are carried out not only willingly but enthusiastically. The essential elements in the marriage are assimilated into the personalities of both parties; no essential element is permanently encysted and shut out of the life of either partner. In such marriage each individual is permitted to approach as near to his objectives as his capacities will allow. There is nothing in the relationship to impede him. Each spouse gives the other freedom, confident that that freedom will never be abused.

Since marriage involves persons other than the couple themselves, social as well as personal criteria of success must be taken into consideration. A successful marriage meets the requirements of the law. It is consistent with the expectations set by the mores. The relationship of the marriage partners produces a "climate" conducive to the healthy emotional development of children. As mentioned earlier, a successful marriage is conducive to the free association of people. To the degree to which a marriage places obstacles in the way of such free association it may be considered unsuccessful. For example, in a religiously or racially mixed marriage, the way that the couple get along together is not the only factor to be considered. If the racial or religious difference prevents in-laws from accepting one another, acts as a barrier between grandparents and child, makes difficult or impossible the establishing of a set of common friends, then, to a degree, the marriage is unsuccessful. An individual marriage is not an isolated phenomenon. It is an integral part of a social mosaic. It is a focus for the crisscrossing of innumerable human interrelationships.

Successful is not synonymous with *happy, ideal, satisfactory,* or *perfect,* although all these terms overlap. No marriage is perfect. Happiness is subjective and individual. It depends in part upon the degree to which achievement approaches expectation. An individual whose expectation was represented by, say, 2 would be unhappy if his achievement was represented by 1. An individual, on the other hand, whose expectation was represented by 1 would be happy if his achievement was also represented by this number. Putting it another way, happiness equals the fraction "achievement over expectation" [Nimkoff, 1934]. A successful marriage is happy, but one may conceive of a happy marriage that is not successful because the standards of the couple are low and their relationship does not meet the criteria set up by society as well as those they set up themselves. A marriage might be happy for one spouse but not for the other. Under such circumstances it could hardly be considered successful. *Ideal* marriage connotes the marriage one most desires, the nearest approach to perfection he can make, and implies that he is satisfied with his lot, knowing that human limitations forbid perfection. It also implies the standard set up by the mores as most desirable. *Satisfactory* connotes varying degrees of good enough, all of them relative to expectations and some of them so closely approximating *successful* as to be practically synonymous with it. A marriage may contain unsatisfactory elements and yet be *workable.*

No criterion of success is sufficient alone. Several must be used in conjunction before any judgment upon a particular marriage may be passed. Marital success and failure are not two entities with the line between them sharply drawn. Each is a matter of degree, and they represent the two ends of a continuum.

Who can judge whether a particular marriage is successful? An outside observer cannot always judge, because he is likely to set up a standard based upon his own tastes and expectations rather than upon those of the couple involved. He may also lack information about the marriage, since at best he can observe only overt behavior and for many items must depend upon the biased observation of husband or wife.

The persons in the marriage cannot always tell whether it is successful because they have nothing to compare it with. If they try to compare their marriage with others, for the latter they fall into the category of outside observer with the limitations mentioned above. They are certain to be biased and to look at their marriage through the colored glasses of their own expectations. Both the outsider and the couple must do the best they can with the knowledge at their command, knowing that even under circumstances most favorable to observation, the final judgment is subjective.

There are actually three norms of success: (1) the ideal set up by society, (2) the type of marriage that society allows to "get by," and (3) the norm set up by each individual as to what he wants from marriage and expects it to be.

With these things in mind let us discuss some of the factors that may play a part in adjustment in marriage—factors that may contribute to success or failure, as the case may be. Some have already been suggested or implied in other parts of this book. In general these factors fall into two groups: those "outside" the individual or the marriage, such as social conditions, and those "inside," such as personality traits or marital processes. We cannot hope to discuss them all because they vary according to time, place, circumstance, and personnel. We shall mention the first group in this chapter and in the next go on to discuss the second.

Factors in the social situation

LEGISLATION

We speak of American marriage as if it were an entity, something uniform throughout the country. Actually we should speak of New York marriage, Missouri marriage, California marriage, and so on through the list, since the institution is defined by fifty-one sets of laws, including the District of Columbia, and is not exactly the same under any two jurisdictions. This variety not only reflects a lack of standards but contributes to confusion and to the inclination to seek the most convenient legislation. If a couple want to marry and cannot conveniently do so in their own state because restrictions are irksome, they may go to another where the law is more lenient. In some states, for example, a couple must wait five days after applying for a license before the wedding may be performed; in others, three days; in others, not at all. Such laws are often influenced by financial considerations. In 1961, for example, Iowa raised the minimum age for marriage and instituted a three-day waiting period. As a result many Minnesotans who formerly would have been married in Iowa were married in North Dakota, which had no waiting period. In 1962 marriages taking place in Iowa dropped almost one-fourth below the number for 1960 [*Statistical Bulletin*, May, 1963]. A similar situation exists relative to seeking lenient divorce legislation.

In many states there is too little checkup on the couple at the time they apply for a license. They may swear to false ages. They may give false addresses. Unless one of them later complains, there is no attempt to ascertain the truth. All but a few states require both applicants for a marriage license to present an affidavit or a medical certificate indicating freedom from venereal disease; but for the most part health requirements are limited to this type of infection.

In a considerable proportion of the states the law permits marriage at so early an age that the individual may not be mature, and preparation for marriage may be impossible. In some states a girl may marry before the age at which she may leave school, get a driver's license, vote, sign a valid contract, or has reached puberty. One gets the impression that legislators drop into any of several attitudes: (1) they consider marriage less important than other aspects of life; (2) they think that marriage requires less maturity and intelligence than voting; (3) they are afraid to tamper with the traditional arrangement; (4) they are more interested in taxes, sewers, and roads; (5) they permit all marriage legislation to be colored by the requirements of the minority of cases, in which marriage occurs because of pregnancy; (6) they do not consider marriage at all. Knowing little about it and caring less, they are content to let their action be controlled by the philosophy of "what was good enough for father is good enough for me." By and large, legislators reflect public opinion. A large portion of the general public is as apathetic, as unconcerned, and as unprogressive with regard to marriage laws as are most legislators.

Marriage laws are an illustration of cultural lag. Modern social conditions are so different from those under which our marriage laws developed that new legislation is needed. But law tends to lag behind the need for change. The result is maladjustment. Many marriage laws are not adapted to the present-day social scene, although progress is occurring. A tabulation of some statutory details may be found in the Appendix.

LACK OF PREPARATION FOR MARRIAGE

Society does not demand or even expect preparation for marriage. Anyone may marry, provided that he seems to fulfill the meager requirements of the law. He may be scatterbrained, immature, and maladjusted. He may know practically nothing about marriage or its responsibilities. He may not be able to carry a normal economic load for a person in his class. He may make an obviously poor choice of partner. He may have preparation so slight that with an equivalent amount occupationally he would be unable to hold a job in a business office or to rise even to the lower limits of mediocrity in a profession. Yet society in its slipshod way assumes toward marriage even of the most poorly prepared the attitude, "Whom God hath joined together let not man put asunder." Success in marriage is assumed to come "naturally." This attitude is reflected in the replies of 1,151 college students who were asked whether success is something that has to be worked for, or whether it comes naturally to those who are in love. The latter answer was the one given by 118.

Preparation in the form of marriage education is gradually increasing in quality and extent and in the consciousness of certain portions of society. The process is in its infancy, however, and still has far to go before it can be said that America prepares its youth for marriage. Anyone who, in any sort of counseling capacity, has contact with young unmarried people or with married couples knows that by the marital board goes tragedy after tragedy, many of which would have been preventable through adequate preparation.

OBSCURANTISM

Until recently there has been a veil of obscurantism cast about marriage and sex. This veil has now begun to lift. Substantial remnants of it are, however, to be observed on every hand. In one sense this obscurantism is part of society's lack of demand for preparation for marriage. In another sense it is more than simply a negative, a lack; it is a definite, positive impediment to preparation. Marriage is the only human endeavor in which ignorance is considered a virtue. In spite of all our supposed open discussion of sex and marriage, there is still an ample element of taboo. Sex is discussed more freely, for example, in casual conversation than it is in many schools. Innumerable families have no program of sex education, or sex education is as unplanned and uncontrolled as the development of Topsy, who "just growed."

In one study of 364 college students it was found that though 70.1

per cent felt that both parents should be responsible for the sex education of children, only 10.4 per cent indicated that both parents were actually the source of their information. When the sexes were considered
separately, it was found that 17.9 per cent of the boys and 54.6 per cent
of the girls mentioned the mother, while 20.5 per cent of the boys and
8.0 per cent of the girls mentioned the father as the source of sex information. In short, these students felt that the sex education of children
should be planned and participated in by both parents, but they indicated
that their own families were disappointing in this respect. Their school
experience, too, had fallen short of their expectations; for though 50.8
per cent felt that the school should assume some responsibility with regard to sex education, only 25.0 per cent indicated that their schools had
done so [Rockwood and Ford, 1945].

When the 1,151 college students already mentioned were asked to
check what they considered the best way to prepare for marriage, the
replies were as follows:

TABLE 3

1. Remain ignorant of marriage	46
Because studying marriage is apt to destroy romance	14
Because there are things no girl should know before marriage	27
Because there is plenty of time after the wedding to learn what one needs to know	16
2. Make a thorough study of marriage relationships and problems	991
By taking a course in college	889
By reading good books on the subject	827
By discussing the subject with parents	715
By discussing the subject with teachers	426
By discussing the subject with friends of your own age	506
3. Miscellaneous replies volunteered by the students and not suggested in the inquiry form included:	
Discuss subject with a physician	23
Discuss subject with fiancé	25

The veil of obscurantism is reflected in these figures. Students
whose replies fall into the first group are not numerous; but the number
is significant. One could expect a larger proportion of the general population to express such an attitude when it is expressed by that number of
college students. In the second group the number of students who want
preparation for marriage but would turn for help to persons other than
the instructor in a special college course indicates that some of these

students feel they cannot get the information they need from parents or other teachers.

Anyone who is at all familiar with the behavior of young people knows that they discuss sex and other marriage-related topics. Then the question to be answered is this: Is it better for young people to discuss such topics with sound information or with poor information, under good auspices or under poor auspices, with older adult leadership or without such leadership? Thoughtful persons dare give only one set of answers, and these spell education.

There is no "pillar of cloud by day or pillar of fire by night" to guide wanderers in the marital wilderness. The only adequate guides are intelligence, information, maturity, and emotional balance. When society realizes that to lift the veil of obscurantism on marriage and sex does not mean to tear back the curtain that shields the intimacies of life from wanton public gaze but rather to substitute knowledge for ignorance, planning for drifting, effort for chance, idealism for superstition, and education for an agglomeration of misinformation, then preparation for marriage will be immeasurably advanced.

Wherever there is a need for remedy, there is a corresponding need for prevention. But remedy is often more dramatic than prevention and therefore receives more attention. With regard to failure in marriage and family life, the need for remedy is apparent and is approached through counseling, social case work, and similar avenues. In this area there is also a need for prevention, which may be approached in part at least through education. If we believe in education, and Americans do, we must believe that education can make a contribution to the improvement of marriage and family life.

PREMARITAL ROMANCE

There is an overemphasis on premarital romance and an underemphasis on marital success, as if the former guaranteed the latter. In movies, magazines, some books, many plays, and in the public's attitude, the boy-meets-girl situation tends to take precedence over the situation of the happy marriage.

There is also in America a glorification of the youthful body. On billboards, in magazine advertisements, on radio and television, in motion pictures—everywhere one turns—the youthful body is brought to his attention. From battleships to citrus fruit, the bathing beauty runs the entire gamut, associating her attention-getting qualities with supposedly less interesting events and objects.

Success in marriage depends upon something more than youthful beauty and the intensity of premarital romance. How much the emphasis on these two things actually affects marriage is difficult to say. There are gullible people who believe everything they hear or see and who look ahead only as far as the wedding. Putting the emphasis on beauty and premarital romance gives a false impression of the factors making for long-time happiness and success. In a subtle way and without either party's being clearly aware of it, many a husband or wife, especially the latter, is a competitor with the more or less standardized youthful beauty that is so widely publicized.

LOW STANDARDS OF SUCCESS

The standards that society sets up for success in marriage are comparatively low and apply mostly to overt behavior. "A man's home is his castle," even if he detests living in it. A couple may have serious conflict and may have no affection for each other. There may be no understanding and no happiness in their relationship. But if they "put up a good front," do not disturb other people, and neither complains to the court, as far as social standards are concerned their marriage passes muster. Society is also inclined to judge too largely in terms of stability; if a marriage lasts it must be good. One can be fairly sure that if a marriage does not last it is not successful. Many that do last are unsuccessful, too.

LACK OF SERIOUS ATTITUDE

In many quarters there is a lack of serious attitude toward marriage. When student groups are asked whether they know about certain marriages, they are much more likely to express knowledge of Ma and Pa Kettle, Maggie and Jiggs, and Dagwood and Blondie than they are to know about the marriages of Robert Browning and Elizabeth Barrett or the Robert Louis Stevensons. Such groups are illustrative of a common tendency, namely, that many people are more familiar with the caricature of marriage than with real instances of happy, successful married life. There are many jokes about marriage and the people involved in it. It is laughed at and held up to ridicule. Unpalatable expressions, such as "getting hooked" and "putting one's head in the noose," lightly describe marriage in terms of its worst actualities rather than of its greatest possibilities.

STEREOTYPES

There are two ways to erect a house. One is the process of adding brick to brick and board to board at the site of building until the structure is completed. The other is to fasten together large sections of prefabricated materials constructed in advance to fit a prearranged plan and delivered ready for use at the site of building. In our working out of a point of view relative to life in the society in which we live, we use, figuratively speaking, a combination of these two methods. We do put together experience with experience, idea with idea, and fact with fact to contribute to the erection of a "structure" partly of our own making.

We also build, in part, with large sections constructed by society and fitted, with few alterations, into the pattern of our thought. These large blocks of concept, attitude, and definition are stereotypes.

Stereotypes are seldom valid. They seldom even roughly fit the facts. They are ready and easy, but lazy, ways of arriving at judgments of other people and of various phases of social life. They standardize the thinking of the uncritical. The "Uncle Remus" stereotype of the Negro is well known. According to this erroneous concept all Negroes are simple, happy-go-lucky, irresponsible, fun-loving folks who have a picturesque accent and vocabulary, who like to dance, sing, and eat fried chicken and watermelon. Some Negroes may fit this pattern; but as a generalization nothing could be further from the truth. Yet this stereotype colors the thinking of many Americans.

Other stereotypes are equally erroneous. The college professor is presumably absent-minded, disheveled, and impractical. Students fall into one of two groups: they are either bookworms or "Joe College" and "Betty Coed" as depicted in collegiate movies. Farmers are hayseedy. Businessmen are interested only in profits and are insensitive to human welfare. Politicians are open to suspicion. Men are brave, strong, impersonal, and independent; women are easily frightened, weak, personal, and dependent. Our frequent and uncritical use of the term *typical* shows to what degree these stereotypes have come to be taken for granted.

There are similar stereotypes relative to home, marriage, family, husband, and wife. So deeply rooted is the stereotype of the American home as a dwelling place that new forms of architecture only slowly attained a foothold, in spite of years of effort. People are assumed to date, fall in love, marry, set up a home, bear and rear children, divide labor between husband and wife, and accept traditional roles, all according to stereotypes. When these stereotypes continue to affect our thinking at the same time that they have become less well adapted to modern conditions, when they define the shape of the hole into which both round and square pegs are expected to fit, when they play a part in determining the criteria by which success and failure in dating and marriage are measured, when they become substitutes for insight, understanding, information, and a desire to plumb more deeply into the possibilities of marriage and family living, then they in turn also become factors which play a part in producing failure.

TRADITION

The Second World War took the form of a conflict between armies and between governments. Basically, however, it was more than that. It was in part the armed phase of a conflict between two ideologies, between two ways of life: the totalitarian and the democratic. This conflict did not start with the war, and it was not resolved by the signing of peace

treaties. It is still going on. It permeates many aspects of life. Some refer to it as a world revolution. Marriage and the family, too, are caught
in the maelstrom. They are passing from a form roughly paralleling dic-
tatorship and government by force to a democratic form of organization.
The patriarchal family of the past no longer exists in traditional form.
Yet some of the ideas and concepts with which present-day marriage is
permeated have been carried over from the marriage of yesteryear. Individuals enter marriage with a generous soaking of tradition. Some of
the traditional ways no longer operate so smoothly as they did. They are
not fully adapted to modern conditions. On the other hand, certain
phases of social life have not changed so rapidly as have others; there
is a carry-over of traditional elements, with which some of the newer elements in marriage conflict. The problem is twofold. In either case, the
result is conflict, transition, and confusion. Here again one may observe
cultural lag.

PUBLICIZING OF FAILURE

Marital failure is played up in the press, and marital success is taken for
granted. Failure is more spectacular, and apparently the public is more
interested in it. Successful marriage is not news. When one sees headlines announcing the divorce of a well-known public figure, he feels as
if he had learned something of importance. It is a subject to talk about.
Just the thought of picking up a newspaper and reading headlines to the
effect that millions of Americans are happily married seems ridiculous,
so far have we taken success for granted and overstressed the significance of failure.

Door of escape — divorce

The ready availability of divorce in this country gives American couples
access to an unprecedented door of escape from marriages which they
consider to be intolerable. The possibility of escape, however, does not
create the desire to escape, though it may contribute to the ease with
which a decision to escape is reached. On the other hand, the desire to
escape does not necessarily open the door. But in any human endeavor
the possibility of remedying errors or recovering from failure plays a part
in determining the attitudes of the persons who engage in the endeavor.
Our collective attitude toward divorce is one factor that colors our collective attitude toward marriage. The exact effect of divorce as a social
phenomenon upon the failure of individual marriages cannot be measured with accuracy. Yet divorce as a social phenomenon is part of the
cultural climate within which marriages occur. Hence divorce may be
discussed as one of the factors in the social situation which have some
bearing on marital adjustment. Divorce is in the news. There are many

misconceptions and misplaced emphases. Many individuals come into contact with it in contemplating marriage to a divorced person or through the marital affairs of relatives or friends. Hence this discussion is presented in some detail.

DEFINITION

Divorce is the legal severing of marriage ties which a court recognizes as having existed. The parties who were formerly married become ex-spouses. In divorce, a bona fide marriage is terminated. Divorce and annulment are not identical. In the latter the court declares a supposed marriage null and void; that is, the court officially recognizes that no marriage existed, though the couple or one of the two thought that it did. After annulment the couple are still single as they were before their "wedding," since they have never really been married. They are not "ex-spouses."

RATE

The rapid rise of the American divorce rate is one of the outstanding phenomena of our recent history. The rate may be stated in various ways, one of the commonest being the ratio of divorces to weddings in a given year. Just after the Civil War there was 1 divorce for every 36 weddings. By the turn of the century, the ratio was 1 to 13. In 1945 it was 1 to 3 [Federal Security Agency, 1949]. It is currently 1 to 4 [U.S. Bureau of the Census, 1964]. This is not equivalent to saying that one in four marriages ends in divorce, since the divorces granted in a given year represent the termination of marriages that, as a rule, occurred before that year. To compare the divorces in a given year with the weddings in the same year is not quite accurate, but it is nearly enough so for our purpose.

Among other ways of looking at the divorce rate are the following. The base for the calculation may be the number of married females in the population. In 1900 there were 4.0 divorces per 1,000 married females. By 1920 the number had doubled (8.0). It was only slightly higher (8.7) in 1940. Immediately after the Second World War it doubled again; and in 1946 it was 17.8. By 1950, because the sudden upsurge of the divorce rate brought about by the termination of many war marriages had spent itself, the number dropped to 10.3 divorces per 1,000 married females [Taeuber and Taeuber, 1958]. By 1961 it had become 9.6 [U.S. Bureau of the Census, 1964].

Another method is to compare the increases in population, weddings, and divorces. From 1867 to 1949 the total population increased roughly 4 times, the number of weddings roughly 4½ times, the number of divorces roughly 40 times [Federal Security Agency, 1951]. In 1961 there were more than 40 million married couples. In the same year there were

414,000 divorces [U.S. Bureau of the Census, 1964]. Hence we see that in that year roughly 1 per cent of existing marriages ended in divorce. A few years earlier this ratio was 1 divorce to every 100 to 125 marriages. At the beginning of the twentieth century, it was about 1 to 250 [Lichtenberger, 1931].

None of these ways of calculating the divorce rate is entirely satisfactory. The first is inaccurate for the reason mentioned, namely, that the divorces granted in a given year ordinarily represent the termination of marriages contracted earlier. The second is inaccurate because it does not take into account such changes as lower death rate and extended life span. The third method does not give consideration to the variation among the types of factors that would lead to increases in population, weddings, or divorces. The last is inaccurate because, though it is true that divorces occur among all the marriages existing at a given time, not just among those new ones contracted during a given year, some of those that do not end in divorce one year may do so at some time in the future. Since the majority of divorces occur within the first ten years of marriage, these inaccuracies may be reduced to some extent by comparing the number of divorces granted in a given year with the average number of weddings occurring in the preceding ten years. On this basis we find that in 1910 the rate was 1 divorce per 10 weddings; in 1920, 1 in 6; in 1930, 1 in 6; in 1940, 1 in 5; in 1946, 1 in 2.5; by 1948, 1 in 4 [*Statistical Bulletin*, 1949]. Currently it is about 1 in 4 [U.S. Bureau of the Census, 1964].

The divorce rate rose steadily until the time of the Second World War. In 1946, due to the breakup of many war marriages and the effect of the war on other unstable marriages, the rate reached an unprecedented peak, the highest point it has ever attained. In that year the marriage rate also reached an all-time high. Since 1946 the divorce rate has declined and has now leveled off to approximately the rate of the immediately prewar years [U.S. Department of Health, Education, and Welfare, 1959]. There is evidence to suggest that unless more factors contributing to the improvement of marriage and family life are introduced, the divorce rate will remain high for some time to come.

The rate is not uniform either throughout the country or in all classes. It is higher in cities than in rural areas, probably because of the weakening of primary group control in the former and also because of the type of persons who gravitate toward the city, where control is weakened. The rate varies inversely with occupational and educational level; that is, the higher the level, the lower the divorce rate, and vice versa [Carter and Plateris, 1963].

Much is said and written about Reno and Hollywood divorces. There is no gainsaying the fact that Reno is a divorce mill. Nevada laws permit divorce after only a very brief period of residence; and the city of Reno makes divorce one of its chief industries. Streets are lined with bars and gambling houses established to help the prospective divorcés forget their troubles. Both in and around the city are places of temporary residence, from tourist camps to dude ranches. Reno is a haven for decree seekers of the upper economic levels. To live there for six weeks and pay the attorneys' fees and other costs is expensive. Reno flashes many notorious and spectacular names through the channels of the news. As a result, it has come to symbolize American divorce. The symbol is inept, and Reno has been overrated. Even with its large and well-publicized divorce business, divorces granted there number only about 1 in 89 [U.S. Department of Health, Education, and Welfare, 1959]. On the other hand, of course, this is a large proportion of the divorces for one town to handle.

Hollywood divorces also often make the news, and they, too, are overrated. Hollywood represents only a small, though highly publicized, segment of the population. The divorce rate for Hollywood personnel is very high, like that for Los Angeles as a whole. On the other hand, there are many Hollywood couples who have been happily married for many years.

A person is not permitted to have more than one spouse at a time, but he is permitted to have any number in succession, provided that the requirements of the law are met. MARRIAGE CHAMP SAYS SHE'S WIFE NUMBER FIFTEEN; SEVENTY-EIGHT AND MARRIED SIX TIMES, SHE WEDS EIGHTY, WHO HAS WEDDED SEVEN; BLONDE REVEALS TEN MARRIAGES; THESE SIX WOMEN HAVE HAD FORTY HUSBANDS; WIVES ARE HIS HOBBY —HAS HAD FOURTEEN—these are headlines of a type not infrequently encountered in newspapers and picture magazines. Ostensibly, our mores uphold strict monogamy. Marital records like these and others that are less pretentious reflect a loophole in the mores permitting what might be termed *serial*, or *progressive, polygamy*.

DIVORCE RATE AND EXTENT OF FAILURE

The divorce rate, high as it is, does not present an accurate picture of marriage failure, although as the divorce rate rises we may assume that its correlation with the failure rate increases. A marriage may be "broken" functionally as well as structurally. Many couples separate without divorce, and many others continue to live together even after their marriages have become no more than the legal ashes of once flourishing relationships. Thus marital failure is more common than the divorce rate suggests. Since in each case of failure at least two persons are affected, the total number whose lives have been colored by unsuccessful marriage would be appalling if it could be ascertained. This is not cause for pessimism, however; it is only an indication of the need for better preparation.

There are numerous reasons for a couple to refrain from divorce when a marriage has failed. (1) They may remain together for the sake of the children. (2) There may be property considerations. (3) The husband's business or professional standing might be jeopardized by divorce. (4) There may be a desire on the part of each not to hurt the other. (5) The divorce may be desired by only one spouse, but he may have no grounds. (6) Habit patterns may be too deeply entrenched. There is the memory of their earlier life together. There may be common interests and common responsibilities. (7) The couple may have the hope that their marriage will be readjusted. (8) They may have the attitude of having made a bargain and holding to it. (9) The woman may remain in an unhappy relationship for the sake of support. (10) There may be moral or religious reasons. (11) There may be love, in spite of their inability to live happily together. (12) They may live in a state that does not permit divorce on any ground to which they could or would resort. (13) There may be fear of publicity, of facing friends, of admitting failure. (14) They may be unable to afford it. (15) They may be separated and, through inertia, grow to accept the *status quo*.

There is a common assumption that the increasing divorce rate actually indicates that more marriages are failing. This is not necessarily true. No one knows how many marriages are unsuccessful today as compared with years ago. Standards were different then. Expectations for husbands and wives were different. Roles were different. Another reason for the assumption that the marital situation is growing worse is that stability is considered a more reliable criterion of judgment than happiness and freedom. Stability is only easier to measure. Although instability may mean unhappiness, stability does not necessarily mean the opposite.

There are more appendectomies today than there were fifty years ago, but this does not prove that there is more appendicitis or that the health situation is growing worse. It shows only that more cases of appendicitis are diagnosed as such and that there are more operations performed to relieve symptoms and save patients from peritonitis. Because a man remains at the same job for life does not prove that he is satisfied, successful, or happy in it. It may prove only that he has found no way of changing his occupation. Suppose, for illustration, that two college roommates are locked in a room. They quarrel. The fact that they do not leave the room is not a test of their friendship. In earlier days there was little for a couple to do about their unsuccessful marriage but grin and bear it. Public opinion frowned upon divorce, and there were few ways for the wife to support herself if she left her husband.

Until recently, South Carolina did not permit divorce on any ground. In 1949 the legislature ratified a new divorce law. The divorce rate in that state was previously zero. It has now risen. This does not prove, however, that the proportion of unsuccessful marriages in that state has increased.

In short, the increasing divorce rate proves only that more couples are escaping from marriages which to them have become intolerable. Modern social conditions have opened the door of escape, and more couples are passing through it.

When a careful observer compares a group of unsuccessful marriages in which there is no divorce with a group ending in divorce, he finds that all the elements characteristic of the latter are to be found in the former, with one exception, namely, the willingness to terminate the marriage in court. Some marriages seem to hold together in spite of elements contributing to failure because the couple are not willing to resort to escape. How, then, can anyone determine how much marital failure there is today as compared with, say, fifty years ago?

Divorce is a symptom or an effect of failure. It is not a cause. Couples resort to the courts only after their marriages have disintegrated. In some cases divorce is a secondary, rather than a primary, effect of maladjustment. For instance, a marriage is unsuccessful because the couple are incompatible. This incompatibility leads the husband to infidelity. The divorce is sought on the basis of adultery.

In considering marriage, we are inclined to do something that we avoid in connection with most other human endeavors. We make the broad assumption and postulate the universal expectation that all marriages should succeed. When some fail, we are surprised and conclude that the institution of marriage is disintegrating. It is in a state of transition but it is not, therefore, breaking down.

This assumption of success is desirable when the individual couple contemplate the future of their own marriage. They should enter it confident that it will be successful and will endure for life. In looking at all marriages taken as a group, however, the prognosis is variation rather than uniformity.

Most human endeavors and characteristics fall upon a normal curve of variability rather than upon a straight line or a fixed point. In college some students fail, others pass with honors, and the majority fall in between the extremes. In spite of the best preparation, individuals fail in their chosen occupations, and many never pass beyond mediocrity. Marriage is no exception to the general rule. Of the marriages contracted in any given year a certain proportion may be expected to fail, a large number will be relatively successful, and some will be outstanding. Because one in four ends in the divorce court, we must not lose sight of the fact that three in four do not.

Social and legal aspects of divorce

IS DIVORCE A SOCIAL EVIL?

Whether or not we decide that divorce is a social evil depends upon the definition given for the term *evil*. If it means something regrettable and to be prevented if possible, then divorce is evil. If, however, *evil* is interpreted as meaning something conducive to disintegration and destruction, then divorce is not such. As we have said, divorce is symptom and effect, not cause. Like a surgical operation, it may be the only means by which a life can be saved. Surgery is regrettable; people would be happier if no one ever had to submit to the scalpel. This does not make surgery an evil. It makes it only something that indicates an underlying "evil." Divorce seems to be an evil to the degree to which we fail to think of expectancy of marital success in terms of the normal curve of variability.

Divorce may be judged in terms of the ideal. Ideally, of course, it would be better if no marriage ever had to be terminated by divorce. On the other hand, divorce may be judged in terms of its alternatives. If no marriage, no matter what the degree of incompatibility, no matter how severe the personality damage to spouse and/or children, could be terminated via a legal route of escape, life for some persons could become unbearable indeed. Individuals could be victimized by the distorted personalities to which they were chained by law. Interpersonal relationships that ought to be conducive to emotional health and personal happiness would be forced to remain rooted in bitterness, conflict, and frustration. Some persons will contend that protection of spouse and children may be accomplished by means of legal separation without divorce. This is only partially true. Legal separation, plus court injunction in some cases, may keep individuals geographically apart, but this will not prevent a family from continuing to reflect the behavior and reputation of one of its members. Also, legal separation does not make possible a new attempt to establish the quality of family life that is approved, even by those who disapprove of divorce.

FACTORS AFFECTING THE RATE

As already implied, the factors affecting the divorce rate are not necessarily the same ones that contribute to marital failure, since divorce is merely the opening of the door of escape from failure. We have said that divorce is a symptom of failure in the individual marriage. The rate is also a symptom of social change. Much of this change has been in the direction of removing some of the outside props that used to hold marriages intact even when they were disintegrating on the inside. Modern marriage is like a tent the stakes of which have been pulled out one by one, each time making it more vulnerable to wind and storm. In earlier times marriages were held together in part by coercion from without. Now when they hold together it is largely through cohesion from within. We shall mention only briefly some of the elements in the social situation that may contribute to the high divorce rate.

A higher standard of living. As the standard of living rises, more people have financial resources sufficient to bear the expense of divorce.

The reduction in the institutional functions of the family.   A husband or a wife is no longer the economic necessity of earlier days. Protection has in part been taken over by the state. Provision for old age rests less upon family and more upon outside agencies. Education is controlled by the state, and a child's formal education is the same whether he has one parent or two.

The higher status of women.   Women have greater freedom of choice and action, including greater opportunity for self-support.

New standards of marital success and new ideals of married life. These new standards and ideals place greater emphasis on personal relations, such as love and companionship. When these are not afforded by a marriage, their absence is deemed adequate excuse for escape.

A decline of religious authority.   Marriages contracted with a civil ceremony are more likely to end in divorce than those contracted with a religious ceremony. This does not mean that an irreligious couple could increase the probability of their marital success by having a clergyman "marry" them. The type of ceremony is significant only to the degree to which it reflects the attitudes of the parties to the union. Those more deeply affected by the decline of religious authority are less likely to succeed, or, at any rate, are more likely to divorce.

More widespread liberalism in thought.   Public opinion toward divorce has changed. The divorcé is no longer considered an individual with a shady past or a doubtful character. People do not look askance at divorce as they used to.

Changed ideas of masculine supremacy.   Women are freer to insist upon their rights and more successful in achieving them. "Love, honor, and obey" has been changed to "love, honor, and cherish" in the typical wedding ceremony. In name only and when the census taker calls is the husband the head of the house. In earlier times, the family had one head; nowadays, it often has none or two.

The growth of cities has broken down primary group control.   In the face-to-face groups of rural areas each individual feels called upon to keep his neighbor on the right track or, at best, to inform the community of his activities. In the city there is more freedom and less interference.

Divorce has become easier to obtain.   Courts have become more lenient toward divorce. Grounds for action have been multiplied. Laws dealing with the matter have been reinterpreted.

Divorce is exploited in the press.   The fact that escape from an un-happy marriage is possible, even easy, is flaunted in the face of the pub-lic. However, the fact that divorce is still news is hopeful. It shows that, in spite of our frequent misconceptions, stable marriage rather than di-vorce is the norm.

The death rate has declined.   The fact that the death rate has declined indicates that some marriages that might have been broken by death end in divorce. When both death and divorce are considered, we find that there were actually more broken homes in earlier days in this coun-try than there are today.

Tendency to cast a false glamor around divorce.   We speak of the "gay divorcée." She is pictured as a woman of experience, subtlety, and wiles. Actually, there is no glamor to divorce. We have been gullible enough to accept at its face value the false front of self-defense put on by some divorced persons who wish to forget their tribulations or avoid the adverse opinion of associates. We have also tended to generalize on the occasional shallow individual whose lack of depth makes him seem superficially happy in a situation that would cause a less frothy one pain and regret.

In the typical divorce case there are two persons whose dreams have fallen in ruins. They have tried again and again after bitter disillusion-ment and disappointment to readjust their marriage, only to fail. They have put off the final irrevocable step until they could no longer tolerate their position. They have become progressively resigned to what seemed like an inevitable finale or have hoped against hope that by some miracle their marriage would be saved. At long last they face the embarrassment and humiliation of a court trial, make accusations and recriminations, and air their private affairs before outsiders. Then, after the decree, when they had thought everything would be rosy, they face a long and trying period of readjustment. "Glamorous" is the last word that one would attach to such persons and events. [See Waller, 1951.]

The kind of people this country is producing.   Generalizing broadly, Americans are comfort-loving. They are impatient with discomfort and inconvenience. They feel that whatever they do not like they have a right to change, either through established channels or by direct action. In spite of their sensitivity to group pressure, they are individualistic, and personal welfare is often given precedence over the welfare of the group. Responsibility is often sidestepped for pleasure. A sense of duty is not so conspicuous as it used to be. There is an inclination to assume that what one is and does has its roots in early experience now beyond the individual's control and hence relieving him, to some extent at least, from responsibility for his own behavior. Americans are generally sympathetic with the "underdog," give help to someone in dire need, lend support to a person or a group in time of unusual emergency or crisis. It is not too difficult to get such attitudes confused with self-concern when one is the "victim" of a marital situation assumed to be caused largely by the other spouse.

War. The Second World War, as indicated in an earlier chapter, brought in its train a very high marriage rate, and many of these marriages were hasty, poorly founded unions. War breeds many ill-chosen marriages. Also, many marriages, like poorly built houses during an earthquake, collapse, whereas they might have endured structurally had there been no war. Long separations during which husband and wife had different experiences, made new contacts, and lost interest in each other contributed to the breakup of many already existing marriages. With its necessary emphasis upon destruction and the insignificance of the individual, war changes the attitudes of some persons toward their responsibilities and toward the values by which they previously lived. In some cases, gaining one's own ends without considering others, or even through hurting them, weighs less heavily upon the conscience than in time of peace. The war also brought about great shifts in population and consequent increased breakdown of primary groups. High wages in war industries gave some persons the funds necessary to obtain divorces and gave others the quick money and, for them, unprecedentedly high income which often lead to loss of balance and perspective. War production provided many opportunities for wives who had not previously been employed to establish a new independence and escape the home.

WHO GETS DIVORCES?

About seven out of ten divorces are granted to wives [U.S. Department of Health, Education, and Welfare, 1959]. A number of possible reasons may be given to explain why more wives than husbands are plaintiffs in divorce cases. (1) In some respects women have more at stake in marriage than do men. They are thus more inclined to feel the sting of failure. (2) There is still enough chivalry in the relationships of the sexes so that, when a couple mutually agree to get a divorce, the husband assumes the blame and lets the wife bring suit. (3) More grounds are available to women in some states. For example, the ground of nonsupport is seldom used by husbands. (4) Courts on the whole are inclined to be more sympathetic with women than with men. (5) If the couple agree upon alimony, the court will more readily stipulate it if the wife is the plaintiff. (6) It may still be somewhat easier for a man to face public opinion. (7) Women have greater freedom in seeking divorce now than formerly and are using this freedom. (8) Men have more contact with the world outside the home and may have more frequent opportunity for infidelity. (9) It is easier for women to go away for a period, say, to Reno, while men's occupational responsibilities are more likely to necessitate their remaining at home. (10) This is an era of traveling men, and statistics show that men who spend much time away from home are more likely to be divorced than those whose occupations permit more home life.

DURATION OF MARRIAGE WITH RELATION TO DIVORCE

In 1960 more than 30 per cent of the divorces were granted to couples married less than four years; more than half occurred in less than eight years [Carter and Plateris, 1963]. Only about 1 in 15 occurs before the end of the first year [U.S. Department of Health, Education, and Welfare, 1959]. These figures show that couples do not rush into divorce as soon as, or with as little provocation as, is commonly assumed or as the exceptional spectacular case seems to indicate. It usually takes time for a couple to discover that their marriage is a failure. After that more time will pass before they bring themselves to the point where divorce is sought as a remedy or escape. The figures also show that many couples wait until their children are grown, for about one-ninth of the divorces occur after twenty years of marriage [U.S. Department of Health, Education, and Welfare, 1959].

Statistics of duration of marriage prior to divorce do not give an accurate picture of marital instability, however. Monahan [1962] refers to the "fragility of marriages." He points out that many couples separate much earlier than they get divorces. The real disruption of the marriage occurs at the time of separation; divorce only finalizes it. He points out also that duration of marriage to separation varies with region, time, social class, presence or absence of children, and frequency of marriage; that is, there is longer duration to separation in first marriages than in remarriages.

CHILDREN AS A DETERRENT

Approximately two-fifths of the divorces are granted to childless couples [U.S. Bureau of the Census, 1964]. When we consider only minor children, we find that the rate for couples with such children is about half that for couples without minor children at the time of the divorce [Statistical Bulletin, 1950]. Does this indicate that children are a deterrent to divorce? In some cases, they are. In other cases, they are not. A child may be a source of conflict as well as a bond. The same factors that operate to make a couple avoid having children may contribute to the failure of their marriage and to their inclination to seek divorce. Furthermore, in many cases in which there are no children the divorce occurred rather early in the marriage, when there was insufficient time to have offspring. There is no way of determining whether such couples would have had children or not. In some cases there is no doubt that children are the reason for a couple's continuing to live together after their marriage has failed. In others, too, children serve as a very absorbing common interest, which binds the couple together and may counteract some of the factors operating to force them apart. There is no way of generalizing, and the statistics are inconclusive. We must beware of the *post hoc, ergo propter hoc* (after this, therefore because of this) fallacy in thinking. It would be the height of the ridiculous to recommend that a couple have a child to prevent their failing marriage from ending in divorce, as if children were a specific for marital ills, unless one were positive that the remedy prescribed actually fitted the needs of the couple in a particular case.

GROUNDS FOR ACTION

Grounds for divorce may be considered from two related points of view. They are the reasons alleged by a person seeking divorce on the basis of which he asserts that he has been injured and claims that a divorce should be granted. Grounds are also the categories of reasons for which the law permits divorce and the courts grant it. Grounds and causes are not necessarily the same, either for divorce in general or for the divorce of a specific couple. Usually what happens is something like this. A couple are incompatible. Their marriage is unsatisfactory. This leads one or both of them to commit some act – such as desertion, nonsupport, or adultery – which is a symptom of maladjustment but does fall within the categories of the law. On this basis one seeks divorce. Or, being incompatible, they may agree that they both want divorce. They then fit their situation into the most convenient legal category so that the plea of one conforms to legal requirements and a divorce may be decreed. In many cases this amounts to a deliberate "trumping up" of grounds to satisfy the court. In New York, for example, where the only ground acceptable is adultery, a couple may agree to get a divorce. Then the husband hires an accomplice and witnesses to assist him in "proving" his "adultery," and a divorce is granted on this ground. For reasons such as these, statistics of divorce grounds do not present an accurate picture of conditions.

The word "give" is often used in connection with seeking a divorce – "His wife won't give him a divorce" – as if one spouse had the legal authority to grant a decree to the other spouse. Of course, neither party has such authority. What is meant in such a case is that one spouse wants a divorce but the other does not. The one who wants the divorce has no grounds upon which to get it. The one who does not want the divorce either has grounds but refuses to use them or refuses to trump up grounds which the other person will not contest.

The disparity between the true causes of divorce and the grounds alleged is both made clear and dramatized by what ordinarily happens in court when divorces are granted. In a typical court in a medium-sized Middle Western town there are eighteen cases on the docket. One by one the plaintiffs appear before the judge. Most of them are women. Two or three "character witnesses" make statements about each one. The attorneys ask such questions as "Did you perform all the duties of marriage?" or "Did you give him any reason to leave you?" Most of the plaintiffs are poor or middle-class folk. The majority have been married longer than five years; one has been married twenty-four years. Only one side of each case is made known. No case is contested. The judge seldom challenges anything a plaintiff says. He depends upon the attorneys to get the facts, though few of these facts are brought out in court. He has no way of getting at the facts himself. The court provides no agency for counseling or for attempting to reconcile the couples. The judge later admits that in his opinion at least half the plaintiffs did not deserve decrees on the basis of the evidence submitted; but he also feels that he was helpless to do anything about it and that refusing them divorces would only make them perjure themselves further and would not effect marital readjustment. He is earnest, honest, and sincere, but he has no background in psychology or sociology. At the end of about two and a quarter hours all eighteen decrees have been granted – an average of one every eight minutes.

Grounds vary from state to state. They have been worked out with more regard for institutional considerations, such as status, support, and rights, than for problems of personality adjustment. We consider love to be one of the major bases for marriage, if not the primary basis. Yet lack of love passes unrecognized as a basis for divorce. In historical studies, contemporary discussions, or critical analyses of divorce there is almost no mention of love. Its presence or absence is almost entirely disregarded in the rendering of court decisions.

Statistically the grounds are changing.

1. *As written in the laws of the several states:* The trend seems to be toward extending the number of grounds.

2. *As alleged in specific cases:* Desertion and adultery as grounds alleged have declined. Cruelty has greatly increased. Just over half the divorces granted nowadays are granted on the specified ground of cruelty. If such grounds as "indignities," as defined, for example, in Missouri and Wyoming, be included as being approximately synonymous with "cruelty" in many cases, the percentage would be increased. Only about 1 divorce in 4 is granted for desertion [Carter and Plateris, 1963], 1 in 85 for adultery. Such figures, however, vary considerably from state to state [U.S. Department of Health, Education, and Welfare, 1959].

The definition of *cruelty* is constantly shifting and is difficult to ascertain with any degree of finality or assurance. *Cruelty* ranges from physical violence to the most ridiculous absurdities. Drummond [1934] cites cases in which divorce was granted on the ground of cruelty for the following reasons: because a wife would not speak for days at a time and, when she did open her mouth, it was only to consume the meals the husband prepared for the family and to complain about his cooking; because the husband required his wife to retire at nine or nine-thirty o'clock; because the husband used Biblical language to insult his wife; because the husband failed to make his children stop playing the saxophone; because a wife claimed that a pet cat had deprived her of her husband's affection. A newspaper article states that a woman is seeking divorce on the ground of cruelty because her husband used her pet goldfish for bait.

READING 8 # WHAT IS CRUELTY?

"Cruelty" as an alleged ground for divorce is becoming increasingly common in this country. Also, the interpretation of the meaning of "cruelty" is becoming more and more flexible. But this problem of meaning and interpretation is not new; it began many years ago, as witness the following, published in 1889.

Few venture to define "cruelty." In the decided cases we find certain actions held to constitute "legal cruelty" that strike one as being slight cause for any such far-reaching effect as an "absolute divorce." Very little reason exists when a divorce is granted because once a husband threw water over his wife and threatened more; because a woman contracted the itch, or other loathsome disease, from her husband; because a crosstempered man struck his wife once, kicked her over seven years later, and went for more than two years without speaking to her; because a man treated his wife coldly, was stingy towards her, neglected her in premature labor, and roughly upbraided her for the noise she made when suffering pain.

Such are some of the instances in which there was bodily injury. "Cruel and inhuman treatment to endanger the life of his wife" is the language of the Iowa statutes, which leads one to expect that there the very highest degree of cruelty only would be allowed as cause; but the court interprets the language thus: "If austerity of temper, petulance of manner, rudeness of language, a want of civil attention, occasional sallies of passion, do threaten bodily harm, they amount to legal cruelty."

Tried to kick her once but failed, used abusive epithets,

From D. Convers, *Marriage and Divorce in the United States*, J. B. Lippincott Company, Philadelphia, 1889, pp. 186–190.

and finally refused to speak for months, this is "cruelty!" Here and there one may still find an effort to confine "cruelty" to bodily harm, but generally it extends to mental suffering. Here the greater part of the decisions point to the pain inflicted by false charges of unchastity. In a Kentucky case the man was rough, "with a vulgar and profane mannerism, had but little attraction for a melancholy and sensitive wife. She knew, however, the man before she married him. They were own cousins. After the marriage she entertained the belief that marriage of cousin with cousin was prohibited by the divine law, and this fact, connected with her bad health and the want of sympathy on the part of her husband, aided greatly, no doubt, in the destruction of her peace and happiness. . . . The husband often spoke uncivilly to her, used the most profane and vulgar language in her presence, neglected her in many instances," but, for all that, made "persistent efforts to bring about a reconciliation;" but all in vain, it was "extreme cruelty."

"Marry in haste and repent at leisure" is well illustrated by the family history shown in a Kansas case, where most of the acquaintance and courtship was by letter! He was cross to her; said she had a "hellish or a devilish tongue;" several times said before her that he "did not believe Bessie (her child) was his child;" sent her, when away, a valentine with an ugly woman feeding a child from a bottle; getting an employe of the post-office to write on the margin, "I like children of my own," and to address it; and on her return refused to receive her; being guilty thus of "extreme cruelty." Or again, for a wife to write and send anonymous letters charging her husband with criminal intimacy with his clerk's wife was such "extreme cruelty" as to gain the husband his divorce.

A husband in a room alone with his wife by indirection charged her with incest and advertised her in the local papers as having deserted him; and this too was "extreme cruelty." "A reasonable apprehension of injury is sufficient" to cause cruelty is so commonly held as to need no references.

To quote a learned judge, "Everybody knows that there may be a refinement of cruelty practised on the part of one of the parties towards the other, unconnected with gross and abusive language or epithets, or with anything personally violent or threatening, which may render the marriage state absolutely intolerable, and the discharge of the duties of married life an impossibility." Under this nearly anything can be cruelty.

This latitude in the interpretation of *cruelty* is not entirely new. Convers, writing in 1889, cites cases in which divorce was granted on the ground of cruelty because a husband threw water over his wife; because a wife contracted the itch from her husband; because a husband had a vulgar and profane mannerism. Nevertheless, there is a tendency for freedom of interpretation to increase.

The statistical change in cruelty as an alleged ground for divorce may show one or more of several things: (1) That courts are becoming more lenient in granting divorce. (2) That divorce is being granted on less serious grounds. (3) That the true causes of marital failure are being recognized and their seriousness acknowledged. If this is true, it means that fewer couples are having to perjure themselves in order to obtain release. (4) That *cruelty* may be more readily established and proved than other grounds. The term is more flexible and permits broader interpretation by the court than, say, *adultery* or *nonsupport*. There is evidence to indicate that most divorces are obtained on those grounds that are the least unpleasant to allege under the law [Carter and Plateris, 1963] according to the "principle of least stigma," as suggested by Broom. (5) That we are taking a more intelligent attitude toward divorce. (6) That courts and the general public are becoming more willing to have divorces granted for incompatibility, though in only three states, Alaska, Oklahoma, and New Mexico, is it included among the grounds for divorce defined by statute. In a few states, courts have considerable discretion in granting divorces for grounds not specifically provided by statute. In the state of Washington, for example, a court may grant a divorce for any ground it considers sufficient, if it is satisfied that the couple can no longer live together. In general, we still make couples lie about incompatibility, disguise it, and squeeze it into the most convenient category of the law. (7) That more is expected of marriage today, that standards of success are rising to a new plane. When expectations are not achieved, escape is permitted. The standards of success are becoming more personal and less institutional.

Effects of divorce upon the individual

EFFECTS OF DIVORCE UPON THE COUPLE

For a more detailed discussion of the effects of divorce upon the couple the reader is referred to books that treat the subject more fully [see list of selected readings]. Here a few remarks must suffice.

For some individuals divorce is jumping from the frying pan into the fire. It does not solve their problem. There is a difference between "solution" and "escape." After the decree and the removal of the immediately aggravating circumstances, the divorcé often feels that he loved his spouse more than he realized, that the situation was not so bad after all, that the divorce was too hasty, and that the decree is regrettable. There are, too, of course, persons from whom divorces are obtained against their will. They may have committed some offense which gives the other person ground for divorce, or they may be disinclined to use a defense, yet they may not want a divorce. For such persons a divorce may be profoundly disruptive.

The divorced person faces several acute problems. He must settle the conflict and rebellion within himself. He must repair wounded pride. He must readjust his habits. Often he does not realize until he is called upon to change them how much a part of his life many habits have come to be. He must reorganize his social relationships and friendships. He must grow accustomed to a new relationship with his children, whether he is separated from them or has them with him without the other parent. He must reorient his sexual life. If the person left alone by divorce is a woman, she must usually arrange for support.

Marriage, even a marriage that is not particularly satisfactory, has a way of becoming part of an individual, part of his life, part of his personality. He develops behavior patterns having his marriage at the core. He cannot readily erase the memories of courtship days and the early years of marriage. The image of the spouse-that-used-to-be plagues him. In the idealization lent by time and distance he may forget the unpleasant aspects of his marriage and magnify those that were pleasant. At best, the divorced individual must go through a period of readjustment. In few cases is it easy. In some instances divorce does solve problems or afford effective escape from those that are insoluble. In other instances the problems are too deep-set to be solved by court decree. The individual, though altering the type of problem he confronts, does not really decrease the intensity of the problem situation.

EFFECTS OF DIVORCE UPON CHILDREN

It is often impossible to separate the effects of divorce, as such, from the effects of the failing home situation because divorce is preceded by marital failure. The child may not be aware of this, however, and sometimes the divorce brings to an abrupt and unexpected end a relationship that he had never questioned. This happens even with persons of college age who, in many cases, are taken aback when parents announce their intention of getting a divorce.

The child of divorced parents is in a position somewhat akin to that of the middle horse in a three-horse team, which is pulled now in one direction, now in another, now in both at once, as it attempts to accommodate itself to the movements of the other two horses. The child is torn between conflicting loyalties. He tries to cooperate with and to understand two persons who are at odds and do not understand each other. If he lives with each of them at different times, he is pulled first one way, then another. In neither home is he prepared for living in the other. He may be inclined to lean more toward one parent, and this leads to disillusionment and disappointment. He lives in a society where home and parents are taken for granted. He has, therefore, to face the attitude of his contemporaries, some of whom may chide him for his equivocal family status. There may be a carry-over of the attitude that divorce is a disgrace, and the child must defend himself against this. He may fear adverse public opinion or loss of prestige. In short, he is likely to develop a feeling of insecurity, and this feeling may lead him to compensatory behavior, which makes for more or less maladjustment. This is not always true. Some children of divorced parents are very well adjusted. There is much to be said for a child's living in harmony and security with one parent rather than in an atmosphere of conflict and insecurity with two.

Let us imagine that the reader's parents have just informed him that they are contemplating divorce. The announcement comes as a surprise. He had sensed that their marriage was not perfect, and now that a divorce is impending he can look back to events of the past and read into them new meaning. He begins to see that the situation was worse than he thought, that it had been crumbling for some time. Nevertheless, he had never suspected a complete break, and the announcement of divorce shocks him. He is confused. Conflict upsets him. He begins to worry. In his mixed-up thinking he makes many trials and an equal number of errors in seeking a way out. No solution he can think of seems to fit. He lies awake at night. He cannot study. He seems to feel life constantly pressing in upon him. His security seems threatened. The world he had always taken for granted, which he had assumed would remain as it was, which was the very foundation of many of the things in life about which he felt sure, is about to collapse. What can he do? There are several things that he may do in an attempt to reorient himself.

He should think first of his parents rather than of himself. They have been unhappy and dissatisfied and are contemplating a move which they believe will make them more content. In some cases they have sacrificed their own happiness and submerged their feelings in order to remain together until the child was old enough to be independent. Whatever harm there may be has already been done. The divorce will be only a result rather than a cause of their unhappiness.

They will still be his parents, no matter where they live. Nothing can change that. They may change their geographic location but they cannot change their relationship to their child. Probably, too, he may still see them, though perhaps not together.

They will need someone upon whom they can depend, since their world, too, is badly shaken. The child may be such a one if he keeps his mind clear and maintains his emotional equilibrium. Certainly, making three persons unhappy will not make two of them happy.

The child must recognize that his parents are adults. He may sympathize with them and help them in any way possible. But it is their problem, not his. No doubt they had a problem long before he was old enough to become aware of it. Without becoming indifferent, he should try to remain objective, detached, and independent. The probability is that the child can play little if any part in the solution of the problem. His age is against him. He is in a more disadvantageous position even than an outsider. If his parents cannot solve their own problem, how can he expect to do so for them? Certainly he cannot solve it through worry. Talking with a counselor may help to clear his thinking and relieve his emotions, however.

The child should not assume the blame for the parents' failure. Looking back at his home life he may recall instances in which he seemed to be the center of their conflict; but in all probability he was only the focal point, not the cause. Even if he were the cause upon occasion, he was no doubt not intentionally so. He may have committed many of the errors of adolescence, but that should not make him assume blame now, for his assumption of blame cannot solve his parents' problem. They probably do not hold him to blame.

Very few divorces are entirely one-sided as to causation. One parent's contribution to the failure seems more apparent to the child than the other's. But the child may accept as a safe working rule that both were at fault in one way or another and that the causation was complex. When two people marry, each assumes a responsibility for the success of their mutual adjustment. When adjustment does not work out as they had hoped, the very fact of their assumption of responsibility makes each partly to blame. The child, however, should avoid placing blame or taking sides unless he is certain of the facts. However sincere parents may be, however they may try to be objective, in a situation as critical as that of divorce their interpretations are unavoidably biased. Naturally the spouse that wants a divorce magnifies the bad and minimizes the good in the marriage, while the one that does not want it does the opposite. Even when both parties want a divorce, the one who acts as plaintiff presents a one-sided picture in court to which the other party through silence implies agreement. The child's responsibility is to understand, not to censure.

The child should also try to realize that his parents' problem in no way reflects upon him. We have passed the day when the child of divorced persons was considered disgraced. He is what he is—no more, no less—no matter what the marital status of his parents.

The child should try to avoid generalizing on the basis of his parents' experience. As has been said in the discussion of maturity, he may take the attitude that their divorce will unalterably distort his future, or he may take the attitude that he will profit by their mistakes.

He should also avoid exaggerating the significance of relatively unimportant things. For example, the divorce may make it impossible for the family to be together on the child's birthday, as has been their custom. The importance of foregoing the birthday celebration may easily be exaggerated, since it may serve as a symbol of the child's reaction to the total situation. Actually, the birthday party is not nearly so important as many other things now to be considered, since the crisis is imminent.

Suggested remedies

Before it is possible to talk intelligently about remedies for the situation in which marriage and divorce are seen to be, the objectives must be made clear. Is the objective to decrease divorce or to increase marital success? The latter would lead to the former, but the former would not produce the latter. If the aim is merely to reduce the number of divorces, this could be accomplished by making divorce more difficult through legal definitions and impediments. That would be to treat symptoms rather than the disease. More stringent divorce laws would not make marriages more successful; they would only prevent escape.

Legalizing divorce by mutual consent has often been suggested, and there is something to be said for it. At present, a couple may marry by mutual consent, but they may not unmarry on this basis. The assumption in prohibiting the latter is that there are considerations of property, children, status, responsibility. The same considerations hold in getting married. A couple may marry by mutual consent and then not fulfill their responsibilities. At present, if one spouse wants a divorce and brings suit against the other on some ground defined by law, the divorce is usually granted. If both parties want a divorce and agree that one will allege certain grounds and that the other will make no defense, their agreement is ordinarily interpreted as collusion. If the collusion is discovered, the court may dismiss the suit. The couple's mutual desire to get a divorce or property agreements made on the possibility that a divorce may be obtained usually do not in themselves constitute collusion, if the divorce action is initiated in the usual manner and on acceptable grounds. For example, a husband who committed adultery might be fully as desirous of having a divorce as the wife who sued him for it; but the fact that they both wanted it would not be collusion. In no case, however, can the couple obtain a divorce merely because they both want it.

In most states, when one spouse sues the other for divorce, it is possible for the defendant to initiate a countercharge to the effect that the plaintiff has also been guilty of an offense that constitutes a ground for divorce. This is termed *recrimination*. Sometimes in such cases the divorce is granted to neither party. This means, in essence, that if one party has committed an offense, a divorce may be granted, but that if both parties have offended and the situation is roughly twice as bad, neither can obtain a divorce. There are exceptions to this condition, however. The statutes of Nevada, for example, include the theory of *comparative rectitude*. If, in an action for divorce in that state, it appears that both parties have committed offenses that constitute grounds for divorce, the court may grant a decree to the party it deems less at fault.

By and large, in order to obtain a divorce under our present system, one party must prove injury by the other, and it must be injury of a type defined by the law of a particular state. A divorce suit savors of adversary litigation. If the couple themselves recognize that they have both been injured, they cannot get a divorce unless they conceal their understanding and perjure themselves in court, to "prove" that one was innocent and the other guilty. This means that in actual practice we already have divorce by mutual consent, but it has not been legalized.

In discussing divorce by mutual consent there is a common tendency to begin with the present system and set it up as a norm. This makes necessary the justification of change. One could just as well, perhaps even better, start with divorce by mutual consent and insist that the proponents of the *status quo* justify divorce granted on the plea of only one spouse when the other may or may not want it. We do not force people to marry, but we do force them to remain married or to become unmarried against their will. Perhaps neither system is entirely desirable to the complete exclusion of the other. What is needed is not divorce either as we have it at present or by mutual consent, but divorce when a marriage has ceased to function for either the couple or society — when it is necessary — whether one or both parties desire it. This implies laws adapted to present needs and interpreted by courts having insight into marital problems. It implies the elimination of an attitude and a system through which modern marriage is squeezed into outmoded forms.

READING 9 **A NEW KIND OF DIVORCE COURT**

In a few words, the *standard* juvenile court substitutes diagnosis and therapy for guilt and punishment. It is more interested in ultimate than proximate cause. It doesn't hold trials to determine the child's guilt or innocence. Its skillful approach is friendly; its aim, to help the child; its criterion, what is best for the child.

It operates within the law but does not confine itself to the law. It invokes the aid of other sciences and disciplines,

From Paul W. Alexander, "The Follies of Divorce: A Therapeutic Approach to the Problem," *Law Forum*, Winter, 1949, pp. 695–711. Abridged and reprinted with permission of the editor and the author.

such as religion, medicine, psychology, psychiatry, sociology, and education. It operates under a judicial officer but does not confine itself to the judge. It employs trained technicians and skilled specialists. Even the judge must make himself into a specialist.

According to Dean Pound it has five characteristics of equity jurisdiction: "(1) It is relatively informal in its procedure. . . . (2) As with all equity jurisdiction it is remedial, not punitive. (3) It acts preventively in advance of commission of any specific wrong-doing. (4) It employs administrative rather than adversary methods. (5) It can adapt its action to the circumstances of individual causes and so achieve a high degree of individualization, which is demanded by justice, if not always by security."

At the same time the *standard* juvenile court appreciates "the importance of the ethics of judicial adjudication, of hearing both sides fully, of acting on evidence of logical probative force, and of not combining the function of accuser, prosecutor, advocate of the complaint, and judge; of a record from which it can be seen what has been done and how and on what basis; and of possibility of review before a bench of judges in order to save fundamental constitutional and legal rights. . . ."

It happens that the court over which I preside handles both divorce and delinquency. Years ago I became aware that we were able to straighten out and do a good repair job upon an impressive majority of the delinquent children; while at the same time, in an appalling proportion of the divorce cases, little, if any, respectable effort was made or opportunity presented to do any kind of a repair job. The juvenile court was a hospital where the ailing behavior of the children was diagnosed and treated; the divorce court was a superficial examination, and burial certificates were issued in the form of divorce decrees.

The American Bar Association committee proposes to transform the divorce court from a morgue into a hospital; to handle our ailing marriages and delinquent spouses much as we handle our delinquent children—for often their behavior is not unlike that of a delinquent child and for much the same reasons. Instead of looking only at the guilt of the defendant, it proposes to examine the whole marriage, endeavor to discover the basic causative factors, and seek to remove or rectify them, enlisting the aid of other sciences and disciplines and of all available community resources.

The fresh approach, the new philosophy would be signified by the very titling of the case; instead of it being *"John Doe v. Mary Doe,"* it would be titled *"In the Interest of the John Doe Family."* There would be no plaintiff, no defendant—only an applicant or joint applicants. The application would be not for divorce but for the remedial services of the state. Petition for divorce would be permitted only after complete investigation and report. The new plan would take over almost bodily the entire philosophy, procedure, and techniques of the juvenile court. As in the juvenile court the criterion (fixed by law as well as philosophy) is "What is best for the child?" so in the divorce court the criterion would be "What is best for this family?"

To do this sort of thing would obviously require a special kind of court which, for convenience, has been called the "Family Court." As Dean Pound points out in speaking of the juvenile court there are strong reasons for not making it a separate court but a branch of the court of general jurisdiction of first instance. It would seem necessary to endow it with the broadest possible equitable, civil, and even criminal jurisdiction. It should have the same dignity and status as the court of general jurisdiction: its quarters should be adequate in size, advantageously located, designed for functional efficiency, equipped, and decorated so as to command respect for the law which it will administer.

Among the reasons for this is that although the family court may deal in dimes while other branches of the court deal in dollars, nevertheless, because it is bound to have so many more clients than the ordinary civil and criminal courts and their problems strike home so intimately into their everyday life, the family court cannot fail to have a greater impact upon the sum total of human welfare and happiness than perhaps all other branches of the court combined.

Like the juvenile court, the family court would require an adequate staff of trained technicians and skilled specialists, such as the social caseworker, psychiatric caseworker, clinical psychologist, psychiatrist, marriage counsellor, and others, and, of course, a proper clerical force.

Most important, the court would require a specialist judge or judges. No court can be expected to rise above its judge. No matter how able a lawyer he may be or how filled with the spirit of altruism, he will have to school himself in quite a number of fields of learning and disciplines for which his legal training and experiences have not prepared him. Among these are social casework, group work, counselling, diagnosis and therapy, several branches of psychology (especially so-called abnormal psychology), penology, criminology, the basic principles of psychiatry, medical casework, community organization, child and family welfare, and some others.

Most of the advantages of having all socio-legal family problems handled by one integrated court are obvious.

There is an additional advantage not apparent to the un-initiated. As previously indicated, marriages fail because of the defects of the spouses. Spouses of this sort who have children are apt to have contact with the juvenile court. Then when they wind up in the divorce court, the judge has before him the complete family record. One year in one such court in as high as 40 per cent of the divorce cases, the family had previously had contact with the juvenile court. The information gleaned from these family records enabled the judge to get at the whole truth and to find the best solution for the family as a whole.

Conversely, as pointed out by Judge Edwin A. Robson of Chicago in a recent study of divorce in Illinois, many young wards of the divorce court are destined, because of the broken family, to become wards of the juvenile court; and like advantages could be expected from combining the two courts.

The principal disadvantage of this type of court is seldom mentioned. In counties with a population of a quarter million or more, the volume of cases, adult and juvenile, and the administrative problem of handling a staff of thirty or forty or more, with an annual budget well into six figures, combine to make the judge work under such relentless pressure that he cannot always give his very best to the clients—who are entitled to an unhurried hearing before an unharried judge. The job can be a man-killer for the judge, but the obvious simple solution would be to have two or more judges for the larger courts.

In the case of the smaller community which would not warrant the establishment of a full-time family court with a full-time specialist judge, it is proposed to take a leaf from the experience in Connecticut and Utah, where state juvenile courts are presided over by three judges who travel from county to county with an office and full-time worker in each county.

In conclusion, I hope no one will get the idea that the foregoing proposals are even a remote attempt at a definite blueprint. On the contrary they should be construed as an invitation for criticisms and suggestions which the American Bar Association committee solicits and promises to consider.

Perfection is desirable. So is unanimity of opinion. We should strive for perfection and we should strive for unanimity, but we had best resign ourselves to the fact that we shall never achieve either. If we wait for either perfection or unanimity we shall wait forever, and that is unthink-able. I reiterate, the time for *fundamental* reform has already been *too* long upon us.

Those who believe that divorce by mutual consent would jeopardize marriage and produce an unprecedented increase in the divorce rate have only to look to the countries where such divorce is legalized. Their rates are lower than ours. Ours is one of the highest divorce rates in the world [United Nations, 1962].

In lieu of more stringent divorce laws some persons have suggested stricter marriage laws. The latter would no doubt prove the more effective. There is also needed more thorough enforcement, both of new laws and of the ones already on the statute books. More thorough premarital medical examinations, more careful investigation of applicants for licenses, more adequate age qualifications, and other similar stipulations would no doubt play a part in preventing ill-advised marriages.

Uniform laws have also been suggested. Certainly even the proponents of variety for the sake of experimentation must admit that variety need not extend from one extreme to another. There can be an approach to uniformity without identity. The greatest danger in making marriage and divorce laws uniform in all states is that uniform laws would represent compromises. As it is, some states are more progressive than others. Compromise would mean the loss of some of the progress secured in the more advanced states. There is no hope of achieving uniformity through Federal legislation, since the Constitution does not give the Federal government authority to regulate marriage and divorce. All marriage and divorce laws are state laws. To get a Federal law the Constitution would have to be amended; and the possibility of obtaining passage of such an amendment is so remote that, at present at least, it is not worth considering.

READING 10 **THE NEW AUSTRALIAN DIVORCE LAW**

Before 1959 each of Australia's six states had its own law of divorce, just as each state in this country does at present. The Australian Constitution provides for commonwealth (federal) laws of marriage and divorce, but no such federal laws had been agreed upon prior to 1959. In that year the Commonwealth Parliament passed the Matrimonial Causes Act. It was put into effect in 1961. A new federal marriage act was put into effect in 1963. The American Constitution does not provide for federal legislation pertaining to marriage and divorce. Nonetheless, greater uniformity of law is needed and progress toward

Excerpted from an address by Hon. Sir Garfield Barwick, Q.C., M.P., to the Parliament of the Commonwealth of Australia on "Matrimonial Causes Bill 1959," *Parliamentary Debates*, May 14, 1959.

this end is taking place. To achieve federal laws of marriage and divorce, the several Australian states had to reach compromises. It is interesting and pertinent to see what kind of provisions emerged from this process. Following are excerpts from the attorney-general's address to Parliament explaining the new divorce law then being considered. References to cruelty, desertion, adultery and other similar grounds for divorce, fourteen of which the new law specifies, have been omitted.

The object of this bill is to give to the people of Australia, for the first time in our history, one law with respect to divorce and matrimonial causes and such important ancillary matters as maintenance of divorced wives and the custody and maintenance of the children of divorced persons. Upon the bill becoming law, Australia, so far as my research goes, will be one of the first countries under a federal constitution to deal comprehensively and uniformly on a national basis with matrimonial causes.

The States' enactments on divorce, as a matter of history, largely rested on the theory that the State may properly grant a decree of divorce or judicial separation where one of the parties has repudiated the marriage, whether expressly or by committing such a matrimonial offence as in the eyes of the public ought to discharge the other from marital obligations. In short, these systems have largely limited themselves to consideration and designation of matrimonial offences and have left all initiative in the matter of divorce with the innocent party.

But there are those who feel that recognition of the importance of family life must itself cause us to seek some way out of the situation that arises when man and wife, without misconduct or matrimonial offence on the part of either, become estranged and break off their relationship beyond all possibility of reconciliation, and out of the other situation where the innocent party refuses to take the initiative and to seek a dissolution, preferring to imprison the other party within bonds which have become meaningless and little more than a provocation. Accordingly, some communities have provided a means whereby two people so placed may be enabled with regularity within the law to start a family afresh with another.

Honorable members will see when they study this bill that the Government has drawn upon both of these ideas in deciding the grounds upon which a marriage may be dissolved; that is to say, both the idea of matrimonial offence and the idea of a definitive and irretrievable breakdown even without an offence.

As I have said, the paramount endeavour of this bill,

as contrasted with the existing laws of the States, is that it seeks to maintain marriage and to protect the family.

The first step to promote sound and strong marriage is the support the bill promises to marriage guidance organizations. I am very conscious . . . of the fact that many marriages go "on the rocks" and founder for want of somebody to assist the parties to overcome their difficulties, to assist the one to understand and to adjust to the other. I have been most impressed in what I have read and by those with whom I have taken the trouble to speak by the efforts in this direction of the marriage guidance organizations. I am sure they have already in this country saved many marriages from breaking down. I think they should be supported. The Government has decided that these voluntary and independent organizations should be encouraged and subsidized. Consequently, in this bill provision is made to approve marriage guidance organizations and to subsidize them, exercising for that purpose some limited supervision of their activities.

I do not hold with the view that this work can be done satisfactorily by people who make it no more than a means of livelihood. The work will best be done by those who, as well as being trained, have a sense of vocation and who, to a large extent, volunteer their good offices in this very skilful and sympathetic task. Consequently, the subsidy is not intended to institutionalize these organizations, but rather is confined to give them that financial support which will assist them in their administration, and to train those who are to perform it.

So that consultation with marriage guidance counsellors can be attended by the utmost frankness and with a sense of security, the bill requires marriage guidance counsellors to take an oath of secrecy, and disqualifies them from giving in any proceedings evidence of what is said in the course of their consultations.

I am conscious that in the early days of married life, particularly amongst younger people, the two personalities which had theretofore no need to consider any one's interest or comfort but their own, must make many adjustments in accommodation each to the other in married life. I would expect that, in this period, marriage guidance organizations, if they earn acceptance, can be most useful. I have felt that if, in this period, it was not easy for either party to commence judicial proceedings to end the marriage there would be a much greater prospect of a more earnest endeavour to make a success of the marriage; and there may be added scope for the services of the marriage guidance organizations. Accordingly . . . this bill provides that, with certain exceptions, no proceedings for dissolution or judicial separation may be commenced within three years of marriage, except by leave of a court. The exceptions relate to conduct which would mostly, if not universally, preclude reconciliation. Leave to commence proceedings under three years may be given only in exceptional circumstances where to refuse would create exceptional hardship on the moving party or where the case is one of exceptional depravity on the part of the defaulting party.

Honorable members will have observed that the limitation upon the commencement of proceedings does not extend to a suit for restitution of conjugal rights. This bill makes provision for such a suit, but it does not allow proceedings for dissolution of marriage to be taken immediately upon a failure to comply with an order for restitution, whatever the time fixed for compliance, as I am bound to say is the present position in the State of New South Wales. This bill permits proceedings for divorce founded on non-compliance with an order for restitution of conjugal rights only where that non-compliance has continued for the full space of one year and, of course, where three years have elapsed since the marriage.

By insisting that only non-compliance with such an order for at least one year will be a ground of divorce this bill has returned the suit for restitution of conjugal rights to its orginal purpose. Under this bill, it will be a procedure in aid of reconciliation. This is particularly so where an order for restitution is sought in the early years of the marriage. Consequently, proceedings for an order for restitution of conjugal rights may be commenced within three years of marriage, but proceedings for dissolution founded on non-compliance with such an order must await the expiry of that three years.

Machinery is provided whereby, if the judge thinks he sees a possibility of a reconciliation, he can make an endeavour to effect it. He has power to adjourn the proceedings, so as to give the parties a period of "cooling-off" and consideration; or he can himself undertake the task of seeing them, with or without their legal representatives, as he sees fit, in an endeavour to find a solution to their difficulties. Alternatively, he can appoint a marriage guidance organization to conciliate, or in special circumstances, he can himself appoint a person of suitable qualifications.

Under these provisions the judge will not be able to compel the parties to go into conference with each other or with him or with any person nominated by him or by a marriage guidance organization. He must have their consent.

To ensure frankness and discussion with complete

security, the bill renders inadmissible in all proceedings anything said or any admission made in the course of the endeavour to effect a reconciliation. Further, a conciliator is required to take an oath of secrecy in the scheduled form. The parties may thus discuss with the utmost frankness and with the utmost of security all their difficulties, and have the assistance and good offices of skilled people in their endeavour to prevent destruction of their marriage and their family life.

The bill provides that where there are children of the marriage no decree nisi for divorce, no matter on what ground granted, may become absolute until the court by order has declared that it is satisfied that proper arrangements have been made for the welfare of the children, that is to say, proper arrangements having in mind the means and circumstances of the parents.

Under this bill any person domiciled in Australia can institute proceedings in any State or Territory, with the sole qualification that for instituting proceedings in a Territory a short period of residence is required, for reasons practical if not indeed constitutional.

There remains for mention a ground upon which there may centre a good deal of attention and discussion. It is ground (m) . . . "that, since the marriage, the parties to the marriage have been separated (whether by agreement, decree or otherwise) for a continuous period of not less than five years immediately preceding the date of the petition and there is no reasonable likelihood of cohabitation being resumed."

The Government has utilized the concept that there is a public interest in allowing dissolution where the parties, perhaps without matrimonial offence on the part of either, were, and have for years been, separated with no prospect of any reconciliation. This ground (m) is the result of that course; not requiring a matrimonial offence to have been committed, nor regarding the commission of such an offence as necessarily preventing relief to the wrong-doing party.

Here, the public interest in family life comes down on the side of allowing each of these separated parties to regularize their relationships or to assume regular relationships in the future. On this view, no sense is seen, in the public interest, in denying the possibility of family life to each when all is irretrievably lost between them. No sense is seen in possibly condemning either or both of them to irregular relationships which, in honour, cannot result in families. Nor is the existing capacity of an innocent party to withhold dissolution indefinitely seen as necessarily just or conformable to the public interest. Western Australian law has contained this ground for some fourteen years and, I understand, it has given satisfaction. The present bill includes this ground, applicable to any separation, whether the separation results from agreement or decree or simply from conduct. The period of separation is five years, with no prospect of a resumption of cohabitation.

The bill provides that the court shall refuse a decree if, in the particular circumstances of the case, the court is of opinion that, by reason of the conduct of the petitioner or other circumstances, it would be harsh or oppressive to the respondent, or contrary to the public interest, to grant the petitioner's desired decree. These phrases will, I think, prove adequate for the courts to prevent any abuse of this ground and to ensure that it is kept to those cases which it has plainly been designed to cover.

In the last analysis, the most effective remedy for the situation in which marriage and divorce now stand is education — the gradual, slow, tedious education of a public, part of which is inert and apathetic and not even aware of the need for preparing people for marriage or for departing from timeworn and threadbare tradition. It is hoped that, coupled with education, counseling facilities will continue to increase and improve. The advancement of marriage depends also upon the raising of the general cultural level and improving the emotional, social, and intellectual adjustment of the individual, for, as mentioned in an earlier connection, marriage can be no better than the people in it.

WHAT DO YOU THINK?

1. What factors in the present-day United States are contributing to the high divorce rate?

2. What factors in the present-day United States are contributing to the failure and breakdown of marriages?

3. What are the pros and cons of legalizing divorce by mutual consent?

4. Should incompatibility as a ground for divorce be legalized in all states?

5. Is divorce a social evil?

6. Which is more likely to be detrimental to children, conflict in the family or the breaking of family ties by divorce?

7. What would happen if all divorce were prohibited by law?

8. What are the pros and cons of having marriage counselors connected with divorce courts?

9. In the present-day social situation, what assets may be found and utilized to increase success in marriage? What liabilities are there? How may these liabilities and their effects be avoided? How may the assets be increased and the liabilities decreased?

10. What community resources may be drawn upon to improve marriage and family life?

11. How may marriage and the family contribute to the improvement of community life?

12. You are the chairman of a special committee of the leading club in your community. The committee's assignment is to work out a marriage and divorce law which the club will try to have passed by the state legislature. What would you include in that law?

13. What are the pros and cons of uniform marriage and divorce laws? Of a Federal marriage and divorce law?

SELECTED READINGS

Association of American Law Schools: *Selected Essays on Family Law*, The Foundation Press, Brooklyn, 1950. A collection of articles on many aspects of the laws pertaining to marriage, divorce, annulment, common law marriage, marriage by proxy, illegitimacy, desertion, divorce "without fault," paternity tests, and the "myth of the innocent spouse."

Barwick, Sir Garfield: "Some Aspects of the New Matrimonial Causes Act," *The Sydney Law Review*, vol. 3, no. 3, pp. 409–438, 1961. An explanation by the attorney-general of Australia of a divorce law passed in 1959 and put into effect in 1961. With this act Australia replaced its state divorce laws with a federal divorce law.

Berelson, Bernard, and Gary A. Steiner: *Human Behavior*, Harcourt, Brace & World, Inc., New York, 1964, chap. 7. The family; sexual behavior; courtship; marriage; divorce. This book is an inventory of scientific studies and an appraisal of what the behavioral sciences have and have not established relative to human behavior.

Blake, Nelson M.: *The Road to Reno*, The Macmillan Company, New York, 1962. A history of American divorce.

Blood, Robert O., Jr.: *Marriage*, The Free Press of Glencoe, New York, 1962, chap. 11. Types of dissolution of marriage; divorce and remarriage.

Bowman, Henry A.: *A Christian Interpretation of Marriage*, The Westminster Press, Philadelphia, 1959, chap. 6. An analysis of Jesus' teachings relative to divorce and remarriage.

Cavan, Ruth Shonle (ed.): *Marriage and the Family in the Modern World,* Thomas Y. Crowell Company, New York, 1960, chaps. 10, 18. Laws regulating marriage and family life; importance of divorce; divorce as an escape mechanism; remarriage; alimony.

Clarke, Helen I.: *Social Legislation,* 2d ed., Appleton-Century-Crofts, Inc., New York, 1957. A discussion of the laws pertaining to marriage, divorce, sterilization, adoption, illegitimacy, juvenile offenders, and similar topics.

Despert, J. Louise: *Children of Divorce,* Doubleday & Company, Inc., Garden City, N.Y., 1962. A child psychiatrist examines the effects of divorce on children and makes suggestions for helping them.

Duvall, Evelyn Millis, and Sylvanus M. Duvall: *Sex Ways in Fact and Faith: Bases for Christian Family Policy,* Association Press, New York, 1961, chap. 6. Divorce and remarriage.

Egleson, Jim, and Janet Egleson: *Parents Without Partners,* E. P. Dutton & Co., Inc., New York, 1961. The story of the beginning of Parents Without Partners, an organization of parents having the responsibility of rearing children singlehanded because of widowhood or divorce; problems faced.

Goode, William J.: *After Divorce,* The Free Press of Glencoe, New York, 1956. A study of the divorce process and of the readjustment problems of 425 divorced women.

Kephart, William M.: *The Family, Society, and the Individual,* Houghton Mifflin Company, Boston, 1961, chaps. 14, 20, 21, 22. Sociolegal aspects of marriage; void and voidable marriages; licensing; common law marriage; divorce; causes and effects of family breakdown.

Kling, Samuel G.: *The Complete Guide to Divorce,* Bernard Geis Associates, New York, 1963. A discussion of many aspects of divorce; answers a great variety of questions.

Kuchler, Frances W. H.: *The Law of Marriage and Divorce,* Oceana Publications, Inc., New York, 1961. A digest and analysis of state laws regulating marriage, divorce, separation, annulment, remarriage, and related topics.

Landis, Judson T., and Mary G. Landis: *Building a Successful Marriage,* 4th ed., Prentice-Hall, Inc., Englewood Cliffs, N.J., 1963, chap. 15. The legal regulation of marriage; void and voidable marriages.

Landis, Paul H.: *For Husbands and Wives,* Appleton-Century-Crofts, Inc., New York, 1956, chap. 18. Divorce and remarriage.

Merrill, Francis E.: *Courtship and Marriage,* rev. ed., Holt, Rinehart and Winston, Inc., New York, 1959, chaps. 22, 24. Divorce: characteristics of divorced persons; adjustment after divorce; remarriage.

Nye, F. Ivan: "Child Adjustment in Broken and Unhappy Unbroken Homes," *Marriage and Family Living,* vol. 19, no. 4, pp. 356–361,

November, 1957. The author says that "the adjustment of children in homes broken by divorce is not more difficult or unsuccessful than in homes broken otherwise."

O'Gorman, Hubert J.: *Lawyers and Matrimonial Cases*, The Free Press of Glencoe, New York, 1963. A study of the pressures brought to bear upon lawyers who handle matrimonial cases; evasion of divorce laws; an analysis of lawyers and clients.

Pilpel, Harriet F., and Theodore Zavin: *Your Marriage and the Law*, Holt, Rinehart and Winston, Inc., New York, 1952, chaps. 1–6, 15–21. A discussion of the variety of laws relating to engagement, marriage, husbands and wives, separation, and divorce. Case material is included.

Ploscowe, Morris: *The Truth about Divorce*, Hawthorn Books, Prentice-Hall, Inc., Englewood Cliffs, N.J., 1955. Alternatives to divorce; grounds for divorce; children and divorce; the need for divorce law reform. Includes many illustrations from case materials.

Rothenberg, Charles: *Postscript to Marriage*, Greenberg: Publisher, Inc., New York, 1946. A discussion of divorce grounds, history, laws, alimony, and who gets the children. Written by a lawyer in layman's language.

Simpson, George: *People in Families*, Thomas Y. Crowell Company, New York, 1960, chaps. 18, 19. Divorce and the divorce prone; divorce and the mental health of children; remarriage. Psychoanalytic emphasis.

Waller, Willard: *The Old Love and the New*, Liveright Publishing Corporation, New York, 1930. An analysis of divorce and readjustment after divorce; the process of alienation.

chapter 11

PERSONAL FACTORS AFFECTING MARRIAGE

IN THIS CHAPTER we shall discuss some of the processes, types of behavior, and personality traits which play a part in making marriage succeed or fail. Or, since success and failure are not distinct entities but rather aspects of a continuum, perhaps it would be more nearly accurate to say that we shall discuss some of those factors the combined effect of which determines the level of adjustment in marriage. We cannot hope to discuss all such factors. There are many which are beyond the scope of this book. Therefore, we shall discuss those about which the reader may, if he will, do something either through self-examination on a conscious level, or through putting them into effect in his marital behavior, or through avoiding them. This is not equivalent to giving the reader an oversimplified "do-it-yourself" manual, "Happy Marriage in Three Easy Lessons." Rather it is keeping in mind the fact that no one book can be "all things to all men." The reader is, therefore, addressed as a person concerned about preparation for his own marriage, not as a social scientist, and therefore presumably motivated to do whatever he can to contribute to its success. Any discussion such as that which follows is unavoidably generalized, suggesting that in working out an individual marriage there is ample room for ingenuity, imagination, and the infusion of the reflections of myriad facets of individual personalities. The cultural framework within which marriages occur exerts some pressure toward similarity of structure. But within that structure a couple have almost limitless flexibility of interrelationship and function. In the following discussion, then, we shall consider some of the factors within marriage that need to be understood in order to further the individual's contribution to such interrelationships and functions.

Conflict is normal

It should be said at once that some conflict in marriage is normal and to be expected. Two personalities could not live in such intimate union without it unless both of them were completely apathetic, accepting the relationship with bovine placidity. Men and women being as they are, each with peculiar aims yet each having to take account of the existence of the other, there is a pull away from, as well as an attraction toward, each other. William Graham Sumner termed the association of the sexes *antagonistic cooperation*. There is much to be said for such a description. Conflict is not always overtly manifest; it may be covert. It does not always mean open quarreling. Nor does it necessarily mean failure. A couple need not give up their marriage as lost the first time there is conflict, tension, or a difference between them. Even the most nearly perfect marriages are much more human, more real, and more earthy than fairy stories. A fairy story is perfect because it is made so; it is a static state of bliss. Romance may be found without instituting a stagnant state of unreality.

A husband and wife need not agree upon everything or even like each other's every trait. It is not only disagreement but the manner in which it is expressed that causes difficulty. They should, however, agree upon basic goals; at least, they should reach a workable compromise concerning them.

In his study of the marital adjustment of 792 couples, Terman [1938] found numerous grievances mentioned by happy, as well as unhappy, spouses. The complaints were more frequent in the latter group, but they were far from absent in the former. To pick a few items from Terman's results, among those most frequently mentioned by the happy husbands and wives were grievances over in-laws, choice of friends, recreation, and respect for conventions; complaints that the spouse was argumentative, critical, not affectionate, nervous, a poor housekeeper, or that she nagged. Among the unhappy couples complaints were common. Yet, when all the couples were asked what they would do about marriage if they had their lives to live over again, more than 80 per cent said that they thought they would not only marry but marry the same spouse.

In Hamilton's [1929] study of 200 married persons some interesting attitudes were revealed. In answer to the question, "What is there in your marriage that is especially unsatisfactory to you?" only 39 men and 25 women said that there was nothing. To the query, "What things in your married life annoy and dissatisfy you most?" 23 men and 21 women said that there was nothing. "Has your spouse any habits to which you object?" was a question to which 45 men and 36 women answered "no" or "nothing serious." "Have you any habits to which your spouse objects?" brought from 33 men and 35 women the response "no" or "nothing serious." When asked what changes the individual would make in husband or wife, 21 men and 14 women said they would make no changes in any of the qualities mentioned in the inquiry. The majority of both men and women found some sources of conflict in their marriages, yet when they were asked whether they wanted to continue living with their spouses, 78 men and 75 women said "yes." When asked whether, knowing what they knew about marriage, they would remarry if they were single, 77 men and 74 women said that they would.

To say that some conflict in marriage is normal does not mean that all conflict present in a given couple's marriage must inevitably remain. Conflict may be removed or ameliorated by the other person's changing, by changing oneself, or by altering circumstances.

An understanding of personality and behavior

Personality may be thought of as the sum total of the individual—his habits, behavior, thought patterns, emotional responses, moods, attitudes, reactions to people and situations, hopes, fears, aspirations, and the myriad other things that make him an individual, a person. To say that an individual *is* a personality is more nearly accurate than to say that he *has* a personality. To say that an individual has "personality" is to refer to something relatively limited, that is, certain desirable traits, such as cheerfulness, enthusiasm, vivaciousness, forcefulness, and so on. These traits, however, are only part of his total personality. Personality includes character. Character is composed of those parts of personality that have to do with value judgments, that is, with judgments of right and wrong, and good and evil. Personality is not quantitative. No one has any more or less than anyone else. Personalities may vary as to type or quality but not as to amount.

Personality may be compared to climate. Florida and Montana have different climates. Some people prefer one, some the other. Florida is better adapted to the raising of some crops, Montana to the raising of others. But we cannot say that one state has more climate than the other. In similar fashion, it is inaccurate to say that one individual has more personality than another.

Strictly speaking, personality is not inborn. In a sense, however, some of its ingredients are. An individual's body structure, the way he is "put together," the way he functions, his temperament, and his aptitudes constitute the equipment with which the newborn child meets and begins to adjust to his environment. His personality becomes a product of the interaction between his equipment and his environment.

A personality may be compared to an iceberg only a small portion of which is visible above the surface of the water. This small portion, however, and the much larger portion hidden from sight below the surface are integral parts of the same mass. An individual's observable, overt behavior represents only a relatively small proportion of his total personality. The rest is there, nonetheless, some portions permanently hidden from view or appearing above the surface only now and then as the waves of circumstance cause the berg to rise and fall in the experiences of life.

Most of us exhibit traits and types of behavior that are not readily changed through our own efforts. What is true of ourselves is also true of our wives, husbands, or fiancés. They, too, are not readily changed. On the other hand, there are traits that may be altered through effort and analysis. Fuller understanding of human reactions may contribute significantly to the improvement of mutual adjustment. If we understand why a person is as he is, that very understanding tends to make our relations with him more agreeable, even though we cannot change him. We may not be able to alter his behavior; but we may alter our interpretation of his behavior, and that in itself is significant. Fuller knowledge also enables us to play a more effective role in directing our own development. Although one may not be able to change all his undesirable traits, he may through knowledge and understanding make the most of his limitations and prevent making undesirable traits worse, more obvious, or more obtrusive.

READING 11 **WHEN DOES AN ADULT NEED TO CHANGE?**

No one can give a dogmatic answer, nor can science. The following tentative suggestions as to when and why an adult might consider change came from clinicians, industrial supervisors, and teachers, who appreciate individual variation but who also realize that adult personalities need to grow.

The most that can be said is that the person who behaves in several of the following ways might suspect that a little change is in order. Not much, just a little! Let us call it continuous development or, as Gordon Allport says, "becoming." Here are some of the signals:

resisting change—An adult may suspect that he needs to change a bit if he finds that he strongly resists change. The one who resents suggestions, holds to his present ways defensively, and clings to a status quo which itself is outdated, is letting himself become so rigid that he cannot change if he has to. Perhaps there is some virtue in a little change for its own sake as one goes along. This is especially

From Robert L. Sutherland, *Can an Adult Change?* The Hogg Foundation for Mental Health, Austin, Tex., revised 1957. Reprinted with the permission of the author and of The Hogg Foundation for Mental Health.

true in a turbulent society in which today's status quo has already changed by tomorrow.

A person can be flexible, humble, and searching, without being blown by the wind. A balance is needed between steadfastness of purpose and lack of bull-headedness — between determination to reach a goal and an ability to work with others to attain it.

systematizing everything — An individual may suspect that a little change is indicated if he discovers that he is getting most of his emotional satisfaction out of a minor virtue, like orderliness. Systematizing things and people is usually thought of as desirable — and it is — but like many other good traits, it can be overdone. Some people who are slaves to their intricate systems and want others to follow suit rigidly, may be dodging the bigger responsibility of granting freedom and initiative to others, even freedom to make their own mistakes. Perfectionism, domination, and oversupervision are wordfellows of close kin.

being an "unorganizer" — A person may need to change if he represents the other extreme — if he is a disorganizer, an unorganizer; if he flutters and clutters when things are awry but clings to his state of confusion. He looks bothered; he is baffled; he yearns for peace and order, but he has not learned to achieve it. He can, though — possibly!

resenting evaluation — He may need to change if he does well the work of the day but resists and resents evaluation. He shies from big ideas and clings to busy work. He likes to dictate letters and especially inter-office memoranda but avoids the assigned task of developing a five-year plan with his department. He thwarts himself and others who need to cope with the future.

dreaming — and more dreaming — On the other hand, if he only dreams and never touches reality, he is first revered as an "idea man" only to be discounted later as a visionary who has lost his sense of proportion and of reality.

damning things — and sometimes people — Some change would help if he finds himself spending much of his time and still more of his emotional energy in damning somebody or something — the Republicans, the Democrats, his company, his job, his community, his competitor, his government, another nationality, race, or religion. Now, all of these need to be criticized, for none is perfect. But a constant habit of criticism develops a sour look, a dour countenance, a permanent furrow in the brow, a voice with a high pitch, or low whine. Negativism, suspicion, and fear can become personality habits quite as much as any other attitude.

worrying—for the "fun" of it—A person may suspect that change is needed if he is a "worrier." He may know that worry uses up whatever it is that the internal glands of secretion produce, and that this is bad for the heart and the liver. But, feeling lonesome without worry, he keeps right on worrying. Then, as if to compound the bad interest, he worries about his habit of worrying. It becomes a vicious cycle, but also an emotionally pleasant one, in a pathological sort of way.

Worry, of course, cannot be dismissed with a turn of the phrase; it is often a symptom of an underlying problem to which the psychoanalyst might give years of attention, or it may be somewhat more superficial—a behavior pattern carried on more as a matter of habit after the original problem was solved or outlived.

sarcasm—for the "sting" of it—Dropping to a lesser problem than worrying, a person may need to change if he is a sarcastic soul. He may know that sarcasm has low utility in human relations; but if he has the habit, he keeps on practicing it. There are two kinds of sarcastic digs: The one made in the presence of another person is often said with a smile as a matter of defense; the other dig, made behind one's back, is often more extreme, sullen, and self-righteous.

nagging—If a person is a nagger, a wire recording of his voice might make him horrified at his own tenseness, unattractive manner, and authoritarian air, but he is likely to repeat the same behavior the next day. Over-supervision may be a form of nagging and vice versa.

procrastinating—The one who covers up indecision and procrastination by thinking he is being democratic—that is, conferring with Tom, Dick, and Sally before acting—needs to look at his rationalization more rationally! The desire to include others in planning is admirable; the humility which permits a person to seek advice is desirable; but the one who queries others must not forget that he, himself, is a person—not just a mirror of other people's fears, ideas, and hopes. If there is some discretion to his life, some consistency to his planning, and skill in using earlier experience, he has a mind of his own, capable of figuring out a line of action, even in a new situation. He confers with others, but also with himself!

making quick decisions—The opposite of the procrastinator may be still harder to live with. The "decisive one" has a mind that clicks, and has a yen for action. In the back of his mind is the picture of an efficient administrator who glances at a problem, sizes it up in a jiffy, and issues a memorandum about its solution before his first thought is dry. He gets things done all right, but, sadly, they often have to be undone. His desire for results makes him insensitive and roughshod. His self-confidence makes him authoritarian and unconcerned about achieving a consensus of opinion among his co-workers who may have a right to be in on the decision and whose cooperation is needed in the action. Can he slow up a bit? Can he develop some empathy, where now there is only compulsion? Can his enthusiasm for a goal be tempered without being curbed? Can he change a little, but remain basically himself, the kind of person without whom little would ever get done? We think so.

running for shelter—The person who by virtue of his managerial or professional position is expected to be helpful to others, but who runs from their problems, is in need of change. Subconsciously, he wants to avoid becoming entangled in another's situation because he is a confused or immature person himself. There are various defenses: He is in too big a hurry to sit down and listen; his efficient secretary keeps the flow of calls and callers moving so fast that no one is at ease to state a problem; he holds people off through the red tape of forms, memoranda, and carbon copies. Persons who come to him leave with their original problem unheeded; in addition, they feel frustrated, apologetic, and guilty for having bothered him. How can this person come to see what he is really doing to others? How can he be the leader of an organization administratively, and be available to hear the human problems which inevitably arise in any large group? This is the dilemma, but because of his own emotional problems, he fails to face it, and, instead, has learned to run and to hide!

making frankness a fetish—Now, what about the person who rests on his honesty? He is so impressed with the importance of what he thinks of as frankness that he may confuse it with cruelty. He considers himself a straight shooter. Such "honesty" can cause him to be hard on himself through condemnation. But he gets still more excitement out of being daringly frank with and watching the pained reactions of others. He is so self-righteous about giving the other person a quick inventory of his faults that the victim is caught off guard and may not fight back. Before our "virtuous" one gets through with his attack, he has expressed not so much the high ethics of honesty as aggression in the form of psychological sadism.

wearing feelings on the proverbial sleeve — Then there is the overly suspicious and sensitive person. Can he develop a little more faith and confidence in others and a slightly thicker skin on himself? In his presence, one has to weigh everything said lest it be taken personally. The sensitive one is quick to fly off the handle because he reads malice into the action of others. His blood pressure rises in self-defense, but how silly is a show of defense when there is no attack!

Can he view life less personally, more objectively? His suspicious tendencies are not superficial, but may reflect an insecurity tracing back to the usual place. Nevertheless, trying a new skill — that of acting toward others as though they were friendly — can lead to some change and can mean success in proving that others are cooperative.

For more persistent problems, psychotherapy, or at least group psychotherapy, may be needed. But new types of group experience . . . may bring out a favorable response in more superficial cases.

clinging to well-earned status — "What is the most common human relations difficulty you encounter?" When this question was asked the head of a firm which specializes in psychological counseling to top management, the answer was unequivocal. "One can always expect the problem of the leader who was responsible for developing the company in the early days but now cannot give up authority and status roles to younger, possibly more able, junior executives," the head of the firm replied. "The man kills himself with overwork, while the junior executives lose interest."

Industry is not the only place where one finds the uneasy person who tries to hold on to the status and responsibility he has earned. "The sense of being replaced" is a hard one to cope with in movie and television stardom, in business, in civic responsibility, and also in the family as children grow up and form families of their own. It is not made easier when the newcomer fails to recognize the accomplishments and continued value of the older leader and thinks of himself as the bright and shining hope of a bogged-down organization.

The problem is compounded by the attention which others give the new person and the new ideas he brings. The older one forgets that he enjoyed this acceptance at one time and that life moves on. Stepping down in responsibility has never been easy for persons living in our competitive culture. There are ways of doing it, ways of preparing for it, new types of service one can render, and even new forms of satisfaction in the expansion and success of the program and of the younger personnel in it. Such a shift in attitude and situation "takes some doing," does not come from simple advice, self-given or otherwise. It is one aspect of the total problem of preparation for retirement which might better be phrased "preparation for continuous growth."

ALL BEHAVIOR HAS A CAUSE OR CAUSES

Perhaps, to be more nearly accurate, we should say that all behavior has antecedents or is the outgrowth of contributing factors. To think in terms of causes as such often leads to oversimplification and mechanism. At any rate, the behavior which an individual exhibits always has roots. These may arise in relatively recent circumstances or may extend to remote childhood. They may go back to important experiences or to relatively insignificant incidents. Physiological processes also are not without their effect. The individual is the product of his experience. This concept, however, should not be oversimplified. Experience should not be thought of only in terms of large segments, such as crises, shocks, family life, college career. It may also be considered in terms of a continuum of change in environment, moods, physiology, contacts, ideas, emotions, and events, extending through more than 85,000 seconds per day and through every day of life. None of this experience is lost.

These two views of experience may be compared with one's contemplation of the human body. The body may be regarded in terms of arms, legs, stomach, other vital organs and apparently unitary parts, with their functions or dysfunctions and injuries considered as single experiences. On the other hand, the body may be thought of in terms of microscopic cells, which in aggregates form organs whose functions and changes may be interpreted as the product of minute influences and infinitesimal physiological processes. Just as the body's functions are the sum total of metabolic changes in untold millions of cells, so the individual's behavior and personality are the end product of innumerable experiences, some great, some small; some remembered, most forgotten.

Since we live in only the instantaneous present, the roots of behavior must of necessity be in the past, except in so far as current physiological processes may affect behavior. An individual may change his attitude toward the past or may through present and future experience alter its products; but he cannot change the past itself. It leaves so indelible an impression upon him that he can change only through building up new patterns of behavior. He cannot change merely by saying so or by having someone else tell him to do so. His experiences may lead him to make a decision involving change, so he seems to alter his conduct by voluntary act of will. Actually, however, he alters his conduct because of his experience. Remote past experience forms a matrix in which more immediate experience serves as the precipitating cause of his present behavior or future changes; but he is still the product of his biography.

When confronted with a new situation, an individual reacts effectively or ineffectively, depending upon how and to what degree the new is related to the old and bound up with experience. The past may have laid upon him a hand so heavy that he cannot accept or assimilate the new — for example, the parent who is opposed to the freedom that is taken for granted by his children. In such a case, the new is resisted because the old has become crystallized, so to speak, and the individual has no interest in assimilating the new. In other instances he may be interested in solving a new problem but be unable to do so effectively because there has been nothing in his experience to which the problem may be related or because he relates the new to aspects of the old which enable him to reach only an inadequate solution. In a specific instance, a woman trained as a nurse and having had considerable hospital experience before marriage is having difficulty in adjusting to the marital situation because she treats her husband as if he were a patient. The firm tones and positive directions effective in caring for the cantankerous sick are resented by the husband, who expects mutual give-and-take and resists her efforts to direct him. There is no doubt of the wife's devotion and good intentions; but she is meeting the marital situation ineffectively because she interprets the new only in terms of the old.

CONDITIONING

In understanding the roots of behavior one fruitful concept is that of *conditioning*. Let us imagine that the reader is about to order dinner in a restaurant. As first course the menu suggests oyster or shrimp cocktail. Next there is a choice of one of the following: roast turkey with giblet dressing, creamed sweetbreads, or lobster. The majority of readers would find no insurmountable difficulty in reaching a decision. Now imagine that rattlesnake meat were substituted for one of the items on the menu. The majority of readers would not only not choose it but would have a strong feeling of revulsion at the very thought of eating it. Yet rattlesnake meat is used as food. It is occasionally listed on restaurant menus. It may be purchased in cans ready for use. Fundamentally, a lobster or an oyster is no more aesthetic, attractive, or respectable than a rattlesnake. Why, then, is one's reaction to the snake so different? The answer is *conditioning*.

A child will reach for a snake as readily as for a rabbit until, through his parents' "no, no's" and cries of alarm, he becomes conditioned against the former; that is, he associates "snake" with withdrawal rather than with reaching. If he were presented with a white rabbit and each time he reached for it his act were accompanied by a terrifying noise (as in some experiments), he would soon associate "rabbit" and terror so that sight of the animal would make him cry and seek to escape. If, in addition to this early experience, he were subjected to a cultural tradition and to a literary and social experience all of which were permeated with the idea that rabbit was not only dangerous but repulsive and a symbol of evil, his attitude toward rabbits would be similar to the attitude toward snakes, and he would have just as great aversion to including rabbit in his diet.

If in an experiment a person is subjected to an electric shock, he jumps. If at the moment of shock a light is flashed and this procedure is repeated a sufficient number of times, the individual becomes so conditioned that the light alone causes him to jump. "Light" becomes associated with "jump" rather than with "shock" and is then a substitute stimulus for the original shock.

It is in this way that many of our responses are built up. Conditioning accounts for most of our fears, tastes, and attitudes. Fears of animals, of high places, of enclosed places, of men, and of women, sex, or marriage develop in this manner. Food tastes are partly the result of conditioning, and in this conditioning custom plays a significant role. Some foods are palatable, others are not so, because of conditioning. The same food may be accepted under one name but may seem disgusting under another. Some foods are called by their biological terms, for example, liver, tongue, heart. These terms when employed in connection with diet are used in a conventional rather than an anatomical sense. "Liver" means something on a dinner plate, not a bodily organ. All one needs to do to show how thoroughly conditioned he is is to mention other foods by their anatomical names. Suppose, for example, the diner mentioned at the beginning of this section, instead of having to choose between roast turkey with giblet dressing, creamed sweetbreads, and lobster, had been confronted with a choice between turkey with viscera, creamed thymus gland, and arthropod. His relish of the dinner would probably be somewhat altered.

An individual may become conditioned through a single experience that leaves an indelible impression or through the repetition of a lesser stimulus, a "dripping faucet" type of experience. One serious accident may make a person fear riding in an automobile. One case of overeating may make a child lose his appetite for a given food. A child's learning not to touch things that do not belong to him comes as the result of repeated "no, no's" or slight punishment, but his learning not to touch a hot stove may be the result of one experience.

COMPLEXES

It is in this way that complexes are built up. A complex is a group or series of connected reactions, set off, so to speak, by a single stimulus, which may have little direct connection with the total response and which produces a response often out of proportion to the intensity of the stimulus. The whole complex may take on the emotional tone of one of the elements in it. Usually the emotional tone is marked.

One explanation for the intensity of the response in such situations is that the individual reacts as if he were reacting to a total situation, whereas he is reacting to only a part of it. If, for example, a complicated situation were represented by *ABC*, these three letters representing the stimuli that act upon him in that situation, and if his total response is represented by *XYZ*, the recurrence of part of the situation, say *A*, may be sufficient to produce *XYZ*. This may happen even when *A* occurs in a different setting from the original one and in combination with other elements, for example, *AEF*.

Everyone has complexes, some good, some not. Let us suppose that the reader receives a letter from his fiancée. Actually, the letter is nothing more than ink on paper, and his reading is merely the interpretation of symbols. But the letter arouses a chain of responses, a complex, the emotional tone of which is out of proportion to the intensity of the stimulus when the latter is thought of as paper and ink. In a way, the letter is a substitute for the fiancée, and the response to the letter is similar to the response to the actual presence of the fiancée, though less intense than that would be. Consider the attitude of some persons in this country toward women's smoking cigars. The sight or the mere thought of a woman with a cigar sets off a complex of ideas, attitudes, and opinions involving not only smoking but often immorality, the "double standard," sin, and religion. The emotional tone of the response is out of proportion to the stimulus.

In almost any group one may readily start a heated discussion by mentioning race, politics, or religion. People often have complexes related to these subjects. Money is another frequent focal point for complexes. So is sex.

If through experience an individual has developed a complex of inferiority, his complex may be brought into play by the slightest stimulus. Someone says something that he interprets as disparaging, or someone looks at him or does something equally insignificant. His response is out of proportion to the intensity of the stimulus. The term *inferiority complex* is much abused, much overworked, and often used very loosely, but it is useful in making clear how a cluster of responses may form around one original response and assume an intense emotional tone.

Not every feeling of inferiority or insecurity indicates an inferiority complex, however. An individual might feel inferior, for example, if he were forced into competition with a person who was obviously superior to him. He might feel insecure in a situation where there was obvious risk. In such cases the feeling of inferiority or insecurity springs directly from an objective appraisal of the factors in the immediate situation and is commensurate with them. His approach to the situation is a direct effort either to prevent unfavorable consequences or to remove causes. When an individual has an inferiority complex, on the other hand, he reacts to an immediate situation as if it were a past situation. He does this because a pattern of response that developed as a result of the past has been carried over, so to speak, in such a way that it may be evoked by situations that have little or no relationship to the original one, and the response is not commensurate with the actual situation. He may even respond as if he were inferior when he is not. Such an individual may attempt to compensate for his assumed inferiority in a way that is directed at neither the inferiority, as such, nor the causes of it. Sometimes his compensation takes the form of a nonverbal alibi, for example, a psychosomatic illness.

If one person is aware of another person's complexes, he may go a long way toward making their mutual relationship more harmonious by setting off the desirable complexes and avoiding the stimuli that set off the others. For example, if a woman has built up a complex of a pleasant, romantic type that may be touched off by flowers, the way is open for her husband to increase their mutual happiness by a very simple means. If, on the other hand, she has built up a complex involving money, sex, or some other aspect of marriage the arousing of which produces tension, aggravation, fear, or equally undesirable responses, the setting off of such a complex may, when possible, be avoided.

Complexes are altered or removed through experience and reconditioning. They cannot be removed by argument or demand. No one can pull his complexes out by the roots and remove them from his personality by act of will alone. Most human beings live more by their emotions than by their intellectual processes, if we may so express it. Consequently, logic and reason are frequently ineffective in influencing behavior.

NEGATIVE ADAPTATION

One aspect of conditioning, in the broad sense, is *negative adaptation*. A stimulus may lose its original effectiveness and fail to evoke any response. A student may become accustomed to noise which at first prevented concentration upon studies. Personal peculiarities which at first were irritating may gradually come to be overlooked. A girl who dislikes housework when it is done in her parental home may overcome this dislike when she does it in her own home. In such cases the response is lost because the stimulus is followed by other stimuli and the first one loses its effectiveness in producing a given simple response. Negative adaptation is one part of personality adjustment. In connection with some aspects of getting along with people, it is something that may be cultivated. In human relations we may sometimes take a lesson from the oyster. Were there no irritating grain of sand that found its way into the oyster's shell, there would be no pearl. The oyster makes it possible to get along with the grain of sand by smoothing over its rough edges until it is no longer irritating.

MORES AND FOLKWAYS

One important factor in the conditioning process is custom or, more technically, the *mores* and *folkways*, which are the accepted customs of the group, the former being considered the more essential and unchangeable. Mores and folkways vary from group to group. They put colored glasses upon each individual reared under their influence, determining in appreciable measure his tastes, attitudes, and point of view. Personality is in part socially determined. Each individual develops in a cultural climate, much of which he takes for granted and accepts without question.

Let us imagine that a student leaves a college building and meets her fiancé, who is making an unexpected visit. When she sees him, she screams, rushes toward him, throws her arms around him, and—they rub noses. Your reaction to this illustration shows how thoroughly conditioned by the mores you are. To rub noses seems ridiculous; to kiss would seem not only more acceptable but more sensible. Yet fundamentally there are no more logical arguments for one than for the other. The difference in attitude that you manifest is due to the fact that you look at the situation through the colored glasses of the folkways.

In similar fashion, the mores and folkways determine to considerable degree our attitudes toward morals, monogamy, etiquette, property, religion, and numerous other things which are part and parcel of our particular culture and way of life. Since the mores and folkways vary from group to group, area to area, and time to time, in associating with other people one must take into consideration those that have played a part in conditioning their behavior.

In a sense, we may think of American culture as being made up in part of elements common to all Americans and in part of numerous subcultures which are different and at times bring their adherents into conflict. It is for this reason that certain types of mixed marriage are difficult. We may think of masculine and feminine subcultures. These, too, are taken for granted. It is partly for this reason that the sexes behave differently, are sometimes in conflict, often do not understand each other, and frequently have a problem of communication, as discussed later.

OTHER ASPECTS OF BEHAVIOR

Without going into detail we may mention some other considerations relative to behavior that have a bearing on marital adjustment.

Behavior is affected by physiological processes. Fatigue, hunger, illness, moods, worry, and the menstrual cycle all leave their mark. Individuals differ in the degree to which their behavior shows the effects of such items and in the degree to which they can voluntarily control them.

People are inclined to become angry or irritated when they are thwarted. Such irritation may be reduced either by decreasing the irritant or by increasing resistance to it.

Each individual seeks to maintain what he considers a satisfactory position for himself in his own estimation and in the eyes of others. If he does not maintain this position through actual achievements, in self-defense he may attempt to maintain it through some means, such as rationalization, projection of blame, aggression, or alcoholic escape, or he may try to protect himself from the expectation of maintaining it through some means, such as hypochondria, withdrawal, or psychosomatic illness.

Observable "surface" phenomena often represent only the symptoms rather than the cause of an individual's behavior. On the other hand, "surface" phenomena are not necessarily a reflection of an individual's underlying attitudes. An expression of anger, for example, may be only an instance of habitual response on the part of a person with a quick temper. It does not necessarily indicate a lack of love. How "surface" phenomena are to be evaluated can be determined only on the basis of insight into a given personality.

An individual cannot be expected to change his behavior unless the situation is provided in which such change can occur.

People are often most easily offended by those closest to them in affection and esteem. The more a personal relationship is idealized, the smaller is the pinprick necessary to deflate it.

If you agree with a person on little things, you may more effectively disagree with him over more important matters. If you regularly disagree with someone over little things, you have already lost part of the battle when it comes to a more important issue because the latter is merely another in a series of items upon which to disagree.

No one is entirely introvert or extrovert. But different individuals may lean to one side or the other of the introvert-extrovert fence. In so doing, they exhibit both different behavior and different needs. One type of individual cannot suddenly be made into the other, no matter how much a spouse may desire such a change.

Whenever possible, it is better to be positive rather than negative—the word "positive" being used in the sense of constructive and complimentary, not in the sense of dogmatic and overconfident, and "negative" in the sense of censorious and depreciatory, not in the sense of a negative reply to a question. An ounce of appreciation it is said, is worth a pound of criticism. Reward is more effective than punishment. Praise is more efficacious than blame. Noticing an individual's successes is preferable to noting his failures. The old saying, "If you can't say something good about a person, don't say anything," may be trite, but it has values as well as limitations. One need not be a Pollyanna; but certainly many unfavorable remarks result in no gain and are better left unsaid. They may be made about inconsequentials, but the remarks themselves are not inconsequential.

Criticism, censure, and blame have their place; but they should be used with discretion. It is only the relatively rare person who can accept criticism impersonally and objectively without resentment, defense, or balking. This is due in part to the double-barreled nature of criticism; an individual reacts to both the fact of criticism and the content of criticism. Constructive criticism is more effective than destructive criticism. When one must use the latter, he usually finds it more readily accepted if he prefaces it with something favorable. Suppose, for example, you have two things to tell a person, one favorable, the other unfavorable. If you begin with the latter, a barrier is immediately erected between the two of you. By the time you have reached the favorable comment the resentment, hurt feelings, and defenses of the other person have already become part of the situation. If, however, you begin with the favorable comment, the way is paved for the unfavorable one, and the criticism is put into a new perspective. The other person feels that you are on his side instead of against him and is more likely to accept the criticism with grace.

To make criticism effective, the other person's goals, motives, and motivations must be taken into account. If the criticism seems like a means of helping him achieve his goals, instead of a means by which his desires are thwarted, he will more readily act upon it.

Nagging is so much more likely to be an expression of feeling on the part of the nagger than an insightful attempt to influence the motivations and to touch upon the goals of the person nagged that it seldom accomplishes what it is presumably intended to achieve. Instead, it may make the other individual more determined to do or not to do what he is nagged about. It makes him fight back, or, if not, he may seek other outlets for his emotions. It makes his emotions accumulate over a long period, only to explode eventually. It may make him seek escape from the nagging situation. It may lead him to immunize himself to everything the spouse says, to give up in desperation, or to be completely defeated. It may make him hypersensitive to whatever the spouse says because there is a carry-over of reaction from one instance of nagging to the next. None of these responses can produce better human relationships or more satisfactory marriage. One cannot change the "inside" of a person by continual hammering upon the "outside." Nagging also reveals the points at which the nagger is vulnerable. It calls attention to the items concerning which he may readily be hurt or irritated.

People more readily accept criticism directed at what they do or say than criticism directed at them as persons. Criticism which amounts to classification is especially likely to be resisted. For example, "What you did was careless" is directed toward an act; "Only a careless person would do what you did" is directed toward a person and amounts to classification. "You spoiled the party by your behavior" is criticism; "You always spoil parties by your behavior" approaches classification. The use of supercharged words, such as "stupid," "lazy," and "selfish," may seem to the person criticized like classification. For example, an individual might react more strongly against being told that he made a stupid mistake than to being told that he made an unfortunate mistake.

Some persons do improve through criticism. Others respond more readily to encouragement. Criticism makes them self-conscious. They then have difficulty in improving, especially if their efforts are witnessed by the person who did the criticizing, and even more especially if that person depreciates their efforts at improvement with further criticism or reminds them of the former criticism as the reason for their efforts.

Suggestions are most effective when given at the so-called "psychological moment," even if that moment has to be waited for or created. It is useless to expect a person to give his full attention and consideration to a suggestion if he is absorbed in something else. He will listen more closely if he himself has asked for the suggestion, and in many cases he may be brought to this point.

Advice is a type of suggestion. Usually advice that is given when not sought is worse than useless. There is no more fruitless activity than the wholesale distribution of advice as if it were advertising handbills. One of the most pointless types of advice is that prefaced by the phrase "If I were you." Obviously I am not you and therefore cannot look at a total situation through your eyes. There is no validity in assuming that what I think would be good for me in your situation would also be good for you. Advice, too, is only advice. It is to be taken or not taken as the other person sees fit. It is not command. The adviser has performed his function when he has given the advice. He is under no obligation to insist upon its acceptance and need not feel personally affronted if it is not acted upon.

Other factors

PERSPECTIVE

If you hold a penny very near one eye and shut the other, you can blot out a roomful of people or the whole panorama of nature. This happens, not because the penny is more important than the people or the landscape, but because something near your eye blinds you to more important objects farther away. You have lost your perspective. If you toss the penny away from you, it becomes an insignificant speck in your field of vision.

In marriage, perspective may be lost. Something close may blind one to something more important. One element in a situation may be fixed upon and magnified to the detriment of the whole.

If an individual fails to see the whole marital situation with its parts in their proper relationships; if he fails to discriminate between essentials and nonessentials, between those things that do and those that do not bear a relationship to the more important and basic elements in the marriage, between those which can damage the marriage and those which are only irritating; if he cannot see the forest for the trees, he has lost his perspective. As time goes on, many couples grow to realize that what upset them at first actually did not affect their marriage. Looking back in retrospect they see that their relationship has been unimpaired. If at first they had discriminated between things of lesser and things of greater significance, their initial concern would have been unnecessary.

Loss of perspective is apparent in those cases in which a couple get to the point where anything that happens in the marriage in a way represents the entire marriage, and conflict over a relatively inconsequential incident can be almost as bitter as if the whole marriage were threatened. In one case, for example, the wife went to the refrigerator to get a drink of cold water. On a shelf she found a can of fruit opened but uncovered. She called her husband and said, "Why do you leave a can of fruit in the refrigerator like this?" He retorted, "Why should I cover it when I'm soon going to eat it?" An argument ensued. Out of the argument grew an evening-long quarrel which the couple considered serious enough to discuss with a counselor the next day.

It is a common opinion that "little things" often make for failure in marriage. The term *little things* may be defined only from a specific point of view. They may be "little" to a casual observer, but not to the couple themselves. Much depends upon the relative significance assigned to them, upon perspective. When perspective is lost, "little things" may damage a marriage. Deriving the suggestion from a hunting situation, someone has said, "If you spend all your time swatting mosquitoes, you will never shoot your moose." Some couples give so much attention to "tremendous trifles" that they miss the essential meaning of marriage.

Overemphasis upon sex in marriage is a symptom of distorted perspective. Sex is not all of marriage, any more than the room in the penny experiment is all copper. The more unsuccessful their sexual adjustment is, the more prominent sex is likely to be in a couple's thinking.

If an individual fails to see himself in relation to the total situation and to his spouse—if, for example, personal desire, selfish whims, and hurt feelings are given precedence over the success of the marriage— he has lost perspective. If the marriage is more important than part of it, what difference does it make who takes the initiative in patching up a quarrel during which perspective has been momentarily lost? In this latter statement, however, the implication is that after the patching up of the quarrel the couple's relationship will be a happy one and the marriage successful. It is conceivable, too, that the relationship as it is or as it would have to be reestablished would not be more valuable than the feelings of one of the parties if the latter were seriously affected. When we suggest that it makes no difference who takes the initiative in patching up a quarrel, we are referring to the ups and downs of normal marriage rather than to the steady trends of alienation which, in some cases, have already led the couple to the brink of disaster.

Failure to think of successful marriage as a goal worth striving for is a symptom of lack of perspective. Unawareness that success requires effort, intelligence, understanding, and idealism and is not incidental and automatic is a symptom. Unwillingness to go more than halfway to achieve success is another.

Working out a successful marriage may be compared with writing a theme. If the theme does not seem perfect after the first attempt, the writer does not tear it up and start anew with an entirely new subject and then repeat this process again and again until a perfect finished product is achieved without revision. Rather, he chooses a topic, works and re-works it, changes words here and there, rewrites sentences and paragraphs, injects new ideas and rejects irrelevant ones until the final product is what he wants it to be and is as well done as his capacities permit.

If successful marriage is a goal worth striving for, it may be set up as a definite objective. Instead of following the path of least resistance, the couple may work toward that objective. Suppose that you are going on an automobile trip. Someone asks you where you are going and you say, "I don't know; I'll tell you when I get there." You step into your car and drive down every well-paved road merely because it is well paved. You may arrive somewhere; you may not. That would not be your plan. First, you would decide upon a destination. Next you would work out an itinerary. Then you would take the roads leading to your destination, even though some were rough, though the driving was sometimes hard, and you had to make some detours. You would not turn back at the first detour or stretch of poor pavement. It is sensible to lay out the best possible itinerary, but that is not the same as following the path of least resistance.

Generalizing on too few instances is an indication of lost perspective. When an individual makes *once* become *always* or *never*, he shows that he does not see the whole for the part. "You never remember a thing I tell you," says the irate wife whose husband has forgotten a single instruction. "You're always spending too much money," says the husband whose wife's latest shopping venture has been expensive. The person who concludes that the inevitable little mistakes of the first years of marriage represent permanent maladjustments has lost perspective — or, rather, has never gained it.

A philosophy of life enabling a couple to meet a crisis is a factor contributing to successful adjustment; its absence is a factor contributing to failure. A mature person knows that sooner or later in everyone's life crises come. Friends and relatives die. Illness occurs. Children are born. Disappointments of one sort or another impose themselves upon existence. The inability to make the best of an unchangeable situation or to tolerate a situation until there is time or opportunity for change may lead to poor adjustment. At times people are called upon to learn to live with insoluble problems. Someone has said, "It takes internal props to withstand external pressure." Someone else has said, "Not all the water in the seven seas can sink a ship unless that water gets inside." A philosophy of life to meet a crisis supplies those internal props and acts as the agency for keeping the water from getting inside.

In a sense, such a philosophy of life is a type of perspective—the whole of life is seen, rather than only some of its parts. When we think in terms such as these, we may think of religion as a type of perspective. So are idealism and a sense of humor. These three things—religion, idealism, and a sense of humor—do as much as any other three factors to enable the individual to see himself in the total life situation and to see the relationships between the whole and the parts.

FOCAL POINTS

If there is tension in a marital situation, anything may become a focal point for conflict, just as crystals form on a string suspended in a saturated chemical solution or just as an "incident" such as the assassination of a government official may, if the stage is set, precipitate a war. The focal point for conflict may be relatively unimportant and may not be the true cause or even closely connected with it. As with an individual, so with a couple, the obvious cause of behavior is not always the real one. Conflict in marriage is very obtrusive to the couple who experience it. If it becomes serious and permeating enough to produce failure, that failure, impending or actual, is extremely important to both husband and wife. Failure in marriage is a "big" thing. Therefore, the couple and less careful observers, oversimplifying, reason that it must have a "big" cause, and they seek for one. Among the most obvious, most tangible, possible "big" causes are such things as children, sex, money, in-laws, religion, and use of leisure time. Sometimes one of these is the true cause of conflict. At other times it is only the hook on which the conflict is hung; and the true causes are numerous subtle influences not so obvious, hence less readily analyzed. Failure is usually the result of a multiplicity of contributing factors rather than the result of a single, simple cause, no matter how important this one cause may seem. Figuratively speaking, marriages that fail seldom "go on the rocks," as is commonly said. They are more likely to be wrecked on piles of sand—the combined and cumulative effect of numerous contributing factors, no one of which alone would be sufficient to produce failure.

Depending upon personalities and circumstances, the same things that serve to bind some couples closer together serve only to wedge others apart. Children, property, money, religion, sex, and numerous other factors may serve either as adhesive or as repellent, depending upon the way the couple react to them. None of these factors can produce conflict unless the couple have attitudes and personality traits that permit conflict to arise. Some marriages succeed while containing elements that contribute to the failure of others. Maladjustment is largely a subjective process, a result of whole personalities reacting to a total situation. The situation alone cannot produce maladjustment.

The *post hoc, ergo propter hoc* (after this, therefore because of this) fallacy in thinking is often found in the analysis of marriage adjustment. In such analysis it is important to be sure that cause and effect are in the proper order. A couple have open conflict over money. Money seems to be the cause of their disharmony. But what personality traits have led them to have conflict over money? Its use may be effect as well as cause. Honeymoon experiences are frequently said to be the cause of a wife's poor sexual adjustment. Sometimes they are. In other cases, however, personality traits that made possible the reactions exhibited in the early days of marriage also play a part in producing the maladjustment. The honeymoon experiences are results as well as causes. Conflict over one thing may itself become a factor in developing reactions which, in turn, make for other conflict. In this way an endless chain of cause and effect springs up. If this chain is not broken at some point and the situation is not reversed or stabilized, the couple grow farther and farther apart. This process is termed *alienation* [Waller, 1951].

Focal points may also be considered in a positive sense. A couple may further their marital adjustment by centering their marriage on meaningful points of interest. This does not imply permanent crystallization. It implies only the employment of a kind of emotional centripetal force that draws them together. For example, a child or their home may be a focal point. So may participation in some such common activity as church attendance or a hobby. A regular ritual of some sort, such as grace at dinner, or a traditional manner of celebrating a special occasion, such as a holiday or birthday, may serve periodically to bring attitudes, memories, aspirations to a focus. A couple with imagination and ingenuity may set up such focal points most meaningful to themselves.

MOTIVATION

One of the most important factors in making marriage succeed is motivation, commitment, the will to succeed. This suggests setting up marriage as a goal toward which the couple will strive, taking care that other goals, perhaps worthy in themselves, such as occupational ambition or child rearing, do not divert the couple's efforts from achieving success in the marriage itself and lead them to relegate marriage to a subsidiary position to that of their other objectives.

Such commitment involves work, not in the sense of employment, but rather in the sense of the expenditure of time and effort for marital success. Such effort entails ego surrender, that is, considering the success of the relationship as being more important than the feelings of the persons in it, self-discipline in channeling one's own behavior, and the application of patience and perseverance to problem solving toward the success of the marriage. It entails ingenuity in providing new experience in marriage so that there is no "letdown" of romance. This does not imply that there must be as much romanticizing in marriage as there is before the wedding. But it does imply that marriage does not inevitably have to involve a loss of enthusiasm and adventure.

The demands of family living make some routine in marriage necessary. But routine should be servant, not master. It should be a means to an end rather than an end in itself. Many educated, intelligent women become what might be called "kitchen-minded." In this state they are mentally and emotionally saturated with housework, and their outlook is bounded by the walls of their dwellings. Everything is submerged in and by housekeeping and the immediate demands of the family. This does not imply that slovenliness is a virtue and is more desirable than system. System implies efficiency; routine implies deadening repetition. Figuratively speaking, romance should not be sacrificed to getting the dishes done.

Men often suffer from the masculine equivalent of "kitchen-mindedness." They become choked by ticker tapes, buried under piles of sales tickets, covered with grease, or deafened by the sound of gears. They "keep their eye on the ball" with such concentration and single-mindedness that they lose sight of other things.

Many husbands and wives grow to take each other for granted. Each one becomes a sort of habit to the other. "Marriage," said Balzac, "must continually vanquish a monster that devours everything: the monster of habit." Habit may destroy spontaneity. It may make husband and wife as unstimulating and as predictable as a perpetual-motion machine. Constant rubbing in one spot may wear the garments of romance so thin that the original cloth is no longer seen because of the patches.

Why should two complex personalities lack variety in their relationship? Monogamy and monotony are not synonymous. Seeking variety in the sense of extramarital flirtations or sexual experience indicates either failure or immaturity. Seeking variety in the sense of discovering new facets of the other spouse's personality, looking for new things that can be done together or old ones that may be revived, makes for happiness and prevents the marriage from falling into a rut of habit. It is possible to have variety in a marriage relationship, rather than a variety of partners where there is only a partially complete relationship with each one.

Romance may be kept alive in marriage by continuing to do the same things that fostered it before marriage, plus the carrying out of new ideas that occur as marriage develops, some of which may more readily be put into effect by the married than by the single.

Habit is not an unadulterated evil, however. Many of its aspects may enrich a marriage. For example, habits of courtesy make any relationship smoother. It is puzzling to know why so many people seem to assume that a wedding ceremony creates the privilege of being rude, that it is a signal for discontinuing toward husband or wife the courtesies that are exhibited toward less meaningful persons.

ACCEPTANCE

As we have seen, the wedding ceremony indicates on the part of each party in marriage an acceptance of the other person as that person is. This does not preclude expectation of growth. It does raise a serious question about the advisability of attempted reform. To accept another person as that person is does not mean that there is never any conflict or irritation in marriage. It does mean that conflict and irritation are kept in proper perspective. Ideally, this acceptance should be complete and unqualified.

In day-by-day living, however, with more or less ordinary personalities, there may be limits to acceptance. The threshold of intolerance is lower in some persons, higher in others. For example, what if there is found a considerable discrepancy between role expected and role played? A man expects his wife to be highly domestic and maternal but finds himself married to a woman who rejects the wife-mother role in favor of a career. A woman expects her husband to be an interested, attentive, affectionate companion but marries a man who is "all business" and is no more romantic than the proverbial "lump on a log." How far can a person be expected to go in accepting such things as impotence, frigidity, infidelity, mental illness, homosexuality, physical brutality, or what is defined as immorality?

Many couples, even with a problem less serious than any of those just mentioned, find themselves at what seems like a crossroad in their marriage; they reach a low point. It appears to them that their marriage has deteriorated to the point where they have almost given up. Yet they still cling to the marriage in the hope that something can be made of it. Their problem is basically a discrepancy between what their marriage is and what they hoped it would be. If they go on as they have been going, the marriage may terminate in failure. On the other hand, they may, if they will, take a new inventory. They may reevaluate the marriage and each other in terms of actual present assets and liabilities rather than in terms of their dreams at the time of the wedding. Often, at this point, if they can accept one another and the marriage as each is, they can work out a good marriage, even though it may not coincide exactly with their earlier, perhaps less realistic, expectations.

This process of reevaluation plus new acceptance combined with more realistic expectations based on greater insight into what each spouse is and what each has to contribute to the marriage is not infrequently called for in a young marriage. This is especially true if the couple knew each other only a relatively brief period and therefore not too well before the wedding. They married with romantic enthusiasm at a high pitch and a great deal of momentum generated by physical appeal. They are carried along for a while but ultimately reach the point where their marriage, if it is to endure, must be put on a more realistic footing. Like opening a Christmas gift in fancy wrapping, they need to strip the unreality from their expectations and look inside to see what they actually have to work with.

Recognition of individual private worlds

Each individual lives in a private world of which he is the center and which is partly his own creation. True, we all live on the same planet, but the earth is not our world. One's own world is one not of sensation alone but also of meaning. Sensations are the raw materials out of which experience is constructed. They are not isolated. Each new one fits into a complex pattern formed of all the individual's experience up to date. Meaning depends not upon sensation but upon interpretation, which in turn rests upon all experience. In a sense, then, the world is a unique "illusion" to each person. Each individual is a unique "illusion" to every other individual. It is for this reason that two persons may react so differently to a third person, for example, parents' reaction to a child, a husband's and wife's reaction to the mother of one of them, the reader's reaction to a possible marriage partner as compared with his parents' reaction to that person.

We know nothing about reality. We know only our experience of it. Let us suppose that several persons are looking at a flower; they are a student in love, one not in love, a florist, a mortician, a botanist, a gardener, an artist, and an African Bushman. Do they see the same flower? They do, in the sense that the light rays passing to each person's eyes are the same for all. "Seeing the flower," however, is not a matter of sensation alone. It involves meaning; and meaning depends upon interpretation colored by previous experience. Furthermore, all that these persons know about the flower is their experience of it. We might say that each person is like a prism through which light passes to form a spectrum. The spectrum depends not only upon the source of light and any interference with the light before it reaches the prism but also upon the shape of the latter, the type of glass from which it is made, and the color of that glass. The individual knows nothing about the source of light. He knows only the spectrum, that is, his experience.

At best, it is possible for one person to penetrate another's world to only a slight degree. Certainly no one but the individual himself can live in it. In a sense, we are all hermits—each partly isolated from other people. This is because only a fraction of one's experience is communicable. Communication depends upon language and other symbols. Of necessity, these are generalizations. Words are definitions determined by common agreement and based upon the assumption that, given a set of circumstances, all human beings will react the same. Therefore, words can express only that part of an individual's experience which he has in common with other people. The same is true of other symbols.

When two persons "see" the "same" color—that is, when the same light rays enter the eyes of both individuals—they may use the same word to express what they "see," for example, "red." There is no way of proving that their total experience is the same. If language is analyzed far enough, eventually it is reduced to words which are indefinable and depend for their intelligibility upon the assumption that all persons have identical experience. When A says to B, "The color I see is red," A is in one sense communicating his experience. In another sense, A is stimulating B to recall his own. Let the reader imagine how he would explain "red" to a man born blind, and he will understand how one person can communicate with another only in so far as there are common elements in their experience. How can one fully communicate what he experiences in looking at a sunset, listening to a symphony, or being in love? After experience has been described and communicated as nearly completely as behavior and all known symbols permit, after it has been subjected to as nearly complete scientific analysis as is possible at present (and probably for some time to come), there is still an incommunicable, indescribable, unanalyzable residue, which is the individual's own and is unique.

Living in a private world gives each individual a unique *frame of reference* that makes all experience relative. Imagine that your stature were decreased by 24 inches. Your world would be altered because your frame of reference would change. Other people would appear in a new light. Doorways, automobiles, houses, and store windows would all seem larger. It would take longer to walk to places. From all objects light would come to your eyes from a different angle. In a crowd you would have a new perspective. You would find yourself better adapted to some sports, less well adapted to others. In some occupations you might be at a disadvantage; in others you might have an advantage over taller persons.

All this would be true as a result of a simple change in stature. One may readily understand, then, how each individual has a unique frame of reference, how each one's experience causes him to look at life through different eyes, and how all new experience is relative. No two persons have an identical total experience. No two have identical personalities. Hence, no two have the same frame of reference.

To these individual differences add sex differences. The world seems different to a woman from what it seems to a man. Occupations, clothes, other people, children, reproduction, homes, and sex — all appear in a different light, depending upon whether the frame of reference is masculine or feminine. It is impossible for one sex to look at life entirely through the other's eyes. Many of the experiences of one are completely foreign to the other, and there is no known method of communication. Take, for example, motherhood. There is no way for a woman fully to explain to a man what it is like to be pregnant or to give birth to a baby. Because of the difference in social pressures and role expectations under which the sexes live and which are ingrained in them from birth onward, it is sometimes difficult, if not impossible, for a man to explain to a woman his attitude toward his job. There is no way for a man to look at either women or other men through a woman's eyes, no way for a woman to look at either men or other women through a man's eyes. There is no way for one sex to know what the other experiences when in love. Under the most favorable circumstances in the best marriages, where there is as nearly complete understanding between husband and wife as is humanly possible, there is still an unbridgeable gulf of sex difference.

COMMUNICATION

Communication is important in marriage. Yet, as suggested above, it is necessarily incomplete. But an awareness of this inevitable incompleteness is itself a contribution to marital adjustment. Unawareness of such unavoidable incompleteness may create an impasse.

One often hears it said that when a couple have a marital problem, they should talk it over. So far as it goes and to the extent to which this implies getting the problem out into the open instead of "bottling it up," this is good. But because of the inevitable incompleteness of communication, discussion is not an automatic solution to all problems. There can be discussion without communication.

When a couple seek counseling help on a marriage problem, each spouse is wont to assume that he or she is stating and dealing with the facts. To a degree this may be true. But actually neither the husband, nor the wife, nor the counselor deals with facts alone. Each spouse gives the counselor not a factual analysis but rather an interpretation of the marital situation. The counselor, then, works partly with facts and partly with such interpretations. It is for this reason, among others, that it is so important, if at all possible, for both spouses to visit a counselor if their marriage is in difficulty, no matter how much one as compared to the other may seem to be at fault.

Because of the incompleteness of communication and their living in private worlds, understanding between husband and wife is also incomplete. It is important to understand that they cannot always understand. When a couple who are motivated to make their marriage succeed reach the end of communication and therefore of understanding, they are called upon to commit an act of faith, an acceptance of difference based on trust, confidence, and love.

READING 12 COMMUNICATION IN MARRIAGE

In marriage we have at least three different problems of communication, although two of them are quite similar. One is the problem of communicating role-expectations so that the spouses are informed about the size and direction of the adjustment they are required to make. Another is to communicate from one spouse to the other the feelings of love and tender emotions that they possibly have for each other, and a third is the problem of communicating feelings of respect and admiration, i.e., giving status.

The importance of the latter two kinds of communication upon satisfaction is evident. It is only the love and respect that are communicated to the mate that are of importance for his satisfaction. However necessary these two kinds of communication are, they do not constitute a very serious problem in marriage. They arise more or less naturally. It would be a more serious problem to hide "love" or respect than to let it shine through in a natural and unreflected way.

The communication of role-expectations is important for the marital satisfaction in the way referred to above. Communication of role-expectations is a necessary prerequisite for adjustment. If the communication is inadequate the spouses do not know what to adjust to, in what direction and how much to adjust.

There is also another way in which communication facilitates marital adjustment. In order to perform the marital interaction efficiently it is necessary for the spouses to be able to predict what the other will do next. Such prediction requires communication of intentions.

Communication of plans and contexts of single acts may also be necessary in those cases where the act is part of a larger role-segment which is perfectly acceptable to

From Georg Karlsson, *Adaptability and Communication in Marriage*, rev. ed., The Bedminster Press, Totowa, N.J., 1963, pp. 37–41. Reprinted with permission of the publisher.

the other spouse, but where the act is dissatisfying to him when it appears out of its context. Thus dissatisfaction may occur unnecessarily because of lack of communication.

With regard to the communication of role-expectations we have to take the following into account. Differences between role-expectations will always occur even in a marriage adjusted in the best possible way. Marital role-expectations are so complex and so varied that it is impossible to hope for a complete correspondence between them. Some expectations will be relatively easy to change and others relatively difficult to change. We may thus distinguish between those role-expectations with regard to which adjustment is expected, and those with regard to which no adjustment is expected.

The formulation of the problem of communication of expectations which is implied by these considerations is obvious. The question is how to communicate as much as possible from the first set of expectations and as little as possible from the second set. Clarification of the situation where no basic opposition of expectations is suspected should also be communicated, of course.

Communicating dissatisfactions in order to enable the other spouse to minimize them is a prerequisite for all adjustment.

However, communicating dissatisfaction which one has already accepted as inevitable would create dissatisfactions also in the other spouse without any compensating increase in satisfaction.

We have enumerated some of the kinds of communication that are of importance in marriage. The basic process of communication, however, is the same in all the different cases. We will therefore first describe this basic process and then analyze to some degree the conditions for its adequate development.

Our problem is not primarily one of transmission of symbols. It is rather a problem of transmitting in some cases certain items of information, namely characteristics of role-expectations, intentions, feelings of love and respect, etc., and in other cases not transmitting them. Our information source is thus producing information items and our measure of information will be taken in relation to these information items.

We suppose that as the marital process goes on information items are created within the spouses. At any time some items will be more clearly felt than others. These items we will call the more *relevant* items at that time. We suppose that at any time the relevant information items are finite and relatively few in number. Thus, it is defensible to use simply the number of elements in the set of relevant information items as measure of the information generated in the source.

In this way we get a change in amount of information generated at different times, which seems natural. At some times information is more pressing than at other times, and thus a greater amount of information is generated.

The type of communication system we are concerned with consists of the following parts:

1. An *information source* which produces information items with certain probabilities.

2. A *selector* which determines whether the items will be transmitted or not.

3. A *sender translator* which translates the information items into symbols.

4. A *transmitter, channel, and receiver*. The transmitter consists of those parts of the body which produce words or any other kind of behavior revealing information items. The channel is the sound and light waves in the air. The receiver is the sense organs receiving these waves. We take all these three operations together as one because they constitute no problem for us. What is of interest to us is what happens before the symbols are transmitted and after they are received. The distortions of communication occurring through operation No. 4 are in our set-up so small, comparatively, that they may be disregarded.

5. A *receiver translator*, which translates the symbols into information items.

6. The *destination* of the communication.

The concepts of information source, selector, translators, and destination are all intervening variables. We have no means of observing them directly. The only excuse for using them is that they facilitate a rational explanation of why communication occurs the way it does. It should be emphasized that we offer this frame of reference only as a possible one. Its usefulness should be proved by testing hypotheses formulated within this frame of reference.

We are dealing here only with the communication in one direction. In the other direction, of course, the whole process is repeated in reverse order.

We start with the information source which is equivalent to the individual spouse with his role-expectations, intentions, and feelings. These things constitute the raw material for the communication and the problem is if and how they are communicated. We may regard the other parts of the communication process as *operations* performed on the information items from the source, resulting in a reduction of the number of items coming through or a distortion of their meaning.

The selector is an operation performed by the communicator. It is put into effect only in those cases, e.g., with regard to role-expectations, where some information would be detrimental. The selector is the operation of determining to which of two sets an information item belongs, those that should be communicated and those that should not, and then transmitting those items that should be communicated.

The sender translator performs the operation of translating the messages into signs which are received by the other spouse as symbols of the message. The translation may be perfect and then no information is lost by the operation. It may also suffer from defects, and then information is lost. One defect is that the translation does not occur at all, either because the sending spouse is incapable of translating the message into symbols or because he is inhibited from performing the operation. The result in both cases is that the message involved does not go through.

Another defect may be that the correspondence between the elements of the message and the symbols sent is deficient. The symbols may have more or less of what is known as semantic inadequacies: rephrasing because of tabus, generalizations, etc. The semantic defects will cause a message other than the original one to come through.

The receiver translator works in a way corresponding to the sender translator, only it is performed by the receiver of the information. It prevents the reception of certain messages which may be called *selective inattention*. It may also change the meaning of some items, which is a semantic distortion corresponding to the one in the sender translator.

The added effects of all these operations are that some items never go through at all because of selection, incapacity and/or inhibition in the sender and selective inattention in the receiver. Some items arrive in a changed form because of semantic distortions in sender and receiver.

The communication will have various degrees of adequacy under different conditions. Some of the conditions which are believed to influence the adequacy of communication will be enumerated.

The efficiency of the selector is dependent upon the quality of the judgement of the selecting person. He has to make a judgement of which items to communicate and which not to communicate, and the effect of the operation depends upon his good judgement. It does not seem too unreasonable to assume that his judgement will be better if he has higher intellectual capacity in general, a greater practical knowledge of how to deal with people, and is emotionally in balance.

When it comes to the translators we have first the sheer incapacity to translate the information into symbols or to understand those symbols. This incapacity is probably of small influence in marital communication. It is most important in verbal communication and so much of the communication in marriage is of a non-verbal nature. To the extent that this incapacity is influential it goes together with the lack of intellectual capacity in general.

The inhibition from communicating and the selective inattention are also parallel mechanisms. Regarding some kinds of information there are social tabus against communicating them or receiving them. This inhibition will vary together with the social background of the spouses. We have also to take into account special psychological inhibiting mechanisms. These may be of a more permanent nature, e.g., neurotic anxiety, or of a more temporary nature, e.g., tensions between the spouses. Tensions may also belong in the more permanent set of mechanisms, of course.

In the selective inattention we have yet another thing to take into account. The selective inattention will increase with the extent to which the receiver is unprepared for the information he receives. Thus, it may be decreased by a change in the communication process itself: introducing preparatory messages and sending each message repeatedly by different signals.

Finally we have to take the semantic inaccurateness into account. It is particularly important in verbal communication. Some of the semantic shortcomings are: undue generalizations, vague terms, unusual terms not defined, rephrasing because of tabus, etc. The semantic disturbances are due to inadequate structure of the symbol system used for the communication but also to lack of experience and mastery of the system. A decrease in the semantic disturbances might also be effected by sending more signals for each item of information, i.e. by rephrasing the information. On the whole, the semantic disturbances probably are of relatively small significance for the marital communication for the same reason that was mentioned in connection with the incapacity to translate: marital communication is non-verbal to a great extent, and semantic inadequacies are chiefly connected with language.

COMMUNICATION PROBLEMS IN MARRIAGE

One of the most common sources of communication difficulty in a marriage relationship is that situation where one spouse *assumes* he knows what the other means or feels by certain actions, words, gestures, expressions, and tones of voice. There is a tendency either to project one's own feelings into one's spouse or to project one's observations of the feelings of others into the spouse. For example, Jane yawns or frowns or smiles absent-mindedly or says "Liberty and justice for all." Bill, her husband, knows what *he* would mean, how *he* would feel, if he yawned, frowned, et cetera, so he *assumes* that is what his wife means and feels. Or, Bill has intimately known, or *thought* he intimately knew, a few other women, like, say, his mother, his sister, and the girl he went steady with during his sophomore year in school. From this vast knowledge of the female sex, he has built up unshakeable convictions about what women mean and feel when they yawn, frown, and so forth. So, though he is *assuming* what his wife means or feels, he actually thinks he *knows* what she means or feels. While I have used a male example of assuming as a block in marital understanding, *you* should not assume that I think this tendency is any less pronounced among women. I do not.

In counseling with couples who have developed communication difficulties in marriage, I emphasize the importance of the *art of asking*. Each spouse is instructed to *ask* his or her mate what is meant, felt, or intended in marital areas where misunderstandings have arisen or threaten to arise. Then after the spouse *explains* what is meant, felt, or intended insofar as he or she can, the other mate is told still *not to assume* that he or she understands. He is told to repeat back to the explaining mate what he understands by the explanation. Then if the mate says: "Yes, that's right," then, and only then, can the partner begin to feel he is on the right track to understanding.

Even after considerable practice in this tedious (though very worthwhile) process of tracking down specific feelings, meanings, and intentions, many husbands and wives still want to generalize. The old habit of assuming easily re-asserts itself. After asking about a few specific matters, many spouses want to generalize about whole universes of feelings for the mate. Such generalizations are often based on what I call the *false principle of logical consistency*.

From Robert A. Harper, "Communication Problems in Marriage and Marriage Counseling," *Marriage and Family Living*, vol. 20, no. 2, May, 1958, pp. 107–112. Reprinted with permission of the editor and the author.

If the wife insists on an orderly living room—no newspapers or magazines on the floor, no crumpled pillows, no strewn ashes—then it logically follows that she should not leave a stream of hair curlers, bobby pins, eyebrow pluckers, open cream jars, vinegar bottles, lemon peels, and nylon stockings in the bathroom. It may logically follow, but logic has very little, if anything, to do with the habits people develop. It is not logical to squeeze the toothpaste tube in the middle instead of the bottom, to check the lock on the door five times instead of once, to soap oneself standing up in the bathtub, to chat lengthily by long distance telephone with one's mother the evening prior to visiting her, and so on. It is not logical, but sane people do such things. One of the most important things for couples to learn is that *feelings*—nonrational and often irrational feelings—and *not logic* are the motives of human actions. If a person will learn to ask himself and his mate what feelings may be served by some apparently silly action, he is apt to come closer to marital understanding than by looking for logic. Some fear, insecurity, or anxiety is undoubtedly being served by his or her absurd little ritual. Tolerance, sympathy, understanding is called for here; not condemnation for illogical inconsistency.

Just as some communications in marriage are marred by the mistaken search for logical consistency, others break down over the *false principle of right and wrong*. A request I have heard hundreds of times from couples is: "Just tell us which of us is right and which of us is wrong." And my answer is that there is no right side or wrong side in marital disagreement—*just different sides*. Differences can often be understood, reduced, compromised, and sometimes even removed. But, before that can happen, we must stop looking for THE RIGHT and THE WRONG. Absolutes are blocks to marital communication—especially absolute rights and absolute wrongs. Instead of judging who is right and who is wrong, let us try to *understand our different feelings*. And when the husband and wife try to understand, rather than judge, they find their differences are less in quantity and in importance.

When the marriage counselor is making such suggestions for improving the couple's marital communication, he is also trying to get the couple to understand and adopt the *basic principle of respect for personality*. For love and companionship to develop and flourish in marriage, communications of all types between husband and wife must be based on *self respect and respect for the mate*. Each spouse must learn to proceed on the fundamental conviction that *nothing* is so important as to warrant the violation of integrity in marriage—his own or his mate's. If communication in marriage is undertaken with the conviction that *we as people are what are important*, compatible co-existence can usually be worked out. Couples must learn to feel that *you and I matter as persons* — not the words we say, not the principle of the thing, not what my mother or your friends or our neighbors think, not what the book or the marriage counselor says. If each of us learns to deal respectfully and lovingly with the you, me, and us of this relationship, meanings will somehow get communicated, marriage will be enjoyable much of the time, and problems will somehow get handled, if not solved.

And this gets us back again to what is the heart of communication as I see it: a situation of safety for the individual to express his true feelings; a sense that the person to whom he is relating genuinely understands his feelings; and the knowledge that in this relationship of safety and understanding, he is truly loved. And what we get, we give. By this I mean that an individual who has experienced a relationship in which safety, understanding, and love are offered (with a counselor, for example) is much more apt to be equipped to offer safety, understanding, and love to others (such as the mate).

My discussion of safety, understanding, and love should not, however, be translated into the belief that either counselors or spouses should strive toward "sweetness and light." *Genuineness* is the most essential component of a successful counselor and a successful spouse. Safety, understanding, and love are sometimes more adequately communicated to a client or a mate, for example, by a sincere expression of annoyance than by a sweet and loving smile. The constantly "gooey-positive characters" are either fakes or fools.

How may communication in marriage be improved? There is no formula, no shortcut, no "quick and easy way." But a few suggestions may be made.

Both the individual who has something to say and the individual who is expected to listen must be motivated to try to improve their mutual communication. Communication is not a one-sided process. There is a difference between talking and communicating.

Listening is an active, rather than a passive, art. One person can facilitate another's speaking or make it more difficult by the way he listens. If attention is diverted or haphazard, if the listener does something like read the paper or drum on the table with his fingers, the speaker's problem is increased. Conversely, the speaker cannot expect full attention if he addresses the listener under circumstances such that the latter cannot give complete attention; for example, a husband talks to his wife as she puts dinner on the table or bathes the baby, and she talks to him when he is sleepy or tense from business worries.

Not even commonly used words necessarily have the same meaning to both persons. Hence it becomes important for each person to seek to learn the other's vocabulary, not only the colloquialisms and special words used but also the shades of meaning and emotional tones of words. For some persons certain words are emotionally supercharged, not only in the sense mentioned earlier in this chapter but also in the sense of being especially unacceptable because they are reacted to against a backdrop of highly individualized personal experience and point of view.

Men and women often use the same vocabulary with somewhat different meaning or connotation because of the masculine and feminine subcultures from which interpretations emerge. Consider, for example, the overtones of meaning of the following words when used by one sex as compared to the other: "cry," "fight," "mother," "wedding," "corsage."

As indicated in an earlier chapter, women are more likely than men to read a personal reference into something said, and men are more likely to make statements intended to have no such reference. If communication is to be improved, both sexes must understand the possibility of having this difference become a factor in a discussion, even though the difference is not universal.

Communication is furthered to the degree that each person is aware of complexes, special sensitivities, fears, values, biases, and points of resistance of the other person so that no unnecessary barriers to communication are introduced. The content of communication may be resisted because of the tone of voice or attitude of the speaker; it is not only what is said but the manner in which it is said to which a listener reacts.

Insight into the other person's inclination to handle facts with accuracy or with exaggeration facilitates communication. So does an understanding of the definition of the topic discussed. Two people can hardly communicate unless they are talking about the same thing.

FEAR

Various sorts of fear may play a part in marital adjustment. Fear of submerging one's own personality in that of the spouse, of loss of liberty, of one's own abilities or, rather, of their lack or inadequacy may elicit reactions that are unfavorable to success.

Fear of losing the affection and fidelity of the other person is common. This is *jealousy*. Jealousy is a fear reaction. There are two shades of meaning for the term. If an individual has an intense desire to preserve something meaningful to him and would defend it against any attempt to destroy it but in fighting for it is confident that he will win, he may be said to be jealous. If, on the other hand, he seeks to preserve something meaningful to him but fears that he will lose and be unable to retain it, he may be said to be jealous in the ordinary sense of the term. The first type of jealousy may be illustrated by a couple's efforts to preserve their home against the insidious attack of some vengeful relative who would destroy their happiness if he could. The second type is that exhibited by the husband who sees another man manifesting interest in his wife and fears that he will be unable to retain her affection and fidelity against the onslaught of a seemingly more attractive person. The husband may not analyze his fear to this extent; but it is present, nevertheless. His reaction may be anger or hate, as far as he is aware of it; but at bottom it is due to insecurity.

Jealousy may be divided into two types upon another basis, namely, (1) necessary or justifiable jealousy—that based upon observation of the behavior of the spouse; and (2) unnecessary or unjustifiable jealousy—that based not upon fact but only upon the insecurity, inferiority feeling, or suspicion of the jealous person. In the first type, the wife may know that her husband is interested in another woman and may feel helpless to hold him. In the second type, the husband has exhibited no suspicious behavior; but because the wife feels insecure, she becomes jealous when he no more than talks with a woman business associate or converses with the woman who sits next to him at a dinner.

For several reasons jealousy is self-defeating. (1) Love and fidelity cannot be forced through suspicion and surveillance. The only love worth having is that which is given freely and voluntarily. (2) The other person resents the lack of trust. (3) Even when justifiable, jealousy is not addressed to the true causes of the infidelity. Therefore, effort which

MARITAL ADJUSTMENT

The basic components of marital adjustment are in some respects unique to the marital relationship, yet they also include many elements common to personality adjustment in general. The personality—behavior patterns, emotional responses, attitudes—of each individual is his own and necessarily differs in some respects from that of another. When these differences conflict, adjustment is necessary. One of the keys to successful marital adjustment lies in whether the individuals or personalities involved approach such problems in a positive or negative way, whether the points of possible conflict are handled in such a way as to break down the relationship or to build it up.

*Jealousy is a fear reaction. The insecure person, fearful
of his ability to retain his mate's affection, may read
unjustifiable meanings into her behavior and become
vindictive, while a mature person may profit from the
same kind of situation. He may recognize her attraction
to other men and admire her for it because he feels
secure in the mutual love of his wife and himself and
such attraction is no threat to him.*

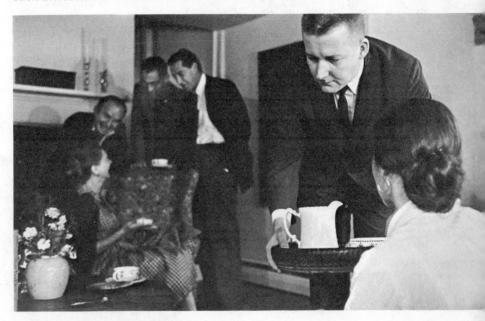

*The husband and wife may find
themselves at different levels of
development in their sexual
relationship. If the partner whose
expectations are not met is quick to
reject the other in disgust, the marriage
will be headed toward failure; if on the
other hand, he is patient and
considerate, the relationship will grow
in scope and depth.*

Even routine and habit may precipitate problems. The husband and wife may become habits to each other and neglect the courtesies and the adventure of mutual discovery that they valued during their courtship, or they may use routine and habit as a framework, a constant factor, into which they continue to bring fresh experience and deepened interests.

During the courtship the wife may have been charmed by her husband's punctuality concerning their dates and shared activities. After marriage she may find it difficult to accept changes in this courtship pattern. She should realize, however, that marriage carries with it new responsibilities and self-expectations as a result of their cooperative union. A realistic acceptance and adjustment to this can help build a successful marriage.

might be directed to the solution of the problem and to readjustment is dissipated without gain. (4) A jealous person is likely to be hard to live with and, therefore, is likely to become unattractive. This may make the spouse lose interest and do exactly what it was feared he would do, thus furthering the end the jealousy was intended to prevent. (5) Jealousy tends to be a symptom of immaturity and is often part of an immature pattern of behavior that is not conducive to happy marriage. (6) Jealousy often involves projection of blame. The jealous person does not say, "I am jealous because I am fearful and insecure." He says, "I am jealous because of what you are doing."

It is not the fact of jealousy alone, but also its expression, that affects a marriage. Expression of it entails criticism, suspicion, questioning,

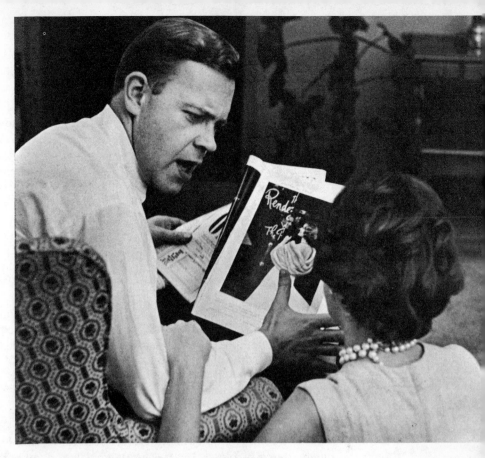

*Money and material goods often have symbolic meaning
to the individual far deeper than their practical
function. A couple may become involved in violent
conflict over money and its use, possibly deciding that
the solution lies in more money, or each partner may
probe the deeper causes of the conflict within himself
and work from there to a solution of the relationship
problem.*

nagging, demands for explanation, displays of temper, moodiness, loss
of respect, attempted domination, restriction of freedom, or any of a
number of other irritating and irksome attributes and experiences.
Sometimes the jealous spouse refuses to believe the truth. The more the
other person tries to explain that there is no cause for jealousy, the more
jealous the first one becomes, insisting that the explanation is only an
attempt to "cover up." Thus the couple sink deeper and deeper into the
quicksand of alienation.

Jealousy, however, may have one mitigating quality that compensates in a minor way for its unpleasantness and may make the bitter
pill easier to swallow. The fact that an individual manifests it may be

an indication that he does not wish to lose the other person, that he wants to preserve their relationship. This thought is worth the consideration of anyone who has a jealous spouse.

If a wife, for example, feels that she is losing her husband and there is a real basis in fact for her fear, she is thrown into a dilemma to know what to do. There is no use in theorizing. The husband may be wrong. The other woman may be unscrupulous. All the wife's venomous thoughts may be justifiable. But that will not solve the problem. No man becomes interested in another woman if his wife is more attractive to him than the other woman. The wife may force him to remain her legal spouse, but she cannot hold him as her husband except through the bonds of personal attraction. If she would retain her husband and preserve the marriage, the wife's only recourse is to compete – compete with the other woman for the affection and attention of her husband. This is the way she won him before they were married. It is the way she must hold him. This will involve studying and remedying the underlying causes of the loss of interest in herself in so far as these apply to her. Most cases of infidelity are two-sided, even though one partner alone is unfaithful. A readjustment of circumstances may be helpful. If possible and advisable, the couple may talk with a marriage counselor.

DOMINATION

The results of actual or attempted domination are relative and depend upon the personalities involved. By and large, however, domination is unhealthful. Some marriages become what might be termed "battles for prestige." The question to which the couple seek the answer is not "How may we work best together?" but "Who will give in?" [Knopf, 1932]

Alfred Adler speaks of a "household run by water power." He refers to a home ruled by a wife's tears. An individual may resort to "illness" in order to dominate a spouse. A wife may become a stickler for etiquette or may use punctuality as a weapon. She may overstress her own weakness and so much admire what her husband does that he becomes burdened with expectations of further success. If the husband does not succeed, the wife blames others for having hindered him. This binds the pair more closely together and gives the wife more power over the husband. Some women marry men who are physically disabled; behind their pretense of pity and sympathy is the wish to dominate.

One not uncommon type of attempted domination is a demand for gratitude. "If it were not for me, you wouldn't be where you are today"; "I've put up with a lot for you"; "Think what you were before I married you." When gratitude is voluntary and spontaneous, it is good for both concerned. When it is demanded, it is likely to become resentment. It throws new light upon the thing done and upon the person who makes the demand.

When the demand for gratitude takes the form of supposed martyr-dom, playing up sacrifices and flaunting them in the face of the other person, it becomes especially insidious. "A sacrifice labeled as such is like a gift with the price tag deliberately left on; it is more of an insult than a compliment" [Wile and Winn, 1929, p. 275].

OVERDEPENDENCE

Marriage is for mature persons; the overdependent, parasitic, clinging-vine type of individual does not fall into that category. Considerable de-pendence of one spouse on the other is natural and desirable. When it reaches the point of evasion of responsibility, failure to make a contribu-tion to the success of the marriage, or inability to carry out one's half of the bargain, it is detrimental.

Overdependence may also be a symptom of immaturity in that it may result partly from narcissism, that is, self-love. A wife, for example, may identify herself with her husband and by inference praise her wise choice of mate by continually calling attention to his virtues. She sub-ordinates herself to him, bowing, scraping, yes-yesing, taking his slight-est wish as a command. To the husband this may become tiresome. If he actually believes that he is all that she seems to think he is, this type of behavior may affect his personality.

What sometimes passes for overdependence may actually be domi-nation. By submission and yielding, by manifesting an apparent need for help and guidance, by expecting another to make one's decisions and assume one's responsibilities, one person may in part control the other's behavior.

"HOMEOPATHIC REMEDIES"

Years ago there was a school of medical thought one of the tenets of which was this: To cure a disease there should be administered a drug which in a healthy person would produce symptoms similar to those of the illness. For example, to cure a fever, the physician would administer a drug that would raise the patient's temperature. This was homeopathic medicine, "homeopathic" being derived from two Greek words meaning "like" and "suffering."

In medical practice homeopathic remedies are outmoded. In mar-riage they should be, but unfortunately they are not. Such remedies in marriage take the form of retaliation in kind. An attempt is made to remedy a maladjustment by deliberately doing what the other person has done, when that proved annoying, instead of seeking and remedy-ing the real cause of the maladjustment. There is a duplication of the undesirable behavior of the spouse. A wife is hurt by something the hus-band does. To remedy the injury and prevent his doing it again, she in-tentionally hurts him. A wife is sarcastic; the husband responds with sarcasm. Criticism is countered with criticism. One attempts to dilute his own offense or error by pointing out that the other does the same thing or something equally bad. A husband is extravagant. To cure him of his weakness for spending money and to show him the difficulties caused by an extravagant spouse, the wife becomes extravagant. This is supposed to balance the budget and also to change the husband's behavior. "Homeopathic remedies" balance neither the financial nor the marital ledger. Two minuses do not make a plus, nor two wrongs a right. Such behavior not only does not alleviate the condition toward which it is directed but has a tendency to multiply irritations, since the number of offensive stimuli as well as the sensitivity of both persons is increased. Each one reacts to the other's action plus the other's attitude.

TENSION

Tension may be defined as a physiological, emotional, or mental state tending to give rise to activity. The activity is not necessarily directed toward removing the cause of the tension. The tension tends to spread from one area of life to others, to be cumulative and to explode with a slight stimulus which may have little or no relation to the cause of the tension. For example, a man has been harried all day by complaining, cantankerous clients. His emotions have been frequently aroused, and fatigue has gradually increased. For professional reasons he has had to maintain an appearance of patience, good nature, and self-control. At the end of the day he goes home. One of the children does some trivial thing to disturb him, and he explodes in a fit of anger. The gun is loaded, and the child pulls the trigger. The explosion is not directed toward removing the cause of the tension, and the stimulus has little relation to the cause.

Some couples are skilled at reading the signs of each other's tension. Others are not. It would not be unthinkable to utilize special signals as a means of letting each other know that unusual tension exists and of appealing to the other for patience and consideration. In "Who's Boss?" one of the films in the Marriage for Moderns Series, as such a signal the wife wears her apron astern and the husband enters the house twirling his hat on his finger. Such signals may seem silly and juvenile, but they are not so silly and juvenile as a pointless quarrel growing out of tension and precipitated by something inconsequential. Also, the use of such simple signals indicates that each spouse is aware of his own tension and hypersensitivity; this is the first step toward an effective handling of the situation.

Tension may be dissipated so that the cumulative effect is prevented and relief is afforded. Every married couple and every individual needs what might be termed *tension relievers*. Often a little ingenuity, like a little oil, is all that is needed to smooth troubled water or prevent friction from wearing down a relationship. A couple may develop techniques for letting off steam as it accumulates, instead of waiting until it blows up their marriage. It is difficult to say just what these tension relievers may be for a given couple because each case is individual. Each couple may through observation, experiment, and the exercise of imagination determine them and put them into effect.

Sometimes, in spite of all efforts at prevention, tension gives rise to quarreling. It is somewhat risky either to recommend or deliberately to plan upon quarreling as a means of dissipating and reducing tension. Only a rare couple are equipped to handle it in that way. There is no way of guaranteeing that both persons will react to it in the same manner. There is too great a possibility of its producing more tension than it was intended to relieve. When and if, however, a couple do quarrel, there are several things which they might try to keep in mind. We might term these "rules" for quarreling. (1) Unless cumulative experience suggests the contrary, each should assume that what the other says and does during the quarrel is the product of the tension involved and is not a true reflection of that individual's personality. (2) Each should assume that whatever judgments he makes during the quarrel are invalid. The judgments upon which action are based should be formed at a time when the individual is relatively calm and has regained his perspective. (3) Both should try to keep the quarrel within bounds. It should not be allowed to spread to aspects of their relationship, their situation, or their personalities that had nothing to do with its origin. (4) A quarrel should be kept private. It should not be allowed to occur in the presence of others, especially children. (5) A quarrel may further a couple's adjustment if, instead of letting it generate ill will and insecurity, the couple forget it when it is over, let bygones be bygones, carry no grudges, and take a step forward in the clarified atmosphere following the storm. (6) Since the marriage is more important than the feelings of either party and in most cases much more important than the difference which precipitated the quarrel, each should be willing to go more than halfway to effect a reconciliation. Sometimes the first step in this direction is easier for the person less at fault because his pride is not so great an obstacle to an apology. (7) The sooner after the quarrel the couple return to the pattern of affection and conversation which characterizes their marriage, the easier it will be; the longer they delay such a return, the more difficult it is likely to be.

In spite of the fact that we pride ourselves on living in a scientific age, most of us do not approach life scientifically. Actually we live in an age in which science is given a great deal of attention and in which science and scientists have produced a technology that is widely enjoyed. But the "average person's" world view and his attitude toward, and interrelationships with, other people are highly colored by assumptions, impressions, tradition, folklore, emotions, and wishful thinking. These are fertile soil in which to germinate tension, argument, and quarreling because they are more likely to befog the need for facts than to lead to an elucidation of them. When two people argue, each one is convinced that he is defending truth. If each could see that he is more likely merely to be supporting an unsubstantiated point of view, less tension would be generated.

IN-LAWS

It is almost a self-evident, universally accepted truth that there are in-laws who are selfish, scheming, shortsighted, prying, interfering, demanding, or malicious. There are those who have not kept pace with the development of their children and fail to realize that the latter have grown up and become independent. There are others who are unselfish, generous, farsighted, and considerate. Some of them grow to be closer to the child-in-law than his own parents have been. Some in-laws make a real contribution to the success of a marriage and help a couple over rough spots in their adjustment. More is said about the first type, and there is a tendency to generalize upon them.

Whenever there is an in-law problem, the young couple as well as their parents are in the midst of it. No person can have in-laws without being an in-law. Not all the friction is precipitated by the older generation. So much has been said about in-laws, so many jokes have been made about mothers-in-law, that they have acquired a regrettable reputation. As a result, young couples often enter marriage on the defensive, with a chip on the shoulder, so to speak, almost daring their in-laws to knock it off. If ever inadvertently or intentionally it is knocked off, the trouble begins.

When a man and woman fall in love and marry, usually each respects the intelligence of the other. If each has been accustomed to thinking that his parents were agreeable people, there is a possibility that he is right. The other partner may, then, make that assumption until the facts prove otherwise.

If there is a bona fide in-law problem, the young couple need first of all to be certain of their perspective. The success of their marriage should be put above everything else, even above attachment to parents. Husband and wife must come first. Otherwise the individual exhibits immaturity, unless the spouse is unbearable and the marriage has hopelessly failed. The situation calls for all the tact, diplomacy, and consideration the couple can command, but it calls for firmness and intelligence, as well.

Understanding the problem faced by the couple's in-laws may help to facilitate adjustment. A family is an in-group; it exhibits cohesion. Even when the members are in conflict with each other, there is an inclination to stand united against external pressure and against members of the out-group. A child-in-law is a member of the out-group. It takes time and requires some readjustment fully to accept him as a member of the in-group. He is considered an outsider, and there are some things that one does not do with an outsider. One does not tell him family secrets. One does not express affection for him without reserve. One does not appear in his presence in a state of dishabille.

The in-law problem is not dissimilar to that of a nation in assimilating immigrants. A nation, too, is an in-group. When an immigrant seeks citizenship, there is a responsibility on both sides. The nation has a responsibility for helping the immigrant understand its ways, its language, its laws, and its people. The immigrant, on the other hand, is expected to make some effort to acquire such understanding and to adapt himself to the nation's pattern of life. If the nation is suspicious of him, thwarts him, or sees nothing good in what he brings to it, or if the immigrant resists the nation's ways, criticizes its pattern of life, or refuses to learn its language, the process of assimilation will be blocked. Similarly, when a young in-law enters a family, if the family refuses to help him become assimilated, resists his overtures of good will, or rejects him as a person, or if the young in-law sees nothing good in the family's way of life, criticizes it, tries to remake it, or is antagonistic to family members, again assimilation will be blocked and the in-law problem will be accentuated.

Parents acquire their natural child when it has no opinions to express, no prejudices, resentments, habits, tastes, or ideas of its own. The child is gradually assimilated into the family and molded by the parents to fit their pattern of life. The child-in-law is precipitated into the family, sometimes unexpectedly, sometimes against the family's will, and always with ideas, tastes, habits, and personality already developed.

Parents may resent the transfer of a child's affection from themselves to another person. There may be a conflict in roles, that is, in the expectations set up by parents and spouse. The parents think of the husband or wife as their child and expect a continuation of the child role, the parent-child relationship. The spouse thinks of the person not as child but as adult, with a specific status and responsibility.

A child is accustomed to having his parents interfere with his doings, ask questions about his plans, speak freely concerning his ideas. He accepts this from them and they in turn accept similar behavior from him. Not so with in-laws, each of whom considers the other a member of the out-group. Furthermore, older in-laws and younger ones have been reared in different eras. Their points of view may differ, and there has been neither time nor opportunity to have the corners worn smooth by constant rubbing of difference against difference, as is the case of parents and children. The mutual assimilation and adjustment of in-laws is not always easy. Anything that can serve to further the process is worth trying. What hinders the process is worth avoiding.

PRINCIPLE OF LEAST INTEREST

This principle was stated, ungrammatically for emphasis, by the late Willard Waller [1951], following a lead from E. A. Ross. Waller applied the principle to the courtship process, but it is also applicable to the marital relationship. According to this principle, when two persons are emotionally involved in a relationship, the conditions of the association will be dictated by and the relationship will be controlled by the person who has the lesser interest in it. The less involved individual can afford to make the greater demands because he has less at stake. The more involved individual is impelled to make more concessions because the discontinuance of the relationship would be more serious for him.

A similar and related but not identical principle is this: If a husband and wife have a pronounced difference in their degree of insight into the marital relationship and in their awareness of each other's needs and of the nature of marriage, that person with the greater insight and awareness often has to make the greater adjustment in order to assure the continuance of the relationship [Waller, 1951]. This may seem at first glance to be unfair. But looking at it realistically, there may be no alternative.

If a relationship is dominated by the person with less interest in it and/or less insight into it, it is clear that in cases where the demands are excessive they contribute to failure. In other cases where the more interested, more insightful person can manage the relationship satisfactorily or can make the required adjustments, there can be success. In any case, however, there is likely to be loss of mutuality.

LAW OF DIMINISHING RETURNS

The law of diminishing returns is ordinarily mentioned in the field of economics. Freely interpreted, it may be applied to marriage. Strictly speaking, what we are discussing may be more nearly like the law of marginal utility. But to the noneconomist "diminishing returns" suggests something that "marginal utility" does not.

In economics this law suggests that as a series of units of a given economic good is acquired or consumed, each successive item in the series, though similar to the one preceding it, is less attractive or less valuable to the collector or consumer. For example, if a man is acquiring real estate, the tenth piece will be less important to him than the first or second piece, and the hundredth piece would be less important still. A similar thing would be true of cars, money in the bank, or clothes. Suppose the reader is very hungry when he sits down to dinner. His first helping is consumed with great relish. The second helping is not eaten quite so enthusiastically as the first. The third, fourth, fifth, and so on, decrease in attractiveness until, if he were put under pressure to eat more and still more, he would eventually be repulsed by the food rather than attracted by it. Yet each helping of food is approximately like the one before it.

The law of diminishing returns is applicable to a number of aspects of marriage. Perhaps its most important application is in connection with the couple's sexual experience. When sex is combined with love and integrated into a growing, expanding marital relationship, the sexual element itself is enriched. True, the couple may note a decrease in frequency of intercourse as time goes on, but this does not necessarily imply a decrease in interest, responsiveness, or meaning.

On the other hand, when sex is divorced from love it is more likely to be subject to the law of diminishing returns. It is at least partly for this reason that couples who marry on the basis of physical appeal which they confuse with love often reach the point where the marriage seems to die, to reach a dead level. Actually some such couples scarcely know each other. They do not have the necessary requisites to build a happy marriage. Some of them do not even have enough in common to quarrel. Such cases not infrequently come to a counselor's attention. When the law of diminishing returns has left its imprint on their sexual relationship, the couple no longer have anything left.

OUTSIDE HELP

Outside assistance may become an important factor in success in marriage because in some cases a couple exhaust their own resources and, though they have a will to succeed, do not know the next steps to take. In many cases of this kind outside help may give them the suggestion, impetus, or reorientation needed. When home remedies fail in marriage, it is good sense to turn to an expert, just as one would in case of an injury or a disease. It is better to do that than to let a marriage atrophy or die in agony.

Friends may, in rare cases, be of assistance. Usually they lack the knowledge required and have too biased a point of view toward the couple. A physician or a clergyman may be of assistance if he is well informed and has some insight into psychological problems and marital adjustment, and if he sees more than the physiological or moral aspects, as the case may be.

In many communities there are counseling agencies where for a nominal fee one may get as nearly expert help as is possible at the present stage of knowledge. A marriage need not be on the brink of failure before a couple visit one of these agencies. For some couples they are educational centers rather than clinics to treat maladjustment. The couple may go for budget help, advice in child rearing, information on contraception, suggestions as to the use of leisure time, or any of a host of similar matters, having as the objective the enrichment of marriage and family life rather than the bare necessity of salvaging them.

One cannot, however, expect a complex adjustment problem to be solved in cliché fashion by a paragraph in a newspaper column or a snap judgment on a radio or television program. The newspaper advice column has a place. It is, in fact, the only agency available to large numbers of young people who are confused and need assistance. It must also be admitted that the writers of newspaper columns recognized the need for preparation for marriage and for aid to those already married before that need was recognized by many educators and members of other professions, some of whom are not yet aware of it. Whenever possible, in cases where counseling is wanted, it is better to turn to a responsible professional counselor who can give the case careful, thorough, individual attention.*

Choice of counselor must be made cautiously. There are persons who set themselves up as counselors but who are unqualified or even outright unscrupulous. Quacks and charlatans may often be recognized by one or more of the following: (1) They make extravagant claims. (2) They make much of asserting that they are able to handle a great variety of problems. (3) They advertise. (4) They stress fees; their fees are high. (5) They demand payment in advance for service not yet rendered. (6) They display diplomas or certificates from unheard-of schools. (7) They profess to have unusual degrees, for example, Doctor of Psychology. (8) When asked about their training and experience, they are vague and evasive. (9) They make snap diagnoses. (10) They put pressure on the client to return for further counseling.

Marriage, religion, and basic values

Students often ask about the role of religion in marriage. They want to know whether its role begins and ends with the initiation of marriage through a religious ceremony. They wonder whether it plays any part in marital adjustment except in connection with certain types of mixed marriage and the education of children. They are curious to determine whether it has any role in the relationship of a couple that is different in either kind or intensity from its role in the lives of individuals not associated in marriage. In short, what part does—or perhaps we should say, can—religion play in marital adjustment?

In discussing the role of religion in marriage, we shall be discussing religion's highest possibilities rather than its worst actualities, what religion can do in marriage under the best circumstances, not what it does under its narrowest and most distorted connotations. We shall be referring to the type of religion and the form of marriage that we know in this country, not to the religions or the marriage systems of the Eastern world. We shall use the term *religion* in its widest, most profound sense, not as meaning various conflicting and divisive creeds and dog-

*The American Association of Marriage Counselors will provide the names and addresses of qualified counselors in various parts of the country. Executive director: Dr. David R. Mace, 27 Woodcliff Drive, Madison, New Jersey.

mas. Many of the things we shall mention are obviously elements of Christianity. Many are also in one form or another elements of Jewish belief.

It must be admitted that whatever role religion plays in marriage must usually be through the channel of individual behavior, since almost everything that affects marriage must in one way or another be accomplished through that channel. Religion colors a person's thinking about standards and values. It plays a part in his decisions concerning what is important in life, what is meaningful, what is worth striving for. It colors his attitudes toward other people and influences his behavior toward them, what he does to or with them, and how he relates himself to them. Religion constitutes a motivation to action. It may permeate a person's philosophy of life. It provides a pattern of ethics, but it is more than such a pattern because it provides also a foundation on which ethics rests. Religion involves more than the way an individual lives because it involves also the central reason for which he lives that way.

Marriage is a special association between two people whose relationship is highly personalized, deeply significant, and profoundly influential upon the personality of each of them. Whatever attitudes toward people an individual holds, whatever lies at the root of his behavior, whatever his habitual treatment of others is, whatever values and standards he considers important, and whatever colors his thinking about life will play a part in the way he reacts to his spouse and to his marriage.

In the discussion that follows, the reader may make his own applications and draw his own inferences. When he does so, he will find that each item mentioned is in one way or another pertinent to the relationship of husband and wife. He may even go beyond the items mentioned, for the role of religion in life or in marriage cannot be exhausted in a few paragraphs.

Religion attributes to the individual a fundamental dignity and worth, irrespective of his personality, age, sex, race, intelligence, social status, or behavior. This does not imply that all personality traits are equally desirable or that the consequences of behavior may be completely disregarded. It does imply that the simple fact of his being human gives an individual a core of importance that demands respect in appraisal of him and consideration in action toward him, no matter what, in a more specific sense, he himself may be or do. Religion suggests that human beings need love most when they are most unlovable. Because religion places marriage so high among human values, it attributes a special esteem to husband and wife as members of a unique association, regardless of the nature of the persons themselves.

Religion places primary emphasis upon the individual as a person rather than upon the things connected with him. The goods that he owns are inconsequential. The resources that he controls are unimportant. What counts most, indeed, what matters at all, is the person himself, the traits that constitute his personality, the values reflected in his character, and the aspirations expressed in his idealism. This does not mean that it makes no difference, for example, whether a man works to support his home and family. In such a case it is not only the money, or its absence, that is important. His attitude toward, and relationship with, these other persons who depend upon him are also important. Religion sets a standard whereby one person is not worthy of greater esteem than another merely because there is associated with him a greater quantity of commonly desired economic goods, or the means to acquire them, than is associated with that other person. A couple's living beyond their means in order to convince themselves and others of their importance becomes, then, a pointless misdirection of effort.

Religion establishes the principle that a person may be judged separate from his acts. His acts are, of course, important. In the last analysis, however, even more important than his acts are the attitudes and motives underlying them. A religiously motivated individual assumes that another person's motives are good unless he has proof to the contrary. He does not guess at motives, with his guessing dominated by mistrust and suspicion. Of all possible underlying motives, the most important, the one that gives rise to most effective action toward human betterment, and the one most fully contributory to deeply satisfying life experience is love, interpreted broadly.

This love is other-person-centered. It is outgoing. It results in forgetfulness of self. It stimulates giving for the sake of the well-being of another rather than in expectation of return. It is expressed through service to others as opposed to the utilization of others for one's own ends. It makes possible the deepest, fullest, most profound sharing of which human personality is capable. Just as the forces of man's mind beat down the walls of time and space and enable him to move freely in the realm of eternity and infinity, so love annihilates the barriers between the "self" and the "other than self" and enables man to identify himself with others of his kind and with the totality of human life. This process does not destroy "self"; it gives "self" a new dimension. It evolves "self" into a new awareness directed not toward a center but toward a circumference. When the individual's dominant motive is love, he becomes not the apex of a triangle upon which the favorable judgments and beneficent activities of others, the spiritual resources of the race, and the cultural accumulations of history are focused for self-gratifying ends. Rather, he becomes the small passage in an hourglass through which the sand of unearned advantage pours into the chamber of human betterment.

Religion appraises persons in terms of their highest possibilities rather than only in terms of their achievements. The individual capable of making judgments of others on the basis of their possibilities gains confidence in people and is optimistic about their improvement. This type of appraisal in marriage enables each spouse to see and bring out the best in the other. Religion places no theoretically insurmountable barrier in the path of a person's improvement. It grants to each individual an unlimited capacity to grow. It binds no one permanently and inextricably to his past.

Religion gives rise to what may be termed "dynamic good will," a constructive, confident attitude toward the potentialities for development to be found in each person, as opposed to what may be termed "passive good will," a tolerant acceptance of the continued presence and essential variability of human beings. A religiously motivated person may recognize the facts and principles of psychology and may be aware of the degree to which experience conditions behavior. Yet he may believe that, at least to a degree, dynamic good will can influence an individual's growth in a direction defined in part by someone whose relationship with him is characterized by reasonable and knowing confidence that such development is not only possible but a *fait accompli* in anticipation. This is different, however, from the blind "faith" of an individual who convinces himself of change in another person without that person's being aware of and responding to this "faith." Such blind "faith" is a substitution of wishful thinking for observation of facts, understanding, sincere confidence, and a two-sided relationship involving rapport and trust. The part that a wife's dynamic good will may play in molding her husband's career is more commonly recognized than the effect of his attitude upon her, but the situation is two-sided.

Religion assumes that all human beings are basically equal, not in their achievements or abilities but in their right to take their places in society and in the family on a similar footing and with similar opportunities for self-development. It assumes that the degree to which people seize upon these opportunities may be restricted by their own personal limitations or failures but that no restrictions should be imposed by the prejudices, greed, or personality distortions of others. It is upon only such a basis that democracy can flourish either in a nation or in a home.

Although religion attributes to each individual a fundamental dignity and worth, it also introduces something of a dualism in this connection. On the one hand, it gives high esteem to the individual as a person. On the other, it suggests humility. When human beings in general are considered as representatives of qualities most basically and universally valid, high appraisal and unlimited opportunity are suggested. When a person thinks of others, he should think in similar terms. When, however, a person thinks of himself, he thinks of his possibilities, but without losing self-respect he tempers his high estimate of human nature with a low estimate of his own achievements and a recognition of his responsibility. The religiously motivated individual recognizes and accepts the equality of all persons. Yet, being aware of the frequency with which he falls short of his own highest expectations, he is patient and generous in his attitude toward the mistakes and shortcomings of others. He does not expect in others what he demands in himself, and he forgives in others what he does not excuse in himself. He believes that in the last analysis forgiveness will contribute to the growth of the other party. He has no fear that forgiveness will be a signal for the other party to take advantage of him.

In these days of numerical analysis, frequency curves, scientific measurement, and quantitative evaluation, religion suggests qualitative evaluation. At a time when actions, events, and natural phenomena are often appraised not upon the basis of their intrinsic character but rather upon the frequency of their occurrence, religion contributes a disregard of numbers. On the one hand, it establishes principles rather than frequency as a valid basis for judgment, especially for judgment of one's own behavior. It is what an individual does and why he does it, not how often he does it, that matter more. Religion creates and sanctions fundamental principles of such nature that a single violation is, in a sense, equivalent to the one vote that can produce a majority or the one act that is equivalent to "once too often." This disregard of frequency does not imply, however, that once an individual has done something, he may as well repeat it over and again because no matter how often he does it he cannot make it any worse. Such a procedure would indicate serious confusion, rationalization, or failure carefully to examine his own motives. On the other hand, in some instances religion condones a disregard of the frequency of another's acts and puts major emphasis upon the person himself, especially if he sincerely desires to improve.

Religion provides life with its broadest, longest, deepest, most penetrating perspective. It gives human life a cosmic frame of reference. It enables man in spirit to overcome the earth-bound limitations of his body. It sets up timeless norms unaffected by the ups and downs of current events or the confusion of temporary affairs. This perspective, this frame of reference, these norms enable man to transcend circumstances, to rise above both the vicissitudes of life and deceiving, counterfeit values. This may in turn lead to spiritual triumph over temporary failure and to enduring patience in the face of trying problems. In short, man may achieve poise through faith.

Man is the only organism aware of his own ignorance. This awareness gives him a certain humility. On the other hand, recognition of ignorance is a type of knowledge. "I know that there is something I do not know" reflects an awareness of truth beyond immediate experience. This awareness gives man a certain confidence in his perpetual reaching for things beyond his grasp. It is one of the factors that make man creative.

Man is not content with the world as he finds it. He embellishes his existence beyond his observations. When the facts are faced, it must be admitted that there are some things that cannot be demonstrated, that verification must often be by inference. Important as it may be to keep one's feet on the ground, the individual who does no more may so shorten his reach that to a degree he ceases to be human. The senses alone are not an adequate guide to life because the experience man gains through them is incomplete. This incomplete experience cannot be the channel through which he arrives at an understanding of and appreciation for the world in which he lives and a satisfying way of life. Man has the unique ability to project his conceptions of the world and of life beyond his immediate experiences and direct observations. In order to make life make sense, man goes beyond his senses. He reads beauty into paint and canvas. He projects patterns onto the universe. He interprets life in terms of meanings. He thinks of other people as imperfect representatives of qualities fundamental to existence. He assumes that life is founded upon a moral structure. He has hope where situations appear hopeless. He maintains faith where experience is incomplete. He encompasses the infinite in his finite mind. He defines indefinables with verifiable concepts. He orients mortal life toward immortality. He projects ideals upon imperfection.

Ideals become, then, not daydreams but an integral part of the reality in which man lives. They form some of the most significant roots of choices of action. They play a role in the defining and establishing of objectives, both distant and immediate. They enable a person to set up goals unattainable in themselves but of such nature that, in a sense, they may be attained through the very process of striving for them. Out of that striving for the unattainable, that devotion to things considered to be permanent, may spring a sense of security that is inexplicable in terms of temporary success alone or merely the length of one's reach. Religion, with its infinite perspective, gives unique validity both to such ideals and to persistent reaching. In this connection, however, we are discussing the ultimate goals of life, not immediate goals so out of keeping with an individual's abilities that striving for them leads only to hopeless frustration, as, for example, an occupational choice for which a person has no aptitude.

Some persons find it difficult to understand how an individual who sets unattainable goals can be happy. They accept at face value the fraction we referred to earlier, namely, $\text{happiness} = \dfrac{\text{achievement}}{\text{expectation}}$. They insist that an individual whose happiness is represented by, say, $2/1$ will be happier than an individual whose fraction is $1/1$ or $1/2$ because the first has achieved more than he had expected while the second has only met his expectation and the third has fallen short. For many aspects of life this argument is valid. But it loses its validity when it is applied to the ultimate goals of life and when a religious element is introduced.

The religiously motivated person sets his expectation at infinity. He thinks in terms of endless and unlimited personal growth toward a perfection that he knows he can never attain. In the light of his infinite expectation his achievement seems meager indeed. He finds himself in the position of a mountain climber who upon ascending one peak widens his horizon so that he sees still higher peaks to be climbed. His achievement seems meager not only in the light of his infinite expectation but also because religion suggests humility. Therefore, the religious person tends to appraise his achievement as approaching zero even as he sets his expectation at infinity. His fraction would be $\frac{zero}{infinity}$, and unless something else were added, this would represent complete and ultimate frustration.

What is added is first a conviction that it is not only achievement that is important but also, and perhaps even more so, commitment. The direction of one's striving qualifies the degree of his attainment. It is more important to feel that one's achievement is zero while striving for the ultimate good than to feel greater attainment while striving for a lesser goal. With this commitment there goes ego surrender. With ego surrender there goes a reduction of other wants and needs for the satisfaction of which many people strive, for example, the desire for money, goods, praise, and status.

A second thing that is added is the religious person's belief that the love of God is infinite and unchangeable and extends to both the deserving and the undeserving, that God's love for an individual is not dependent upon that person's achievement. Believing this, a religious person continues his efforts to improve, not in order to make God love him more, for God's love cannot be forced, earned, or purchased, but rather because he loves God and has confidence that God loves him. He accepts God's love as infinite and constant, not as limited and variable, and knows that nothing he can do can compensate for it. But because of the happiness that the assurance of God's love gives him, the religious person continues to do all that he can, counting everything that he does as nothing in comparison to what he receives. Therefore, a religious person can be happy in spite of his fraction, zero achievement over infinite expectation.

A parallel to this distinction between the *in order to* and the *because of* approaches to living may be found in the role played by love in marriage. Upon what basis shall I assume that I shall be loved by my marriage partner? Is it because I do so many things for that person? Love in marriage cannot be forced, earned, or purchased either. If I think that it can, I am likely to assume that the other person has an obligation to love me and that the more that I do the more I should be loved. Shall I be loved by my marriage partner because I am so lovable? If I make that assumption, I express such conceit that I would be unlovable. I may safely expect to be loved by my marriage partner because that person is so loving—so loving that he or she finds it possible to love me in spite of all my shortcomings. Then I do things selflessly to make that person happy not *in order to* be loved but *because* I love and am loved. Here again religion introduces a dualism, for when I consider why I love my marriage partner, my reason is not that I am so loving but that the other person is so lovable. In a successful marriage the process is two-sided and works both ways. The result is that each person makes a continuous and growing contribution to the happiness of the other without expectation of return except in the deep, abiding joy that comes from giving. With commitment to this principle goes ego surrender. With ego surrender goes a reduction in the number and type of things that can be interpreted as threats to self or to marriage.

On the one hand, religion plays a part in reducing and eliminating destructive conflict within the individual, between one individual and others, and between an individual and the nonhuman elements in his environment. It produces a peace of mind, "the peace of God which passeth all understanding," important not only in and for itself but because of its contagious nature. By its focusing upon things bigger than self, religion plays a part in reducing the discomfiture, discouragement, anxiety, and confusion arising from personal problems. Again because of this focus, it makes possible working together for a common end without comparison of one person with another and even without measurement of the contribution of a given individual. It aids in eliminating competition because success in moving toward a common end is felt to depend upon each one's doing his full share in the light of his capacities rather than upon one's doing more than another. Such working together can produce a oneness second to none in human life. On the other hand, religion may intensify constructive conflict, for it sharpens the individual's determination to struggle against those elements in life that distort personalities, frustrate worthy purposes, and sacrifice one person to the selfish interest of another.

Religion plays a part in the integration of personality around basic values. It makes for consistency of behavior because it provides constant points of reference against which behavior may be judged and toward which it may be directed. Like a magnetic pole it keeps the needle of man's aspirations pointed in the direction of the highest and best he knows. Thus religion affects decision making. If every time an individual makes a decision, great or small, he must make a new judgment concerning his over-all goal, each decision may assume major proportions and precipitate conflict within him, especially if he makes decisions that are inconsistent with each other. If, on the other hand, he commits himself once and for all to a central purpose, each new decision assumes lesser importance and is made in the light of his commitment. Thus conflict is reduced and consistency promoted.

Religion contributes a set of values in which the gratification of the senses appears relatively insignificant. Yet religion gives importance and esteem to natural phenomena. At the same time that it depreciates sensual satisfaction as an end in itself and divorced from other values, it does not condemn natural processes on the mere ground of their existence.

It reduces tension, anger, hatred, annoyance, irritation, and similar responses in a twofold manner: It changes one's attitude toward the cause by altering the significance of that cause in the light of higher values and broader objectives. It changes one's reaction by making consideration, patience, and self-discipline more important in the light of one's attitude toward other persons.

WHAT DO YOU THINK?

1. What is personality? How does it originate and develop? What factors cause it to change? Can an adult change?

2. Does heredity play any part in the development of personality?

3. Does a newborn child have a personality? An unborn child? A lower animal?

4. What suggestions would you give students to help them get along better with members of their own sex and with members of the opposite sex?

5. What are the similarities and differences between getting along with a roommate and getting along with a husband or wife?

6. If each individual lives in a private world, how can a person know what another person means when he says, "I love you"?

7. What suggestions would you give a couple to help them improve their communication with each other in marriage?

8. What is your reaction to the statement: "Since all behavior has a cause and each person is the product of his biography, one should never be angry, disappointed, or impatient no matter what another individual does"?

9. An individual has a spouse who is very sensitive and does not accept criticism well. But this individual has a justifiable criticism to make of this spouse. What suggestions would you give such a person?

10. To what extent do desirable motives justify or excuse undesirable behavior?

11. An individual has a fiancé who exhibits some very annoying personality traits. The individual assumes that these traits will change after the wedding. What suggestions would you make?

12. What factors, other than those mentioned in this chapter, play a part in making marriage successful or unsuccessful?

13. A married couple are interested in religion. They know that religion may be a contributor to more meaningful living. They feel that religion may also be a resource that may be drawn upon in making marriage more meaningful. What suggestions would you give them?

14. What is the full significance of the statement: "Some conflict in marriage is normal and is to be expected"?

15. What suggestions would you make to an individual who has a very jealous spouse? To the spouse?

16. By what means may tension be reduced or removed?

17. How may in-law relationships be improved?

18. What are the pros and cons of making education for marriage and family living a required part of the curriculum in high schools and colleges?

19. In this chapter it is suggested that sometimes that spouse dominates a marriage relationship who has the lesser interest in it or the lesser insight into it. In such a case, what suggestions would you give the other spouse?

20. Does the law of diminishing returns apply to anything in marriage besides the physical aspect of sex?

21. List some focal points, other than those mentioned, that might play a part in making marriage succeed or fail.

SELECTED READINGS

Baber, Ray E.: *Marriage and the Family*, 2d ed., McGraw-Hill Book Company, New York, 1953, chaps. 6, 7. The changing emphasis on love in marriage; the difficulty of classifying causes of conflict; authority in marriage.

Beasley, Christine: *Democracy in the Home*, Association Press, New York, 1954. "This book attempts to clarify the basic concepts of democracy and to offer some practical, down-to-earth methods of applying these concepts to family living."

Bee, Lawrence S.: *Marriage and Family Relations*, Harper & Row, Publishers, New York, 1959, chaps. 12, 13, 15, 16. Early adjustments in marriage; patterns of faulty and of productive marriage.

Bell, Robert R.: *Marriage and Family Interaction*, The Dorsey Press, Inc., Homewood, Ill., 1963, chap. 11. Marital adjustment.

Bernard, Jessie, Helen E. Buchanan, and William M. Smith, Jr.: *Dating, Mating and Marriage*, Howard Allen, Inc., Cleveland, 1958, chap. 8. Dealing with differences in marriage. Includes many case-documentary materials.

Blood, Robert O., Jr.: *Marriage*, The Free Press of Glencoe, New York, 1962, chaps. 9, 10, 12, 13, 16. Marriage as a system of roles; role con-

flicts and their resolution; maintaining love in marriage; how to reduce tension; decision making; the power structure in marriage; division of labor in the home; religion in family living.

Burgess, Ernest W., Harvey J. Locke, and Mary Margaret Thomes: *The
Family*, 3d ed., American Book Company, New York, 1963, chaps.
13, 14, 15, 18, 22. Factors in family unity; measuring success in marriage; predicting success; marital conflict; family relations in the
middle and later years.

Cavan, Ruth Shonle: *American Marriage*, Thomas Y. Crowell Company,
New York, 1959, chaps. 12, 18. Adjustment in marriage; communication in marriage; in-laws — how to live with parents and in-laws in
their home, in the young couple's home.

―――(ed.): *Marriage and the Family in the Modern World*, Thomas Y.
Crowell Company, New York, 1960, chaps. 13, 17, 24. In-laws and
grandparents; the wife and the husband's occupation; why marriages fail; infidelity; alcoholism and the family.

Denton, Wallace: *The Role of the Minister's Wife*, The Westminster
Press, Philadelphia, 1962. An examination of the special problems
faced and the adjustments required.

DeWit, Gerard A.: *Symbolism of Masculinity and Femininity*, Springer
Publishing Company, Inc., New York, 1963. A report of a pilot study
of word associations. Males and females of three age groups were
used as subjects. The "psychological symbolism of the sexes from
adolescence to adulthood." The "symbolism of the sexes pertains to
symbols representing the conception of the male or female person . . . a masculine or feminine way of existence. . . ." This is
different from symbolism in the Freudian sense.

Duvall, Evelyn Millis: *In-laws: Pro and Con*, Association Press, New
York, 1954. A study of the sentiments and experiences of 5,020 men
and women forms the basis of this exploration of in-law relationships.

―――and Reuben Hill: *When You Marry*, rev. ed., D. C. Heath and
Company, Boston, 1962, chaps. 10–12. What holds marriages together? What happens when there are crises? Common conflicts in
marriage.

"Executive Staff and Distaff," *Dun's Review and Modern Industry*,
vol. 69, no. 4, pp. 70ff., February, 1957. The responsibilities and role
of the executive's wife; attitudes; personal qualities needed. This
report grew out of a management clinic in which six young wives of
business executives listed "characteristics of today's successful
business wife."

Karlsson, Georg: *Adaptability and Communication in Marriage*, rev.
ed., The Bedminster Press, Totowa, N.J., 1963. "This book is a first
attempt to bring order and theory to our knowledge about satis-

factions and dissatisfactions in modern marriage. It also takes a critical look at the methods used to predict marital happiness." For the more advanced student.

Kohut, Nester: *A Manual on Marital Reconciliations*, Adams Press, Chicago, 1964. "A substantial number of marriages alleged by the partners and supposed by the attorneys and divorce courts to be broken, lifeless or irreparable are not in fact completely or irreversibly broken." The author is a lawyer. He believes people should not give up too easily on marital reconciliation.

Kolb, William L.: "Family Sociology, Marriage Education, and the Romantic Complex: A Critique," *Social Forces*, vol. 29, no. 1, pp. 65–72, October, 1950. The author's thesis is that "when the criteria for marriage developed by the family sociologist and marriage educator are judged by the complex of ultimate values embodied in the Western European tradition, these criteria reveal themselves to be nondemocratic and neglectful of the values of the dignity and infinite worth of the individual. . . ."

Koos, Earl Lomon: *Marriage*, rev. ed., Holt, Rinehart and Winston, Inc., New York, 1957, chaps. 10, 11, 15. Criteria of adjustment in marriage; interaction and morale in marriage; in-laws.

Krech, David, Richard S. Crutchfield, and Egerton L. Ballachey: *Individual in Society*, McGraw-Hill Book Company, New York, 1962, chap. 8. An analysis of communication: process and problems; meanings of words as related to sex, personality, and culture.

Landis, Paul H.: *For Husbands and Wives*, Appleton-Century-Crofts, Inc., New York, 1956, chaps. 6–9. Patterns of adjustment in marriage; "happiness versus problem-solving attitudes"; trouble areas; religion and marriage.

———: *Making the Most of Marriage*, 2d ed., Appleton-Century-Crofts, Inc., New York, 1960, chaps. 18, 19. Do all couples find adjustment difficult? "Women adjust most." In-laws. Quarreling as an adjustment device.

Le Masters, E. E.: *Courtship and Marriage*, The Macmillan Company, New York, 1957, chaps. 11–16. Research on in-laws. "In-laws: Friends or Enemies?" Factors in marital adjustment; religion in marriage; social class and marital adjustment.

Levine, Lena: *The Modern Book of Marriage*, Bartholomew House, New York, 1957. The author is a gynecologist, psychiatrist, and marriage counselor of wide experience. The book covers a wide range of topics, including sex, women's fears, jealousy, infidelity, artificial insemination, etc.

Levy, John, and Ruth Munroe: *The Happy Family*, Alfred A. Knopf, Inc., New York, 1938, chaps. 1–6. Factors affecting marital adjustment.

Mace, David R.: *Marriage: The Art of Lasting Love,* Doubleday & Company, Inc., Garden City, N.Y., 1952. "In what I have written here I am concerned not so much with the scientific as with the artistic, aesthetic, emotional approach to marriage." Discusses early weeks of marriage, how to handle quarrels, keeping marriage healthy, the art of married love, and jealousy. The author is executive director of the American Association of Marriage Counselors.

Magoun, F. Alexander: *Love and Marriage,* rev. ed., Harper & Row, Publishers, Incorporated, New York, 1956, chap. 11. Emotional adjustments in marriage; irrational behavior versus integrated, adaptive behavior; in-laws; money; other problem areas.

Martinson, Floyd M.: *Marriage and the American Ideal,* Dodd, Mead & Company, Inc., New York, 1960, chaps. 17–19, 21. Marital adjustment, self-realization in marriage; maintaining marriage.

Merrill, Francis E.: *Courtship and Marriage,* rev. ed., Holt, Rinehart and Winston, Inc., New York, 1959, chaps. 12–15, 20, 21. Extensive analysis of roles in marriage; marriage interaction and adjustment; frustrated roles.

Peterson, James A.: *Education for Marriage,* 2d ed., Charles Scribner's Sons, New York, 1964, chaps. 13, 18, 20. Early adjustments in marriage; personality changes after the wedding; religion in the family; descriptions of types of religious organizations and their relation to marital adjustment; the democratic family; the contribution of conflict to family cohesion.

Waller, Willard: *The Family: A Dynamic Interpretation,* rev. by Reuben Hill, Holt, Rinehart and Winston, Inc., New York, 1951, chaps. 13–16, 23. Changes in personality after the wedding; bases of conflict in marriage; clash of egos; processes and forms of conflict; in-laws; productive quarrels; marriage solidarity; the process of alienation; criteria of success.

Winfield, Louise: *Living Overseas,* Public Affairs Press, Washington, D.C., 1962. Presents the problems of families but also discusses the special problems of wives called upon to live in an overseas environment.

See also references on adjustment to military life at the end of Chapter 12.

CAMPUS AND
SERVICE MARRIAGE

AS INDICATED IN AN EARLIER CHAPTER, Americans today are marrying earlier than at any previous period in history. In addition to this decline in age at the time of the wedding, however, many young marriages are occurring under one or both of two sets of unprecedented circumstances, namely, military service for males as a "normal" expectation in time of relative peace, at least at a time of no open armed conflict, and also the extension of higher education both for a longer period of time and to greater numbers than ever before.

These two sets of circumstances impose certain problems on young marriages. To some degree they entail threats. Yet neither set of circumstances gives any indication of being temporary. Both are apparently here to stay, at least in so far as readers of this book are concerned. As a consequence, arguments of the recent past, which originated at a time when both sets of circumstances were relatively new in their present form, need to be reevaluated in the light of present observations. This does not imply that the problems are eliminated or even reduced by the mere fact that the circumstances continue to exist. It does imply that the solution to such problems will come through facing them, not through acting as if they were no part of the current picture, and as if present-day young marriages were occurring in the societal situation of a quarter of a century ago.

The fact that the young "service marriage" and the "campus marriage" are relatively new in no way excuses the hasty judgment, evasion of reality, and inadequate planning which sometimes inaugurate them.

Nor does this fact excuse rationalization of the circumstances in the light of which they occur as being so overwhelming that the couple are helpless either to prevent or to solve the problems generated.

In appraising both "service marriage" and "campus marriage," broad generalizations become meaningless. To be helpful the appraisal must be particularized. The question is not, "Can such marriage be made to work?" The question is, "Can this particular couple, with their particular objectives, assets, and liabilities, in their particular situation, make such marriage work?" Much depends upon the quality of persons involved. Here, for example, is a young man who is unmarried. He has a high IQ. His parents subsidize him so generously he does not have to earn any money during his college days. He is in excellent health. Yet he is on scholastic probation because he does not maintain a required grade level. Here, on the other hand, is a young couple both of whom are employed because they are completely on their own financially. They have two children and are expecting a third. The wife is concerned lest labor start during the final examination period. They participate in extra-curricular activities, are very happily married, and are both maintaining a commendable grade level.

Campus marriage

Two to three decades ago only an occasional college or university student married and remained in school. This was especially true of undergraduates in "arts" colleges. There was widespread skepticism, and some outright opposition, relative to both students' ability to handle successfully the education-plus-marriage situation and the advisability of letting them attempt it. Some administrators were convinced that an appreciable proportion of married students in an undergraduate student body would somehow constitute a threat, a disrupting influence. In some schools there was discrimination as well as skepticism. For example, married students were not permitted to participate in school-sponsored athletic events, could not live in dormitories or fraternity or sorority houses, were not allowed to hold offices in campus extracurricular organizations.

Today much of this earlier resistance to campus marriage has disappeared. Only traces of it remain. Administrators have found that many students can successfully combine marriage and college education and that married students are not only not a source of campus disruption but may contribute to campus stability. Yet in some schools married students are relegated to inferior housing, and there is a sort of unexpressed attitude to the effect that "you married of your own free will. Therefore, if you have any problems due to the fact that you're married, don't expect us to help you solve them."

NUMBER OF MARRIED STUDENTS

In the fall of 1963, 22 per cent of all college and university students (about 26 per cent of males and 16 per cent of females) were married and living with their spouses. These percentages, therefore, do not include students who were married but whose spouses were absent, for example, in military service. Of students attending full time (registered for twelve or more hours during the average school week), 12 per cent were married (of males about 15 per cent, of females 6 per cent). Of those attending part time (taking fewer than twelve hours during the average school week), almost 55 per cent were married (59 per cent of males, almost 47 per cent of females) [U.S. Bureau of the Census, 1964]. Since estimates suggest that more than 4 million students were enrolled in institutions of higher learning in 1963, these percentages represent considerable numbers of young people. Even taking into account the fact that many part-time students are older and decided to attend college after having been married, figures such as those above suggest that in general married students take longer than single students to get degrees.

There are several possible explanations for the differences in the percentages for the two sexes as indicated above. As a group, males are more likely than females to go through college. Males are also more likely to work for advanced or professional degrees. Male students, as a group, are older than female students. There are some married male students whose wives already have their undergraduate degrees. Many married girls drop out of school because of childbearing or in order to contribute to family support while their husbands are students.

Since present-day college education is so closely tied in with occupational training for many students, males and females are subjected to somewhat different social pressure toward getting degrees. There are males who drop out of college because they cannot handle satisfactorily the combined task of marriage, study, and earning. On the other hand, there are males whose motivation toward completing a degree is increased with marriage. Generalizing, this increased motivation is more likely to be seen in the male than in the female because the male is subject to the social expectations associated with family support and standard of living.

In contrast, after her wedding, many a girl loses her motivation for getting a degree. She may see a less apparent connection between her college work and her new role as wife-homemaker than her husband sees between his studying and his occupational objective. She may become absorbed in her new responsibilities. She may feel that her husband's burden would be lightened if she got a job. She may find it inconvenient to get to classes at times when she would prefer to be doing something domestic. Since she is under neither social nor occupational pressure to get ahead in the sense in which her husband is expected to get ahead occupationally, she may fail to see the importance of continuing her education. She may feel that when she married, she "arrived." Overlooking the relationship between education and satisfaction in living, she may feel that it is pointless to continue to work for a degree when she is already where she wants to be. Her motivation gradually slips away. She drops out. If her dropping out means that eventually her husband will continue to grow while she marks time, an educationally mixed marriage may develop, though it was not such a mixed marriage at the time of the wedding.

This matter of dropout gives concern to school administrators as well as to students. Precisely how common it is is not possible to ascertain because, when students drop out of college, the reasons for their doing so are not always readily apparent, and precipitating causes may be confused with basic causes. But we may be sure that, among students who might otherwise receive their degrees, a higher dropout rate, like reduced academic load and hence a longer period required for a degree, as already mentioned, is one of the costs of the increase in the number of campus marriages.

Using the word "costs" as it is used in the sentence above implies an assumption to the effect that college education is a value. Some would challenge such an assumption; and it must be admitted both that the majority of young people do not attend college and that there are many individuals who are not equipped to benefit by the type of learning experience which college provides. Nonetheless, for those young people who do go to college, we may assume that such education is considered a value by most. A degree is a worthy objective. Marriage is also a worthy objective. The concept of cost arises when one such objective is sacrificed for the achievement of another such objective.

Dropping out is sometimes followed by projection of blame in later life. For example, suppose a girl drops out in order to get employment so that her husband may graduate. In later life, when she has forgotten how eager she was to leave school but feels different from the wives of her husband's professional associates because she has no degree, she may project the blame onto him. Or suppose a male student drops out because his wife becomes pregnant and must give up her job and there is no way for the family to be supported except through his efforts. He gets an immediately well-paying but blind-alley job. As the years go on the men who would have been his professional associates move ahead in the field in which he would prefer to be working. He begins to feel like a "might-have-been." It would not be difficult for him unintentionally to project blame for his failure onto the wife and child. The accusation "if it hadn't been for you" can be devastating for a person to live with.

Other considerations in connection with campus marriage are as follows.

AGE AND MATURITY

After the Second World War, when the great influx of veterans into the colleges occurred, a rapid increase in the frequency of campus marriage took place. The arrival of veterans on the campus was not the only factor causing this increase, but it was undoubtedly one contributing factor. Many of the veterans were older than the previously typical undergraduate. Hence many of the married students were older. No figures are available for comparing the ages of married students then and now. But it would be safe to guess that with the increase in the number of campus marriages the picture has changed somewhat. Many current campus marriages involve relatively young students. Some of them are immature. It goes without saying that the age and maturity level of the persons participating in a marriage, campus or otherwise, plays an ample role in the success or failure of that marriage.

STATUS

An individual's or a couple's place in the college scheme is an important consideration so far as marriage is concerned. Contrast these two cases with respect to advisability of marrying. One case involves two seniors who plan to marry in March and who will graduate in June. The other case involves a seventeen-year-old freshman girl and an eighteen-year-old sophomore boy who plans to go through medical school. They met in September and plan to marry during the Christmas vacation. Both of these would be considered campus marriages.

GRADES

When the increase in campus marriages began, grade studies made in certain schools suggested that, as a group, married students earned higher grades than unmarried students [Riemer, 1947]. In evaluating such studies one might well wonder whether sufficient weight was given to two factors, namely, the ages of the students studied and the fact that grade studies must of necessity be made on students who are in school rather than on ex-students who for one reason or another dropped out of school or on persons who might have become students had there been nothing in their situations to prevent their doing so. There are cases in which marriage has provided a student or a couple with a sense of security, motivation toward study, and time free from pressures of dating, and thus contributed to the improvement of grades [Schroder, 1963]. On the other hand, there are students whose grades suffer because of marriage. The research data are not conclusive [Samenfink and Milliken, 1961]. Certainly no one would seriously suggest marriage as a way to raise one's grades.

In the statistics mentioned earlier in this chapter, note was made of the difference between married students and unmarried students with regard to number of hours carried. Reduced academic load and therefore a longer period of attendance in order to accumulate enough credit for a degree is apparently a not infrequent accompaniment of campus marriage.

HUSBAND'S MOBILITY

In some occupational fields a beginner, even though he has a professional degree, is expected to be able to move about from one location to another. It is a method used by many large companies to find the proper niche for promising young men and to train them in the intricacies of the organization. In some instances an unmarried man may be moved about more readily than a married man, and the former is more amenable to such mobility. A married man may give more weight to income, housing, schools, and similar items than to the opportunity presented when such moving is suggested. In some cases wives object to moving because they want to remain near parents, or they just get one apartment arranged to their liking when they are called upon to leave it and start over on another, or they do not like the prospect of living in the community in which the husband's new job would be located, or for any of a number of similar reasons. Hence, a girl contemplating a campus marriage might well give serious consideration to the question of whether she would help her husband or hinder him in the critical early days of his career.

There may also be a problem of academic mobility. Even when a mistake has been made, a married male student may not feel free to change his major or his field of professional training, especially if such change would involve loss of credit and his wife or economic need puts him under pressure to get his degree as soon as possible.

ATTITUDE OF PARENTS

Parental approval and good will is an asset to be preserved, if possible, in any marriage. Campus marriage is no exception. In many cases parents disapprove of a marriage when one or both of the couple are students, whereas these same parents would be more likely to approve if the young couple were not students. No matter how this may be explained —as cultural lag, failure to understand present-day trends, conservatism, fear of dropout, insight, concern, love—it represents part of the reality of the situation within which campus marriage occurs. This is not meant to imply that, no matter how old or how mature the young couple may be, the judgment of their parents must be the final determining factor in whether or not they marry. It is meant to imply that parental judgment is not to be lightly disregarded as if it had no bearing on the marriage.

Here again there is the problem of possible cost as one worthy objective is weighed against another worthy objective. Some couples confuse the importance of the time of marriage with the importance of the fact of marriage and in so doing sacrifice parental good will that might have been preserved if the wedding had been postponed to a later date.

FINANCES

In a campus marriage there is not only the problem of sufficient income per se but a correlative, and sometimes more sensitive, problem of who depends upon whom for what and for how long. We shall discuss this latter problem later.

Many campus couples exist upon minimum financing. Some have learned how to economize, how to stretch their income, how to do without things they want but do not need, how to budget, how to have recreation at low cost, and how to make some of the things they cannot afford to buy. To arrive at such a solution to the problem of finances requires the cooperation and understanding of both husband and wife. It cannot be achieved by one spouse while the other continues to act as if he or she were still single.

In some schools married students have "taken the bull by the horns" and themselves organized means of meeting part of the problem of living costs. For example, in one university community, merchants have been approached to allow discounts to married students, and merchants are cooperating. In another school, the married students formed a co-operative and by this means could purchase staple articles at wholesale prices by purchasing them in quantity. Cooperative baby-sitting plans are widely used. In some cases records are kept and a given sitter is credited with the hours used in caring for someone else's child. In turn the sitter has a similar amount of time due him from the "pool."

It may be true, as some suggest, that some colleges are paying too little attention to the special needs and problems of married students. On the other hand, it may also be true that married students, as a group, could through cooperation, ingenuity, and effort contribute to the improvement of their own lot. Many of them wait for something to be done for them. Others industriously work on the solution of their own problems, failing to recognize that if more than one-fifth of the student body in many colleges and universities is married, this constitutes a group of persons who can, if they will, solve at least some of their problems by mutual aid.

In any discussion of the financial problems of campus marriage the question of parental subsidy is certain to be raised. Should or should not parents contribute to the support of the campus couple? Should they be expected to do so?

Parents who willingly subsidize a son or daughter as a single student may refuse to continue such subsidy after the student marries. Others equally willingly continue subsidy after the wedding. Some increase it. In a few cases the two sets of parents and the campus couple work out a cooperative plan.

In those cases in which parents refuse to contribute to a child's support after the latter marries, one wonders whether there is merely bias expressed or a basic principle involved. Parents often act as if it were the latter. They draw the line of support very sharply at the wedding— "When you marry, don't expect any more help from us."

On the one hand, the parents have a point. A couple should, if possible, be independent when they marry. On the other hand, the attitude that suggests the drawing of such a sharp line of demarcation at the wedding is one that emerged from social conditions of the past. It does not take fully into account the new phenomenon represented by the extension of higher education, often interrupted by military service, which extension parents themselves approve and encourage. It is easy to assert that young people should wait to marry until they have completed their formal schooling. One might more hopefully have expected this assertion to be a deterrent in earlier days when few attended college. But when one is discussing more than 4 million college students who represent almost a cross section of the population rather than a select elite, and who constitute a democratized student body whose objective is largely education for immediate practical use, occupationally or otherwise, rather than intellectual pursuit for its own sake, one must expect life to go on. One cannot expect all 4 million students to postpone marriage until they have completed their degrees when for some this means four to eight years of training beyond an undergraduate degree. This is in no way intended as meaning that parents should subsidize every campus marriage. It implies only a new evaluation of an old assumption. A similar new evaluation would be appropriate for those husbands who accentuate the problem of family financing by resisting a subsidy which the wife's parents are able to afford and willing to continue.

It may be noted that parental subsidy does not necessarily mean regular allowance. It may take the form of special gifts, aid in time of financial stress, such as at the birth of a child, or payment of special costs, such as insurance premiums. It must also be noted that in any case of parental subsidy, no matter what form it takes, the gain is not worth the cost if the subsidy is accompanied by parental interference in the young marriage, if the subsidy is so generous and can be anticipated for so long in the future that the young couple grow to depend upon it and therefore lose their ambition and in a sense become pauperized, or if the young husband cannot accept the subsidy without a feeling of resentment or inadequacy yet the wife's parents insist upon continuing it.

Whether parental subsidy of campus marriage is desirable or undesirable is still an open question. No universal generalization can answer the question. In some cases it has worked out well; in others, poorly. In many cases it has not been tried. Whether it is good or bad, whether it should be more common or less common, the fact remains that at present not all parents favor it. The young person contemplating campus

SOME SPECIAL PROBLEMS OF CAMPUS MARRIAGE

Students enter college with a number of expectations; they hope to accomplish certain things. This often includes the expectation of making friends, among whom the student often hopes to find a marriage partner. But academic achievement, cultural enrichment, and career preparation are also part of the picture. So when two students fall in love and consider marriage, they do well to examine again their original objectives in the light of such plans.

The time of the wedding is different from the fact of the wedding. In setting a wedding date careful plans should be made which may be difficult when the couple are deeply in love. What differences are there between the factors involved for sophomores and those for seniors, between a career in medicine and one in merchandising?

marriage must face the reality of the present, as well as the hopes of the future. Unless he is sure of his own parents' willingness and ability, and the willingness and ability of his fiancée's parents, to subsidize a contemplated marriage, the reader would be buying a grab bag if he married and depended upon the continuation of allowances for support.

Subsidized marriage is not something new and untried. There is some reason to believe that in this country the present period is the first in which marriage has not been subsidized. In earlier times, a girl usually entered marriage with an ample hope chest and often with a dowry. When a man married, his father gave him some land, stock, and equipment, and friends and relatives assisted in the building of his house. This was a form of subsidy and it worked—a fact which neither proves nor disproves that the same plan would be satisfactory in our present-day money economy.

Under the best of circumstances many little things come up to cause irritation in marriage. Consider the ways in which the cramped living quarters of married students can make tension-relieving efforts more difficult. What steps might the couple take to cut down possible points of friction in such a situation?

PLANNING

Whether or not campus marriage succeeds depends in large part on the quality of planning with which it is inaugurated. Some students make plans which "look good on paper" but which cannot function effectively under any circumstances other than those anticipated at the time of the planning. There is no allowance made for the unexpected. There is not enough flexibility to permit the plan to be adapted to altered conditions. The plan is such that, if one element breaks down, the entire plan collapses. Only part of the marital situation, rather than all of it, is taken into account; the couple do not foresee the total job to be done. There is no reasonable assurance of the couple's attaining all of their objectives; there is the likelihood of their having to sacrifice one objective — marital success, academic degree, parental good will, or having children — for another, as mentioned earlier. For example, the couple's income will depend largely upon the wife's continuing to earn. If she becomes pregnant and has to give up her job, the plan collapses because no allowance

Many students receive some subsidy from their
parents toward academic or living expenses or
both. The fact of marriage often affects the
subsidy and the attitudes of the parents. While
there are some advantages of continued parental
financial help, there are also dangers. The usual
adjustment when parental subsidy is discontinued
is for each partner to assume the traditional role
of wage earner or homemaker to some extent.
Sometimes these traditional roles are reversed.
What additional sacrifices and unfamiliar
compromises must often be made by each partner
under such circumstances?

   With the great increase in married students,
the attitudes of college administrations are
changing toward greater acceptance of such
students' participation in campus life. In addition,
many colleges offer special counseling help to
married students. On the large campus there may
even be some possibilities for cooperative aid.
To what extent is the role of married students
limited in your college? Are there ways in which
they have advantages in campus activities?

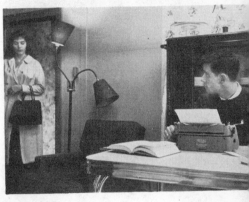

Sometimes circumstances make it seem necessary to the couple for one or
both of them to drop out of school short of the degree toward which they had
been working. There are some immediate possible consequences of this
action, but in what ways may the future life of the couple and its socioeconomic level be affected? Consider the adults you know of your parents'
generation who did not finish college and their evaluation of its effect on
their lives.

Even the most carefully laid plans require flexibility, and undergraduates planning marriage must be prepared for unexpected developments. What adjustments are involved, for example, if the wife should become pregnant? When career-plan changes prolong education?

is made for such an eventuality. Or the couple do not take into account the total job to be done, namely, earning, housekeeping, possibly child care, and academic work. They assume the same sort of division of labor that they could safely assume if the husband were a full-time bread-winner and the wife a full-time homemaker-mother; but such an assumption in their case is invalid.

A good plan is one which (1) is realistic and includes a critical appraisal of the couple's assets and liabilities; (2) takes into account the total job to be done and includes a mutually agreeable means for doing this job; (3) is flexible enough to be adapted to changing circumstances but sufficiently rigid and strongly enough motivated to withstand the ups and downs of day-to-day trials and errors; (4) is not so critically vulnerable at one point that the success of the entire plan rests upon the achievement of one part of it; (5) gives the couple some assurance of getting what they want; (6) at least to a reasonable degree eliminates conflict among their objectives so that these objectives, as mentioned above, are not set in opposition to each other in a way which permits one to be jeopardized by another. Most students enter college with serious intent. They hope to obtain an education, including for many of them occupational training. Their occupational ambitions ordinarily are geared to a high level of expectation. At the same time they hope someday to marry and establish a new family. Some consider the possibility of meeting a possible future marriage partner through campus contacts. Most of them are interested in maintaining a happy relationship with their own parental families and are hopeful of establishing an equally happy one with their new families-in-law when they marry. They want the social experiences which ordinarily accompany campus life. None of these objectives becomes any the less important merely because a young couple fall in love.

SECURITY

Marriage can provide a unique type of security, but it cannot provide such security unless there already exists a sound and secure relationship between the two persons before the wedding. In other words, marriage cannot transmute insecurity into security; it cannot make security "out of whole cloth." It is not per se the solution to the problem of the couple one of whom does not want to return home or the couple who are afraid that during summer vacation or after the graduation of one of them they

A man's mobility is often one consideration of an employer, who recognizes that a single man is freer to move than a married man. Evaluate the ways in which family responsibilities can limit choice of beginning jobs and career opportunities. To what extent does the wife play a role in her husband's job selection?

will drift apart. Marriage also provides the possibility of a solution to the problem of sexual tension. But it is not to be thought of merely as a solution to this problem. Some persons recommend early marriage as a means of solving the problem of premarital sexual intercourse. Such a recommendation is oversimplified and is often based on a disregard of other important considerations.

SPECIAL STRESSES

One of the basic reasons for which campus marriage presents a problem to many persons, both to the individuals in it and to others, is that they make the erroneous assumption that campus marriage is merely young marriage that happens to occur in a college milieu. This assumption leads to expectations that may be appropriate for ordinary marriage but are not appropriate for campus marriage. There is a discrepancy between expectation and reality. The result is special stress, special pressure.

Campus marriage is young marriage, but it is not merely young marriage that happens to occur in a college milieu. In some respects it is a new type of marriage because it entails factors hitherto relatively unknown to the degree to which they are now found. The sooner this fact is recognized, the sooner progress will be made in improving campus marriage. We shall stop trying to fit the square peg of stereotype into the round hole of social change. Counseling has revealed some of the special "pressure points" in campus marriage, and the following are among them.

Reprinted from "U.S. News & World Report," published at Washington, D.C.

READING 14 **EARLY MARRIAGE AND CAMPUS MARRIAGE**

The following are excerpts from "A New Look at Early Marriages," an interview with Dr. Margaret Mead, noted anthropologist.

Q Do you look for this trend toward youthful marriages to go on, and snowball—or will people get over it and start marrying later?

A I don't think we know yet. We don't know what the full price is, for society, of frowning so heavily on anyone remaining unmarried. We haven't begun to discover what that means in a shortage of educated people and a shortage of adventurous and creative people.

We don't know how many younger boys and girls may look at the marriage of their brothers and sisters who are older than they are and decide that they were trapped—that they were married too early; that they aren't having any fun. There is a whole series of decisions that might be made by young people looking at older brothers and sisters.

There are decisions that might be made by the official worriers of the country, who are beginning to give reports on what's happening. We might have a sufficient shift in economic conditions—a little less prosperity, a little belt-tightening—to make a difference.

Or we might be called upon to make more of a defense effort than we are making at present, so that more of our young men were taken into the armed services and made unavailable for early marriage.

Q What seems to account for this trend to get married while still in college?

A There are a whole lot of different causes that have been identified.

For the last 25 or 30 years we've had a great deal of agitation along the lines that adolescents are sexually mature, and that a society that denies them a sex life until sometime late in their 20s—or, in some societies, even into their 30s—is going against nature.

Now, from time to time we're in favor of nature and at other times we're against it. As far as sex is concerned today, we think we're in favor of nature, and we think sex is good for you and you ought to have it, under licensed and domestic conditions, from the time that you're just technically physically mature until you're 80.

This general notion about sex—which has developed in this country in the last 25 years—means, of course, we disapprove now of any form of single blessedness. We suspect any form of single-minded dedication. We are running very short of religious orders on which many important institutions in this country have been based. We have to import nuns from other countries, for example, to teach schools and run hospitals because this whole country now believes that marriage—that regular sex life inside marriage—is physiologically necessary for everyone. This has been one factor in these college marriages.

Another factor is that everybody is doing things younger today. They're not only getting married younger. They're piloting planes younger. If we look at what our young men are expected to do in war, we realize that we're putting a tremendous strain on young people.

This pressing down on young people, into premature responsibilities, is not confined only to marriage.

Q Besides the emphasis on youth and sex, does anything else encourage these early marriages?

A A third factor, I think, is that World War I, then the depression, then World War II and, finally, the Korean War have all discouraged the adult world—the people who are the parents of these kids. The parents have felt, "We want you to have some fun now. Take some enjoyment in life while you can get it. The future is totally uncertain."

The fear of atomic war—which is not being faced but is only being felt as a vague shadow—also is the sort of thing, just as war itself, that drives young people into "snatching" at happiness out of a sense that it's going to disappear if not taken.

Q Which is more important in causing college marriages — the ideas that drive young people, or those that drive their parents?

A The parents are driven into conniving with the youngsters in early dating, and early "going steady." They push the boys, as well as the girls, into courtship as early as possible and underwrite the marriage. This is what is happening to the parents.

At the same time, the young people have this feeling that they're living in a world where the future is very uncertain, so they might as well get what they can now—a husband, a wife, children, a house in the country.

Q What about the colleges' part in all this? Before World War II, universities often would expel students who got married—

A Especially girls. A married girl was supposed to be very, very disastrous in a dormitory. This was based on all sorts of assumptions about the state of mind of the other girls in the dormitory—and what it would do to them to have a married girl among them who was going to give them information not otherwise available. And some boys' colleges had the same rules.

Q What was the basis for that attitude?

A For boys, it was related to the fact that they lived in dormitories that were supposed to still be under supervision. For girls, a married woman was supposed to corrupt the unmarried.

Q Do you think that was a realistic idea?

A I think the idea was mainly traditional. It was only in the late part of the nineteenth century that, for example,

Cambridge dons [faculty members] of any age were allowed to marry. A lot of our university traditions stem from monastic conditions. A great deal of this protection for young men and women was based on a different set of premises from those we would base it on today.

Q What do you think about the comment by a dean of students at a large U.S. college that college years are man-hunting and girlhunting years anyway?

A That is true in this country now. It isn't what those years have been in the history of civilization. It isn't quite certain we can call this civilization.

Q What has happened? Is it considered old-fashioned to want a little time to think about marriage?

A It's not fashionable at present, partly because in this country we've built this tremendous opposition to the intellectual by our high-school system, and we've expanded our colleges to include more and more of the people that once went only through high school.

So we now have, actually, a high-school standard of intellectual life on our college campuses, and this is combined with a very strict vocationalism among the young people—many of them already burdened with wives and children or husbands and children—who demand from colleges instead of a chance to think, or a chance to find themselves, a chance to become qualified for some job that will give them security and permit them to support this family that they either have or are going to have very soon.

Q Is that desirable?

A Intellectual life demands some kind of postponement of this early domesticity. Early domesticity has always been characteristic of most savages, of most peasants and of the urban poor. But most civilized societies—we have to remember—have only had a very small group of people who had any intellectual life, a very small group who went to universities.

In European history it has been the young men of the elite classes who were trained as philosophers, as priests, as statesmen and writers. They have been permitted to postpone responsibility while they had a chance in some reasonably protected environment to think, and to make friends with other young men of their own age and class, and discuss things and develop and change their minds and explore. This is the thing we're cutting out in this country.

Q What about the young wives? Are they usually other students or are they—

A There's a pretty good tendency in this country for people to marry within their same social-economic-educational group, so these are not the landladies' daughters that the traditional Oxford and Cambridge student occasionally married to his sorrow.

On the other hand, these young wives don't have much chance to study any further, and, if they marry before they finish college and the husband goes on to a professional career, the chance of their not belonging to the same educational level as their husbands by the time they are age 30 is pretty high.

Q What happens if there are babies while they are still in college?

A If there are babies, it means, you know, the father's term paper gets all mixed up with the baby's bottle. This was fine in the GI days when young fathers learned to enjoy their babies, and they lived in trailers with a baby and a doctor's dissertation and a bed arranged in a row within a very narrow space. The fathers got interested in their babies and began enjoying them. We now have a tremendous crop of young fathers who enjoy their babies, often more than their mothers do.

Babies are, in fact, very engrossing objects. They've engrossed women for hundreds of thousands of years, and it now looks as if they were going to engross men, too. And the question is, is anybody going to have time to pay attention to anything else?

Q "Anything else" being the husband or the wife?

A No, no. "Anything else" being sports, statesmanship, art, science, exploration of outer space. Those are a few of the other little things we're going to have to work on in the next quarter century.

Q Should men be more concerned with those things than women?

A They have been traditionally. In human society achievement has always been something that men did. It didn't make any difference what it was.

I've worked in societies where something you might call "dressing dolls" on rather an elegant scale is something that men do. But if it's something that men do, it's achievement. If it's something that women do, it isn't achievement. And one can relate this to the fact that women, after all, do have the task of producing the babies initially, giving more time and attention to them than the husbands do, and they are tremendously satisfied by it. Producing a whole human being is a very satisfactory thing to do.

Meanwhile, men have crossed rivers, built ocean liners, built airships, built empires and scientific systems and written great works. And now, if we're going to have both men and women devoting all their time to infants, it's a little problematic what's going to happen to the world.

Q Do you think there will be lasting effects on the country, as a result?

A Early student marriage is domesticating boys so early they don't have a chance for full intellectual development. They don't have a chance to give their entire time, not necessarily to study in the sense of staying in the library — though libraries are pretty well deserted today except in ivy-clad, one-sex colleges, or where the libraries are good dating spots — but in the sense that the married students don't have time to experiment, to think, to sit up all night in bull sessions, to develop as individuals.

This is not only important for the intellectuals, but also the boys who are going to be the future statesmen of the country and lawyers and doctors and all sorts of professional men; even men studying for the ministry don't have time to think about theology because they're busy going home to look after the baby.

There is a tendency to substitute easy domesticity for a period of stretching one's intellectual and ethical muscles before one settles down.

Q How about the girl's intellectual development? Is a college marriage likely to have bad effects for her, in your opinion?

A Yes, I think it's bad for women, too, because it's in high school and college that you learn to make friends, and making friends is as important for women as it is for men. It's as important in all the terms I've discussed for men — to find out what you think about, how your mind works, whether you can write poetry or not or whether you want to go out and run for the Senate. These are all things that one ought to thresh out with members of one's own sex at about the same age level.

Also, with our present differential death rate — and there doesn't seem to be any reason to hope that this will be stopped very quickly — not the way we're making young men take responsibility now — a great proportion of American women are going to outlive their husbands. They're going to live in a world as populated by women as a convent was once populated by women, and they had better learn to make friends with them before they get married or they're going to be very lonely afterwards or very useless.

Q Are the student marriages lasting? Is a marriage at, say, 22 or 23, following graduation from college, more likely to be successful than a marriage in college?

A I don't think we know. A great many of these early marriages—if they have children very early—sometimes seem to be surviving reasonably well, as far as the mere survival of the marriage is concerned.

The fathers, as I said before, enjoy their children very much, and take a lot of care of them. So that they may get caught in a kind of mutually happy nest-building which I don't think is very good for the country because it cuts us off from a lot of talent, but it is a perfectly contented setup for the nestlings.

Q Is the fact that the college man is supported by his wife an added tie to the marriage—or an added strain?

A I don't think it's a good thing at all, because I don't think any American young man really feels he's a man if he's supported by his wife. So, he lets her support him, turns her into his mother, whom he is more willing to have support him, and, when he gets whatever degree she's supporting him for—especially if there are no children— he's very likely to leave.

Q Is that what happens?

A That is what is said to be happening and I've tried it on audiences all over the country, and the audiences agree that this is what's happening. We haven't any nationwide statistics on the subject.

We even have colleges giving certificates to the wives for pushing their husbands through college. But how many men want to be married to women who pushed them through college—you know, there may be some, but it isn't exactly in line with our existing American cultural ideals.

Reversal of role. In many campus marriages the wife is the primary, sometimes the only, breadwinner. In some cases the husband resents this reversal of role and is uneasy under it. He may feel guilty. He could accept support from his wife if he were incapacitated. Such support would be socially approved. But he is able-bodied; and commitment to getting a degree does not carry the traditional weight carried by physical need. Under the circumstances it might appear logical for him to give a good deal of time to housework, but this he is not necessarily able or willing to do. His wife resents this because she has to carry a double load. There are also cases in which conflict arises because of the wife's resentment of the fact that the husband is not earning enough. Being less appreciative than he of the importance of his degree, she would like him to leave school and get a job so that she may stop working. This he will not do.

Aspiration level.   When an individual compares where he is with where he thinks he ought to be relative to standard of living, his definition of the latter will naturally affect his degree of acceptance of the former. The unmarried student thinks of his present standard of living as temporary, not entirely of his own making (although of his own choice because of his subordination of standard of living to academic achievement), the best that he and/or his parents can do under the circumstances, and something that will change when he gets his degree. His standard of living is not radically different from that of many students about whom he knows. A considerable amount of minimum living on very limited income is commonly accepted among students.

The married student, on the other hand, when comparing his present standard of living with that which he feels he ought to have, is sometimes less likely to fit himself into the general college picture and more likely to compare what he has with the standard of living of the general married group in his socioeconomic class. He operates within a different framework. His present situation, then, seems replete with limitations and deprivations and is less likely to be accepted without stress and strain. For example, an unmarried girl who would get along well on a minimum standard financed by her parents and/or her own employment may be discontent with the same standard when financed in part by a husband because being married gives her a different aspiration level on the basis of which she appraises her present standard and finds it wanting. Similarly, a male student may get along well with minimum income while he is unmarried and dating but shift his basis for comparing where he is with where he thinks he ought to be when he marries and is called upon to provide a standard of living for a wife and perhaps children in a way which reflects upon him as a man. These are broad generalizations, to be sure, by no means applicable to all married students, but such cases do come to light.

Parental expectation.   When there is complete or partial reversal of role as suggested above, the wife's parents sometimes contribute to family conflict by continually nagging their daughter with the insinuation that her husband "is not doing enough." This may be an expression of their disapproval of their daughter's having contracted a campus marriage, or it may be an indication of their lack of understanding that campus marriage is different from the type of marriage to which they are accustomed.

Wife's responsibilities. Many a campus wife carries an unusually heavy load of responsibility. She may be a student herself, have employment, do housekeeping, and take care of one or more children. Even when she herself is not a student, her load may be heavy. In some cases this one-sidedness stems from lack of cooperation on the part of the husband. But in other cases it is not entirely his fault. If he is a poor or average student and has to struggle to maintain his grades but is determined to get a degree, he may literally not be able to help his wife as much as either of them would like. It is difficult for some campus wives to understand this and to accept a heavy load of responsibilities and yet have so little in the way of material goods and comforts to show for it. In some cases the total load is more than one person can carry successfully. If, in such a case, the husband criticizes the wife for neglecting part of the load, say certain aspects of housework, her resentment may be bitter indeed.

Child care. Many campus couples are faced with the necessity of providing care for very young children while the parents are in class or at work. Sometimes this results in relatively unprecedented arrangements which emerge from the ancient truth that "necessity is the mother of invention." For example, one couple arranged their two class schedules so that one could be at home while the other attended class. But the college provided only ten minutes between classes. So one of the spouses would take care of the baby while the other went to class. Then the parent-sitter would take the baby to a halfway point on the way to class to be met by the other parent who was on the way home from class and took the baby back to the apartment.

In the country at large, most gainfully employed married women who have children drop out of employment while their children are very young, returning to work after the children have entered school or become somewhat independent. In 1960 only about one woman in five with preschool-age children worked outside the home [Nye and Hoffman, 1963]. On the other hand, in 1961 about one employed mother out of three had a child under six years of age [U.S. Women's Bureau, 1962]. Comparative figures are not available for campus wives. But it would be safe to guess that here may be found one of the pressure points in campus marriage. When the husband is a student is the time that the wife's income is most desperately needed, and this is often the very time that her children are of preschool age. In other words, some campus wives must of necessity cope with a situation which the great majority of wives have found reason and means to avoid, namely, gainful employment during the early years of their children's lives.

Parental subsidy.   This point has already been mentioned. It will bear a second reference. Many a conflict in campus marriage arises from some situation positively or negatively associated with parental subsidy. No amount of theorizing on the part of the young couple to the effect that they ought to be independent of their parents increases their income. No amount to the effect that parents ought to help reduces the couple's financial needs. No amount of similar theorizing on the part of the parents decreases the young couple's expenses. The campus couple may be caught between the pressure of tradition and customary expectation—on their own part as well as on the part of others—on the one hand, and the struggle for existence, on the other. But in their case the struggle for existence is not imposed upon them in the ordinary sense of the term. It arises from their own decision to marry and at the same time attend college. There are two hypothetically escapable elements in the situation, namely, the determination to continue their education and the determination to marry. They could, if they would, leave school, have a customary marriage, and live "normally." Or they could postpone marriage. Neither, of course, will they do. Yet these hypothetically escapable elements color the problem of parental subsidy, both in the giving of subsidy and in the receiving of it. In some cases they make the parents more than usually reluctant to give it. In other cases they make the campus couple reluctant to accept it. If the young couple were actually reduced to a simple, elemental struggle for existence, and both they and their parents recognized it as such, the problem of parental help would be greatly modified, if indeed it did not disappear.

Academic pressures.   There are pressures involved in breadwinning, but they have been recognized and accepted since time immemorial. Family life is to a considerable extent adapted to them. For example, the meal schedule, recreation plans, vacation trips, place of residence, and similar things are determined in part by the requirements of a man's and/or a woman's job. The pressures imposed by academic work, when compared to those above, are both atypical and irregular. They are not widely understood and accepted. As a result, there are campus wives, who are themselves not students, who are irritated by and come to resent the husband's attention to study. If the couple have no children and the wife is gainfully employed, she may want to leave the home for social contacts and recreation in the evening, which is the only time the husband has for study. When final examinations, bar examinations, and similar special pressures enter the picture, the wife may fail to understand the husband's increased preoccupation, tension, irritability, and fatigue, and interpret his behavior as an indication of lack of interest in her.

Similarly, there are wives who have as great determination to complete their education as their husbands have. Yet some husbands fail to understand this. If the husband also depreciates the importance of a woman's education, thinking of it as something casual which she can readily give up without regret at the slightest whim, the stage is set for his misunderstanding the effect of academic pressures upon her.

A problem may arise when a husband spends a good deal of time studying with friends at night. He may do this because he finds it helpful. Yet the wife may fail to understand. On the other hand, the husband may rationalize as necessary spending time studying with friends when actually it provides a means of escape from his wife.

In cases in which the husband is a student and is employed and the wife is a student and/or is employed, their schedules involving times of arising and retiring, times of greatest busyness and preoccupation, leisure time may coincide so infrequently that they seldom talk together at length without a feeling of pressure or without distraction. Communication suffers. Sometimes even their sexual adjustment is affected.

In some cases, when husband and wife are both students, there is competition for grades. This is often intensified if they are both in the same course or class; at times it becomes especially acute when the wife receives higher grades than the husband. Some husbands accept the wife's higher grades with admiration for her. Others, however, find her success more than they can tolerate, and conflict ensues. In one case, such competition was brought to an unusually sharp focus when the husband took a given course the first semester and the wife took the same course with the same instructor the second semester. She deliberately set out to get a higher grade than her husband had gotten – and she did, a fact of which she kept her husband reminded, much to his annoyance. Of course, with the attitudes underlying this sort of behavior, there would no doubt be conflict no matter which spouse deliberately set out to get and then received higher grades.

Temporariness. Much that is included in the experience of the campus couple is temporary. For example, they struggle for an education, knowing that when they have completed it they will start again, perhaps "at the bottom." Young couples like to establish homes, to accumulate household goods, to improve or even to buy their place of residence. The campus couple often have substandard housing. They cannot afford to purchase many household items both because they do not have the money and because they know that they will have to pay for moving them later. They often take little interest in improving their place of residence because they know they will not live in it very long. Young couples like to begin building a circle of mutual friends. The campus couple know that any friends they make will in all probability be left behind, or will leave them behind, when education is completed. But as we shall see, this temporariness, though it may constitute a problem, may also suggest one approach to a solution of a problem.

MAKING CAMPUS MARRIAGE SUCCESSFUL

Assuming maturity, an adequate period of acquaintance, a wise choice of marriage partner, and similar items that play a part in the success of any type of marriage, the first step in making campus marriage successful is to recognize it for what it is. This implies that the couple understand that there is a discrepancy between the stereotype of young marriage and campus marriage. There is a difference between common expectations and actual reality. Campus marriage entails special stresses, special "pressure points."

The next step is to accept the fact that campus marriage involves such special "pressure points" and plan and act accordingly. This may be more easily said than done in some cases, but it is possible for a couple to do it, too. In doing it one of the most helpful factors is an understanding of the relative temporariness of many of the special problems involved. In appraising their marriage and each other, the couple may differentiate between the permanent and the temporary in their situation and by the same token decide which aspects of their marriage call for permanent decisions and which for tentative ones. If they can hold on until education is completed, then they may emerge into a more nearly conventional type of marriage in which roles are more nearly customary, traditional expectations are more nearly within reach, and their temporarily thwarted hopes may more readily be realized.

Marriage and military service

With "service marriage" as with campus marriage, generalizations are meaningless. Appraisal must be particularized. The question is not whether couples can marry successfully before or during the man's military service. The question is, "Can this couple, with their particular personalities, in their particular situation, marry successfully in the light of the man's military service?" Here again there are certain items that may be assumed as having a bearing on marital success, for example, maturity, an adequate period of acquaintance, a wise choice of marriage partner, careful planning, and facing reality. In addition, there are a number of other considerations, as follows.

Separation. Fear of separation leads some couples to marry sooner than they might otherwise have done. In the face of possible separation, it is not difficult to rationalize infatuation as being love and a brief period of acquaintance as being adequate for no other reason than that the couple have no more time together. They then marry because of the military service rather than in spite of it. This distinction is an important one. A couple who marry prematurely because of the service are not on so solid ground as the couple with long-time plans who have carefully weighed and assimilated the prospect of service and marry in spite of it.

Young couples sometimes fear that unless they are married they will lose each other during an extended separation. They might recognize at least two facts: first, marriage per se, without previously existing security in their relationship, will not guarantee that they will not lose each other; second, they might ask themselves, "If we do not have the requisites for surmounting the problem of separation without marriage, do we have what it takes to make marriage succeed under immediate circumstances, if at all?" In most cases a couple who lose each other because of circumstances ought to be happy that they discovered in time the limitations of their love.

Extended separation is difficult for a young marriage to weather. If enough time has elapsed after the wedding for the couple to establish their marriage, separation is one thing. If, on the other hand, they have only time for a honeymoon after the wedding, they may not have enough time to establish themselves in marriage sufficiently securely to withstand the pressure of separation. Separation removes the couple from the benefit derived from the support of the social pattern in the formative days of their marriage.

Young couples often assume that if they are married and the husband is in military service, they will naturally be allowed to live together, or at least to see each other often. In some cases, of course, such is true. In others it is not; and changes can be made without notice. There are some posts to which a man cannot take his wife and others to which he would not even if he could. The problems of either being separated or being together may be accentuated by the presence of a baby.

Being together. Even when the couple are permitted to live together, problems are not necessarily eradicated. There is sometimes only inadequate housing near military posts. In some cases housing is crowded and dwellings must be shared by more than one couple. Housing on a given post may be more nearly adequate but may still fall short of the couple's expectation.

When there is overcrowding around a military post, there is often inadequate recreation. There is much competition among wives for fewer jobs than there are women to fill them.

Branch and term of service. It is clear without explanation that there are differences among the various branches of the service as to the desirability of a man's being married and also the possibility of the couple's being able to work out satisfactory living arrangements and plans for being together. The anticipated term of service also makes a difference.

Rank. As a group, college students are accustomed to freedom of choice in their social contacts and in planning and participating in social activities. Some of them, especially girls, have difficulty in accepting the military rank system and the rigid lines of social demarcation emanating from it. Because of his training in ROTC, a student may enter military service as a commissioned officer. This differentiates him from the enlisted man. Nevertheless, both his relatively low rank and his income result in lines between himself and his wife and higher-ranking officers and their wives at a given post. The enlisted man and the noncommissioned officer are even more clearly on lower levels in the military caste system.

Finances. In the young service marriage finances are a common problem. Even when provision is made for the husband's maintenance, there is no similar provision for the wife's maintenance. Income, including pay plus allowances, tends to be low relative to current costs of living. Around some military installations, where the wives of younger personnel must live off the post and rents and other costs are high, the problem of finances may be particularly acute. The author has participated in special training programs involving about five hundred military chaplains. They report that one of the commonest family problems coming to their attention is that of money management.

Anticipation of excitement. Some girls assume that accompanying a husband while he is in service will lead to travel, excitement, and adventure. In some cases this is true. In many others, however, travel is limited to moving from one post to another in this country with something less than the zest and excitement of a vacation tour.

Civilian versus professional. It is not safe for a couple, the man of which is in the service temporarily, to generalize on cases of couples the men of which are in the service on a permanent professional basis. Be cause the latter type of couple can work out a satisfactory adjustment, knowing that they are in the service for a good part of their lives, does not necessarily mean that a young couple in the service for a brief period can do equally well with the same degree of acceptance.

Change. Some men go through a term of military service exhibiting no change. Others change for the better. Some change for the worse. Aside from changes that may be described as above, there is a possibility of change in attitude toward a given person. Young persons often change their attitudes toward one another while they are in the same college. Certainly some do so during periods of separation. It would be unrealistic to expect thousands of young men to go through an experience as different from civilian life as military service is and yet not have some of them change. Probability of change would depend in part on degree of maturity and length of acquaintance or duration of marriage at the time of entering the service.

Expectations for marriage.   The couple should not expect marriage to do for them what marriage is not equipped to do. The fact of marriage alone cannot create security in a relationship where insecurity existed before. It cannot sustain a couple during an extended separation. It cannot make lonely people less lonely. It is not a complete substitute for actual contact and companionship. Marriage may help in some cases, but it is not to be considered a prescription to counterbalance the effects of military service.

Planning.   Because of the assurance that a man's term of military service during relative peace is limited as to time and risk, a couple can have reasonable assurance that they can, if they will, project their plans for marriage beyond the period of service. This means that they can afford to plan carefully, whether they decide to marry before or during the term of service or decide to postpone marriage until after the completion of it. Upon the quality of such planning, and the degree of facing of reality which it includes, depends much of their probability of success.

WHAT DO YOU THINK?

1. Should parents be permitted to subsidize young marriages? Campus marriages? Should parents be *expected* to subsidize such marriages?

2. Some persons say that if college students want to marry, that is their privilege, but they should not expect special consideration from parents or college administrations. What is your reaction to such a point of view?

3. What suggestions would you make to a campus couple to help them handle more effectively the special "pressure points" in their marriage?

4. What are the arguments for and against campus marriage? Service marriage?

SELECTED READINGS

Bernard, Jessie, Helen E. Buchanan, and William M. Smith, Jr.: *Dating, Mating, and Marriage,* Howard Allen, Inc., Publishers, Cleveland, 1958, chap. 6. Campus marriages. Includes many case-documentary materials.

Cavan, Ruth Shonle (ed.): *Marriage and the Family in the Modern World,* Thomas Y. Crowell Company, New York, 1960, chap. 11. An appraisal of the married undergraduate; adjustment of married students; housing; "Why I am glad I didn't marry while in college."

Jerome, Sally, and Nancy Shea: *The Marine Corps Wife,* Harper & Row, Publishers, Incorporated, New York, 1955. What a wife needs to know to adjust to military life.

Koos, Earl Lomon: *Marriage,* rev. ed., Holt, Rinehart and Winston, Inc., New York, 1957, chap. 18. Marriage and military service; some of the problems.

Land, Elizabeth, and Carroll V. Glines: *The Complete Guide for the Serviceman's Wife,* Houghton Mifflin Company, Boston, 1956. What a wife needs to know about the military service.

Landis, Judson T., and Mary G. Landis: *Building a Successful Marriage,* 4th ed., Prentice-Hall, Inc., Englewood Cliffs, N.J., 1963, chap. 11. College marriage; marriage and military service.

Lantz, Herman R., and Eloise C. Snyder: *Marriage,* John Wiley & Sons, Inc., New York, 1962, chap. 15. Problems of campus marriage; role conflicts.

Pye, Anne Broscoe, and Nancy Shea: *The Navy Wife,* 3d ed., Harper & Row, Publishers, Incorporated, New York, 1955. What a wife needs to know to adjust to military life.

Shea, Nancy: *The Air Force Wife,* rev. ed., Harper & Row, Publishers, Incorporated, New York, 1956. What a wife needs to know to adjust to military life.

———: *The Army Wife,* 3d ed., Harper & Row, Publishers, Incorporated, New York, 1954. What a wife needs to know to adjust to military life.

chapter 13

SEX IN
MARRIAGE

SEX IS NATURAL. Were there no sex, there would be no marriage. Therefore, a sexual element is to be expected in marriage. It is this element that makes marriage different from other enduring human relationships. Sex is by no means the whole of marriage, but it is basically important. At times it is underemphasized; at other times it is overemphasized.

Sex and personality adjustment

Satisfactory adjustment sexually and in other ways (if they may be separated for purposes of discussion) go hand in hand, reacting one upon the other. Where there is failure, either may be cause or effect, depending upon circumstances. If the couple's adjustment in general is unsatisfactory, there may be a sexual element at the root of the difficulty. On the other hand, unsatisfactory sexual adjustment may be the result of nonsexual factors. Success in either increases the probability of success in the other, but neither guarantees the other. Often sexual maladjustment is blamed for marital failure when it may be only one among several causes or the result of the factors that are working together to make the marriage fail. Under such circumstances sex may become the hook on which the couple hang their marital wraps, so to speak.

Sexual adjustment and personality adjustment are aspects of a single process. There is not one problem of adjusting personalities in marriage and another separate one of sex. Sex in marriage is not a simple physical act, distinct in itself. It is one component of a complicated whole, ramifying through other elements, which in their turn ramify through it, a thread of changing hue inextricably woven into the warp and woof of life.

NATURE OF SEX

As has been said before, the physical aspects of sex are important, but sexual experience is more than physical. Sex in marriage contains emotional, ideal, other-than-physical elements which in a way are more important than the physical elements as such. In sexual union there is not only the contact of bodily organs but also the contact of personalities.

Just as it is incorrect to think of sex as only physical, it is also incorrect to think of it as only psychic or platonic. The physical element can be neither avoided nor denied. It is the matrix out of which the psychic elements grow and is simultaneously one of their most potent means of expression. There is no sound reason for assuming, as some do, that the "purpose" of sexual union in human beings is only or primarily reproduction. Reproduction is often a result of sexual intercourse and for many married couples it may be a motivation. But the sexual relationship between husband and wife may play so ample a role in producing satisfaction, happiness, and personality development and in enriching the couple's marital existence that it goes beyond procreation. It is creative as well as procreative.

In animals the function of the sexual act is reproduction. Animal mating is a transitory, fleeting experience, often limited to one or more brief periods during the year. In man sexual experience is not limited either to the act itself or to a specific time. It is part of an extension process of growth and new discovery. In its broadest sense it is one of the most fruitful sources for some of the deepest, richest satisfactions known. Assuming that sex is for reproduction alone is like assuming that, since we depend upon eyesight to move about and to make a living, seeing is for practical purposes only, and there should be created no beauty beyond the line, form, and color necessary for self-maintenance. It relegates man to the level of the lower animal and denies him the ability to take the raw materials of nature and out of them fashion a work of art.

We may think of the sexual urge as "instinctive," that is, as the product of inborn behavior patterns. We cannot, however, leave sexual adjustment in marriage to "instinct" because the biological urge is overlaid with tradition, habits, and attitudes all of which make it more complex than the mating instinct of lower animals and, at the same time, more subject to inhibition, repression, and perversion. Instead of the sexual act's being a simple, automatic, biological reaction for which no training is necessary and which training could not improve, in its most highly developed form in man it becomes a complex type of behavior which depends not only upon physical desire and its satisfaction but also upon ideas, ideals, the influence of custom, past experience, and the attitude of husband and wife toward each other. It is as different from the mating of lower animals as the building of a home is different from the construction of a nest, as the composition of a symphony is different from the automatic warbling of a bird.

An understanding attitude toward reactions

MUTUALITY

In Chapter 1 the conclusion was drawn that, owing partly to biology and partly to training, men and women are different but complementary. It may, therefore, be assumed that they both derive satisfaction from a complementary relationship. We cannot say that they derive identical satisfaction because their experiences are not comparable. This complementariness is most nearly complete in sexual union. Hence, in such union there are potentialities for deep satisfaction for both parties. The complementariness is not complete if the union is on a physical basis only. Its potentialities cannot be realized unless there are overtones of other less tangible but equally real qualities.

Stating that sexual union is the most nearly complete complementary relationship for a man and a woman and that it contains great possibilities for satisfaction for each is obviously equivalent to saying that sexual experience is not masculine only, as is sometimes assumed. It is a shared experience and a sharing process. It is mutual. Women have natural sexual desire, just as men do, although it may take a somewhat different form and be aroused by different stimuli. When a woman does not experience such desire, there are two probable explanations. (1) It has been trained out of her. It has been so overlaid with inhibitions that it cannot find expression. She has built up, or has had built up for her, a wall about herself so effectively corralling natural impulses that they have ceased to demand exercise. (2) There has been nothing in her experience up to date to arouse her desire. She is, as we say, "unawakened." Some women remain so until their experiences with loving husbands bring to the fore an urge that they were not aware could exist. There are women who have a sexual urge but do not recognize it as such. Some refuse to admit what they feel. But there are relatively few women who for some basic, underlying, physiological cause are completely devoid of sexual interest. Unfortunately our cultural tradition has all too frequently taught that women should be neuter, that sex is not "ladylike," and that sexual union is a masculine prerogative for masculine satisfaction to which a woman is bound to submit. There could be nothing further from the truth.

This is not equivalent to saying that all women have an equally ardent interest in sexual experience or an equal responsiveness to sexual stimuli. The sexual urge, like all things natural, falls on the normal curve of variability. Some women, like some men, are more passionate; some are less so. There is the possibility for all gradations from greatest to least. At best, it is difficult to say that a woman who seems sexually cold is therefore unable to respond, even though we think in terms of inhibitions rather than physiology. All that may safely be said is that under a given set of circumstances she does not exhibit interest and seems unresponsive. Under other circumstances she might be different. Furthermore, sexual unresponsiveness is almost always the result of multiple causation. There is no one thing, no one condition, that will invariably produce it.

Let us go back for a moment to a point mentioned above. Young women are sometimes worried about their sexual adequacy. In their reading or in discussions they have learned that women experience a sexual urge, just as men do. These girls have never experienced anything that they identified as sexual desire. Often they are not averse to a controlled amount of affection and fondling on the part of boys, and they like to date. They have come to feel that they are "undersexed" or that they will be unable to respond to a husband in the way they vaguely realize that women can.

A girl of nineteen, for example, lets boys kiss her occasionally but has no inclination to be more intimate. She likes to date and associate with boys but prefers to go out with many different ones rather than to limit herself to one. Her girl friends have told her how boys arouse them. Both boys and girls tell her she is undersexed. She has heard that a woman may experience sexual desire, but she herself has never been conscious of any such urge. As a result, she has worried about her condition until she has almost reached the conclusion that she is abnormal and unfit for marriage. Her attitude toward sex is somewhat naïve, perhaps, but on the whole it is healthy and there do not seem to be any special fears, inhibitions, or aversions. Nevertheless, she cannot imagine herself as ever being intimate, even with a husband whom she might love. Her failure so to picture herself is due to her inability to anticipate anything that is entirely foreign to her experience and for which she has no conscious desire.

There is nothing the matter with such a girl. She is neither abnormal nor undersexed. She is unawakened. Up to date, there has been nothing in her experience to cause her to react in a way that she can identify as sexual or to feel a desire of a specifically sexual nature. She finds pleasure in being with boys and in having them kiss her. This is a broad, generalized type of sexual experience, but she does not think of it as such. There are many girls like her. They are just as normal as the girls who have more readily identifiable sexual desire or response. They need not worry about their condition. The probability is that after they fall in love and marry they will eventually find themselves as responsive as any, allowing, of course, for individual variations. When they marry, however, such girls should not insist upon maintaining their former attitude. They should permit themselves to move on to new experiences. In one case a girl who had been unawakened before marriage found herself very responsive with her husband. Yet for two years after the wedding she cried each time intercourse occurred because early in life she had been taught that only "bad" women were passionate, and she continued to have feelings of guilt.

To say that the unawakened girl will probably be responsive in marriage is not the same as saying that the girl with strong inhibitions and feelings of repugnance, to whom sex is something to be repressed or suppressed, and who is conscious of reacting against it, will become equally responsive. Such a girl may try to rethink the whole subject, may examine her past to learn if possible why she feels as she does, and may talk the matter over with some informed and understanding counselor who may help her reach a new attitude. She may change her attitude, too, when she begins to think of sex specifically in terms of a relationship with a husband whom she loves, rather than thinking of it in a more or less general and abstract way.

Girls exhibit interest in boys and curiosity about sex just as boys show interest in girls and are curious about anatomical differences and reproduction. Sex seems natural to a child until distortions of the educative process make it appear otherwise. It is a strange side light upon our culture that some natural processes are accepted as they are with no implication of good or bad, while others equally natural are highly colored with moral or aesthetic condemnation.

Attempting to shut sex out of one's life does not raise one to a higher plane of existence, as some people suppose. It only relegates one to a more incomplete and more arid existence. In the last analysis, sex cannot be shut out. Whether it finds natural expression or not, no matter where it is put, from one extreme of manifestation to the other, it will play a part in affecting the individual's life and must be taken into account. If it is repressed or avoided, it is still not without its effect. One may as well try to rule out metabolism.

WOMAN'S REACTION

Generalizing, even though a woman is not inhibited and has not attempted to shut sex out of her life, the arousing of her natural desire is less spontaneous than is the case with a man and depends to great extent upon her husband, his expression of affection, his own desire, and his insight, understanding, and skill as her lover. A man may be compared to starting a fire with dry tinder and dry wood. The materials may be carelessly thrown together, and one match is enough to make them leap into flame. Arousing a woman may be compared to starting a fire in the rain. The materials have to be put together carefully. The match has to be shielded after it is struck. The new little flame must be protected, perhaps even fanned, until the heat generated is sufficient to overcome the dampness. Only then will it burn untended, and even then it may easily be extinguished. This is not true of all women. As we have said, there are variations among them as to the strength of their impulses. This is more likely to be true early in a marriage than later and is certainly true in the case of the unawakened girl discussed above. Before marriage, a man may be more conscious of sexual desire, and his interest tends to be more specific. Later, if the couple's adjustment is successful, the wife may be as clearly aware of her urges as the husband is of his. In some cases the wife is more passionate than the husband and desires more frequent intercourse than he does.

Until they have had satisfactory sexual experience, women as a rule do not have a problem of control comparable to men's. Hence, they have a somewhat different situation to cope with before marriage.

Because sex is feminine as well as masculine, women as well as men can reach a climax of satisfaction in sexual union. In man there is a dual reaction, namely, orgasm, which is a neuromuscular response, and ejaculation, which is the discharge of seminal fluid containing the sperm cells. Actually the two reactions typically occur so nearly simultaneously that they are thought of as one. In women there is nothing equivalent to ejaculation. There are lubricating secretions, but they do not involve special sensations, as does ejaculation. Women can, however, achieve orgasm. This has no relationship to the production of egg cells, which are secreted at the rate of, roughly, one per month, irrespective of sexual intercourse. Nor is there any established relationship between orgasm and conception, as is frequently assumed. In women, the orgasm is sometimes referred to as a "nervous explosion" during which accumulated tension is released, and there are muscular contractions and relaxations and sensations of touch. This all proves very pleasurable and satisfying both physically and emotionally. To describe what a man or woman actually feels under such circumstances to a person who has had no similar experience is impossible. The important thing is that the reader realize that orgasm in women can occur, not that a detailed analysis of it be given.

The intensity of this reaction in sexual union varies from individual to individual, and there may be a difference between husband and wife. It is not necessary that all persons react equally intensely. As long as the experience is agreeable to both husband and wife and both find satisfaction, relaxation, and happiness in it, it may be considered relatively adequate.

Some women never achieve full sexual satisfaction. This does not prove that they are unhappy in their marriages. Nor does it indicate an absence of love. A husband and wife may love each other, but their sex adjustment may be incomplete. Nor does absence of orgasm or infrequent orgasm indicate that a wife does not enjoy sexual intercourse with her husband. Research reveals that a considerable proportion of wives report that they enjoy intercourse yet seldom or never reach orgasm [Wallin and Clark, 1963].

Some women never achieve any satisfaction in their sexual life. Such women not only miss the pleasure and happiness that their relationship with their husbands might produce but often must endure what to them is uninteresting or repugnant. They may be psychologically virgin, though not so anatomically. They tolerate sex; they do not really experience it. Others become physically and emotionally aroused but fail to reach orgasm. Instead of their finding pleasure and release, their experience ends only in nervous tension, restlessness, disappointment, or irritation.

No woman should leap to the conclusion that occasional failure will be dangerous. Either type of woman—the one who is indifferent, inhibited, repressed, unresponsive, or the one who is responsive but whose experience tends habitually to be incomplete, unsatisfying, and productive of tension rather than relief of tension—may usually be assisted in making a more adequate adjustment if she, and perhaps her husband, will consult a marriage counselor. Although a woman of the first type may have no interest in improving her own adjustment, she should for the sake of her husband at least make the effort. If sexual union is the most completely complementary experience possible for a husband and wife, it is obvious that it cannot be full and rich if the wife's participation is fragmentary.

RIGHTS AND DUTIES

Sexual intercourse is sometimes considered a masculine right and feminine duty. This attitude was more common in the past, but it has not yet disappeared. It is still reflected in the laws of some states, where a man may demand that his wife submit to his advances and may divorce her if she refuses. This duty-right attitude is cold, one-sided, unromantic, uninteresting, and unchallenging as compared with the attitude that sex is a mutual experience, entailing mutual satisfaction and the expression of affection, trust, and desire by both parties rather than the imposition of rights and the unwilling performance of duty.

In a sense, a right is established at the wedding, but only in the sociological and legal sense. It is better to think of the situation as presenting opportunities for both persons rather than to think of it as a trap for the woman or a bargain by which she agrees to submit to masculine demands in return for which she gains status and security. Any man who enters marriage with the intention of demanding his rights shows plainly the shallowness of his attitude toward his wife. He is more than old-fashioned; he is medieval.

SUCCESS AND FAILURE

As already explained, the achievement of the deepest, most lasting satisfaction in sexual union is not "natural" in the sense of being "instinctive." It is an art. An art requires time, patience, thoughtfulness, perseverance, and understanding for its fullest development. Interest and urge are "instinctive," but human beings have worked out means of expression that are more than automatic and that transcend the "natural." Sex has been raised to the plane of creative achievement.

Since this is true, a couple should not be discouraged if success is limited or absent at first. Few couples reach the greatest possible success immediately or in the early days of marriage. The sexual relationship of husband and wife is not merely a series of isolated, unrelated incidents. It is a growing relationship which becomes deeper and richer as time goes on. There is no reason to assume that the achievement of the first success is the end and goal and that there is nothing to look forward to or to strive for. As they grow older, the couple grow closer to each other in this as well as in other ways.

They need not be disappointed if they never reach perfection in their sexual life. Human beings never reach perfection in anything; at best, they merely approach it. They may strive for it but never actually expect to attain it. If the couple are successful a good proportion of the time, that is about all that one can expect. If in rare instances a couple approach more closely to the perfect ideal, so much the better. Most couples, even though very happily married, will fall short. This is not the equivalent of being content with mediocrity, but there is a real danger in setting an impossible, unattainable goal.

Even in those cases in which a couple's sexual experience does grow richer, the zest and tumultuousness of the early years of marriage may gradually change from pounding breakers to the more deeply flowing currents of later married life. No loss accrues in such a transition; there is only change. There may be gain. If, for example, as time passes a couple find that sexual intercourse becomes less frequent, that does not necessarily indicate that there is less interest or that their relationship is not successful. It implies only that after the first dash from the starting line they are finding their stride and that sexual intercourse in the more specific sense is becoming part of a greatly broadened mutual experience.

In developing a new skill or new art, the novice makes many errors. In learning to walk, skate, play tennis, swim, drive a golf ball, or bid a bridge hand we perpetrate so many mistakes that after mastering the necessary technique we look back in embarrassed retrospect on the immensity of our previous ignorance and the incredibility of our original awkwardness. We do not let our mistakes defeat us; nor do we stop with them. We overcome them. We correct them. A newly married couple are novices confronted with the problem of learning a new art and acquiring a new skill. They are almost certain to make mistakes at first. They may feel that their ignorance is stupendous and their clumsiness colossal. They need not leap to conclusions and defeat themselves. They may learn by their mistakes. With patience, understanding, intelligence, self-analysis, an ample amount of love, and a liberal sprinkling of a sense of humor, errors may be corrected. To give up in defeat because sexual adjustment is not complete at the very beginning and because in their mutual experience there are mistakes is just as unnecessary and foolish as it would be to lie prone for the rest of one's life because one fell down the first time he tried to walk. Each successful sexual union plays a part in conditioning both husband and wife so that success in the future becomes easier. Hence, care, patience, intelligence, perspective, and a will to succeed pay large dividends in terms of long-time happiness.

In almost all cases in which there are difficulties that prevent adequate sexual adjustment, those difficulties are matters of attitude and habit rather than of anatomy. There are relatively few cases of structural defects that prevent sexual harmony, and most of these may be discovered in a premarital medical examination and remedied by medical treatment. A couple who have unusual handicaps or hindrances should not conclude that these are irremediable until every resource, including professional counseling, has been drawn upon.

The great majority of couples have no difficulties at all, except perhaps the normal readjustments involved in making any transition such as that from single life to the new experiences of marriage. These require only time, patience, and intelligence. We do not mean to imply that a couple should direct their attention toward nothing but possible difficulties. Quite the opposite is true. They should think of the joys of their experience together and the building of a successful relationship. Nevertheless, if there are difficulties, these should be faced frankly and objectively.

In working out a satisfactory sexual adjustment, husband and wife may help each other considerably. Each may help the other understand reactions and attitudes. The wife may explain to the husband what pleases and what displeases her. Reticence or secrecy based upon false modesty, conceit, or ignorance is one of the most effective obstacles to success.

WHAT A WIFE SHOULD UNDERSTAND

When she enters upon marriage and begins a new phase of her emotional life, there are several things that a woman ought to understand. First of all, she should realize that hers is not the only problem. Her husband has one, too. It is that of helping her to the best start and making her experience as rich as possible. In a sense he has her and her problem. She should help him as much as she can. She must also realize that she has married a man, not a neuter organism. He is a masculine being with strong masculine impulses. He has good intentions, but he may have little finesse and may possibly lack complete understanding of her, her reactions, or the sexual relationship. Whatever generalizations he has gathered from books, discussions, friends, or counselors must be applied and adapted to specific individual circumstances. He must observe his wife's reactions and contemplate her attitudes. He could not possibly have read about her in a book. She must, therefore, give him time to learn. She cannot expect too much at first. Together they may work out an adjustment. One beauty of the experience is that it is worked out together and that it cannot be taken cut and dried from a textbook. What they finally evolve is, therefore, uniquely their own. Some men know more than others, but the wife should at least give her husband the benefit of the doubt. It is not at all unknown for what would otherwise have developed into a satisfactory adjustment to be nipped in the bud because the wife was too ready to draw unwarranted conclusions.

The wife should also be aware of the fact that some men have a tendency to become angry, irritated, or impulsive when their desires have been aroused only to be thwarted, especially if the frustration is the result of what seems to the man to be an arbitrary and unreasonable denial on the part of the wife. We are not suggesting that the wife should always be submissive, but only that she should be prepared to understand.

A wife needs to understand, too, that, though a man's sexual experience may appear to be largely of a physical nature, it also includes a considerable degree of ego involvement. A man derives some pleasure from sexual intercourse whether or not his wife is responsive. But his experience is intensified if she responds because he knows he has contributed to her pleasure. If, over a long period, she is unresponsive and he grows to feel that he is imposing himself on his wife, especially if she lets him know that she feels it is an imposition, he may eventually come to avoid intercourse or even become impotent and be unable to perform the sexual act. Assuming that a husband has any sensitivity at all, he wants to feel enthusiastically accepted by his wife both as a man and as her sexual partner. If she rejects him as the latter, she can defeat him.

A situation that gives rise to fear is not necessarily inherently fearful. An experience that produces a feeling of aversion is not always inherently repugnant. For example, one person attempts to ride horseback, is thrown, picks himself up, tries again, and eventually learns both to enjoy it and to do it well. Another person tries to ride, is thrown, and thereafter is afraid not only of riding but also of being near horses. Two individuals are reared on a farm and later go to live in a large city. One yearns to be back in the country, finally buys a farm, and commutes. The other so thoroughly dislikes the country that he refuses to go there even for a vacation. One girl, aged ten, is frightened by a man's approaches and for the remainder of her life is fearful of sex and afraid of men. Another girl, victim of the same sort of situation, has a healthy, optimistic attitude toward sex, falls in love enthusiastically, and has a happy marriage. If a wife who has inhibitions and fears associated with sex can come to see that it was not sex alone but rather her reaction to some situation involving sex that made her as she is, she may more readily change her attitude toward her relationship with her husband. It will also help if she can understand that her husband does not represent the situation that gave rise to her attitudes. Rather he represents a new situation the elements of which are referred to in the same terminology but with new meaning. If a wife's attitudes prevent her from finding sexual experience satisfactory or, in other cases, prevent her from being glad that she does find it satisfactory, she should direct her resentment toward her own attitudes or their source rather than toward her husband.

Occasionally it happens that, because of what she has read or heard or because of her own interest and impulses, the wife expects to have her first sexual experience almost immediately after the wedding, only to find that her husband seems to lack interest. She may be not only interested but eager to consummate their relationship, to enter a new adventure together, and to express her love for her husband. His attitude disappoints her, hurts her pride, and worries her, for she wonders why he feels as he does. Fortunately, there are few cases of this sort. It is more common for the man to be more interested than the woman. If, however, a bride does find herself in such a predicament, she should not leap to conclusions before she has ascertained the real cause.

There are a number of possible explanations for the husband's apparent attitude. He may actually lack interest, or his natural sexual desire may be weak or lacking. Such men are rare, however. The husband may fear sex or consider it disgusting, unclean, or sinful. Such men, too, are rare, much rarer than women who have similar attitudes. He may think that sexual intercourse is for reproduction only and try to avoid it because he does not feel ready to assume the responsibility of a family. Any of these first three attitudes an observant girl could probably detect before marriage. He may be afraid of his own ability to measure up to what is expected of him as a husband. He wants their relationship to be as nearly perfect as possible, and he underestimates his own adequacy. Such a man needs encouragement and trust. Criticism or hysterics will not help him. Because of the strain of a large wedding and its accompaniments, he may be fatigued. He may be shy, nervous, or embarrassed. He may be showing consideration for his wife. He knows she is tired. He feels that it is better that they become accustomed to being together at first and that their new relationship be approached gradually. This is always a possibility. The safest assumption for the wife to make is that this represents her husband's attitude unless and until she has reason to believe otherwise. Although it usually does, there is no good reason for assuming that a couple's first sexual union must occur on their wedding night, just because that is traditional. There may be sound reasons for postponing it. The tradition developed in a period when sexual intercourse was considered a masculine prerogative to which a passive and disinterested wife was forced by custom to submit.

WHAT A HUSBAND SHOULD UNDERSTAND

Just as there are various things that the wife should realize, so there are several of which the husband should become aware. He must understand that he has married a woman, a feminine being who will react as a woman and not as a man. Probably she has had no experience. In some cases she scarcely knows what to expect in marriage. She may be ignorant of some of the most elementary and fundamental facts. There are educated girls who are ignorant of masculine anatomy and do not fully understand the anatomy and functions of their own bodily organs. Many girls do not know how men react. Many are unaware that sex is a feminine as well as a masculine experience and that women as well as men may derive satisfaction from it. If the wife has gathered any general knowledge from reading or discussion, she, too, must apply this to the individual situation. She may have good intentions and be anxious to do the right thing and to please her husband, but she may not understand fully what is involved. She too must be given time to learn.

If the wife is a woman who before marriage was conscious of no desire that she indentified as sexual, that desire will not be created by the wedding. Some men act as if the ceremony were all that is necessary to transmute an unawakened girl into a passionate wife. They fail to understand that this transformation depends upon the husband, not upon the ceremony.

A husband should realize further that his wife is more inclined than he to have inhibitions and fears centering around sex and its expression. Sometimes her fear is vague. At other times it is more specific, and sexual intercourse recalls a fear situation that occurred early in her life, in the recalling of which she again experiences emotions similar to those that she felt at the time.

It is easy for a woman to let her attitude toward sexual union be influenced by her attitude toward menstruation. If she has painful periods, she may let this fact color her attitude toward sex in general. After puberty a girl is more likely to associate her genital organs with pain and with a process of which she is half ashamed and that she seeks to conceal, while a boy is more inclined to associate his with pleasurable sensation. Menstruation and sexual union, though somewhat related anatomically, are two distinct processes.

A girl may, as we have already suggested, fear pregnancy or child-birth and let this color her attitude toward sexual relations. Such a fear may be ameliorated by securing advice on the control of conception from an informed physician and following that advice carefully, intelligently, and cooperatively. Dependence upon hearsay, advice of friends, advertisements, or incomplete knowledge is definitely to be avoided. Reliable control of conception may not remove a wife's fear of child-birth because that fear probably has its roots deep in her past. But it will remove the necessity for letting the fear affect the couple's relationship, and the woman may so consider it. She may believe that sex is for reproduction only and wish to avoid it unless she feels ready to have a baby. She may fear the pain of her first sexual intercourse. Girls frequently hear greatly exaggerated accounts of the pain that a bride suffers on her wedding night, or they listen to old wives' tales of one sort or another. As a result, they come to develop an entirely unnecessary and ill-founded fear. We shall consider the matter of pain later.

In order to make this discussion of inhibitions and fears more concrete, let us cite a few cases of college girls in whom one or more of these attitudes may be found. The first is a girl of nineteen. Her parents are separated and, though she sees her father occasionally, she feels that she does not really know him. Her home life is not too pleasant. Her mother is very conservative and has never told the daughter anything about sex. Recently, a sister married several months after becoming pregnant. The mother's attitude toward marriage is unhealthy, and she has talked against it to the daughter. The girl has a genitourinary disease of long standing that has necessitated frequent painful treatment. She has concluded that if sexual union involves any pain similar to that which she suffers in these treatments, she wants to avoid it. For a long time she thought little of sex, but now she has fallen in love and wants to make her marriage successful. She is aware of the importance of sex in marriage and does not want to marry until her point of view has changed; for, because of the above influences, she has developed an attitude that is a mixture of indifference and disgust. She cannot understand why or how a couple could bring themselves to have intercourse. At the same time, she is not averse to having her fiancé show affection for her.

Another girl comes for a conference because she is worried about something that she heard in a discussion with other students. Her parents are very strict, and her mother has taught her that all men are bestial. In the discussion she discovered that several girls have a similar opinion and so fear marriage. She herself is afraid. All her life she has wished that she were a boy and regretted that her freedom was restricted. She likes to date and says that she hopes some day to marry. At the same time, she says she does not like men. Menstruation is very painful for her. She has such a dread of the pain of childbirth that she herself is aware of the need for changing her attitude. She has gathered considerable misinformation about the pain of first sexual union and wonders whether a girl can be happy in marriage if she takes no interest in sex.

A girl of eighteen feels that she is in love with a boy who seems to fit her ideal. She says that as far back as she can remember she has had a fear of sex. Until she was about seventeen she had no clear idea as to what sexual intercourse is. At that time she acquired some incomplete information from a girl of her own age. Previously, she had known that babies sometimes resulted from sexual union, but she did not know why or how. She was fairly sure that kissing would not produce pregnancy but had a vague idea about a girl's becoming pregnant if a boy came too close to her. She has never felt any specific sexual desire and cannot imagine having sexual intercourse with a husband. She feels that sex is for reproduction only, and she is, therefore, opposed to the use of contraceptives. She has heard something about the pain of first intercourse but does not understand any reason for it. She has developed a fear of sex in marriage because she does not know what to expect and because she has heard exaggerated tales.

Attitudes such as these may make marital adjustment difficult, especially if in the early days of marriage something occurs that the girl does not understand and that seems to bring her fears to a focus. But attitudes are acquired, and they may be changed. Back of each one there is an underlying cause, some experience or educative process out of which the attitude grew. Discovering the underlying factors and looking at them from the vantage point of greater maturity and fuller information usually leads to dispelling what otherwise might become a cloud hanging over a marriage. This is especially true if the girl herself realizes the need for change and takes the initiative in talking with someone who can help her.

If the girl marries before change occurs, the husband is presented with a real challenge to all the patience and understanding of which he is capable. If he handles the situation correctly, he may play an important role in assisting the wife to change her point of view and to move to a less inhibited, less fear-ridden level of existence. If, however, he bungles his opportunity, he may set deeper the fears that impede their adjustment.

In addition to the attitudes mentioned above, many women, and some men, have inhibitions in connection with the exposure of their own bodies or feel embarrassed at witnessing that of others. Some girls, about to be married, express more uneasiness at the prospect of seeing the husband unclothed than at the prospect of being seen unclothed themselves. These inhibitions, too, are the result of conditioning, of training, and the latter is highly colored both by girls' need for self-protection and by convention. Convention still prohibits complete exposure of the body under many conditions. But marriage alters circumstances. What is prohibited among the unmarried is not only acceptable but expected between husband and wife. There is no conventional restriction on their bodily exposure. If one or the other carries into the marriage relationship inhibitions having their origin in the premarital standard, that person is doing something fundamentally not different from insisting upon swimming fully clothed because a bathing suit is not appropriate apparel for a shopping trip or a formal reception.

If a husband understands that his bride may be more concerned over the bodily exposure of both persons than he can appreciate, he will approach such exposure with tact, patience, and consideration. If a bride understands not only that her husband is likely to take bodily exposure for granted but also that he is "visual-minded" and that his is not the wanton gaze of "men" but rather the observation of the man whose love for her and idealization of her make her attractive in his sight, the man into whose care she placed her happiness at the time of the wedding, she may anticipate bodily exposure with more insight and less apprehension.

Some problems in adjustment

FEAR OF PAIN

A couple's first sexual union sometimes involves slight pain for the wife. The pain may be accompanied by slight bleeding. This is due partly to the fact that the opening of her genital tract, or more specifically the external aperture of the vagina, is partially closed by a membrane called the *hymen.* If the lining of the vagina is dry because of a paucity of lubricating secretions which accompany responsiveness, this fact may contribute to the wife's discomfort. During the first act of intercourse the hymen is stretched and, in infrequent cases, torn slightly so that a few drops of blood escape. Girls often hear exaggerated accounts of this process or those based upon rare instances in which a husband is brutal or based upon the experiences of an exceptional woman whose attitudes or anatomy made sexual union inordinately difficult. There is also a residue of an attitude toward first sexual intercourse that originated in an earlier period in history when sex was considered a masculine prerogative and a feminine duty, when there was no idea of mutuality, when it was not unknown for a man to be unnecessarily rough and hasty in order to "prove" that his wife was virgin. As a result, some girls come to fear their first sexual intercourse.

It cannot be emphasized too strongly or too often that such a fear is absolutely unfounded and unnecessary. Granting that the husband is something better than a savage, the pain, if there is any at all, will be very slight and of very brief duration. In many cases there is no pain whatever. If there is any, the woman should realize that it is the pain of transition, of growth, of moving from one stage of existence to a more mature one. It is natural pain. It might be compared with the pain of cutting teeth—not that it feels like teething, but there are similarities as to naturalness and significance. No one would deliberately enter adult life with his milk teeth or with no teeth at all because the cutting of permanent ones is a painful process (usually more painful than the stretching of the hymen). Neither should a woman allow herself to become conditioned against sexual experience or let her first experience precipitate fears and inhibitions just because there may be slight and temporary discomfort. The bleeding, if there is any at all, will be insignificant. It may be compared to "pink toothbrush," so alarmingly presented in advertisements. "Pink toothbrush" may be an indication of pyorrhea. It is much more likely to be the result of inconsequential puncture of the gums by a bristle of a stiff toothbrush, something that most people experience at one time or another.

The process of stretching the hymen is similar, in some ways, to that of putting on new kid gloves. If the gloves are carefully worked onto the fingers the first few times they are worn, they gradually stretch until they accommodate themselves to the wearer's hand. The same gloves forced on hastily and roughly will tear instead of stretching.

In rare instances a wife's fear reacts upon the muscles of her genital organs, causing them to contract so vigorously that the very pain she is afraid of is increased. She then finds herself in a vicious circle: the more she fears the experience, the greater is the pain; and the greater the pain, the more she fears it. If she can be brought to accept the experience without resistance, the cause of discomfort will be removed. In instances still more rare some anatomical defect prevents intercourse. In either case, or we might say in any case in which there seems to be unusual difficulty, in which the pain is experienced more than once or twice or in which the bleeding persists, a physician should be consulted at once. Practically all such difficulties can be remedied. Even in these unusual and extreme instances there is no cause for alarm. Above all, the wife should not let the temporary inconvenience color her attitude toward the whole future of her marriage. She should be careful here, as in regard to menstrual pain, not to confuse normal elements with abnormal ones.

There is considerable variation among women as to the extent, toughness, and elasticity of the hymen. Typically there is an opening in it large enough for the menstrual discharge but not large enough, without stretching, for sexual intercourse. In some girls the hymen is so slight as to be almost nonexistent. In others it is heavy and inelastic, and the aperture is small. In some cases there are two or more small, sometimes almost microscopic, openings. In rare instances, the hymen has no opening and completely closes the entrance to the vagina so that there can be no menstrual discharge, though menstruation does occur. The hymen has been known to return to a seemingly virginal state after having been stretched in sexual intercourse. In many cases the hymen is stretched by accident, by sports activities, by the use of the tampon type of menstrual protection, during a medical examination, or manually at a physician's suggestion. Consequently, the condition of the hymen is no certain, never-failing indication of the virginity or nonvirginity of a woman presumably virgin at the time of marriage. A husband who hastily concludes that his bride has had previous intercourse because she has neither pain nor bleeding as a result of their first sexual intercourse betrays his ignorance of anatomical variations and reflects an outmoded attitude. So does a responsive girl who fears, or the husband of such a girl who concludes, that if she exhibits responsiveness the first time they have intercourse, it will seem to indicate that she has had previous sexual experience and is not virgin.

PREMARITAL MEDICAL EXAMINATION

Partly because of the possibility of slight discomfort experienced by some women in their first sexual intercourse and partly because of the relatively remote possibility of there being some unusual anatomical condition, some girls prefer to have the hymen stretched by a physician before marriage. An examination of this membrane and the physician's recommendation as to what should be done about it may be made part of the premarital medical examination, part of which is a pelvic, including a vaginal, examination. We may go further and say that this is one of the purposes of that examination. If the physician concludes that it is advisable, the membrane may be stretched mechanically or manually or, in some cases, cut. The pain associated with the latter process is so slight that only a local anesthetic is necessary. If this is done, the entire process becomes associated with the impersonal atmosphere of the physician's office rather than with the husband and the honeymoon. Some women prefer this; others do not. If it is done by a physician, however, the fiancé should be informed so that there can be no possibility of his concluding that his bride is not virgin.

Since the chief function of the premarital medical examination is preparative rather than prohibitive, it is recommended that both man and woman have the examination. They may go to the same physician at different times or to different physicians. In either case, they should choose one who understands the problems of normal marriage. He should be aware of the newer developments in this field of medicine and be interested in this type of problem. He should also be willing to take time to talk with the couple and answer their questions. If the couple go to different physicians, they might do well to visit specialists, the man going to a urologist, the woman to a gynecologist or obstetrician. This will be a bit more expensive, but it may be worth the extra investment. A girl who contemplates such an examination with embarrassment should realize that to the doctor she is a patient, not a woman. His attitude is strictly impersonal. It is unlikely that she will present him with anything new or anything he has not observed many times before. She may also simplify her problem by choosing a woman physician.

Several hundred years ago, when the practice of midwifery in Europe was taken over by men, these first obstetricians were known as "male midwives." At that time there was so high a premium upon feminine modesty, especially in the upper class, that women insisted that during delivery they be completely draped in sheets and the obstetrician deliver the baby only by his sense of touch without ever seeing any part of the woman's genital anatomy [Findley, 1933]. Nowadays a woman who insisted upon such a procedure during delivery would not be able to find an obstetrician to accede to her wishes, and she would be considered eccentric, to say the least. It is taken for granted that an obstetrician will examine a woman's anatomy both before and during delivery. There is need for similar acceptance and objectivity relative to the premarital pelvic examination. Unfortunately, however, there are some women whose attitude still reflects the false modesty of the distant past — to their own detriment.

Even if a girl does find it difficult to have a premarital pelvic examination, she may well ask herself this question: "Which is better, to have such an examination in spite of hesitation and embarrassment, or possibly, at the time of first intercourse, to confront an anatomical problem which neither she nor her husband is equipped to solve?"

The examination should occur far enough in advance of the wedding to make it possible to carry out the physician's recommendations without excessive haste, to read what he suggests, and to return to him for further discussion. If they choose their physician carefully, a couple may feel free to ask him about anything that they do not understand in connection with sexual adjustment and reproduction. There will probably be a number of points growing out of the examination or their reading that will not be fully clear or on which they desire further information. No matter what they may have read or gathered from other sources, it is often advisable for them to talk through with the physician the matter of sexual adjustment. They should not consider the matter closed until they have had answered all the questions that they feel the need for asking. In most cases one of these will pertain to control of conception, and on this the physician may make recommendations. Such discussion may also facilitate their own communication relative to sex later.

THE HUSBAND'S RESPONSIBILITY

Premarital examination and even stretching of the hymen by the physician do not relieve the husband of his responsibility in initiating his wife into the new realm of sexual experience or the woman of the responsibility for cooperation and the development of an enlightened attitude. If the husband considers her initiation as a chore to be hurried through in order more quickly to make possible the unimpeded satisfaction of his own desires, he not only shows his ignorance of marriage, sex, and feminine reactions but also exhibits toward his wife an attitude of exploitation that is inconsistent with mutuality and sharing. By the exercise of gentleness and patience, by the sacrifice of his own immediate pleasure if necessary, the husband may carefully lay a foundation for a happy, satisfactory relationship for the future. If he is blinded by the surging impulses of the moment, he may for temporary gain pay the price of lifelong failure and incompleteness. Roughness, haste, selfishness, and thoughtlessness in the early days of sexual adjustment may produce a severe psychological trauma, leaving permanent scars upon a marriage and an unbridgeable gulf in the husband-wife relationship. With their attitude toward sex and their ignorance of a woman's reactions and of what successful adjustment in marriage requires, some men are in the position of a person who is employed for a job but fails to inquire what the job involves. With pick and shovel on his shoulder, he reports for work, thinking of the contractive power of his biceps, only to find that he is to do watchmaking and that the requirements are patience, finesse, delicacy of operation, and lightness of touch. Other men are like an individual who is presented with a fine violin. He assumes that the only matter to be considered is the fact of possession and that possessing the instrument is all that is necessary to prepare him to play it. Hence, whatever he does to it ought to produce music as long as he enjoys doing it. Fortunately, not all men—not even most—are like this. It is mentioned not to frighten the woman reader but only to make the man reader sharply aware of his role and responsibility.

There is no reason for a young husband to hurry to demonstrate his potency. No doubt his wife will eventually appreciate masculine vigor, but she expects it to be mingled with a generous admixture of love, understanding, and consideration. Neither *masculinity* nor *virility* implies riding roughshod over a finely balanced and delicate relationship.

In the last analysis, a man has no reason to take pride in his virility. That is a gift of nature, which he has had no part in creating. He may, however, take pride in his ability to give his wife satisfaction and happiness in the broadest sense. That is an achievement of which he may well be proud because it is an art of his own making.

As the demonstration of masculine virility is nothing for a husband to be proud of, so unnatural reserve and false modesty are nothing to which a wife may turn as a source of pride. It is no more womanly to be inhibited and emotionally undeveloped than it is manly to be bestial and inconsiderate. The best adjustment for either person is a balance between intelligent restraint and the unhampered expression of natural desires, from which the artificially imposed unnatural impediments have been removed.

FEAR OF MARRIAGE

Unmarried girls sometimes worry about marriage, especially the sexual aspects of it, because they wonder what happens immediately after the wedding when the couple are for the first time alone as husband and wife. Only a few years ago the reader, if a college girl, would have been extremely embarrassed if a boy had kissed her. At that earlier date she could not have imagined that there would ever be a time when she would be happier in the companionship of a particular man than with anyone else, and that she would place him before even her own parents in her affection. Now during her engagement, however, not only is she unembarrassed by his caresses but she desires them and would be disappointed if he did not express his affection for her in a tangible, physical way. The transition to the increased intimacy of marriage is equally natural. One step in that transition, the specific act of sexual intercourse, is perhaps more clear-cut than other aspects of the process. But there will be no sudden crisis or cataclysm to shock or surprise, no experience that cannot readily be anticipated and imagined, assuming, of course, that the girl has made a wise choice of husband. There will be only the next natural step to something growing out of, and built upon, previous courtship experience, not something entirely new and different. The difference will be one of degree as well as of kind of experience.

DIFFERENCES BETWEEN MEN AND WOMEN

Since men and women are different physically, one might expect to find a difference in their sexual behavior. In men the sexual impulse may be brought to a sharp focus within a short time and is somewhat localized in the genital organs. In women it tends to be more diffused and generalized and involves more of the entire body. The genital organs are involved, of course, but not nearly so exclusively as in the male.

The vagina is not so sensitive to either pain or sexual stimulation as is commonly assumed. However, there is an area in the vagina which is sensitive to stimulation. The muscles surrounding the vagina are sensitive to stimuli [Kegel, 1952]. The labia at the entrance to the vagina are sensitive. There is universal agreement neither as to the role played by the vagina in orgasm nor as to whether the vagina or the clitoris is the primary seat of orgasm [Oliven, 1955]. Evidence suggests, however, that the clitoris is at least one of the primary seats of sexual stimulation and response in the female. (See the diagram on p. 551.) On the average the clitoris is about the size of a small bean. It is buried in the soft tissue just above the entrance to the vagina. Most women are unaware of its presence as an organ, although they may be aware of its location as an area of stimulation and response in sexual intercourse or masturbation. Occasionally a woman who has a clitoris that is larger than average becomes aware of its presence when it responds to stimulation. Structurally the clitoris is like a rudimentary penis. It is to the penis of the male what the rudimentary breast of the male is to the developed breast of the female. The rudimentary breast and the clitoris in the male and female, respectively, constitute a clear-cut instance of overlap, or blending, of sexual characteristics due to common embryological development, as discussed in an earlier chapter. In structure the clitoris is homologous to (that is, derived from the same source and similar to, but not identical with) the penis. It has a glans, a spongelike interior, a similar nerve supply. Unlike the penis, however, it has no passage through it and therefore has no function in either secretion or excretion. For this reason and because the female produces nothing comparable to the seminal fluid, there is no ejaculation in the female.

In response to sexual stimulation the clitoris becomes tumescent, that is, enlarged, because of an increased blood supply in the spongy internal tissue. There is no universal agreement as to whether this tumescence is a true erection, as in the case of the penis. There has been a widespread assumption to the effect that there is true clitoral erection. Recent research by Masters and Johnson [Winokur, 1963], however, casts doubt on this assumption and suggests that the clitoris responds to sexual stimulation "in specific vasocongestive patterns, just as do the vaginal barrel, labia, breasts, etc.," but that it is a fallacy to define this as erection. What appears to be erection of the nipples of the breasts in response to stimulation or as a result of temperature change is due to the contraction of smooth muscle fibers and is not true erection [Haagensen, 1956]. Research indicates that the clitoris is slower to respond than the penis [Winokur, 1963]. The specific terminology to be applied to the reaction of the clitoris is not so important for our purpose as the fact that the clitoris does respond to sexual stimulation in a way not dissimilar to that of the penis and that the clitoris is at least one seat of sexual response in the female.

For a woman sexual intercourse is more likely to be part of a larger experience, in which ideal elements play an important role. This is not to say that a man's experience is limited to the physical, for his, too, may be more comprehensive. But in his reactions the physical is more clear-cut and specific. In men sexual desire is aroused by both internal and external stimuli, whereas in women it is more subject to external influences, though internal ones play a part. Both sexes respond to such stimuli as sight of each other, verbal expressions of affection, and physical contact. Both have memory and imagination, the man having an advantage in this respect. Such factors affect a man more readily and more quickly than they affect a woman. In addition, a man is subject to an internal stimulus, namely, the accumulation of seminal fluid in the seminal vesicles. (See Chapter 15.) If one could divide the sex drive into segments, one might say that an important part of it in a man is the desire for relief from this accumulation of fluid. There is nothing in a woman's experience quite analogous to this. She may be subject to nervous or muscular tension, but no more so than a man. Because this urge for release is foreign to a woman's experience, it is impossible for her fully to understand how a man feels when his sexual impulses have been aroused. As a couple's sexual experience together develops, however, the wife becomes increasingly responsive to external stimuli and more consciously sensitive to internal ones.

Because external stimuli play so large a part in her reactions, her dependence upon her husband is little short of complete. On the other hand, a man derives some pleasure from the emission of the seminal fluid under almost all circumstances. His sexual experience is far from complete unless it, too, has in it the other-than-physical elements; but because of the explicit nature of his physical response, he may easily be betrayed into concluding that sexual experience is entirely physical and exclusively masculine. Furthermore, because of this accumulation of fluid, the ease with which it is evacuated, and the pleasure derived from that process, a man is less dependent upon his wife for physical satisfaction than she is upon him. As a result, unless he is enlightened, he is likely to be swept away by his own desires, forgetting her and her dependence upon him. The greatest satisfaction for both persons comes when the climax is reached simultaneously, or approximately so, by both husband and wife. The next best thing is for the wife to reach it first. If the husband reaches orgasm first, he may help the wife to reach it through manual or other stimulation.

By and large, women are slower to reach orgasm in sexual intercourse and also slower to "subside" afterward. Sometimes this latter period is referred to as the "afterglow." The metaphor is taken from a sunset – the sun has gone down but the sky is still red. A man's reactions are more likely to be very quick and to end more or less abruptly. Shortly after orgasm he may be almost overcome by overwhelming sleepiness. If he yields to this sleepiness, from her point of view deserting his wife when she desires attention, reassurance, affection beyond the momentary culmination of orgasm, ecstasy may be followed by devastating disappointment. When this happens repeatedly, some women conclude that they are being "used" because the man seems interested only in his own satisfaction. In some cases masculine ignorance in this connection is scarcely less than appalling.

Sexual intercourse usually should not take place until both persons are ready for it. This implies more than just willingness on the part of the wife. A woman needs preparation for sexual union – some women more, some less – and usually she needs more earlier in marriage than later after she has had satisfactory experience. Such preparation is not a mechanical thing. It is a direct outgrowth of frequent expression of affection and trust intensified periodically as a direct preface to a culmination in intercourse. In this process, especially in its final stages, there should be no barrier, physical or otherwise, between husband and wife. No parts of the body need be considered subject to tabu so far as tactile contact is concerned. Any act or expression that furthers the process is acceptable and desirable, provided that (1) it does not cause injury, pain, or disgust to either party; (2) it does not indicate or produce a fixation at a low level of adjustment; (3) it does not make either person feel guilty; (4) it does not become a permanent and regular substitute for normal sexual intercourse; (5) it leads up to and eventuates in normal sexual intercourse. But even such generalizations cannot be assumed to be universally applicable. There may be couples to whom they do not apply. In mentioning their sexual behavior couples often say something to this effect: "We do thus and so. Is this right? Is it good?" In the last analysis, whatever the husband and wife do together—*anything*—provided that it is mutually agreed upon and not imposed by one upon the other, and provided also that it remains private and does not become a social problem involving other people, is right and good. There are no rules but their rules, no standards but their standards.

No matter what one may think about sex before marriage, there is nothing more moral or more "right" than sexual intercourse in marriage. The very impulses and desires that need to be inhibited before the wedding need lack of inhibition afterward. It would be strange indeed if in a relationship as intimate as marriage special sensitivities containing great potentialities for mutual satisfaction had to be excluded. A man is more inclined than is a woman to be amenable to, and tolerant of, this sort of freedom, especially at first. Many a woman needs time to acclimate herself to a situation in which all bars are down, even though the other person is the man she loves.

PREPARATION

In preparing his wife for sexual intercourse, much depends upon a husband's skill as a lover, his so-called and much written about *technique*. The term does not imply merely maneuvers or manipulations. It implies a thorough understanding of everything necessary to make his wife's, and consequently his own, experience the fullest possible. Often the word is used in a too narrow sense. Frequently it is assumed that some mechanical process is all that is needed or that such a process supersedes and replaces love, affection, trust, and the other qualities that make marital relationships deep and rich. If one were to take some books on this subject at their apparent face value, one might assume that overnight any man could become a great lover and sweep any woman, whether she loved him or not, to supreme and incomparable heights of ecstasy by the mastery of some sleight of hand. Nothing could be more misleading. Maneuvers and manipulations without love, affection, and understanding are like the ability to blend colors with keen eye and nimble fingers while lacking the vision, inspiration, and insight of the true artist. Technique is important but not all-important. When a couple's relationship is successful, technique is only one of the factors to which credit is due. When it is unsuccessful, only part of the blame may be put upon this aspect. The sexual act to be complete must involve meaning as well as sensation. Meaning has a permanency about it that sensation lacks, and this cannot be produced by technique.

Much is sometimes made of the so-called "positions" in intercourse. Some writers list, divide, subdivide, classify, and even diagram, several dozen of them. It must be admitted that a variety of positions in intercourse is possible. Which ones are best for a particular couple they may discover through experimentation. But to many a young person contemplating marriage, such listing makes intercourse seem like an engineering problem, whereas it should be a spontaneous expression of love, affection, and desire, with the emphasis on abandonment and oneness, not on posture. A list of positions for kissing could be worked out similar to that for intercourse. But we assume that persons in love will discover ways to embrace without making a choice from a catalogue of postures – and as a matter of fact they do.

It is true that much may be gained from reading and discussion, and some of the prerequisites for sexual harmony are readily learned. There is, however, no standard technique, no universal formula. Individual differences, attitudes, background, fears, relative intelligence, depth of affection, irritating circumstances, personality traits, understanding of anatomy, and similar items must be taken into account. A couple must work out what to them is an acceptable relationship, not only on the basis of stock information and injunction but also by exploration, experimentation, variation, ingenuity, and discovery. This latter process is in itself one means toward successful adjustment over a long period. Love-play in marriage should be spontaneous and contain many subtleties. For a husband always to make a direct sexual approach to his wife not only shows that he does not understand her reactions but is likely to make her avoid him because at the time he is more fully prepared for sexual intercourse than she. He may also defeat his purpose if he gives her the impression that every time he expresses affection for her in any way he expects intercourse inevitably to follow or if after intercourse there is a period during which he seems disinterested and unaffectionate. She should not be made to feel that intercourse is a price that she must pay for love or that it constitutes a prelude to apathy.

In this preparatory play and in intercourse a woman does not, as is sometimes supposed, have an entirely passive role. As her inhibitions fade, she may follow her impulses when she becomes aware of them.

In the early days of marriage she needs most of all to abandon herself to her husband and to lose herself in this new experience with him. For some women that is more readily said than done because all their lives they have been taught not to abandon themselves, and to make a complete rightabout-face is not easy. When a woman stands "before God and these witnesses" and takes a man as her "lawfully wedded husband," solemnly promising to love and cherish him, to forsake all others for him, and to cling to him in sickness and in health, for better or for worse, so long as they both live, she is placing her future in his hands and ought to be willing to go the whole way and lose herself with him in a new experience that represents the epitome of trust and devotion and the acme of mutuality.

A woman derives pleasure from yielding to the man she loves, a pleasure as remote from masculine experience and understanding as the physical aspect of a man's experience is remote from a woman's comprehension. Responsive girls often experience a foretaste of such yielding in their reactions to boys' expressions of affection before marriage. In trying to describe this experience for which there is no special vocabulary, a girl may say, "When he kisses me, I get butterflies in my stomach," or "When he kisses me, my knees turn to water." These are yielding responses. A boy does not get "butterflies in his stomach" or have his "knees turn to water." He becomes more like a coiled spring. Such girls have a great asset in their capacity and readiness to yield and in their derivation of pleasure from it, if their responsiveness is controlled, directed, and selective until it can have fullest expression in marriage. They should be glad for it, not ashamed of it. That same responsiveness, however, becomes a liability when it is not understood, when it is uncontrolled and unselective, or when it is unaccompanied by good judgment.

Above all, a woman should not worry about technique, especially at first. As time goes on she will discover how she may most effectively participate. If she focuses her attention upon details, women's reactions being diffused as they are, she puts the emphasis exactly where it does not belong. What we are saying, however, applies to specific sexual union. In the matter of responding to her husband's love-making a wife should and usually does resort to all the subtleties that she employed in courtship. There is no logical or adequate reason, biological, psychological, ethical, or otherwise, why a wife should not take an active part in a couple's love-play, even going as far as taking the initiative.

Sexual adjustment in marriage is not unusually difficult of achievement. Neither does it come automatically, without intelligence, effort, or understanding. Further to allay the fears of those who may feel that such an achievement is beyond the realm of possibility and quite beyond their resources, we may generalize to this extent. Except in those relatively rare instances in which unusual physical defects or uncommonly strong inhibitions or fears make successful sexual adjustment abnormally difficult, any healthy, intelligent couple who are in love and are happily married otherwise may work out a satisfactory sexual adjustment if they persevere and approach the problem sensibly, even though at first there may seem to be obstacles in their path. Some couples have no problems at all; satisfactory sexual experience comes to them as easily and naturally as their mutual love. Others have minor problems, readily solved. Relatively few, even extreme cases, are entirely hopeless [Friedman, 1962].

OTHER CONSIDERATIONS

Several miscellaneous considerations bearing upon sexual adjustment may be mentioned briefly.

1. Both husband and wife should have some knowledge of the anatomy and physiological reaction of both self and the other person. Included in this knowledge is the fact that in response to sexual stimulation internal secretions lubricate the vagina. To the degree to which the wife accepts sexual intercourse this process is facilitated. It may also be supplemented by means of a lubricating jelly. If the couple's reading has not answered all their questions, they may, as has been suggested, talk with the physician at the time of the premarital medical examination.

2. In their sexual life there should be no mechanical regularity as to time, place, or frequency. Spontaneity furthers romance; mechanism destroys it. Usually sexual union should be mutually desired before it is consummated, allowing for the difference in degree of preparation needed by husband and wife and taking into account the fact that accumulation of seminal fluid creates a problem for the husband but not for the wife. If she understands this latter point, sexual intercourse may be considered mutually desirable, even though the wife is not sufficiently aroused to reach orgasm.

Young persons often wonder about the danger of too frequent intercourse. There is no such danger as long as the experience is mutually desirable and as long as it is followed by a sense of well-being, repose, relaxation, calm, and oneness rather than a sense of regret, repugnance, guilt, or excessive fatigue. A woman may repeat intercourse over and again, and some women report a series of orgasms. Because of the ejaculation of the seminal fluid, Nature puts a brake on the male. He may be able to repeat ejaculation several times within a brief period, but the possibilities are far from limitless.

3. An attitude of leisure is important. Haste, like mechanism, is defeating. At the time of intercourse a couple should have the attitude that for the time being this is the most important thing in life, in the broad sense. They should not consider it something to be hurried through because other things are waiting to be done.

4. Physical cleanliness will bear reference, since it is just as important in marriage as in dating—perhaps even more so because physical contact becomes more intimate.

5. A young couple should be able to have privacy when they want it. Inquisitive neighbors, obtrusive relatives, a feeling of general uneasiness because of the possibility of intrusion or because of thin-walled apartments—all make adjustment difficult. If privacy is not possible, it is in many cases advisable to change residence. It is better to have an inferior residence, if necessary, than an inferior relationship.

6. Fatigue often hinders adjustment. It cannot always be avoided in daily life, but the relation between fatigue and sexual adjustment may be understood and kept in mind.

PERIODICITY

Many women manifest *periodicity of sexual desire*. Both sexes exhibit variations in intensity of interest and desire, not only from individual to individual but in the same person at different times. These latter variations depend upon fatigue, other interests, bodily functions, proximity of husband and wife, and frequency and recency of intercourse. Superimposed upon this irregular series of changes in the individual, there is in many women a more nearly regular cyclical or rhythmic change, which bears a relation to the menstrual cycle. One might say that the man is like a lake; he exhibits waves or calm. The woman is more like an ocean; in addition to waves and calm she exhibits tides. Some women are conscious of no such periodicity. Others experience a heightened desire just before menstruation, just after menstruation, before and after, midway between periods, or at some other time relative to the menstrual cycle. In some the periodicity is regular and recurs each month; in others it is irregular. Whether this variation in interest is physiologically, psychologically, or otherwise conditioned is irrelevant here. If it exists, it is important in marriage.

G. V. Hamilton [1929], in making a study of 100 men and an equal number of women, found that 61 of the men had observed a periodic variation in their wives' sexual interest and that 73 of the women had been conscious of such variation in themselves. Katherine Bement Davis [1929], in a questionnaire study of some 2,200 women, found that among 1,000 who were unmarried, 272 had been aware of this periodicity of desire in themselves, and of a similar number of married women, 171 had been conscious of it. The discrepancy in these figures may be due, as Dr. Davis explains, to the fact that there was some difference in the questions on the two inquiry forms. Dr. Hamilton's methods of study were different from those of Dr. Davis, and his group was smaller. Either of these factors may account for the difference in results of the two investigators. A large proportion of the wives studied by Terman [1938] indicated an awareness of periodicity. Benedek and Rubenstein [1942] report a similar phenomenon. Ascertaining the exact number of women who are conscious of this cyclical change in their sexual interests is not so important as recognizing that a considerable proportion of women do experience it. A given husband is confronted with the problem of understanding one wife, not with a problem in statistics.

There are only two means by which a husband may understand his wife in this particular regard: observation and information. He may observe her carefully to see whether there is any variation in her attitudes and responses during the menstrual cycle. No one can furnish him with information about his wife, however, except the wife herself. She may help her husband by carefully noting her inclinations, and she need not hesitate to let her feelings become known to him. Both husband and wife may learn how to detect and recognize each other's needs and desires, as well as feel free to make their own desires known. This need not always be done by direct statement. There are other more indirect and subtle means known to anyone who is less than completely naïve in the matter of making love.

This discussion of periodicity of desire is not meant to imply that sexual intercourse is possible or advisable only at those relatively infrequent intervals when a woman experiences a heightened sexual interest. It does imply that at various times a different approach is necessary and there may be various degrees of responsiveness. There may, too, be times when a woman is not only less interested but when intercourse may be repugnant to her. At such times a husband cannot expect his wife to respond to his advances.

It is interesting to note in passing that, in women who are aware of the periodicity of sexual desire, heightened interest does not always coincide with that phase of the menstrual cycle when the ovum is released and conception is possible. This may be another bit of evidence to add weight to the argument of those who maintain that the function of sex is not primarily reproduction. In lower animals reproduction is the function of sexual union; and among mammals periods of increased desire on the part of the female and the release of the ovum, and thus the possibility of conception, coincide.

PREMENSTRUAL TENSION

For some women there is a brief period during the menstrual cycle during which they feel depressed or irritable. Hamilton [1929] found that of the 100 women, 68 had periods of depression, 71 had periods of increased irritability, and others felt "physical letdown," fatigue, or nervousness. Fluhmann [1957] says that though estimates as to the number of women who have premenstrual tension vary, a reasonable compromise estimate would be 60 per cent. Other writers [Novak, 1944; Hoffman, 1944; Hamblen, 1945; Gill, 1943; Greenhill, 1945b, 1961; Fluhmann, 1957; Bowes, 1956; Kessel and Coppen, 1963], in discussing premenstrual tension, also mention headache, anxiety, restlessness, inability to relax, inability to concentrate, depression, emotional outbursts, crying spells, hypersensitivity, unexplainable fears, imperative ideas, exaggeration of trifles, and loss of inhibitions. Evidence suggests that there is a relationship between menstruation and premenstrual tension and accident-proneness. In one study, 52 per cent of a group of women involved in accidents had their accidents during menstruation or the four days immediately prior to it [Dalton, 1960]. In another study, it was found that 62 per cent of violent crimes committed by women were perpetrated in the premenstrual phase of the menstrual cycle [Morton, Additon, Addison, Hunt, and Sullivan, 1953]. Some women want to hurt someone. Such feelings usually pass in a day or so. In a sense, they are uncontrollable. At least the feelings are uncontrollable; their expression may be restrained to some degree. Here again observation and information are necessary to enable the husband to understand the wife and for her to understand herself. Certainly a woman need not take undue advantage of this situation because she gets the impression that statistics justify any behavior and that she is the victim of uncontrollable forces. If a wife does experience these periods of depression or irritability, her behavior may be more than usually unpredictable, and a husband needs to understand this fact. If she feels impelled to hurt someone, the most convenient victim is her husband. He must learn that some days each month are "off the record." They are days when nothing counts and nothing is held against the wife. If a husband is not aware of this, he may wonder why the loving wife of yesterday, for whom he cares so much and who expressed her affection so warmly, has seemed to make a rightabout-face and, without apparent provocation, cut him to the quick today. Tomorrow her mood will probably have passed. She may wonder why she felt as she did and be sorry for it; but at the time she may have enjoyed her cruelty. No husband should leap to any conclusion concerning his wife's attitude toward him until he has carefully ascertained the relation of that attitude to her menstrual cycle. No wife should conclude that her attitude toward her husband during such a period of depression or irritability is permanent or represents her "true self." A woman's "true self" is what she is over a period of about twenty-eight days, not what she is at a given moment. Generalizing somewhat, we may say that during a large part of a woman's life her body is at any given time in some phase of a cycle.

During the period immediately preceding menstruation many apparently normal women have an increase in body weight varying from about 2 to occasionally as much as 15 pounds. This increase in weight is manifested in generalized swelling, in swelling of the hands and feet, in puffiness of the face and eyelids. Some women complain of feeling bloated. They are aware of a noticeable increase in girth, and their clothes feel tight. This swelling is due to water retention in the body tissues, not in the bladder, which, in turn, is due to retention of certain salts. Such retention of water and salts is considered by some investigators to be at least one of the factors contributing to premenstrual tension, but there is not universal agreement on this point [Bruce and Russell, 1962]. Symptoms may be relieved by limiting fluid intake, eating a salt-free diet, and taking a diuretic, that is, a drug which causes an increase in urination [Fluhmann, 1957; Bowes, 1956]. Treatment should, of course, be prescribed by a physician.

ADJUSTMENT

We have been setting a comparatively high standard and discussing the better type of adjustment. Suppose that a person marries an individual who does not do all that we have suggested. Either husband or wife may or may not be able to attain a high degree of success. If the individual who is not well adjusted is aware of this fact, he may see a counselor, acquire further information, or analyze himself in so far as his knowledge permits. In most instances there is little to be gained by talking the problem through with friends or other laymen. The probability is that they know no more than the individual himself and are prone to generalize on one case, which is usually their own. Above all, neither one of the spouses needs to leap to the conclusion that the situation is hopeless and that immediate separation or divorce is the solution.

If it is the wife who is incompletely adjusted and the husband realizes this but she does not, he may adopt any of several courses: (1) try new methods of approach or allow more time for courting her; (2) talk the problem over with her to see whether he is doing something that displeases her; (3) suggest that she seek counseling help; (4) compromise, if it seems impossible for the wife's adjustment to become fully successful, as sometimes success comes after many years of marriage—a couple should not give up easily, especially if the wife is eager to succeed or if their relationship is partly or occasionally complete; (5) examine time, place, and circumstances to determine whether there are obstacles to success to be found in the general environment; (6) suggest that there be a medical examination to determine whether there are physical defects; (7) talk the problem over with a trained counselor. If, after all these resources have been drawn upon, the adjustment seems incomplete, the couple may continue to do the best they can. Partial failure in sexual adjustment may be an explanation, but it is not an excuse, for a husband's (or a wife's) extramarital promiscuity.

If it is the husband's role that is faulty or inadequate, the following suggestions may be of use to the wife. (1) She may help him to learn more about their relationship, if he is the type of man willing to learn and is amenable to suggestion. She may explain her own reactions to him. At the same time she must remember that very few men exactly fit a textbook pattern; some men express themselves in one way, some in another. (2) If the husband seems hasty and a bit rough and sexual intercourse seems rather frequent, the wife may rest assured that in all except rare cases time will, at least in part, remedy these conditions. (3) She may consult a trained counselor about her specific problem. Generalizations are not adequate. (4) Reading may help if the couple are open-minded and willing to learn and if there is mutual understanding. (5) In the earlier part of marriage, the one solution for many a problem is time to learn.

The best preparation for successful sexual adjustment in marriage is the development of a healthy, balanced attitude, free of unnecessary and unfounded inhibitions and fears, together with the acquisition of sound, reliable information. No matter how much the couple have read or may pride themselves upon knowing, it is still often advisable for them to talk through the whole matter of sexual adjustment with a trained counselor so that they may think in terms of specifics rather than in terms of generalities. There is no single book that can be guaranteed to give them all the information that they need. In many ways every couple's mutual adjustment is unique.

WHAT DO YOU THINK?

1. What is the significance of the statement: "Sex is a means of communication"?

2. Which factors in the present-day social situation further, and which retard, young people's preparation for successful sexual adjustment in marriage?

3. What do you consider wholesome and unwholesome attitudes regarding sex?

4. What is meant by the phrase "the conditioning of sex through childhood experiences"?

5. How may a couple determine what is "right" and what is "wrong" in the sexual aspect of marriage?

SELECTED READINGS

Bassett, Marion: *A New Sex Ethics and Marriage Structure,* Philosophical Library, Inc., New York, 1961. A discussion of woman's sexual nature; an examination of the marriage relationship.

Blood, Robert O., Jr.: *Marriage*, The Free Press of Glencoe, New York, 1962, chap. 18. Sex in marriage; varieties of sexual experience.

Butterfield, Oliver M.: *Sex Life in Marriage*, Emerson Books, Inc., New York, 1952. A discussion of sexual adjustment in marriage.

Calderone, Mary Steichen: *Release from Sexual Tensions*, Random House, Inc., New York, 1960. Deals with the function of sex in the life of the child, adolescent, and adult. Sex problems of the widowed and divorced are discussed.

Cole, William Graham: *Sex in Christianity and Psychoanalysis*, Oxford University Press, Fair Lawn, N.J., 1955. Interpretations of sex in Christianity, historical and contemporary; the Freudian interpretation.

Kephart, William M.: *The Family, Society, and the Individual*, Houghton Mifflin Company, Boston, 1961, chap. 16. Sex in marriage; the "female myth"; the sexual nature of male and female; the extent of sexual maladjustment.

Landis, Judson T., and Mary G. Landis: *Building a Successful Marriage*, 4th ed., Prentice-Hall, Inc., Englewood Cliffs, N.J., 1963, chap. 17. The sex factor in marriage.

Landis, Paul H.: "Don't Expect Too Much of Sex in Marriage," *Reader's Digest*, pp. 25–28, December, 1954. An appeal to keep sex in perspective.

——: *For Husbands and Wives*, Appleton-Century-Crofts, Inc., New York, 1956, chaps. 10, 11. Sexual adjustment in marriage; realistic sex expectations.

Le Masters, E. E.: *Modern Courtship and Marriage*, The Macmillan Company, New York, 1957, chaps. 17, 18. Sexual adjustment in marriage.

Martinson, Floyd M.: *Marriage and the American Ideal*, Dodd, Mead & Company, Inc., New York, 1960, chap. 20. Sexual expression in marriage.

Simpson, George: *People in Families*, Thomas Y. Crowell Company, New York, 1960, chap. 10. Sexuality in marriage; some sexual disorders. Psychoanalytic emphasis.

Stone, Abraham, and Lena Levine: *The Premarital Consultation*, Grune & Stratton, Inc., New York, 1956. What is involved in the premarital examination; questions that might be discussed with the physician.

Stone, Hannah M., and Abraham Stone: *A Marriage Manual*, rev. ed., Simon and Schuster, Inc., New York, 1953. Written by a husband and wife, both physicians. In question-and-answer form as if a couple were talking with their doctor. Responsible, accurate, reliable explanation of sex and reproduction.

chapter 14

THE USE OF
MONEY AND
LEISURE TIME

IN ONE BRIEF CHAPTER we cannot hope thoroughly to explore two aspects of marital adjustment so important as the use of money and the use of leisure time. This section proposes only to call to the reader's attention the importance of these problems. We shall make a few suggestions. But the chief objective is to make the reader aware of the need for turning to more specific and detailed sources of information and for drawing upon his own resources of experience and ingenuity in seeking for a practical, workable plan for meeting two inescapable aspects of marriage.

The use of money

Studies of marital adjustment do not agree as to the relationship between size of income and degree of happiness or success. In the study of 200 individuals made by Hamilton [1929], 50 husbands whose annual income was more than a given amount were compared with 50 whose income was less than that amount. As to happiness in marriage, they were distributed approximately the same. Terman [1938] found no significant correlation between income and happiness in his study of 792 couples. Burgess and Cottrell [1939], in studying 526 couples, found that adjustment seemed better when income was moderate than when it was either low or high, but they do not regard their results as conclusive. Weeks [1943] and Goode [1951] found an inverse relationship between economic level and divorce rate; the higher the level, the lower the rate, and vice versa. Even more important than the quantity of the money per se are the couple's attitude toward it and the use to which it is put. Few families ever have what they consider to be enough money.

The use of money may serve as a binding factor for a couple, affording common interests and establishing common goals. It may also be a focal point for, or a cause of, conflict. One couple may find happiness on an income identical in amount with that of another couple who are suing for divorce because of it.

Amount of income and its relation to happiness are also relative to expectations. If both husband and wife are accustomed to a modest standard of living, or if they are committed to an occupational field in which monetary returns are typically low, they may never hope for a large income. If, however, their expectations run higher than their possible income, the amount of the latter may be a thorn in their flesh.

The use of money is more of a problem for the modern young couple than it was for their ancestors because in our national economy money has come to play a larger role. There is an increased distance between production and consumption. In earlier days, for many economic goods the producer was also the consumer. This is now more likely to be true in rural districts than in cities. As the distance between producer and consumer lengthens, goods exchange hands more frequently, and this necessitates the use of a medium of exchange, namely, money. In earlier days the problem confronting a couple was how to organize time, labor, and natural resources to produce the goods that they consumed. Nowadays their problem is to apportion income so that they may consume the goods someone else produces. There has been a shift from making a living to earning a living. Besides, there has been built up a continuously increased variety of opportunities for consumption, and evidence of consumption is more commonly employed as a criterion in appraising people than is evidence of production. At the same time, there has developed a continually more specialized function for the individual whose single source of income depends upon his taking an infinitesimal and highly specialized part in the almost infinitely subdivided scheme of production.

With indulgence for oversimplifying somewhat, this point may be illustrated by a diagram (Figure 6). In this diagram, the consumer goods are the same in both periods. But in the earlier period the individual converted raw materials ABC into consumer goods $A_1B_1C_1$. Today the individual earns money through work X, then apportions his income and purchases consumer goods $A_1B_1C_1$.

The budget is a distributing agent. Like a dam, it holds back the undirected flow of the river in order to turn the waters into channels that supply power generators so that electric current may be provided now here, now there, as needs arise. It should be considered as a plan for obtaining what is wanted rather than as something negative — a restriction on spending.

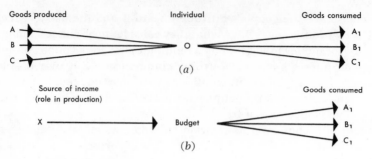

Figure 6. The changes in the economic aspects of marriage: (*a*) in earlier times, (*b*) today.

COOPERATIVE PLANNING

Formulating a budget and putting it into effect should be a cooperative undertaking in which husband, wife, and children participate. No one in the family should be put into the position of an employee who must have a requisition slip signed by his superior before he may get the supplies he needs. Each member of the family should be considered a shareholder with voting power relative to his age and experience and varying according to the decisions to be made. One way to prevent extravagance and careless use of money is to give an individual responsibility. This may be temporarily expensive, but it pays for itself in the end.

A man's salary check is made payable to himself. For this reason, many men assume that they alone earn that salary. If the wife cares for the home, children, and husband; is an expert in consumption; makes social contacts that assist the husband in his profession or broaden family experience; is a companion who enriches his life, stirs his ambitions, aids him in his work, gives him something to work for, they earn the income jointly. This is implied in the concept of community property as recognized in the Federal law which permits a couple to make a joint income tax return, using only the husband's income as a base but thereby reducing the total tax to be paid.

The fact that a wife earns no money at homemaking does not indicate that homemaking has no monetary value. Also when one thinks in terms of purchasing power rather than a sum of money, one may readily see that a wife may, through careful spending, raise the purchasing power of each dollar that her husband earns.

Not all wives are of the type described above. Some men earn their salaries in spite of their wives rather than with their help. Points of view must be adjusted to relationships observed. We are thinking in terms of the attitudes of the about-to-be-married. They should enter their new relationship with the idea of joint enterprise, joint earning, and joint spending uppermost in their minds.

METHODS OF HANDLING INCOME

There are several possible methods of handling the actual spending. This is related to, but not identical with, the formulation of the budget. Not all ways are of equal merit. Each couple must decide for themselves which way is best adapted to their attitudes, abilities, and temperaments. (1) One person may handle all money. (2) One may handle all and give the other a personal allowance. (3) The husband may handle some items, the wife others. (4) The husband may handle some items, the wife others, and in addition each may have a personal allowance. (5) One may handle regular expenses, such as rent and utilities, both drawing upon a joint bank account for personal expenses. (6) They may at the beginning of each week or month, depending upon how their income is received, apportion their money for various items, paying some immediately and putting into special envelopes the sums reserved for others. For example, rent, utilities, and so on, may be paid immediately; money for amusements, clothing, laundry, and similar items may be placed in marked envelopes to be used as needed. Special envelopes for this purpose may be purchased at slight expense. (7) In place of envelopes, which necessitate having money around the house, checks may be written in advance, to be cashed when necessary. If the couple have an inclination toward simple bookkeeping, a lump sum may be left in the bank but apportioned to various accounts in a small ledger. Then, as money is spent for any particular item, it is deducted from the balance in that special account in the family books. (8) Other schemes will suggest themselves to the reader who has the determination to keep finances under control and the ingenuity to make control not only effective but interesting.

So far as marital happiness is concerned, the actual method of handling income is not so important as the means by which the couple arrive at the employment of that method. For example, one couple get along very well with the wife handling the bulk of the income and the husband having a personal allowance. Another couple with the same plan have continual conflict. The difference is that the first couple arrived at their plan by mutual agreement. The husband is content to have the wife handle finances. The wife is skillful in doing so and gladly accepts the chores involved. In the second case, however, the wife is unskilled but nonetheless insists upon a one-sided plan, and the husband's ego is continually rubbed raw by the abrasive implication of his incompetence. A similar situation might exist with a plan that appears desirable "on the surface." For example, a wife lacks both skill and interest in handling records. The husband, an accountant, insists that she participate in record keeping. She would be glad to have him take over.

The important point, then, is not the method of handling income per se so much as it is the means by which the method is chosen. If the method is agreeable to both marital partners, almost any method can be made to work successfully. If, on the other hand, the method represents an imposition upon one partner by the other, through either insistence or irresponsibility, and it is therefore reluctantly tolerated rather than willingly accepted, any method can give rise to conflict.

If the couple do adopt a plan by which one partner is responsible for the greater part of the record keeping, it is wise to set up an over-all record system so that in case of the death of the one partner the other will have a ready reference for comprehending and carrying on family finances. Such an over-all record might include details on regular expenditures, insurance policies and premiums, items to be included in an income tax statement, notes due, savings and investments, and similar items. Some husbands also work out a statement, as nearly accurately as they can, of what regular income the widow can depend upon, including income from investments, insurance, social security, and so on. It is most discouraging for a bereaved spouse to be immersed in financial confusion in the grief-stricken, apprehensive period of early widowhood.

AN EXPERIMENTAL BUDGET

We suggest that the reader work out a budget to see, among other things, how many channels there are through which income ordinarily moves, that is, how many drains there are upon it. This is often a revelation to the young person whose parents have taken care of most expenses, whose allowance has come with little or no effort and has been reserved for current personal expenses. In working out an experimental budget, the amount of income should be kept relatively small unless the specific amount upon which the budget is to be based is already known.

In a budget for a young, childless couple the following items are possible inclusions.

Food
Clothing:
  Wife
  Husband
Rent
Water
Light
Laundry and Cleaning:
  Furnishings
  Clothing
Medical and dental costs
Insurance:
  Life – wife
  Life – husband
  Health and hospitalization

House furnishings:
  Additions
  Repairs
  Replacements
Fuel:
  For heating
  For cooking
Taxes:
  Income – Federal
  Income – state
  Personal property
  Real estate
  Sales
  Other
Social security

Fire
Other
Service (maid, etc.)
Toilet articles — beauty
 treatments, hair-cuts
Church and charity
Travel
Fares — taxis, buses
Amusements, recreation
Gifts
Education
Dues to organizations
Automobile:
 Payments on cost
 Insurance
 Gas and oil
 Repairs
 License — state, city
 Tax
 Accessories
 Other

Savings:
 Savings account
 Investments
Telephone and telegraph
Stationery and postage
Books, magazines, papers
Tobacco
Candy, beverages, etc.
 (unnecessary foods)
Debts:
 Principal payments
 Interest
Loans to others
Miscellaneous:
 Films
 Flowers
 Hobbies supplies
 Pets
 Sports equipment
 Other

Amounts allowed for various items will vary according to time, locality, type of residence, and individual interests and needs. Financial planning for a baby may be included if the reader so desires. Many items, such as clothing and insurance, are not paid monthly; but in an effective budget monthly allowance should be made and amounts set aside for them so that when payment is made it represents a summation of monthly averages. Some items, for example, maid service, may be followed by a zero. It is important, however, to include such items in order to see which holes in the sieve will be closed as well as those that will be open.

In this experimental budget the reader should reach a balance; there are to be no debts or overdrafts. There is not to be too great dependence upon gifts. Already-existing debts, assured wedding gifts, shower gifts already received, savings already in the bank, the purchase of furniture — all these must be considered. The reader may find it difficult to balance this budget on a relatively small income, as suggested, and many things that he has previously taken for granted in his standard of living may have to be omitted. He should face the facts. If he balances the budget with wishful thinking, he is only postponing and amplifying his inevitable impact with reality.

After the reader has made a budget on the basis of a relatively small income as suggested, he may make another as he would like to see it, but keeping the income at a reasonable level. Then the two budgets may be compared. The items showing the greatest discrepancy will probably be those that will have to be watched most closely in order to make the actual budget balance with the lower income.

When the reader has seen, through experiment, what it means to balance a budget, he will be more than ever interested in securing expert information and professional hints on· this problem. There are many useful books and pamphlets available.*

Whatever budget is made for experimental purposes in advance of marriage is in a sense generalized. A budget cannot be laid out in its final form in advance, except roughly. It must grow out of experience. A couple make a budget, try it for a while, then revise it. As the second one is found not to fit here or there, another is made, and so on, until experience has been sufficient to enable them to make one to which they may adhere for some time. Even then, however, it will change as income changes and as new needs arise or old ones are satisfied.

There is no standard budget, no distribution of income that will automatically fit every couple's needs. Published materials help, but they alone cannot solve a couple's problem. To expect them to do so would be the same as to expect every man to wear the same size mail-order suit. In order to make a budget work at all, a couple should list in advance probable needs and wants in so far as these are predictable, leaving a margin for the unpredictable. They should look not only weeks but months and years into the future. They should think of wants and needs not only in the economic sense but also in the emotional and social sense.

A budget need not be considered absolutely inflexible. As unpredictable needs or opportunities arise, it may be adjusted to them. Furthermore, the couple must expect to make mistakes. The budget is a tool, a means to an end. It is not an end in itself and should not become master rather than servant. It should not be so much in evidence at all times that it becomes a source of irritation, thus defeating its own purpose. It can become a bone of contention, a cause of friction, a source of conflict. But so can a hand-to-mouth handling of income. Therefore, this is no argument against budgeting.

No item in the budget may be increased without decreasing some other item, assuming that income remains constant. This fact seems self-evident, but there are many who overlook it.

If income varies from month to month, as, for example, a physician's fees do, a conservative estimate may be made and the standard of living scaled to that. There is then the possibility of carrying over a surplus rather than a deficit to future months.

CONSUMPTION

Merely apportioning income is not enough. Purchases need to take account of quality and quantity. Often the things costing least are most

*Inexpensive, useful pamphlets may be obtained from the U.S. Government Printing Office, Washington, D.C.; The Household Finance Corporation, Dept. IF, Prudential Plaza, Chicago, Ill.; The Women's Division of the Institute for Life Insurance, New York City; and similar sources.

expensive when all factors are considered. The couple need to take a long-range point of view. The budget is only the plan of attack; it is not the actual spending of money.

Both husband and wife are consumers, and modern economic conditions are putting an ever-increasing responsibility upon the consumer. This is especially true of the wife, since ordinarily most of the family purchasing falls to her. A girl may well ask herself this question, "Would I marry a man only as well prepared to earn money as I am to spend it?" One of the modern wife's chief functions has become her role as specialist in consumption. By careful buying to lower expenses, she may raise the relative family income. As we said in another connection, some of the wife's traditional functions have been taken away from her. What can she substitute in their stead? Expert knowledge of consumption is one answer to this pertinent question. Consumer education is spreading rapidly in this country. There are many aids at her disposal. She may make a distinct contribution to family life by taking advantage of them.

LIFE INCOME

The couple may think in terms of life income rather than only monthly or weekly income. For the unmarried, especially the unmarried girl, this suggests learning something about the life income to be expected in various occupations or in that to be followed by the man she plans to marry.

Take, for illustration, the matter of savings. A couple may feel that they can save nothing immediately after marriage because expenses are so high and income so small. As years go on and income increases, they raise their standard of living, so saving remains just as difficult as it was at first. Expenses encroach upon resources, and the fact that they save little or nothing seems reasonable and is readily rationalized. Suppose that they think in terms of life income. They may think of amounts expressed in six digits. The actual sums are not so important as the recognition that any couple ought to be able to save something out of amounts of those dimensions.

It is better to save first and spend what remains than to spend first and plan to save what is (or is not) left. Instead of saving merely to save, that is, for saving's sake, it is better to do so for a specific purpose. Save to spend.

INSURANCE

Insurance is important but is too complex a topic to be dispatched in a few paragraphs. There are many reliable agents who can fit a couple's insurance to their needs and in the process educate them in the intricacies of the subject. There are also numerous books about it. Probably every couple should have some insurance. None should be so overloaded with it that their budget becomes top-heavy and the life blood is drained out of their income.

Insurance may be considered as protection, saving, or postponed spending, as the case may be and according to the types of policies purchased. As a couple's income grows, it is wise to increase the husband's insurance especially, since financial obligations will increase and the wife will accustom herself to a higher standard of living, which would make it difficult for her to drop back to a lower standard in the event of the husband's death.

Insurance is a means invented by society to spread the burden of crisis over a large proportion of the group and over a long period for the individual. If any insurance company were faced with the necessity of paying in full and at one time all its outstanding policies, it would have to fail, for its resources would be inadequate. It is because many individuals continue to pay in, while the company pays out to relatively few, that insurance is possible. Also, for the privilege of using an individual's money a little at a time an insurance company assumes the burden of helping him or his family meet a crisis. The individual or the family can afford to pay out money in small sums, whereas the demands of an emergency could not be met. It is the part of wisdom for a couple to avail themselves of this civilized method of preserving the individual and his family from the vicissitudes of existence.

HOUSING

The question of whether to rent, buy, or build a home is one that cannot be answered dogmatically in a general discussion. Much depends upon the couple's resources, their probable financial future, the type of community in which they reside, the housing available there, comparative costs, the question whether the husband's work may necessitate moving to another community, the availability of funds for mortgages, and interest rates. There are certain advantages in owning a home. There are also advantages in renting. The problem should be approached intelligently and cautiously. It should not be solved hurriedly or prematurely. While living for a few years in rented dwellings a couple may learn how to use their income and what they would desire in a home of their own, without hastily binding themselves to obligations that they cannot bear or to a house that they will learn later does not fit their tastes and needs.

RECORDS

A budget cannot be made to work effectively unless some record of expenditures is kept. Inexpensive forms for such records may be purchased. The probability is that in most cases budget and expense record will not agree exactly because during the month some small item has been overlooked or some little error made. This need not be a source of worry. The couple need not expect to balance their accounts to the penny. If there is a fair approximation between the budget and the expense record — say within a dollar or two — that is usually close enough.

CREDIT

Installment buying has its good points as well as its much-discussed bad ones. It should be used with great discretion, for it can make a couple as closely and inextricably bound to the credit company as a tenant farmer is bound to his landlord. Installment buying may be like a guest who arrives bearing gifts, only to remain for years and become dependent upon the family. It is expensive because the purchaser must pay for two things rather than one: (1) He pays for the article purchased. (2) He pays a carrying charge.

A carrying charge is interest figured on a total purchase. The interest is added to the purchase price and the sum divided by the number of monthly payments to be made. At first glance a carrying charge may seem to be the same as ordinary interest; but the carrying charge is higher even when it is stated as the same rate.

Suppose a person borrows $600 from a bank on a promissory note due in 12 months at 6 per cent interest. At the end of the year he pays the $600 plus $36 interest, a net interest cost of $36. During the entire year he owed, and therefore had the use of, all of the $600. Now suppose he pays off the loan in 12 monthly installments but the bank charges him interest only on what he owes. At the end of the first month he pays $50 plus $3 interest because during that month he owed $600. At the end of the second month he pays $50 plus $2.75 interest because during that month he owed only $550. During the third month he owes only $500, and his interest is $2.50. During the twelfth month he owes only the last $50, so the interest for that month is only $0.25. The total interest, or net cost for the year, is $19.50.

Now suppose he makes a $600 purchase and there is a 6 per cent carrying charge. The total amount he owes, then, is $600 plus $36. He pays off the loan in twelve $53 installments. But since the principal decreases each month but the amount of interest does not, on what he still owes he pays a higher rate of interest each month. The twelfth month, when he owes only $50, he still pays $3 interest – a rate of 72 per cent. By this carrying-charge method he pays $16.50 more interest than in the second plan mentioned above.

Credit, when used properly, is a boon to the consumer. It is obvious, however, that cash purchasing is not only less expensive but subject to more immediate and effective control. When a couple start out on a credit basis, it is often difficult for them to shift to a cash basis, since in any given month they must bear double expense for a given item – the payment for the past month and the reserve of cash for the month to come. Also, if one buys at stores that permit charge accounts, the probability is that he pays a carrying charge, whether or not that is stipulated. When the store management allows credit, that necessitates larger outlays of capital and more extensive bookkeeping. Someone, too, must pay for the purchases of those who fail to pay. As a result, the company that sells for cash can afford to do so at lower prices. Cash purchasing may also yield a discount. The retailer can afford to allow this because, having the cash on hand, he can purchase more goods for sale and in this way increase his turnover and, hence, his profits.

PSYCHOLOGICAL CONSIDERATIONS

Budgeting is not a financial or mathematical problem alone. It is a psychological problem, as well, involving choices, tastes, motives, standards, and self-discipline. It is a matter of the head as well as of the pay envelope or the pocketbook, so to speak. It is a way of thinking as well as a plan for spending.

In one sense we budget income; we decide how it will be apportioned according to wants and needs. In another sense, we budget wants and needs, since income is fixed and these two other factors are variable. The budget is in a way like a camera shutter, which determines how much light (satisfaction of wants and needs) shall pass through the lens (income) and affect the film (individual).

There is a difference between wants and needs. Rationalizing makes it easy to confuse them. Therefore, it is wise to allow for a "cooling-off period" when contemplating a purchase, especially if it is the purchase of a relatively expensive item. In this way, impulse buying may be avoided. There is also a tendency for wants to become needs as the standard of living advances. For example, for the middle- or upper-class family an automobile, formerly a luxury, has become a necessity, at least if a given standard is to be maintained. The same is true of cosmetics, radios, television, college education, good music, travel, and in some communities, boats.

In budgeting, one is faced with the problem of buying things versus buying "states of mind." Conspicuous expenditure tends to run rampant. Many people try to "keep up with the Joneses." "Keeping up with the Joneses" means the purchasing of things that may be seen and compared. Another indication of conspicuous expenditure and the common awareness of comparisons is the widespread use of the term *status symbol* and its application to economic goods. The term applies to other things, too, of course. But its use with reference to purchasable commodities indicates our sensitivity to social competition and our assumption that possessions and status are closely correlated. In fact, we are as inclined to believe that possessions create status as we are to believe that they reflect it. Many individuals of grandiose exterior are rather shabby and drab internally. The reverse is often true, too. The problem confronting the young couple of limited income is where to draw the line between the purchase of things and the purchase of experiences and "states of mind."

ADAPTING TO A LOW STANDARD OF LIVING

Ordinarily a couple cannot expect to maintain a standard of living equivalent to that of their parents. Occasionally they have a higher standard, especially if they both work. But ordinarily the standard is lower—at least at first—no matter how adequate their education and occupational training. This is due not only to the relative size of income but also to the fact that early in marriage expenses for furniture, professional equipment, and so on, are high. The parents have had time to take care of the overhead involved in having a home and family, but overhead must come out of the young couple's current income. When they marry, then, the couple are likely to find that they must revise the spending habits that they took for granted before the wedding. As mentioned in an earlier chapter, such revision of spending habits may be called for not only in the sense of stepping down from the parents' standard of living but also in the sense of having to shift from a premarital standard determined on an individual basis to a marital standard involving the sharing of income.

This probability of temporarily lower standard of living need not prove discouraging. Young couples who have everything given to them miss something. They miss the exhilarating satisfaction of creating something that is their own, that they have planned for and worked for together. This planning, working, striving, and sacrificing together for common ends can prove to be one of the most effective binding forces that a couple experience. Nevertheless, this is no argument for hasty, ill-prepared, premature marriage on the basis of the rationalization that the greater the struggle, the greater the benefits.

The use of leisure time

Leisure time may be defined as time that is free from economic pursuits, including homemaking. It is time in which the individual has greater freedom of choice as to how it shall be employed. Modern social conditions have increased the amount available to both sexes. They have also created new opportunities and new problems.

Young couples frequently are not aware of the importance of the use of leisure or of the fact that its use may constitute a problem in marriage. An opinion often expressed by students is that, if a person has leisure, he will know what to do with it and there is no use talking about it. Experience proves that many do not know what to do with leisure time. They pass time instead of using it. They spend it instead of investing it. The expression "kill time" is indicative of a not uncommon attitude. The use of time is important in marriage because it is usually in their nonworking hours that husband and wife are most closely associated. Their leisure-time pursuits contribute, for good or ill, to the development of their personalities and their mutual relationship. Those pursuits may serve as common interests or as points of departure for conflict. They may increase tension or dissipate it. They may preserve romance or allow it to atrophy. It is not essential that all these pursuits should represent common interests. In marriage it is important that there be individual interests as well as those held by both partners.

Modern social conditions have not only increased the amount of leisure, they have made its use more important, since in the present-day world many individuals engage in occupations that play little or no part in rounding out their personalities and enriching their lives. Modern conditions have increased opportunities for beneficial use of leisure by making it possible cheaply and easily to multiply recreation facilities.

READING 15 **THE AMERICAN FAMILY AND TIME**

Among the dimensions of family time choice, there is ample evidence that families fail to consider time factors in depth prior to making choices. Selecting a place to live may be taken as an example. Many people select a house or an apartment without realizing the inevitabilities of the choices they have made about living. In order to provide his family with "a decent place to live," to raise his children behind a velvet curtain, as Mildred Morgan says, the man of the dream house agrees to sacrifice a portion of his day in commuting. He makes a time choice based solely on the time it will now take him to get to work and get home again at night. He realizes that his commuting will cause him to lose time with his family. But that "decent place to live" is his target.

In many cases, he fails to realize that his commuting —his time choice—in all likelihood will separate him socially from his office or factory colleagues. His immediate home neighborhood and the contacts in the community his wife makes will condition his circle of friends. His time choice means that he has accepted the time choices of others—with consequences far more profound than merely additional commuting time.

Once he has arrived at work by train, bus, or bumper-to-bumper car pooling, he faces a round of time studies and retraining programs to keep up with the changing demands of his job. He faces on all sides the bustle of

From Wallace C. Fulton, "The American Family and Time," *Journal of Marriage and the Family*, vol. 26, no. 1, February, 1964, pp. 6–9. Reprinted with permission of the editor and the author.

competition—for promotion, production, profit—guided by that universal: Time is Money.

If he gets concerned about struggling upward just to stay where he is, he might turn to the time management literature. These sources will tell him—in no uncertain terms—that he can learn to do the routine things in his life by habit. He will learn that such habit formation is all-important, for it means that his attention can be in other times or places than those of the task at hand. All of this because, as the time managers say, his goal is to multiply his output.

Increased output can mean that he can have the opportunity to invest in idling and its joys to the degree that he is managing his time effectively at other times. It is almost as if one must apologize for "just sittin'." Time-harassed, he will be told, "Decide now to plan your development for the next three months. Now is the time to act, gain time and grow."

One may shudder at this kind of formula time-finding, but articles of this sort can be found with fair frequency in the mass-circulation periodicals. They are reminiscent of that compulsive quatrain once taught in grade schools:

Good, better, best
Never let it rest
Until your good is better
And your better best.

Obviously, the time-press is not an exclusive problem of working men. Back at the dream house, wives and mothers are caught up in their own special time problem. They are constantly being told how fortunate they are to have so many labor-saving devices their mothers never had. They may have the equipment, but they still have no time, partly because that equipment is time-consuming when it is operating and even more so when it is not and requires waiting for the repairman.

Furthermore, little notice has been taken of the new responsibilities of the contemporary housewife. *Parent's Magazine* once did a first-rate job of detailing the demands on women. To briefly summarize the list: She is expected to keep her home clean and attractively decorated and furnished, to serve economical and attractive meals, to foster physical and emotional well-being in her children, in many cases to make clothes for the children and herself, to help improve the schools, to help raise money for causes, to become active in community organizations, to learn more about the United Nations and countries at large, to be a glamorous wife, to be conscientious about getting the children and her husband and herself to church regularly, to be a den mother, to create a proper cultural atmosphere for the children, and to add something to the family income if she can.

This incredible list does not take into account yet another time problem, that of intrusion of the technical age. A modern household is dominated by the schedules of every member of the family. Buses, schools, and commuter trains interfere with the quiet breakfast gathering of the family.

Like their parents, children too are subject to time pressure. A major change is the growing phenomenon of academic competition, reaching down now into the lower elementary grades, apparently because a college education is being viewed almost as a universal necessity.

Youngsters are early impressed with the value of high grades and are encouraged to spend a considerable amount of time on homework and extra study. At the same time, the "cultural atmosphere" which *Parent's Magazine* mentioned as a maternal responsibility frequently consists of special trips to museums, concerts, and plays, as well as private art and music lessons. All of these reduce the amount of "just-with-the-kids" kind of time.

The talented child often presents special time considerations. All-out efforts are frequently made to make sure that his talent is nurtured—even if that private lesson on Saturday afternoon rules out the chance for family fun, the only time during the week when all other members of the family are free.

These few illustrations of family time choice make it evident that all members of the family are both the creators and the victims of time pressure. These examples dealt largely with "committed" time, things people are obligated to do. But everyone has a certain amount of uncommitted time each week which he can use—to a limited extent—as he individually wishes.

According to one researcher, many Americans do their most conspicuous consuming during uncommitted time. The better life for them is a new and bigger boat, an electric rotisserie for last year's barbecue outfit, a new car that does everything but pay for itself. The things many Americans now want cost money. Money costs work. Work costs time. And this may well explain the reason many workers use their free time to hold a second job, to join the growing army of moonlighters. Their uncommitted time goes toward acquiring greater consuming power.

Others, in substantial numbers, are using their uncommitted time to return to handicrafts and the fine arts— for reasons, perhaps, of greater significance than those in the consumption realm. Some people *need* to be creative: they may experience an innate, wordless, deep-felt need to halt the rush of time by exerting the privilege of creativity to create something that can remain constant, unchanging. As the creator changes, the creation persists to memorialize a feeling in a given moment of time. Creativity, then, can serve as a sort of rebuttal to time pressure and, particularly, to what time destroys. This is a fairly elaborate hunch, but the intense devotion busy people can give to creativity, especially when they create just for themselves, suggests significant implications.

Still others are using their uncommitted time to turn to community service. Indeed, the phenomenon of volunteerism in America has probably achieved a higher order of organization and consequence than anywhere else in the world. Volunteer activity may very well serve as a substitute source of satisfaction and power, denied on the job or in the home. Since participation time is the way toward power, the active participant does not have to seek power. It will be thrust on him in the guise of responsibility. "Time is Money" may be the universal in business, but in community service, time is power. In part because of the satisfaction and power derived from community service, people are often willing to give large amounts of time. They will do so, even if it means – as it does – that family time will suffer.

Some would argue that community service is not rightly classified as an activity involving uncommitted time. Despite present-day time pressure, community service or citizenship activity is something which, according to this writer's bias, responsible adults really have no choice about. Never has there been in our history such desperate need for men and women of intelligence and dedication, men and women who will knowingly sacrifice family time to answer a plea to action for larger purposes of awesome urgency.

Such a plea may appear to be in conflict with basic American beliefs about family life. But the very fact that choice can be discussed documents the obligation to help extend the rights of *all* choice to *all* people. It is imperative to help families accept the fact that they live within a larger framework, that they must make a personal sacrifice of time to help produce a great age. The only alternative is the collapse of the upward striving of mankind.

In terms of time choice and citizenship, there is reason for optimism. There is heartening increased concern by man for his fellow man. Never has the world seen so much interest in the underprivileged, diseased and poverty-stricken.

This is not a simple matter to explain, and it is forbiddingly difficult to encourage families to act so that they will give up some of the comfort of the family circle. But the challenge to explain and to encourage is urgent.

Great as the contribution of many modern developments may be, they have also a debit side. They make the ordinary individual a passive rather than an active participant. Radio and television programs, motion pictures, and commercialized sports are predigested or "canned" recreation for the audience, and the latter takes them sitting down. Thrills and adventure, love and pathos, achieving success and outwitting villains are all experienced in vicarious fashion and absorbed without effort. Commercialized recreation by and large is also held to the level of greatest popular appeal, with little allowance for individuality. Along with this growth in passive participation has developed the large-scale production of facilities for active participation in certain pursuits. Photography, for example, has become a widespread hobby. Golf equipment is relatively cheap, and municipal golf courses have made this sport available to thousands. Interest groups and publications centering around collecting have added to both the quantity and the quality of this diversion. Examples of active-participation pursuits, organizations devoted to them, books on how to engage in them, and instructional opportunities for learning more about them are found on every hand and are almost endless in variety. It would have to be a rare individual indeed who could not find something to his liking.

LEISURE–TIME PHOTOQUIZ

Represented in the following photos are a number of activities. In each photo, what elements would you rate as:

(1) Amusement

(2) Recreation

(3) Re-creation

(4) Not leisure time

Why do you rate them thus? In each, describe the ways in which the participation is passive or active. To what extent do the activities suggest that the participants have explored their community resources? Resources within themselves? Which activities offer the greatest possibilities for development of interests and enrichment of personality?

1

3

2

4

5

6

The problem of the use of time is one of consumption. The total amount of time at anyone's disposal is limited. Only a fraction of this total is leisure. The problem becomes one of using to best advantage the limited resources at hand. The situation is in some respects similar to that which obtains with respect to natural resources, such as coal, iron, and oil. The same is true of income. If part of an individual's resources is used for one purpose, that part cannot also be used for another. Certainly this can be said of time. The individual must make choices.

7

8

1

9

In order most effectively to use time, the individual may budget it just as he budgets income. This implies not deadening regularity but planned distribution. A husband's schedule is often more rigid than a wife's because of the difference in occupational pressure, unless, of course, she too is employed. It is important that the wife budget her time so that she and her husband will have leisure together. If she does the unpostponables first, she can readily adjust her schedule so that leisure-time pursuits may be included. If, on the other hand, she has an inclination to do postponables first, she may find that there are things she must do when her husband is free.

The married woman's problem is not one of having her housework all done and then trying to find something to fill the remainder of her time. Hers is a problem of including outside interests and pursuits in a

11

14

12

13

busy schedule. It is not only a problem of using leisure time but also one of creating it at the most opportune intervals.

One is tempted to be almost dogmatic concerning the married woman's use of leisure and to say that no woman can be as good a wife by devoting her entire life to housework and the demands of her family as she can be if she devotes an ample portion of her time to outside pursuits. Everything she does to contribute to the development of her personality and the enrichment of her life makes an indirect contribution to the life of her home and family provided that it is not so time consuming that home and family are neglected. The same is true of the husband. The couple's task is not only to maintain or create a dwelling. It is also to create and maintain a set of attitudes and relationships. The woman who claims to feel guilty when she takes time from her

15

household duties for recreation does not conceive of homemaking in its broadest terms. It would be more appropriate for her to feel guilty when she allows household duties to prevent her from participating in recreational activities.

There is a difference between amusement, recreation, and recreation. Each has its place, but they are mentioned here in the order of increasing significance. The more re-creative leisure-time pursuits are the more beneficial. Many re-creative interests are not amusing at all. Community service, for example, is a splendid leisure-time activity, but it is not classed as amusement or recreation.

It is difficult to suggest leisure-time pursuits for the individual or the couple because the possibilities are as varied as human nature and as numerous as members of the population. Churches, temples, and social service agencies are fertile fields for constructive, useful activity which will benefit both the donor and the recipient. One may collect something – anything, from paper-match covers to rare antiques. Collecting is more than merely accumulating objects. It is a door through which one may pass to broader knowledge and wider social contacts. Pets are fascinating to some people. They range from goldfish to tame lions, and the gamut of their procurement runs from the five-and-ten-cent store to foreign expeditions. Music has almost unlimited possibilities, not only in individual participation but in family participation and community organization. Any group of persons able to read music may form an orchestra. Whether or not anyone but themselves listens to their playing is inconsequential. Reading, a reading diary, a collection of excerpts or poems may abound in interest. A handful of people may organize a community theater if they have sufficient interest and are not afraid of work.

Hobbies are almost unlimited, both in variety and in scope. There is much to be said for hobbies in which husband and wife have a mutual interest. Gardening may be made a year-round, as well as a seasonal, pursuit. Handwork of all sorts may be inexpensive and is fascinating. One young woman has for a period of more than three years prepared and served one new dish every day. She has sampled regional recipes, those of foreign lands, and those requiring unusual ingredients. Not only has her hobby proved interesting, but she has added a number of useful dishes to her repertory, pleased her friends, earned an enviable reputation, and had many an hour of fun with her husband. A woman of seventy has been writing for years. Nothing she has written has ever gone farther than the wastebasket, but writing has enabled her to express something and has enriched her life. Children draw before they write; yet few of us develop the earlier tendency.

To derive enjoyment from an activity one does not have to be an expert. Certainly one cannot expect to produce a masterpiece the first time he makes an attempt. In fact, it is not necessary or even important that he should ever produce anything outstanding. The important thing is to do something creative. It is not necessary to have a great amount of money to make a beginning. Ingenuity is more important than dollars. One may make a modest start.

In developing a leisure-time pursuit the individual should follow his own inclinations; he should not copy someone else's choice. He may do what someone else does also, of course, but that does not necessarily imply copying. Instead of limiting himself to the usual, let him try something out of the ordinary if he has the inclination to do so. There is no good reason why his hobby should not be entirely unique, as long as his interest is sincere and he does not pursue it for notoriety and attention.

It is worth while to develop several hobbies, since many are seasonal or intermittent. Having several will enable one to associate with more people. Too many would lead to superficial sampling, and this is as bad as having none at all.

In every community there are untold opportunities for the use of leisure time; every individual can, if he will, find something to his liking. The first step is to make an inventory of resources both within and outside oneself, and the next is to use these to best advantage. Many individuals are defeated before they begin because they expect leisure-time interests to be furnished ready-made or to spring into being without effort, self-examination, or an attempt at discovery of resources.

One source of conflict in marriage is boredom. When two people are bored, they may magnify little things in their relationship because their perspective is distorted. Little things occurring in a setting of interesting activities and imaginative, enthusiastic approaches to life are more likely to remain little things. But the same little things occurring in a setting where there is little to contrast them with or draw attention from them may loom large and out of proportion to their importance. Also, open conflict over them may break the monotony. It is difficult to understand how intelligent, educated people with all their faculties can be bored in present-day America, where all about them are opportunities for interesting pursuits. Yet the fact remains that some of them are bored, and their marriages often suffer because of their boredom. One place where a start can be made in making life and marriage more interesting is in the imaginative, creative use of leisure time.

WHAT DO YOU THINK?

1. On what basis should a couple decide how and by whom their finances will be handled?

2. What are the pros and cons of budgeting?

3. What is the significance to marriage of the fact that we live in a money economy?

4. What is the difference between wants and needs? When do wants become needs? What factors accelerate this process?

5. A girl is accustomed to a high standard of living. She marries a man whose income is considerably lower than her father's. What suggestions would you give such a couple?

6. In the above situation, the girl's parents are very generous and frequently give the young couple money. The husband objects. What suggestions would you give the couple?

7. What are the various types of insurance? Which would you suggest that a young couple with limited income buy?

8. Some students say, "There is no point in discussing a wife's use of leisure time. If she has leisure time, she will know what to do with it." What is your reaction to this statement?

9. How may a wife be sure that she will have leisure time when her husband does?

10. A newly married couple have a low income and a small apartment. The wife is not employed. What suggestions would you give the wife regarding leisure time?

11. A young husband discovers that his wife does not know how to use money and is somewhat extravagant. What suggestions would you give him? Her?

SELECTED READINGS

Baber, Ray E.: *Marriage and the Family,* 2d ed., McGraw-Hill Book Company, New York, 1953, chap. 12. The economic aspects of family life; the budget; insurance and savings.

Bell, Norman W., and Ezra F. Vogel: *A Modern Introduction to the Family,* The Free Press of Glencoe, New York, 1960, chap. 12. How the family influences consumer behavior; purchasing consumer goods in the United States today.

Bernard, Jessie, Helen E. Buchanan, and William M. Smith, Jr.: *Dating, Mating, and Marriage,* Howard Allen, Inc., Publishers, Cleveland, 1958, chap. 7, "Money: Master or Servant?" Includes many case-documentary materials.

Black, Hillel: *Buy Now, Pay Later,* William Morrow and Company, Inc., New York, 1961. A discussion of current consumer credit practices; points up uses and abuses.

Blood, Robert O., Jr.: *Marriage,* The Free Press of Glencoe, New York, 1962, chaps. 14, 17. Family financial management; major expenses; insurance; "domesticated leisure."

Cavan, Ruth Shonle: *American Marriage,* Thomas Y. Crowell Company, New York, 1959, chaps. 14, 15. Money management; purchasing; insurance and medical care; credit; investments.

———— (ed.): *Marriage and the Family in the Modern World,* Thomas Y. Crowell Company, New York, 1960, chap. 15. Family finances.

Cohen, Jerome B.: *Decade of Decision* (pamphlet), Health Insurance Institute, New York, 1961. How to plan a life insurance program to meet the needs of the insured; health insurance.

————and Arthur W. Hanson: *Personal Finance Principles and Case Problems,* rev. ed., Richard D. Irwin, Inc., Homewood, Ill., 1964. Principles and practices of financial management.

Consumer Bulletin: Consumers' Research, Inc., Washington, N.J. A monthly publication.

Consumer Reports: Consumers Union, Mt. Vernon, N.Y. A monthly publication.

Donaldson, Elvin F., and John K. Pfahl: *Personal Finance,* 3d ed., The Ronald Press Company, New York, 1961. Principles and practices of financial management.

Fishbein, Morris, and Ruby Jo Reeves Kennedy (eds.): *Modern Marriage and Family Living,* Oxford University Press, New York, 1957, chap. 21. Home management; financial management and budgeting; how can planning be done?

Fitzsimmons, Cleo: *Consumer Buying for Better Living,* John Wiley & Sons, Inc., New York, 1961. A guide to improved purchasing.

Household Finance Corporation, Dept. IF, Prudential Plaza, Chicago, publishes inexpensive pamphlets on money management and purchasing.

Landis, Judson T., and Mary G. Landis: *Building a Successful Marriage,* 4th ed., Prentice-Hall, Inc., Englewood Cliffs, N.J., 1963, chaps. 20–22. Family financial planning; insurance; purchasing; credit; "getting your money's worth."

Landis, Paul H.: *For Husbands and Wives,* Appleton-Century-Crofts, Inc., New York, 1956, chap. 12. Money management and budgeting.

Le Masters, E. E.: *Modern Courtship and Marriage,* The Macmillan Company, New York, 1957, chaps. 19, 20. Family finances; suggestions for saving; housing; cars; insurance; installment buying.

Linton, M. Albert: *How Life Insurance Can Serve You,* Harper & Row, Publishers, Incorporated, New York, 1958.

Oliver, Bernard J., Jr.: *Marriage and You,* College and University Press, New Haven, Conn., 1964, chap. 13. Financing marriage; conflict over money.

Peterson, James A.: *Education for Marriage,* 2d ed. Charles Scribner's Sons, New York, 1964, chaps. 17, 19. Family finances; family recreation; movies and television.

Phillips, E. Bryant, and Sylvia Lane: *Personal Finance,* John Wiley & Sons, Inc., New York, 1963. Principles and practices.

Springer, John L.: *Making the Most of Your Income,* Prentice-Hall, Inc., Englewood Cliffs, N.J., 1961. A guide to the handling of family finances.

Troelstrup, Arch W.: *Consumer Problems,* 2d ed., McGraw-Hill Book Company, New York, 1957. Discussion of various aspects of money management and consumer purchasing.

U.S. Government Printing Office, Washington, D.C., publishes inexpensive pamphlets on money management and purchasing.

Women's Division, Institute for Life Insurance, New York, publishes inexpensive pamphlets on money management.

part 4

FROM MARRIAGE
TO FAMILY LIVING

With the present-day American emphasis upon the individual, we are often inclined to think of persons as independent, somewhat isolated units who live in groups by choice and may accept or reject the influence of those groups at will. Actually people do not live this way. Each individual lives as a member of each of a network of clusters. Only within limits may he choose which clusters. Only within very much narrower limits may he choose whether he will be affiliated with clusters at all. For example, he may choose the occupational group with which he will affiliate himself. He may decide to be a member of this or that religious organization. He may live in the country or in the city. In his adult life he could even live on an island of which he was the only inhabitant. But with respect to some of the groups that are most influential in molding his personality, for example, his sex group and his family, he has no freedom of choice at all. The first and most basic group is the group into which he is born, his family. The family, not the individual, is the nuclear unit in society. On the other hand, parents as well as children are members of families, but their membership comes through decision to marry and through biological processes that are at least partially under their voluntary control. As a couple move from marriage to family living, both sides of this coin become apparent. Hence it is appropriate that we consider the process by which children are produced and what happens to human interrelationships as a result.

chapter 15

REPRODUCTION

IF ONE WERE ASKED to choose that thing in the universe which had greatest relative potentiality, he could advance reasonable arguments for choosing the fertilized human egg (*zygote*) — that almost microscopic bit of protoplasm that constitutes the beginning of the new human individual and is smaller than the period at the end of this sentence. Here is a potential that dwarfs the awesome release of nuclear energy, that makes the explosion of a supernova seem like pointless force, that renders all the radiation of the sun in a measure subordinate to itself, as means is subordinate to end. For perhaps a billion years Nature has been working to perfect the organism that arises from that fertilized egg and the determiners of hereditary traits which that egg contains — determiners passed to it in unbroken succession from countless generations of ancestors and to be passed on to countless generations of descendants.

Contained within the zygote are also the regulators of a pattern of growth that is complex beyond comprehension. Two hundred billion times the egg multiplies itself between fertilization and birth, trillions of times between fertilization and adulthood, by a process involving not only increase in numbers but also specialization of form and function and a continuous series of interrelated changes, a chain reaction, extending from fertilization to death. It is a pattern that produces multiplicity and diversity but also unity, as the multicelled body behaves as an entity.

Start with an almost microscopic zygote. "Add" nothing but food, water, salts, oxygen, and other nonliving materials. Give it a few years in a favorable environment, and we find it falling in love, establishing enduring relationships, creating beauty, contemplating values, seeking truth, and asking, "Who am I? Where did I come from? Why am I here? Where am I going?" All the art, literature, government, science, ethics, philosophy, and religion that we know spring from that zygote. All the reachings and searchings that characterize the human mind and spirit are, in a sense, contained within it.

When we think in terms of potentiality plus parental expectation rather than merely in terms of size, shape, and structure, we see that from the moment of fertilization the zygote is a human individual. For the first nine months it lives and grows in complete darkness, continuously submerged in water, and, during the latter part of the period, upside down a good part of the time. This it can never do again. From the moment of fertilization it is a separate organism, living within its mother, to be sure, but never part of its mother. In a sense, the zygote controls the mother's body more than it is controlled by her body. It is her body that changes to adapt itself to the zygote, while the zygote takes advantage of the adaptations. When we take into account the difference in size, it is not surprising that the means by which the zygote communicates to the mother's body that fertilization has taken place is not completely understood. This is an oversimplification of the situation to dramatize the relationship. When at last the baby emerges from the mother's body, ordinarily by forces that she neither voluntarily initiates nor can willfully control, it is already a highly complicated and well-developed individual, endowed with a unique ability to learn and a unique capacity to grow. This is the miracle of human reproduction.

It is around this miracle of reproduction that a couple may build their perspective relative to having children. Cost, inconvenience, and obstetrical detail need not blind them to the essential process and its meaning. It is as participant in this miracle that a woman, especially, finds profound fulfillment. Since reproduction requires the participation of both husband and wife and literally a part of each is necessary for fertilization to occur, one may readily see what an exhilarating, fascinating, and satisfying experience having a child may be for a happily married pair.

CHROMOSOMES AND GENES

The nucleus of each cell in the body contains *chromosomes*, on which are located *genes*. The genes are complex molecules (deoxyribonucleic acid, referred to as *DNA*) and are the determiners of hereditary traits. For each such trait exhibited by the organism, with some exceptions, there are two genes or sets of genes, one received from each parent. In the *somatic (body) cells* there are forty-six chromosomes (twenty-three pairs), while in the *gametes* (sex cells—*ova* and *spermatozoa*) there are only twenty-three chromosomes, one member of each pair. Thus in order to re-create the twenty-three pairs found in each body cell, two gametes must unite.

Cells increase in number through a process of division (*mitosis*); that is, each cell divides to form two cells, these two to form four, and so

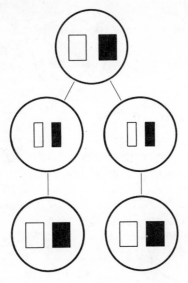

Figure 7. Schematic representation of mitotic cell division.

on. Each chromosome is longitudinally double [King, 1962]. When the cell divides, each chromosome splits lengthwise and one-half goes to each new cell, where it duplicates itself. Thus each new cell has the same chromosome content, the same genetic constitution, as the original cell. This process is shown schematically in Figure 7, where the number of chromosomes is kept to one pair to make the illustration simpler.

After division each half-chromosome develops into a whole one, which has the same relative genetic content (genes) as the half. Each new cell is, therefore, like the original cell as far as chromosome content is concerned. Since all body cells have a common origin in a single cell, all must have the same chromosome content.

In the formation of the gametes, however, the chromosomes, instead of splitting into halves, act as units. One whole chromosome of each pair goes to one new cell. The other whole chromosome goes to the other new cell. The number of chromosomes in each new cell is reduced to half, and the process is termed *meiosis,* or *reduction division.*When two cells unite in fertilization, the original number of chromosomes is restored. This process is shown schematically in Figure 8.

For each hereditary trait exhibited by the organism there are, with some exceptions as mentioned above, at least two genes. Since chromosomes act as units in the formation of the gametes, only one of the genes for a given trait is carried by a gamete. The chromosomes may be "shuffled" and "dealt" to the gametes as playing cards are shuffled and dealt to players. The statistical probability of two gametes having identical genetic content may be compared with the probability of a player's re-

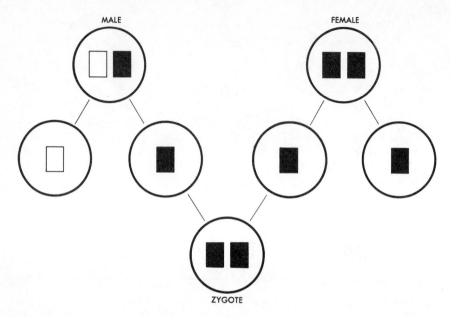

Figure 8. Schematic representation of reduction division and fertilization.

ceiving two identical hands after two separate shufflings and deals, assuming that on each deal he received half of the fifty-two cards. His chance would be expressed in figures of astronomical magnitude. Since this same enormous number of possible combinations of genes is found in the gametes of each parent and the number of gametes also is colossal, one may readily see why, even with all the millions of people in the world, there are no two exactly alike. (One-egg twins have the same genetic constitution.)

THE GAMETES

An *ovum* (plural, *ova*), or female gamete, commonly called *egg,* is globular and is about 1/200 inch in diameter. It is just visible to the naked eye; but relatively few ova have been seen. All the ova needed to produce the population of the world — more than 3 billion — could be contained within the shell of a hen's egg [Hartman, 1962]. At that, ova are the largest single cells in the body and are 60,000 times the volume of sperms. A clump of 60,000 sperms would be just visible to the naked eye [Hartman, 1962]. In an egg such as a hen's, the ovum itself constitutes only an infinitesimal fraction of the whole; the rest is food material for the developing embryo. There is no correlation between the size of the ovum and body size. The ova of rabbits, whales, dogs, gorillas, pigs, and cows, for example, all have approximately the same dimensions.

Sperms (spermatozoa), or male gametes, are minute and are shaped, roughly, like tadpoles. There is an oval head approximately 1/5,000 inch long, a middle piece, and a comparatively long tail, making the total length about $\frac{1}{500}$ inch. The more than 3 billion sperms needed to produce the population of the world could be accommodated in a container about the size of a peppercorn [Hartman, 1962].

Ova are nonmotile; that is, they cannot move by their own power. Sperms, however, propel themselves by lashing their tails in much the same way as a tadpole swims. Relative to their size, they get about fairly well, moving approximately $\frac{1}{7}$ inch per minute. Since each sperm is about $\frac{1}{500}$ inch long, this means that it swims 500 times its length in 7 minutes. A human being walking at an average pace covers about 500 times his height, or approximately $\frac{1}{2}$ mile, in 7 minutes. Relative to their size, sperms swim about as fast as we walk.

Organs and processes in reproduction

THE PRODUCTION OF SPERMS

Sperms form in minute tubes within the *testes (testicles)*, which are two oval-shaped organs suspended in the *scrotum*. These tubes are coiled and would total several hundred feet in length if straightened out. Among the tubes lie the *interstitial cells* that produce the male hormone, *testosterone*, which plays a part in masculinization. The temperature within the scrotum is 2.5 to 4.5°F lower than body temperature [Albert, 1961]. Were it the same, sperm formation could not take place. While the sperms are still immature, they pass, by ciliary action, from the tubules in each testis into the corresponding *epididymis* (a tightly coiled tube about twenty feet long) [Hartman, 1962]. Here, and to some extent in the lower portion of each *vas deferens*, they are stored [Hotchkiss, 1944; Oliven, 1955; Bishop, 1961]. They are not stored in the *seminal vesicles*, as was formerly supposed. During their sojourn in the epididymis, according to Bishop [1961], the sperms acquire the capacity for motility and are capable of movement but remain in a quiescent state.

The *seminal fluid (semen)* is a whitish, viscous mixture composed principally of the secretions of the *prostate gland* and seminal vesicles. At least the vesicular portion of it is stored in the seminal vesicles [Lowsley, Hinman, Smith, and Gutierrez, 1942; Oliven, 1955; Price and Williams-Ashman, 1961]. During sexual excitation the spongy interior of the penis becomes engorged with blood, causing the organ to increase in both size and rigidity and enabling it to enter the vagina. During orgasm, the sperms are moved up through the vasa deferentia by *peristalsis* (waves of muscular contraction) and enter the *urethra*. At this point, through a delicately timed mechanism, they are mixed with the seminal fluid which is being ejaculated (discharged) [Oliven, 1955]. At this time the sperms become active; but whether this activity is the result of stimulation by the seminal fluid or some other factor is not certain [Bishop, 1961].

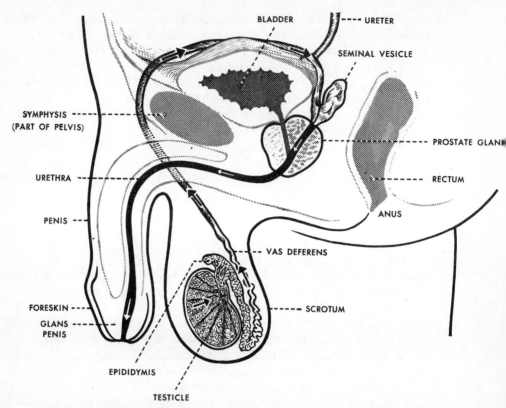

Figure 9. Male genital organs.

Seminal fluid is ejaculated during sexual intercourse. It may also be discharged during masturbation and periodically is discharged spontaneously during sleep, as mentioned in an earlier chapter.

Sperms are produced in prodigious numbers. In a single ejaculation of seminal fluid (about a teaspoonful) there may be hundreds of millions of sperms. Yet, compressed together, they would occupy a space equivalent in size only to the head of a pin. In a single ejaculation, then, there are often more than enough sperms, if every one were used, to produce a population larger than that of the United States.

Once discharged, the sperms move in all directions and diffuse through the vagina. Ordinarily some pass into the uterus; but by what specific means this is brought about is not yet fully known. Various explanations have been suggested, but all rest upon hypotheses that are as yet unproved. It has been said that the sperms swim against currents. If there were some subtle attraction exerted by the ovum, sperms would not enter the uterus when there was no ovum to be fertilized; yet this is known to occur. It has been suggested that electrical charges orient the sperms toward the cervix. It has also been suggested that some of the seminal fluid is ejaculated directly into the uterus. There is no conclusive evidence to prove that there is suction produced by the opening and closing of the cervix during orgasm, as some suggest, though later contractions of the muscular walls of the uterus and tubes may play a part. In fact, conception can take place as a result of rape or in cases in which the wife is frigid and no orgasm occurs. It is hypothetically possible that some sperms are forced into the uterus through the movements of the genital organs in sexual intercourse.

How long sperms live after leaving the body is still unproved. Assuming that there are no unusual environmental conditions, estimates as to the life of the sperms within the female genital tract vary. The period during which they remain effective is relatively brief, probably not more than twenty-four to forty-eight hours.

THE PRODUCTION OF OVA

Ova are produced in the *ovaries*, two oval-shaped organs 1 to 2 inches long situated on either side of the *uterus*. Formation of ova occurs only in prenatal life. Before birth most of them degenerate and the total number is very much reduced. There are about a million immature ova in the

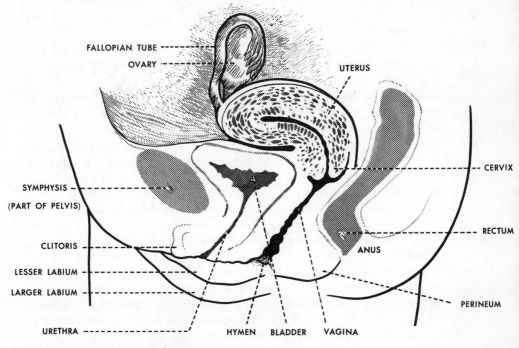

Figure 10. Female genital organs.

ovaries of a newborn female infant. By age seven this number has been reduced to about 300,000. Fewer than 500 are ovulated during a typical woman's reproductive life. There is no evidence that new ova are formed after birth as is sometimes assumed [Baker, 1964].

Ordinarily, ova mature, or "ripen," one at a time in response to a hormone produced by the pituitary gland. During the maturing process the ovum migrates toward the surface of the ovary and becomes surrounded by a fluid, which eventually bulges out the surface tissue of the ovary, forming a blisterlike prominence about the size of half a small cherry. This is the *Graafian follicle,* which secretes a hormone (*estrogen*) which brings about preliminary changes in the uterus in the process of that organ's preparation for the reception of a zygote. At length the follicle bursts, and the ovum is discharged. This release of the ovum is termed *ovulation* and on the average occurs about once in twenty-eight days.

After ovulation, the lining cells of the Graafian follicle undergo change and form the *corpus luteum* (yellow body), which secretes a hormone (*progesterone*) which carries still further the preparation of the uterus for pregnancy. If pregnancy occurs, the progesterone secreted by the corpus luteum holds the uterus in a condition favorable to sustaining it until this function can be taken over by hormones secreted by the placenta. Eventually the corpus luteum degenerates, leaving a small scar on the surface of the ovary. This also occurs in the menstrual cycle, which will be discussed later.

After the ovum leaves the ovary, its life is subject to as much conjecture as is the life of sperms. Probably its effective life, the period during which it may be fertilized, is not more than a few hours, the probable maximum being twenty-four. The ends of the tubes in close conjunction with the ovaries divide into fingerlike projections (*fimbriae*) which, at the time of ovulation, are activated to come into even closer contact than usual with the ovary. There is also evidence to suggest that the muscles in the wall of the tube may contract and relax, developing suction similar to that in a vacuum cleaner, and that by this suction the ovum is drawn into the tube [Engle, 1952]. Both the fimbriae and the interior surface of the tubes are lined with tiny, hairlike protuberances (*cilia*) which have the capacity to move with a whiplike motion. They move more vigorously toward the uterus than toward the ovaries on the return stroke. Thus a current is set up. The ovum, which has been released from the ovary, is drawn into the tube near which it has been released and starts its migration toward the uterus. The ovum is moved along by the cilia, much as a ball might roll over a lawn if the blades of grass could move the ball. The passage through the tube has a diameter only about as large as a broom straw, but that is ample for the movement of the egg.

The ovum is moved along also by tubal peristalsis, that is, waves of muscular contraction in the tube [Greenhill, 1960]. One may envisage the process of tubal peristalsis by imagining a marble in a rubber hose. By pressing the walls of the hose with one's fingers at the back of the marble and sliding the fingers along, one may move the marble. The entire journey from ovary to uterus requires a variously estimated period of about three to seven days. Unless it has been fertilized, the effective life of the ovum will have ceased before it has reached its destination.

FERTILIZATION

Fertilization is the union of sperm and ovum. It ordinarily takes place in one of the Fallopian tubes. Sperms are usually deposited in the vagina near the relatively small entrance to the uterus (external *os* in the *cervix*, that is, the small end of the uterus). They immediately begin to swim in all directions in the vagina. Some pass into the uterus and into the tubes. In one deposit of seminal fluid, even though it may contain several hundred million sperms, many will never enter the uterus. Of those that do, many will enter the wrong tube. Many are likely to be defective, to die shortly after being deposited, or for some other reason to make little or no progress in the direction of the ovum. Only relatively few will actually reach the egg. Hence, typically, a large number of sperms must be deposited for fertilization to occur. It used to be assumed that, since the ovum as released from the ovary is surrounded by cu-

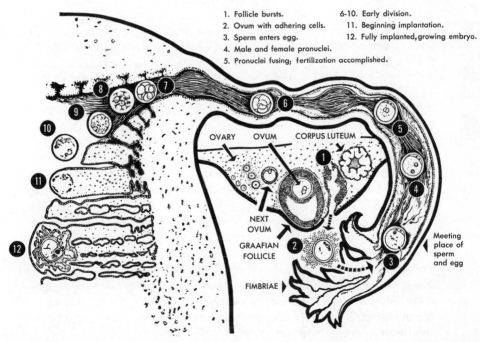

1. Follicle bursts.
2. Ovum with adhering cells.
3. Sperm enters egg.
4. Male and female pronuclei.
5. Pronuclei fusing; fertilization accomplished.

6-10. Early division.
11. Beginning implantation.
12. Fully implanted, growing embryo.

Figure 11. The journey of the ovum (enlarged) from ovulation to implantation.

mulus cells from the follicle, a large number of sperms had to reach the ovum and produce sufficient enzyme to digest away enough cells so that one sperm could reach the ovum proper. Now the pendulum has swung in the opposite direction, to the view that a single sperm carries enough enzyme to make a path for itself in reaching the ovum [Blandau, 1961].

When a sperm meets the ovum, its head penetrates the latter's outer wall, and its nucleus fuses with the nucleus of the egg, reestablishing the twenty-three pairs of chromosomes. After one sperm has penetrated the ovum, ordinarily other sperms are prevented from doing so. Only one sperm can fertilize the ovum. If, by chance, more than one sperm enter the ovum, the latter dies. Since the life span of both the sperms and the ovum is relatively brief, it is obvious that, for fertilization to occur, the sperms must be deposited very near the time of ovulation. At the time of fertilization the new individual's sex and hereditary traits are determined. After fertilization the zygote continues its journey through the tube to the uterus, in the wall of which it implants itself.

Conception occurs through *insemination* (entrance of sperms into the female genital tract). Insemination may be by natural means or by artificial (mechanical) methods in those instances in which natural means fail or there is need for special control. Artificial insemination will be discussed later in this chapter.

Parthenogenesis. Parthenogenesis is the process by which an ovum develops without having been fertilized. It is known to occur naturally among some lower animals and has been brought about experimentally with some such animals. There is no authenticated instance of human parthenogenesis. How, then, may reports of "parthenogenesis" be explained?

Parthenogenesis might be presumed in a case of pregnancy following coitus interruptus and due to sperms in the preejaculate (see p. 601). There is also another possibility. If conditions of moisture, temperature, acidity-alkalinity, location of the ovum in the tube, and number and vigor of sperms were unusually favorable, sperms contained in seminal fluid deposited at the external entrance to the vagina (for example, in "heavy petting" which was just short of intercourse) might pass an intact hymen, through the vagina and uterus, and into the tube. Under such circumstances fertilization could occur in a woman still technically virgin because the penis had never penetrated the vagina in sexual intercourse and the hymen, therefore, remained unaltered [Oliven, 1955; Sjövall, 1964; Friedman, 1962; Stone and Stone, 1953]. Occasionally a case is reported in which a physician is convinced, but, of course, cannot prove, not only that the above occurred but also that the sperms passed through the fabric of underclothing.

DEVELOPMENT OF THE FETUS

After fertilization, the zygote continues its migration through the tube to the uterus. Before it reaches the latter, it has already begun to divide, first into two cells, then into four, eight, sixteen, thirty-two, and so on. During the very early stages, however, it does not increase in size. When it reaches the uterus, it remains free for a period. Then, after several days, it embeds itself in the wall of the uterus, which, through hormone action, has been prepared for its arrival. This process of implantation is accomplished through corrosive action, the zygote dissolving the tissues of the uterine wall and burying itself. In this process the zygote literally digests some of its mother's tissue as food.

As the cells of the zygote continue to multiply, some become specialized to form the *placenta*, the roots, so to speak, through which the fetus receives its food and oxygen supply. These will be described later. Other cells form the *umbilical cord*; still others, the *fetus* proper. Many students have difficulty in visualizing this process because they think of the placenta and the cord (also the amnion) as being part of the mother. Fetus, cord, and placenta make up one unit (see Figure 15). They develop from the zygote in much the same manner as the leaves and branches, trunk and roots of a plant develop from a seed, though, strictly speaking, there are important differences between a zygote and a seed.

Let us carry further the comparison of the zygote with a seed, a comparison which must be made with caution. The most favorable place for a seed to grow is in a specially prepared garden plot. But a seed can grow, at least for a while, anywhere that its roots can find nutriment—the lawn next to the garden plot, a crack in a walk, or a pile of debris. Similarly, the most favorable place for the zygote to grow is in the uterus. But it can grow, at least for a while, anywhere that its "roots" (*villi*) can find food, water, and oxygen. The most common nonuterine location of growth is in one of the Fallopian tubes. A tubal pregnancy is one form of *ectopic* pregnancy. Other forms are rare but do occur. In some cases, for example, the ovum is fertilized before it reaches the tube [Berlind, 1960], even before it leaves the ovary in occasional instances [Greenhill, 1955], or a tubal pregnancy ruptures but the embryo does not die and continues to develop outside the uterus in the abdominal cavity. In such cases, the placenta may be attached to the ovary, the outside of the uterus, ligaments, or other abdominal organs. "Abdominal" pregnancies rarely continue to full term, but instances have been known. In these, of course, the child must be delivered by Caesarean section. The purpose of this discussion is not to emphasize ectopic pregnancy. But often the unusual highlights the usual, and these infrequent cases of extrauterine pregnancy highlight the fact that fetus, placenta, and cord constitute a unit.

Prenatal development extends through approximately nine calendar months. During this period the following changes occur. Figures and stages mentioned represent averages. Allowance must be made for variation in individual cases.

End of first month.   By the end of the first month the embryo is about ¼ inch long. It weighs only a small fraction of an ounce. Many organs have begun to form, but the embryo does not look human. At this early stage, only an expert could distinguish a human embryo from that of a lower animal. Blood has begun to form. What will develop into the heart has already begun to pulsate.

End of second month.   The embryo is now about 1¼ inches long. It now weighs about ¹/₁₄ ounce. The organs have continued their development, and some have assumed their permanent functions. Budlike projections that will form the limbs are noticeable, but fingers and toes are not yet completely formed. The tail has shrunk and will soon disappear, except for a few bones at the lower end of the spine (*coccyx*), which are embedded in other tissue. The face begins to look more nearly human. The embryo may move slightly, but this movement is not detectable by the mother or her obstetrician. Genital organs have appeared and, if the embryo is aborted and carefully examined, the sex may be ascertained. After the second month the new individual is termed a *fetus* rather than an embryo.

End of third month.   The fetus now weighs about an ounce and is approximately 3 inches long. Arms, legs, hands, fingers, toes, and ears are formed. Nails have begun to form. The fetus appears definitely human, but the head is very large in proportion to the rest of the body. Teeth have begun to develop in sockets in the jawbones. Vocal cords are formed.

End of fourth month.   The weight is now 5 to 6 ounces, and the length is 6 to 8 inches. This latter represents about one-third the height at birth. The head is still disproportionately large. The heartbeat is audible through a stethoscope. Limb movements may sometimes be felt by the mother. The body of the fetus is covered with a downlike coat (*lanugo*), which in most cases disappears during the eighth or ninth month. Eyebrows and eyelashes have appeared. The skin is reddish and somewhat transparent. The skin ridges, which in later life will make fingerprints possible, have already formed.

End of fifth month.   The fetus now weighs about 1 pound and is 10 to 12 inches long. Nails are well formed. Head hair has appeared. A mixture of fatty secretion and dead skin cells forms a cheesy covering (*vernix caseosa*) on the surface of the body. Fetal movements may be clearly

1. Four weeks menstrual age

4. Two and one-half months (from rear)

2. Six weeks

3. Seven weeks (from rear)

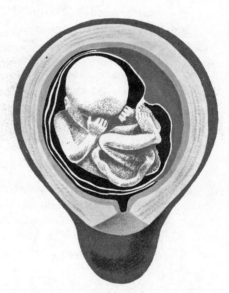

5. Three and one-half months

Figure 12. Early development of embryo and fetus.

felt by the mother. If born at this time, the fetus will survive only a few moments at best.

End of sixth month. The weight is about 2 pounds and the length about 14 inches. The child may live for a few hours if born at this time but has only an extremely slight chance of survival.

End of seventh month. The weight has increased to about 3 pounds and the length to about 16 inches. A child born at this time has a fair chance of survival.

Eighth and ninth months. The weight increases by this time to about 7 to 8 pounds and the length to about 20 inches. The lanugo disappears. Body organs have assumed their permanent functions in most cases. The skin is reddish. The eyes are bluish in color, but their final tone cannot be predicted. Fatty tissue has formed under the skin so that the fetus looks less wrinkled than in earlier months. The vernix caseosa may persist even until birth at full term.

It may be seen by reviewing what has been said above that the fetus gains about 80 per cent of its weight after the fifth month and about 50 per cent during the last two months. A child born at the end of the eighth month has a good chance of survival, much better than at the end of the seventh month, in spite of the common superstition to the contrary. In fact the closer to full term (nine months) the birth occurs, the better are the chances of the child's living.

During a good part of prenatal life the fetus goes through processes similar to those through which it will go after birth. As we have already indicated, it moves its limbs. It swallows some of the amniotic fluid, which is then absorbed through the walls of the digestive tract much as food and water will be later. It takes shallow "breaths," drawing small amounts of amniotic fluid into the lungs. It excretes small amounts of urine. It has alternate periods of activity and rest and may even wake and sleep as it does after birth.

DURATION OF PREGNANCY

Pregnancy usually lasts 270 to 280 days (40 weeks; 9 calendar months). Conception cannot occur unless there is an ovum to be fertilized. Thus conception usually occurs somewhere in the middle of the menstrual cycle. This point will be discussed more fully later. It is impossible to ascertain the exact date of fertilization, even though the exact date of fruitful insemination is known, since time is required for the sperm to reach the egg. A variation of a few days in the length of pregnancy is neither unusual nor abnormal. It is, therefore, impossible to forecast the exact date of the child's birth.

A physician who promises delivery on a predetermined date because he plans to go on his vacation or because the couple want the child born on a holiday, or for some similar reason, is either deceiving the couple or planning to resort to induced labor. The latter is not considered by some physicians to be the best obstetrical practice when there is no acceptable medical indication for it [Greenhill, 1960].

The nine-month period is considered full term. Delivery of the child after seven months of prenatal development (that is, during the eighth or ninth month) is considered premature. Ordinarily any child born before term or weighing less than 5½ pounds is considered premature. Before the end of the seventh month delivery is termed *abortion*. The term *miscarriage* is commonly applied to spontaneous abortion.

Not uncommonly there are reports of unusually long pregnancies. A pregnancy can continue for a relatively brief period beyond the typical 270–280 days. But this overtime period cannot ordinarily be extended for very long because the placenta begins to degenerate [Greenhill, 1961]. Reports of unusually long pregnancies are subject to errors of calculation. For example, a woman has a baby eleven months after her last menstrual period. She assumes an eleven-month pregnancy. Actually she had a normal nine-month pregnancy preceded by two months of amenorrhea.

FETAL PROTECTION AND FOOD AND OXYGEN SUPPLY

As the fetus grows, the uterus enlarges to accommodate it, expanding from a small, pear-shaped organ about 3 inches long and weighing about 2 ounces to an oval organ about 15 inches long and weighing about 2 pounds. Fitting snugly against the inside surface there develop several membranes. The one that will concern us is the *amnion*, which, like the placenta and umbilical cord, arises from the zygote and is thus part of the fetus rather than part of the mother. What is left of the amnion after delivery is expelled with the placenta and cord as afterbirth. Inside the amnion are 1 to 4 pints of amniotic fluid. In this fluid the fetus is suspended. At first it floats about, anchored by the placenta and cord. As it increases in size it fits more snugly inside the uterus. The fetus, then, in a sense has an aquatic existence.

Earlier in this chapter it was stated that when the zygote implants itself in the wall of the uterus, it continues to divide, and some of the cells form "roots," so to speak. These "roots" multiply eventually, forming the placenta, a disk-shaped organ which when fully developed is 7 to 9 inches in diameter, is about 1 inch thick in the middle, and weighs about 1 pound. Strictly speaking there is a maternal as well as a fetal portion to the placenta, namely, the changed tissue of the uterus at the site of attachment (*decidua basilis;* see Figure 13). But for our purposes we shall consider the placenta only as being part of the fetus. On the side in contact with the uterine wall, the placenta is covered with thousands of rootlike projections (*villi*), which branch out in all directions and ramify through the tissue of the uterus. The area of a smooth disk 9 inches in diameter is approximately 64 square inches. The branching and re-branching of the villi increase the area of the uterine side of the placenta to some 70 square feet, about four times the skin area of an adult [Schumann, 1936]—a fact that is important when we consider that this means 70 square feet of absorption surface for food, water, and oxygen.

The villi are loops of blood vessels. These converge to form several

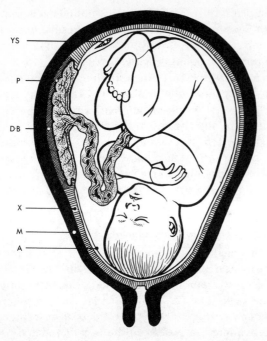

YS

P

D·B

X

M

A

Figure 13. Full term fetus in uterus: *YS*, yolk sac; *P*, placenta; *DB*, decidua basilis (the portion of the endometrium, that is, the lining of the uterus, to which the placenta is attached); *X*, decidua vera (the remaining portion of the endometrium); *M*, muscular wall of uterus; *A*, amnion.

large vessels (two arteries and one vein), which extend through the umbilical cord to the fetus. The cord is about 2 feet long and ½ inch in diameter. It is twisted into a spiral by the uneven growth of the blood vessels and the movements of the fetus.

There is no direct connection between the blood stream of the mother and that of the fetus. The fetus manufactures all his own blood; he gets none from his mother. His circulatory system is a "closed circuit." The villi protrude into the *lacunae* ("lakes" of blood in the wall of the uterus). All food material that reaches the fetus must pass through the membranes of the villi. The process may be compared roughly to the absorption of water through the roots of a plant in an ivy bowl. Waste products pass in the opposite direction and enter the mother's blood stream through the membranes of the villi. The actual process of the food's passing through the membranes is not difficult to understand when one stops to realize that all food passing into his own blood stream must be in solution and pass through the membranes of his intestinal tract and his own blood vessels, since there is no direct, open-ended connection between blood vessels and intestines. Oxygen is absorbed from the mother's blood just as food is. One writer, Barron [1960], refers to the placenta as the "fetal lung." Thus the fetus can live without breathing.

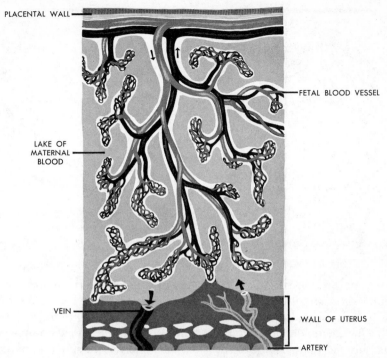

PLACENTAL WALL

FETAL BLOOD VESSEL

LAKE OF MATERNAL BLOOD

VEIN

WALL OF UTERUS

ARTERY

Figure 14. Highly magnified, diagrammatic representation of placental villi.

The fetus lives in a controlled environment, and little that occurs in the outside world seriously affects him. Temperature is controlled by the mother's body temperature. Food and water are filtered through the membranes of the villi. The amniotic fluid acts as a shock absorber and distributes pressure evenly over the body of the fetus. Most disease germs are filtered out by the membranes of the villi. Only relatively few bacteria can pass from mother to child, and these not in every case. The organisms producing syphilis and tuberculosis do sometimes penetrate the defenses.

Viruses can pass from mother to fetus through the placenta. In a study of 1,915 cases of mumps, measles, polio, and other viral diseases, Kaye and Reaney [*Obstetrical and Gynecological Survey*, October, 1962] found abnormalities in the babies in 86 cases (4.5 per cent) and abortion in 115 cases (6 per cent). In a study of 94 cases of mumps, Hyatt [*Obstetrical and Gynecological Survey*, October, 1961] found that 15 per cent of the babies were aborted or stillborn and that 16 per cent had congenital defects. The virus causing smallpox can affect the fetus [Villee, 1960]. The fetus is much more vulnerable to such diseases during the first trimester (three months) of pregnancy. After that the disease is unlikely to cause damage unless, of course, it precipitates spontaneous abortion or premature delivery.

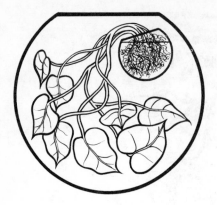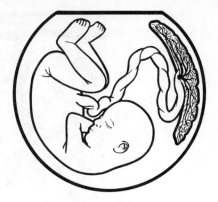

Figure 15. Fetus, cord, and placenta compared to a plant. (Adaptation from sculptured birth series by Dickinson and Belskie in "Birth Atlas," Maternity Center Association, New York.)

In very rare cases fetuses have been affected when the mother was vaccinated for smallpox. But the number of such cases is so small that there is no reason for women to fear vaccination [Eastman, August, 1961]. There is evidence to indicate that a female fetus may be masculinized by hormones administered to the mother during pregnancy [Greenhill, 1960]. Too much anesthesia during childbirth may cause the reactions of the fetus to be depressed to the point where breathing is affected. Narcotic drugs may pass through the placenta to the fetus. Thalidomide, a synthetic drug used as a sedative, tranquilizer, and sleeping tablet, caused several thousand cases of severe malformation (*phocomelia*, a condition in which arms and/or legs are malformed or absent) before it was discovered to be the causative agent and was subjected to control [Greenhill, 1962; Taussig, 1962]. The effects on the fetus of the mother's smoking are not clear; but there is some evidence to suggest that the babies of mothers who smoke have, on the average, a lower weight at birth than the babies of nonsmokers [Greenhill, 1960; Savel and Roth, 1962]. Alcoholic beverages, when used in moderation, appear to have no effect on the fetus [Speert and Guttmacher, 1956]. Alcohol used to excess, however, may have a depressant effect unfavorable to the fetus's normal functioning after birth.

In recent years *rubella* ("German measles"), a viral infection, has come into prominence as a cause of fetal abnormalities. If the mother has rubella during the first trimester of pregnancy, there is a chance that her baby will be affected. If she has it during the first two months, the chance is greatly increased. If she has it after the third month, the chance is markedly decreased. The most common consequences of rubella are fetal death, deafness, cataracts, heart conditions, and mental deficiency caused by damage to the central nervous system [Mayes, 1963]. Because of shortcomings in the method of investigating this problem, earlier reports suggested that the chances that the child would be defective were about nine in ten. As a result, many physicians advised therapeutic abortion. Now it appears that a woman's chances of bearing a normal baby are about nine in ten. In other words, generalizing broadly and keeping in mind the increased risk if rubella is contracted during the first two months of pregnancy, the situation is the reverse of what it was originally assumed to be. As a result, physicians are now more reluctant to recommend therapeutic abortion, though such abortions are sometimes performed [Greenhill, 1959; 1960; 1962; 1963; Campbell, 1961]. Some physicians recommend exposing all young girls to rubella before they marry so that immunity may be established.

If the maternal blood does not afford the fetus the food materials he requires, parasite that he is, he will "eat" his mother. Not that he literally ingests her, but he will draw upon her tissues for his own growth. However, it is not true, as some persons believe, that a woman must lose "a tooth for every child." The fetus does not take calcium from the mother's teeth. Besides, the woman may regulate her diet so that the child is supplied with the food, salts, calcium, and other substances that he needs. There is little, if any, relationship between the amount of food a mother eats and the size of her baby. If she overeats because she believes she must "eat for two," the excess is stored in her own body as fat; it is not transferred to the baby. On the other hand, she cannot keep the weight of the baby down merely by reducing the quantity of food consumed unless she reduces it to the point of starvation [Bourne and Williams, 1953]. The size of her baby is determined largely by heredity, the development of the placenta, and the duration of the pregnancy.

One may readily understand why a woman gains weight during pregnancy. There is a tendency for fat to be deposited. The breasts enlarge, preparatory to supplying the baby with food. The fully developed placenta weighs 1 to 2 pounds, the enlarged uterus about 2, the amniotic fluid 1 to 4, and the child itself, when it has reached full term, 7 to 8.

MATERNAL IMPRESSIONS

Can the baby be affected by what the mother does, sees, or thinks during pregnancy? There is a common superstition that it can. The following "instances" of maternal impressions are typical. As is common during pregnancy, a woman developed a persistent craving for a particular food (termed *pica*), in this case, cherries. At the market she found that cherries were unavailable, because out of season, and therefore she could not buy any. When the baby was born it had a growth "just like a cherry" on its upper lip. A woman was chopping wood, holding a small ax in her right hand. The ax slipped and cut her left hand. She grasped her left hand with her right one to stop the bleeding. When her baby was born it had no fingers on its left hand.

There is no way known by which such experiences can affect the fetus. What actually happens in cases of "observed" maternal impressions and birthmarks is probably this: A child is born with some particular trait or later exhibits certain behavior. The mother wonders about the trait and seeks for an explanation. During her nine months' pregnancy she is almost certain to have had some experience into which she can read what she thinks should be there. Then by turning the situation around she has an "explanation" of the trait. If the child has no birthmark, no explanation is required, so the woman's experiences during pregnancy are not recalled.

SEX DETERMINATION

The sex of the fetus is determined by the combination of chromosomes in the fertilized egg. Other factors may play a role, in some cases, in causing the individual to shift from one side of the sexual fence to the other or to fall into an equivocal position somewhere between maleness and femaleness. Nevertheless, at the moment of fertilization the pattern is usually set.

With regard to the chromosomes of sex determination, all ova are alike; they all bear what is termed an X chromosome. Sperms bear either an X or a Y chromosome. The Y chromosome is somewhat smaller than the X. When in the process of fertilization an XX combination is produced, the individual develops into a female. An XY combination produces a male. In the X and Y chromosomes there are genes other than those determining sex. The Y chromosome, however, contains fewer of these than the corresponding X chromosome. Therefore, in the male certain traits are the result of the action of one gene alone, while in the female these traits are the result of two genes acting together. Hence, some traits tend to be sex-linked and occur much more frequently in males than in females.

Sex determination in the genetic sense is not the same as ascertaining the sex of the fetus. Guttmacher [1933] mentions a number of supposed "tests" used for this purpose. According to these "tests," if the baby kicks on the mother's right side, it will be a boy; if it kicks on her left side, it will be a girl. A boy is "carried high"; a girl is "carried low." Loss of hair by the mother indicates a girl; more profuse hair growth, a boy. A boy is more active than a girl. If the mother develops a preference for sweet foods, the baby will be a girl; a preference for sour foods indicates a boy. Boys are believed to cause more nausea. As Guttmacher points out, all such "tests" are without foundation in fact.

Until recently there was no accurate means of ascertaining the sex of the fetus in the uterus. The difference between male and female heartbeat is not reliable, since there is so much overlapping. This is true also of fetal size. If the fetus is aborted after the first six or so weeks of pregnancy, sex may be ascertained, but such a fetus, of course, dies. Before the end of six weeks of pregnancy the cells that will form the gonads (testes or ovaries) are undifferentiated, and the genital organs exhibit the same development in both sexes; hence the sex of the fetus cannot be ascertained by examining these organs.

It is now known [Eastman, 1960] that in the somatic cells of the female there is a dark mass (*nuclear chromatin*) that is not present in the cells of the male. The presence or absence of this mass may be established through microscopic examination by the end of the second week of embryonic life. But, of course, no such examination could be made at this early stage unless the fetus were aborted. During prenatal development, fetal skin cells flake off and remain in the amniotic fluid. By midpregnancy such cells may be examined by withdrawing a small quantity of amniotic fluid from the uterus by means of a hypodermic needlelike instrument which is introduced into the uterus through the abdominal wall. This procedure is termed *paracentesis*. But this method is not without risk, and, as far as a given woman is concerned, the procedure is out of proportion to what is learned, so the end hardly justifies the means.

Means for controlling the sex of the child are as fantastic as some of the "tests." GIRL IS BORN IN ACID TEST TO FIX SEX, reads a newspaper headline. The article goes on to say that the use of an acid douche will ensure the birth of a girl; an alkaline douche, the birth of a boy. A theory expounded in some quarters holds that if the wife is "dominant," the child will be a girl; if the husband is "dominant," the child will be a boy. Another theory states it a bit differently, holding that the sex of the child is dependent upon the degree of masculinity and femininity in both persons. Such theories have no basis in fact, although there is some evidence to suggest that the relative health of the parents may play a part. At the present stage of scientific knowledge there is no practical means by which the sex of the child may be controlled.

Signs of pregnancy

When a woman has reason to believe that she may be pregnant, she wants to know the facts as soon as possible so that she may plan accordingly. There are several types of symptoms that may aid in diagnosing her condition. These are termed *presumptive* and *positive* signs. Disregarding for the moment the conditions in the mother's body that make tests for pregnancy possible (and even these may be produced by factors other than conception), the relationship between mother and baby may be dramatized by pointing out that the presumptive signs of pregnancy are exhibited by the mother, while the positive signs are exhibited by the baby. There are even cases of "false pregnancy" (*pseudocyesis*), in which hormonal factors or emotional factors, such as a great desire for a baby or a deep fear of having one, cause a woman to exhibit some of the signs of pregnancy when she is not pregnant at all.

READING 16 **LIFE FORCE: A REPORT OF A CASE OF FALSE PREGNANCY**

"This pregnancy is no different from my others," said the Oklahoma housewife mildly. Physicians had indeed found that their 27-year-old patient had just about all the obvious signs of a four-month pregnancy. What flabbergasted them was the knowledge that two years before, she had undergone a hysterectomy, and thus could not possibly have conceived.

Last week the University of Oklahoma Hospitals reported that rarely in medical annals has the poignant phenomenon of false pregnancy—pseudocyesis—survived such odds of matter over mind. Pseudocyesis is older than Hippocrates, has affected subjects from seven to 79. Modern medicine knows it as a mental condition, arising from emotional needs so intense that they lead to suppression of menstruation, distention of the abdomen, enlargement of the breasts, and morning nausea. Most cases involve psychotic women with a feeble grasp of reality. But this patient was not psychotic. Her perceptions were normal; she knew all along that the operation had barred her from reproduction.

Maternity clothes. Her trouble, as the physicians analyzed it, sprang from her intense desire to be "a whole woman." At 13, she developed chronic diabetes. After her first marriage at 18, diabetes complicated the birth of her only child, who was delivered by Caesarean section. Married again at 19, the girl insisted on a second pregnancy against the wishes of both her physician and new husband. The result was a stillborn delivery in the fourth month, followed by the hysterectomy.

Depressed after the operation, she tried vainly to adopt a second child. She lost interest in housework, devoted hours to playing with her daughter, sometimes reversing their roles. When her husband became interested in a more mature woman, she quickly seized upon pregnancy as the

Courtesy TIME: copyright Time, Inc., 1958.

only means of keeping her home and self-esteem. Last year she developed all the symptoms of pseudocyesis, including the same sharp decrease in the insulin required to control her diabetes that she had experienced in her real pregnancies.

Labor pains. She readily consented to psychiatric treatment at a University of Oklahoma hospital. Physicians found her responsive, warm in temperament, of high average intelligence — and inexplicably able to subsist on only six insulin units per day against her normal daily dosage of 30 to 40. After only five weeks of treatment, she appeared fully prepared mentally to end her strange charade. The only question seemed to be how to do it without social embarrassment. Her solution: she returned to the hospital in ordinary clothes after a weekend pass, told fellow patients that she had aborted spontaneously while at home.

Yet the symptoms of false pregnancy stayed on. Three weeks later, still in the hospital, she awoke with severe "labor pains." Not until the "labor pains" had continued for 24 hours did her "pregnancy" finally end, five months after it began. Next day her insulin need promptly rose. At last she gave away her maternity clothes and went home, where she is now living with her husband and child.

PRESUMPTIVE SIGNS

Temporary cessation of menstruation. This is one of the first signs noticeable, but it is not reliable, since factors other than pregnancy (for example, illness, tumors, nervous shock, experience highly colored with emotion, or change of climate) may interrupt the menstrual cycle. Worry about possible pregnancy may cause menstruation to be delayed or cause a period to be missed. Some women are so irregular that an occasional rather long delay is not unusual.

Since it takes several months for the fetal and the maternal portions of the placenta to fuse, and since the ovary sometimes continues to function after conception, it is possible for menstruation to continue for a month or two after the beginning of pregnancy. When this occurs, the flow is usually scanty. In some instances, bleeding due to other factors is mistaken for menstruation.

Morning sickness. About a third of pregnant women have marked symptoms of nausea. About a third have occasional or mild symptoms. The other third have no symptoms at all [Greenhill, 1955]. Morning sickness may be relieved by medication and usually disappears by the end of the third month. Some cases are due to physiological changes, but there is reason to believe that others are the result of suggestion. If a woman has heard that illness accompanies pregnancy, she may expect it and have her expectations fulfilled through the machinations of her own mind. If she fears pregnancy, that too may contribute to her illness.

Increased frequency of urination.   This is due to congestion in certain blood vessels.

Increased vaginal secretion.   This is especially noticeable in women who have previously had considerable vaginal discharge.

Changes in the breasts.   Slight pain, a sense of fullness, increased size of nipples, increased pigmentation around the nipples, secretion of a fluid termed *colostrum*, increased size of breasts, prickling or tingling sensations, increased blood supply so that blood vessels may be seen under the skin – these are all symptoms accompanying pregnancy but are not positive proof that conception has occurred.

Changes in the vaginal lining.   The lining becomes congested and bluish in color.

Enlargement of the abdomen.   This occurs rather late for diagnosis in ordinary cases and may be due to some factor other than pregnancy, for example, a tumor.

Softening of the cervix.   In the nonpregnant state, the cervix is firm.

Changes in the form, size, and position of the uterus.   As pregnancy progresses, the uterus becomes larger, less pear-shaped and more nearly globular, and at first tends to slope forward more than ordinarily.

Intermittent uterine contractions.   At about the end of the second month the uterus begins to contract at irregular intervals (Braxton Hicks contractions). These contractions may be detected by the obstetrician but are not felt by the mother. Since no dilation of the cervix accompanies these contractions, they do not constitute true labor.

Ballottement, or repercussion.   The fetus is at first too small, and late in pregnancy too large, for this sign to be used; but between the sixteenth and the thirty-second week the physician may, during an examination of the woman, feel the floating fetus rebound against the wall of the uterus. [Greenhill, 1955].

Basal body temperature. The basal body temperature is the body temperature of an individual upon waking in the morning. It tends to be maintained at a relatively high level during pregnancy. A level of 98.8 to 99.9°F, maintained for more than sixteen days, is highly suggestive of pregnancy. Diagnosis of pregnancy based on body temperature is accurate in 97 per cent of cases [Greenhill, 1955]. In order to use this method, however, records of temperatures must be kept both before and after conception, and other possible causes of fever must be ruled out.

POSITIVE SIGNS

The positive signs of pregnancy are certain evidence of its occurrence, since these signs can be produced by no factors other than a live fetus.

Movement of the fetus in the uterus. This movement is noticeable for the first time usually during the fourth or the fifth month, that is, about halfway through the pregnancy. The fetal movements are often vigorous and may be distinctly felt by the mother. In advanced pregnancy they may be seen by an observer.

Fetal heartbeat. This is audible to the physician by means of a stethoscope, usually at about the fourth month. The rate varies from 120 to 160 beats per minute, which is about twice the mother's rate under normal conditions. Thus the two beats may be distinguished.

The shape of the fetus. This may be felt through the abdominal wall.

The appearance of the fetus in an X-ray photograph. This method of diagnosis is possible only late in pregnancy after other signs have appeared. Therefore, it is usually unnecessary. X-ray studies are sometimes made before delivery, however, to determine the size of the fetal head relative to the opening in the mother's pelvis or to assist in the diagnosis of multiple pregnancy. Such studies should supplement, not replace, careful clinical observation. Exposure to X rays for photographic purposes is not to be confused with exposure for therapy or the careless exposure of technicians.

Tests for pregnancy

The positive signs are observable only when pregnancy is well advanced. The presumptive signs are not conclusive, and few of these are observable during the early stages. The importance of some means of diagnosing pregnancy very shortly after it begins is apparent. This means has been provided by pregnancy tests.

The placenta produces several hormones, one of which is termed *chorionic gonadotropin* and is referred to as *CG*. Through the process of metabolism and excretion, CG passes into the urine of the pregnant woman, where it is detectable by about the tenth day after ovulation. Since CG is produced by the placenta, it is found only during pregnancy. Also, since it is produced by the placenta rather than the fetus, its presence indicates only a functioning placenta, not a live baby [Hon, 1961].

In biologic tests for pregnancy, urine from a woman presumably pregnant is introduced into a test animal. If the woman is not pregnant, there will be no CG present and the animal will not respond. If the woman is pregnant, CG will be present and the animal will respond as follows [Hon, 1961]:

The A-Z (Ascheim-Zondek) mouse test. Five immature white mice are used. Into each mouse urine is injected subcutaneously three times a day for two days. Then, 100 hours after the first injection the ovaries of the mice are examined. If corpora lutea have formed, the test is positive. Although all tests are subject to error and false positives are possible, typically a positive test indicates that the woman is pregnant. The A-Z test has a high degree of accuracy. It is no longer widely used, however, because of the long interval that must elapse before the result is available and also because of the difficulty of keeping on hand a large number of test animals.

The Friedman rabbit test. A mature female rabbit that has been isolated from males for three to four weeks is used. The urine is injected into a vein in the external ear. Forty-eight hours after the injection, the rabbit's ovaries are examined. If ruptured Graafian follicles are found, the test is positive. A positive reaction may be found in twenty-four hours. If it is not, this does not prove that the woman is not pregnant, and a reexamination should be made at the end of forty-eight hours. The Friedman test has the high degree of accuracy of the A-Z test with the advantage of having the results available sooner. It is, however, relatively expensive because of the cost of keeping the animals on hand.

The rat hyperemia test. Two immature female white rats are used. The urine is injected subcutaneously. After sixteen to twenty-four hours the animals' ovaries are examined. Accuracy is reduced if the animals are examined earlier than this. If the test is negative, the animals' ovaries will appear small and pale or slightly pinkish. If it is positive, the ovaries will appear enlarged and entirely reddened or covered by red spots because of their increased blood supply (*hyperemia*). The major disadvantage of this test is the difficulty of interpreting the condition of the ovaries. High accuracy can be maintained only by skilled technicians.

Frog and toad tests. Various species of frogs and toads of both sexes are used. When the urine of a pregnant woman is injected into a female animal, it causes her to lay eggs. When it is injected into a male animal, it causes him to produce sperms. There is variation in the time required for these tests, depending upon the animal used. But in some cases positive results have been available in as little as three hours. There is not so high a degree of accuracy in these tests as in those using mice, rabbits, or rats because frogs and toads are less sensitive than these other animals, and their sensitivity exhibits seasonal variations.

The margin of error in these biologic tests is due to several factors. Test animals sometimes vary in their reactions. Too early administration of the test, too great dilution of the urine, or keeping the urine too long before injecting it may affect results. As suggested above, there are seasonal variations in the sensitivity of frogs and toads. Foreign substances in the urine may affect the test animal.

Occasionally urine specimens are mixed up in a laboratory. In rare cases complications in the woman may cause the test to be positive when she is not pregnant or negative when she is. As mentioned earlier, a positive test does not prove that the fetus is alive; it indicates only that some of the placental tissue is alive. The placenta may live after the death of the fetus, but the death of the latter follows promptly upon the death of the former. In some cases the test may be positive after childbirth or abortion, since enough of the hormone remains in the mother's blood so that it passes into the urine.

Other tests for pregnancy. Chemical tests to determine the presence of CG or the increase in hormones produced by the mother during pregnancy have been devised, but none has the accuracy of the biologic tests. A similar observation may be made of the colostrum test. Colostrum is a substance secreted by the breasts. A subcutaneous injection of colostrum causes a nonpregnant woman to develop a reddened and swollen area on the skin, a wheal, like that caused by some insect bites. This wheal persists for more than an hour. In early pregnancy the injection causes a whitish wheal which disappears within an hour. Experiments have been made with other tests. In one type, serum instead of urine is used. In another type, hormones are administered orally. Since the dosage is limited, a condition of hormone withdrawal is produced. If the woman has vaginal bleeding following this procedure, she is assumed not to be pregnant. If she has no vaginal bleeding, she is assumed to be pregnant. This test causes nausea in a few women. It cannot be used safely if the woman has cancer of the breast or genital organs. The perfect test for pregnancy has not yet been devised. All known tests involve a margin of error or are contraindicated in some cases. Up to date, no test has been found which entirely replaces the biologic tests mentioned above [Hon, 1961].

Childbirth

Some two weeks before the onset of labor, the fetus shifts its position so that it is lower in the pelvis and has started to enter the birth canal. This process is termed *lightening*. In some cases, at about this time there are irregular contractions of the uterus, termed *false labor*. When the fetus has reached full term, that is, when it has reached its full prenatal development, complicated factors not fully understood cause the uterus to contract, and labor begins. During pregnancy the uterine muscle cells increase, not only in number but also in size, to prepare the organ for its role in expelling the fetus. As the uterus contracts, pushing the child against the cervix, the latter dilates until it is practically effaced for the time.

Labor may be divided into three stages: first stage—from the beginning of contraction (not of dilation, since in many cases dilation is under way before labor starts) to the complete dilation of the cervix; second stage—from this point to the birth of the child; third stage—from the birth of the child to the expulsion of the afterbirth and the final contraction of the uterus. In the first stage the pains accompanying contraction are, at the beginning, slight and rather far apart (twenty minutes or more). As labor progresses, they occur closer together in an increasingly rapid rhythm. As contraction proceeds, one side of the amniotic sac ("bag of waters") is forced by pressure to protrude through the opening in the cervix. At length the sac bursts and some of the amniotic fluid is discharged. In some cases this discharge is the announcement of the onset of labor. If the membrane ruptures prematurely (*dry birth*), the cervix may be dilated too rapidly. In some cases the onset of labor is announced by a somewhat bloody vaginal discharge, the "show," caused by the loosening of the mucous plug which is normally found in the cervix; but such discharge may occur before or after the onset of labor and is, therefore, not a reliable indication.

The average (mean) duration of labor in American white women is about thirteen hours for first babies and about eight hours for subsequent deliveries. Such figures must be interpreted with caution, however. The average (mean) is derived by including all labors, those that are longer than average as well as those that are shorter. It may, therefore, be misleading. The modal duration of labor, that is, the length that occurs most frequently, is about half the mean, or about seven hours for first births and about four hours for subsequent deliveries.

There is not severe pain during the entire labor. During the early part of the first stage of labor the pain is relatively mild. It increases in intensity as labor progresses and the contractions of the uterus become stronger and closer together (every two to three minutes). The pain becomes more severe during the second stage of labor, which lasts an hour or so, though there is, of course, considerable variation among

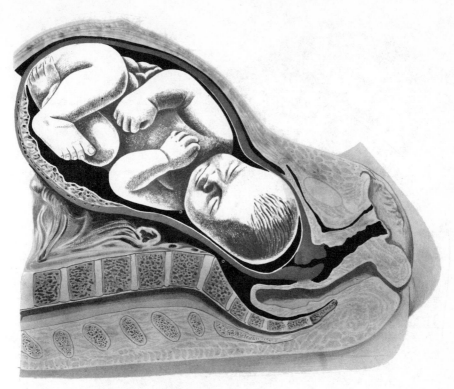

Figure 16. Fetus at term before beginning of labor.

women. Put differently, a woman in a normal delivery with her first child can be expected to pass through the second stage in no more than twenty to thirty pains, and in some cases less than twenty. The number may be expected to be reduced in subsequent deliveries. The pain of labor reaches its crest when the baby's head passes through the external opening of the vagina and emerges from the mother's body. This passage is usually accomplished in one strong expulsive movement, and the process lasts only a few moments. The pain of the third stage of labor is usually not severe, and the mother may experience only a drawing sensation. Ordinarily this stage is relatively brief [Greenhill, 1955].

As labor progresses from first through second stage, the child moves slowly through the birth canal, pushed along by the contractions of the uterus. Progress is not continuous, however. When the uterus contracts, the child is moved forward. When it relaxes, the child slips back, but not so far back as he was moved forward. Progress is made, therefore, by alternate forward and backward movements in increasingly rapid rhythm, until at the very end it is predominantly forward. The tissue of that portion of the uterus that is normally the cervix, but is now more

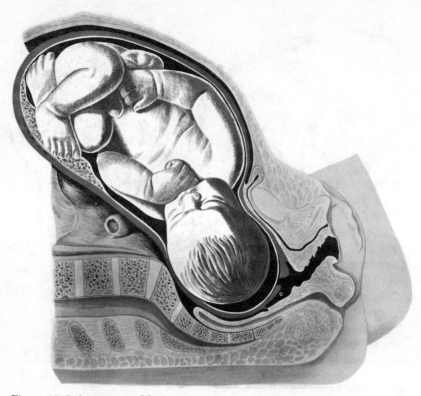

Figure 17. Labor: cervix dilating.

or less indistinguishable from the rest of the organ except for the open-ing, moves up over the child's head. In about 95 per cent of cases the baby enters the birth canal head first. In the other 5 per cent he enters feet first, buttocks first (breech presentation), or in some other manner. One of the problems in such deliveries is that the umbilical cord, instead of passing from the child's abdomen past the feet to the placenta, passes between the child's head and the wall of the birth canal. Hence it may be subjected to so much pressure that the child's oxygen supply is cut off. In some instances in which there is not a head presentation the obstetrician may turn the child in the uterus. This process is termed *version* and may be done by external manipulations or by the doctor's working through the vagina.

The child's head is almost as broad as its shoulders. Owing to the relatively large proportion of cartilage and small proportion of bone in its skeleton, its whole body is somewhat flexible. The head is more rigid than most parts, but even the head yields somewhat to pressure. At times a child's head is pressed slightly out of shape during the birth process (*molding*). This is often a matter of concern to young couples

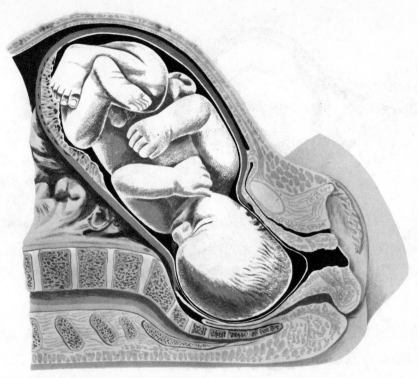

Figure 18. Labor: cervix completely dilated. Note amniotic sac.

who have just had their first baby. They conclude that it is abnormal, not knowing that nature takes care of this problem and that, unless there has been some complication, the head will soon reshape itself.

The child's head must pass through the opening in the mother's pelvis, and the fit is close. For this reason it is most important for the mother to have the obstetrician measure her pelvis as soon as she becomes pregnant, if he has not done so before. When he knows what to expect, he may prepare for it. Later X-ray photographs may be taken if this procedure seems to be indicated. In a sense the child's head is like a cat's whiskers. Any opening through which the head will pass will accommodate the rest of the body. Hence, after the head is born the rest is relatively easy, and the body is rapidly expelled.

There is evidence to show that during pregnancy, especially in young women, owing to a softening of the cartilage, there is a degree of relaxation in the pubic joint (the place at which the pelvic bones meet in the fore part of the body) and that this relaxation permits a slight increase in the gap between the bones. This process prepares the pelvis for childbirth. Opinions differ, however, as to the extent to which this condition influences the course of labor. The probability is that in most cases the

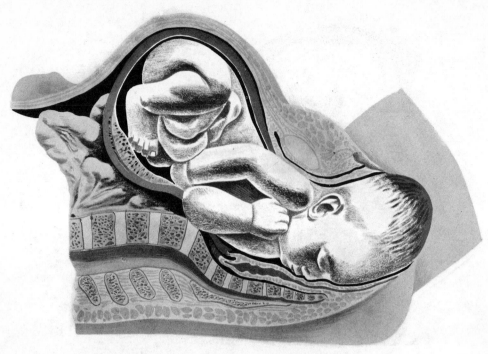

Figure 19. Labor: head begins to appear. Note rotation of head.

influence upon labor is relatively minor. We can be sure that the pelvic bones do not open in the manner of a drawbridge to permit the baby to pass through without resistance.

In addition to the resistance afforded by the rather snug fit of the birth canal, during childbirth the child's head meets three points of resistance, namely, the cervix, the mother's pelvis, and the muscles surrounding the external opening of the vagina. If these muscles are unyielding and if in pressing against them the child's head is subjected to too great pressure for too long, the blood supply to the brain may be reduced to the point of damage to brain tissue due to oxygen deprivation. There may also be damage to the mother. The obstetrician may facilitate the child's progress and relieve the pressure on its head by one or both of two procedures. He may use obstetrical forceps, whose function is as much to protect the child's head as to facilitate its movement through the muscular ring. The other procedure involves an incision in the muscle tissue surrounding the entrance to the vagina. Such an incision is made under anesthesia and is termed an *episiotomy*. Its function is to increase the size of the vaginal opening and permit the ready passage of the child through it. It is safe and constitutes a small price in maternal discomfort for the protection and safety of the baby.

In recent years the vacuum extractor (sometimes referred to as a

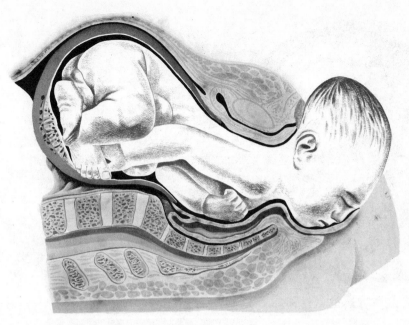

Figure 20. Labor: head turns upward.

ventouse) has been given some publicity as a possible alternative to the obstetrical forceps. This device consists of a suction cup which fits onto the crown of the baby's head. By this means the obstetrician may assist the baby's passage through the birth canal. The vacuum extractor has been used more widely in Europe than in this country. There is a good deal of difference of opinion among American obstetricians as to its value and safety. In some cases, it has been used with success. In others, babies have been injured, as they have been with forceps [Greenhill, 1961, 1962, 1963; Eastman, 1960, August, 1961, 1962, 1963; Thompson, 1962; Chalmers, 1963].

In extreme cases, when the passage of the baby through the mother's bony pelvic opening is impossible or would entail too great risk, or when the uterus does not contract properly and is ineffective, Caesarean section may be used. A Caesarean section is an abdominal operation in which the uterus is opened surgically and the child is removed from the mother without passing through the birth canal. Ordinarily the obstetrician can predict whether such an operation will be necessary, and plans may be made accordingly. Sometimes, however, he elects to let the mother go through trial labor to see whether she can be delivered normally. If she cannot, a Caesarean section is then performed. Childbirth is a natural process. Caesarean section is not, and it involves risk, as any major operation does. In skilled hands the outcome is usually favorable, especially when the operation is planned, and it is also

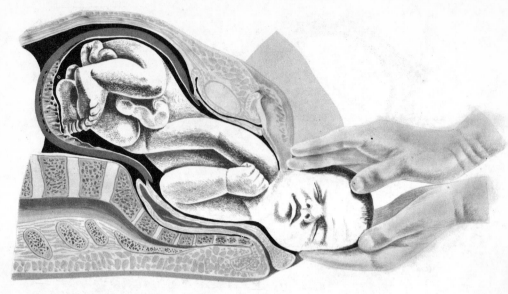

Figure 21. Labor: birth of shoulders.

usually fraught with less risk than an extraordinarily difficult delivery. Caesarean section is not, however, as some persons suppose, a simple means of avoiding normal delivery. Caesarean section also involves risk to the baby. Babies born by means of Caesarean section have a higher mortality rate than babies born by the natural vaginal route. A woman may have several Caesarean sections without any unfavorable consequences. Some physicians used to recommend that, if a woman had two living children, she be sterilized during her third Caesarean section. But attitudes on this matter are changing, and today fewer physicians are inclined to make such a recommendation.

Normally the child cries as soon as it is born; in some cases, as soon as the head is born. In rare cases the child cries while it is still in the uterus. This cry fills the lungs with air. If the child does not cry spontaneously, oxygen or a mixture of carbon dioxide and oxygen is introduced into its respiratory tract. This method usually resuscitates the infant. Violent manipulations, such as swinging by the feet, immersion into hot and cold water alternately, and pulling on the tongue, belong to a past era and have no place in modern obstetrics.

Immediately after it is born, the baby is identified. This is accomplished by placing something around its neck with identification on it, taping something to its back, recording its palm prints, recording its footprints (which are easier to obtain with a newborn infant than are palm prints), or a combination of methods. Recently a new method of identification has been developed [Fields, Falls, Warren, and Zimberoff, 1960]. It was found that each baby's ears are unique in form and that the

ears of different babies can be distinguished from one another. The
method involves photographing the baby's ear, the mother's fingerprint,
and other pertinent data all at one time so that complete identification
is available on one photographic print. The umbilical cord is bound or
fastened in two places near the baby's body. This is not done until the
cord has stopped pulsating, however, showing that circulation of blood
through the placenta has ceased. If it is done too soon, more blood than
the baby can afford to lose may still be in the placenta and cord. The cord
is then severed between the ligatures. The stub of cord attached to the
child's body eventually drops off, leaving a small scar. To prevent infection, antiseptic substance is put into the infant's eyes.

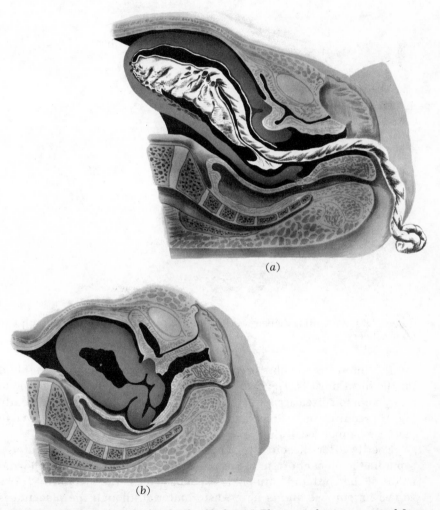

(a)

(b)

Figure 22. Labor: uterus after birth of baby. (a) Placenta almost separated from
uterus; (b) uterus after expulsion of placenta.

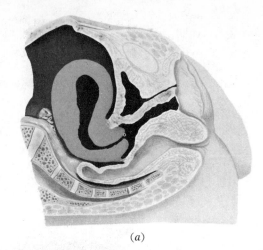

(a)

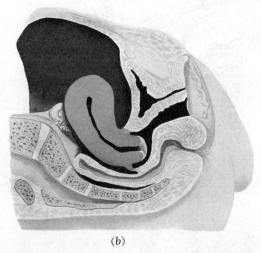

(b)

Figure 23. Uterus after delivery: (a) fifth day after delivery; (b) fourteenth day after delivery.

It is interesting to note in how many ways Nature prepares the child for the birth process. His body is flexible. He is temporarily immune to many common diseases. He can live longer than an adult without breathing. He requires no food for a day or two. He is relatively insensitive to pain. He cannot recall the experience.

Shortly after the birth of the child the contractions of the uterus separate the placenta from the uterine wall, and the placenta, with what is left of the cord and amnion, is expelled. This is the afterbirth. It has served its purpose and is now waste material, though the placenta is carefully examined to make sure that no portion of tissue has remained in the uterus to serve as the seat of infection or to cause hemorrhage.

When the afterbirth has been expelled, hormones cause the uterus to contract, squeezing the ends of the blood vessels together and preventing bleeding.

From this point on for about six weeks, the mother goes through a period of recuperation, during which the genital organs gradually assume approximately their original size and shape. Recovery is usually rapid and proceeds without mishap if the woman follows the physician's instructions. If she does so, there is no reason why she should have a permanently protruding abdomen or become permanently overweight.

RELIEF OF PAIN

An uninformed person could get the impression from current discussion that there are various types of childbirth and that a woman must choose among them when she has a baby. We hear of childbirth without pain; "natural childbirth," that is, childbirth without anesthesia; childbirth without fear; childbirth without risk. There is considerable confusion as to just what each of these implies. At times one type is assumed to be synonymous with another.

A reliable obstetrician will do what he can do with safety to make a woman comfortable during labor and delivery; but he cannot safely guarantee the complete absence of pain in every case. At the present stage of knowledge, there is no drug or combination of drugs that can eliminate all the pain of labor with complete safety in all cases. Excessive anesthesia may also injure the child. Therefore no woman should make impossible demands of her obstetrician, and no obstetrician should make promises that he cannot safely fulfill.

Generalizing, there are three types of drugs used for obstetrical pain relief: *anesthetics*, which produce other insensibilities, even unconsciousness, as well as insensitivity to pain; *analgesics*, which produce insensitivity to pain without affecting other sensibilities; and *amnesic agents*, which produce forgetfulness. These drugs are administered in the following ways:

1. Hypodermic injection.
2. Paracervical block, in which an injection is made into the tissue on either side of the cervix.
3. Pudendal block, in which injections are made to block the nerves supplying the lower part of the vagina and the surrounding area.
4. Inhalation of a gaseous substance.
5. Spinal anesthesia, in which the anesthetic drug is introduced into the space between the spinal cord and the bony structure of the spinal column. *Saddle block* is one type of spinal anesthesia.
6. Continuous caudal anesthesia, in which a flexible needle to which a tube is attached or a small plastic tube is introduced into the space between the spinal cord and the bony structure of the lower part of the spinal column and taped into position, permitting the introduction of

the anesthetic drug a little at a time by a "continuous drip" method. This procedure makes possible a degree of control of the quantity of drug introduced that is not possible with spinal anesthesia. Female students who have never borne a child often have difficulty in visualizing this process and may be somewhat taken aback at the idea of having such equipment taped to the lower part of the back. Women who have had continuous caudal anesthesia do not find this a problem. The reader must remember that we are discussing pain relief, not pain production.

7. General anesthesia.

Exactly what drugs are to be used and how they are to be administered is a decision that must be made by the obstetrician and/or anesthesiologist in each case. Generalization is impossible. The decision will depend upon the woman's preferences, the physician's preferences and special skills, the woman's condition and reaction to certain drugs, the hospital staff and equipment available, and other similar considerations. All known methods of pain relief have advantages and disadvantages. None is perfect.

Much has been written in recent years, some of it prematurely and some irresponsibly, about anesthesia in obstetrics. Popular writers have often given the impression that the day is at hand when all women will be spared all the pain of labor by a simple, universally applicable, absolutely safe technique. Unfortunately, such is not the case. Varieties of spinal and caudal anesthesia have been given special publicity because of their dramatic effects. When continuous caudal anesthesia is successful, it is very good. However, it cannot be used in all cases. Some women cannot tolerate the drugs employed. Its administration requires special skill. It can be administered safely only in an adequately staffed and equipped hospital; it is not to be used casually. The patient must have a trained person in constant attendance. Some women complain of headaches after having had spinal anesthesia. There is an element of risk involved, and for this reason some obstetricians do not recommend its general use [Greenhill, 1963]. In obstetrical anesthesia and analgesia encouraging steps forward have been taken, but the final answer has not yet been found. This is, however, no reason for a woman to fear childbirth; as we shall see, for a woman in good health having a baby is one of the safest things she can do. Her answer to the questions about anesthesia is to choose a competent obstetrician.

"Natural childbirth" implies labor and delivery without anesthesia or analgesia or with a minimum of either, as advocated by Dr. Grantley Dick Read and others. There are women who prefer this method, and some report that the birth of the baby was an exhilarating experience. The advocates of "natural childbirth" have performed a service in calling attention to the importance of physiological preparation through exercise, relaxation, and improvement of health in general and psychological preparation through increased understanding, acceptance, and elimination of tension and fear. But "natural childbirth" is neither universally applicable nor universally desired. We must beware thinking of any method as *the* method and must think in terms of what is best for a particular woman under particular circumstances. Otherwise, what might be a helpful addition to the art and science of obstetrics becomes a cult that may do more harm than good.

Hypnosis has been used successfully to relieve the pain of childbirth in some cases. It has certain advantages, especially where the woman cannot tolerate anesthetic drugs. On the other hand, not all women can be hypnotized with equal success. Even for those who can be hypnotized, a time-consuming period of preparation is necessary. Hypnosis should be employed only by qualified individuals who have had proper training in its use. Such training must involve more than mere proficiency in hypnotic techniques. There must also be sufficient knowledge of psychiatry and of symptoms of mental illness to enable the hypnotist to recognize those cases in which hypnosis would be dangerous. In obstetrics, then, hypnosis, though a helpful tool in some cases, has limited usefulness [Eastman, February, 1962].

An interesting device for the relief of the pain of labor is the recently developed decompression suit [Greenhill, 1959, 1962; Heyns, 1963]. This suit consists of a dome-shaped decompression chamber constructed of plastic and steel and fitted over the woman's abdomen. Air is then drawn from the chamber, reducing the inside pressure to about one-fifth the external atmospheric pressure. This exerts a sucking force on the abdomen, causing it to bulge out. Thus the uterus is permitted to rise forward unopposed by the tense abdominal wall. In this way less uterine energy is expended, and both fatigue and pain are reduced. The decompression suit has been used with some success, but results have not been consistent enough to justify its use as a routine measure to replace other methods of pain relief [Greenhill, 1963].

Even in cases in which no anesthetic or analgesic is employed and the birth occurs with none of the benefits of modern medical science, the pain of childbirth is soon forgotten. It is difficult to remember any pain. A woman may remember her reactions to the pain, but to recall the actual experience of pain is quite another matter. In the fascinating experience of seeing the newborn offspring, nursing it, caring for it, and planning for its future, the mother quickly forgets the inconvenience of pregnancy and the pain of labor. Many women plan for a second child before leaving the hospital with the first one.

The pain of childbirth should not be approached in the light of old wives' tales or in the light of the experience of an individual woman who happened to have a difficult labor. It should be approached in the light of modern science and should be put into correct perspective. The pain may be the most immediately obvious aspect of childbirth while the process is going on, but it is not the most important aspect. The important thing is that the woman has produced a new being, part of herself, part of her husband, a being to which she will become more closely attached than to any other individual except her husband. For her fiancé, one of her parents, her husband, or a friend, a woman would voluntarily suffer because the values involved would be greater than the discomfort. For her child, once born, she would suffer, and die if need be. Even the father, whose relation to the child is less intimate, would suffer for it or die to save it. Why, then, should a woman fear to suffer for her child for a period less than a day, when her entire life and that of her husband will be made immeasurably richer by her experience, when that experience represents a step in the creative process by which she introduces into independent existence a creature uniquely her own? Furthermore, pain and risk are not necessarily correlated. The more the woman dissociates them in her thinking, the more readily she can accept the pain.

Childbirth without fear is a possibility for every woman who is willing to face the facts intelligently, maturely, and squarely, for the very simple reason that there is no longer anything to fear. Many of the attitudes that some women have toward childbirth have their roots in the past when having a baby was a "descent into the valley of the shadow." But those days are gone forever. Having a baby is now one of the safest things a woman can do. Childbirth without risk has been all but completely achieved.

When we include all the women who have babies in and out of hospitals, all those who have inadequate as well as adequate prenatal care, all those who have poor care at delivery as well as those who have skilled care, all those having illness or defect during pregnancy or at the time of delivery as well as the healthy ones, all those who have miscarriages or criminal abortions as well as those who carry their babies to term, all ages and all races, we find that in 1963 the over-all mortality rate for causes associated with pregnancy and childbirth was about 3 per 10,000 live births as compared to 61 per 10,000 live births in 1915, the first year for which data are available [Statistical Bulletin, September, 1961, 1964]. During 1960 the rate for white women at ages 20 to 24 was only 1.4 per 10,000 live births and did not exceed 2.0 per 10,000 in any age group under 30. The rate among colored women is about four times as high as that for white women [Statistical Bulletin, September, 1961]. This reduction in maternal mortality is one of the most dramatic but least publicized advances in modern medicine. Twenty years ago the rate was many times what it is today, and that was about the period in which the reader was born and in which the mother of the reader acquired the attitudes which, in some cases, she passed on to her child.

Obstetrical practice is continually improving. Medical students and nurses are being better trained. Hospital facilities are being improved and extended. More and more agencies, both public and private, are directing their attention to better prenatal care, better care both during and after delivery. More people are being educated in the hygiene of pregnancy and are being taught both what to expect in pregnancy and what to seek in the way of care. Premarital examinations are increasing in both frequency and quality. Use of X rays makes possible the detection of conditions that may give rise to difficulty in labor. Improved methods of diagnosis, immunization, and treatment make it possible to prevent more of the complications that arise during pregnancy as a result of diseases present before pregnancy began. More is being learned about antibiotics and other drugs. Anesthesia, analgesia, and methods of treating hemorrhage are being improved. More physicians are specializing in obstetrics. All this plus the experience of some communities leads to the prediction that the maternal mortality rate can be still further reduced.

The reader, or his wife or wife-to-be, will probably begin her child-bearing in her late teens or early twenties, a favorable time. Like 95 per cent of the women who become mothers, she will be attended by a physician, perhaps by a specialist in obstetrics. Like more than 90 per cent of mothers, she will be delivered in a hospital. She will have adequate pre-natal and postnatal care. She will know enough about pregnancy and childbirth to follow her physician's instructions and to be cooperative. In short, in the light of what was said above, she will have childbirth without risk. She may, therefore, have childbirth completely without fear.

Perhaps by reading between the lines of a few letters written by women still in the hospital after the birth of their babies we may gain insight into the relative values of joy and pain. These letters express not exceptional but typical attitudes. The women who wrote them give no indication of thinking of their recent experience as a forbidding "descent into the valley of the shadow." The reason there are not more such documents is that few women write them, not that only a few women feel this way. The women who wrote these did not know at the time that they would be read by anyone except the friends to whom they were addressed. Hence there was no reason for being anything except straightforward and sincere. There is no evidence of polishing the facts for publication. Personal details are omitted from these restatements; the rest is in their own words. Mrs. A writes:

At last the great "Johnny" has arrived. Can you believe it? "He" is a lovely girl—nicer and sweeter than any other in the nursery. She is just too precious for words. I am so proud of her and you should see my husband: he just beams all over. It's just as if he had a halo around his head. I love him so very much. Just wait until you fall in love and see what sensations and thrills really are. He and the baby are all my life now. I can hardly wait to get out to take care of them.

The hospital is lovely. I just lie here and push a button and my every wish is gratified. The nurses are wonderful and are so sweet and patient.

The baby weighed seven pounds, eleven and three-quarter ounces. She is still slightly pink but is toning down a bit. She is strong enough to hold her little head up and pushes away with her hands when they bring her to nurse. She honestly chews so hard I am sore; but that little mouth is so sweet I just love to have her touch me.

I guess I had a rather hard time with labor but my husband was with me until the last forty minutes. They would give me ether and then my husband would say, "Can you see me?" and I would answer, "Yes." Then the doctor would say, "Can you see *me*?" and I would say, "No." I can't remember that at all but they told me about it afterward. When I came to, I couldn't realize that it was all over and I had a daughter.

Mrs. *B* writes:

First I must apologize for staying away from the nice dinner you prepared for us Sunday. I really intended to come but I had other very important business on Sunday.

Now I can get down to business and *rave*! That boy is simply marvelous and I can see a new life for —— [the husband] and me. It's even more wonderful than I thought it would be and you know I've been thrilled for nine months.

The baby looks like —— [husband] – has black hair, big feet and big hands – and is the sweetest baby in town. I'm so happy I have to cry a little every once in a while. It still seems too good to be true. I only hope that someday you will celebrate a blessed event. It's worth all the pain and all the sacrifice; it's wonderful. And Dr. —— is a great man and a great doctor. I almost felt like kissing him.

I am still on my back and writing is rather difficult. . . .

Mrs. *C* writes:

Your letter came this morning. Gee, but I'm happy. Now don't let me start raving over my boy. Did I ever say I wanted a girl?

Now I'll tell you about him this once and God forbid that I become one of those raving mothers. He's fat enough to be cute. His little cheeks hang over a bit. His blond hair is a bit mouse-colored but is going to curl. His hands and feet are exactly like ——'s [husband's]; his ears and nose are mine; and the rest of him seems to be all his own. His nails were so long at first that he scratched his face; but now he has had a manicure and only slaps his mother because she does not have enough to satisfy his appetite. Today I hope to accomplish that.

For the first two days I was a bit worried about his IQ. They say a newborn baby knows only one thing and that is how to nurse. Well, he didn't even know that or at least he didn't give a care; but last night he learned his lesson and now the rest is up to me.

Miss —— is the old maid superintendent of the hospital. When I was starting into labor, she dropped in to see me. I asked her to tell me the proper technique for reacting to the pains in order to get maximum results. She just laughed and said, "Now that's a question to ask an old maid." I said, "I mean, theoretically." She did tell me very clearly just how one was supposed to do it. I followed it as nearly as I could and I know it hastened things.

The doctor was certainly pleased with the outcome. I think he was a bit worried. He wouldn't give me enough dope to deaden a flea. Afterwards he said, "I knew you'd forgive me in the end." Just think—twenty-four hours after I saw you I was back in my room on an "ether jag" with an eight-pound baby in the nursery.

When you have your baby—wherever you go and whomever you have to deliver you—have confidence in your doctor. Forget every worry; that's half the battle. I may be insane but if that man said, "If I cut off your left ear, your eyesight will never dim," I'd believe him and say, "O.K., go ahead."

Here it is 10:20 and I have not finished the letter I started at the crack of dawn. There is certainly not a dull moment here.

Mrs. *D* writes:

A week ago today I gave birth to a darling baby boy. I'm so thrilled about him that you'd think I was the first one ever to have a baby. I'm writing you about it now because I want to tell you how thankful I am for the discussions we had in class and for the opportunity of reading those letters from women who had just had babies. [Mrs. *D* is referring to the three letters above.] They made things so much easier for me mentally. I kept thinking of how they felt about it when untactful people would say to me, "You'll find out that it's not easy, etc., etc." One mother had the grace to say, "Oh, the pain—that's the first thing you forget." And that is what you can tell the girls that I say, too.

I'll admit that the first day I wondered whether I could ever have any playmates for my son (I'd like four, in all); but in another twenty-four hours I couldn't remember how terrible the pain was. Anyway, what's a half hour or so of pain when you get a lifetime of happiness for it? I don't think a child would want a woman for his mother if she couldn't stand that much for him. My son's daddy is in the Air Corps in Europe. It wasn't as nice having him gone at this time but at least he didn't have to pace the floor while he waited for me.

Mrs. *E* writes:

Before I became pregnant, my knowledge of the actual birth of a baby consisted of a few old wives' tales and bits of information from friends. After I was sure of my pregnancy, I became much more aware of the actual truth about childbirth. I realize that the more you know about something, the less you fear it, and believe that it is very important for a woman who is going to have a baby to know as much as possible about it.

My experience during labor and childbirth was a happy and somewhat humorous one. My labor began with the show of blood. As soon as I noticed it, I called my doctor and was told that labor would soon follow. Then I called my husband out of his Saturday morning class. He raced home as quickly as possible, and, like most expectant fathers, he was very excited. At this time my pains were not very severe. I was anxious but not afraid because I knew what to expect.

Sunday morning I felt fine and decided to go to church. I passed up Sunday School because I didn't feel like sitting through two services. The contractions continued during the service and were a little more painful. After church, we ate out since I didn't feel like cooking. We spent the afternoon timing the contractions and taking a long walk around the campus. By eight o'clock Sunday evening, after the pains had occurred at three-minute intervals for two hours, my husband called the doctor who agreed to meet us at the hospital.

My clothes for the hospital had been packed for two weeks, so we went directly to the hospital. By one A.M. Monday the pains were much more severe and labor progressed slowly and continued throughout the night. Monday morning I sat up, combed my hair, and fixed my face between contractions. I don't remember anything after that, but my precious son was born at 11:14 A.M. that Monday morning.

Mrs. *F* writes:

Our third little girl was born last Saturday night at 7:10 P.M. She weighed 6 lb. 5 oz. and looks just like her daddy. She is bald on top with a fringe of red fuzz, very much like Jiggs in the funny paper. Jennifer is another Read method baby — this time completely successful. I had her without anesthetic or sedative of any sort. I came to the hospital Friday night about 10 P.M., after my water broke, and then did nothing until Saturday afternoon about 2:30 P.M. Then my labor began. I called my husband and he came and stayed with me in my room during the first part. I relaxed easily with the pains and about 5:30 I went back to the labor ward. I relaxed well until the very end of the first stage when the pains became too strong to relax with. During the last few first stage pains, which were very sharp, I took a deep breath and held it till it passed. With the first second stage "pain" all pain ceased entirely and a new feeling began, a good "bearing down" feeling which was entirely painless. I was rushed to the delivery room after I announced that the second stage had begun and the baby was coming fast. The doctor asked me not to bear down while he rushed into his gloves, and I was surprised to find that I could control when the contractions would come. When he was ready I bore down good and the baby was born. I immediately popped up on an elbow and saw him lift her up. She made a few noises and was laid across my tummy and I watched while the cord was tied and cut. She was then carried to a table to be wrapped in a blanket and I was asked to lie back down and push once more. I popped up again to see the afterbirth and about that time the baby gave a good loud yell. The nurse brought her over for me to see once more before they took her to the nursery. By that time I was cleaned up and ready to leave, so the doctor gave me a hand to sit up and I slipped off the table and walked out in the hall. I didn't feel at all weak and wanted to walk to my room; but my bed was already at the delivery room door so I climbed up and got a ride to my room. My husband was waiting there and as I rolled through the door I said, "Hi, honey. I'm hungry." Then I told him we had another daughter. While he went to round up some crackers for me to eat, I used the telephone by my bed to call some of my friends and tell them we had a girl. They were all amazed to hear me. I felt wonderful and got up several times during the night. I've been up and around ever since. I don't feel at all as if I'd had a baby and I am the happiest person in the world. The Read method worked so beautifully all the way that there was no need for fuss. There was nothing about any of it that I couldn't bear perfectly well and I was totally fascinated by every minute of it. I could have a dozen more just like it — but this is the end.

LACTATION

For a brief period after the birth of the child the mother's breasts secrete colostrum, a substance that may have food value for the child and acts as a mild laxative but is not true milk. Colostrum is usually supplemented with water given by bottle. True milk appears in two to five days. Breast feeding is on the decline in this country [Eastman, June, 1963]. Pediatricians are not as insistent upon it as they used to be. This is due in part to increased knowledge of infant nutrition and in part to improvement in prepared formulas. But breast feeding has by no means lost all of its proponents. Many pediatricians recommend it. Some psychologists, psychiatrists, anthropologists, and similar specialists feel that the method of infant feeding is influential in the psychosocial development of both mother and child. Montagu [Eastman, June, 1963], an anthropologist, in discussing breast feeding, mentions the "psychophysiological benefits" conferred upon mother and child by their "continuing symbiotic relationship" and calls breast feeding "very important for their further development." Some women derive a special satisfaction from breast feeding. Others do not. Some feel guilty when they cannot or do not nurse their babies. Such a feeling of guilt is unnecessary and inappropriate. It stems from attitudes of the past rather than from present-day knowledge of child rearing. Some mothers are reluctant to nurse their babies because they fear permanent breast enlargement and impairment of appearance. If a woman follows her physician's instructions, such a fear is groundless.

Contrary to common assumption, it is possible for a woman to become pregnant while nursing. Menstruation may start, or conception may occur without the reinstitution of the menses. About one-half of nursing mothers menstruate within three months after delivery; about four-fifths menstruate before the cessation of lactation [Schumann, 1936]. The return of the menses tends to be delayed by nursing, however. In a study of 2,885 patients of Johns Hopkins Hospital it was found that one-fourth of the white women and one-third of the Negro women became pregnant within twelve months after delivery. Of the whites 36 per cent and of the Negroes 47 per cent were still nursing their babies when conception occurred [Guttmacher, 1937].

MULTIPLE BIRTHS

What is a couple's chance of having more than one baby in a given pregnancy? In the period 1951 to 1957, in this country, there were approximately 300,000 plural births in which at least one child was born alive (a number that is lower than the number of multiple pregnancies). This was a ratio of about 1 plural birth in 100 live births. Twins occurred about once in 95, triplets about once in 11,000 and quadruplets about once in 900,000. There were no births of quintuplets during that period [Statistical Bulletin, January, 1960]. Quintuplets are born only rarely,

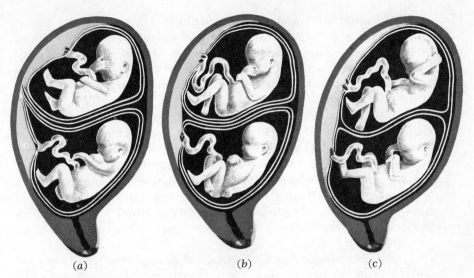

(a)   (b)   (c)

Figure 24. Twinning. (a) Two-egg twins: two placentas; each fetus with two sacs; amnion inside and chorion outside; sex may be different; fraternal twins. (b) Two-egg twins: two placentas have merged; each fetus has both membranes, amnion and chorion; sex may be different. (c) One-egg twins: one placenta; each fetus with inner sac (amnion); single outer membrane (chorion) envelops both; same sex; identical twins. (Adapted from sculptured birth series by Dickinson and Belskie in "Birth Atlas," Maternity Center Association, New York.

about once in 40,000,000 births. There have been authenticated births of sextuplets, but in no case have they lived. There has been one authenticated case of septuplets (seven babies), but they did not survive [Greenhill, 1955]. Reports of births involving more than seven babies must, at least to this point, be considered folklore.

Plural births vary with the age of the mother. For teen-age mothers the ratio is 6 in 1,000. The ratio increases for each age group until it reaches 16 in 1,000 for mothers aged thirty-five to thirty-nine [*Statistical Bulletin*, January, 1960].

Twins are of two types: one-egg (monovular, monozygotic, so-called "identical") twins, and two-egg (binovular, dizygotic, so-called "fraternal") twins.

About one-third of all twins are of the former type. One-egg twins are produced when the zygote has developed into a cluster of cells which breaks apart or, later, into a hollow sphere of cells in which two centers of growth appear where ordinarily only one occurs. Such twins are, in a sense, parts of the same individual. They have the same genetic constitution, are thus always of the same sex, and resemble each other very closely; but, being subject to prenatal and postnatal environmental influences, they are not so nearly identical in appearance and behavior that they cannot be distinguished by persons who know them well. Sometimes they are "identical" in the sense of being alike. At other times they are "mirror images" of each other; for example, one twin's right hand is like the other's left hand. Whether they are "identical" or "mirror image" depends upon factors involved in the twinning process, such as the time and plane of cleavage in the cluster of cells. When the cleavage is incomplete, conjoined twins, commonly referred to as "Siamese," result. Such twins are rare. In many cases they die before or soon after birth. If they live, they may or may not be separable through surgery, depending upon where and how they are joined and what organs they have in common. According to Hertig [1960], most one-egg twins have one common placenta with two amnions and two cords. A minority have two placentas, which may or may not be fused. Very rarely one-egg twins are found in the same amniotic sac [Timmons and de Alvarez, 1963].

Two-egg twins are produced when two ova are released at one time and fertilized by two sperms. They are not produced by having two sperms fertilize one ovum, as is sometimes assumed. Two-egg twins may be of the same or of different sex. They have different genetic constitutions and are no more closely related than any two children having the same parents. They have two placentas, but these sometimes fuse, making classification difficult and at times leading to error. Two-egg twins have two amnions and two cords.

The individual children in a multiple birth are usually smaller than the child in a single birth, but their combined weight is usually greater than that of the single child. The former is due in part to the fact that in the majority of cases multiple births occur prematurely. There seem to be indications that a tendency toward twinning, especially two-egg twinning, is hereditary; but the evidence as to the pattern of such inheritance is not clear. Marriage of twins increases the hereditary tendency.

It is ordinarily assumed that the sperms which fertilize the two ova in the production of two-egg twins are deposited during the same act of insemination. Could such twins be produced by sperms from different acts of insemination, provided the inseminations occurred during the brief period in which the two ova released at one time of ovulation were fertilizable? This process is termed *superfecundation*, and the answer to the question is in the affirmative. Two-egg twins can even have different fathers if a woman has sexual intercourse with two men within a brief time span or if, as we shall discuss later, a mixture of the seminal fluid of the husband and that of a donor is used in artificial insemination.

An odd case was taken to court in Baltimore in 1960 [Eastman, February, 1961]. The man in question admitted intercourse with a woman who had borne twins. Blood tests indicated that he could have been the father of one twin but not of the other. The woman claimed that she had had intercourse with no other man during the period in which the twins must have been conceived. The judge ruled that her statement was insufficient. Since the man could not have been the father of one twin, the final verdict was "not guilty," and he was ruled to be the father of neither twin.

Ordinarily twins are born with a relatively brief time interval between them. How are reports of unusually long intervals to be interpreted, for example, a report of two babies born to the same mother 56 days apart [Eastman, February, 1961] and another by Drucker, Finkel, and Savel [*Obstetrical and Gynecological Survey*, 1961] of two babies 65 days apart? Are such babies twins in the ordinary sense? Or do they represent another type of multiple pregnancy, termed *superfetation*? In superfetation one pregnancy is started and then, after a time interval sufficient to permit another ovulation, a second pregnancy is started by means of fertilization effected by a sperm from a later insemination. Until the first is terminated, the two pregnancies progress concurrently. Superfetation has been produced experimentally in lower animals [Greenhill, 1959]. It is highly doubtful that it ever occurs in humans and has never been authenticated beyond all question.

Family planning: conception control and the spacing of children

Most couples want children and, under favorable circumstances, have them. Hence, conception control does not necessarily imply that a couple will remain voluntarily childless. Conception control implies only that a couple have the number of children that they want when they want them, when they are ready for them, at sufficiently long intervals to permit the wife to maintain good health and to give birth to healthy babies. In short, conception control implies parenthood by choice rather than parenthood by chance.

Conception control implies any method by which sperm and ovum are prevented from uniting, that is, any means by which fertilization is prevented. This is biologically, sociologically, philosophically, ethically, and legally different from induced abortion. Abortion is a means of birth control, but it is not a method of conception control. Sterilization and reliance upon the "safe period," or "rhythm," are, however, intended to control conception. Contraception of various types is also a means toward this end.

REQUIREMENTS FOR MEANS OF CONCEPTION CONTROL
Whatever may be the means of conception control that a couple employ, it is essential that the chosen means shall fulfill the following requirements: (1) It should be relatively effective, that is, as effective as modern medical science can make it. No method is entirely foolproof. The methods most commonly recommended by informed physicians and

reliable clinics, when used with intelligence and care, are nearly enough 100 per cent reliable to make possible the removal of all fear of unwanted pregnancy. (2) It should be relatively easy to use, simple, and readily understood. (3) It should be readily available and relatively inexpensive. (4) It should be aesthetically acceptable to both parties and repugnant to neither. (5) It should permit normal, satisfactory, successful sexual intercourse. (6) It should have no harmful results. It should contain or entail no chemical or mechanical irritant that may give rise to infection or poisoning. (7) It should be temporary, in the sense that its use may be terminated at will, unless for some special reason the couple desire sterilization.

Calderone [1964] states three "contraceptive axioms" : "1. *Any* method . . . is more effective than *no* method. 2. The most effective method is the one the couple will use with the greatest consistency. 3. Acceptability is the most critical factor in the effectiveness of a contraceptive method."

Many of the highly advertised and widely sold "feminine-hygiene" products are intended as contraceptives but are sold under another name to allow them to slip through the loopholes of the law. Many of these products are ineffective. Some are outright dangerous to health and life. A normal, healthy woman does not need "feminine hygiene" for cleanliness. Internal organs need no cleansing, and external ones may be adequately cleansed with soap and water.

Books of directions accompanying commercially sold "feminine-hygiene" products are oversimplified. They make insufficient allowance for individual variations in anatomy and sensitivity to chemicals. To rely upon them is about as sensible as to purchase eyeglasses from a mail-order house or in a five-and-ten-cent store. Conception control should be adapted to the individual couple by a reliable, well-informed physician upon the basis of his knowledge of the couple's anatomy and needs. It should not be used upon the recommendation of friends, drugstore clerks, advertisements, or oversimplified publications.

There is no longer any question as to whether we shall or shall not have, practice, or permit conception control. It is already here on a large scale. The problem is one of improving use and eliminating abuse. It is extending among all classes. Its continued advance depends upon deep-set economic forces. Once a people have discovered how to raise their standard of living by regulating the number of offspring, the extension of that knowledge is inevitable and irresistible. It can be slowed down, but it cannot be halted.

In order to understand how conception control functions, we must understand how ova and sperms are produced and how fertilization takes place, as already discussed. We must also understand the nature of the menstrual cycle.

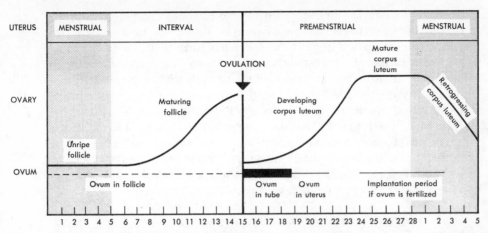

Figure 25. Schematic representation of the menstrual cycle.

MENSTRUAL CYCLE

Let us assume that ovulation occurs but that fertilization does not follow. The Graafian follicle secretes a hormone (*estrogen*) which causes
certain changes in the uterus. After the ovum has been discharged from
the follicle, the cells of the latter undergo change, forming the corpus
luteum (yellow body). The corpus luteum secretes a hormone (*progesterone*) which causes further changes in the uterus and prepares this
organ for the reception of the zygote. One of the changes is that which
occurs in the blood vessels in such a way that small "lakes" of blood
(lacunae) are formed within the wall of the uterus. This process of preparation requires about two weeks. If fertilization does not occur, the
preparations are for naught and are consequently eliminated. The corpus
luteum degenerates and finally ceases to function. As a result, the hormone (progesterone) which was secreted and which sustained the uterus
in its receptive, prepregnant state is withdrawn. This causes the lining
of the uterus (*endometrium*) to break down and loosen itself from the
uterine wall. The lining and some of the blood from the lacunae and
blood vessels are discharged. This is menstruation. Getting rid of the
preparations for pregnancy requires several days, and then the cycle
begins over again. Thus we see that it is not ovulation that causes menstruation. Menstruation is caused by the withdrawal of the hormone
(progesterone) secreted by the corpus luteum, which in the event of fertilization would continue to be produced for a while until the placenta
began to secrete a hormone with a similar function.

In some cases a type of menstruation occurs without there having
been ovulation and the formation of a corpus luteum with its resulting
hormone. Such menstruation is termed *anovulatory* and is the result of

estrogen withdrawal, the Graafian follicle forming and being absorbed without bursting to release the ovum. The difference between the two types of menstruation is shown in summary form in Table 4.

The length of the menstrual cycle varies in different women. Often for some time after puberty the cycle is irregular. Then, as the girl matures, a rhythm is established. When women are considered as a group, the length of this rhythm falls on the normal curve of variability. Twenty-eight days, the ordinarily assumed cycle, is the one that falls near the middle of the curve. In one study it was found that about 10 per cent of the women had cycles ranging in length from 6 to 23 days; about 10 per cent, ranging from 35 to 409 days; the great majority (about 80 per cent), ranging from 24 to 34 days [Greenhill, 1957].

TABLE 4 STEPS IN THE MENSTRUAL CYCLE

Ovum matures.
Follicle forms.
Follicle secretes estrogen.
Estrogen changes uterus.

ovulatory	*anovulatory*
Follicle bursts (ovulation).	Follicle does not burst (no ovulation).
Corpus luteum forms.	Follicle absorbed.
Corpus luteum secretes progesterone.	Estrogen withdrawn.
Progesterone changes uterus.	Menstruation.
Corpus luteum degenerates.	
Progesterone withdrawn.	
Menstruation.	

In the individual woman the length of the cycle may vary from time to time for various reasons. Most women are regularly irregular, if we may so express it for emphasis. Hartman [1936] cites a study showing that only 0.7 per cent of cases were "absolutely regular"; 10 per cent varied from 1 to 3 days; 30 per cent, from 4 to 7 days; 44 per cent, up to 10 days; 56 per cent, 11 or more days. Hartman later [1962] refers to a "regular" cycle as one varying no more than 6 days and states that about 75 per cent of women have such cycles; the other 25 per cent have cycles even more irregular. One early investigator, Fraenkel [Hartman, 1962], made a statement which has now become classic relative to the study of the menstrual cycle: "The only regular feature of the menstrual cycle is its lack of regularity." Another investigator, Holt [Hartman, 1962], has said, "Not the slightest evidence pointing toward perfect regularity has so far produced even a single exceptional individual." He goes on to say that if such a perfectly regular individual is ever found, "she will constitute a true medical curiosity."

When we think only in terms of time sequence, we see that ovulation and menstruation alternate (assuming ovulatory cycles). But when we think in terms of cause and effect, we must think of menstruation as following ovulation, not of ovulation as following menstruation. Yet, in seeking to predict the time of ovulation, a woman may erroneously think of menstruation-ovulation, since she knows the dates of her last menstrual period but not the date of ovulation. This error is made easier to commit by the fact that in numbering the days of the menstrual cycle, the day on which menstruation begins is considered the first.

Ordinarily menstruation begins about two weeks after ovulation, no matter how long the cycle. In other words, the preovulatory phase of the cycle (the period between menstruation and ovulation) is much more variable than the postovulatory, or premenstrual, phase of the cycle (the period between ovulation and menstruation). Here again, however, there is both wide variation among women and variation in the cycles of any given woman. The two-week period mentioned above represents a broad generalization based upon averages. Hartman [1962] cites studies based on different methods of ascertaining the date of ovulation which indicate that ovulation may occur on any day of the menstrual cycle from the fourth onward and which suggest that the preovulatory phase may vary from a few days to several months and the postovulatory phase from less than a week to almost a month. Young [1961a] points to evidence suggesting that ovulation may even occur during menstruation. Fluhmann [1957] states that, in twenty-eight- to thirty-day cycles, ovulation may occur at any time from the seventh to the twenty-first day.

Various attempts have been made to pinpoint the time of ovulation. Among them are measurement of the hormones in women's blood or urine, microscopic study of the corpus luteum, study of changes in cells from the vagina, examination of uterine tissue and activity, correlation of artificial insemination and conception, studies of the pregnancies of the wives of military personnel home on short leaves, records of pain which may possibly be associated with ovulation, studies of intermenstrual bleeding, and the correlation of ovulation and basal body temperature.

Some women experience pain in the region of the ovaries at about the time of the menstrual cycle when ovulation might be expected to occur. Some of these women claim that the pain alternates from side to side in alternate months. Such pain is referred to as intermenstrual pain, or *mittelschmerz*. Since the opening of the follicle to release the ovum requires only a few moments, intermenstrual pain can hardly be produced only by the actual momentary bursting of the follicle. But data do suggest that it is associated with the over-all process of ovulation [Hartman, 1962].

Some women experience intermenstrual bleeding, that is, vaginal bleeding, at about the time ovulation might be presumed to occur. Such bleeding is caused by the fact that there is an increased blood supply in the woman's ovaries and uterus at the time that the follicle ripens. This blood supply produces congestion in the wall of the uterus, resulting in the leakage of a small amount of blood into the uterus through the lining of that organ, but without any break in that lining. This is the sort of bleeding which occurs in nonmenstruating mammals, such as dogs in "heat," and which pet owners often erroneously assume is menstruation [Hartman, 1962].

There is some correlation between ovulation and a woman's basal body temperature (BBT). BBT is the temperature taken immediately upon waking in the morning, before the woman gets out of bed or has anything to eat or drink. As soon as she begins to move about, her temperature rises slightly. The temperature must be taken by a special or clinical thermometer and read to within tenths of a degree. Differences between the lowest and highest temperature in a given menstrual cycle must be at least 0.4°F to be considered significant [Hartman, 1962].

Presumably the estrogen secreted by the growing follicle is a temperature depressant and causes the woman's BBT to fall as ovulation is approached. Her BBT reaches its lowest point at about the time of ovulation. Then the progesterone secreted by the corpus luteum causes the BBT to rise. This is termed the *thermal shift*. The BBT remains at the higher level until about the time of menstruation [Hartman, 1962]. If pregnancy occurs, the BBT remains at a relatively high level.

BBT records are difficult to interpret because they are not so clear and regular as an oversimplified explanation seems to suggest. There is much variation among women and in a given woman during a series of cycles. BBT and ovulation do not always coincide [Farris, 1956; Greenhill, 1954]. There are many factors, other than those involved in the menstrual cycle, which can cause a change in body temperature.

As intimated in an earlier chapter, menstruation is a natural, normal function and ordinarily is not exceedingly painful, though it may be accompanied by a brief period of depression, fatigue, or irritability. Painful menstruation (*dysmenorrhea*) is a consequence of some dysfunction, some maladjustment, which should be clearly distinguished from the function itself. Dysmenorrhea may be the result of hypersensitivity of the lining of the uterus, too tightly closed cervix, unusual flexion of the uterus backward or forward, atrophy of the uterus, tumors, inflammation of organs adjacent to the uterus, infection, congestion due to constant standing, disorders of the endocrine glands, allergies, constipation, and other similar contributing factors. It may also be due to subtle psychological factors, for example, resistance to the fact of being a woman. Many cases of dysmenorrhea may be relieved by adequate medical treatment. A woman subject to painful periods should see her physician. She should not depend upon patent medicines purchased on the recommendation of advertisements or clerks in drugstores.

Menstruation is not only natural and normal but, if we may personify Nature for a moment, is given special attention as a somewhat exceptional phenomenon. It is limited to human beings and some of the primates. In all other instances, bleeding is an indication of trouble. Menstrual bleeding is an indication of good health. In other instances, the blood clots to stop the bleeding. Menstrual blood does not clot in the usual way, thus permitting the bleeding to continue.

THE "SAFE PERIOD," OR "RHYTHM"

In constructing a diagram, Figure 26, to represent the fertile and infertile or "safe" periods in a woman's menstrual cycle, broad generalization and oversimplification are unavoidable. In this figure, M indicates the period of menstruation proper, about four days. At O, ovulation occurs. The ovum is thought to be fertilizable for a maximum of twenty-four hours. But even though the day of ovulation might be ascertained, the moment of this occurrence cannot be pinpointed, and there may also be some variation in the effective life of ova. Hence two days have been allowed as the period during which the ovum might possibly be fertilized. This two-day period is designated as OY. Sperms deposited in the woman's genital tract are thought to have an effective life of twenty-four to forty-eight hours. Here again an extra day has been allowed for possible variation. Sperms deposited during the three-day period XO may live long enough to fertilize an ovum released at O. Sperms deposited during OY would be present at the same time the ovum is present. The period XY, then, represents the fertile period, and the period YX the "safe period," since there is no ovum to be fertilized during this period.

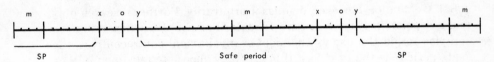

Figure 26. Phases of a twenty-eight-day menstrual cycle to show the so-called "safe period": M, the period of menstruation proper; O, ovulation; XO, period during which sperms deposited might live long enough to fertilize ovum released at O, OY, period during which ovum is possibly fertilizable; XY, fertile period; Y, point after which there is no fertilizable ovum present; YX, "safe period."

Theoretically, then, every woman has a "safe period" during each menstrual cycle. The problem is to know when it occurs. There are so many variables involved that determination is impossible with completely constant accuracy and in all women.

Means of ascertaining the time of ovulation have been discussed. At the present stage of knowledge, all such means have limitations [Greenhill, 1960, 1961; Hartman, 1962]. Furthermore, they are more useful in indicating that ovulation has occurred than in predicting when it will occur and are, therefore, more helpful to couples who want to determine the fertile period in order to have a child than to those who want to determine the infertile period in order to avoid having one. For these two types of couples failure has different consequences. The former may simply try again to carry out their plan. But the latter are called upon to abandon one plan and adopt another. What is needed to make the "safe period" safe is an accurate means of predicting the time of ovulation.

The menstrual cycle may vary from month to month in a given woman. Even though she may keep a record for several months and may seem to be regular, there is no way for her to know that she will be regular in the future. The irregularity of women as a group has already been discussed.

No one knows precisely how long sperms and egg live and remain effective. Surely there is no way of determining this for a given woman each time there is a possibility of her becoming pregnant.

It is impossible to ascertain precisely how long it takes sperms to make their way to the ovum, since this may vary from time to time and depends in part upon anatomy and conditions within the female genital tract, such as the mucous plug in the cervix and the vitality of the sperms. The "safe period" is useless during the interval between delivery of a baby and the reestablishment of menstruation. This interval may be of several months' duration.

Theoretically every woman has a "safe period," but practically, because of the variables involved, the "safe period" is not entirely safe. A significantly higher failure rate is reported by couples who employ the "safe period" than by couples who employ the most effective methods of contraception [Freedman, Whelpton, and Campbell, 1959; Hartman, 1962]. We cannot, however, dismiss it arbitrarily. Further research may make dependence upon it more reliable. For couples whose religious scruples forbid the use of chemical or mechanical contraceptives, the "safe period" is the next best thing. If they choose to rely upon it, they should keep careful records of the woman's menstrual periods and discuss the problem with a physician. They should not depend upon oversimplified printed tables or guidebooks.

In addition to the uncertainty of the method, there is another argument against relying upon the "safe period" to prevent conception. Relying upon the "safe period" means that the couple's sexual life is regulated by the probability and avoidance of conception, that is, by the calendar, rather than by their mutual interest, love, and desire.

COITUS INTERRUPTUS

Coitus interruptus is incomplete intercourse. It is sometimes referred to as *withdrawal*. In coitus interruptus the penis is withdrawn from the vagina just before ejaculation, and the seminal fluid is discharged outside the woman's body. This is an ancient and widely known method of conception control. It is the type mentioned in the Old Testament (Gen. 38:8–10). It is unreliable because it requires precise timing and a very high degree of self-control on the part of the male. When the point of orgasm-ejaculation is reached, involuntary muscular contractions occur that are not subject to voluntary control. Also, before the ejaculation of the seminal fluid, there is a discharge of a small amount of glandular secretion (the *preejaculate*) of which the man is unaware and the function of which is apparently lubrication and/or acid neutralization. The preejaculate may also contain sperms. Ordinarily the number of sperms in the preejaculate is not large enough to effect fertilization, but fertilization by this means is possible. Coitus interruptus is likely to be less satisfactory to both sexes than is complete intercourse.

MECHANICAL CONTRACEPTIVES
These contraceptives are of several types. Many couples use a combination of both mechanical and chemical methods to prevent sperms from reaching the ovum.

Diaphragm. This is a shallow, cuplike device made of soft rubber with a flexible spring embedded in the outer edge. It fits snugly against the wall of the vagina and covers the cervix. It is made in a variety of sizes and must, therefore, be fitted by a physician. When used with a jelly or cream which both seals the contact between diaphragm and vaginal wall and also kills sperms, it forms an effective barrier to the sperms' entering the uterus.

Cervical cap. This device is smaller than the diaphragm and fits directly over the cervix. It is made of plastic or rubber, the former having certain advantages. The cervical cap, like the diaphragm, is used in conjunction with a jelly or cream and must be fitted by a physician.

Condom. This is a rubber sheath which fits over the erect penis. At ejaculation, the seminal fluid is retained in the condom and does not enter the vagina.

Other blocks. Jellies, creams, or suppositories which melt at body temperature and spread through the vagina are sometimes used as barriers. Foaming substances may be introduced into the vagina for a similar reason. A sponge placed in the vagina at the entrance to the cervix is sometimes used, often in conjunction with a jelly or cream. None of these barriers is as effective as the diaphragm, cervical cap, or condom. Intrauterine devices are sometimes used. But opinions differ as to whether such devices are dangerous because of possible irritation to uterine tissue; and some women do not retain them.

CHEMICAL CONTRACEPTIVES

Spermicides. Creams, jellies, foaming tablets, aerosol foam, and suppositories have a spermicidal (sperm-killing) function as well as that of providing or improving a mechanical barrier to sperms, as mentioned above. Used alone, however, they are not so effective as combination methods.

Spermicidal solutions used for douching are often dangerous because of the chemicals employed. Douching is primarily a means of removing sperms from the vagina rather than a means of killing them. At best it is not highly effective because sperms may enter the cervix before the douching can be accomplished.

Ovulation inhibitors, oral contraceptives. Naturally secreted hormones suppress ovulation during the latter part of the menstrual cycle and during pregnancy. It has been found that synthetic, progesterone-like substances will also inhibit ovulation.

The regimen for the use of this type of contraceptive is as follows. On the fifth day of her menstrual cycle, counting the first day of menstruation as day number one, a woman begins taking a series of pills. She takes one each day for twenty days; and regularity and consistency are very important. After the twentieth pill she takes no more that month. Typically she will menstruate within a week after taking that twentieth pill. On the fifth day after the onset of menstruation she begins another series. Between menstrual periods she does not ovulate. Hence conception cannot occur. If the woman discontinues taking the pills entirely, she will begin to ovulate again.

Oral contraceptives are very effective. Pregnancies occurring when they are used are due to failure to follow instructions. In some women there are side effects, such as nausea, fatigue, weight gain, and breast tenderness. In the presence of conditions such as tumor of the breast or genital tract, their use is not recommended. Nor should they be used by mothers who are nursing their babies. Since oral contraceptives are relatively new, there remains the unanswered question concerning their long-term effects. Greenhill [1962, p. 389] says, "The one concern which I have . . . is what latent or late effect the oral contraceptives may have on the pituitary gland and on the ovaries when they are used for a number of years." Eastman [February, 1962, p. 164] says, ". . . I am opposed to the indiscriminate use of drugs with widespread systemic effects when local agents are equally effective. . . . This very simple but expensive contraceptive is often prescribed to suit the convenience or the whim of a patient or to save office time, and none of these indications in my mind is justifiable." A year later Eastman [February, 1963, p. 145] says, "In prescribing progestational agents for oral contraception, I feel we must continue to remember that we are profoundly affecting the physiology of the individual. . . . For the present, I see no reason to change my opinion that these drugs should be used only as a medical emergency when more direct mechanical methods are . . . impossible."

In other words, promising as they may appear to be, oral contraceptives have not yet been proved to be the final step in the search for an ideal contraceptive. In addition to medical considerations there are sociomarital considerations that have up to this point been given relatively little thought. The oral contraceptive, to a greater degree than any other contraceptive known, presents the possibility of a wife's controlling conception without her husband's being aware that she is doing so. We can only speculate on what the ultimate reverberations of this fact may be, especially in those marriages involving a Catholic husband and a non-Catholic wife. If oral contraceptives become available, surreptitiously or otherwise, to unmarried women, a new vulnerability for men will be created. In cases of premarital intercourse in which the woman assures the man that there is no risk of pregnancy because she is using an oral contraceptive, he will have only her word that she is not only using it but meticulously following the proper regimen of use.

OTHER FORMS OF CONTRACEPTION

Investigation continues into other possible means of contraception. One involves antizygotic agents, that is, substances which inhibit the development of the zygote during its passage through the Fallopian tube. Another involves antispermatogenic agents, that is, substances which inhibit the production of sperms. Still another avenue of approach is found in the possibility of immunizing women against sperms or against the formation of the placenta by innoculating them with sperms. But these methods are still in the experimental stage [Nelson, 1963, 1964].

THE LEGAL STATUS OF CONTRACEPTION

There are thirty-four states which have laws that are in some way applicable to contraception. In some, the law prohibits advertising or regulates the distribution of contraceptives but does not prohibit their use or prescription. Only in Massachusetts and Connecticut is there legal restriction on medical practice relative to contraception or medically supervised contraceptive services, such as clinics. Only in Connecticut is there legal prohibition of the use of contraceptives, and attempts are now in process to have this unenforceable prohibition declared unconstitutional [Calderone, 1964].

STERILIZATION

Sterilization, although not a form of contraception, is a means of conception control. It may be voluntary or involuntary. There are numerous ways by which it may occur, for example, overexposure to X rays, castration, removal of the ovaries (oöphorectomy), cryptorchidism, and disease. The methods commonly employed in effecting voluntary sterilization are *vasectomy* in the male and *salpingectomy* in the female.

Vasectomy involves the tying and cutting of the vasa deferentia, the tubes through which the sperms pass from the epididymes (see Figure 9, p. 550). The vasa deferentia are near the surface of the scrotum. They are readily accessible to the physician through a small, superficial incision on either side. Under local anesthesia this incision is made, and the tube on either side is tied and then cut. This provides a barrier, a "roadblock," to the passage of sperms. Since the interstitial cells in the testes which secrete the masculinizing hormone remain undisturbed, vasectomy produces no change in the man's physique, secretion and discharge of seminal fluid, sexual drive, or capacity to have intercourse. The only change is the absence of sperms in the seminal fluid. Hence, vasectomy and castration are radically different and must not be confused. Hypothetically, vasectomy may be reversed by rejoining the cut ends of the tubes and assuring that the internal passageway is unobstructed. But this reversal cannot be accomplished successfully in all cases. The sperms, which continue to be produced in the testes and are prevented by the "roadblock" from passing through the tubes, are absorbed by the body.

Salpingectomy involves the tying and cutting of the Fallopian tubes (see Figure 10, p. 551). The tubes are accessible to the physician only through an incision in the abdominal wall. In spite of this fact as compared to the superficial incision in the scrotal wall in vasectomy, in some cases in which a couple seek sterilization the husband insists that his wife rather than he have the necessary operation. He confuses sterility with lack of masculinity or mistakenly assumes that in vasectomy his sexual capacity will be altered.

Salpingectomy provides a barrier, a "roadblock," to the passage of the ovum and sperms through the tube and prevents them from meeting. Since the ovaries remain undisturbed, it produces no change in the woman's physique, sexual interest, or sexual capacity. In fact, her interest in sexual intercourse may be increased if it was previously colored by fear of unwanted pregnancy. Ova prevented from passing through the tube are absorbed. As in the case of vasectomy, hypothetically salpingectomy may be reversed. But reversal is not readily accomplished, would involve a second abdominal operation, and would be less likely to be requested than in the case of vasectomy because so large a proportion of sterilizing operations on either partner are sought because of some condition in the wife or her pregnancies which makes conception inadvisable and which is not likely to change after the salpingectomy.

Until recently, as mentioned earlier, obstetricians commonly recommended that a woman have a salpingectomy during her third Caesarean section, especially if she already had two living children. Some obstetricians still make such a recommendation. Others feel that with modern obstetrical and surgical skill available to her, a woman may safely have more than three Caesarean sections [Greenhill, 1961] and, though salpingectomy may be recommended in some cases, such a recommendation should not be routine.

Infertility

There is confusion with regard to the terminology employed to describe childlessness. Some persons use "fecundity" to indicate the capacity to have children, "subfecundity" thus meaning reduced capacity, and "fertility" to indicate actually having children, "infertility" thus meaning childlessness. Others employ the terms with the definitions reversed: "fertility" is used to refer to the capacity to have children, with "relative infertility" meaning reduced capacity, and "fecundity" used to indicate children born. In either case, "sterility" indicates zero capacity, hence no children. We shall use "fertility" and "infertility" as meaning capacity and "childlessness" as meaning the absence of children. Childlessness may be voluntary or involuntary.

The proportion of couples involuntarily childless is variously estimated by different investigators. Probably the proportion is at least 10 per cent. Their childlessness is due to some condition in the husband, in the wife, or in both. Ordinarily it is the result of several factors operating in conjunction.

Involuntary childlessness is commonly referred to as "sterility." Actually, only part of the cases are due to this cause, if the term is used in the strict sense. It is better to speak of relative fertility and relative infertility. The population is not divided into two distinct groups one of which is fertile and can produce offspring and the other of which is sterile and cannot do so. The ability to produce offspring falls on the normal curve of variability, as do all human traits, and consequently ranges from very high fertility on the one hand to absolute sterility on the other.

Relative infertility may be temporary or permanent, remediable or irremediable. Many couples experience a brief period during which conception does not occur even though no contraceptive measures have been taken, for the time elapsing between the wedding and the birth of the first child is commonly one to two years.

Among the factors contributing to infertility are chance, age, general health, certain infectious diseases, tumors, overexposure to X rays or radium, removal of the genital organs, relatively low fertility in both spouses, genetic incompatibility (a condition in which the genes contain lethal, that is, death-producing, factors which kill the zygote), excessive acidity in the female genital tract, hormone deficiency, infantile genital organs, abnormal position of the uterus, too tightly closed cervix, obstruction in the cervix, closed Fallopian tubes, or too few or defective sperms. When there are fewer than 20 million sperms per cubic centimeter of seminal fluid, relative infertility may result. A lower sperm count does not render conception impossible but does make it less likely. Cases have been found in which pregnancy occurred when the husband's sperm count was between 1 million and 10 million [Greenhill, 1961]. A similar thing may be said if a man produces a high percentage of defective sperms.

Another factor contributing to infertility in women is anovulatory menstrual cycles. As we have seen, a kind of menstruation can occur without ovulation. Some women have more such cycles than do others. There is evidence to suggest that the average fertile woman ovulates normally only about 85 per cent of the time, and a healthy woman may have three or four anovulatory cycles per year [Young, 1961a]. It would be safe to assume, then, that some women have an even higher incidence of anovulatory cycles.

During the menopause, a woman's fertility decreases. When the menopause is complete, she is infertile. During the menopause, a woman may have anovulatory menstrual cycles. On the other hand, she may possibly continue to ovulate occasionally without her ovaries producing enough hormone to bring about menstruation when it is withdrawn. Some women cease menstruating rather abruptly at the onset of the menopause. In others the menstrual discharge gradually diminishes in quantity. In still others the menstrual periods become farther and farther apart until they cease altogether. Because of this last possibility, which might mislead a woman into concluding that the menopause was complete, when it was not, and the possibility that a woman may continue to ovulate without menstruating, and thus conclude that the menopause was complete, some women dispense with conception control and have unexpected pregnancies late in life—sometimes twenty or more years after the birth of the last previous child.

If a woman has her ovaries removed (oöphorectomy) for medical reasons, she will have the equivalent of abrupt, immediate menopause. Her physician will give her hormone therapy to assist her body in making the necessary transition. In popular parlance, surgical removal of the uterus, tubes, and ovaries is referred to as a "complete hysterectomy." Strictly speaking, however, "hysterectomy" refers to the removal of only the uterus.

In males one cause of infertility is *cryptorchidism*. The testes develop within the body cavity. During the seventh and eighth prenatal month they descend into the scrotum, where the temperature is low enough to permit the formation of sperms. If the testes do not descend normally by the time puberty is completed and nothing is done medically or surgically to effect their descent, the male may be sterilized by his own body heat. Also, a high percentage of undescended testes are abnormal; that is, they are undescended because they are abnormal, not abnormal because they are undescended [Scott, 1961].

It is variously estimated that factors in the husband contribute to involuntary childlessness or are the sole cause of the condition in 20 to 50 per cent of cases. The exact proportion is not so important as the fact that husbands are much more frequently at "fault" than some of them have known or have been willing to admit.

Through careful diagnosis by a medical expert the contributing factors in infertility may in many instances be discovered. Once these factors are discovered, remedy is possible in a large percentage of cases. The first step for the couple who want a baby and have been unsuccessful in having one is to visit a specialist, explain their situation and marital history, and follow his advice. If they are serious about wanting a child, he will suggest that they submit to a series of examinations and tests. The process may be long and perhaps expensive, depending upon the readiness with which causal factors are discovered and corrected. Complete cooperation of the couple—both of them—is essential.

With the ego that tradition has built up in men and with their customary confusion of masculinity and fertility, some husbands are offended when it is suggested that they may be at fault. Some even object to examination and testing. Such behavior is absurdly juvenile, for there is no necessary relationship between masculinity and fertility, and a man cannot increase his fertility by refusing to measure it.

Some physicians suggest that the husband be tested first. The tests for him are easier of administration than those for the wife. If there are found in him factors that may contribute toward the couple's infertility, the physician may begin to remedy these and thus possibly save the couple much time and expense. The tests for the wife are more extensive and require more time. To start with her might involve a long and expensive procedure, only to find at last that the husband was responsible anyway.

There is a not uncommonly held theory to the effect that some cases of relative infertility are "cured" by adoption. The assumption is that the infertility is caused by a combination of delicately balanced factors. As the couple try unsuccessfully to have a child, the tension which increases tips the balance in the direction of infertility. Then, at long last, they adopt a child. This turns their attention away from their infertility and concern. Thus tension is reduced, and the balance is tipped in the direction of fertility. Soon after adopting a child, the wife becomes pregnant. In one study made some years ago [Perkins, 1936], it was found that in 273 cases of adoption, 200 of the adoptive mothers who had never been pregnant before had a child within an average of thirty-nine months after the adoption and within ten years after the wedding. But does this prove that fertility was increased by the adoption? Or would they have become pregnant anyway in a period that long? Undoubtedly some women become pregnant soon after adopting a child. But recent evidence does not support the view that there is a cause-and-effect relationship between adoption and conception, at least not in most cases. There may be exceptions. The percentage of previously childless women who become pregnant after adoption is not greatly different from the percentage of such women whose infertility is ended spontaneously without adoption [Greenhill, 1961, 1962; Weinstein, 1962; Aronson and Glienke, 1963].

Abortion

It is impossible to gather complete and accurate data on the frequency of abortions. One estimate is that there are at least a million abortions annually in this country, of which a minimum of about 30 per cent are criminal. Only a small proportion, variously estimated to be from 1 to 5 per cent, are therapeutic [Rosen, 1954]. One investigator [Calderone, 1958] estimates that the actual number may be as low as 200,000 or as high as 1,200,000. Another investigator, Potter [Greenhill, 1959], estimates that each year a million fetuses die before delivery and another million are destroyed in criminal abortion. There is no way of being certain of the accuracy of such estimates. But we can be certain that the annual number of abortions is very large.

As implied above, abortions are of three types:

1. *Therapeutic*, that is, induced by a physician, usually after consultation with at least one other physician and ordinarily in a case in which continuation of the pregnancy would endanger the life or seriously impair the health of the mother, though such abortions are sometimes performed for psychiatric, eugenic (fetus may be defective), humanitarian (cases of rape), or socioeconomic reasons. Such an abortion is legal and may be performed in a hospital. Actually, with modern antibiotics and chemotherapy there are relatively few cases in which a therapeutic abortion is indicated literally to save the life of the mother. Therapeutic abortion on psychiatric grounds appears to be growing more common, but opinions differ as to whether abortion on such grounds is justifiable. In one study it was found that the condition of many psychotic patients was not made worse by allowing their pregnancies to progress to full term and that in some cases the women showed improvement. On the other hand, the condition of some psychotic women was made worse by abortion. Sim [*Obstetrical and Gynecological Survey*, 1963], who made this study, sums up his attitude in one sentence: "There are no psychiatric grounds for the termination of pregnancy."

2. *Spontaneous*, that is, an abortion that occurs because of some condition in the mother or fetus and without deliberate interference; such an abortion is commonly termed *miscarriage*.

3. *Criminally induced*, that is, an abortion brought about through deliberate interference with the pregnancy when the reason for such interference is the desire or convenience of the mother rather than some condition that is considered an indication for therapeutic abortion.

It is difficult to determine accurately the relative proportions of criminal and spontaneous abortions because in order to evade the law many criminal abortions are mentioned as having been spontaneous. In some states the mother is legally as guilty as the abortionist and hence is likely to claim that she had a miscarriage. If the mother induces the abortion herself, technically she commits a criminal offense. If, however, she says she miscarried, it is difficult to prove the contrary.

There are many factors that may play a part in causing spontaneous abortion. One of them is a defective fetus. Thus such abortion is not always an unmixed tragedy. In one study, 48 per cent of aborted fetuses were found to be abnormal. In another study, 46 per cent were abnormal. In still another, it was found that 80 per cent of the fetuses aborted at the end of the first month were defective, and half of those aborted in the second month were defective. In the third and fourth months, only about 12 per cent were abnormal [Greenhill, 1944]. Broadly speaking, about one-third of the fetuses in spontaneous abortions are defective [Greenhill, 1948]. Greenhill [1945a] estimates that there are at least five times as many deformed fetuses among those aborted as there are deformed babies among those born at full term. The proportion may be even higher than this, since by no means all aborted fetuses are subjected to examination. As mentioned above, Potter [*Obstetrical and Gynecological Survey*, 1963] concludes from her studies that there are "probably well over a million spontaneous abortions" each year in this country, that "most of them result from abnormal development of the embryo or villi," and that, if those that occur so early that the woman is unaware or uncertain that she was pregnant are included, the number would be "in the neighborhood of four to five million." Some occur so early that the woman is not even aware that she has been pregnant and assumes that she has had an unusual menstrual period. Such very early abortions are sometimes referred to as *silent abortions*.

Every woman who has a criminal abortion thinkingly or by implication makes a value judgment concerning the nature and importance of human life. She must either admit that in abortion at any fetal age a human life is destroyed or she must draw a line at some arbitrary point in fetal development on one side of which the fetus is considered human, while on the other side it is not. For thoughtful persons, the drawing of such a line presents a difficult problem. Some individuals draw the line at the moment of fertilization. Some draw it at the point at which the fetus looks human. Others draw it at the point of viability, that is, the point at which the fetus could continue to live outside the mother's body. Some draw it at the point of birth, whether this is premature or full term. Others insist that any organism at any age is human if it has human parents. Still others assert that, since pregnancy is not comparative, that is, a woman is either pregnant or nonpregnant, she cannot be more pregnant or less pregnant at any time during pregnancy; she is pregnant with a human being whether this be in the first minute after fertilization or in the last minute before birth.

There may be psychological consequences of criminal abortion because the woman cannot make a permanent, unequivocal decision at the time the abortion is performed and later feels regret or guilt. There is a variety of physiological consequences of criminal abortion. Because of the use of antibiotics and chemotherapy, fatal infection is not so common as it used to be. Improved means of controlling hemorrhage have reduced but not eliminated death from this cause. In a study of abortion deaths in New York City [Helpern, 1959], it was found that "what one encounters most at the present time is the case in which there is immediate or rapid death as the result of the method utilized, usually by crude, ignorant, nonmedical persons." These cases include deaths from "gross overdosage of intravenous barbiturates administered for anesthesia," from inhalation of chloroform, from air embolism (air in the circulatory system) resulting from the injection of air into the uterus through the use of a douche or syringe, from "hemorrhage and shock resulting from crude instrumentation, with laceration and perforation of vagina, uterus, cervix, intestines, and mesentary," and from "injections of irritating and corrosive fluids into the uterus." In this study it was also found that "there were more deaths from crudely performed criminal abortion, some with very severe injury, among single women, who in desperation are more apt to expose themselves to the crude abortionist than are married." In addition to the women who die as a result of criminal abortion, there is an unascertainable number who become ill or sterilized, or who have menstrual disturbances or complications in future pregnancies.

The physiological risk is greater in criminal abortion than in therapeutic abortion chiefly because of the type of person who performs the operation and the conditions under which he works. He knows that he is violating the law and medical ethics. He knows, also, however, that in most instances he is protected, since the woman wishes to keep the abortion secret. The criminal abortionist feels no responsibility for the health of the woman because his reputation depends not upon his skill and success as a surgeon but upon his willingness to violate the law. He is interested in dollars rather than patients and may be unable to make a legitimate living. He may not even be a physician. For example, in one case coming to this writer's attention the abortionist was a laundress. The abortionist cannot take the woman to a reputable hospital. Hence, the operation is performed in an inferior hospital, in a hospital controlled by the abortionist or his associates, in his office, or in his residence. To protect himself, not the patient, he may work without the assistance of a nurse. For the same reason he may not permit the patient to know his identity or have anyone accompany her. His instruments are often not carefully sterilized. His techniques are frequently crude and unskilled. Since his practice is illegal and undercover, he is not subject to control by the American Medical Association and feels no responsibility for maintaining the high standards of that organization. After the operation, the woman usually goes directly back to her place of residence, since the abortionist supplies no convalescent care.

Partly because of the manner in which abortionists function and partly because state laws, though defining criminal abortion as a punishable offense, often almost protect abortionists by making their apprehension difficult, few abortionists are convicted. Part of this failure to apprehend abortionists is due to the apathy of a public which may become greatly exercised over a newspaper headline announcing one homicide, especially if the victim or the perpetrator is a famous person, but seems largely disinterested, partly because uninformed, when American mothers annually destroy several times the number of lives that the atom bomb destroyed at Hiroshima or perhaps a number broadly comparable to that of all Americans killed in all the wars in which this country has participated in its entire history.

Sometimes it is assumed that safe criminal abortion may be achieved through the use of abortifacient drugs. They are usually purchased on the basis of hearsay, advertisements, or the recommendation of clerks. Many of these drugs are not only ineffective but dangerous. Some of them may cause serious injury or death. Often a woman is willing to do almost anything to induce abortion. She or her "boy friend" or husband purchases a package of abortifacient. She takes the recommended dosage and nothing happens. This makes her panicky, and she increases the dosage until at length she becomes ill. Even then she may not abort, since there is reason to believe that ordinarily a pregnant woman will not abort as the result of using drugs unless the fetus is dead or unless there is some physical condition that makes abortion easy or imminent or the dosage is great enough to be definitely dangerous to her well-being.

Contrary to common assumption, criminal abortion is found primarily among married women rather than as a means of terminating premarital pregnancies. Some investigators estimate that 90 per cent of such abortions are performed on married women. This is due in part, of course, to the fact that more married than unmarried women become pregnant.

Some persons maintain that a woman ought to have the right to make a free decision regarding the deliberate termination of her pregnancy, whether or not there are medical indications for such termination. They maintain that the fact that the fetus is at no time actually a part of the mother's body is a technicality because the pregnancy certainly affects her body and, therefore, she ought to be able to decide what the condition of her body will be. To support their point of view, these persons point to the experience of countries where abortion has been legalized. They say that the risk in legal abortion is far lower than that in criminal abortion, that we are going to continue to have abortion whether or not it is legalized, and that therefore the United States should follow the lead of these other countries and make abortion legal.

Others maintain that abortion at any stage of fetal development involves the destruction of a human organism. Therefore, there is no more justification for legalizing such destruction at one stage of development than at any other, and a woman has no more right to destroy a fetus merely because it is inconvenient for her to continue the pregnancy or she does not want the baby than she has to destroy a newborn baby for a similar reason. The persons taking this position point to the experience of the same countries as those mentioned above, noting that legal abortion is not without risk and regret [Greenhill, 1960].

The problem is not an easy one. There is danger of falling into a trap of oversimplified, capsule solution. It involves ethical and philosophical as well as legal considerations. Is the fetus a human organism or is it not? If it is not, what is it and when does it become human? If it is, who has the right and upon what basis to decide whether it is to live or die? Is pregnancy only a personal or familial condition or is it also a societal situation involving a new member of the state? The degree to which the state is to be permitted to regulate individual conduct through restrictive legislation is a continuing issue. Most people would agree that the more individual behavior affects one or more other persons, the more it may justifiably be regulated by law and that the state has a right to protect any of its members from offense by other members. But where does abortion fit into this picture? The law permits therapeutic abortion for medical reasons. Is the condition of a woman's body more important than her total life situation? The problem calls for a great deal more careful thought than has been given to it up to date.

Artificial insemination

Artificial insemination is the process of transferring seminal fluid from the male to the female by mechanical means rather than by sexual intercourse. The seminal fluid is ejaculated during masturbation or incomplete intercourse into a glass container. This fact has given rise to the term *test-tube baby*. The fluid is then redeposited in the vagina at the entrance to the cervix, or sometimes directly into the uterus, by means of a syringelike device. It is done at the request of the couple in cases in which the husband has low fertility, there is some anatomical condition making natural insemination difficult, there is some eugenic consideration, such as the husband's carrying an undesirable hereditary trait, or some similar reason. There is no way of ascertaining how frequently it occurs, since physicians' records are not made public.

Artificial insemination is of two types. In one type the woman's husband provides the seminal fluid. This type is referred to as *AIH* (artificial insemination – husband). In the other type an anonymous donor, to whom the couple are also anonymous, is chosen by the physician and provides the seminal fluid for remuneration. This type is referred to as *AID* (artificial insemination – donor). Some physicians mix a small quantity of the husband's seminal fluid with that of the donor. Then, if the woman conceives, there is no way of proving which man is the father of the child. Such a procedure, it is claimed, facilitates the husband's acceptance of the child and eliminates legal problems that might arise relative to the child's being the husband's heir. Other physicians feel that AID should be performed only with carefully chosen, mature couples and that with such couples subterfuge is unnecessary. In cases of AID, legal complications may be avoided by the husband's adoption of the child. But adoption involves court procedure and a degree of publicity which many couples want to avoid. Hence, they simply keep the fact of artificial insemination secret and present the child to relatives and friends as their natural offspring.

Artificial insemination has been common practice in animal breeding for some time. It facilitates control of such breeding and eliminates the necessity of transporting large and often valuable breeding stock. It also enables a given male to sire more offspring than he could sire by means of natural insemination. In recent years animal seminal fluid has been quick-frozen and shipped to owners of females, who then thaw it, dilute it, and use it in artificial insemination. This suggests a question: Could human seminal fluid be quick-frozen and used in artificial insemination? The answer is in the affirmative. It has been done both in AID and as a means of concentrating the sperms from several samples of seminal fluid when a husband has a low sperm count. Normal children have resulted from such frozen-semen insemination. Up to date, however, the number of such children has been small [Greenhill, 1959; Farris, 1956; Guttmacher, 1960; Bishop, 1961]. Frozen bull sperms have been stored for as long as six years and regained their motility when thawed [Bishop, 1961]. It is not beyond possibility that there will someday be semen banks in much the same way that there are now blood banks, permitting a further extension of currently employed methods of assisting childless couples [Hartman, 1962].

Rh factor

The Rh factor is a substance found in the blood. It derives its name from the fact that it was discovered during the course of experiments to learn what happened when the blood of one species was introduced into another. One type of animal used in the experiments was the Rhesus monkey. An individual in whose blood the Rh factor is present is designated as Rh-positive. One from whose blood it is absent is designated as Rh-negative. Actually, there are several Rh factors. But we shall generalize and discuss them as if there were only one and say that about 85 per cent of the white population is Rh-positive. Nonwhite races appear to be almost entirely Rh-positive. There are also other types of mother-fetus blood incompatibility, but Rh incompatibility has received a good deal of publicity in recent years.

Whether an individual is Rh-positive or Rh-negative is determined by heredity. Rh-positive is dominant; Rh-negative is recessive. This means that an individual's blood will be Rh-positive if he receives two positive genes from his parents or if he receives one positive gene and one negative gene. At the present stage of knowledge, there are no tests to distinguish between these two types of Rh-positive, though helpful evidence may sometimes be obtained from an analysis of an individual's family tree. Actually, there are more than one pair of genes involved, but again we shall generalize. In order to have Rh-negative blood, the individual must receive two negative genes. As we saw earlier in this chapter, when sperms or ova are formed, the pairs of chromosomes, and hence pairs of genes, separate. Therefore, the following combinations are possible, letting a plus sign (+) indicate a positive gene and a minus sign (−) indicate a negative gene.

The proportions given in Table 5 apply to large numbers of families. A particular couple of the type indicated in situation 6, for example, might, by chance, have all negative children.

The instance in which the Rh factor ordinarily can cause a problem is that indicated in situations 4 and 7 in Table 5, that is, the mother is Rh-negative, the father is Rh-positive, the child is Rh-positive. But in fewer than 10 per cent of such cases does the problem actually arise [Allen and Diamond, 1957].

Although it is generally true that there is no direct connection between mother and fetus, that the placental "roots" (*villi*) are part of a closed fetal circulatory system and merely extend into, but do not connect with, the mother's blood stream, there are exceptions. There are cases in which there is a breakdown of the placental barrier, possibly due to premature aging of the placenta [Greenhill, 1958]. The entrance of the fetal blood cells into the maternal circulation during the third stage of labor is also a possibility [Roberts, 1957]. In such cases, there is an actual interchange of blood between fetus and mother. The amount of

TABLE 5   POSSIBLE RH-POSITIVE–RH-NEGATIVE COMBINATIONS

father	mother	offspring	
1. ++(positive)	++(positive)	all++	(all positive)
2. ++(positive)	+−(positive)	1/2++;1/2+−	(all positive)
3. +−(positive)	++(positive)	1/2++;1/2+−	(all positive)
4. ++(positive)	−−(negative)	all+−	(all positive)
5. −−(negative)	++(positive)	all+−	(all positive)
6. +−(positive)	+−(positive)	1/4++;1/2+−;1/4−−	(3/4 positive; 1/4 negative)
7. +−(positive)	−−(negative)	1/2+−;1/2−−	(1/2 positive; 1/2 negative)
8. −−(negative)	+−(positive)	1/2+−;1/2−−	(1/2 positive; 1/2 negative)
9. −−(negative)	−−(negative)	all−−	(all negative)

interchange need not be very great to produce an effect. In situations 4 and 7 in Table 5, the Rh factor can cause a problem only if such interchange occurs.

When an individual is vaccinated for smallpox, a small amount of vaccine, a foreign substance, is introduced into his blood stream. His body reacts to this foreign substance and produces chemicals termed *antibodies*. The antibodies remain in the individual's blood stream for some time. If the organisms that cause smallpox find their way into his blood stream, the antibodies destroy them. Hence, he is immunized against the disease. In immunizing an individual against typhoid fever, however, a series of "shots" is required. After each "shot," the concentration of antibodies in the individual's blood stream is increased. After only one "shot," there are not enough antibodies to produce immunity. After three "shots," there are enough.

When an Rh-negative mother has an Rh-positive fetus and there is a breakdown of the placental barrier permitting an interchange of blood between mother and child, the mother's body may react to the Rh-positive blood of the child as to a foreign substance and produce antibodies. It is as if the mother were vaccinated against the blood of her baby. The result is a type of sensitization termed *isoimmunization*. When the antibodies from the mother pass back, presumably through the placenta, into the blood of the fetus, having been formed to protect the mother from the fetus's Rh-positive blood, they damage red cells in that blood. Because of this damage, the condition in the child is termed *hemolytic* (blood-damaging) disease. Since the part of the fetal blood damaged is the red cells and the condition causes the fetus to produce immature red cells (erythroblasts) at a rapid rate, the disease is termed *erythroblastosis foetalis*.

Even when the mother is Rh-negative and the fetus is Rh-positive and there is a breakdown of the placental barrier, permitting an interchange of blood, and the mother's body reacts to the baby's blood, she is not likely to produce enough antibodies in one pregnancy to affect the child. Several exposures are needed. The situation is similar to that in immunization against typhoid fever. The above statement must be qualified. It is the number of pregnancies, not the number of live-born children, that must be considered. For example, if a woman has two spontaneous abortions or stillbirths before she bears a live baby, so far as the Rh problem is concerned she would count three pregnancies. If an Rh-negative woman had a transfusion of Rh-positive blood, antibodies would be produced that would give her a "head start" on her first pregnancy. Since the Rh factor was discovered in the early 1940s, there are women of childbearing age who may have had such a transfusion.

The antibodies produced by the mother damage the baby's red blood cells. As a result of this damage, a chemical (*bilirubin*) is released and accumulates in the baby's blood. This chemical is a pigment, and its presence produces a yellowish skin discoloration (jaundice). Since the red cells carry oxygen, damage to them reduces the oxygen-carrying capacity of the fetal blood. Hence the child may exhibit symptoms of anemia. The combined effect of the anemia and the chemical (bilirubin) may cause brain damage with resultant mental retardation or cerebral palsy. It may even cause death. Since the red cells are formed in the liver of the fetus, this organ may enlarge in an effort to produce cells more rapidly than they are damaged [Allen and Diamond, 1957]. At the other extreme, the child's symptoms may be very mild and involve no more than a brownish discoloration of the milk teeth which disappears when these teeth are replaced by permanent ones.

The Rh factor is something to be understood and taken into account when the blood types of the parents are such that a problem may arise. This factor is, however, not as fearsome as was first thought. The publicity accompanying its discovery set into motion a fear that has not yet been allayed. Part of the reason that the Rh factor need not be feared as much as was originally thought is the fact that methods of detecting the problem by measuring the concentration of antibodies in the mother and methods of treating babies that have been affected have been greatly improved. The principal means of treating the baby is an exchange transfusion during which, a little at a time, the baby's Rh-positive blood is replaced or partially replaced with Rh-negative blood.

The use of Rh-negative blood in such cases is puzzling to many students. Several things must be kept in mind. The first problem is to give the baby blood that will function in the presence of the antibodies which passed to him from his mother. Since the antibodies are designed to damage Rh-positive blood cells, the baby is given Rh-negative blood. He will not react to this blood by the production of antibodies, since it is the Rh-negative individual who reacts to Rh-positive blood, not vice versa. Furthermore, the transfused Rh-negative blood will not produce antibodies in reaction with the baby's Rh-positive blood, since the antibodies are not formed in or by blood but in the spleen, liver, bone marrow, and/or lymph nodes [Carpenter, 1956]. The baby, being Rh-positive by heredity, will continue to form Rh-positive blood which will gradually replace the Rh-negative blood with which he was transfused.

Sometimes, when it is likely that the baby will be erythroblastotic, the obstetrician induces labor so that the child is born early. Such induction of labor does not prevent erythroblastosis, but it does prevent some stillbirths [Allen and Diamond, 1957; Scott, 1963].

If the situation discussed above is reversed, that is, if the mother is Rh-positive, the fetus is Rh-negative, and there is a breakdown of the placental barrier, why is the mother not affected by antibodies produced by the fetus? There are several reasons. First, an immature organism usually has a lower capacity to produce antibodies than does a more mature one [Carpenter, 1956]. Second, the difference in body size, and hence in quantity of blood (with resultant dilution), would make a difference. Third, there is no possibility of an accumulation of antibodies in the fetus through successive pregnancies.

Choosing an obstetrician

The importance of adequate prenatal care for the prospective mother cannot be overemphasized. Her health, both present and future, and her baby's well-being hinge in large measure upon her care during pregnancy. There are many useful books and pamphlets on this subject, and the reader is urged to refer to them. The woman's best protection, however, is a competent obstetrician.

The obstetrician should not be chosen only for his ability to diagnose and treat disease. Pregnancy is not a disease. He should be chosen primarily for his ability to handle cases of pregnancy. What is significant is the number of successful deliveries he has to his credit, not the number of operations or the number of occasions on which he has let women reach the brink of disaster only to save them in the nick of time.

Preferably he (or she) should be a physician equipped to handle the pregnancy from the first visit to the care of the mother after she leaves the hospital. He need not be able singlehandedly to meet all emergencies; that is too much to ask of any physician. But it is essential that he be able to recognize and detect emergencies and be willing to call in a consultant if necessary.

The obstetrician's personality is important, since his contact with the prospective mother is somewhat intimate. She should not be forced to have a physician whom she dislikes and with whom she cannot get along. His training is important. So is the extent of his experience. Does he have enough obstetric cases to gain experience? Does he let himself become so busy that he must resort to time-saving techniques, such as induction of labor or use of forceps, unnecessarily and for his own convenience rather than for the patient's good? Is he so busy that he delegates so much to nurses that the peculiar relationship between obstetrician and mother is rendered unsatisfactory? "The obstetrician who depends upon the obstetrical nurse to follow his patients in labor and who wishes to be called only when delivery is imminent is not practicing obstetrics in the best sense of the term; he is a doctor who delivers babies. . . . No analgesia can take the place of considerate and conscientious care by the obstetrician. . . ." [Crampton, 1961]. Does he keep abreast of new developments? Is obstetrics his special interest, or is it only incidental in a general practice? Will he, indeed may he, take his patients to a reputable hospital? Learning to which obstetrician the wives of other obstetricians go for their own deliveries may be helpful. All these considerations are more important than his age.

A problem not infrequently faced by young couples is that of choosing a physician soon after having settled in a new community, before sufficient time has elapsed for them to become thoroughly acquainted. In such cases, information may be gathered from friends or from persons at the husband's place of employment. The local hospital may yield some data. The couple may write to their physician in their home town and ask him to recommend someone.

Before the couple put their case in the physician's hands, they should talk it over with him. Let them remember that they are employing him, not he them. They have a right to know what his techniques are, how many visits he will recommend before delivery, what care he will continue after delivery, to what hospital he takes his patients, what is his attitude toward induced labor, what he does concerning relief from pain, and what the total cost will be.

Once the obstetrician is chosen, he should be told everything relevant to the case. No detail, no matter how insignificant it may seem to the couple, should be withheld. Questions should be freely asked. Any obstetrician worth his salt would rather have the couple ask innumerable questions than let a clue remain hidden which, if revealed, might prevent complications.

Once the obstetrician is chosen, too, his instructions should be followed faithfully, explicitly, and thoroughly. The couple should never let other people's advice supersede the doctor's instructions. If they do not like the way he handles their case, they may change obstetricians. But as long as they accept a particular physician's services, they should cooperate to the utmost and have complete confidence. Such confidence is a *sine qua non* of good obstetrical procedure. Both physician and patient may play a part in establishing the rapport demanded by the nature of their relationship.

Pregnancy and the couple's adjustment

We are accustomed to saying that such and such a woman is pregnant. In one sense that is correct; in another it is not. It would be more nearly accurate to say that there is pregnancy in the family. Pregnancy is in many ways a social condition. It certainly involves both husband and wife; it also involves their relatives, the mores, and the laws of the state.

Motherhood and baby care begin not at birth but at conception. A woman is a mother for nine months before her child is born and should act and be treated as such. The father's case is similar. His responsibility and new status do not begin with the passing out of cigars.

READING 17 BECOMING A FATHER

Even in an era of small families, girls receive instruction and practice in motherhood from their days of doll-play until their first children arrive. Indeed, baby-sitting may furnish better training—when girls can see and critically compare the procedures of many mothers—than comes merely from caring for their own younger siblings. Child study groups, nursery schools, magazines and books, and the whole informal complex of advice given by relatives and friends—all the standard resources of family life education are concentrated on the young mother after practice becomes reality.

But what of the boys who are just as surely to become fathers? Does it not seem likely that they are almost as conscientiously educated out of fatherhood as girls are educated into motherhood?

Boys tend early to be discouraged from playing with dolls. They are encouraged to vest their thinking about the future primarily in preparation for employment. Their toys, their reading, their commercial entertainment, the ways in which they are implicitly guided in school all seem to work against their preparation for parenthood.

It is not surprising therefore that the stereotype of the expectant father awaiting word at the hosptial is of a nervous, embarrassed, and helpless goof. While his wife is typically radiant with joy and the congratulations of friends, he is the butt of numerous reflections on his ineptitude and his loss of boyish irresponsibility. Thereafter the stereotype persists, in the bumbling Jiggs or Dagwood who has to be cajoled into adult behavior by his wife and

From Nelson Foote, "Becoming a Father," *The Bulletin on Family Development*, vol. 3, no. 1, spring, 1962, pp. 7–9. Reprinted with permission of the editor and author.

children. All too often this humorous caricature is not too far from reality, although in reality the immature father is far from funny. Particularly when a father tries to compensate for parental incompetence by displays of petty tyranny or physical domination, the consequences of his deficiency can be frustration—sometimes cumulatively tragic—for all concerned.

Far more will be contributed to child development in our society by raising the level of parental competence than by further increments of attention to the preparation of girls for motherhood. The first condition for any improvement in preparation for fatherhood, of course, is recognition that vast improvement is possible. Much useful research could well be done, mostly of descriptive and comparative varieties, which would simply demonstrate how far short most fathers fall from exercising the quality of parenthood exercised by their wives. Obviously such illumination of the present situation does not gainsay the greater time mothers have to spend with children. Nor does it imply that the parental role of the father is or should be identical with that of mothers. Proper criteria for evaluating the competence of fathers as fathers could well receive as much attention as has been spent by laymen and professionals in deciding how a good mother should behave.

We take for granted that the character of a girl has much to do with whether she will make a good mother. But we also take for granted that merely to possess a wholesome character is not enough. There are many things for a mother to learn to do if she is to play her role with credit and success. Moreover, she must be motivated by the desire to be a good mother, if she is to master all the know-how, and is also to master the obstacles in her environment that may interfere with her performance of this role.

But if motherhood can be learned, it can be taught. And if motherhood can be taught, so can fatherhood. The day is far off—although maybe within our lifetime—when every boy who graduates from high school will be well prepared for fatherhood. Nonetheless that far-off goal can serve as a guide in taking the many more modest intermediate steps along the way.

Instead of devoting resources primarily to persuading the reluctant, probably the right move at present—after demonstrating the gap between what is actual and what is possible—is for professional people concerned with family life education in the community to work first with those who are not reluctant. It sometimes seems a little easier, paradoxical though it sounds, to go on preaching to the hard of heart or hearing, than to show the way to those who are ready to start. Yet if the already-willing can make progress in a desirable direction, then this may be all it takes to persuade the reluctant.

So the question comes down to whether young men can be demonstrably trained for better performance of the role of father than they would otherwise be able to display. Here is the point at which, if family life education proves that it can really make a difference, it will make a tremendous leap forward. Such a demonstration would eventually bring parent education from the status of a women's leisure activity to being a serious masculine activity as well. There has been some progress in drawing men into Parent-Teacher Associations, but largely with a view to utilizing their support for higher education budgets in the community.

The popular caricature of the bumbling father who is patronized by wife and children would lose its validity as a symptom of a disturbing trend if a counter trend toward a more competent fatherhood were vigorously developed.

The father can be a heroic as well as a comic figure. The father as the strong protector is a traditional role that is as strongly welcomed by wife and children as ever, even though occasions for its display may occur more rarely than in the past. The father as wise judge is also a traditional role that gets less exercise today, but the reason is not that the need is less for wise judges and advisers. The reason is that the role of expert has gotten confounded with the roles of judge and adviser. The authority of the judge and adviser in human relations is not based on the expertness of the encyclopedist, but on the recognition by the judged and the advised of his wisdom. Somehow the rise of professional expertness of all kinds has intimidated many fathers in exercising this kind of authority and responsibility, and has encouraged many children to discount and defy them. It is possible both to train fathers in the exercise of judgment and to increase their confidence in exercising it in real life. Quite incidentally family life education has the task, not an extremely difficult one although an important one, of clarifying those situations where personal limitations do exist and professional expertness is the appropriate recourse.

The father as hero and the father as judge are only two manifestations of the role of the father which evoke respect rather than ridicule. Many others occur as well, and could recur more often if family life education takes on the task of training for more competent fatherhood.

Having a baby is a joint enterprise from the very beginning. The father's physiological role may not be so prominent as the mother's, but he has indispensable psychological and economic functions. The husband suffering the throes of becoming a parent is made the butt of many a joke. Much humorous discussion and literature are directed toward the "care and treatment" of expectant fathers. The father's situation is anything but a joke. A child needs two parents, and the father has a responsibility. There are many things that he may do to make the wife's nine months of pregnancy more enjoyable. He may assist with the housework or employ someone to do it. He may make certain that he and his wife do interesting things in their leisure time. He may prepare for the baby's coming by making things for the nursery. He should understand what is occurring so that he may help his wife follow the doctor's instructions and will know what to do in case an emergency arises. Together he and his wife may attend prenatal classes in infant care which are becoming increasingly available in many communities. The wife is likely to be more than ordinarily dependent upon him, and he can do much to color her attitude, favorably or unfavorably, toward both the present and future pregnancies. Some pregnant women develop temporary personality traits that make them somewhat difficult to live with. It is important that the husband understand this fact and adjust himself accordingly.

Not the least of the father's functions is economic. Babies cost money. When the total cost of the child is taken into consideration, reckoning from early pregnancy through infancy, childhood, adolescence, to young adulthood, and including all expenses borne by parents from the initial doctor's fee to college education, the picture is breathtaking. Each time a couple have a child, the financial responsibility they assume is roughly equivalent to that involved in purchasing a new home.

A question that often arises in connection with the prospective father is whether he should be in the delivery room (as distinguished from the labor room) when his baby is born. Some hospitals and obstetricians will permit him to be present; others will not. Much depends upon the attitude of the wife. If his presence would reassure her, he may be useful. If his presence would cause her to worry, he would be less than useless. Some men want to witness the birth; others do not. Some feel that witnessing it makes the child seem more their own, since they are more nearly participators.

There are arguments against the husband's being present at the delivery. He may get in the way of doctor or nurses. Typically the delivery room is not equipped to accommodate observers. He may become emotionally upset and conclude that the doctor is not doing all he can. He may have little or no background for interpreting what he sees and hence may misinterpret it. If he presumes to give the doctor suggestions, he becomes a nuisance. He carries germs and shakes them off onto the delivery-room floor or spreads them through the air. Through long strain he may faint. Doctor and nurses have more important duties than reviving an unconscious father. Medically speaking, he is usually of little or no help.

Unless her obstetrician advises to the contrary, a woman may with some exceptions pursue her regular activities, including housework, during pregnancy. There are many sports in which she may engage, though she may not usually ride horseback, dive, or do similar things that are more or less violent in character. Sexual intercourse may be engaged in unless there are special considerations for which the obstetrician advises against it. In a healthy pregnancy, in which there is no abnormal condition of fetus, uterus, or placenta, the fetus is not readily dislodged, and spontaneous abortion is not brought about by the ordinary activities or life.

If the woman is employed, however, adjustments in her work may be indicated, depending upon the nature of her occupation. In discussing women in industry, McCall and Trace [Greenhill, 1961] point out that pregnancy often reduces a woman's work efficiency. It may play a part in shortening her span of concentration. As the uterus enlarges, the woman becomes more vulnerable to accident. Chronic fatigue is to be avoided. Among women in industry, spontaneous abortion occurs at about the same rate as in the general population unless working conditions involve noxious materials. But among the infants of such women, the mortality rate is almost twice as high as among the offspring of housewives if the women stop work before the end of the twenty-eighth week of pregnancy and almost three times as high if they work beyond that time. They suggest that minimum standards should provide that women not work for six weeks before, and two months after, delivery.

For her own morale, as well as for the benefit of persons who observe her, a pregnant woman should keep herself as attractive as her resources permit. If the husband realizes how near clothes are to the ordinary woman's heart and knows that her morale depends in part upon her appearance, he will encourage her to keep attractive during pregnancy, even though it may mean extra expense when the couple are saving for the baby.

Another question that is sometimes raised concerns the extent of the father's participation in infant care. Many modern fathers participate with enthusiasm. Others feel that infant care is the mother's responsibility. Still others, never having had experience with infants, are afraid of their own child. They feel awkward in holding it and fear that they will hurt it. The question of the father's participation in infant care is not one only of the contribution he can make to such care. It is also one of the contribution that such care can make to him. What will he miss if he does not participate? There is evidence to suggest that the human mother has no "maternal instinct" in the strict sense of the term but that through handling, fondling, caring for, and nursing the baby she very quickly learns to love it. Of course, this process is greatly facilitated if the woman wants a baby very much and eagerly anticipates having it. Also, in every culture there is a pattern of expectation which colors the rearing of girls and orients them in the direction of motherhood. Certainly there is no paternal instinct. The father, too, learns to love the child through anticipation, caring for it, and fondling it. Furthermore, the day-to-day development of an infant is a fascinating process. As the baby's world expands and he becomes aware of more and more of his environment, many a modern father wants to be part of that world from the beginning with a strong affectional bond between himself and the child already established. He does not want to wait and then be introduced into the child's world later merely because infant care is time- and energy-consuming.

Adoption

It is estimated that there are 100,000 adoptions yearly in this country. The demand for babies far exceeds the supply. Each year more than a million couples apply to agencies to adopt a child—a ratio of 10 applications to each child placed [Kurtz, 1960]. Often a couple must wait a year or more after making an application before receiving an infant. Older children are less in demand and easier to obtain.

Adoption is no longer considered an act of charity through which a homeless child is given maintenance. It is deemed a privilege for the adoptive parents as well as for the child. The future welfare of all concerned is taken into consideration. Not only is the child chosen; the adoptive home and parents also are chosen. Actually, in recent years the concept of "adoptability" has changed. Formerly the emphasis was upon finding a child for a family. Now the emphasis is upon finding a family for a child [Kurtz, 1960]. The staffs in the better agencies insist upon meeting the prospective adoptive parents, investigating their social and economic position, and sending a special investigator to see the home and talk with friends. In this way adults and child are "fitted" to each other. Race, religion, intelligence, nationality, education, and cultural background of natural and of adoptive parents are matched in so far as this is possible. So carefully is this done in some cases that the child actually looks like the new parents and could easily pass as their own offspring.

Usually the agency collects all available facts pertaining to the child's background. These are kept on file. Some agencies reveal as much as the adoptive parents wish to know. Others hold that the less the new parents know the better off both the child and they will be, since knowing the child's background may lead them to "read into" his behavior something that is there only in their own imagination. In general, trusting the staff of a reliable agency is a better safeguard than knowing the necessarily incomplete data on the child's origin. The identity of natural parents is usually not revealed to adoptive parents, and vice versa. Hence there is very little chance of the former's appearing at an inopportune time to upset the child's adjustment. When the baby is left with the agency, all claim to it is relinquished.

No defective child is offered for adoption without the prospective adoptive parents' being apprised of the defects. They are not obliged to accept the baby if they do not want it. In the better agencies all children remain in a temporary home for observation, medical attention, and testing for at least a brief period before being placed.

When the child is taken by the prospective adoptive parents, it is on probation, so to speak, for a time—from several months to a year. If during this period before the final papers have been signed it develops any defects not observable in infancy, it may be returned to the agency. Few babies are returned, since many defects may be observed very early in life and there is but slight chance of others developing. A couple who adopt a child run very slight risk of receiving one who is defective—certainly no more risk than in having one of their own, and probably less. When they adopt a baby, they can at least see what they are getting.

Experience proves that adopted children love and are loved as much as natural ones. The biological parents, if anything is known about them, are strangers; if nothing is known of them, they are merely words and a source of mild curiosity.

In the rearing of the child, his adoption should be made a natural part of his life, something that he takes for granted. He should be told of it as soon as he is able to understand. He should not, however, be reminded of it in a disparaging way. No gratitude should be demanded, and his shortcomings should never be blamed on the fact of adoption. Some foster parents speak of their "adopted child" or "chosen child." In this way the child grows up with the idea of adoption accepted casually and without shock. Cases are known in which a child has boasted to his playmates, "I was chosen because my parents loved me, but yours had to take you." In one case in which a couple had adopted several children, two of them were overheard discussing a new friend, who was the natural child of her parents. "Let's not tell her that we're adopted," they agreed, "it might make her feel bad."

When the child is reared believing that he is his adoptive parents' natural offspring and then, when partly grown, learns about his adoption, he may experience a shock that shakes the foundations of his personality. This is especially likely to happen when he acquires the facts indirectly, suddenly, and without preparation. His world collapses. Things he thought most secure become insecure. He is forced to read-just his whole point of view and outlook upon life. He is not the person he thought he was. He may begin to feel inferior and insecure or become cynical and pessimistic.

Let us imagine a person of college student age who was adopted but did not learn about it until adolescence or later. The open wounds or scars of shock are still observable. What may he do? He is not changed by the knowledge that he was adopted. He should be flattered that his adoptive parents were sufficiently eager to have a child and that he was so attractive to them that they voluntarily chose him and devoted themselves to him. A person feels no inferiority because of having been chosen to become husband or wife instead of being born to this status. In fact, by most people the marital relationship is held in greater esteem than consanguinity (blood relationship). The adopted youth should be gratified that he has brought his adoptive parents happiness. In many ways, life does not depend so much upon biological relationships as it does upon those that are personal and social. Although one's biological relationship to adoptive parents is not what it is to his natural parents, the other relationships are the same with the former as they would have been with the latter. There is no need for the adopted child to worry about his background, for he would probably not have been chosen had there been any apparent defect. As far as his carrying possible heredi-tary defects is concerned, he may rest assured that he knows only slightly less about his ancestry than he would know if he were ac-quainted with his parents and grandparents. We inherit from all our an-cestors. Yet few of us know more than a handful of related persons from the two or three most recent generations.

WHAT DO YOU THINK?

1. A young couple move to a new community because of the hus-band's occupation. Soon the wife finds herself pregnant. How may the couple go about finding and choosing an obstetrician?

2. What may a wife do to make pregnancy an enjoyable experi-ence? What may the husband do for the wife?

3. A pregnant wife fears the pain of childbirth. She insists that her obstetrician guarantee her completely painless delivery. What sugges-tions would you give her?

4. When should a zygote, embryo, or fetus be considered a human being?

5. Each month a girl has severe menstrual cramps. She takes a pain-relieving drug which is widely advertised and commonly used for

this purpose, but she does not know what the ingredients of the drug are. She hesitates to go to a physician because she is afraid he will suggest a pelvic examination. What suggestions would you give her?

6. What are the pros and cons of various health-insurance, medical-care, and hospitalization plans relative to pregnancy?

7. What do you think of having community classes for prospective mothers? For prospective fathers? How might such classes be organized, and what should they include?

8. Who or what should determine how many children a couple have and when they have them?

9. Should everyone be permitted to have children? On whom, if anyone, should restrictions be placed? Why? How? What restrictions?

10. A couple say they want to marry young so that they may "grow up" with their children. What are the pros and cons of such a point of view?

11. How would a couple go about adopting a child in your state?

12. What are the pros and cons of adopting a child?

13. Is there ever any justification for adopting a child through any means other than a recognized, reputable adoption agency?

14. What are the similarities and differences in the concepts implied in the following terms: birth control, conception control, contraception, prevenception, family limitation, family planning, spacing of children, planned parenthood, abortion, sterilization?

15. What should be included in the laws relating to contraception?

16. A couple who are about to be married find that the woman is Rh-negative and the man is Rh-positive. What suggestions would you give them?

SELECTED READINGS

Bates, Jerome, E., and Edward S. Zawadzki: *Criminal Abortion*, Charles C Thomas, Publisher, Springfield, Ill., 1964. A discussion of many aspects of abortion and abortionists, with case histories.

Blood, Robert O., Jr.: *Marriage*, The Free Press of Glencoe, New York, 1962, chap. 19. Family planning: ethics, methods, child spacing, and contraception in practice.

Calderone, Mary Steichen (ed.): *Abortion in the United States*, Paul B. Hoeber, Inc., New York, 1958. Criminal abortion in the United States: methods, risks; therapeutic abortion in the United States; legal aspects of abortion; abortion in the Scandinavian countries.

Cavan, Ruth Shonle (ed.): *Marriage and the Family in the Modern World*, Thomas Y. Crowell Company, New York, 1960, chaps. 20, 21. Heredity: what a child can and cannot inherit; defective children;

Rh factor; twins; the first child; adoption. "Should you have a baby the first year?"

De Merre, Leon J.: *The Female Sex Hormones*, Vantage Press, Inc., New York, 1964. The author is a biochemist who prepared this book "to try to bridge the gap between incomplete and erroneous conceptions . . . and strictly scientific findings that are not accessible to the public." Discusses the endocrine glands, menstruation, hormones, pregnancy tests, breast feeding, and sex determination. Readable, not highly technical, and not overpopularized.

Duvall, Evelyn Millis, and Sylvanus M. Duvall: *Sex Ways in Fact and Faith: Bases for Christian Family Policy*, Association Press, New York, 1961, chaps. 13–15. Family planning: needs, goals, and progress; abortion: medical and social review; voluntary sterilization.

Eastman, Nicholson J.: *Expectant Motherhood*, 3d ed., Little, Brown and Company, Boston, 1957. Discusses pregnancy, childbirth, and motherhood.

Freedman, Ronald, Pascal K. Whelpton, and Arthur A. Campbell: *Family Planning, Sterility, and Population Growth*, McGraw-Hill Book Company, New York, 1959. A study of family size in different social groups; use of contraception; attitudes toward contraception; the influence of religious belief, education, occupation, etc., on the use of contraception. The study is based on interviews with 2,713 young married women.

Gilbert, Margaret Shea: *Biography of the Unborn*, rev. ed., Hafner Publishing Company, Inc., New York, 1963. A detailed but nontechnical account of the development of the fetus.

Guttmacher, Alan F., and the editors of *Consumer Reports: The Consumers Union Report on Family Planning*, Consumers Union of U.S., Inc., Mt. Vernon, N.Y., 1962. "A guide to contraceptive methods and materials with a special section on infertility and what to do about it."

———, Winifred Best, and Frederick S. Jaffe: *Planning Your Family*, The Macmillan Company, New York, 1964. "The most comprehensive and up-to-date handbook on conception and contraception ever made available to the general public." Nontechnical. Includes material on infertility, abortion, and sterilization, as well as contraception. Dr. Guttmacher is one of the leading authorities in this field.

Hamblen, E. C.: *Facts about the Change of Life*, Charles C Thomas, Publisher, Springfield, Ill., 1949. A nontechnical discussion of the menopause.

Landis, Judson T., Thomas Poffenberger, and Shirley Poffenberger: "The Effects of First Pregnancy on the Sexual Adjustment of 212 Couples," *American Sociological Review*, vol. 15, no. 6, pp. 766–772, December, 1950.

Levine, Lena, and Beka Doherty: *The Menopause*, Random House, Inc.,

New York, 1952. A nontechnical discussion of the menopause.

Meaker, Samuel R.: *Preparing for Motherhood*, The Year Book Medical Publishers, Inc., Chicago, 1956.

Merrill, Francis E.: *Courtship and Marriage*, rev. ed., Holt, Rinehart and Winston, Inc., New York, 1959, chaps. 17, 18. Reproductive roles and cultural norms; contraception; prenatal roles of husband and wife.

Monsma, John Clover (ed.): *Religion and Birth Control*, Doubleday & Company, Inc., Garden City, N.Y., 1963. Twenty-one medical specialists discuss contraception, sterilization, therapeutic abortion, natural childbirth, and artificial insemination.

Montagu, Ashley: *Human Heredity*, 2d ed., The World Publishing Company, Cleveland, 1963. A general discussion of heredity, with special emphasis on human heredity and also with emphasis on environmental influences: ". . . not only does the environment regulate the the expression of genetic potentials but also it is in every instance capable of affecting the basic structure of those potentials." Includes a "census of inherited disorders" in humans.

Newman, Horatio Hackett: *Multiple Human Births*, Doubleday & Company, Inc., New York, 1940. Discusses many aspects of multiple births: causes, kinds, "Siamese" twins, and the Dionne quintuplets; the psychology and behavior of twins.

Newton, Niles: *Maternal Emotions*, Paul B. Hoeber, Inc., New York, 1955. A study, by a woman psychologist, of women's attitudes toward sex, menstruation, pregnancy, childbirth, breast feeding, baby care, and men.

Oliven, John F.: *Sexual Hygiene and Pathology*, J. B. Lippincott Company, Philadelphia, 1955, chap. 15. The philosophy and methods of contraception.

Palmer, Rachel Lynn, and Sarah K. Greenberg: *Facts and Frauds in Woman's Hygiene*, Garden City Books, New York, 1938. A critical discussion aimed at caution in the purchase and use of drugs claimed to "cure" dysmenorrhea and other feminine disorders, dangerous drugs used as abortifacients, fake sterility "cures," and related topics. Although the book was published some time ago and some of the products mentioned may no longer be available, it still suggests an appropriate caution relative to products that are now available.

Pilpel, Harriet F., and Theodore Zavin: *Your Marriage and the Law*, Holt, Rinehart and Winston, Inc., New York, 1952, chaps. 8, 9, 11–13. The legal aspects of adoption, artificial insemination, birth control, abortion, and sterilization.

Quay, Eugene: "Justifiable Abortion: Medical and Legal Foundations," *The Georgetown Law Journal*, vol. 49, no. 2, pp. 173–256, winter, 1960; no. 3, pp. 395–538, spring, 1961; reprinted by the Family Life Bureau, National Catholic Welfare Conference, Washington, D.C.

An analysis of the medical, legal, and historical aspects of "justifiable abortion," which is a broader term than "therapeutic abortion" and includes abortion for such possible reasons as rape. A résumé of state laws is included.

Rainwater, Lee: *And the Poor Get Children*, Quadrangle Books, Inc., Chicago, 1960. A study of sex, contraception, and family planning among the working class.

Raymond, Louise: *Adoption and After*, Harper & Row, Publishers, Incorporated, New York, 1955. Questions regarding adoptive parents; adjustment in the family; telling the child of his adoption; adoption of the older child.

Read, Grantley Dick: *Childbirth without Fear*, rev. ed., Harper & Row, Publishers, Incorporated, New York, 1953. A discussion of natural childbirth by the man whose name has become almost a synonym for the term.

Reed, Sheldon C.: *Counseling in Medical Genetics*, 2d ed., W. B. Saunders Company, Philadelphia, 1963. Material designed to answer frequently asked questions about human heredity.

Rosen, Harold (ed.): *Therapeutic Abortion*, The Julian Press, Inc., New York, 1954. Medical, psychiatric, legal, religious, and anthropological aspects of therapeutic abortion.

Scheinfeld, Amram: *Human Heredity Handbook*, J. B. Lippincott Company, Philadelphia, 1956. A nontechnical discussion.

———: *The New You and Heredity*, rev. ed., J. B. Lippincott Company, Philadelphia, 1950. Discusses many aspects of human heredity: physical traits, aptitudes, personality traits, etc.

Simpson, George: *People in Families*, Thomas Y. Crowell Company, New York, 1960, chap. 17. Planned parenthood; contraception; the "reproductive revolution." Psychoanalytic emphasis.

Smith, I. Evelyn (ed.): *Readings in Adoption*, Philosophical Library, Inc., New York, 1963. A series of articles on principles and values, assumptions underlying adoption practices, unmarried parents, and adoption methods and agencies.

Speert, Harold, and Alan F. Guttmacher: *Obstetrical Practice*, Landsberger Medical Books, Inc., New York, 1956. Written to meet the needs of the general medical practitioner who is called upon for obstetrical care; but it is not too technical for the layman who has some knowledge of the anatomy and physiology of reproduction. Discusses all aspects of pregnancy and childbirth. Answers many questions.

Thoms, Herbert, Lawrence Roth, and David Linton: *Understanding Natural Childbirth*, McGraw-Hill Book Company, New York, 1950.

Weber, Laura E.: *Between Us Women*, Doubleday & Company, Inc., Garden City, N.Y., 1962. Written by a woman physician for women. The objective is to answer women's questions about prenatal care, pregnancy, childbirth, and postnatal care.

chapter 16

FAMILY LIVING

Functions of the family

The family has several functions:

1. As suggested in the introduction to this section, it is the basic, nuclear unit in society. Statistically, society is composed of individuals. These individuals, however, are not entirely separate one from another. They occur and function as members of clusters of individuals. Some of these clusters are biologically produced and cohesive. Some are culturally produced and cohesive. The family is an outgrowth of both types of factors. The family is characterized by mutual aid and protection. It is an agency for the preservation and transmission of the cultural heritage of the group. In some cultures "family" suggests a structure different from that found in this country, but the central function is the same.

2. The family is a socially approved means for the production, nurture, rearing, and socialization of children. In our culture it is also a means of identifying children.

3. The family develops parents. As the family is a means of socializing children, so it is also a means of maturing and stabilizing parents. There are as great opportunities for personal growth in having children as there are in being children. In this "age of the child" there is some inclination to overlook the fact that parenthood as an end in itself is as important as parenthood as a means of child production and rearing. Parents are not merely adults who devote a part of their lives to the rearing of children who, in their turn, will devote their lives to the rearing of children, ad infinitum. Parents are people who, perhaps as much as anyone, receive, or can receive, through giving. Social theorizers who

speculate on the comparative values of child rearing in the family versus child rearing by the state often base their arguments only on the welfare of the child. They do not think of parents and forget what might happen to them under some untraditional scheme.

In fulfilling these functions the present-day American family is confronted by new conditions and new demands. With increased urbanization there has been extensive proliferation of the number and types of groups, or aggregates, with which an individual may be affiliated. Some of these compete with the family for his time, interest, support, and loyalty. Individuals are drawn away from the family in a great variety of directions. Generalizing broadly, in earlier times there were more demands on the individual for the good of the family. Now there are more demands on the family, not only for the good of the individual, but also for the welfare of the myriad nonfamily clusters of which the individual is a member.

The present-day American family is "losing" its members, not only because of the centrifugal force mentioned above but also because of the increasing fragmentation of the extended family with a corresponding decrease in the centripetal force which previously bound the family together. In earlier days an extended group of "blood" relatives, including even remote cousins, thought of themselves as "family" in a way less commonly found today. In those earlier times a greater variety of relatives often shared the same dwelling or were closely associated residentially. Grandmothers, maiden aunts, and similar persons often played a part in the family economy, helped with the housework, cared for children, and contributed to their own support through useful service. The rapid rise of the baby-sitter and the difficulty many couples have in finding responsible sitters show how far from this earlier arrangement we have moved. In earlier days, when a son married, he and his wife often settled near his parents, perhaps on a portion of their land. Many homes were occupied by the same family generation after generation, giving children a type of "roots" that present-day apartments, small dwellings, and mobility no longer afford.

In earlier days, an individual could be, or at least often was, to a considerable degree appraised on the basis of his family membership. The reputation of his family was projected onto him in a way that is no longer found. Nowadays, especially in large metropolitan communities, there is so much acquaintance among individuals who know little or nothing about each other's families that such family-based evaluation is seldom possible. Family status is not "inherited" in the way it used to be.

In earlier times, children, like older persons, had a place in the family economy, doing chores and in larger numbers than today leaving school relatively early in order to earn. Now children tend to be "mouths to be fed" rather than "hands to work." In this sense the aged are becoming more like children. They, too, are becoming "mouths to be fed" rather than "hands to work." Society in general and the family in particular have only begun to solve this growing problem.

One of the functions of the family is the transmission of the cultural heritage of the group from one generation to the next. But in rapidly changing times and the complexities and cross currents of present-day American society, what cultural patterns and what values are to be transmitted? In the rearing of children, how insistent should parents be in adhering to the attitudes and standards of yesterday, how adaptive and permissive in accepting the shifting norms of today or anticipating the emerging patterns of tomorrow?

Contributing to this dilemma is the rapid evolution of new pressures being brought to bear on the processes of attitude formation and behavior-pattern determination. In earlier times such pressures grew largely and more or less directly out of the life of the family and the community in which the family lived, with the addition, of course, of ideas derived from reading, the mingling of people, immigration, travel, and social theorizing. The new and highly influential factor today is the introduction of mass media of communication that were hitherto unknown. Media such as movies, radio, and television in a sense make each family a miniature "melting pot" for the ideas, norms, and cultural patterns of the entire world, not just of the community in which the family is situated. But these media also intrude into the family pressures, suggestions, subtle germinal ideas, and behavior patterns which do not come from the life of the community in which the family lives but in many instances are artificial, synthetic, false, and at best presented for profit by a few individuals who are remote from the family and unconcerned about it. It is not surprising that parents wonder about child rearing and that some families fall short in performing their functions.

One function of the family which has come into prominence, but not into existence, in recent years is its contribution to the mental health of its members. The family more than any other single agency lays the foundation for mental health or illness, for good or poor adjustment to life. Therefore, in the discussion of child rearing which follows, considerable attention will be given to the role of the family in meeting children's needs.

Child rearing

For several decades there has been so much said and written about the problems of child rearing, with much profit to be sure, that many parents have come to feel worried and harried. They are badgered by this theory or that. The pendulum of "the right way to do it" swings first one way, then the other. Harassed parents try to keep pace with the swing or feel guilty when they fail to do so. Some have conflict with their own parents or parents-in-law because of differences in attitude and method that arise from generation to generation. "Pick up the child when it cries." "Don't pick up the child when it cries." "Show the child affection." "Don't show the child affection." Should there be scheduled feeding or demand feeding? Or shall we call the latter "self-regulatory feeding"? So it goes. Some modern young parents accept, rear, and enjoy their children with a natural but responsible casualness that would make the "patternizers" of the recent past throw up their hands in horror.

The rearing of children may be approached with greater confidence and relaxation and with less apprehension and tension if several points are recognized:

1. There is no single method of child rearing that is *the* way. Various methods are effective with different parents, different children, under different circumstances. Method should be individualized. There is no over-all or catchall method that applies equally well to all cases. One may readily note in observing children one knows that there may or may not be a complete correlation between quality of personality and the method of rearing which contributed to it. This generalization applies, of course, within reasonable limits and to more or less deliberately chosen methods of child rearing, not to every influence or condition under which children grow. Even when the latter is included, however, the correlation between quality of personality and the life conditions from which the personality emerged is far from complete.

2. No child is reared without some problems. The path of parent-child relationships is never perfectly smooth. It is never possible to predict in advance, and therefore to prepare for, every circumstance that will arise. Parents are called upon to do the best they can in a dynamic relationship involving ever-changing circumstances within which there is interaction between growing organisms each of which is in many ways unique. Much as the parents may know about children and family living through study or experience, part of the time they must "play by ear." Study and experience are useful assets, but they are not guarantees of flawless child rearing.

Any problem that parents have with a particular child is in all probability not unique. It is almost certain to have been faced and solved—or lived with—by other parents. Sometimes an erroneous assumption of uniqueness leads parents to be unnecessarily pessimistic about a given problem.

The definition of a "problem" is ordinarily formulated by the person who has it rather than the person who is it. Parents speak of "problem children." But children refer to "problem parents." We may safely guess that there are as many of the latter as there are of the former. It depends from which side the issue is raised.

3. Usually to become seriously maladjusted a child must be subjected to a chronologically extended and circumstantially extensive

distorted pattern of development. Serious maladjustment in children is not ordinarily produced by occasional, isolated parental mistakes that occur within a healthy pattern of parent-child relationships.

4. Someone has defined a child as "potential with a push." A personality has an "internal push" toward normal development, just as the body has a built-in "mechanism" which directs its changes toward physical health. One aspect of child rearing is to stay out of the way of the child's natural maturation. This does not imply letting the child "run wild." It implies only that personality develops by an "unfolding" as well as by an educative process.

5. Parents alone cannot provide everything a child needs for his development. A child is reared by a multiplicity of agencies. The older he becomes, the greater the number of these becomes. To some extent parents can control the selection of such agencies or modify their influence on the child. But the parents' possibilities in this regard are not limitless. This by no means implies lack of parental effort or concern. It does imply understanding and acceptance of the inevitable and the importance of providing a child early with a foundation of experience, learning, and security upon which he may evaluate such extraparental influences.

One is tempted to make a broad generalization. Under dissection its shortcomings are readily discernible. But as a point-of-departure principle for those approaching parenthood it may prove tranquilizing. The generalization is this: If parents love a child and let him know that he is loved, if they provide him with opportunities to grow as an individual and as a member of society and stay out of the way of his natural development, if they keep the door of communication open at all times for all topics, then they may make some mistakes in child rearing without seriously damaging the child, and the child will be prepared to meet and evaluate the extraparental influences with which he comes into contact.

CHILDREN'S NEEDS

With the above in mind let us turn our attention to some of the needs of children. Whether these are biologically or culturally determined will not be our problem. They are discussed because in the last analysis successful child rearing is the process of successfully meeting children's needs with reference to the needs of others and within the cultural framework of a given society.

In many respects the needs of children and the needs of adults are similar, at least in so far as a verbal description of them is concerned. Hence in reading the following discussion of children's needs the reader may ask himself, "Which are also needs of adults? How can such needs be met in marriage? What contribution can one spouse make toward meeting the needs of the other?"

Some needs are universal. Others are individual. If a child's needs are not met in helpful, constructive ways, he may resort to damaging, destructive ways of meeting them.

Security. If an infant is held and then suddenly deprived of support, he becomes terrified. This is one of man's few "instinctive" reactions. It suggests that the need for security is present in human beings from the very beginning of life. "Insecurity" is used as a catchall explanation of numerous personality traits and types of behavior, especially when not all the factors in a given situation can readily be diagnosed. The concept has considerable usefulness and validity, nonetheless. Throughout his life the individual does those things which, according to his particular frame of reference, will produce security or avoid insecurity.

A child is not born with a feeling of security; he acquires such a feeling through experience. He learns it first from his parents through their manner of treatment of him. A young child's world is almost completely filled with the processes of functioning physiologically, growing, and learning. Because his experiences are limited and the cumulative total is small, each separate experience constitutes a relatively larger part of the whole, so to speak, than is true with an adult. For example, eating is an insignificant part of an adult's total life activity, whereas it is a very significant part of a young child's. Similar experiences are not in the same proportion in child life as in adult life. Furthermore, both needs and behavior are more elemental in a child than in an adult. As a result, some things which adults take for granted are more fascinating, more poignant, and more meaningful to a young child and are, therefore, more likely to be a source of learning for the child than for the adult. In the light of this it may readily be seen that such things as feeding, fondling, cuddling, and holding a child, which an adult often mistakenly assumes are more or less incidental, may lay the groundwork for the child's feeling of security. Such experiences leave an indelible, though usually not recalled, impression on the child. Such a simple procedure as a mother's holding her baby snugly in her arms, or a father's holding the baby in his even stronger arms, is one of the roots of a child's feeling of security. It is no accident that hymns and other religious utterances sometimes refer to the "arms of God" in an attempt to present a figurative description of the type of security which an individual may derive from religious faith.

A child may also develop a feeling of security through being trusted, being accepted, being recognized for achievement, sharing in family activities and secrets, and in similar ways. Some of these will be discussed in the paragraphs which follow.

In order to have a feeling of security a child must be helped to develop it. It must emerge from activities which the parents initiate but through which the child responds to the parents and through his response grows. It cannot be provided "secondhand." It cannot come through activities that the parents initiate but which the child resists or which deprive him of the opportunity to grow. For example, parental overprotection, which is presumably designed to make the child secure, at least in the physical sense of the term, actually ultimately gives him a feeling of insecurity. The reason for this is that, when the parents are overprotective, the child is deprived of an opportunity to learn and the parents rather than the child meet a present-life situation. Hence the child is not equipped to get along without the parents. Ultimately this eventuates in insecurity.

New experience. In order to grow, and some would say in order to be happy, an individual needs new experience. In a way new experience and security may be at odds with each other. The individual grows and matures as he learns to feel secure in new experiences and new situations. It goes without saying that for some persons new experience adds zest to living. Others are more content with a more nearly changeless *status quo.* One problem parents face in this age of passive recreation and the common question, "Where do we go?" rather than, "What do we do?" especially in large cities, is that of how to provide a child with growth-producing new experience within limits of reasonable safety and control.

READING 18 **RESULTS OF INFRINGEMENT UPON MUTUAL RESPECT**

The ideal balance of family attitude is one of mutual respect. Such a balance exists in a family "when each member is respected in his right to achieve the masteries and pursue the satisfactions of his developmental level until the pursuit infringes on the right of another family member to do the same." The following are common consequences of parents' departure from mutual respect and of infringement upon a child's rights.

OVERSUBMISSION: Parent capitulates to the child's immature whims and demands without sufficient regard for his own rights and needs.

Child's Usual Response: Excessive demands, temper outbursts when demands aren't met, impulsiveness, little consideration for others.

From *Feelings and Their Medical Significance,* W. Hugh Missildine (ed.), vol. 2, no. 11, November–December, 1960, pp. 3–4. Reprinted with permission of Ross Laboratories, Columbus, Ohio.

OVERCOERCION: Parent directs and redirects child's activities without sufficient regard for the child's right to initiate and pursue his own interests and activities.

Child's Usual Response: Undue reliance on outside direction, dawdling, forgetting, procrastination, day-dreaming, active or passive resistance.

PERFECTIONISM: Parent withholds acceptance until the child's behavior is more mature than can be comfortably achieved at his current developmental level.

Child's Usual Response: Striving, overserious preoccupation with physical, intellectual or social accomplishment, self-devaluation.

NEGLECT: Parent has little time for, consideration of, or awareness of a child's right to interested assistance at each level of his development.

Child's Usual Response: Incapacity to form close, meaningful relationships with others, or to get satisfaction from them. Often impulsive, because the child has no close relationship to utilize for learning controls.

HYPOCHONDRIASIS: Parent morbidly centers attention on functions or organs that are objectively healthy, or anxiously exaggerates minor ailments and sensations.

Child's Usual Response: Excessive complaining and anxiety about sensations, minor ailments and organ functions.

OVERINDULGENCE: Parent constantly showers the child with goods and services without regard for the child's needs.

Child's Usual Response: Boredom, blasé behavior, lack of initiative or capacity for persistent effort.

DISTRUST: Parent anticipates failure or inadequacy in the child's body, character or performance.

Child's Usual Response: Self-belittling, tendency to gravitate toward the characteristic which is the object of distrust.

REJECTION: Parent grants the child no niche of acceptance in the family group.

Child's Usual Response: Bitter, hostile, anxious feelings of isolation, self-devaluation.

PUNITIVENESS: Parent excessively vents his personal aggressions on the child, the parent often thinking that this represents discipline. Or, the parent may be from a family culture which insists that hurting children is part of the correct method of child rearing.

Child's Usual Response: Behavior which invites punishment, longings for retaliation, self-devaluation.

SEDUCTIVENESS: Parent consciously or unconsciously stimulates the child's sexual feelings.

Child's Usual Response: Premature and excessive preoccupation with sex, hostility, guilt.

Self-preservation. "Self-preservation," we say, "is the first law of life." In human beings it involves more than physical self-preservation. As we saw in an earlier connection, self-preservation includes also preservation of the "self," the "I," which makes every person different from every other. Each person has a private world, a world partly of his own making, which he seeks to preserve and protect but which he himself may alter as his interpretations of experience change. If life as he finds it is too complex for him, he may manufacture an unreal "world" which, from his point of view, is a more satisfactory explanation of his experiences than is the world of reality.

Love. The individual has a need to love and to be loved. In early years the individual's love in both the giving and the receiving is self-centered. As he matures his love more and more reflects concern for the "other than self." A child learns to love through being loved. But this does not happen through his always being the center of attention and the recipient of love. He must also learn concern for others, for without such concern he cannot learn to love. All of us know of cases in which children have become so accustomed to receiving love without learning to give it that they remain self-centered persons all their lives.

Children of both sexes seek and need affection from parents of both sexes. In our culture the major breakdown in this four-way giving and receiving of affection is often to be found in the relationship of father and son, especially after the latter has ceased to be a small child and has become a boy or man. The traditional standard of manliness in this country discourages kissing as an expression of affection between two post-pubertal males. Some fathers are so sensitive to this prohibition that they are reluctant to kiss even very young sons.

But there are ways other than kissing through which father and son may show affection for one another. A paternal arm across a boy's shoulders, a slap on the back, or a son's hand upon his father's arm may express deep and warm affection. Some fathers and sons find a partial solution to the problem of expressing affection in acceptable masculine ways through what might be termed a playful or nonthreatening negative rather than a direct, positive approach, for example, a punch in the chest, wrestling, and "horseplay." Some have worked out a special vocabulary of terms that are ordinarily used in a highly derogatory sense, but when used upon each other, with a special meaning known to father and son, these same words become terms of endearment. There are also, however, some fathers and sons who have retained kissing as an expression of affection even into the sons' adulthood. Their kissing may occur only on special occasions and it is typically not mouth-to-mouth kissing. It is more likely to occur in private than in public. But the important point is that in some cases it does occur.

Belonging. The individual needs to identify himself with others and have a sense of belonging to a group. The first and most natural group to which he belongs is the family. When this sense of belonging is undermined, the child naturally feels insecure. He may turn to persons other than the family to satisfy his needs. Unwanted children often exhibit such behavior. It is important, in disciplining a child, to be certain that the child is given the impression that it is his act and not himself that is rejected by the parent.

As the child matures, he forms affiliations with groups other than the family. This is especially apparent in the teens when the pressure of the peer group becomes almost irresistible. At this stage of development the child is often inclined to give more weight to the judgments of his contemporaries than to those of his parents. This may not be carried to such an extreme that parents' judgments are given no weight at all. But if parents do not understand this phase of their child's development, they may accentuate the very process they deplore. The young adolescent is under tremendous pressure to conform to the ways of the peer group. If parents do not make some concessions in this process, they may "lose" the child completely. Perhaps the wisest plan is to make concessions on less important things and "hold the line" on a few essentials. In so doing, parents may well try to distinguish between those things the child wants to do which may be damaging or dangerous and those which are merely different from the way the parents think they should be done. In one case, crinoline underskirts were "all the rage" in a fourteen-year-old girl's peer group at school. The girl naturally wanted a crinoline underskirt. The mother objected to it because she thought it was silly. Mother and daughter had come to an impasse. Both communication and rapport had broken down. The mother was so concerned that she sought special counseling help. The mother had made an issue of the underskirt all out of proportion to its importance.

An individual can best achieve a sense of belonging when he accepts some responsibility for the group to which he belongs. In present-day urban and suburban living, with its breakdown of primary groups and the consequent dispersal of loyalties, this is not always easy to arrange in the family. It may be achieved, however, by such means as participation in household tasks, sharing family recreation and pleasures, and, within the limits of the individual's ability to understand, sharing in family problems and troubles. In some cases parents deprive a child of an opportunity to share in the total life of his family by shielding him from all the unpleasant aspects of family living.

Communication. Man is a communicating mammal, and the individual's life is inextricably interwoven with the lives of others through communication. One aspect of belonging is communication. As mentioned earlier, the fact that each person lives in a private world makes communication incomplete, but there is no way to solve this problem completely. A problem that parents can solve is that which arises when they themselves arbitrarily thwart a child's communication because of their own lack of interest in what the child wants to communicate or because they feel that the content of the communication is inappropriate, as, for example, when a child is rebuffed for asking a question regarding reproduction. Once the door of communication is closed, the latch and hinges soon become rusty, and in many cases it becomes difficult if not impossible to reopen it.

Keeping the door of communication open, however, is not always accomplished without problems. One father complained that his children had learned that he disciplined them for their misdeeds less severely or not at all when they told the truth. He felt that at times they "worked" him. But in weighing the pros and cons, he concluded that keeping the door of communication open, retaining good rapport with his children, and in this way having greater opportunity to help them think through their behavior and develop self-discipline, was more important than his disciplining them in every instance, even if they did "work" him on occasion.

Sense of achievement. Typically human beings have a desire for recognition. In children recognition and a sense of achievement are closely related. Mature individuals may more readily separate them. If a child does not get the recognition he needs under desirable auspices, he may seek it under undesirable auspices.

Because of this combination of needs, namely, for achievement and for recognition, the typical individual likes to feel useful. Sometimes

CHILDREN'S NEEDS

When a married couple first consider having children, they are largely concerned with their own needs: to be like other couples, to enrich their daily lives, to perpetuate themselves through their offspring. Once the family is started, however, the needs of the children assume an extremely prominent position. There is always some conflict between the parents' own healthy needs and those of the children, and each family must work out its own balance.

The child needs the warmth and affection of his parents.

helping a child to feel useful increases rather than decreases the work of the parent, for example, when a little girl wants to help her mother bake a cake. But it is worth an investment of time and effort, for in feeling useful the child not only satisfies a need per se but also strengthens his ties with the family group.

Reaching out. As we have seen, man is the only organism that reaches out beyond his immediate experience. He does this in numerous ways, two of which are creative imagination and religious faith. As an individual matures, his reaching out should mature. Yet many persons' religious faith stops developing at a childish level. This is due in part to the fact that one factor in the extension and maturing of faith is the process of probing the unknown with penetrating questions. If parents assume, as some do, that questioning and faith, doubting and believing, are antagonistic rather than complementary, a child's fluid reaching out may be thwarted by crystallized dogmatism and fear. When a child questions what parents assume to be established truth, the parents may well be

The child needs the
freedom to explore
and experience new
sensations . . .

and the freedom to make
a few safe errors.

The child needs clearly defined
limits which he can understand.

*The child needs a parent's explanation
of questions that puzzle him . . .*

assured that, if it is truth, the child, like themselves, will come to accept it; if it is not truth after all, he has the right to discover this.

Children's creative imagination is sometimes not so carefully channeled as that of adults; and the children themselves cannot always distinguish between the imagined and the real. This leads some parents to confuse the child's imaginings with dishonesty. They punish him for the latter and eventually cripple the former.

In American culture conformity is considered a virtue. In some cases in which recognition and prestige are given to outstanding individuals, it is quantitative difference rather than qualitative difference that is recognized. The outstanding individual is "like everyone else, only more so." For example, the high school valedictorian, the beauty queen, the best of this or that is often basically a conformist; the individual may exhibit no true originality, no true creativity.

Parents are not free of pressure toward conformity where their children are concerned. Many psychological tests, personality rating scales, tables of one sort or another, norms for children of a given age, the grade level system in schools, and so on, though useful, subtly suggest conformity. Hence parents sometimes sacrifice a child's individuality by molding him so that he will conform instead of releasing him to be creative. This does not imply letting him become so out of step with his peers that he fits nowhere into the social scheme or letting his personality become maladjusted. It does imply helping him develop the creativity inherent in every normal personality.

and the privacy to contemplate those answers.

When we compare the number of young children who have insatiable curiosity, who make works of art which, though crude, are creative, who play-act, who make up stories about imaginary characters, who sing songs they have composed, beat out a rhythm or dance spontaneously, with the number of adults who are creative in similar ways, we realize that somewhere between childhood and adulthood conformity has overshadowed creativity and originality.

Growth and development. We said earlier in this chapter that personality develops by an "unfolding" as well as by an educative process. This implies that the individual goes through stages of development. Within broad limits these stages are similar for all persons. Not all individuals, however, pass through the same stage or reach the same point at the same age. Each individual has his own "built-in" pattern and rate of growth.

Generalizing somewhat, each stage of growth is typified by certain forms of behavior. For example, most children creep before they walk. Many suck their thumbs in their early years. Sometimes behavior at a given stage seems to the parents to represent retrogression, or backsliding, as compared to a previous stage. For example, some children develop reasonably satisfactory table manners in their early years but revert to infantile eating habits temporarily at about the onset of adolescence, much to the despair of their parents. It would help parents to realize that, unless there are special factors at work to produce something in the nature of a fixation in the child, stage-typical behavior is ordinarily not habit-forming. This means that stage-typical behavior is something into which the child grows but out of which he also grows. Take for example, thumb-sucking. Parents torture their children with foul-tasting drugs, mechanical devices, threats and punishment, and torture themselves with concern and anxiety to stop this practice. Unless, as is true in some cases, the child is pressing his thumb against his palate in such a way that he pushes his front teeth forward, the practice is harmless. Almost all children grow out of it. Being stage-typical behavior, it is usually not habit-forming.

One reason that parents often persist, even in the face of continual failure, in trying to alter stage-typical behavior through instruction, nagging, threat, punishment, and a free exuding of their own tension and anxiety is that they fear that whatever a child is permitted to do in his early years he is likely to continue to do throughout his life. If the child runs out of the house unclothed, they fear that he will become a nudist. If a little boy wears his sister's clothes while play-acting, the parents wonder whether he will become a transvestite. If a child leaves toys lying around, the parents fear that he will be careless about leaving his clothes strewn around after he is married. They fail to realize that it is not so much leaving things around at an early age and because of a

*The child needs
peer relationships . . .*

his parents' acceptance of his own world . . .

*and especially the security and happiness
of family companionship.*

brief interest span that makes an adult careless but rather the fact that
someone, either through constant haranguing or through picking up
after the child, teaches him that he has no responsibility in this regard,
that somebody will assume his responsibility for him.

The direction of a child's development is determined in part by
factors within himself. Part of his development, however, is determined
by the pattern and framework of life into which he grows. This framework is provided in part by the family. In other words, in a given respect the child may not at first conform to the family pattern. Since,
however, the direction of his growth is not predetermined, he may grow
in one direction as readily as in another. The family pattern, then,
is the framework within which he will grow. For example, a little child
has no appreciation of courtesy. He is born uncivilized, and the process
of civilization takes time. If the family provides him with a pattern of
habitual courtesy, he is likely to become courteous. If on the other hand
the family provides him with a pattern of habitual lack of attention to
courtesy, he is likely to become discourteous. In order to accomplish
the former, the family must continue to provide the pattern of courtesy
even while the child is too immature to be expected to exhibit the courtesy of an adult.

If parents do not exhibit consistency in establishing the pattern into
which they expect the child to grow, it is not surprising when the child

disappoints them. For example, many parents see no need to be courteous with a little child. Yet they are irritated when their child is discourteous with them. Some parents see nothing wrong with telling a child untruths. Some thoughtlessly embarrass a child in front of his companions. Some are impatient when a child wants to talk with them and they tell him they do not have time to talk. Then when the child is reluctant to leave his play when his parents want to talk with him, they consider him disobedient. Sometimes parents punish a child when he honestly reports some misdemeanor. Then they wonder why the child becomes dishonest. Some betray a child's confidence, then wonder why he ceases to confide in them. Some assure the child that he is trusted, then spy on him.

Inconsistency is also apparent in those instances in which parents disagree on the handling of a child. The child soon learns to "play" one parent against the other or to seek the approval of the parent who is more lax in giving permissions or in meting out punishment.

A child's learning is the result of three processes, namely, experience, maturation, and instruction. Parents sometimes fail to distinguish between the last two processes, with the result that they expect a child to learn through instruction before through maturation he has reached a point where this is possible for him. Instruction is to no avail until learning readiness has been achieved through growth. For example, a child aged one could not be taught to read no matter how good his instruction. If instruction is started too early, that is, before readiness has been established, it will be ineffective. If instruction is continued after readiness is established, the child may learn quickly; but he would have learned by about the same time if instruction had been delayed until readiness was established. In fact, the child will learn some things without instruction merely through his own maturation.

This failure to distinguish between maturation and instruction, especially verbal instruction, may be made clear, perhaps, by means of a parable. A certain man planted a seed. He was very eager to have the seed grow into a plant that would bear fruit. Every day he addressed first the seedling, then the plant, saying, "I want you to bear fruit. Please do so." At last, one day, the plant did bear fruit. The man said, "See, I told you I could teach the plant to bear fruit." All the people said, "What a wonderful teacher he is. He has taught the plant to bear fruit." This is not meant to imply that there is no place for verbal instruction in child rearing. But there is often too much dependence upon verbal instruction and too little insight into the process of maturation. Sometimes, as in the parable above, the former is given credit more appropriately due to the latter. Also, when there is too great dependence upon words, a child may immunize himself to verbal exhortation so that words intended to eventuate in learning result only in an increased resistance to verbal injunction. His parents then may as well "save their breath."

Being an individual. No two children are identical, not even "identical" twins. Each child is unique. Each has his own rate and pattern of growth, allowing for broad similarities at different stages of development, as mentioned above. Each has his own temperament. Each has his own abilities and aptitudes. Yet these facts do not keep some parents from trying to make children alike, or from seeking to make a child into a replica of a parent, or from attempting to squeeze a square peg into a round hole. Wise parents set their expectations for a child according to the child's ability to achieve, not according to the achievements of other children or according to some arbitrary and unreasonable parent-imposed standard. For example, among the college educated there is often such a premium put upon academic achievement in children that a child who is a "muscle learner" rather than a verbal learner is looked down upon and may be forced to attempt success in a field for which he has no aptitude. A boy who might do very well as a mechanic is forced through parental pressure to work for a university degree, with the result that the child becomes an unhappy, maladjusted failure who is subtly rejected by his parents.

A similar problem is found in the situation in which parents expect a child to enter a given occupation because of family tradition, parental leanings, or to serve as a vicarious success for a parent who was prevented by ability or circumstance from entering the occupation of his choice. College and university counselors meet many of this type of student—a kind of living human sacrifice to thwarted parental ambitions.

Consider both the parental attempt to squeeze the square peg into the round hole and the effect of the parents' effort to keep their son immature in the following statement by a university senior, aged twenty-three, who was on scholastic probation. Said he, "I want to go into teaching. But my father is a physician, and his father was a physician. My parents insist that I go into medicine. I'm not interested in medicine, and I'm having trouble in my science and math courses. Mamma says that if I don't make my grades, she won't let me use the car."

If a child is to be an individual, he cannot be expected to agree with his parents on everything. He has a right to make his own judgments, within, of course, limits of ability and safety, as mentioned earlier.

If each child is to be considered an individual, no child should be penalized for something he cannot possibly control. Sometimes, for example, a child is discriminated against because he is the eldest child in the family, because he is less attractive in appearance than other children in the family, because, as indicated above, he lacks some ability that is prized by his parents, or because of his sexual classification. For example, the parents discipline their son severely, but they are more lenient with their daughter. One of the most devastating experiences for a child is to be a second-class citizen in his own family because his parents consider another child their favorite.

A child is a child. He is not a small adult. Therefore, he should not be expected to act like an adult; or perhaps we should say the child should not be expected to act as an adult is expected to act. For example, a child may be intelligent; but this fact does not necessarily make him reasonable under given circumstances. He cannot be expected suddenly to change his behavior merely because someone older than he tells him to change it. He does not have, indeed cannot have, the foresight of an adult. A child is naturally somewhat selfish. He must gradually learn to be generous. He cannot be expected suddenly to exhibit adult altruism.

Independence. A child, like a ship, is to be launched. Some parents are like the proverbial man who carefully built a boat in his garage only to find that the boat was too large to pass through the garage door and hence never reached the water. Launching a child into adult independence is a prolonged, carefully planned process. It necessitates as much development on the part of the parent as on the part of the child. Many a parent who is a "good" parent for an infant remains the parent of an infant psychologically even when the offspring has grown to adulthood. The result is actual or attempted "apron strings." When the time comes that a child can get along without his parents because he is an independent young adult, the parents may well take pride in their achievement. Many parents, however, make the day of the child's independence a day of sorrow.

Facing reality. In so far as it may be safe to do so, a child may be allowed to learn from his own experiences rather than from instruction. He needs to learn to face and, if possible, to accept the consequences of his acts. For example, he will learn more about the use of money by being allowed to spend his money unwisely and thus being deprived of something he wants than he will learn through verbal instruction.

Children are sometimes allowed to evade reality in such a way that the child is started on the road to emotional maladjustment. For instance, a child is permitted to rationalize, alibi, and shirk responsibility to such an extent that he grows to assume that this is the way life is to be lived.

Discipline. Children need discipline. It is one method of learning. It can give a child a sense of security when it defines his limitations, that is, the framework within which he can operate. Many a parent has had the experience of having a child "push" him to the point of exasperation. Then the parent "blows up," the air is cleared, the child is given a definition of his area of operation, of his limitations, and peace and harmony are restored. Discipline can also give a child a sense of security when it helps him to get past previous misbehavior and to get rid of a sense of guilt growing out of it.

To fulfill its function, discipline need not always be negative; it may also be positive. In fact, whenever possible it should be positive. Teaching a child to save or to cooperate in household tasks is as much part of discipline as is punishment. One of the common errors in child rearing, as in other areas of life where one person seeks to modify the behavior of another, is the assumption that the elimination of small vices results in the production of large virtues. A series of "don'ts" may be necessary on occasion; but it does not necessarily follow that in place of the behavior modified by the "don'ts" will be put behavior that is positive and constructive.

In order to accomplish its purpose and to be appreciated by a child, discipline must be fair and not too harsh. It should also be appropriate to the misdeed. Sometimes parents make a child dislike what is fundamentally a good thing because they use that good thing as punishment. For example, one of the greatest satisfactions in life is that which comes from work. Work, providing that it is honest and useful, deserves to be respected. If, however, parents impose work on a child as a means of punishment, it is not surprising that the child may grow to dislike it. This is especially true of certain household chores.

Nagging is ineffective as discipline for several reasons. It permits the child to evade the consequences of his behavior with only a tongue-lashing as punishment, and to the tongue-lashing he may readily immunize himself. Nagging exposes the vulnerable spots of the nagger. It provides the child with an effective weapon for penalizing the parent.

To spank or not to spank—that is the perennial question in any discussion of discipline. On the one hand are those who deplore any suggestion of corporal punishment or penalizing physical contact between parent and child. On the other hand are those who consider spanking a form of communication. Arguments are presented on either side.

Evidence [Sears, Maccoby, and Levin, 1957] indicates that spanking often does not accomplish what it is intended to accomplish. Its good effects, if any, are likely to be temporary; its harmful effects may be permanent. It is not a substitute for true discipline because it involves learning through fear rather than through trust. It is negative rather than positive. Not all children respond to spanking in the same way. Some are humiliated and embittered by it and become resentful. The parent-child relationship may break down.

Earlier in this chapter the importance of consistency in child rearing was stressed. What about the matter of consistency when parents teach a child that striking his playmates is not the most desirable way of getting along with them and that under no circumstances is he ever to strike his parents; yet the parents strike the child?

Spanking is more likely to be a means of relieving parental feelings than an effective means of training a child. In some families it is a last resort, implying that it occurs when a parent is "at the end of his rope" because of tension, fatigue, or frustration. Spanking is often a reflection of ignorance; the parent knows no better form of discipline. It may be an expression of rejection of child by parent or an outgrowth of aggression. In some families spanking is the principal means of discipline used, and in such cases it is especially harmful.

What was said above is not meant to imply that a child's personality will be permanently warped if his parents spank him occasionally. Parents, being human, have their "weak moments." In the complexities of family living they are not always free of fatigue and tension and do not always govern their every act by carefully considered theory. A happily married couple may have a bitter quarrel, knowing that in so doing they fall short of their own ideal of marriage. They regret what has happened and try to avoid it in the future. In like manner a parent may have an occasional similar experience with a child. It is important that the parent realize that he has resorted to a procedure that falls short of the ideal and ought to be avoided and that he has solved nothing. To assume that spanking is the best form of discipline is like assuming that quarreling is the best way to achieve adjustment in marriage.

Acceptance. Overlapping several of the items already indicated but deserving separate mention is the need for acceptance. Each individual wants to be accepted for what he is, if possible as he conceives himself to be. Such acceptance is found in probably its purest form in the family where a child is loved by his parents without damaging comparison with other children and without regard to whether or not he deserves to be loved. Lack of such unqualified acceptance, as for example, in the case of a mentally retarded child, creates one of the most critical problems of childhood.

There is another aspect to acceptance, namely, acceptance of oneself. This implies learning to live with one's limitations. It also implies acceptance of one's sexual classification and its attendant role. An individual cannot, of course, accept his own sexual classification unless he can simultaneously accept the classification of the opposite sex. In learning to accept his sexual classification the individual develops a concept of his sexual role. Somehow, too, he must learn to fit his sexual impulses into the societal pattern. This suggests the need for sex education.

Sex education

NATURE AND OBJECTIVES
Sex education is the process of teaching an individual to understand and accept himself as a whole person and as such to relate himself to other people in a healthy, constructive, and meaningful manner. In a bisexual

world this includes the individual's understanding and accepting his own sexual classification and behavior plus his understanding and accepting the sexual classification and behavior of members of the opposite sex. It includes his learning to fit his natural sexual impulses into a satisfactory societal pattern. One of the central objectives of child rearing is the achievement of a balance between socialization and conformity to the societal structure, on the one hand, and individual freedom, growth, and realization of innate potential, on the other. Nowhere is the need for such a balance more apparent than in connection with sex education.

In order to achieve the above, the individual needs factual information, to be sure. But he needs much more than factual information, especially that minimum regarding genital anatomy and physiology commonly referred to as "the facts of life." The individual needs to understand sex not as a limited facet of life that is somehow regrettably superimposed upon more desirable aspects of living, as sex is often represented. He needs, rather, to understand sex as a way of life. In order to do this, in addition to acquiring sound factual information he must develop healthy attitudes, carefully weigh values, thoughtfully impute meaning to sexual behavior, and establish creative interpersonal relationships. Whatever values he accepts relative to sex should be consistent with the value system upon which his individual life is being built and with the value structure of the society within which he lives.

Time to begin.   "When should I start to give my child sex education?" is a question asked by many parents. Actually, there is no time to "start," just as there is not a specific time to start to teach a child to be honest or to be a good citizen. We assume that the teaching of honesty and citizenship will be an integral part of the child's learning from birth onward. So it should be with sex education.

If we may "stretch" a point for emphasis, we may say that sex education begins before birth—not in the sense of verbal communication with the fetus, but in the sense of sex education's having its roots in the attitudes of the parents toward the process by which the child was conceived.

Communication versus telling.   Some parents assume that they can avoid giving a child sex education by telling him nothing about sex. They assume that lack of verbal instruction means lack of communication. The opposite is true. When the parents give the child no verbal instruction, they communicate to him that sex is a topic so mysterious, so unpalatable, and so difficult to discuss—for them—that he had better seek information elsewhere.

Parental behavior in the home is also a means of communication whether or not anything is said about sex. The child soon learns through observation that there are differences between the sexes both as to anatomy and as to role. He cannot help but observe whether or not his parents are affectionate with each other, whether they accept their roles with enthusiasm or resistance, and a host of similar items. Such observations constitute part of sex education.

Parents who do not give a child verbal instruction might well wonder about such questions as these: Will ignorance protect a child from misinformation, shock, perhaps even tragedy? What is a child to think if his parents give him the impression that sex is "bad" and then his mother becomes pregnant and the child knows that the parents have engaged in a process they feel is unfit to be discussed?

BODILY EXPOSURE

A young child takes his anatomy for granted, at least until he is taught otherwise. Sooner or later he discovers his genital organs. This discovery is part of his exploration of his world. To a little child everything he encounters is new and interesting. Things and experiences no longer interesting to adults are fascinating to the young child because the entire world is new to him, and he explores it with all the equipment Nature provides him for sensing and perceiving. In so far as it is possible to do so, he uses all his senses in his observations. He touches the soft fur of a rabbit with exuberant delight. He listens to the ticking of a watch with rapt attention. His horror-stricken, germ-conscious parents find him putting anything movable into his mouth. His curiosity is insatiable. He performs simple experiments, such as holding the family cat by the tail, to see what will happen.

In the course of such a process of observation and experimentation the child discovers his genital organs. He then proceeds to learn more about them, how they are constructed, what sensations he has when he handles them. He soon learns that there are two types of people in the world, male and female, and his interest and curiosity extend to the differences between them. So he proceeds to satisfy his curiosity. Since all normal children have this curiosity as to how the sexes are constructed, it is not unusual for two children of opposite sex to make their observations simultaneously. To them such a thing is as natural as tasting a new food.

Let us imagine two children, a boy and a girl, four years of age. They are playmates. They are curious about the differences in their genital organs. In a corner of the garage they set about satisfying their curiosity. By happenstance the mother of the little girl enters the garage to get something out of storage at just the moment that the two children are observing each other's genital organs. The mother becomes very wrought up. She sends the little boy home with an excited stream of invective following him like a swarm of angry bees. She hurries her daughter into the house. The little girl cannot avoid getting the impression that something terrible has occurred, that her mother is deeply disturbed, that she herself has committed an act which, at least in her mother's judgment, classifies her as "bad." There are girls who reach marriageable age still bearing the scars of such an experience.

How much better it would have been if the little girl's mother had treated the situation as natural and inoffensive. Perhaps the children need some help in understanding what is acceptable behavior in our society, what is "family" and what is not. But they are not to be condemned, frightened, and punished for adult fears and inhibitions projected onto the natural behavior of childhood. They are not to be traumatized through shock into acquiring a sense of guilt that is felt first only by the parent.

In connection with the question of bodily exposure on the part of family members within the home, opinions differ widely. There are parents who believe that every effort should be made to protect all family members, especially parents, from even the casual gaze of others. Such parents dress behind closed doors, bathe behind carefully inculcated "no trespassing" warnings, and become upset at accidental exposure. On the other hand there are parents who treat bodily exposure within the home as natural and to be taken for granted by family members. They draw a distinction, however, between observation of genital anatomy and observation of sexual behavior. When all the pros and cons are considered, and assuming that the parents do not make a cult of nudity, it seems clear that the more nearly natural bodily exposure within the home is taken to be, the healthier the child's attitude toward such exposure will be. When parents are overly meticulous in preventing children from observing the parents' bodies, the children's curiosity is increased, or at least certainly not decreased, and is more likely to lead to attempts to satisfy it outside the home under auspices unknown to parents and in situations permitting no questions to be asked.

Bodily exposure in the home can be just as "forced" as artificial barriers can be. There are times when any individual, child or adult, seeks privacy. Such privacy should be respected by all family members. But an occasional demand for privacy is not the same as an over-all fear of bodily exposure.

One problem giving concern to many women, even some of those who are relatively uninhibited in the matter of bodily exposure within the home, is that of whether or not a child, especially a boy, should be permitted to see the mother unclothed when she is wearing external menstrual protection. Menstruation is as natural as any other bodily function. In these presumably modern times there is no need to read into it the connotations of mystery, shame, and uncleanliness that were associated with the process in the past. Sooner or later the child will learn about menstruation. If the mother is sufficiently objective about it to permit him to do so, he can understand and accept it without emotion or undue curiosity even at an early age.

CHILDREN'S QUESTIONS

There is widespread agreement to the effect that a child's questions concerning sex and reproduction should be answered, not evaded. In no way, either by act or implication, should the child be made to feel that an honest question about something which is natural to him is inappropriate or "bad." One reason for which some parents avoid a child's questions, with a show of emotion on the part of the parent, is that the parent, not the child, is embarrassed to discuss the subject. To cover up this embarrassment the parent repulses the child with an assertion that that sort of question should not be asked.

Before a parent can answer a child's question intelligently, he must ascertain what the child has asked. The real question may not be readily apparent in the verbal statement of it. This is illustrated in the well-worn story about the child who rushed up to his mother and said, "Mother, where did I come from?" The mother thought, "This is it," and launched into a long, previously prepared dissertation on reproduction. The child tried to interrupt, but the mother would not permit him to do so. When the mother finally finished, feeling that at last she had done successfully what she had long anticipated with apprehension, the child exclaimed, "But Mother, that's not what I meant. Billy down the street says he came from Chicago, and I wanted to know where I came from."

In answering a child's question, the parent must consider the child's readiness to understand. A preschool child is not prepared to understand an explanation that would be more appropriate for a medical student. The child needs to be told only as much as he can absorb at the time. One is reminded of the little girl who said, "I don't like to ask Mother questions like that because she always tells me too much." If the parents keep the door of communication open, the child will return to the same question over and over again as he grows older. Each time he can be given further detail. No matter how many times the child repeats the same question, the question should be answered.

There are some persons who feel that a child's questions concerning sex or reproduction should be answered immediately upon being asked. In general this is a satisfactory working principle. But in the complexity of family living it is not always possible to meet ideal standards, and parents should not feel guilty or inadequate, as some do, when they fall short, especially if the over-all parent-child relationship is healthy. For instance, if we may exaggerate to make a point, a father need not feel guilty if he does not stop carving the Thanksgiving turkey and let the guests wait to be served just so he can answer the question of a child who has chosen this inappropriate moment to ask why babies have fathers. He can tell the child that he will discuss the question later. Then he keeps his word and does discuss it later.

VOCABULARY

There are different schools of thought regarding what vocabulary is best in teaching children about sex and reproduction. At one extreme are the advocates of technical, scientific, medical terminology. Every anatomical part, every physiological process is to be called by the correct technical term. At the other extreme are the adherents of the "do-do, da-da" point of view. Everything is to be described in the most evasive type of "baby talk" so that camouflage of the natural is as nearly complete as human ingenuity in manufacturing new vocabulary will permit. Sometimes this process is carried to such an extreme that communication is limited to parent and child because no one else knows the meaning of the terms the two of them have concocted.

Neither of these extremes is entirely consistent with ordinary day-to-day living in our culture. Adults do not refer to every anatomical part and every physiological process by its correct technical term at all times regardless of circumstance. Neither do they use only substitute vocabulary. Common parlance represents a compromise, a combination of technical and substitute vocabulary. Some of the latter is conventionalized.

The fundamental problem is one of communication, of imparting information, of imputing correct meaning, of facing rather than evading facts. There is also the correlative problem of avoiding giving the child a false impression. One of the commonest instances of such a false impression is using an unpalatable term to mean menstruation.

ACCEPTING ONE'S SEXUAL CLASSIFICATION

If, as suggested earlier, one of the objectives of sex education is to help a child to accept his sexual classification, parents must find a way to teach girls to accept with understanding such natural female functions as menstruation and childbirth. Yet many a girl is not helped toward such acceptance either because her parents engender a negative attitude in her or because they do nothing to engender a positive one. Since children learn by observation and "contagion" as well as by verbal instruction, many a girl "picks up" a negative attitude during her observation of her parents' treatment of each other or through chance remarks made by one parent or the other and not intended as instruction for the girl. For example, the child is affectionate. She seeks warmth, security, and attention from other people. She seldom or never sees her father kiss her mother. Without reasoning it out, she begins to feel that, if that is what a woman can expect from a man, she regrets that she is female. She hears her mother make a remark about menstruation or hears her complain because she is pregnant again. Mother and daughter are doing dishes while the husband-father reads the paper. Mother complains about the lack of cooperation on the part of the man, but, instead of particularizing her complaint so that it is directed to a certain act on the part of a given man, she generalizes and says something to the effect that women have to do chores while men can relax. Translated, this is equivalent to telling the daughter that it is better to be a man than to be a woman.

The acceptance of one's sexual classification is not a problem limited to girls. Boys more readily, perhaps, at least in our culture, accept their maleness than girls accept their femaleness. But some parents thoughtlessly allow such acceptance to become an assumption of prerogative. In their effort to make a son a "real man" they permit the development of the idea that to be manly means to exploit girls, to sow "wild oats," to have premarital sexual exploits, sometimes with complete disregard of the fact that someone else's daughter may have to reap the "wild oats" their son sows. Instead of emphasizing respect for girls and de-emphasizing the "wild oats" approach to manliness, they lightly approve the latter on the ground that "boys will be boys" and thereby unwittingly detract from the former. In the last analysis what constitutes manliness differs with time, place, circumstance, and cultural demands. There is a wide gulf of difference between being an aboriginal, primordial male who gives free rein to natural impulses and a modern, civilized man who lives by a standard of values.

MASTURBATION

The day is past when masturbation was referred to as "self-abuse," just as the day is gone when nocturnal emissions were termed "pollutions." Masturbation is such a widespread phenomenon of childhood that attitudes toward it should be evaluated with this fact in mind. Studies show that in young males masturbation is reported as being just short of universal, and an appreciable majority of young females are reported as at some time engaging in the practice.

In the natural inclination to explore both their environment and their bodies most children sooner or later discover that their genital organs are endowed with special sensitivity and that in the stimulation of these organs pleasurable sensation can be produced. If the child does not become acquainted with this fact through his own curiosity, he is likely to learn it from other children.

Contrary to common assumption, there is no evidence to prove that masturbation per se is physically harmful. Masturbation, as such, which involves only sexual self-stimulation, should be carefully distinguished from the dangerous practice of a girl's inserting some object into her vagina either in an attempt at masturbation or merely through curiosity.

Anyone would agree that such insertion of sharp, unclean objects is dangerous; and physicians are not infrequently called upon to remove such objects, sometimes after injury has caused infection or hemorrhage.

Masturbation may become psychologically damaging to the degree to which the child is led to develop a sense of guilt associated with it. Such a sense of guilt is instilled by parents or others who appraise the practice in terms of sin or immorality. Some churches appraise it in such terms.

Parents have been known to try to prevent a child, especially a son, from masturbating by threatening the child with consequences that the parents know will not follow but which place upon the child an unbearable burden of fear and guilt. For example, one mother told her young son that, if he persisted in masturbating, his genital organs would fall off. Another told her son that masturbation would make him insane. Such untruths can do a child incalculable harm.

"What should I do if I discover that my child masturbates?" is a common question asked by parents. There are a number of things such parents might do.

1. Relax. The child will do himself no harm.

2. Do not make an issue of it. Do not "read into" it something which is not there. Do not connect in the child's mind the act of masturbation with parental emotional upset, threat, and condemnation.

3. Recognize that childhood masturbation tends to fall into the category of stage-typical behavior, which does not ordinarily eventuate in permanent habits over which the individual has no control. Most persons either stop masturbation when they grow older, especially after marriage, or modify its frequency and practice it through choice subject to voluntary control. It does not dominate their lives, as parents often fear it will.

4. Sometimes masturbation is a symptom of a problem which does call for parental attention. For example, if a child masturbates excessively because he is bored and lonely and has learned that masturbation is something he can do with pleasure and by himself, the provision of companionship and interesting activities may meet a need for him and make the masturbation less "necessary" to him.

5. Do not drive the practice "under cover" by threat of punishment. If a child is inclined to masturbate, he will find a time and place to do it. If his parents threaten him for doing it in one place about which they know, he will find another that is less likely to be discovered by them.

6. Do not expect a child to discontinue a pleasurable practice by an act of will, a level of determination and self-discipline that would do credit to an adult.

7. Keep the door of communication open. There is no reason why a child should not be able to discuss his masturbation with his parents just as he would discuss any other type of behavior. Such discussion

should be permitted, not forced. That is, the child rather than the parents should take the initiative, though the parents might suggest the possibility of discussion. Children in some families do take such initiative because the parents have set up no barrier between themselves and their child. A child who voluntarily discusses masturbation with his parents pays them a profound compliment. They should not "let him down." A child could hardly be expected to take the initiative in discussing with his parents something which he knows in advance they condemn and will condemn him for doing.

SEX EDUCATION IS UNAVOIDABLE

As suggested earlier in this chapter, sex education is unavoidable. Parents cannot avoid giving a child sex education by avoiding verbal instruction relative to sex. A child learns through other channels besides that of verbal instruction. There is a difference between instruction and communication. Parents' choice is not between sex education and no sex education. Their choice is between good sex education and poor sex education. No matter what they do or do not do, say or do not say, the child receives his first, and sometimes his most indelible, sex education from them.

Family development

The family is a dynamic institution. It changes in slow, evolutionlike fashion as part of over-all cultural change. Each family, too, is dynamic. It changes as the number, ages, needs, and behavior of family members change and as the family as a group adapts itself to fluid circumstances. No matter where the family is found, in whatever area, class, or culture, at whatever period in history, certain broad similarities are to be observed in the stages through which it passes, just as there are broad similarities in the stages through which individuals pass in their development from infancy to old age. This universal similarity among families has given rise to the concept of the *family life cycle.* The stages of this cycle overlap but are nonetheless distinguishable, much as the stages in the development of an individual overlap but are distinguishable; for example, infancy, childhood, adolescence, adulthood, middle age, and so on, may be thought of as stages of development, even though each merges imperceptibly into the next and there is no clear-cut line of demarcation between them. In order for a family to move successfully through the several stages of the family life cycle, it must complete the *developmental tasks* at each stage. A developmental task, in the life of an individual or a family, is a task which arises at a given period of life, the successful completion of which leads to happiness and to success with later tasks, while the failure to complete it leads to unhappiness, social disapproval, and difficulty with later tasks [Havighurst, 1953].

SOME NEGLECTED AREAS IN FAMILY—LIFE STUDY

Most of the forces playing upon the contemporary family have made for the individualizing of the life of its members, and this fact has correspondingly influenced the literature dealing with family life. Important as this individualistic emphasis may be, the essential fact remains that a family is a project in group living, and the stability of the family calls for the promotion of techniques in the cooperative functioning of its members.

There are two places where the family spends most of its time as a group. They are the dining room and the living room. The relative importance of these two varies, but it seems safe to say that for most American families, the dining room takes first place. It is here that the family members meet regularly, repeatedly, and in intimate participation with each other.

From this it follows that the family meal is a recurrent and fundamental aspect of the family's life. And what happens is more than a dietary procedure. It is while seated around the table that the family is at its greatest ease, both physically and psychologically; is held together for definite periods of time; becomes engrossed in common objectives; and has fewer distractions than at most other times. There are, to be sure, many purposes which the family meal is made to serve in the life of the family. Firsthand studies made under the auspices of the William T. Carter Foundation at the University of Pennsylvania identify four common types of family meals.

1. Some are hurried meetings which appear to be regarded by the family personnel as unavoidable periods of family refueling. Food tends to be served as if eating were a mere physiological compulsion, and gulped as if the time required were a wasteful form of biological maladjustment. Conversation is scant, often blunt and direct, and the meal is terminated as soon as possible.

2. Other family meals are devoted largely to recurrent domestic warfare. The children are taken to task for past or present misdeeds, parents quarrel with each other, the food is criticized or its preparation is depreciated. There are families in which few meals are completed without a family quarrel, or without some member of the family

From James H. S. Bossard, Eleanor S. Boll, and Winogene P. Sanger, "Some Neglected Areas of Family-life Study," *The Annals of the American Academy of Political and Social Science*, no. 272, November, 1950, pp. 68–76. Abridged and reprinted with permission of The American Academy of Political and Social Science.

leaving the table in tears, anger, or disgrace. Or there is constant nagging about table manners.

3. Some family meals, particularly at selected class levels, become occasions for interesting conversations. Information on various topics is exchanged; triumphs, disappointments, and various other experiences are shared; family programs or projects are evaluated; public issues are discussed; and intellectual interests tend to be stimulated. All, even the children, are encouraged to take part. Each one who participates is recognized for what he or she contributes to the group discussion.

4. Still other family meals become occasions for family rituals. They are characterized by order and impressive decorum. Prayers may be said by way of prelude, candles may gleam, mother may preside as conventionalities are observed, there are servants perhaps to serve the food, and coffee in the living room may follow. The meal here becomes a "private communion" for the members of the family group.

The specific nature and role of the family meal in any particular home is a matter both of circumstance and of choice. In one respect, it is the product of the kind of people that compose the family—their occupations, and their attitudes toward life and toward one another; but in many ways, the family meal becomes a factor which determines the foregoing in some measure. Families make family meals what they are, but it is equally true that family meals make families what they are.

To emphasize the family meal as a factor in family stability means that conscious thought should be given to its systematic cultivation. This involves, of course, many things. The physical setting of the family meal is important. It can be served now in the dining room, then perhaps on the lawn, or on a card table before an open fire or window. Particular occasions, such as birthdays, family days, and holidays, may be observed with special meals, and at special places. Attention to impressive details, like eating by candlelight, the use of colorful china, color combinations of food, and dining room furnishings, is possible in many—perhaps most—families in this country today. Finally, there is the creation of "atmosphere," with attention to the observance of etiquette. This, assuredly, is available to everyone.

FAMILY MODES OF EXPRESSION

Language is so important a factor in human relationships that it is difficult to understand why its role in family life should have been neglected so generally. Language is many things that are basic in family life. It is a form of behavior, and a particularly revealing one, for each individual member of the family; it is the medium of their interaction; and it is the vehicle through which ideas and attitudes are transmitted. In addition, it is also a form of behavior for the family as a whole, and it is this organic aspect that is being emphasized here.

A study of family conversation in eighty-two families, made by the Carter Foundation, reveals a number of striking facts. First, most families show a specific totality or pattern which is characteristic of that particular family. This pattern is a product of many aspects of the family's life – the occupations of its members, their religious affiliation, the geographic areas in which they have lived, their social status, their age and sex, and the like. As a pattern, it reveals the life, past and present, of the family. For this reason the pattern is persistent and distinctive for any given family.

It is striking to observe, in thus studying objectively a number of family patterns of conversation, how readily they can be typed. For instance, some families talk chiefly about themselves: their experiences, achievements, misfortunes, plans, and problems. Other families, by way of contrast, talk mostly about persons or events outside of the family. As these conversations are reduced to written form and analyzed, it is noteworthy how largely they are of one kind or another in the foregoing respect.

Similarly apparent is the contrast between family patterns of conversation that are analytical or evaluating. The first-named are those which consist chiefly of the analysis, description, and interpretation of persons, objects, or events. The interest is to tell about the subject under discussion. One has something to tell here, and the overtones may be those of humor, mystery, drama, or simply recording. Over against this type is that where the underlying motif is that of passing judgment. Motives are impugned, purposes are evaluated, persons and events are "placed in their proper light." These are the family conversations devoted to "talking about someone." Comments are chiefly critical, depreciatory, belittling. The boss is flayed, a competing neighbor's child is depreciated, the teacher is criticized, a social rival is ridiculed, a relative is castigated, a public official is denounced, the children are nagged, or the food is declared unpalatable.

Somewhat akin to this latter type is the pattern where conversation comes to be a kind of exhibitionism, or showmanship. The emphasis is not so much on expressing a thought as on giving a performance. The aim may be at cleverness, and may achieve that purpose or degenerate into mere smart-aleckiness; or the conversation may partake of the nature of a sadistic performance, where the purpose of hurting expresses itself in cutting speech; or the objective may be primarily that of holding the floor, so to speak, with a juggling of verbal balls, sometimes of gold but more often of tinsel. In most cases, this type of speech seems designed basically to call attention to the speaker, and may be related to a deep-seated inferiority complex.

Other contrasts in these family patterns of conversation are to be found in their tonal qualities. At one extreme are those conversations which abound with "snarl words," and much of the talk consists of spasmodically throwing verbal bits at one another as one throws sticks at a dog. In contradistinction are those family conversations which suggest a Sunday afternoon symphony concert. Instead of loud noises, wrangling, and constant interruptions, there is a quiet and polite exchange of ideas, even allowing for disagreement in conviction. People are allowed to finish a sentence. Even the children are allowed these courtesies.

One important by-product of this study is the impression one gains of these patterns as unconscious, even if persistent, habits of family living. That is to say, the families studied had no awareness, seemingly, of the extent to which their patterns of conversation conformed to a given type. There was no awareness or thought either of their nature or of their role in the development of the child members or in the relations between the adult family members. One cannot but be impressed with the possible human salvage that could be achieved by some judicious attention to the cultivation of family language patterns. One wonders, too, what the diversion of but a minor part of current instruction in family living to family patterns of conversation might accomplish in this respect.

HOUSEHOLD PETS

One in every four big-city families has a dog. Dogs are found in three out of every four farm families. The dog population of the United States was estimated in 1948 at 20,000,000, an all-time high. Cats are about half as popular as dogs. Approximately three out of every five families in the country as a whole have either a dog or a cat. In addition, all sorts of other animals, ranging from ducks to snakes and from lion cubs to lizards, serve as household pets. Not only are these animals found in a majority of American households, but, as is obvious to every observer of the family scene, they constitute an integral part of the family's life. The lack of recognition of their role in the literature on the family constitutes one of its most glaring omissions.

One study published several years ago, and based on a collection of original case studies, explored the various ways in which dogs affect the lives of family members. Briefly summarized, the conclusions of this study follow.

1. The dog is an outlet for our affection. This is its basic service and the chief reason for its presence in most homes. The manifestations of this affection may vary from an occasional friendly cuff to the most tender solicitude, but in most families it is open and frank, with general agreement that the dog receives more attention and affection than any other member of the family.

2. The dog serves each family member according to his or her particular need. This relationship often develops a deep and abiding quality, as evidenced in numerous tributes of older adults to the canine companions of their youth.

3. The dog contributes to the development and integration of the family the challenge of a continuing responsibility, and this obviously is one of life's major and maturing experiences.

4. The dog is one of the best vehicles for parents to use in the training of children in toilet habits. Self-discipline evolves as an accessory before the fact of imposing a discipline upon someone else.

5. The dog is possibly the best available vehicle for parents to use in the sex education of their children. Promiscuity and its results for the female dog present a natural opportunity to discuss similar tendencies, and problems, in the human female.

6. The dog is a satisfactory victim of personal needs for ego gratification and ego satisfaction. When things have gone wrong, in the office, at the club, or on the playground, and you feel like taking it out on someone, there is Waldo waiting for you.

7. Akin to this is the fact that the dog satisfies the very human longing or desire for power. The wish to dominate someone seems fundamental, and the dog offers an outlet that may save other members of the family.

8. A dog accustoms one to the idea of the normality of physical processes, thus making for the lessening of certain inhibitions in the area of natural and intimate family contacts.

9. By the time one has walked a dog a few months, one is sure to have increased markedly the range of one's acquaintances, even in the most impersonal city neighborhood. A dog thus serves as an effective social aid, particularly for the younger members of the family.

10. Similarly, a dog serves as an effective and continu-

ing subject of family conversation, particularly helpful because he stands mute. In many families marked by intellectual aridity or perennial tensions, such service may be of major importance.

11. Finally, a dog offers companionship, to each according to his need. And in the contemporary small family, with its individualized life and the mobility of its members, this function often meets a real need.

To all save the hopelessly esoteric, it should be obvious that household pets are an integral part of many family groups, enriching the range of their activities, broadening the scope of their responsibilities, integrating the relations of their members, and promoting the family hygiene.

FAMILY RITUALS

In analyzing family life from within, our attention came to focus some years ago upon certain forms of family behavior so recurrent as to suggest the term "habit," and yet having aspects of conscious rigidity and a sense of rightness not generally associated with mere habit. We have come to think of these as family rituals, and, speaking specifically, we define them as patterns of prescribed behavior, arising out of family interaction, which are directed toward some specific end or purpose, and which acquire rigidity and a sense of rightness as a result of their continuing. Thus conceived, rituals develop in connection with many aspects of family life, but cluster chiefly around such things as holidays, anniversaries, meals, vacations, religious worship, and collective ways of using leisure time.

Our study of family rituals covers a period of about eighty years and includes data from almost four hundred families. Some of the conclusions which emerge from this material are as follows. (1) Family rituals have been an integral part of family life during the entire period included in the study. (2) They seem quite definitely to be on the increase. (3) An increasing proportion of these rituals have to do with the secular rather than the religious. (4) Education and economic ease make for their development, but decreasing size of the family unit acts contrariwise. (5) Obvious differentials exist on the basis of social class. Lower-class rituals tend toward expediency; as one moves upward, classwise, they are more concerned with the niceties of living.

But the outstanding conclusion is that of ritual as a relatively reliable index of family integration. Family rituals tend to unify the diverse elements of a family group into a harmonious unit. They both reflect and promote the common interests of the members of the family as a group;

they stimulate a sense of group participation; they foster family pride; they encourage refinements in personal relations; they serve to control the behavior of family members; they are an incomparable medium through which newcomers, such as children, are grooved into the pattern of family life. Most of the rituals which we studied arose as group efforts to achieve some common purpose. The trend from the authoritarian to the democratic family, which modern students have emphasized increasingly in recent years, facilitates the development of this type of ritual and increases its importance as an index of family organization. This naturally leads to the final phase with which this article deals.

THE FAMILY COUNCIL

The family council, as a more or less formalized meeting of a family group and with regulatory powers over its members, seems to be as old as the human family. In primitive societies, and in the earlier stages of civil society, its organization was more formal and its powers were more prescribed. It had a relatively high status among various immigrant groups coming to this country, and particularly so among the French who settled in Louisiana. In contemporary times, with the prevalence of smaller family groups and with the greater role of public agencies in family matters, a more simplified and informal type has come to prevail.

In terms of formalized definition, then, the modern family council may be regarded as a gathering of the family group to discuss matters of common family interest, to advise, deliberate, and if possible agree. Its basic implications are that the family is a unified group of interacting personalities, in which each member has his rights, roles, and responsibilities. Occasionally one hears of modern family councils which are organized on a more pretentious basis, with a definite time, place, and procedure, with rules and regulations. Father may be the presiding officer; there is a secretary to keep a record of the proceedings; decisions are made formally by majority vote. More and more, however, the contemporary family council dispenses with formalities of this kind and becomes an informal get-together of the family group for joint discussion of its common problems.

There are at least five reasons for a growing emphasis on the family council and its role in the promotion of stability in the contemporary American family. First is the decline in the size of the family, thus permitting greater ease in family conference and fuller voice to all its members, with particular reference to the younger ones. Second is the growing isolation of the immediate family, which eliminates the interference of relatives. Next is the decline of parental authority, particularly the domination of the father, and the rise of the democratic idea as applied to family group living. Fourth is the growing diversification in interests and occupations of the family members, which makes for increased richness, variety, and at times conflicts in the family background. Finally, one needs to recall here the growing emphasis in family life upon the personality development of its members, particularly its child members.

Based on current uses of the family council, certain tentative conclusions concerning its values are stated here in summary form. (1) It may serve to acquaint all members of the group with the family's needs and problems. Personal problems are merged into a group problem, and each may see his or her problems and needs both in relation to those of each other member and also in relation to those of the group as a whole. (2) Wiser decisions are possible because all members can present pertinent information and particular interests. (3) There is the important fact that group decisions tend to be supported by group authority. The authority of the group is more acceptable than the authority of just a single member. (4) Emotionally, perhaps the most significant value inherent in the family council idea is the sense of security which it may give to the individual family member. Here is not just a family into which he is born and in which he must remain, subject to regimen and complete conformity. This is *his* family, in which he has his say and in which he co-operates in doing his part. The successful family council involves a strong "we feeling," a sense of belonging, of oneness and unity with the family.

Duvall [1962] discusses the several stages of the family life cycle with the developmental tasks to be completed at each stage. The following is a very much condensed résumé of that discussion.

1. *The beginning family: establishment phase.* This stage starts with the wedding and continues until the first pregnancy. The developmental tasks of this stage include the establishment of a home and a pattern of living together as a couple and as members of an extended family and community.

2. *The beginning family: expectant phase.* This stage starts with the awareness of pregnancy and continues until the birth of the first child. The tasks of this stage include the reorganization of the home, the

budget, the couple's various interpersonal relationships, and their philosophy of life to prepare for the arrival of the baby.

3. *The childbearing family.* This stage begins with the birth of the first child and continues until this child is thirty months old. Developmental tasks include adapting living arrangements to the needs of a young child. (Some refer to this process as "childproofing" the home.) They also include meeting new expenses, reworking patterns of husband-wife responsibility, establishing new systems of communication and new interpersonal relationships with each other and with relatives, and fitting into the community as a young family.

4. *The family with preschool children.* This stage involves the couple's learning to rear their children at the same time that they continue to develop as a couple, meeting new costs and new responsibilities.

5. *The family with school children.* This stage involves such developmental tasks as helping children to grow, providing for each family member's needs, learning to cooperate together as a family, and relating the family to a community.

6. *The family with teen-agers.* In this stage the needs of all members put new demands upon the family. Sometimes needs conflict. New patterns of money usage and communication must be worked out. Family responsibilities may be shared in a new way. The husband and wife, as well as each child, have need for continued development as persons. The parents also are called upon to develop a point of view consistent with teen-age values and activities.

7. *The family as a launching center.* This stage marks the beginning of family contraction. During this stage the children are prepared for leaving home to become independent and to establish new families. The parents must prepare themselves for this and for a renewal of their relationships as a couple.

8. *The family in the middle years.* In this stage the couple are called upon to readjust their living conditions, to adapt themselves to the "empty nest," to develop new or pursue already established interests and friendships. During this stage many couples draw closer together.

9. *The aging family.* This stage involves making satisfactory living arrangements for the declining years, learning to live on retirement income, maintenance of meaningful contacts with friends, children, and grandchildren, provision for illness, developing a philosophy that will enable the individual to face bereavement, and finding new and reaffirming old meanings in life.

Our purpose in mentioning this succession of stages in the family life cycle with the developmental tasks of each stage has been to emphasize the importance of looking ahead. To make family life successful, parents as well as children must develop and mature. A "good" parent is actually a series of "good" parents, each having different responsibilities and performing different functions at various levels of development. Preparation for marriage means more than preparation for a wedding and for the first part of marriage. It means preparation for a way of life that in the great majority of cases characterizes a couple for as long as they both live.

WHAT DO YOU THINK?

1. What needs that are observable in children are also needs in adults? How may such needs be met through marriage?

2. What suggestions would you give to a couple whose needs were in conflict?

3. What is the significance of the statement: "The family is the nuclear unit in society"?

4. Mention some human needs other than those referred to in this chapter.

5. What should be the relationship between father and son relative to the expression of affection as the son grows older?

6. Some present-day theorists insist that children need love but adults do not. What is your reaction to such a point of view?

7. A teen-ager and his or her parents do not agree with regard to certain aspects of the child's behavior. The child wants to conform to the standards and expectations of the peer group. The parents insist upon other standards. What suggestions would you make to the teen-ager? To the parents?

8. Are there any questions or topics which a child should not feel free to discuss with his parents?

9. A child is reared in the faith of his parents' church. The parents take such faith for granted. To what degree should the child be allowed or encouraged to question such faith?

10. In this chapter it is asserted that each child has his own "built-in" pattern and rate of growth. If this be true, where and how may a line be drawn between letting the child "be himself" and insisting that he conform to societal norms and expectations?

11. What is the full significance of the statement that a child represents "potential with a push"?

12. To what extent and on what types of issues should a child be permitted to disagree with his parents?

13. What are the pros and cons of corporal punishment for children?

14. What does it mean to accept one's own sexual classification?

15. What is meant by the phrase "creative interpersonal relationships"?

SELECTED READINGS

Aldrich, C. Anderson, and Mary M. Aldrich: *Babies Are Human Beings*, 2d ed., The Macmillan Company, New York, 1954. The growth and development of children, each according to his own pattern and rate.

Baber, Ray E.: *Marriage and the Family*, 2d ed., McGraw-Hill Book Company, New York, 1953, chaps. 8, 9. Some common difficulties in child rearing; obedience and discipline; truthfulness and lying; projection of parents' ambition on children; acquiring sex attitudes.

Berelson, Bernard, and Gary A. Steiner: *Human Behavior*, Harcourt, Brace & World, Inc., New York, 1964, chap. 3. Behavioral development in children. This book is an inventory of scientific studies and an appraisal of what the behavioral sciences have and have not established relative to human behavior.

Bro, Marguerite Harmon: *When Children Ask*, rev. ed., Harper & Row, Publishers, Incorporated, New York, 1956. Aids in answering children's questions on reproduction, religion, and other topics.

Bruch, Hilde: *Don't Be Afraid of Your Child*, Farrar, Straus & Co., New York, 1952. "A guide for perplexed parents." "The purpose of this book is to help parents find their way in the perplexing maze of changing and contradictory advice about better psychological care for children."

Cavan, Ruth Shonle (ed.): *Marriage and the Family in the Modern World*, Thomas Y. Crowell Company, New York, 1960, chap. 22. Principles of positive parent-child relationships; parenthood as a crisis; men's feelings about prospective fatherhood and their reactions to the birth of a baby; the family council.

Duvall, Evelyn Millis: *Family Development*, 2d ed., J. B. Lippincott Company, Philadelphia, 1962. A full discussion of the family life cycle and developmental tasks.

Farber, Bernard: *Family: Organization and Interaction*, Chandler Publishing Company, San Francisco, 1964, chaps. 8, 9, 11, 12. Interaction between generations; the family's role in socialization; competence in interpersonal relationships; mental health in the family.

Fishbein, Morris, and Ruby Jo Reeves Kennedy (eds.): *Modern Marriage and Family Living*, Oxford University Press, Fair Lawn, N.J., 1957, chaps. 30–32, 37. The growth of children; adoption—legal and social procedures; the family council as a means of dealing with family problems.

Gruenberg, Sidonie Matsner (ed.): *The Encyclopedia of Child Care and Guidance*, Doubleday & Company, Inc., Garden City, N.Y., 1954. Covers many topics and answers a variety of questions.

————: *The Parents Guide to Everyday Problems of Boys and Girls*, Random House, Inc., New York, 1958. The author has had wide experience in the field of child rearing and welfare.

Iscoe, Ira, and Harold W. Stevenson (eds.): *Personality Development in Children*, University of Texas Press, Austin, 1960. "Penetrating observations on the personality development of children by six nationally known authorities."

Kenkel, William F.: *The Family in Perspective*, Appleton-Century-Crofts, Inc., New York, 1960, chaps. 11, 14–17. The family function of socialization; child rearing, past and present; the family life cycle.

Kirkendall, Lester A.: *Sex Education as Human Relations*, Inor Publishing Company, Inc., New York, 1950. A modern approach to sex education by a man who has had wide experience in this field.

Landis, Paul H.: *Making the Most of Marriage*, 2d ed., Appleton-Century-Crofts, Inc., New York, 1960, chaps. 26–28, 30. An evaluation of the democratic family. Is parenthood necessary for marriage happiness? What is the best time to have the first baby? Is family size important? Child rearing patterns; the family life cycle.

Langdon, Grace, and Irving W. Stout: *The Discipline of Well-adjusted Children*, The John Day Company, Inc., New York, 1952. Changes in discipline since 1880. The book is based on what 414 parents of well-adjusted children reported that they did in rearing them.

Lerrigo, Marion O., and Helen Southard: The Dutton Series on Sex Education, E. P. Dutton & Co., Inc., New York, 1956. This series of little volumes is designed for both parents and children. The material is graded and is sound. The titles in the series are as follows: *Parents' Privilege* (what parents should tell children three to eight years of age); *A Story about You* (for the child nine to twelve years old); *What's Happening to Me?* (for the teen-ager); *Learning about Love* (for young people sixteen to twenty); *Sex Facts and Attitudes* (for adults who have responsibility for the sex education of children or young people).

Levy, John, and Ruth Munroe: *The Happy Family*, Alfred A. Knopf, Inc., New York, 1938, chaps. 7, 8. "All children have difficulties." Child rearing and family living.

Martinson, Floyd M.: *Marriage and the American Ideal*, Dodd, Mead & Company, Inc., New York, 1960. Family planning; preparing for parenthood; the first baby; the growing child; the adolescent in the home; the family and the community.

Menninger, Karl: *Love against Hate*, Harcourt, Brace & World, Inc., New York, 1942, chap. 2. The frustrations of childhood and their effects on adult life.

Miller, Daniel R., and Guy E. Swanson: *The Changing American Parent*, John Wiley & Sons, Inc., New York, 1958. A study of the child rearing attitudes and practices of the parents of almost 600 children. Includes a discussion of changes in child rearing from the middle of the eighteenth century to the present.

Oliven, John F.: *Sexual Hygiene and Pathology*, J. B. Lippincott Company, Philadelphia, 1955, chaps. 2, 3, 7, 9. Sex education; nudity in the home; masturbation.

Parsons, Talcott, and Robert F. Bales: *Family, Socialization and Interaction Process*, The Free Press of Glencoe, New York, 1955, chap. 2. The family's role in the socialization of the child.

Patton, Robert Gray, and Lytt I. Gardner: *Growth Failure in Maternal Deprivation*, Charles C Thomas, Publisher, Springfield, Ill., 1963. The report of a clinical study of the influence of family disturbance and the deprivation of normal parent-child relationships on children's growth; the effects of early environment and sensory deprivation (mothering) on growth.

Sattler, Henry V.: *Parents, Children and the Facts of Life*, Doubleday & Company, Inc., Garden City, N.Y., 1956. A manual on sex education for parents and teachers written by a Catholic priest.

Schwartz, Alvin: *A Parent's Guide to Children's Play and Recreation*, Crowell-Collier Publishing Co., New York, 1963. A discussion of toys, games, etc.; the use of trips in children's education; how to introduce a child to good music, etc.

Sears, Robert R., Eleanor E. Maccoby, and Harry Levin: *Patterns in Child Rearing*, Harper & Row, Publishers, Incorporated, New York, 1957.

Sullenger, Thomas Earl: *Neglected Areas in Family Living*, The Christopher Publishing House, Boston, 1960. A compilation of articles on a variety of topics, including family rituals, the family meal, household pets, the family council, roles, and crises.

U.S. Government Printing Office, Washington, D.C.: *A Healthy Personality for Your Child* (catalogue #FS3.209:337). An inexpensive pamphlet on child development.

———:*Infant Care*, an inexpensive pamphlet.

Whitman, Howard, *Let's Tell the Truth about Sex*, Farrar, Straus & Co., New York, 1948. "In the present volume I have avoided the cataracts of disagreements and schisms among the experts. Instead, I have tried to integrate and correlate the great areas of *agreement*." The sex education of children.

Woods, Sister Frances Jerome: *The American Family System*, Harper & Row, Publishers, Incorporated, New York, 1959, chap. 9. Parent-child relations; learning parental roles; social class differences in child rearing. The author is a Catholic nun and a sociologist.

EPILOGUE

WE HAVE BEEN DISCUSSING marriage in terms of what it is and, to some extent, in terms of what it can be. May we be permitted one brief excursion into the area of ideals and values over and above those of the ordinary relationship, into the realm of what marriage *can* be and, as a matter of fact, has been for some? We shall not be talking about impossibilities. We shall be talking only about the fulfillment of the potentialities that marriage holds.

In discussing the possibilities inherent in music, art, or any other product of creative achievement, we recognize human limitations. This does not imply that such discussion must be kept at the level of "rock and roll" or the comic strip. It need not be assumed that because the charwoman strikes flat notes while singing at her scrubbing there could never be a great symphony, such as the *Eroica*, or that because the "man in the street" cannot build even a garage there could never be a Parthenon.

Assuming, and correctly, that there are values in any stable marriage, it must be recognized that in some marriages there is a plus element. For the discussion of this plus element we turn to the poet as well as to the scientist. Often poets "see" things that escape scientists because the former are more likely to be interested in whole experience and in meaning, while the latter are more often chiefly interested in structure and function, cause and effect.

Marriage can give an individual a sense of having reached that for which he has hoped and striven ever since he first became aware of the fact of sexual difference. Men and women are "geared up" for marriage from early life.

Marriage can afford normal and adequate expression of some of the deepest, richest, and finest things in life. It can give a sense of completeness, of oneness, permitting a spouse to make an intimate part of his own life values that he could not achieve alone and personal qualities that he himself does not possess.

My perfect wife, my Leonor,
Oh heart, my own, oh eyes, mine too,
Whom else could I dare look backward for,
With whom beside should I dare pursue
The path gray heads abhor?

For it leads to a crag's sheer edge with them;
Youth, flowery all the way, there stops—
Not they; age threatens and they contemn,
Till they reach the gulf wherein youth drops,
One inch from life's safe hem! . . .

My own, confirm me! If I tread
This path back, is it not in pride
To think how little I dreamed it led
To an age so blest that, by its side,
Youth seems the waste instead?

My own, see where the years conduct!
At first, 'twas something our two souls
Should mix as mists do; each is sucked
In each now; on, the new stream rolls,
Whatever rocks obstruct.
          "By the Fireside," *Robert Browning*

Marriage can give one the sense of identifying himself with a growing process, which begins—not ends—with the wedding and becomes richer as time goes on.

It exhibits, not the tumultuous emotions of dating, but something deeper. Dating is the ripples along the shore. This sort of marriage is the great tides that sweep the ocean. Dating is the glare of the sun. Marriage is the infinite horizon, where sky and earth blend into the eternal vastness.

One morning as Robert Browning stood by the window thinking of his work and waiting for the breakfast dishes to be cleared away so that he could use the table for writing, Elizabeth, his wife, thrust something into his pocket and slipped out of the room. In surprise, he drew out a sheaf of papers and began to read. An hour later he was still standing there, still reading, his eyes wet with tears, as one after another of her *Sonnets from the Portuguese* bore to him an expression of his wife's love, which reached a climax in these lines:

How do I love thee? Let me count the ways.
I love thee to the depth and breadth and height
My soul can reach, when feeling out of sight
For the ends of being and ideal grace.
I love thee to the level of every day's
Most quiet need, by sun and candlelight.
I love thee freely, as men strive for right.
I love thee purely, as they turn from praise.
I love thee with the passion put to use
In my old griefs, and with my childhood's faith.
I love thee with a love I seemed to lose
With my lost saints. I love thee with the breath,
Smiles, tears, of all my life; and, if God choose,
I shall but love thee better after death.

Marriage can give one a sense of being part of life in a larger way, a sense of oneness with life, a feeling that "This is one of the reasons I am here and alive, one of the fundamental reasons for which I was born." It enables one to feel that here is something that can be placed first, something to which he would willingly give his all. It enables one to lose himself in something bigger than himself, not because he is submerged in it or by it, but in such a way that his own life becomes richer for having lost self in that larger thing.

Marriage can make for focus rather than dissipation in life. It can redirect urges, impulses, and ambitions toward the highest things we know.

Marriage can give a sense of attainment similar to the satisfaction derived from any creative achievement. In art, beauty is created by relationships, not by isolated units and pigments. Paints in pots are not beautiful. It is only when they are blended, mingled, and interrelated through time and skill that beauty is created.

The raw materials of love are yours—
Fond hearts, and lusty blood, and minds in tune;
And so, dear innocents, you think yourselves
Lovers full-blown.

Am I, because I own
Chisel, mallet, and stone,
A sculptor? And must he
Who hears a skylark and can hold a pen
A poet be?

If neither so, why then
You're not yet lovers. But in time to come
(If sense grow not duller nor spirit dumb)
By constant exercise of skill and wit,

By patient toil and judgment exquisite
Of body, mind, and heart,
You may, my innocents, fashion
This tenderness, this liking, and this passion
Into a work of art.

                "Epithalamion," *Jan Struther**

    Marriage affords the opportunity to give someone else happiness. "When two people love each other," wrote Guy de Maupassant, "nothing is more imperative and delightful than *giving*; to give always and everything, one's thoughts, one's life, one's body, and all that one has; and to feel the gift and risk everything in order to be able to give more, still more."

    Marriage yields the satisfaction of having another individual depend upon one emotionally and gives the realization that oneself is a major factor in that person's world. It gives untold opportunity for sharing and for being shared with; joys, sorrows, experiences, thoughts, ideas, things owned are all enhanced by such sharing. Life acquires new meaning when it is lived for and with another. Enlargement of life comes from knowing another individual so thoroughly that one's own capacity to live is doubled.

    Marriage can give one the feeling of never being alone at any time or anywhere. Young lovers walking hand in hand have a sense of nearness, a feeling of being where they want to be. There may be a similar feeling in marriage, but in a broader, deeper sense and in a way that transcends distance and makes husband and wife seem together though apart. It gives the individual an emotional mooring post, a goal and direction for life. It gives him the sense that someone is always "there" to be relied upon, no matter what else seems uncertain and insecure.

Go from me. Yet I feel that I shall stand
Henceforward in thy shadow. Nevermore
Alone upon the threshold of my door
Of individual life, I shall command
The uses of my soul, nor lift my hand
Serenely in the sunshine as before,
Without the sense of that which I forebore,—
Thy touch upon my palm. The widest land
Doom takes to part us leaves thy heart in mine
With pulses that beat double. What I do
And what I dream include thee, as the wine
Must taste of its own grapes. And, when I sue

*In *The Glassblower and Other Poems*. Reprinted by permission of Harcourt, Brace & World, Inc., New York.

God for myself, he hears that name of thine,
And sees within my eyes the tears of two.
"Sonnets from the Portuguese,"
Elizabeth Barrett Browning

Every human being needs someone to believe in him—not necessarily for achievement, but for contentment and happiness. Each needs someone who knows without being told, someone who sees beneath exteriors. Marriage brings such a one.

There are also in you and in me,
As in everyone else, things lacking,
A particular weapon
You cannot lay hands on;
But it happens always, luckily for us,
That I can lay hold of that weapon,
That your garden is alive with those flowers,
And that we go, without asking, the one to the other
To take what we need.

You are well aware of my wants
And of my weaknesses;
They turn to you unabashed,
You receive them and love them;
And I equally love yours,
Which are a part of your strength.

And so each of us . . .
Goes and may go with assurance,
Because of a hand which is ready,
At the least peril, to turn and take hold
Of the wandering arm of the blind man
That you become, or that I become,
Like everyone else, from time to time.
"A Book of Love," *Charles Vildrac**

*Translated from the French by Witter Bynner.

APPENDIX

The tables on the following pages are greatly condensed. They are intended to give only the general picture and to show the great variety among the laws of the various jurisdictions. Classification of laws in such tables cannot be entirely accurate, since terminology varies from statute to statute, laws are not codified in the same way in all states, and courts interpret statutes in various ways. The reader who wants more detail and greater accuracy concerning the laws of a given state should consult one of the more extensive analyses available.

MARRIAGE LAWS

	Minimum age				Medical certificate (or affidavit)	Days waiting before ceremony	Mixed marriage prohibited—white with		
	With parental consent		Without parental consent				Negro	Oriental Mongolian	American Indian
	Male	Female	Male	Female					
Alabama	17	14	21	18	Both	0	x		
Alaska	18	16	21	18	Both	3			
Arizona	18	16	21	18	Both	0	x	x	
Arkansas	18	16	21	18	Both	3	x		
California	18	16	21	18	Both	0			
Colorado	16	16	21	18	Both	0			
Connecticut	16	16	21	21	Both	4			
Delaware	18	16	21	18	Both	1	x		
District of Columbia	18	16	21	18	Both	4			
Florida	18	16	21	21	Both	3	x		
Georgia	17	14	21	18	Both	5(b)	x	x	x
Hawaii	18	16	20	20	Both	3			
Idaho	15	15	18	18	Both	0	x		
Illinois	18	16	21	18	Both	1	x		
Indiana	18	16	21	18	Both	3	x		
Iowa	18	16	21	18	Both	3			
Kansas	18	16	21	18	Both	3			
Kentucky	18	16	21	21	Both	3	x		
Louisiana	18	16	21	21	Both	3	x	x	x
Maine	16	16	21	18	Both	5			
Maryland	18	16	21	18	Both	2	x	x	
Massachusetts	14	12	21	18	Both	3			
Michigan	18	16	18	18	Both	3			
Minnesota	18	16	21	18	Neither	5			
Mississippi	(d)	(d)	21	18	Both	3	x	x	
Missouri	15	15	21	18	Both	3	x	x	
Montana	18	16	21	18	Both	5	x	x	
Nebraska	18	16	21	21	Both	0			
Nevada	18	16	21	18	Neither	0	x	x	x
New Hampshire	14	13	20	18	Both	5			
New Jersey	18	16	21	18	Both	3			
New Mexico	18	16	21	18	Both	0			
New York	16	14	21	18	Both	1			
North Carolina	16	16	18	18	Both	0	x		x
North Dakota	18	15	21	18	Both	0	x		
Ohio	18	16	21	21	Both	5			
Oklahoma	18	15	21	18	Both	3	x		
Oregon	18	15	21	18	Both	7			
Pennsylvania	16	16	21	21	Both	3			
Rhode Island	18	16	21	21	Both	5			
South Carolina	16	14	18	18	Neither	1	x		x
South Dakota	18	16	21	21	Both	0	x	x	
Tennessee	16	16	21	21	Both	3	x		
Texas	16	14	21	18	Both	0(c)	x		
Utah	16	14	21	18	Both	0	x	x	
Vermont	18	16	21	18	Both	5			
Virginia	18	16	21	21	Both	0	x	x	x
Washington	(a)	15	21	18	Male	3			
West Virginia	18	16	21	21	Both	3	x		
Wisconsin	18	16	21	18	Both	5			
Wyoming	18	16	21	21	Both	0	x	x	

(a) Male under 21 may marry with parental consent but no minimum age specified.

(b) Unless both parties 21 or older; or parents of girl give consent if she is under 18.

(c) Except 3-day waiting period for those requiring parental consent.

(d) No minimum specified.

ANNULMENT GROUNDS

	Fraud	Force—duress	Insanity—feeble-mindedness	Impotence—physical incapacity	Non-age	Prohibited degree of relationship	Previous marriage existing	Color—race	Concealment of previous mge. or div.	Misrepresentation of condition of life	Concealment of life	Concealment of pregnancy	Not married by proper authority	Unchastity	Venereal disease	Imprisonment for life	Felony conviction	Disappearance	Mistaken identity	Epilepsy	Habitual drunkenness	Habitual use of drugs	On probation or parole	Both parties paupers	Leprosy—loathsome disease
Alabama	x		x		x	x	x	x																	
Alaska	x	x	x		x	x	x																		
Arizona	x		x		x	x	x	x	x	x	x														
Arkansas	x	x	x	x	x	x																			
California	x	x	x	x	x			x																	
Colorado	x	x	x	x	x	x	x																		
Connecticut			x				x						x												
Delaware	x	x	x	x		x	x	x							x						x	x	x	x	x
District of Columbia	x	x	x	x	x	x	x																		
Florida							x	x																	
Georgia	x	x	x			x	x																		
Hawaii	x	x	x	x	x	x	x																		x
Idaho	x	x	x	x	x	x	x																		
Illinois			x				x																		
Indiana	x		x		x	x	x	x																	
Iowa			x	x	x	x	x																		
Kansas	x		x		x	x	x																		
Kentucky	x	x	x		x	x	x								x										
Louisiana		x				x	x	x											x						
Maine			x			x	x							x											
Maryland	x					x	x	x						x											
Massachusetts			x			x	x	x																	
Michigan	x	x	x			x	x	x							x				x						
Minnesota	x	x	x			x	x	x																	
Mississippi							x	x																	
Missouri			x			x	x	x											x						
Montana	x	x	x	x	x	x	x																		
Nebraska	x	x	x	x	x	x	x	x																	
Nevada	x		x			x	x	x																	
New Hampshire			x			x	x	x																	
New Jersey			x	x	x	x	x																		
New Mexico						x	x																		
New York	x	x	x	x	x	x	x	x								x	x								
North Carolina				x	x	x	x	x																	
North Dakota	x	x	x	x	x	x	x																		
Ohio		x	x			x	x																		
Oklahoma			x			x	x	x																	
Oregon	x	x	x			x	x																		
Pennsylvania						x	x																		
Rhode Island																									
South Carolina			x			x	x	x																	
South Dakota	x	x	x	x	x	x	x	x																	
Tennessee	x	x				x	x	x																	
Texas				x	x	x	x	x																	
Utah			x		x	x	x	x							x								x		
Vermont	x	x	x	x	x	x	x																		
Virginia			x			x	x	x																	
Washington	x	x	x			x	x	x																	
West Virginia			x	x	x	x	x	x							x	x	x	x							
Wisconsin	x	x	x	x	x	x	x																		
Wyoming	x	x	x		x	x	x	x																	

NOTE: In some states certain types of marriage are prohibited or considered void but are not listed as voidable, hence they are not included in this table. What may be grounds for annulment in some states may be grounds for divorce in others.

State	Residence required	Adultery	Desertion – abandonment	Cruelty	Conviction – felony imprisonment	Impotence – physical incapacity	Habitual drunkenness	Habitual use of drugs	Insanity	Nonsupport	Willful neglect	Woman pregnant (by another man) at marriage	Unnatural behavior	Violent temper or behavior	Living apart	Previous marriage existing	Fraud	Disappearance	Under age of consent
Alabama	1	x	1	x	x		x	x	5	x		x	x						
Alaska	1	x	1	x	x	x	x	x	18 mo.	x		x							
Arizona	1	x	1	x	1	x	x			x		x			5				
Arkansas		x	1	x	x	x	1		3	x					3	x			
California	1	x	1	x	x		1		3		1								
Colorado	1	x	1	x	x	x	x	1	3	1					3				
Connecticut	3	x	3	x	x		x		5								x	7	
Delaware	2	x	2	x	x		2		5	x						x			x
Dist. of Columbia	1	x	2		x										x	x			
Florida	6 mo.	x	1	x		x	x	x						x		x			
Georgia	6 mo.	x	1	x	x	x	x		3			x					x		
Hawaii	1	x	6 mo.	x	7		x		3	x					5				
Idaho	6 wk.	x	x	x	x		1		6		x				5				
Illinois	1	x	1	x	x	x	2									x			
Indiana	1	x	2	x	x	x	x		5	2									
Iowa	1	x	2	x	x		x					x							
Kansas	1	x	1	x	x		x		5		x								
Kentucky	1	x	1	x	x	x	1		5			x		x	5	x			
Louisiana		x	x	x	x		x			x					2				
Maine	6 mo.	x	3	x		x	x	x		x									
Maryland	1	x	18 mo.		x	x			3						3				
Massachusetts	3	x	3	x	5	x	x	x		x									
Michigan	1	x	2	x	3	x	x			x									
Minnesota	1	x	1	x	x	x	1		5						x				
Mississippi	1	x	1	x	x	x	x	x	3			x				x			
Missouri	1	x	1	x	x	x	1					x				x			
Montana	1	x	x	x	x		x		5	x									
Nebraska	1	x	2	x	3	x	x		5	x									
Nevada	6 wk.	x	1	x	x	x	x		2	1					3				
New Hampshire	1	x	2	x	x	x	2			2					x			3	
New Jersey	2	x	2	x															
New Mexico	1	x	x	x	x	x	x		5	x		x							
New York		x																	
North Carolina	6 mo.	x				x			5			x	x		2				
North Dakota	1	x	1	x	x		1	x	5	x									
Ohio	1	x	1	x	x	x	3			x						x	x		
Oklahoma	6 mo.	x	1	x	x	x	x		5	x		x				x	x		
Oregon	1	x	1	x	x	x	1		3							x	x		
Pennsylvania	1	x	2	x	x	x	x									x	x		
Rhode Island	2	x	5	x	x	x	x	x		x									
South Carolina	1	x	1	x			x												
South Dakota	1	x	1	x	x		1		5	x									
Tennessee	2	x	2	x	x	x	x			x		x				x			
Texas	1	x	3	x	x				5						7				
Utah	3 mo.	x	1	x	x	x	x		x	x					3				
Vermont	6 mo.	x	3	x	x				5	x					3			7	
Virginia	1	x	1		x							x	x						
Washington	1	x	1	x	x	x	x		2	x					5		x	x	
West Virginia	1	x	1	x	x		x	x											
Wisconsin	2	x	1	x	3	x	x			x					5				
Wyoming	60 da.	x	1	x	x	x	x		2	x		x			x				

NOTE: Numerals refer to years, unless otherwise specified.

DIVORCE GROUNDS (Continued)

	Prohibited degree of relationship	Divorce out of state by other party	Mental incapacity	Force – duress	Venereal disease	Attempt on life of other person	Woman's unchastity	Public defamation of other party	Indignities	Man's vagrancy	Physical malformation preventing intercourse	Joining religious sect renouncing mge.-cohab.	Refusal to cohabit	Gross marital behavior	Woman's refusal to move to new residence	Incompatibility	Void or voidable marriage	Fugitive from justice	Feeble-mindedness – epilepsy
Alabama									x				x			x			
Alaska																			
Arizona									x										
Arkansas																			
California																			
Colorado																			
Connecticut																			
Delaware																			5
District of Columbia																			
Florida	x	x																	
Georgia	x		x	x															
Hawaii																			
Idaho																			
Illinois					x	x													
Indiana																			
Iowa																			
Kansas																			
Kentucky				x	x	x	x				x	x							
Louisiana						x		x										x	
Maine																			
Maryland	x																		
Massachusetts																			
Michigan		x																	
Minnesota																			
Mississippi	x																		
Missouri									x	x									
Montana								x											
Nebraska																			
Nevada																			
New Hampshire													x	x					
New Jersey																			
New Mexico																x			
New York																			
North Carolina																			
North Dakota														x					
Ohio		x																	
Oklahoma																x			
Oregon									x										
Pennsylvania	x			x					x										
Rhode Island														x				x	
South Carolina																			
South Dakota														x					
Tennessee						x			x						x				
Texas																			
Utah																			
Vermont																			2
Virginia						x													
Washington			x	x					x										
West Virginia																			
Wisconsin																			
Wyoming									x	x									

BIBLIOGRAPHY

Adler, Alfred: *What Life Should Mean to You*, Little, Brown and Company, Boston, 1937.

Albert, A.: "The Mammalian Testis," chap. 5 in William C. Young (ed.), *Sex and Internal Secretions*, 3d ed., The Williams & Wilkins Company, Baltimore, 1961.

Aldrich, C. Anderson, and Mary M. Aldrich: *Babies Are Human Beings,* 2d ed., The Macmillan Company, New York, 1954.

Alexander, Paul W.: "The Follies of Divorce: A Therapeutic Approach to the Problem," *Law Forum*, pp. 695–711, winter, 1949.

Allen, Fred H., Jr., and Louis K. Diamond: *Erythroblastosis Fetalis*, Little, Brown and Company, Boston, 1957.

Aronson, Howard G., and Carl F. Glienke: "A Study of the Incidence of Pregnancy following Adoption," *Fertility and Sterility*, vol. 14, no. 5, pp. 547–553, September–October, 1963, abstracted in *Obstetrical and Gynecological Survey*, vol. 19, no. 1, pp. 158–159, February, 1964.

Baker, T. G.: "A Quantitative Cytological Study of Germ Cells in Human Ovaries," *Proceedings of the Royal Society of Medicine*, sec. B, vol. 158, pp. 417–433, October 22, 1963, abstracted in *Obstetrical and Gynecological Survey*, vol. 19, no. 4, pp. 700–701, August, 1964.

Barron, Donald H.: "The Placenta as the Fetal Lung," chap. 4 in Claude A. Villee (ed.), *The Placenta and Fetal Membranes*, The Williams & Wilkins Company, Baltimore, 1960.

Barwick, Sir Garfield: "Matrimonial Causes Bill 1959," *Parliamentary Debates*, May 14, 1959, Commonwealth Government Printer, Canberra, A.C.T., Australia.

Baum, Gregory (ed.): *The Ecumenist*, vol. 1, no. 2, pp. 23–25, December, 1962.

Bell, Howard M.: *Youth Tell Their Story*, The American Youth Commission of the American Council on Education, Washington, D.C., 1938.

Benedek, Therese, and Boris B. Rubenstein: "The Sexual Cycle in Women," *Psychosomatic Medicine Monographs*, no. 3, pp. 1–2, The National Research Council, Washington, D.C., 1942.

Berlind, Melvyn: "The Contralateral Corpus Luteum: An Important Factor in Ectopic Pregnancy," *Obstetrics and Gynecology*, vol. 16, no. 1, pp. 51–52, July, 1960.

Bernard, Jessie: *Remarriage*, Holt, Rinehart and Winston, Inc., New York, 1956.

Bishop, David W.: "Biology of Spermatozoa," chap. 13 in William C. Young (ed.), *Sex and Internal Secretions*, 3d ed., The Williams & Wilkins Company, Baltimore, 1961.

Blandau, Richard J.: "Biology of Eggs and Implantation," chap. 14 in William C. Young (ed.), *Sex and Internal Secretions*, 3d ed., The Williams & Wilkins Company, Baltimore, 1961.

Bonnar, A.: *The Catholic Doctor*, P. J. Kenedy & Sons, New York, 1952.

Bossard, James H. S., Eleanor S. Boll, and Winogene P. Sanger: "Some Neglected Areas in Family-life Study," *The Annals of the American Academy of Political and Social Science*, no. 272, pp. 68–76, November, 1950.

Bourne, Aleck W., and Leslie H. Williams: *Recent Advances in Obstetrics and Gynecology*, McGraw-Hill Book Company, New York, 1953.

Bowes, Kenneth (ed.): *Modern Trends in Obstetrics and Gynecology*, Paul B. Hoeber, Inc., New York, 1956.

Bowman, Henry A.: *A Christian Interpretation of Marriage*, The Westminster Press, Philadelphia, 1959.

Breckinridge, Sophonisba: "The Activities of Women outside the Home," in *Report of the President's Research Committee on Social Trends*, pp. 709–750, McGraw-Hill Book Company, New York, 1933.

Bremer, Johan: *Asexualization*, The Macmillan Company, New York, 1959.

Bromley, Dorothy Dunbar, and Florence Haxton Britten: *Youth and Sex*, Harper & Row, Publishers, Incorporated, New York, 1938.

Broom, Leonard, and Philip Selznick: *Sociology*, 3d ed., Harper & Row, Publishers, Incorporated, New York, 1963.

Browning, Elizabeth Barrett: *Sonnets from the Portuguese*, Thomas Y. Crowell Company, New York, 1933.

Browning, Robert: "By the Fireside," in *The Complete Poetical Works of Robert Browning*, The Macmillan Company, New York, 1927, pp. 245–248.

Bruce, Joan, and G. F. M. Russell: "Premenstrual Tension: A Study of Weight Changes and Balances of Water, Sodium, and Potassium," *Lancet*, vol. 2, no. 7250, pp. 267–271, August 11, 1962, abstracted in J. P. Greenhill (ed.), *The Year Book of Obstetrics and Gynecology*, 1963–1964 Year Book Series, The Year Book Medical Publishers, Inc., Chicago, 1963, p. 446.

Burgess, Ernest W., and Leonard S. Cottrell, Jr.: *Predicting Success or Failure in Marriage*, Prentice-Hall, Inc., Englewood Cliffs, N.J., 1939.

—— and Paul Wallin: *Engagement and Marriage*, J. B. Lippincott Company, Philadelphia, 1953.

Burkhart, Roy: *From Friendship to Marriage*, Harper & Row, Publishers, Incorporated, New York, 1937.

Burma, John H.: "The Measurement of Negro Passing," *American Journal of Sociology*, vol. 52, no. 1, pp. 18–22, July, 1946.

Butterfield, Oliver: *Love Problems of Adolescence*, Bureau of Publications, Teachers College, Columbia University, New York, 1939. Reprinted with permission of Emerson Books, Inc., New York.

Calderone, Mary Steichen (ed.): *Abortion in the United States*, Paul B. Hoeber, Inc., New York, 1958.

—— (ed.): *Manual of Contraceptive Practice*, The Williams & Wilkins Company, Baltimore, 1964.

Campbell, Maurice: "Place of Maternal Rubella in the Aetiology of Congenital Heart Disease," *British Medical Journal*, vol. 1, no. 5227, pp. 691–696, March 11, 1961, abstracted in *Obstetrical and Gynecological Survey*, vol. 16, no. 4, pp. 473–475, August, 1961.

Carpenter, Philip L.: *Immunology and Serology*, W. B. Saunders Company, Philadelphia, 1956.

Carter, Hugh, and Alexander Plateris: "Trends in Divorce and Family Disruption," *Indicators*, August, 1963, U.S. Department of Health, Education, and Welfare.

Chalmers, J. A.: "The Vacuum Extractor," chap. 8 in R. J. Kellar (ed.), *Modern Trends in Obstetrics*, Butterworth, Inc., Washington, D.C., 1963.

Christensen, Harold T.: "Studies in Child Spacing: I—Premarital Pregnancy as Measured by the Spacing of the First Born from Marriage," *American Sociological Review*, vol. 18, no. 1, pp. 53–59, February, 1953.

————: "Child Spacing Analysis via Record Linkage: New Data plus a Summing Up of Earlier Reports," *Marriage and Family Living*, vol. 25, no. 3, pp. 272–280, August, 1963.

———— and Hanna H. Meissner: "Studies in Child Spacing: III—Premarital Pregnancy as a Factor in Divorce," *American Sociological Review*, vol. 18, no. 6, pp. 641–644, December, 1953.

Clemens, Alphonse H.: *Marriage and the Family*, Prentice-Hall, Inc., Englewood Cliffs, N.J., 1957.

Convers, D.: *Marriage and Divorce in the United States*, J. B. Lippincott Company, Philadelphia, 1889.

Conway, Bertrand L.: *The Church and Eugenics* (pamphlet), Paulist Press, New York, 1929a.

————: *The Question Box*, rev. ed. (pamphlet), Paulist Press, New York, 1929b.

Cox, Ignatius W.: *Birth Control, Birth Controllers and Perversion of Logic* (pamphlet), Paulist Press, New York, 1936.

Crampton, C. B.: "Uncomplicated Obstetrics: A Revaluation," *Connecticut Medicine*, vol. 25, no. 5, pp. 279–283, May, 1961, abstracted in *Obstetrical and Gynecological Survey*, vol. 16, no. 5, pp. 607–609, October, 1961.

Dalton, Katharina: "Menstruation and Accidents," *British Medical Journal*, vol. 2, no. 5210, pp. 1425–1426, November 12, 1960, abstracted in *Obstetrical and Gynecological Survey*, vol. 16, no. 3, pp. 404–405, June, 1961.

Davie, Maurice R.: *Negroes in American Society*, McGraw-Hill Book Company, New York, 1949.

Davis, Katherine Bement: *Factors in the Sex Life of Twenty-two Hundred Women*, Harper & Row, Publishers, Incorporated, New York, 1929.

Dickinson, Robert Latou, and Lura Beam: *The Single Woman*, The Williams & Wilkins Company, Baltimore, 1934.

Doress, Irving: "The Problem of Early Marriage," *The Bulletin on Family Development*, vol. 2, no. 1, pp. 20–23, spring, 1961.

Drake, St. Clair, and Horace R. Cayton: *Black Metropolis*, rev. ed., Harper & Row, Publishers, Incorporated, New York, 1945.

Drucker, Paul, Jerrold Finkel, and Lewis E. Savel: "Sixty-five Day Interval between the Births of Twins," *American Journal of Obstetrics and Gynecology*, vol. 80, no. 4, pp. 761–763, October, 1960, abstracted in *Obstetrical and Gynecological Survey*, vol. 16, no. 1, pp. 43–44, February, 1961.

Drummond, Isabel: *Getting a Divorce*, Alfred A. Knopf, Inc., New York, 1934.

Duvall, Evelyn Millis: *Family Development*, 2d ed., J. B. Lippincott Company, Philadelphia, 1962.

Eastman, Nicholson (ed.): editor's comments, *Obstetrical and Gynecological Survey*, vol. 15, no. 5, October, 1960; vol. 16, no. 1, February, 1961; vol. 16, no. 4, August, 1961; vol. 17, no. 1, February, 1962; vol. 17, no. 2, April, 1962; vol. 17, no. 5, October, 1962; vol. 18, no. 1, February, 1963; vol. 18, no. 3, June, 1963.

Ehrmann, Winston: *Premarital Dating Behavior*, Holt, Rinehart and Winston, Inc., New York, 1959.

Eichler, Lillian: *The Customs of Mankind*, Doubleday & Company, Inc., Garden City, N.Y., 1925.

Engle, Earl T. (ed.): *Studies on Testis and Ovary, Eggs and Sperm*, Charles C Thomas, Publisher, Springfield, Ill., 1952.

Family Court Center, Toledo, Ohio: "Annual Report," 1953.

Farber, Seymour M., and Roger H. L. Wilson (eds.): *The Potential of Woman*, McGraw-Hill Book Company, New York, 1963.

Farris, Edmond J.: *Human Ovulation and Fertility*, J. B. Lippincott Company, Philadelphia, 1956.

Federal Security Agency: *Vital Statistics of the United States, Part I*, 1949.

——: "Summary of Marriage and Divorce Statistics: United States, 1949," *Vital Statistics – Special Reports*, vol. 36, no. 2, June 5, 1951.

Fields, Charles, Hugh C. Falls, Charles P. Warren, and Manuel Zimberoff: "Ear of Newborn as Identification Constant," *Obstetrics and Gynecology*, vol. 16, no. 1, pp. 98–102, July, 1960.

Findley, Palmer: *The Story of Childbirth*, Doubleday, Doran & Company, Inc., New York, 1933.

Fluhmann, C. Frederic: *The Management of Menstrual Disorders*, W. B. Saunders Company, Philadelphia, 1956.

Folsom, Joseph (ed.): *Plan for Marriage*, Harper & Row, Publishers, Incorporated, New York, 1938.

Foote, Nelson: "Becoming a Father," *The Bulletin on Family Development*, vol. 3, no. 1, pp. 7–9, spring, 1962.

Ford, John C., and Gerald Kelly: *Contemporary Moral Theology*, vol. 2, The Newman Press, Westminster, Md., 1963.

Freedman, Ronald, Pascal K. Whelpton, and Arthur A. Campbell: *Family Planning, Sterility, and Population Growth*, McGraw-Hill Book Company, New York, 1959.

Fremantle, Anne (ed.): *The Papal Encyclicals*, New American Library of World Literature, Inc., New York, 1956.

Friedman, Leonard J.: *Virgin Wives*, Tavistock Publications, Ltd., London, 1962.

Fulton, Wallace C.: "The American Family and Time," *Journal of Marriage and the Family*, vol. 26, no. 1, pp. 6–9, February, 1964.

Gebhard, Paul H., Wardell B. Pomeroy, Clyde E. Martin, and Cornelia V. Christenson: *Pregnancy, Birth and Abortion*, Paul B. Hoeber, Inc., New York, 1958.

Gill, Merton M.: "Functional Disturbances of Menstruation," *Bulletin of the Menninger Clinic*, vol. 7, no. 1, pp. 6–14, January, 1943.

Glick, Paul C.: *American Families*, John Wiley & Sons, Inc., New York, 1957.

Goldin, Hyman E.: *Hamadrikh: The Rabbi's Guide*, Hebrew Publishing Company, New York, 1939.

Good, Frederick L., and Otis F. Kelly: *Marriage, Morals and Medical Ethics*, P. J. Kenedy & Sons, New York, 1951.

Goode, William J.: "Economic Factors and Marital Adjustment," *American Sociological Review*, vol. 16, no. 6, pp. 802–812, December, 1951.

——: *After Divorce*, The Free Press of Glencoe, New York, 1956.

Greenhill, J. P. (ed.): *The 1943 Year Book of Obstetrics and Gynecology*, The Year Book Medical Publishers, Inc., Chicago, 1944.

——: *Obstetrics in General Practice*, 3d ed., The Year Book Medical Publishers, Inc., Chicago, 1945*a*.

——: *Office Gynecology*, The Year Book Medical Publishers, Inc., Chicago, 1945*b*.

—— (ed.): *The 1945 Year Book of Obstetrics and Gynecology*, The Year Book Medical Publishers, Inc., Chicago, 1946.

——: *Obstetrics in General Practice*, 4th ed., The Year Book Medical Publishers, Inc., Chicago, 1948.

——: *Obstetrics*, 11th ed., W. B. Saunders Company, Philadelphia, 1955.

—— (ed.): *The Year Book of Obstetrics and Gynecology, 1954–55*, The Year Book Medical Publishers, Inc., Chicago, 1954; *1957–58* (1957); *1958–59*

(1958); *1959–60* (1959); *1960–61* (1960); *1961–62* (1961); *1962–63* (1962); *1963–64* (1963).

Groves, Gladys H., and Robert A. Ross: *The Married Woman,* Greenberg: Publisher, Inc., New York, 1936.

Guttmacher, Alan Frank: *Life in the Making,* Garden City Books, New York, 1933.

————: *Into This Universe,* The Viking Press, Inc., New York, 1937.

————: "The Role of Artificial Insemination in the Treatment of Sterility," *Obstetrical and Gynecological Survey,* vol. 15, no. 6, pp. 767–785, December, 1960.

Haagensen, C. D.: *Diseases of the Breast,* W. B. Saunders Company, Philadelphia, 1956.

Hacker, Helen Mayer: "The New Burdens of Masculinity," *Marriage and Family Living,* vol. 19, no. 3, pp. 227–233, August, 1957.

Hamblen, E. C.: "Endocrinology of Women," Charles C Thomas, Publisher, Springfield, Ill., 1945.

Hamblin, Robert L., and Robert O. Blood: "Pre-marital Experience and the Wife's Sexual Adjustment," *Social Problems,* vol. 4, no. 2, pp. 122–130, October, 1956.

Hamilton, G. V.: *A Research in Marriage,* Albert & Charles Boni, Inc., New York, 1929.

Harper, Robert A.: "Communication Problems in Marriage and Marriage Counseling," *Marriage and Family Living,* vol. 20, no. 2, pp. 107–112, May, 1958.

Hart, Hornell, and Ella B. Hart: *Personality and the Family,* D. C. Heath and Company, Boston, 1935.

Hartman, Carl G.: *Time of Ovulation in Women,* The Williams & Wilkins Company, Baltimore, 1936.

————: *Science and the Safe Period,* The Williams & Wilkins Company, Baltimore, 1962.

Havighurst, Robert J.: *Human Development and Education,* Longmans, Green & Co., Inc., New York, 1953.

Helpern, Milton: "The Problem of Criminal Abortion," *Quarterly Review of Surgery, Obstetrics, and Gynecology,* vol. 16, no. 4, pp. 231–234, October–December, 1959, abstracted in *Obstetrical and Gynecological Survey,* vol. 15, no. 3, pp. 369–371, June, 1960.

Hertig, Arthur T.: "Pathological Aspects," chap. 8 in Claude A. Villee (ed.), *The Placenta and Fetal Membranes,* The Williams & Wilkins Company, Baltimore, 1960.

Heyns, O. S.: "Theory and Application of Abdominal Decompression," chap. 9 in R. J. Kellar (ed.), *Modern Trends in Obstetrics,* Butterworth, Inc., Washington, D.C., 1963.

Hoffman, Jacob: *Female Endocrinology,* W. B. Saunders Company, Philadelphia, 1944.

Hon, Edward H.: *A Manual of Pregnancy Testing,* J. & A. Churchill, Ltd., London, 1961.

Hoskins, R. G.: *The Tides of Life,* W. W. Norton & Company, Inc., New York, 1933.

Hotchkiss, Robert Sherman: *Fertility in Men,* J. B. Lippincott Company, Philadelphia, 1944.

Hotep, I. N.: *Love and Happiness,* Alfred A. Knopf, Inc., New York, 1938.

Hyatt, Herman W., Sr.: "Relationship of Maternal Mumps to Congenital Defects and Fetal Deaths, and to Maternal Morbidity and Mortality," *American Practitioner,* vol. 12, no. 5, pp. 359–363, May, 1961, abstracted in *Obstetrical and Gynecological Survey,* vol. 16, no. 5, pp. 656–657, October, 1961.

Kane, John J.: *Marriage and the Family,* Holt, Rinehart and Winston, Inc., New York, 1952.

Kanin, Eugene J.: "Premarital Sex Adjustments, Social Class, and Associated Behaviors," *Marriage and Family Living*, vol. 22, no. 3, pp. 258–262, August, 1960.

——— and David H. Howard: "Postmarital Consequences of Premarital Sex Adjustments," *American Sociological Review*, vol. 23, no. 5, pp. 556–562, October, 1958.

Karlsson, Georg: *Adaptability and Communication in Marriage*, rev. ed., The Bedminster Press, Totowa, N.J., 1963.

Kaye, Bernard M., and Burnell V. Reaney: "Virus Diseases in Pregnancy: Prevention and Fetal Effects," *Obstetrics and Gynecology*, vol. 19, no. 5, pp. 618–622, May, 1962, abstracted in *Obstetrical and Gynecological Survey*, vol. 17, no. 5, pp. 654–655, October, 1962.

Kegel, Arnold H.: "Sexual Functions of the Pubococcygeus Muscle," *The Western Journal of Surgery, Obstetrics and Gynecology*, vol. 60, no. 10, pp. 521–524, October, 1952.

Kellar, R. J. (ed.): *Modern Trends in Obstetrics*, Butterworth, Inc., Washington, D.C., 1963.

Kessel, Neil, and Alec Coppen: "The Prevalence of Common Menstrual Symptoms," *Lancet*, vol. 2, no. 7298, pp. 61–64, July, 1963, abstracted in *Obstetrical and Gynecological Survey*, vol. 19, no. 1, pp. 146–149, February, 1963.

King, Robert C.: *Genetics*, Oxford University Press, Fair Lawn, N.J., 1962.

Kinsey, Alfred C., Wardell B. Pomeroy, and Clyde E. Martin: *Sexual Behavior in the Human Male*, W. B. Saunders Company, Philadelphia, 1948.

———, ———, ———, and Paul H. Gebhard: *Sexual Behavior in the Human Female*, W. B. Saunders Company, Philadelphia, 1953.

Kirkendall, Lester, A.: *Premarital Intercourse and Interpersonal Relationships*, The Julian Press, Inc., New York, 1961.

Knopf, Olga: *The Art of Being a Woman*, Blue Ribbon Books, New York, 1932.

Komarovsky, Mirra: "Cultural Contradictions and Sex Roles," *American Journal of Sociology*, vol. 52, no. 3, pp. 184–189, November, 1946.

Kurtz, Russell H. (ed.): *Social Work Year Book*, National Association of Social Workers, New York, 1960.

Landis, Judson T., and Mary G. Landis: *Building a Successful Marriage*, 4th ed., Prentice-Hall, Inc., Englewood Cliffs, N.J., 1963.

Leach, William H.: *The Cokesbury Marriage Manual*, 2d ed., Abingdon Press, Nashville, Tenn., 1945.

Leyburn, James G.: *Frontier Folkways*, Yale University Press, New Haven, Conn., 1935, quoting Olive Schreiner, *Thoughts on South Africa*, p. 193, T. Fisher Unwin, London, 1923.

Lichtenberger, J. P.: *Divorce: A Social Interpretation*, McGraw-Hill Book Company, New York, 1931.

Locke, Harvey J.: *Predicting Adjustment in Marriage*, Holt, Rinehart and Winston, Inc., New York, 1951.

Lord, Daniel A.: *Don't Marry a Catholic* (pamphlet), The Queen's Work, St. Louis, 1952.

Lowsley, Oswald Swinney, Frank Hinman, Donald R. Smith, and Robert Gutierrez: *The Sexual Glands of the Male*, Oxford University Press, Fair Lawn, N.J., 1942.

Lunde, Anders, Carl Ortmeyer, and Earl Huyck: "Trends in Marriages, Births, and Population," *Indicators*, U.S. Department of Health, Education, and Welfare, March, 1963.

Markun, Leo: *Mrs. Grundy*, Appleton-Century-Crofts, Inc., New York, 1930.

Mayes, Bruce: "The Effect of Rubella on the Fetus," chap. 11 in R. J. Kellar (ed.), *New Trends in Obstetrics*, Butterworth, Inc., Washington, D.C., 1963.

McDanald, Eugene C., Jr., Bert Kruger Smith, and Robert L. Sutherland: *Self-acceptance* (pamphlet), The Hogg Foundation for Mental Health, University of Texas, Austin, 1962.

Meyer, Fulgence: *I'm Keeping Company Now* (pamphlet), Paulist Press, New York, 1934.

Miller, D. F.: *Can Mixed Marriages Be Happy?* Lignorian Pamphlets, Redemptionist Fathers, Lignori, Mo., 1960.

———: *Program for Catholics in a Mixed Marriage,* Lignorian Pamphlets, Redemptionist Fathers, Lignori, Mo., 1961.

Missildine, W. Hugh (ed.): *Feelings and Their Medical Significance,* vol. 2, no. 11, pp. 3–4, November–December, 1960, Ross Laboratories, Columbus, Ohio.

Monahan, Thomas P.: "When Married Couples Part: Statistical Trends and Relationships in Divorce," *American Sociological Review,* vol. 27, no. 5, pp. 625–633, October, 1962.

Montagu, M. F. Ashley: *Adolescent Sterility,* Charles C Thomas, Publisher, Springfield, Ill., 1946.

Morton, J. H., H. Additon, R. G. Addison, L. Hunt, and J. J. Sullivan: "A Clinical Study of Premenstrual Tension," *American Journal of Obstetrics and Gynecology,* vol. 65, no. 6, pp. 1182–1191, June, 1953.

Nelson, Warren O.: "The Physiology of Reproduction and Its Relation to the Regulation of Fertility," *Marriage and Family Living,* vol. 25, no. 1, pp. 74–80, February, 1963.

———: "Areas of Research in the Physiological Control of Fertility," in Mary Steichen Calderone (ed.), *Manual of Contraceptive Practice,* The Williams & Wilkins Company, Baltimore, 1964, pp. 260–263.

Nimkoff, M. F.: *The Family,* Houghton Mifflin Company, Boston, 1934.

Novak, Emil: *Textbook of Gynecology,* The Williams & Wilkins Company, Baltimore, 1944.

Nye, F. Ivan, and Lois W. Hoffman (eds.): *The Employed Mother in America,* Rand McNally & Company, Chicago, 1963.

O'Brien, John A.: *Why Not a Mixed Marriage: A Plain Answer to a Common Question* (pamphlet), Paulist Press, New York, 1937.

Oettinger, Katherine Brownell: "Illegitimacy Problems: A 1962 Priority," in *Proceedings of the Conference on Unwed Mothers,* pp. B-1–B-8, The Social Hygiene Society of D.C. and Mt. Vernon Place Methodist Church, Washington, D.C., 1962.

Ogburn, W. F., and M. F. Nimkoff: *Technology and the Changing Family,* Houghton Mifflin Company, Boston, 1955.

Oliven, John F.: *Sexual Hygiene and Pathology,* J. B. Lippincott Company, Philadelphia, 1955.

Perkins, H. F.: "Adoption and Fertility," *Eugenical News,* no. 21, pp. 95–101, 1936.

Pillay, A. P., and Albert Ellis: "Sex, Society and the Individual," *The International Journal of Sexology,* Bombay, India, 1953.

Pope Pius XI: *Encyclical Letter on* Casti Connubi (pamphlet), Paulist Press, New York, 1930.

Pope Pius XII: *Moral Questions Affecting Married Life: The Apostolate of the Midwife* (pamphlet), Paulist Press, New York, 1951.

Population Reference Bureau: *Annual Report, 1962,* Washington, D.C.

———: *Population Bulletin,* vol. 19, no. 2, March, 1963, Washington, D.C.

Potter, Edith L.: "Defective Babies Who Die before Birth," *Clinical Pediatrics,* vol. 1, no. 2, pp. 73–74, November, 1962, abstracted in *Obstetrical and Gynecological Survey,* vol. 18, no. 2, pp. 240–242, April, 1963.

President's Commission on the Status of Women: *American Women* (report), Washington, D.C., 1963.

Price, Dorothy, and H. Guy Williams-Ashman: "The Accessory Reproductive Glands of Mammals," chap. 6 in William C. Young (ed.), *Sex and Internal Secretions*, The Williams & Wilkins Company, Baltimore, 1961.

Pruemmer, Dominic: *Birth Control* (pamphlet), Paulist Press, New York, 1934.

Quay, Paul M.: *Contraception and Marital Love*, Family Life Bureau, National Catholic Welfare Conference, Washington, D.C., 1961.

Ramsey, Glenn V., Bert Kruger Smith, and Bernice Milburn Moore: *Women View Their Working World* (pamphlet), The Hogg Foundation for Mental Health, University of Texas, Austin, 1963.

Riemer, Svend: "Married Students Are Good Students," *Marriage and Family Living*, vol. 9, no. 1, pp. 11–12, February, 1947.

Roberts, G. Fulton: *Comparative Aspects of Haemolytic Disease of the Newborn*, William Heinemann, Ltd., London, 1957.

Robson, J. M.: *Recent Advances in Sex and Reproductive Physiology*, 3d ed., McGraw-Hill Book Company, New York, 1947.

Rockwood, Lemo D., and Mary E. N. Ford: *Youth, Marriage and Parenthood*, John Wiley & Sons, Inc., New York, 1945.

Rosen, Harold (ed.): *Therapeutic Abortion*, The Julian Press, Inc., New York, 1954.

Rosenbach, A. S.: "The All-embracing Dr. Franklin," The Rosenbach Company, Philadelphia, 1932, quoted in Bernard Stern, *The Family Past and Present*, Appleton-Century-Crofts, Inc., New York, 1938.

Samenfink, J. Anthony, and Robert L. Milliken: "Marital Status and Academic Success: A Reconsideration," *Marriage and Family Living*, vol. 23, no. 3, pp. 226–227, August, 1961.

Savel, Lewis E., and Edward Roth: "Effects of Smoking in Pregnancy: A Continuing Retrospective Study," *Obstetrics & Gynecology*, vol. 20, no. 3, pp. 313–316, September, 1962, abstracted in *Obstetrical and Gynecological Survey*, vol. 18, no. 1, pp. 62–64, February, 1963.

Scheinfeld, Amram: *Women and Men*, Harcourt, Brace & World, Inc., New York, 1944.

Schmiedeler, Edgar: *Marriage and the Family*, McGraw-Hill Book Company, New York, 1946.

Schroder, Ralph: "Academic Achievement of the Male College Student," *Marriage and Family Living*, vol. 25, no. 4, pp. 420–423, November, 1963.

Schumann, Edward A.: *A Textbook of Obstetrics*, W. B. Saunders Company, Philadelphia, 1936.

Scott, James S.: "Developments in Haemolytic Disease of the Foetus and Newborn," chap. 5 in R. J. Kellar (ed.), *New Trends in Obstetrics*, Butterworth, Inc., Washington, D.C., 1963.

Scott, L. Stuart: "Unilateral Cryptorchidism: Subsequent Effects on Fertility," *Journal of Reproduction and Fertility*, vol. 2, pp. 54–60, February, 1961, abstracted in *Obstetrical and Gynecological Survey*, vol. 16, no. 5, pp. 704–706, October, 1961.

Scott, Martin J.: *Marriage* (pamphlet), Paulist Press, New York, 1930.

Sears, Robert R., Eleanor E. Maccoby, and Harry Levin: *Patterns in Child Rearing*, Harper & Row, Publishers, Incorporated, New York, 1957.

Sim, Myre: "Abortion and the Psychiatrist," *British Medical Journal*, vol. 2, no. 5350, pp. 145–148, July 20, 1963, abstracted in *Obstetrical and Gynecological Survey*, vol. 18, no. 6, pp. 884–886, December, 1963.

Simpson, George Eaton, and J. Milton Yinger: *Racial and Cultural Minorities*, rev. ed., Harper & Row, Publishers, Incorporated, New York, 1958.

Sjövall, Elisabet: "Coitus Interruptus," in Mary Steichen Calderone (ed.), *Manual of Contraceptive Practice*, pp. 202–206, The Williams & Wilkins Company, Baltimore, 1964.

Speert, Harold, and Alan F. Guttmacher: *Obstetrical Practice*, Landsberger Medical Books, Inc., New York, 1956.

Statistical Bulletin, vol. 30, no. 4, April, 1949; vol. 31, no. 2, February, 1950; vol. 32, no. 4, April, 1951; vol. 37, May, 1956; vol. 38, March, 1957; vol. 41, January, 1960; vol. 42, January, 1961; vol. 42, September, 1961; vol. 44, May, 1963; vol. 44, July, 1963; vol. 45, January, 1964, Metropolitan Life Insurance Company, New York.

Stone, Hannah M., and Abraham Stone: *A Marriage Manual*, rev. ed., Simon and Schuster, Inc., New York, 1953.

Stone, Joseph L., and Joseph Church: *Childhood and Adolescence*, Random House, Inc., New York, 1957.

Struther, Jan: *The Glassblower and Other Poems*, Harcourt, Brace & World, Inc., New York, 1941.

Stuber, Stanley I.: *A Primer on Roman Catholicism for Protestants*, Association Press, New York, 1953.

Sumner, William Graham, and Albert Galloway Keller: *The Science of Society*, Yale University Press, New Haven, Conn., 1927.

Sutherland, Robert L.: *Can an Adult Change?* rev. ed. (pamphlet), The Hogg Foundation for Mental Health, University of Texas, Austin, 1957.

Taeuber, Conrad, and Irene B. Taeuber: *The Changing Population of the United States*, John Wiley & Sons, Inc., New York, 1958.

Taussig, Helen B.: "A Study of the German Outbreak of Phocomelia," *Journal of the American Medical Association*, vol. 180, no. 13, pp. 1106–1114, June 30, 1962.

Terman, Lewis, M.: *Psychological Factors in Marital Happiness*, McGraw-Hill Book Company, New York, 1938.

―――― and Catherine Cox Miles: *Sex and Personality*, McGraw-Hill Book Company, New York, 1936.

"The Teen-age Mother," *Population Profile*, June 3, 1962, Population Reference Bureau, Washington, D.C.

Third Plenary Council of Baltimore: *A Manual of Prayers for Use of the Catholic Laity*, P. J. Kenedy & Sons, New York, 1930.

Thomas, John L.: *Marriage and Rhythm*, The Newman Press, Westminster, Md., 1957.

Thompson, Spencer G. (ed.): *Pediatric Currents for General Practice*, vol. 11, no. 5, May, 1962.

Time, April 21, 1958, p. 44.

Timmons, J. Daniel, and Russell R. de Alvarez: "Monoamniotic Twin Pregnancies," *American Journal of Obstetrics and Gynecology*, vol. 86, no. 7, pp. 875–881, August 1, 1963.

Tobin, T. E.: *When Is Rhythm Allowed?* Lignorian Pamphlets, Redemptionist Fathers, Lignori, Mo., 1962.

Tyler, Leona E.: *The Psychology of Human Differences*, 2d ed., Appleton-Century-Crofts, Inc., New York, 1956.

United Nations: *Demographic Yearbook 1961*, New York, 1962.

U.S. Bureau of the Census: *Census of Population: 1940, The Labor Force, Employment and Family Characteristics of Women*, 1940a.

―――― : *Census of Population: 1940, The Labor Force, United States Summary*, 1940b.

―――― : *Census of Population: 1960*, vol. I, *Characteristics of the Population*, part 1, *United States Summary*, 1960a.

―――― : *Historical Statistics of the United States, Colonial Times to 1957*, 1960b.

―――― : *Population Characteristics*, Current Population Reports, ser. P-20, no. 129, July 24, 1964.

―――― : *Statistical Abstract of the United States*, 1964.

U.S. Department of Health, Education, and Welfare: *Vital Statistics of the United States, 1959,* vol. I, 1959.

U.S. News and World Report, June 6, 1960.

U.S. Public Health Service, National Office of Statistics: "Marriages and Divorces: United States and Each State, Alaska, Hawaii, Puerto Rico, and the Virgin Islands (U.S.), 1955," *Vital Statistics — Special Reports,* vol. 46, no. 12, July 23, 1957.

U.S. Women's Bureau: *Who Are the Working Mothers?* leaflet no. 37, rev. 1962.

Vildrac, Charles: *A Book of Love,* translated by Witter Bynner, E. P. Dutton & Co., Inc., New York, 1923.

Villee, Claude A. (ed.): *The Placenta and Fetal Membranes,* The Williams & Wilkins Company, Baltimore, 1960.

Vincent, Clark E., *Unmarried Mothers,* The Free Press of Glencoe, New York, 1961.

Walker, Kenneth, and Eric B. Strauss: *Sexual Disorders in the Male,* The Williams & Wilkins Company, Baltimore, 1941.

Waller, Willard: *The Family: A Dynamic Interpretation,* rev. by Reuben Hill, Holt, Rinehart and Winston, Inc., New York, 1951.

Wallin, Paul, and Alexander L. Clark: "A Study of Orgasm as a Condition of Women's Enjoyment of Coitus in the Middle Years of Marriage," *Human Biology,* vol. 35, no. 2, pp. 131–139, May, 1963.

Weeks, H. Ashley: "Differential Divorce Rates by Occupations," *Social Forces,* vol. 21, no. 3, pp. 334–337, March, 1943.

Weinstein, Eugene A.: "Adoption and Fertility," *American Sociological Review,* vol. 27, no. 3, pp. 408–412, June, 1962.

Wile, Ira S., and Mary Day Winn: *Marriage in the Modern Manner,* Appleton-Century-Crofts, Inc., New York, 1929.

Williams, J. Paul: *What Americans Believe and How They Worship,* Harper & Row, Publishers, Incorporated, New York, 1952.

Winokur, George (ed.): *Determinants of Human Sexual Behavior,* Charles C Thomas, Publisher, Springfield, Ill., 1963.

Young, Hugh: *Genital Abnormalities, Hermaphroditism, and Related Renal Diseases,* The Williams & Wilkins Company, Baltimore, 1937.

Young, William C.: "The Mammalian Ovary," chap. 7 in William C. Young (ed.), *Sex and Internal Secretions,* 3d ed., The Williams & Wilkins Company, Baltimore, 1961a.

—— (ed.): *Sex and Internal Secretions,* 3d ed., The Williams & Wilkins Company, Baltimore, 1961b.

——, Robert W. Goy, and Charles H. Phoenix: "Hormones and Sexual Behavior," *Science,* vol. 143, no. 3603, pp. 212–218, January 17, 1964.

NAME INDEX

Trace, R. J., 85, 623
Troelstrup, A. W., 542
Turner, E. S., 170
Tyler, L. E., 16, 33, 695

Vildrac, C., 679, 696
Villee, C. A., 561, 687, 691, 696
Vincent, C. E., 152, 170, 696
Vogel, E. F., 84, 541

Walker, K., 200, 696
Waller, W., 91, 111, 170, 196, 220, 316, 370, 394, 415, 440, 454, 696
Wallin, P., 128, 151, 301, 316, 490, 688, 696

Warren, C. P., 578, 690
Weber, L. E., 630
Weeks, H. A., 516, 696
Weinstein, E. A., 608, 696
Whelpton, P. K., 600, 628, 690
Whitman, H., 674
Wile, I. S., 435, 696
Williams, J. P., 253, 324, 696
Williams, L. H., 563, 688
Williams-Ashman, H. G., 549, 694
Wilson, R. H. L., 22, 84, 690
Winch, R. F., 196
Winfield, L., 454
Winn, M. D., 435, 696

Winokur, G., 15, 504, 696
Witkin, H. A., 17
Woods, F. J., 674
Woolf, V., 80

Yamomura, D. S., 250
Yinger, J. M., 207, 252, 694
Young, H., 14, 696
Young, L., 17
Young, W. C., 20, 597, 606, 687, 694, 696

Zavin, T., 394, 629
Zawadzki, E. S., 627
Zimberoff, M., 578, 690

SUBJECT INDEX

Catholic - Protestant marriage, sterilization in, 233–234
therapeutic abortion in, 234–235
validity of, 228–229
wedding, validity of, 230–231
Cervix, dilation of, during childbirth, 572
CG, 570
Character, nature of, 397
Charivari, 336–337
Childbirth, 572–589
afterbirth expulsion of, 580–581
breech presentation in, 574
Caesarean section, 577–578
cervix, dilation of, 572
child, identification of, 578–579
passage through birth canal, 573–576
colostrum, secretion of, 590
episiotomy, 576
forceps, use of, 576
lactation, 590
lightening, 572
maternal mortality, 584–585
menstruation after, 590
molding of child's head during, 574–575
natural, 581, 588–589
pain, relief of, 581–584
decompression as means of, 583
hypnosis as means of, 583
points of resistance, child's head and, 576
premature, criteria of, 558–559
pubic joint, relaxation of, 575–576
ventouse, use of, 576–577
version during, 574
Childlessness (see Infertility)
Children, campus marriage, care of, in, 476–477
divorce, as deterrent to, 372–373
effects of, on, 278, 378–381
growth pattern, 254–255
mother's gainful employment, effects of, on, 67–68
needs of, 635–653
communication, 641
discipline, 651–653
love, 639–640

Children, needs of, security, 636–637
rearing of, 633–635
in Catholic-Protestant marriage, 236
mutual respect in, 637–639
Chivalry, difference between sexes, 12
Choice of marriage partner (see Marriage partner, choice of)
Chorionic gonadotropin, 570
Chromosomes, 15
number of, 546
and sex determination, 564
Climacteric, male, 200
Clitoris, nature and sensitivity of, 503–504
Coitus interruptus, in artificial insemination, 612
conception control, as means of, 600–601
and parthenogenesis, 554
Collusion, 381
Colostrum, as food for newborn infant, 590
pregnancy, as sign of, 568
in test for, 571
Common interests and choice of marriage partner, 182–183
Common law marriage, 327
Communication, in child rearing, 641
in family living, 663–665
limitations on, 420–421
in marriage, 420–429
improvement of, 428–429
in sex education, 654–655
between sexes, 12
Comparative rectitude, 382
Complementariness of sexes, 5–7
in marriage, 7
meaning of, 5–6
reciprocity, relation to, 6
roles, relation to, 34
simultaneity, relation to, 6
Complex, nature of, 406–407
Conception control, 593–605
in Catholic-Protestant marriage, 231₄–236
coitus interruptus as, 600–601
contraceptives, chemical, 602–603
mechanical, 601
oral, 602–603
and premarital pregnancy, 156
"feminine hygiene," 594

Conception control, legal status of, 603
meaning of, 593
and premarital medical examination, 180
requirements of means of, 593–594
"safe-period," 599–600
and women's freedom, 72
Conception during lactation, 590
Conditioning, of behavior, 404–408
mores and folkways, role of, in, 408
and negative adaptation, 407–408
Conflict in marriage, normal, 396–397
Consensus during wedding, 326–327
Conspicuous expenditure, 526
Contraception (see Conception control)
Corpus luteum, formation of, 552
and progesterone, secretion of, 552, 595
Counseling, marriage, in Australia, 388–390
as factor in adjustment, 441–442
Cruelty as ground for divorce, 375–377
Cultural lag, marriage laws as examples of, 356–357
and married women's gainful employment, 59
nature of, 59
Culture, internalization, 27
sex differences, relation to, 18–19, 21–29
Custom (see Mores)
Cryptorchidism, 604, 606–607

Dating, Catholic-Protestant, 230
failures in, as marriage failures, 116–117
importance of, 115–116
as preparation for marriage, 117–122
and social change, 117
Death rate, difference between sexes, 9
and divorce rate, 370
infant, for illegitimate children, 162–163
(See also Maternal mortality)
Deoxyribonucleic acid and genes, 546
Desertion as ground for divorce, 39

Development, differences between sexes, 9
Developmental tasks in family life cycle, 661, 669–671
Diminishing returns, law of, 440–441
Discipline, children, need for, 651–653
Division of labor, by sex, 35–36, 38
  breaking down, 42
Divorce, Catholic attitude toward, 236–237
  children, as deterrent, 372–373
  effects on, 278, 378–381
  collusion, 381
  comparative rectitude, 382
  couple, effect on, 377–378
  court, 382–386
  definition of, 363
  grounds for, 373–377
    in Australia, 387–391
    cruelty as, 375–377
    desertion as, 39
  marriage, duration of, with relation to, 372
  failure in, relation to, 365–367
    as symptom of, 367
  for love, as effect of, 38
  mixed, relation to, 218–222
  by mutual consent, 381
  Protestant attitude toward, 331–332
  rate, 363–367
    and age at marriage, 309
    in earlier times, 36
    in early marriage, 309
    factors affecting, 368–371
    and gainful employment of married women, 62–63
    and premarital pregnancy, 163
    in remarriage, 218
  recrimination, 381–382
  remarriage after, churches, attitude of, 331–332
    possible problems in, 219–222
  remedies suggested for, 381–391
  as social evil, 367–368
  to whom granted, 371–372
DNA and genes, 546
Double standard and premarital sexual intercourse, 137

Dysmenorrhea, causes of, 598

Economic element, in choice of marriage partner, 185–186
  in mixed marriage, 210–211
Elopement, 337
Engagement, 291–303
  broken, 300–303
  dating during, 295–297
  function of, 291–292
  intimacy of, 293–295
  length of, 292–293
  monopoly during, 295–297
  problems to be faced during, 299
  revealing past, 299–300
  rings, pins, "drops," 297–299
Episiotomy, 576
Erythroblastosis foetalis and Rh factor, 615–616
Estrogen, function of, 552
  secretion of, 552, 595
  withdrawl of, and anovulatory menstruation, 595–596
Eunuch, characteristics of, 15, 19–20
Expectation of life, difference between sexes, 9
Experience, sexually colored, 27

Family, background, in mixed marriage, 211–216
  and success in marriage, 178–179
  conversation, patterns of, 663–665
  council, 668–669
  developmental tasks, 661, 669–671
  functions of, 631–633
    institutional, and divorce rate, 369
  as in-group, 438–439
  life cycle of, 661, 669–671
  living, pattern of, and married women's gainful employment, 64
  meals, 662–663
  pets, 665–667
  rituals, 667–668
Father, role of, 41–42, 619–621
Fear, of marriage, 503
  as reason for singleness, 106
  marriage adjustment, as factor in, 429–434
  of pregnancy and childbirth, 496

Fear, of sex as reason for singleness, 105–106
Femaleness, nature of, 20
Femininity, and hormone balance, 16, 20
  nature of, 20–21
  sports, relation to, 8
Fertility, adoption, relation to 607–608
  menarche, relation to, 255
Fertilization, 553–554
Fetus, appearance of, in X-ray photograph, as sign of pregnancy, 569
  development of, 555–563
  factors affecting, 561–564
  maternal impressions, 563–564
  protection of, food and oxygen supply of, 559–563
  sex of, ascertaining, 564–565
    nuclear chromatin, 565
    determination of, 564
  as sign of pregnancy, heartbeat of, 569
    movement of, 569
    shape of, 569
  size of, factors determining, 563
Fixation, emotional, 260–261
  parent, 275–277
Folkways (see Mores)
Friedman test for pregnancy, 570
Frog and toad tests for pregnancy, 571

Genes, nature of, 15, 546
Genital organs, development of, 13–14
  homologous, 14
Glands, endocrine, as cause of sex differences, 15–16, 19–20
Golden weddings, number of, 353
Gonads, relation to sex differences, 15–16, 19–20
Graafian follicle, estrogen, secretion of, by, 552, 595
  formation of, 552
Guilt as reason for singleness, 106

Hair, difference between sexes, 9
Hemolytic disease and Rh factor, 615–616

Vernix caseosa, 556
Version during childbirth,
574

Wed, 332, 334
Wedding, 317–332
  bride given away, 329–
    330
  ceremony, 321–332
  church and state, interest
    of, 318–319
  consensus, 326–327
  cost of, 319
  customs, 332–337
    as survivals, 332
  date of, 320
    and bride's menstrual
      period, 320
  golden, number of, 353
  marriage, adjustment in
    implied, 330
  preparation for, 320
  purpose of, 317–318
  ring, 334–335
  as sacrament, 324
  secret, 337–340
  size of, 319
  state of being, established
    during, 327–329
  term, meaning of, 332
  validity of, 326–327
Widowhood, difference be-
  tween sexes, 9
  mixed marriage, relation
    to, 218–222

Wife, evaluation of, criteria
  for, 35
  role of, 47–57
    relation to husband's
      occupation, 48
    as specialist in con-
      sumption, 523
Women, married, gainful
  employment of,
    49–69
  arguments for and
    against, 65–69
  children, effect on,
    67–68
  and comparative
    prestige, 62
  and cultural lag, 59
  division of labor,
    breakdown in, 61,
    63
  and divorce rate, 62–
    63
  and intersexual com-
    petition, 61
  and marriage part-
    ner, new expecta-
    tions for, 63–64
  number of women
    employed, 49–51
  and occupational dis-
    crimination, 62
  pattern of family life,
    64
  problems emerging
    from, 59–65

Women, married, gainful
  employment of,
    reasons for, 51–59
    competition, 53
    masculine ideol-
      ogy, 53
    money economy,
      51–53
    necessity, 57
    opportunity, 51
    personal desire,
      58–59
    standard of living,
      57–58
  and status of women,
    62
  and upward mobility,
    64
  position of, in U.S., re-
    lation of individual
    to, 73–74
  role of, 22–27
    factors complicating
      choice of, 48
    separability of ele-
      ments of, 48
  sexual classification,
    dissatisfaction with,
    30

Zygote, characteristics of,
  545–546
  implantation in uterus,
    555